W9-AYB-706

EDUCATION
87/88

Editor

Fred Schultz
The University of Akron

Fred Schultz, professor of education at The University of Akron, attended Indiana University to earn a B.S. in social science education in 1962, an M.S. in the history and philosophy of education in 1966, and a Ph.D. in the history and philosophy of education and American studies in 1969. His B.A. in Spanish was conferred from the University of Akron in May 1985. He is actively involved in researching the development and history of American education.

A Library of Information from the Public Press

Cover illustration by Mike Eagle

The Dushkin Publishing Group, Inc.
Sluice Dock, Guilford, Connecticut 06437

The Annual Editions Series

Annual Editions is a series of over forty volumes designed to provide the reader with convenient, low-cost access to a wide range of current, carefully selected articles from some of the most important magazines, newspapers, and journals published today. Annual Editions are updated on an annual basis through a continuous monitoring of over 200 periodical sources. All Annual Editions have a number of features designed to make them particularly useful, including topic guides, annotated tables of contents, unit overviews, and indexes. For the teacher using Annual Editions in the classroom, an Instructor's Resource Guide with test questions is available for each volume.

PUBLISHED

Africa
Aging
American Government
American History, Pre-Civil War
American History, Post-Civil War
Anthropology
Biology
Business/Management
China
Comparative Politics
Computers in Education
Computers in Business
Computers in Society
Criminal Justice
Drugs, Society and Behavior
Early Childhood Education
Economics
Educating Exceptional Children
Education
Educational Psychology
Environment
Geography

Global Issues
Health
Human Development
Human Sexuality
Latin America
Macroeconomics
Marketing
Marriage and Family
Middle East and the Islamic World
Nutrition
Personal Growth and Behavior
Psychology
Social Problems
Sociology
Soviet Union and Eastern Europe
State and Local Government
Urban Society
Western Civilization,
    Pre-Reformation
Western Civilization,
    Post-Reformation
World Politics

FUTURE VOLUMES

Abnormal Psychology
Death and Dying
Congress
Energy
Ethnic Studies
Foreign Policy
Judiciary
Law and Society
Parenting
Philosophy

Political Science
Presidency
Religion
South Asia
Third World
Twentieth-Century American
    History
Western Europe
Women's Studies
World History

Library of Congress Cataloging in Publication Data
Main entry under title: Annual editions: Education.
    1. Education—Addresses, essays, lectures.   I. Title: Education.
LB41.A673   370'.5   73-78580
ISBN 0-87967-674-4

Fourteenth Edition

Manufactured by The Banta Company, Menasha, Wisconsin 54952

Editors/ Advisory Board

To The Reader

In publishing ANNUAL EDITIONS we recognize the enormous role played by the magazines, newspapers, and journals of the *public press* in providing current, first-rate educational information in a broad spectrum of interest areas. Within the articles, the best scientists, practitioners, researchers, and commentators draw issues into new perspective as accepted theories and viewpoints are called into account by new events, recent discoveries change old facts, and fresh debate breaks out over important controversies.

Many of the articles resulting from this enormous editorial effort are appropriate for students, researchers, and professionals seeking accurate, current material to help bridge the gap between principles and theories and the real world. These articles, however, become more useful for study when those of lasting value are carefully *collected, organized, indexed,* and *reproduced* in a *low-cost format,* which provides easy and permanent access when the material is needed. That is the role played by *Annual Editions.* Under the direction of each volume's *Editor,* who is an expert in the subject area, and with the guidance of an *Advisory Board,* we seek each year to provide in each *ANNUAL EDITION* a current, well-balanced, carefully selected collection of the best of the public press for your study and enjoyment. We think you'll find this volume useful, and we hope you'll take a moment to let us know what you think.

Annual Editions: Education 87/88 represents a synthesis of popular and academic viewpoints concerning the major issues affecting educational development in North America. The essays in this fourteenth edition are taken from both trade and professional publications in order to capture in a single volume the most comprehensive profile of what is being thought and said about current educational issues. The views of students, parents, teacher educators, courts, in-service teachers, and pre-service teachers are considered.

The volume addresses the following concerns: (1) the implementation of proposed reform measures for improving the quality of education; (2) the proclamation of the intent to move toward the medical model of national board certification of teachers in the United States; (3) the effort to begin competency examinations for state certification of teachers; (4) the awareness that, as the Rand Corporation and other research agencies have predicted, a major shortfall in the supply of fully certified teachers is already apparent in certain curricular areas and a major general shortage of qualified teachers is expected by the year 1990 or 1991; and (5) the question of who will fund these proposed changes.

The renaissance in the critical historical reassessment of the North American experience in education which has been under way since 1960 continues. Never has there been a more exciting or challenging time to be involved in the educational system. Great opportunities, as well as great challenges to human and economic resources, are open to everyone. The revisionist critiques of American history in the field of education continue to develop from different ideological perspectives. The reinterpretation of the historical bases of the present crises or reform rhetoric in the current literature on education is furthering the development of broader and more accurate perspectives on which to base educational policy decisions. The quality of professional dialogue has been uplifted as educators are taking renewed critical assessments of their goals and values. More balanced, mature, and incisive analyses of how the situation today compares or contrasts with other crises in the educational past contribute valuable information about problems that may stand in the way of progress in educational development.

Every effort is made to stay in touch with movements in educational studies and with the social forces at work in the schools. Members of the Advisory Board contribute valuable insights to the editorial process. The production and editorial staff at the Dushkin Publishing Group coordinates this effort. Through this process we collect a wide range of articles on a variety of topics relevant to education in the United States and Canada. The articles are then carefully reviewed for their relevance to the topics or themes dominating current public and professional concerns regarding the state of education.

There are basic criterial guidelines for each selection. An article must address at least one major issue in education which concerns those who work in educational systems or those who are served by such systems. In addition, articles in the volume should provide a general overview of the topics which they address. Economic and political forces, forces or pressures in educational systems themselves, and government policy makers, all affect the formation of the national agenda for debate regarding educational policy issues. The dialogue among those who represent these forces contributes to the depth and intensity of educational debate. All of these factors are considered in determining the relevance of material for inclusion in the volume.

Nine units form topical bridges for the exploration and appraisal of current controversy regarding the adequacy of goals, policies, and programming in the various North American educational systems. The units deal with issues related to perceptions of professional and public opinion regarding the condition of education, the reform movement and the struggle for excellence in education, controversies surrounding commission and individual reports on the quality of schooling, alternatives in educational development, morality in education and discipline problems in schools, equality of opportunity in the field of education, special educational needs, the profession of teaching today, and the future of North American education.

We are always interested in improving the quality of each *Annual Edition.* Let us know your opinions of the book and your views on what can be done to improve it by filling out the article rating form on the last page of the volume. We will sincerely try to respond to your concerns.

Fred Schultz

Editor

Contents

Unit 1

Perceptions of Education in America

Five articles examine the present state of education in America. The topics covered include school reform, relationships between families and schools, the future of teaching, and the current public opinion on public schools.

Unit 2

Continuity and Change in Education

Five selections discuss the effects of technological change, equal opportunity, and the reorganization of school programs on current American education.

The topics in italics are developed in the article. For further expansion please refer to the Topic Guide and the Index.

Unit 3

The Struggle for Excellence: Striving for Higher Achievement

Five articles discuss the current aims for excellence in American education. Topics include problems concerning school reform, teacher preparation, and competency testing.

The topics in italics are developed in the article. For further expansion please refer to the Topic Guide and the Index.

Unit 4

Morality and Values in Education

Four articles examine the role of American schools in
teaching morality and social values.

The topics in italics are developed in the article. For further expansion please refer to the Topic Guide and the Index.

Unit 5

Discipline Problems in the Schools

Four articles consider the necessity of judicious and
effective discipline in the American classroom today.

The topics in italics are developed in the article. For further expansion please refer to the Topic Guide and the Index.

Unit 6

Equal Opportunity and American Education

Five articles discuss the current state of equality and opportunity in the American educational system. Educational policies, the history of school desegregation, as well as the long-term effects of school desegregation are some of the topics considered.

Unit 7

Serving Special Needs and Individualizing Instruction

Six selections examine some of the important aspects of special educational needs: mainstreaming, single-parent families, latchkey kids, child abuse, student-student interaction, and drug problems.

The topics in italics are developed in the article. For further expansion please refer to the Topic Guide and the Index.

Unit
8

The Profession
of Teaching Today

Four articles assess the current state of teaching in
American schools. Topics include historical background
on major teaching issues, teacher education, and what
elements make an effective teacher.

Unit
9

A Look to the Future

Three articles look at the future of education in
American schools. Curricula for the future,
demographic changes, and educational reform are
considered.

Topic Guide

This topic guide suggests how the selections in this book relate to topics of traditional concern to education students and professionals. It is very useful in locating articles which relate to each other for reading and research. The guide is arranged alphabetically according to topic. Articles may, of course, treat topics that do not appear in the topic guide. In turn, entries in the topic guide do not necessarily constitute a comprehensive listing of all the contents of each selection.

TOPIC AREA	TREATED AS AN ISSUE IN:	TOPIC AREA	TREATED AS AN ISSUE IN:
Academic Freedom	24. The Courts and Education	"Discipline" in Schools	20. Research Evidence of a School Discipline Problem
Alternatives in Education	6. What Can Schools Become?		21. Good, Old-Fashioned Discipline
	8. The Best Prep School in Town		22. Discipline Is Not the Problem
	9. A National Survey of Middle School Effectiveness		23. Help for the Hot-Tempered Kid
	10. A Good School	Education as a Field of Study	1. The Proper Study of Education
Behavior Management	5. The 18th Annual Gallup Poll of the Public's Attitudes Toward the Public Schools	Effective Teaching	38. Profile of an Effective Teacher
	9. A National Survey of Middle School Effectiveness	Equality of Opportunity	8. The Best Prep School in Town
	20. Research Evidence of a School Discipline Problem		24. The Courts and Education
	21. Good, Old-Fashioned Discipline		25. School Desegregation Since *Brown*
	22. Discipline Is Not the Problem		26. A Long-Term View of School Desegregation
	23. Help for the Hot-Tempered Kid		27. The Bilingual Education Battle
Bilingual Education	27. The Bilingual Education Battle		28. Sexism in the Schoolroom of the '80s
Child Abuse	33. Child Abuse and Neglect	Excellence	4. Who Will Teach the Class of 2000?
Civic Education	16. The Great Tradition in Education		11. Changing Our Thinking About Educational Change
	17. Moral Education in the United States		12. Sustaining the Momentum of State Education Reform
	19. Reopening the Books on Ethics		13. The Carnegie Report
Collective Bargaining	35. The Making of a Profession		14. Educational Ideals and Educational Practice
Competency Testing	13. The Carnegie Report		15. Huffing and Puffing and Blowing Schools Excellent
	14. Educational Ideals and Educational Practice	Families and Schools	3. The Fourth R
	35. The Making of a Profession		8. The Best Prep School in Town
Control Theory	22. Discipline Is Not the Problem		30. Single-Parent Families
Courts and Education	24. The Courts and Education		31. Checking In
	27. The Bilingual Education Battle		33. Child Abuse and Neglect
	29. "Appropriate" School Programs		34. Kids and Drugs
Creativity	8. The Best Prep School in Town	Future of Education	4. Who Will Teach the Class of 2000?
	37. Teachers Aim at Turning Loose the Mind's Eyes		39. Schools of the Future
			40. The Education of Children
			41. Curriculum in the Year 2000
Desegregation	24. The Courts and Education	Homework	8. The Best Prep School in Town
	25. School Desegregation Since *Brown*		10. A Good School
	26. A Long-Term View of School Desegregation	Kids and Drugs	34. Kids and Drugs

Perceptions of Education in America

Perceptions of America's educational heritage are derived from past experiences. The formal educational institutions and the professional educators who serve them have been under critical examination at all levels of society. Thought and opinion regarding education arises from or is influenced by many factors, such as individuals' experiences with schools; the economic and social circumstances in which people live; the relative success or failure of persons in their work careers, whether they work or study in or out of the educational system; the political climate of the times and the extent to which persons in government at the local, state, provincial, or federal levels choose to focus on educational issues and public policies affecting education; the impact of the opinions of prestigious private foundations, organization, and individuals when they make recommendations for improving the quality of schooling or teaching as a profession; and the points of view and the manner of presentation of views on educational issues conveyed by the mass media. The interests of parents, students, teachers, school administrators, and those who must formulate and guide state or provincial educational policy are somewhat different. Within any national public there are many smaller publics whose special interests require the maintenance of continuous and open dialogue for the just or fair development of national educational policy. John Dewey documented this reality brilliantly as far back as 1927 in *The Public and Its Problems.*

Citizens today seem very interested in the quality of schooling. Many recommendations for change in the preparation of teachers have been offered by formal reports since 1983. Both the equity and the quality agendas for improving the effectiveness of America's schools are much more pertinent today than they were in Dewey's time. The perceptions of educators and students on such issues are sometimes very different from those of persons in business or politics. Furthermore, there are distinct sets of interests in society when it comes to assessing either public or private educational systems. Although there have been many changes and successes in recent years in the quality and effectiveness of schooling in some areas, the educational system has not always been successful in communicating these changes to the general public.

This unit opens by taking a look at what constitutes the proper study of education—a topic that is still debated throughout North America. In recent years great advances have been developing in teacher education. As these changes are implemented in response to public and professional concerns for quality in teacher education, spirited debate on what ought to be the best way to study education will, no doubt, continue.

The primary emphasis of the unit is on the basic differences between myth and reality in public opinion about the schools. According to some writers, signs of qualitative improvement in schooling have been apparent in the last three years. Further, the many national reports and individual analyses of the effectiveness of the nation's schools have sparked intense self-examination and critical reviews of existing school curricula among the beleaguered incumbents of state and provincial educational systems. Experts look forward to fundamentally significant changes in the content of schooling in the next fifteen years. These changes have already begun to develop in many areas. For instance, concern for a more scientific and technological knowledge base is evident, commitment to teaching basic literacy and computer literacy have never been stronger, and the national certification of teachers in the United States has been adopted by the American Association of Colleges for Teacher Education (AACTE). Many other changing perceptions of what is needed in the schools as well as in teacher preparation have already received vital support from educators, large private foundations, educational administrators, and corporate and political communities.

People are recognizing that a national shortage of teachers is developing in many teaching areas. Prestigious research think tanks such as the Rand Corporation have predicted a major national teacher shortage in the next few years. The result is a decrease in the number of persons entering the teaching profession at the same time that most states either already have or are developing plans for competency examinations for teachers. The educational reformers and the various commission and foundation reports on the state of the schools are calling for "career ladders" for teachers, more traditional subject matter orientations in the process of becoming certified as a teacher, and specific efforts to recruit more intelligent persons into a teaching career (for example, by offering them higher salaries). There is a fundamental tension in all of this. Many teachers believe that the authors of the various commission reports are not aware of the enormity of the problems they face daily in their classrooms. One such problem involves the family. There are calls for more effective communication between families and schools as well as for a realization of the importance of reinforcing family values in schools. Although it is recognized that the structures of North American families have changed, there is renewed hope that schools and families of all kinds will work more effectively together. Closer school-community relationships must be established through cooperation among students, families, and teachers.

While it is true that many teachers are discouraged by difficult teaching conditions, others are optimistic about the public's new awareness of the necessity of adequately rewarding good teachers for their efforts and of increasing the social prestige and status of teaching as a profession. Also, there is great hope in the vitality and courage of the young people who are preparing to become teachers. They are embracing the calls for change and reform in the educational system. They are bringing the gifts of idealism and youth to the task of improving the schools. They are, for the most part, supporting the proposals for "career ladders," competency testing, and qualitative commitment to teaching as a profession. The profiles of the new teachers that are emerging will be a source of pride to the nation. All of these matters are reflected in the essays that follow.

Looking Ahead: Challenge Questions

What is the line of argument in George Kneller's essay on the proper study of education? How can the study of education be compared to the study of other disciplines? Do you agree or disagree with his comparisons and conclusions? Why or why not?

What is the difference between myth and reality in American education? Have the public schools done anything right? If so, what? If not, why not?

What are the best ways to get a true portrait of the present state or condition of education?

How can families be more directly involved in the schools? What family values ought to be related to the activity of schooling? Is this possible? How could teachers better assist parents or guardians of students in the education of their children?

What are the characteristics and attitudes of future teachers toward educational change?

What are the major crises affecting American teachers today? How can teachers help themselves? How can the public help them?

What are the principal concerns of the general public regarding the quality of conduct of schooling today?

What is the functional effect of public opinion on national educational policy development?

What generalizations can you draw from the Gallup Poll data on public perceptions of the public schools?

THE PROPER STUDY OF EDUCATION

George F. Kneller

**Keynote Address, Annual Meeting of the
American Educational Studies Association,
Milwaukee, Wisconsin, 3 November 1983**

My topic tonight is the proper study of education or what makes education an academic discipline. I shall have little to say about the process or the profession of education, about schooling or pedagogy. My purpose is to illuminate our common endeavor and justify its place along with other disciplines in the university curriculum, especially at the undergraduate level. My text is taken from Alfred North Whitehead: "We are only just now realizing that Education requires a genius and study of its own." Much that I say will not be new to you, but I believe my message is more timely now than ever, and I hope it will encourage you to make our study the discipline it ought to be.

First, let me propose three definitions. By a **discipline** I mean an intellectual enterprise with a domain of phenomena, a body of data, concepts, and theories, and a set of techniques for gaining, validating, and applying knowledge. Neither the domain nor the techniques need be unique. Psychology and sociology alike study human beings, often in the same way, and economics possesses few techniques and no general method of its own. By a **discipline of education** I mean a field of study embodying the knowledge we use to understand intellectual, moral, and emotional development. By a **theory of education** I refer to a set of mutually consistent or coherent propositions derived logically or plausibly from assumptions about the proper nature and purpose of education. A theory of curriculum, for example, is a set of propositions about the kind of curriculum appropriate to the sort of education assumed to be desirable.

Why should we be concerned to establish education as a discipline? There are many reasons. First, to raise the standing of education as a study in the academic world,

where, due largely to variable scholarship, it still is underappreciated. Second, to remind other disciplines of the educational importance of what they research and teach. Third, to puncture the peculiar notion that since everyone has been educated, anyone's opinion of education is as good as anyone else's. Fourth, to remind educationists that their intellectual endeavor certainly is the equal of any other and conceivably the most useful of all. Fifth, to stress the importance of studying aspects of education that are not the central concern of other disciplines—aspects such as curriculum, instruction, control, and administration. Sixth, to clarify the changes in meaning that occur when concepts and propositions are imported into education from other disciplines. Finally, to counter public disillusion with schools of education and teachers and administrators generally. I realize that this disillusion is part of a general distrust of all public services, but much of the blame for it originates in the uncertain status of educational studies.

Some people deny, and others doubt, that education can be an autonomous discipline. The skeptics doubt whether the subject matter of education can be unified, since so much of it comes from other disciplines with different aims, content, and research methods. My reply is that all disciplines relevant to education are more alike than different, and it is the likenesses that count. Furthermore, no discipline is wholly autonomous. Psychology and sociology come together in social psychology; there also are psychohistory, psycholinguistics, and physiological psychology. Physics expands into biophysics, astrophysics, geophysics, and physical chemistry. A discipline is unified and autonomous to the extent that it

From *AESA News and Comments*, Vol. 14, No. 2. March 1984. Reprinted by permission.

can direct its subdisciplines while receiving information from them. Education not only takes from other disciplines, it gives to them. It will become more disciplined to the extent that it influences research and teaching in other disciplines through the knowledge it alone provides.

Critics also contend that the study of education is undisciplined because its subject matter is not organized hierarchically by means of theories and concepts indigenous to education. These critics assume that a discipline of education must model itself on mathematics and the natural sciences. But not even the human sciences, still less the humanities, possess anything like this degree of logical structure. Take the study of English, which encompasses an impressive array of subdivisions, including language, literature, composition, stylistics, and, very often, speech and communication. Does anyone doubt that English is a discipline? Yet its subject matter, like that of education, is loosely structured with no laws and very few theories that all its practitioners accept.

In recent years courses in education increasingly have been moved to the graduate or professional level, and for several reasons: (1) Many faculty members in other fields have raised doubts about the academic qualifications of education as a substantive discipline. (2) The emphasis on practical pedagogy, characteristic of these courses, was not regarded as suitable to the undergraduate experience. And (3) Education courses were taken almost exclusively by students intending to become teachers; they failed to appeal to undergraduates generally. It is a sad commentary on our profession, and on our subject matter, that we have been unable to include in the undergraduate curriculum the study of education as a substantive discipline and therefore have failed to interest the rank and file of students in a subject that is as important to them as any they take. Too many educationists have agreed with other faculty that, unlike standard subjects, education cannot profitably be studied by undergraduates generally. Too many members of our profession seem to have agreed with other faculty in the mistaken notion that education and pedagogy are synonymous. It is almost like saying that physiology and medicine or economics and management are one of the same.

Unlike other professional studies, education has largely ignored the disciplines that are basic to it. Medicine draws on biology and chemistry; law, on ethics and politics; engineering, on mathematics; management, on economics. What disciplines are most basic to education? They are the humanities; history, philosophy, literature, and certain aspects of cultural anthropology. History chronicles the growth of ideas, methods, and systems of education; philosophy proposes and refines educational ideas; literature communicates these ideas; and anthropology interprets education in the light of cultural values and expectations. These disciplines are most basic because education at heart is a normative enterprise. It is concerned with principles of right action according to cultural norms.

True, many people speak of a "science of education." If by this they mean empirical studies undertaken to determine what they think are the most effective ways to teach, design curricula, and administer schools, they may be using the term correctly. But if they mean the study of educational phenomena as if they were natural phenomena, the term is misused. Just think what a naturalistic science of education would be like. It would attempt to formulate laws and theories explaining, predicting, and controlling the educational process, not only in this country but throughout the world. It would provide data that were precise and value-free. Yet can you imagine a time when all of us will agree precisely on what education should be and

do? Granted, natural scientists disagree among themselves, and the behavior of subatomic particles seems much like the behavior of human beings. They don't sit still long enough to be measured; their behavior so far is not entirely predictable; and everytime you think you have nailed things down well enough to establish a law of subatomic behavior, the phenomena open up again into a new cosmic universe, and experimentation is renewed. But most disagreements among natural scientists eventually are resolved by observation and experimentation of and with phenomena that can be controlled and measured, whereas empirical evidence never will resolve the debate between those who believe in school prayer or school vouchers and those who do not. Their disagreement is not about scientific fact but about values. Since, as I have said, education intrinsically is a normative endeavor, in that it seeks to realize ideals, and since ideals are what we disagree about, the study of education always will be subject to controversy and therefore never reducible to a naturalistic science.

What shall we say of the human sciences, especially psychology and sociology? After a hundred years of imitating the natural sciences, what can the human sciences offer to education? Not long ago, on the TV show Firing Line, William F. Buckley gave Wilson Riles a list of 5 prime factors in any educational encounter: (1) skill of the teacher; (2) parental influence; (3) student intelligence and attitude; (4) learning environment; (5) student socio-economic environment. Buckley asked Riles to rate these factors on a 100-point scale according to their relative importance as determined by scientific research. Riles hesitated and asked for the question to be repeated. It was. After thinking for a moment, Riles said he could not rate the factors quantitatively. Why not? We do not have the evidence, he replied. And he was right. We do not. Think of it! After spending hundreds of millions to measure educational priorities, we still have no real answers. And we never shall. Quantitative research never will answer Buckley's question or the really pressing questions of education.

Despite prodigious efforts and enormous expenditures of money, human scientists have produced no universal laws or theories that are either scientific or precise. Instead, psychology and sociology offer partial regularities, ideosyncratic taxonomies, and tendency statements the fiduciary basis for which is both weak and elusive. I have time for only one example. In the once fashionable field of aptitude-treatment interactions psychologist Lee Cronbach spent 18 years seeking stable interactions between instructional treatments and student characteristics. Finally he told the American Psychological Association, "Once we attend to interactions, we enter a hall of mirrors that extends to infinity." Any interactions Cronbach said he had identified soon changed along with changes in the social environment. Does it any longer make sense to look for laws? No, says Cronback. "Taking stock today, I think most of us judge theoretical progress to have been disappointing. Many of us are uneasy with the intellectual style of psychology." He therefore proposed a more modest goal, to "seek insights into social relations and pin down the contemporary facts" in each generation. Instead of laws, then, we have insights; instead of theories, data. Now we educationists can always do with data, provided we bear in mind the perspectives from which they were gathered. But if we want insights, I think I can show you better sources than either psychology or sociology.

Most people in education realize that the human sciences have failed to deliver on their promises. What bothers me is that these people seem untroubled by the relentless grip psychology exerts on educational thought and practice. Throughout the country legislators, swayed in part by educationists, make educational psychology a requirement for teaching licenses; they ignore history, philosophy, and other humanities. They seem convinced that for prospective teachers the only source of reliable knowledge about human behavior, or the mind, or teaching and learning, is educational psychology. How long must we endure this charade? I recently glanced through some university catalogs and found that courses in educational psychology outnumbered all courses in history, philosophy, comparative education, and foundations put together. There isn't enough substantive knowledge in educational psychology to justify this disproportion, and what knowledge there is often can be found in more suitable form in the humanities. Psychology no doubt has yielded some useful information, but many theories, such as those of interest, readiness, transfer of training, social promotion, developmentalism and discovery learning have done more harm to education than good, not only because the research supporting them was ill-conceived and poorly executed but also because the theories themselves were not directly applicable or relevant to classroom teaching and learning. Psychology and sociology are of value to education only if the educationist first adopts a theory of education and then finds a school of psychology or sociology compatible with the theory. If you begin with psychology or sociology, as many do today, and read off what you think are their implications for education, you are lost.

Cultural anthropology is another story. It is the most fruitful of the human sciences for the study of education because it is an interpretive and descriptive science **par excellence.** Why do I say this? First, anthropologists use the method of participant observation. They look into the minds of those they study and seek to comprehend their view of the world. Their aim is to understand people, not to predict their behavior, much less to control it. Next, anthropologists explore education cross-culturally, both within nations and among them. In comparative education especially they investigate the aims, methods, and institutions of education as cultural emanations. Third, anthropologists investigate education in its entirety, studying not only schooling but also education by parents, peers, media, and other agencies, as well as both formal and informal learning. Fourth, and of special importance in this country, anthropologists give us valuable information about race and ethnicity. In our richly multicultural society educators and educationists must come to grips intellectually with an extraordinary array of cultural ideas, practices, and products.

Finally, anthropology acts to correct psychological generalizations about, for instance, the alleged universal character of the development of the human mind as advanced by such as Piaget and Kohlberg with their sequential stages. The growth of the mind is seen by anthropologists as dependent to a large degree on cultural habits, demands, and language use acquired in early life. Critical factors in the development of mind, therefore, cannot be universalized by applying the standards of a single culture, or race, or socio-economic group, or even of Western civilization; much less by standards acceptable within the domain of psychological experimentation generally, but by the special situation of particular subjects in time, place, and circumstance. I do not say that psychologists are unaware of the necessary impact of cultural environments and symbolic representations, as

Howard Gardner's FRAMES OF MIND testifies; but if psychology is to be of greater use to education, especially in a multicultural society, it must be supplemented by anthropology. However, as I have shown in my own work in this field, one can tell what is relevant in anthropology only with the aid of a theory of education compatible with a theory of cultural anthropology. Because in my view cultural anthropology is a human science of greater scope and meaning for education than either psychology or sociology, I would recommend, if I were an administrator and my budget were frozen, that offerings be decreased in psychology and increased in anthropology.

Any scholar wishing to understand his discipline must study its history. I have no time to discuss how different historians have interpreted the past, much as these interpretations recently have reached the front pages of our news media. Instead, I will make just two points. A knowledge of educational history will reveal that although styles may change, along with ways of doing things, new and challenging discoveries of substance are likely to occur only infrequently. In education the lifespan of most innovations has been short, thus leading to Kneller's Law: "The more highly innovative the institution, the shorter the life of the innovations within it." We must bear in mind that any educational reform springs from tradition. The so-called "frontiers" of knowledge, the "breakthroughs" and "cutting edges" that we so often cite, always have a hinterland of preconceptions by which we determine, through critical experience over time, what has proved valuable and what has not. If history does nothing else, it provides us with that critical experience. My second point has to do with the present decline of interest in history **per se,** which may be due in part to its unfortunate dilution into social studies—unfortunate because the product is scraps of information too often lacking perspective or structure and resulting in a sacrifice of the narrative form, continuity, and chronological development that characterizes history as an autonomous discipline. Seen from the perspective of education, which deals intimately with human reality and aspirations, history is a humanity, not a social study, and certainly not an empirical social science. After examining all kinds of research over many years, I am convinced that historical evidence is more relevant to the study of education than evidence from psychology or sociology. Again, however, this evidence is useful only if interpreted in the light of an educational theory, together with a compatible theory of history.

I have said that to determine what another discipline can contribute today to education, you need a theory of education and a theory of the relevant discipline. In both cases this theoretical understanding comes mainly from philosophy, which examines the foundations of all disciplines. There is philosophy of mathematics, philosophy of science, philosophy of religion, philosophy of psychology, very much needed, and, of course, philosophy of education. In all cases philosophy clarifies the concepts and assumptions these disciplines take largely for granted. In the case of psychology, for example, philosophy considers what the mind is, what an action consists of, and how thought and action are to be understood. Particular schools of psychology assume they have the answers to these questions, and they press ahead with their research. But since, as philosophers have shown, the questions have not been answered, research findings often conflict and are confused. The classic debate between Rogers and Skinner shows how two psychologists argued from empirical evidence to entirely different conclusions, so that the debate came to turn on philosophic assumptions about what psychologists should be doing.

Although in my view philosophy is the discipline most relevant to education, since, like education, it is concerned with knowledge, ethics, and values, many educationists tend to dismiss it as impractical and elitist, and students suffer accordingly.

Most scholars in education are aware of philosophy's importance, so I will confine myself to three points which appear to be insufficiently recognized. First, philosophy's contribution to educational research. Nothing is more indispensable to a research project than its basic conceptualization. Unless the questions and hypotheses are clearly conceptualized, the conclusions will be ambiguous and of no theoretical or pratical use. In fact, they well may damage education. Philosophy also acts to correct educational research by ascertaining, for instance, how far a classification scheme is logically coherent, whether a generalization is empirically informative or tautological, and what form an educational theory should take. If philosophy did nothing more, its contribution to research alone would be testimony to its practicality.

Perhaps even more practical, and less elitist, is philosophy's relevance to test validation. I will cite a concrete example. In wide use today is a test for critical thinking composed by two eminent psychologists. It fails of its purpose, for neither the tasks nor the test results differ significantly from either tests for general intelligence or examinations normally given to high school students to measure their assimilation of course content. Worse, the authors do not seem to know the difference between the truth or falsity of propositions and the validity or invalidity of inferences. Thus in one exercise the test taker is told, "Examine each inference. . .and make a decision as to its degree of truth or falsity"—as if truth and falsity were matters of degree and the result of local inference. Again, the test fails to make the crucial distinction between questions that are self-contained and questions that require the use of information not in the questions themselves. Thus in one section the test taker is asked to judge whether each of a series of arguments is strong or weak. The questions are said to be self-contained, for the directions state, "Judge each argument separately on its own merit; try not to let your personal attitude. . .influence your evaluation." Yet both questions and the arguments answering them are political and social. One question asks, "Should the US government take over all the main industries in the country, employ all who want to work, and offer the products at cost price?" The so-called "merits" of these arguments clearly depend on one's political views. Arguments that appear strong to a conservative will appear weak to a liberal and vice versa. In response, my own gratuitous recommendation would be that the test taker, faced with any such test, attack the questions rather than try to answer them, and thus more truly reveal a capacity for critical thinking. Now I am not saying that test validation is something only a study of philosophy can provide, but simply that a study of philosophy can be of considerable help, because its very substance is conducive to performing the task. May I add that since the whole business of educational testing has been monpolized by psychologists, they should study more philosophy or let people in the humanities take over what now intellectually is a faltering and not very productive enterprise.

Third, philosophy contributes to the development of theories of education, for without theory, practice hardly can be justified. In generating theories philosophy has been fecund. Recently, for example, philosophy has given us a theory of education seen as an initiation into worthwhile activities rather than simply as an entree into society or the world of work. It has given us a theory of curriculum based on forms of knowledge in contrast to one of personal and social adjustment. And only recently we have been given a theory of the educational system encompassing all major aspects of schooling as they related to one another. Philosophy of itself does not avoid the concrete or the specific. For instance, in an article in the **Journal of Education**, Winter, 1983, pp.5 - 11, Paulo Freire has given us a theory of the very act of reading. As an example of philosophic phenomenology applied directly to an educational problem, you will find nothing more incisive or insightful. Again, if I were an administrator and my budget were frozen, and psychology courses outnumbered humanities courses, I would take from psychology and give to philosophy, thus making both the discipline and the practice of education more authentic and reflective.

Under any consideration I still would make room for courses in literature and education. The neglect of literature by educationists is incomprehensible. Like the historian, the philosopher, and others in humane studies, the creative writer gives us knowledge of how to live. The writer embodies knowledge of human beings and education in a tale that moves our imagination and emotions as well as our intellect. Writers make us see and feel what it is like to educate and be educated in different times and places. Charles Dickens, for example, portrays some 28 schools and refers to several more. He also depicts a dozen types of coercion in child training. In **Women in Love** D.H. Lawrence, a former elementary school teacher, gives us a riveting portrayal of a lesson seen by a school inspector. Especially since World War II education has become the central theme and setting of many novels. For portraits of teaching, learning, classroom interactions, and the joys and miseries of childhood and adolescence, we can do no better than study such works as Muriel Spark's **The Prime Of Miss Jean Brodie**, John Horne Brown's **Lucifer with a Match**, Frances Patton's **Good Morning, Miss Dove**, Herman Wouk's **Marjorie Morningstar**, and many others I could name.

Ezra Pound called writers the "antennae of the race." Often they reveal aspects of education that the educationist has ignored or misconceived. With their imagination, empathy, and verbal skill, writers invariably are more subtle, insightful, and, yes, accurate than academic researchers. Evan Hunter's **The Blackboard Jungle**, for instance, tells us more about the causes and phenomenology of school violence than any sociological study I have seen. E.L. Braithwaite's **To Sir with Love** does the same thing for race prejudice. Through his integrity and understanding, a black teacher gradually wins the hearts, and minds of his class of hostile white students, who ultimately learn from him as they do from no other teacher. Or take an episode from Irwin Shaw's **Rich Man, Poor Man**. Rudy's French teacher catches him sketching her in the nude. Asked to explain, Rudy replies that he is illustrating a construction he has just learned: "Je suis folle d'amour" (I am madly in love). The teacher, outraged, calls Rudy's father to school. The father stands up for his son. The drawing, he says, does not degrade the teacher but expresses the youth's normal sexuality. Where in the field of scientific research can you find an educational dilemma treated as sensitively as this? If students in education are looking for instant gratification, I would say they will get it by studying educational literature.

I have cited novels. Now led me read a little poetry. For D.H. Lawrence, again, students are not alone in their spirit of rebellion. . .against a school, a class, a teacher, or everybody. Here are some unusual but insightful lines on a teacher's rebellion against his students. The verses have a humor all their own.

1. PERCEPTIONS OF EDUCATION IN AMERICA

What does it matter to me if they can write
A description of a dog or if they can't?
What is the point? To us both, it's all my aunt!
And yet I'm supposed to care, with all my might.
I do not, and will not; they don't and that's all!
I shall keep my strength for myself; they can keep theirs
as well.
Why should we beat our heads against the wall
Of each other? I shall sit here and wait for the bell.

What teacher honestly can say he or she never has felt this sense of resignation? And shouldn't our students of education be asked to face up to the moods of surrender and helplessness that teachers so often are compelled to endure?

There are other forms in literature. The drama "The Crisis in Central High," for example, shows how a teacher in Little Rock, Arkansas, becomes embroiled in the 1957 showdown over integration in her high school. Every issue of this racial crisis is debated passionately yet realistically, and the teacher herself becomes a model of courage and commitment in the face of mass hostility and resentment. Literature also includes biology and essays. You can reach into Gilbert Highet's **The Immortal Profession,** for example, and there find the inner nature of our mutual enterprise portrayed with such discernment and intuitive power as to cast a shadow on the usual academic attempt. I know that the human sciences are seeking accurate knowledge of education to replace what they regard as the impressionism of the humane studies. But as the decades pass and this goal recedes, it looks more and more like a mirage. So for knowledge that is reliable, memorable, and absorbing, for knowledge that touches the heart as well as the head, and for knowledge that increasingly should be a fundamental element in the discipline of education, we should turn to literature. If a benefactor were to ask me what chairs to endow for a department of education, I would recommend joint appointments in education and history, education and philosophy, education and cultural anthropology, and education and literature. Just think what such appointments would do for the prestige of education as a discipline or even for teacher education. Psychologists would face competition, for once. And if some, as I hope, went out of business, funds might be provided to retrain them for something more useful.

One benefit that should result from establishing a discipline of education is greater agreement on the essential content of a first or basic course, variously called introduction, foundations, or principles. The kinds of content and methods of teaching this course today amount to Heinz's 57 varieties, with results that have done little for the cause of education as a serious and stable disciplinary study. Some teachers treat the course as an orientation to the separate subdivisions and branches of education. Others use the problems or topics approach. In favor of both approaches is the fact that they help the student to choose the phase of education which he or she would like to study further. Against these and similar approaches is the fact that they do little to help the student see education as a whole. They seem to aim at an evermoving target.

For reasons I have given, I would construct a first course out of content treated both in education and related disciplines. My ideal syllabus would comprise four main areas of education interconnected with aspects of the four disciplines I have mentioned. The areas would be education's relation to the culture and subcultures, educational control and administration, curriculum theory, and teaching and learning. The disciplines again would be history, philosophy, anthropology, and literature, together with selected information from the human sciences. I would start with a unit in history to supply the background for the topics to follow, thus eliminating the need for historical data later. My second unit would focus on cultural factors introduced in the first unit. It would include educational aspects of such topics as acculturation, cultural change, and ethnicity, all treated largely within cultural anthropology. My third unit, drawing mostly on philosophy, would provide the skills needed to analyze concepts and arguments and appreciate the task of theory construction. It would be concerned especially with aims, values, and the constituents of knowledge. Units 2 and 3 could be interchanged. My fourth unit would center on human development, on the actions and aspirations of persons involved in education. It would treat theories of human nature as they bear on education and would draw principally on philosophy, literature, and psychology. Topics would include the nature of intelligence, imagination, and creativity. Especially for students interested in teaching, it would deal with the profession of education, its rewards and duties, its rights and responsibilities.

The four units would interlock. Literature, for example, would be treated in units other than unit 4. Problems of administration and control would be dealt with throughout the course. I would pay special attention to curriculum theory, which, more than any other area, justifies education's claim to be considered a distinct discipline. Through knowledge in this area we can demonstrate that education is the prime and arguably the only discipline mainly concerned with what to learn, how to learn, and what it means to have learned something. It also is the only discipline likely to do justice to the vital role of education in social and intellectual life. For example, in her latest work, THE TROUBLED CRUSADE, Diane Ravitch gives a superb account of the crucial issues in American education since World War II, including the students' disruption of their own universities, the increased involvement of the courts in education, the fall in intellectual standards, and the ongoing struggle between the view that the prime task fo formal education is to transmit a common body of knowledge and values and the view that education is a vehicle for social change. The chances of this remarkable book's even being studied outside courses in education are slim. Yet it is one of the dozen or so books published in recent years with which students and faculty alike should be familiar, whatever their speciality, since they all are involved in education.

If undergraduates acquired nothing more, they would benefit from at least one course that explained in some depth what the intellectual experiences of their college careers involved. Most undergraduates seem quite ignorant of the many meanings of such terms as thinking, learning, knowing, and analyzing. One question frequently asked by even my best students is, What is a concept? What does it mean to conceptualize? Many of you have experienced the incredulity with which even graduate students greet the news that there are half a dozen different ways of knowing and similarly of learning. My students never have failed to be impressed, for example, with Harry Broudy's essay "mastery." It outlines some nine steps in the process of mastery learning, from mere repetition to the final step of creating new knowledge on the basis of what has been learned. This is light years removed from the study of learning in psychology.

I offer my syllabus simply as an illustration of the ideas I have presented this evening. Any syllabus, however, should take into account the reasons I have given for making education a discipline in its own right. It is painfully clear that while we are constrained to draw on other disciplines, we have come to depend on them too much. We have said, for example, that the best educational philosopher, psychologist, historian, sociologist, is one who got his or her degree in the related discipline rather than in education. We have hired such people with little or no teaching experience at the pre-college level and slight knowledge of differences between their discipline and education. Yet when did you last hear of other departments appointing an educationist to their staff? We have a serious problem here: specialists in other disciplines are taking jobs away from specialists in education, and we remain unconcerned. I am a philosopher but I also am a worker and a businessman, and I am concerned about the fate of education both as a discipline and a profession. As such, I propose some sort of collective agreement, to the effect that all future appointments in education of specialists in other disciplines be contingent on a similar number of appointments of educationists in related disciplines. I have no hard data to prove my point, but I would wager that with this agreement in force, places for over a hundred educationists would become available that now are awarded to interlopers from other disciplines.

Granted, my syllabus embraces a broad range of subject matter; but I see a first course as an overall introduction to the basics of a discipline of education rather than as a selection of topics limited by a particular teacher's academic background. To the shame of our profession, many teachers have built their syllabi around their dissertation topic, or special interest, or around material from popular paperbacks dealing mostly with problems of immediate and short-term interest. My syllabus may not appeal to such teachers, but for quality of content and intellectual rigor it matches any syllabus in the university curriculum. Again I must stress that the subject matter I propose is not limited to, or even geared toward, the preparation of teachers, any more than courses in sociology are intended to prepare social workers, or courses in English to prepare writers and journalists. The purpose of courses in the discipline of education is to provide knowledge and understanding of education and to challenge students of all specialities to think more deeply and more imaginatively about education as a highly desirable part of their academic experience. There would be an added benefit. Some excellent students not originally planning to be teachers might decide to become candidates, thus broadening the base for selection and consequently raising the quality of our teaching personnel. This broadened base becomes all the more important when we consider that in the next ten years, according to the State Superintendent of Public Instruction, California alone will need 150,000 more teachers.

One final question: Should undergraduates be allowed to major in education? I used to reject the idea on the grounds that majors in education were or would be studying something essentially professional rather than theoretical and academic. But I now am convinced that such a major, organized as a discipline in its own right, is as good an academic major as any, and is eminently suitable for those who lean toward no particular subject. For such students, as well as for others, a major in education would have lasting value, if only because most students become parents interested in the education of their children, all become payers of school taxes, and many vote on educational issues. If those who publicly are concerned with educational matters were to study education formally, in the manner described here, I believe the intellectual level of debate would rise appreciably, and so, presumably, would the standard of schooling.

In my opening statement I said that my message was especially timely today. It is timely because educational reform once again has become the talk of the nation, with all sorts of people getting into the act. I can conceive of no more auspicious occasion for concerted action. Your colleagues now will be more amenable to change, and you should approach them when their resistance is low. I do not claim that my proposal is a panacea, but I hope I have shown that it is at least a step in the right direction—toward the enhancement of education as a mature, responsible, and autonomous university discipline, not in any way less deserving, and in some ways more deserving, then disciplines already in the curriculum.

False Premises, False Promises: The Mythical Character of Public Discourse About Education

Too many political and community leaders subscribe to images of reality that have little to do with the available evidence about the nature of public education, says Mr. Hawley. Consequently, our hopes for reform are jeopardized.

Willis D. Hawley

WILLIS D. HAWLEY (George Peabody College for Teachers of Vanderbilt University Chapter) is dean of the George Peabody College for Teachers and a professor of education and political science, Vanderbilt University, Nashville, Tenn.

CURRENT DEBATES about educational policy have an Alice in Wonderland quality to them. At all levels of government, too many political and community leaders seem to be both perpetrators and victims of images of "reality" and of probable futures that do not square with the best available evidence about what has happened in U.S. education and what strategies are most promising for improving it in the years to come.

Everyone concerned with improving schools rejoices in the attention that education has received over the last couple of years. At the same time, we should be concerned about whether the foundation of motives and beliefs on which new structures are being built can support the hopes being raised. False premises lead to false promises.

At the base of the education reform movement lies the conviction that the quality of U.S. public schools has deteriorated. As the National Commission

 From *Phi Delta Kappan*, November 1985, pp. 183-187. Reprinted by permission of Phi Delta Kappan and the author.

It is a short leap
from the belief that
schooling has worsened
to the conclusion that
the policy initiatives
of the immediate past
are the culprits.

on Excellence in Education put it, "We have, in effect, been committing an act of unthinking, unilateral educational disarmament." Virtually the only evidence cited by those who assert this decline is the admittedly long-lived drop in scores on the Scholastic Aptitude Test (SAT). But one purpose of the SAT is to assess students' capabilities to learn, rather than to judge what has been learned. Thus SAT scores, as the test's designers have always warned, are poor measures of school effectiveness.

Richer and more appropriate evidence on the overall success of our schools shows a more complicated and uneven picture of positive and negative changes in student performance over the last several years, depending on the subject in question and the age of the students being tested. In general, it appears that schools are more effective than they were a decade or two ago in the lower grades and for the top 5% to 10% of high school students but less effective for most students in the middle grades and in high school. The negative and positive changes are usually small in any case — 1% to 3% in each direction.[1] These modest changes seem to reflect changes in curricula and spending more than changes in basic capabilities. Moreover, the meaning of changes in test scores is unclear, because the differences in the student populations studied at different times are seldom taken into account in the analytical comparisons.

It does seem clear that high school students in the 1960s took more rigorous academic courses than did students of a generation later (though the "tightening" of the curriculum is now proceeding apace).[2] But if changes in the rigor of the curriculum explain many of the negative comparisons with earlier periods, this is a commentary on our goals — not on the effectiveness of

schools per se. It has gone almost unnoticed in the popular press and in the national reports on school reform that the population of U.S. secondary schools throughout the late Sixties and the Seventies was increasingly composed of students from low-income families, who tend to score lower on tests of achievement and aptitude than did the typical college-bound students who took the tests a generation ago. Moreover, this trend continues, which means that schools must improve just to keep their students' test scores from declining.

I want to be clear that I am not arguing that our schools are as good as they need to be. They are not. But the policy implications of the premise that our schools have fallen from some former state of grace are very different from those one would derive from belief that our schools, overall, are as good as they have been but that this is not good enough for the challenges we now face. In the first case, the solution lies in shaping up the schools, cutting out incompetence, and making incremental improvements. The view that we need to be better than our previous best, on the other hand, dictates that we worry less about defining limits and setting standards and more about investing in new capabilities and reshaping basic ways we go about the facilitation of student learning.

It is a short leap from the belief that schooling has worsened to the conclusion that the policy initiatives of the immediate past are the culprits. This in turn leads to the conviction that we cannot achieve quality and equity at the same time. To be sure, most of the national reports urging new commitments to excellence in education note that we must continue to serve the needs of all students. But the rhetoric is not matched by specific proposals. The truth is that, overall, efforts to improve equal educational opportunity have not failed, nor have they diminished the quality of other programs. Certainly our hopes that new educational programs would eliminate achievement differences and social inequalities have not been realized. But early childhood interventions,[3] compensatory education,[4] and programs for the handicapped[5] have improved the school performance and life chances of the children they serve. One *simple* indicator is that, in areas of the U.S. in which federal programs were most fully implemented, test scores have risen at a faster rate than in the rest of the nation.[6] Furthermore, the presence of

special programs in a school or classroom generally does not have a negative impact on the students who are not served by the program.[7] To be sure, there is debate about the efficacy of many programs for the disadvantaged and the handicapped, but it must be beyond dispute that we now know how to structure such programs so that, on average, they will be more effective than they have been in the past.

The idea that we have neglected the education of the gifted and talented because we have focused our efforts on low-achieving youngsters is another myth that does not fit the evidence. It is almost certain that more public money is spent on programs aimed at the most academically talented students today than a generation ago. For example, the proportion of students taking Advanced Placement courses has increased, as has the overall performance of these students on college placement tests.[8] And, as noted, the very top students today do as well on tests of ability and achievement as they ever did. The truth is that we have seldom addressed adequately the needs of the small proportion of our student population that is intellectually gifted.

If our high schools are our biggest problem — as most critics of the schools agree — it is worth noting that policies to insure equal educational opportunity (not including desegregation efforts) have been focused on elementary school students. Ah, but what about desegregation? Surely, as many of our political leaders assert, this is a policy that has diminished the overall quality of our schools. Wrong again.

The available research shows that minority youngsters more often than not benefit academically from desegregation and that white youngsters do not lose ground.[9] Moreover, the positive effects of school desegregation can be increased by helping teachers deal effectively with a diverse student population through such practices as cooperative learning, peer tutoring, and home-based reinforcement.[10]

And what do those who have experienced school desegregation have to say about it? Though one could never know by reading the popular press or listening to cocktail party conversations, *most* parents, both black and white, describe their children's experience in the schools to which they were bused in positive terms.[11] The first generation of youngsters to have experienced desegregation from the first grade on is just now entering college. Though they are increasingly unlikely to see themselves as liberals, a majority of them favor busing as a means to achieve desegregation.[12] In addition, the research shows that school desegregation tends to reduce racial prejudice and to increase racial integration of jobs, neighborhoods, and higher education.[13]

There are a number of other current misconceptions about public education that reduce our capacity — and disposition — to make sensible public policy. Let me add just a few more of my favorites:

• tracking and remedial pull-out programs help low-achieving youngsters develop self-esteem;[14]

• retaining children another year in a grade they have not mastered improves their achievement in the long run;[15]

• vocational education is important to the long-term job prospects and earnings of most youngsters who experience it;[16]

• we can prescribe curricula that teachers will not change when they do not understand or believe in the goals and substance of the prescriptions;[17]

• most parents have been or are unhappy with the public schools their children attend;[18]

• merit pay is an important management tool in private industry;[19]

• adding more time to the school day or the school year is a cost-effective way to improve student test scores;[20] and

• over the next few years, the demand by employers for more mathematicians, computer experts, and scientists will outstrip the capacity of our schools to educate such high-tech workers.[21]

As we will see below, this list of popular myths is in no way complete. Exceptions rather than rules seem to shape the images that dominate public discourse about education. In the arena of educational policy, just as in Alice's Wonderland, the distinction between fantasy and reality is difficult to determine. In such a world, sensible priorities for improving our schools are not easily established.

WHEN PUBLIC decisions are made on the basis of myths such as those outlined above, it should not be surprising that we end up with policies that are essentially regulatory and punitive (more tests, new course re-quirements, stricter state controls) rather than policies that fundamentally enhance the capacity of the schools to be productive. A case can be made, of course, for some standard-setting and for holding both students and teachers accountable. But such policies are limited and, ultimately, limiting, because they build neither new capabilities nor our confidence in public education.

If the aim of schooling is to produce learning, then the basic means of production is the teacher.[22] It follows that the reform movement should focus on enhancing the competence of teachers and fostering their effectiveness. This is not because teachers are the problem, but because schools can only be as good as those who teach in them. Moreover, in the next few years it seems almost inevitable that there will be a significant shortage of qualified teachers unless substantial changes in policy occur. Indeed, we already have shortages in many districts and in some fields. These problems will worsen, in part because of new reforms being proposed, such as class-size reductions and new course requirements. Without a good supply of qualified teachers these and other reforms will be empty promises. For example, given that we cannot staff the courses we now require, we can only be dismayed at new regulations in many states that increase the number of math courses students *must* take, since these regulations are usually unaccompanied by significant efforts to increase the supply of qualified math teachers.

What might be done to insure that our children will have good teachers? Several currently fashionable proposals hold little prospect of upgrading the teaching force. Merit pay plans, in themselves, will reward existing distributions of talent. The loan-forgiveness programs adopted by several states seem to be having little effect on the recruitment of more-able students to teaching.[23] Contrary to popular belief, increasing the number of subject-matter courses taken by undergraduates or increasing the time preservice teachers spend in conventional practice teaching will not increase teaching effectiveness in most cases.[24] Meanwhile, testing teachers' skills in reading, writing, and computing will help eliminate incompetence in these areas, but it will scarcely insure effective teaching.

Further evidence of our inability to confront reality and develop public policies that have some chance of improving the quality of our schools comes from the current agenda for improving teacher education. On the one hand, policy makers seem intent on defining what prospective teachers should study and on setting minimum standards for academic performance. On the other hand, the dominant proposal coming from teacher educators would add another year — sometimes two — of preentry training to the requirements for becoming a teacher. These proposals, which are being made in the face of an impending shortage of teachers, will almost certainly reduce the quantity — and perhaps the quality — of those who enter teaching. Moreover, the advocates of extended programs often seek substantial subsidies from the government in order to *maintain* the numbers and level of aptitude of current teaching candidates. But the cost to the public of such subsidies could easily exceed $3 billion a year, and there is not a shred of evidence that this investment will improve student learning.[25]

WHAT STRATEGIES for improving education *do* hold promise? We have three types of choices. First, we can significantly increase teacher salaries. Second, we can improve the effectiveness of teachers, especially by creating working conditions that are conducive to good teaching. Third, we can rethink the way we structure the teaching profession.

It seems unlikely that we will do what needs to be done to improve teacher salaries significantly. A major impediment to making the necessary commitment may be the widespread, but unsubstantiated, belief that those who enter teaching today are much less academically able than their counterparts a decade or more ago. Most of the evidence on this point derives from studies showing that the SAT scores of 18- and 19-year-olds who say that they wish to teach have declined more rapidly than the scores of their peers who say that they wish to pursue other professions. But this evidence tells us little about the abilities of those who actually teach. First, there is no meaningful relationship — at least so far as research can tell — between teaching effectiveness and scores on the SAT or similar tests.[26] Second, more than 50% of the high school seniors who express an interest in teaching never receive a teaching certificate; the least able of these students never complete college, and students who transfer into teacher preparation programs during college are appreciably more talented academically than the majority of those who drop out.[27] Third, because there has been a teacher surplus for some time, most school systems have been able to screen out the least able of those who are certified to teach. I do not wish to labor this point, but we have here another example of the myth-spreading character of public discourse about education that contributes to the propensity of public policies to reflect and communicate fear and anxiety rather than pride and confidence.

Teacher salaries, which have never been good, have declined in recent years relative to the average salaries of other professional occupations.[28] (That there is no clear evidence of a decline in the quality of teaching speaks volumes about teachers' commitment to their work.) A sense of impending doom may lead us to improve teacher salaries somewhat in some states. Indeed, many of the states that have recently taken action to improve teacher salaries are at the bottom of the average salary rankings. But optimism, not a sense of doom, is the only way to justify the size of the investment that is necessary to raise the status of the teaching profession to the level we say we want for it. Current talk about the need to increase teacher salaries does not begin to match ambition with commitment.

Paul Peterson estimates that, if teacher salaries are to keep pace with inflation and with expected salary increases in other professions and at the same time to regain the relative salary position teachers held in 1970 (which wasn't all that good), average teacher salaries in current dollars would have to increase by 36%.[29] This calculation parallels a recent study by Charles Manski, showing that, to bring the minimum combined SAT score of teachers up to 1,000 — a figure that a good many reformers say they want to attain — teacher salaries would have to increase by 35% to 40%.[30]

It is doubtful that the nation is willing to pay such costs. The public school population is becoming poorer, and fewer households than ever before have school-age children. Moreover, the myth that our teachers are not as bright as they used to be diminishes the likelihood that salaries will be increased or that such minimal increases as occur will attract candidates who have other, more attractive career options.

Unfortunately, what is now myth may soon seem like prophecy. Although the academic quality of those who have recently *entered* teaching is probably not much different from the academic quality of those who taught today's policy makers, this will surely change as the emerging teacher shortage reaches dire proportions. Not only will school systems have fewer good prospects among whom to choose, but the states — as they have always done in past periods of shortage — will lower their standards. If we assume that we will not make the needed investment to make teacher salaries truly competitive, it is all the more important to consider how teaching can otherwise be made more attractive to able candidates.

A second strategy we could pursue to improve teaching is to improve the conditions under which teachers teach. Among other things, this would require transferring nonteaching tasks to others, insuring order in the schools, increasing peer interaction, and linking valid evaluation of teacher performance to opportunities for professional improvement. These strategies should be augmented by involving parents in their children's education and developing more competent school administrators. In these and other ways we could encourage teachers to teach their best, but such strategies by and large have not been the focus of the policy agendas of most governments or a part of the texts of the numerous national and state commission reports.

The third way we might try to improve teaching would be to restructure the teaching profession. Some movement has already taken place in the creation of career ladder plans and the provision of easy entry to the profession for talented people who might be interested in short-term teaching positions. These steps are significant, but they may not go far enough.

It may be necessary to move away from the idea that all teachers start at the same point and have the same general mix of responsibilities throughout their careers. It may be necessary to find different ways of preparing individuals to teach that rely more heavily on internships, to differentiate salaries by field, and to allocate more resources to the professional development of those teachers who show both a commitment to and an aptitude for teaching. If we want to attract able people to teaching, we will have to provide them with opportunities to shape their work and be adaptive, things that may be difficult to do if teacher evaluation systems embody narrow definitions of effective teaching. If we are going to raise teach-

> The central task of educational improvement is to increase the capacity of the schools to be better than they have ever been.

er salaries significantly, we will find it necessary to be more selective about the conditions under which we reduce class size and to look to technology to increase productivity. If increased productivity is to lead to higher salaries, we may have to measure productivity in terms of learning, so that students can advance academically without the constraints of the graded structure of schools.

Let me conclude by restating my argument. We pay so little attention to the available evidence about the nature of school problems that we have cause to fear for the future of public education. The promises we make to ourselves about what we ought to do for the schools often are not accompanied by financially feasible proposals that research and experience suggest have a reasonable chance of bringing about the changes we seek. To the extent that the public and its elected representatives see the public schools as a disaster made worse by the things we have tried to do in pre-reform years, it seems likely that further regulation — in the form of tests, rules, oversight, etc. — will be the dominant reform strategy. Like the investor who perceives that an industry has become less productive, taxpayers may show little willingness to invest money or time in schools that they believe show little promise of achieving excellence.

The central task of educational improvement is to increase the capacity of the schools to be better than they have ever been. If we do not succeed, the reform movement will have been a failure. But few will blame the reformers; most will blame the schools. If that happens, not only will the so-called window of opportunity close, but the foundation of public education will have been weakened — perhaps beyond repair.

1. PERCEPTIONS OF EDUCATION IN AMERICA

1. Archie E. Lapointe, "The Good News About American Education," *Phi Delta Kappan*, June 1984, pp. 663-67; F. Joe Crosswhite et al., *Second International Mathematics Study: Summary Report for the United States* (Washington, D.C.: National Center for Education Statistics, May 1985); Willard J. Jacobson and Rodney L. Doran, "The Second International Science Study: Results," *Phi Delta Kappan*, February 1985, pp. 414-17; and Gilbert Austin and Herbert Garber, *The Rise and Fall of National Test Scores* (New York: Academic Press, 1982).

2. Daniel P. Resnick and Lauren B. Resnick, "Standards, Curriculum, and Performance: A Historical and Comparative Perspective," *Educational Researcher*, April 1985, pp. 5-20; and *On Further Examination: Report of the Advisory Panel on the Scholastic Aptitude Test Score Decline* (New York: College Board, 1977).

3. Irving Lazar and Richard B. Darlington, *Lasting Effects After Preschool: A Report of the Consortium for Longitudinal Studies, Final Report* (Denver: Education Commission of the States, October 1978).

4. Benjamin D. Stickney and Virginia R. L. Plunkett, "Closing the Gap: A Historical Perspective on the Effectiveness of Compensatory Education," *Phi Delta Kappan*, December 1983, pp. 287-90; Launor F. Carter, *A Study of Compensatory and Elementary Education: The Sustaining Effects Study, Final Report*, Vol. V (Santa Monica, Calif.: Systems Development Corporation, January 1983); and H. Carl Haywood, "Compensatory Education," *Peabody Journal of Education*, July 1982, pp. 272-300.

5. James J. Gallagher and Rune Simeonsson, "Educational Adaptations for Handicapped Children," *Peabody Journal of Education*, July 1982, pp. 301-22.

6. Roy Forbes, "Test Score Advances Among Southeastern Students: A Possible Bonus for Government Intervention?," *Phi Delta Kappan*, May 1981, pp. 332-35.

7. William W. Cooley and Gaea Leinhardt, "The Instructional Dimensions Study," *Educational Evaluation and Policy Analysis*, vol. 2, 1980, pp. 7-25; and Michael A. Knapp et al., *Cumulative Effects of Federal Education Policy on Schools and Districts* (Menlo Park, Calif.: SRI International, 1983).

8. Resnick and Resnick, "Standards, Curriculum, and Performance. . . ."

9. Robert Crain and Rita Mahard, "Research on Minority Achievement in Desegregated Schools," in Christine Rossell and Willis D. Hawley, eds., *The Consequences of School Desegregation* (Philadelphia: Temple University Press, 1983), pp. 103-25.

10. Willis Hawley et al., *Strategies for Effective Desegregation* (Lexington, Mass.: D. C. Heath, 1983).

11. Louis Harris, "Majority of Parents Report School Busing Has Been Satisfactory Experience," *Chicago Tribune*, 26 March 1981. Similar Harris surveys in 1979 and 1983 show similar findings.

12. Cited in *Higher Education and Public Affairs*, 28 January 1985.

13. Janet W. Scholfield and H. A. Sagar, "Desegregation, School Practices, and Student Race Relations Outcomes," in Rossell and Hawley, pp. 58-102; and Jomills Henry Braddock II, Robert L. Crain, and James M. McPartland, "A Long-Term View of School Desegregation: Some Recent Studies of Graduates as Adults," *Phi Delta Kappan*, December 1984, pp. 259-64.

14. Willis Hawley and Susan Rosenholtz, "Good Schools: What Research Says About Improving Student Achievement," *Peabody Journal of Education*, Summer 1984, pp. 76-77, 94-96.

15. C. Thomas Holmes and Kenneth M. Matthews, "The Effects of Nonpromotion on Elementary and Junior High School Pupils: A Meta-Analysis," *Review of Educational Research*, Summer 1984, pp. 225-36.

16. National Commission for Employment Policy, *The Federal Role in Vocational Education: Sponsored Research* (Washington, D.C.: National Commission for Employment Policy, 1981).

17. Hawley and Rosenholtz, pp. 101-3.

18. See the annual Gallup Polls published each September in the *Phi Delta Kappan*.

19. Edward Lawler, *Pay and Organizational Development* (Reading, Mass.: Addison-Wesley, 1981).

20. Henry Levin, "About Time for Educational Reform," *Educational Evaluation and Policy Analysis*, Summer 1984, pp. 151-63; and Nancy Karweit, "Should We Lengthen the School Term?," *Educational Researcher*, June/July 1985, pp. 9-15. 9-15.

21. Russell W. Rumberger, *The Potential Impact of Technology on the Skill Requirements of Future Jobs*, Project Report No. 84-A24 (Stanford, Calif.: Institute for Research on Educational Finance and Governance, November 1984); and Higher Education Panel, *Student Quality in the Sciences and Engineering: Opinions of Senior Academic Officials* (Washington, D.C.: American Council on Education, March 1984).

22. If this point needs justification, see Hawley and Rosenholtz, Chap. 1.

23. Irene K. Spero, "The Use of Student Financial Aid to Attract Prospective Teachers: A Survey of State Efforts," testimony before the Subcommittee on Postsecondary Education, Committee on Education and Labor, U. S. House of Representatives, 31 July 1985.

24. Carolyn Evertson, Willis D. Hawley, and Marilyn Zlotnik, "Making a Difference in Educational Quality Through Teacher Education," *Journal of Teacher Education*, May/June 1985, pp. 2-12.

25. This argument is developed more fully in Willis D. Hawley, "Breaking Away: More of Something a Little Better Is Too Much and Not Enough," in Eva Galambos, ed., *New Directions in Teacher Education* (San Francisco: Jossey-Bass, forthcoming).

26. Evertson, Hawley, and Zlotnik, "Making a Difference. . . ."

27. Thomas A. Lyson and William M. Falk, "Recruitment to School Teaching: The Relationship Between High School Plans and Early Adult Attainments," *American Educational Research Journal*, Spring 1984, pp. 181-93; and *Tomorrow's Teachers* (Washington, D.C.: Applied Systems Institute, January 1985).

28. Linda Darling-Hammond, *Beyond the Commission Reports: The Coming Crisis in Teaching* (Santa Monica, Calif.: Rand Corporation, July 1984).

29. Paul E. Peterson, *Economic and Political Trends Affecting Education*, paper presented to the Association of Colleges and Schools of Education in State Universities and Land-Grant Colleges and Affiliated Private Universities, Denver, February 1985.

30. Charles F. Manski, *Academic Ability, Earnings, and the Decision to Become a Teacher: Evidence from the National Longitudinal Study of the High School Class of 1972*, Working Paper 1539 (Cambridge, Mass.: National Bureau of Economic Research, January 1985).

The Fourth R: The Repatriation of the School

Brigitte Berger

Brigitte Berger is Professor of Sociology at Wellesley College. This article is taken from Challenge to American Schools: The Case for Standards and Values, *edited by John H. Bunzel. Copyright © 1985 by Oxford University Press, Inc.*

It is an undeniable fact that parents all over the world, regardless of race, ethnicity, religion, and social class, are concerned with the well-being and progress of their children. No other social concern activates and, at times, even enrages people more than this. Across all cultures and throughout history parents have gone to great and extraordinary lengths to search for what they deem to be optimal or, at least, tolerable situations for their children to grow up and prosper in. American parents are no exception to this rule. In twentieth-century America parental preoccupations with the welfare and advancement of their children have been linked in a singularly close, albeit ambivalent, way to schools as the most decisive instrument for the realization of these expectations and hopes.

For this reason the short shrift given to the role of the family in the most recent commotion over the dismal state of the nation's school is a puzzling omission in the rousing call for the reform of schools, the reaffirmation of excellence, and the restoration of discipline. To be sure, amid the outpouring of reports, books, and articles on the current crisis in American education, one still comes across the customary genuflection before this much abused social institution. Supreme Court pronouncements, presidential speeches, and sundry statements from the non-elite press of the nation are replete with declarations about the primary role of parents in the upbringing of their children. Yet to the powerful axis of educators, policymakers, and pundits of the media—a formidable political-education establishment, by any measure—the affirmation of the family's role in the education of its children is more of an embarrassment than a serious recommendation. Although more conservative groups are straining to revive the role of parents in education, they have little to offer beyond attempts to resurrect a more pragmatic education ideology and to channel negligible tax sums in their direction.

 n this case as in others, it seems sufficient for those who dominate the public discourse to pay ritualistic obeisance to a dimly remembered ideal. To the "real" task at hand, however, the family is held to be largely inadequate and irrelevant. The insistence upon the pivotal role of families in the education of their children—a view maintained by a minuscule group of public individuals, in any event—is quickly shunted aside, ridiculed, and conveniently labeled hopelessly reactionary, if not worse. This contradiction between paying lip service to the importance of the family and the continued disregard of its role in education runs through most of the current publications and discussions. The national attention is fixated on forces active in the system of public education. Reform is firmly linked to visible, clearly identifiable educational measures that, it is hoped, will make a difference: curricular reform, length of school periods, teacher competence, and the means to be provided by the government to finance all of this. The customary politicalization of any and all issues of critical importance has served to polarize the discussion of these measures as well. In the public debate the battlelines have been drawn between the education establishment, on the one hand, and a loose, not fully crystallized coalition of more conservative groups, on the other. They are interlocked in constant battles over education ideology, jurisdiction, legislation, and public funding. In such a struggle the family figures only marginally. This may be partly due to dismal experiences in recent attempts to use or, sometimes, to circumvent or replace the family in public policy efforts. It may also be partly due to the intractable nature of the family. Hence, it typically serves as a convenient legitimation for whatever point happens to be on the political agenda. The situation created in this manner, however, tends to obfuscate what has always moved and continues to move the large majority of Americans to

whom the education of their children is neither a liberal nor a conservative issue.

In what follows, I shall argue that the role of the family has been sorely misunderstood and misinterpreted. What has been misconstrued in particular is the past and present role of the middle-class—or, in the European use of the term, bourgeois—family. Variously described as a victim as well as a culprit, it has been deplored and vilified. The middle-class family is neither victim nor culprit. More than any other social institution, it has been the carrier of modernization. Insofar as modern industrial, democratic society is inextricably entwined with this kind of family, a convincing argument can be made that the perpetuation of our free and active society requires its persistence. It has been accepted that education, and a particular kind of education to boot, plays a vital role in all of this. It has yet to be more adequately recognized that education in and for our kind of society is peculiarly dependent upon those sentiments, behaviors, and values that typically arise and are fostered in the cultural milieu of the middle-class family.

I shall argue, too, that this kind of family has persisted despite the many attempts to weaken and to dismantle it. In fact, the middle-class family today continues to thrive in all walks of life, albeit in a more or less unofficial fashion. Its ethos, it practices, and its values are recognized to be beneficial, and they remain the norm for the great majority of Americans—ethnic, black, "old stock," and immigrant. They are certainly appreciated by those disgruntled and despondent parents who are alienated from the wasteland of the public schools. There are persuasive reasons why this is so.

Finally, I shall try to show that there exists good evidence that the link between educational success and the values and practices characteristic of middle-class family life has already been made by the many parents who try either to gain greater control over what goes on in public education today or to seek refuge in private schools. The increased attractiveness of private schools to the affluent sector of America's cities and suburbs, the continued, though troubled, allegiance of ethnic Americans to parochial schools,

the attraction of parochial schools for non-Catholic inner-city minorities, the mushrooming of Christian "alternative" schools in various regions of the country, and the not-to-be-underestimated and growing number of "survival" and "grass-roots" schools in the minority sector of American society are all symptoms of this trend. It may well be that a parental revolt against proposals of school reform that disregard the parents' role is not merely a fantasy of pessimists.

Recent scholarly research examining the vast transformations that have taken place in the societies of the West has illuminated the degree to which these cataclysmic changes in the economy, polity, and social structure are rooted in the life of the Western nuclear family.[1] Comprising only parents and their children, it was small and mobile enough to allow individuals to participate in the modernization process; at the same time, it was tightly knit enough to make this participation humanly tolerable. Amid a general separation between the public sphere of work and politics and the private sphere of the family, a domestic life of the family was invented in which concern for individual members, and in particular for children, moved into the foreground. A socialization pattern emerged that is characterized by a close relationship between parents and children, greater parental influence, and a greater emphasis upon individualization. Long before the enthronement of modern society, the Western nuclear family fostered mind-sets and values that were instrumental in bringing about the modernization of economic, political, and social institutions. Above all, it fostered far-reaching changes in human consciousness. So, for instance, "rationalization," one of modernization's driving forces, may be sought in the patterns of socialization of such a family.

This process occurred in western Europe over a period of a few hundred years.[2] It has by now become part and parcel of the history of modernization. It can show how the family and the economy changed in tandem and how the individual was liberated from traditional confines inside and outside of the family. This kind of historical scholarship can further demonstrate how the new family sensibilities and values merged with new ideas of property in the rise and eventual domina-

tion of the middle class as a new social stratum. It should be noted that during the period of consolidation of the middle-class structure, the new family ethos was often linked to religion: to Puritanism, Presbyterianism, and, later, Methodism in England and in the American colonies; to Calvinism and Jansenism in France; to Pietism in Germany.

At least since the late eighteenth century, the history of the West is, in a very basic sense, the history of the middle classes and its culture. The great historical transformations of the subsequent two centuries, which, in aggregate, have produced what we call modernity, have been overwhelmingly the product of this class. Since the triumph of the middle class (in the major countries of the West, that is), this class and its culture have been identified with the status quo, against which any rebel worthy of his salt tried to define himself. It is therefore important to understand the revolutionary character of this class and of the type of family that is its carrier.

The middle-class family was an institution—in the nineteenth century as well as in subsequent years—uniquely suited both to providing a "haven" and sustenance for its members and to socializing and motivating them for participation in the many activities in the larger society. Linked to this was the concern for education, both as a general social value and as something for one's own children. It should be added that the effective raising and educating of children became *the* great mission of this type of family. Everything had to be organized, planned, and executed in accordance with this mission. Since the "bourgeois virtues" originating in the middle-class household are also central to education, a few words may be necessary here. It can be agreed that hard work, discipline, diligence, attention to detail, and a systematic cultivation of willpower are core elements of middle-class culture. Others are decency, reliability, politeness, respect, and fairness. Some of these virtues appear maudlin to the modern mind. Perhaps they should not.

Since all of these elements of this new sensibility are based upon a pronounced individualism, there always exists the potential for their distortion or radicalization once the constraining and balancing influences of family and religion are removed. As the many opponents of the middle class never cease to point out, the same traits described here in positive and beneficial terms may well turn into something very different: selfishness, pettiness, narrowness, avarice, competitiveness, bigotry, oppressiveness, and philistinism. Such an escalation, as I have argued in a different context, is precisely what happened in recent decades.[3] What previously was held in balance now appear to be sets of irreconcilable alternatives: rigid stability against mindless innovation, crass egotism against self-abandonment to a community, adventurism without moral constraint (taking *all* risks) against fearful passivity legitimated by an absolutist morality (willing to take *no* risks at all) and so on. With this loss of balance, the enormous civilization-building power of the middle classes is undermined and threatened, and the very notion of a middle-class society is thrown into question.

At the same time, in spite of these ever-present dangers, it should also be recognized that the middle-class family has a unique potential to provide the social context for the formation of stable personalities ("strong characters") and autonomous individuals, who are ready for innovation and risk taking in a society undergoing historically unprecedented transformations. It also has the potential to provide a balance between individualism and social responsibility, between "liberation" and strong communal ties, between acquisitiveness and altruism.

There is one further dimension that has to be emphasized here: these middle-class virtues are, in principle, accessible to everyone. No one social class or group can be the sole proprietor of hard work, discipline, frugality, and willpower. The opposite vices —idleness, intemperance, and self-indulgence—can also be avoided by anyone who sets his mind to it. In other words, the bourgeois ethos, reinforced by strong religious morality, was from the beginning a democratic and egalitarian one. These were precisely the virtues that the middle-class family sought to inculcate forcefully in its children, and it is a peculiarly shortsighted vision that perceives the forcefulness of this socialization as "authoritarian" or "repressive."

A good argument can be made that the acceptance of the middle-class ethos by large numbers of people was crucial to their move up the social ladder. The social mobility patterns of the industrial societies of the West during the past one hundred years give further evidence to the legitimacy of this claim. It is not surprising, therefore, that those today who are concerned with the future of their children continue to abide by the middle-class ethos, in spite of the many countervailing trends. It may also not be accidental that this ethos finds particular resonance among the working class, among the lower-middle class and immigrants, and, of late, among a sizable segment of America's minorities as well. Convinced that social mobility is won through personal efforts, the great majority of Americans today cite parental encouragement, a good education, ambition, and plain hard work as keys to success.[4] Most ordinary Americans are still convinced that the traditional middle-class family life provides the best context for the development of the desired personality traits. The middle-class family and its values are still perceived as an important and necessary precondition for success in education and life.

It is important to understand that many of the forces of modernization have been particularly unkind to the family. Gradually at first, yet with increasing rapidity in the course of the twentieth century, the family was removed from the central position it had once held, and was demoted to an ever-more subordinate place. This demotion process becomes dramatically visible in the area of education. To be sure, the transformation of the economy robbed the family household of its traditional integrative basis; and urbanization, the apogee of the modernizing process, had lasting consequences for the patterns of human habitation and interaction as well. But the growing process of institutional differentiation that stripped the family of its earlier unchallenged functions in the nurture, care, and socialization of its individual members, and the concomitant transfer of ever-larger chunks of its socializing and educational tasks to institutions outside of it as well as increasingly beyond its control, presented the family with the most massive challenge yet.

It may well be argued that the expansion and eventual autonomy of the eduational system is part and parcel of the modernizing process. The increasing sophistication of the core elements of modern society demand a high level of preparation and education on the part of its citizens. In view of the family's limitations in meeting these essential tasks, a highly specialized and professionalized educational system becomes necessary. However, the complexities of the American situation, accentuated by the great variety of cultural, ethnic, racial, and religious groupings, determined this process to a considerable degree. The real and assumed needs of the children of immigrant families and groups held to be "marginal" to American society have always been the special focus of American schools, be they public, parochial, or private. Above all, the emphasis on equality that is deeply ingrained in the American experience charges education and the schools with becoming, in Horace Mann's words, "the great equalizers of the conditions of man." The paramount purpose of American schools, and of the public schools in particular, many contend, is to liberate children from the emotional, intellectual, and moral confines of their family background. It may thus be argued that an increase in equality of opportunity is directly related to a decrease in the power of the family over its members.

This is not the place to recapitulate the philosophy and history of the American public schools.[5] In the context of the argument pursued here, it need only be observed that as the twentieth century unfolded, the antifamily thrust in education became more and more pronounced. No later than the early 1960s, this thrust received powerful reinforcements from a variety of concerns about the ability of an open society like ours to raise its children for today and for the future. It was argued that in an ever-more industrialized and specialized American society the family had fewer and fewer chances to socialize and prepare its children and adolescents. In particular, as they found themselves spending larger chunks of their days and longer periods of their lives in educational institutions with other youngsters of the same age, they became increasingly susceptible to the actions and approval of other youngsters of the same age with whom they shared life in this separate social structure, cut off from adult society and far removed from adult responsibilities. At the same time, it became evident that this peer society was dominated by a distinct culture, characterized by its own norms and expectations. As a consequence, many observers agreed, the home receded in importance in the life of the young. Parents were diagnosed to have fewer abilities to mold their children. In this socialization vacuum, in which children were largely left to be brought up by their peers in an atmosphere pervaded by subtle opposition to the norms of adult society, the process of "making human beings human" was held to be on the verge of breakdown. The need to counter these destructive tendencies became a priority on the national agenda of the early 1960s. The proposals that emerged varied in their emphases.

Educators felt increasingly inclined to take adolescent society as a given and use it to further the ends of education. This soon extended to younger children as well. Since children and adolescents spent much of their time in educational institutions anyway, the locale of the school and a school curriculum constructed around a "society of peers" was considered by many to be a fortunate instrument. Some thought it still worthwhile to involve parents in a yet-to-be-constructed socialization model for America's children.[6] The Head Start program, initiated at about that period, may serve as a case in point. Regardless of emphasis, however, a general turning away from the family became a widely accepted reality, if not among parents, then at least

among the intellectual elite of the country. For a while it seemed as though American schools were turned into immense laboratories. The result of all these activities in behalf of the nation's young amounted to nothing less than an all-out attack against the family's socialization activities.

The factors determining the success or failure of a family in the socialization of its children are so subtle and intangible that they become practically indiscernible. One difficulty in assessing the family's role in education arises from the existence of a voluminous and controversial body of literature, which makes it almost impossible to arrive at unequivocal answers. In reviewing some of this literature, one is struck by the vagueness about the process by which parental behavior is linked to educational effects in even the best of research.[7] When it comes to the bulk of the literature, one is inclined to observe that measures to get at the "intangibles" in parental behavior are often crude and unsophisticated. Furthermore, it is frequently unclear what precisely is being measured. In this case as in others, fuzzy studies, unsecured theories, and competing and contradictory intellectual frames of reference make for a confusing situation. This is not to say that there has been some sort of conspiracy against the family on the part of researchers. But as hosts of researchers began to put the many socialization functions of the family under close scrutiny, it was found to be wanting in virtually every respect. The family now was questioned in the totality of its functions in general, and in its formal as well as informal ones in particular.

Formal functions are those that include the physical protection of children, their feeding, clothing, and supervision. Of the many informal functions, ranging from emotional solace and sustenance to mutual affection, sympathetic understanding, and similarly benign sentiments, the most important ones within this context are those discussed earlier: the inculcation of cognitive propensities, and of all those emotions and motivations that are customarily linked to success in school and beyond. Ethnic and racial minorities and "the poor" in particular, with their distinct family arrangements and pronounced cultural mil-

ieus, were soon declared to be defective and in need of intervention. But middle-class families, too, were examined and found to be inadequate and, in some instances, even destructive of their children. There soon emerged a general public perception that in a rapidly changing world the American family was no longer able to protect and socialize its children. In a society like America that is propelled by strong impulses toward doing good, particularly when the welfare of children is at stake, public perceptions are soon translated into policy. Whereas in earlier decades social policies related to poor and weak families had been aimed at assisting them to care for their children, now the family as an institution became the target. Programs originally designed to aid families were increasingly replaced by ones that sought to find substitutes for the family and finally to replace it. To be sure, there were many other forces working against the family as well. For example, the liberating feminism turned women away from home and children, and the shift in sentiments within the intellectual elite and America's suburban upper-middle class signicantly added to the attack against the family.

It is very difficult to identify those aspects of family life and family practices that make a difference in the socialization of a child and to estimate the extent of the difference. Many claims made in one frame of analysis are put into doubt, if not directly contradicted, in another. Moreover, what was frequently thought to be at issue at one point, ceases to be so at another. For instance, the small family, which had for many years been advocated and marketed by powerful agencies and programs as crucial for educational achievement, was later held responsible in the predicted rise of an increasingly "narcissistic" American personality type, one unable to relate, share, and cooperate. The discussion over the importance of a stable family underwent a similar shift. As ever-more homes were found to be unstable, broken, or in the process of breaking up, the "disastrous effects" of this situation upon children stirred the nation at midcentury. More recently, however, arguments—and, of course, data—have replaced the earlier discussion that now support the trend of "going it alone." And as befits such a shift in perception, there was a linguistic shift as well: debates over the "broken home" were conveniently reformulated into debates over the needs of "single parents." As questions about the implications of working mothers for their children moved into the forefront of public attention, as debates over "favorable" parental attitudes ("child-centered" or "disciplinarian") proliferated, as disputes over "proper" paternal roles ("companionable" or "authoritarian") became commonplace, and as, finally, issues over children's rights versus parental responsibility became a legal concern, the problematization and the politicalization of all aspects of family life reached a degree not previously known in American history. The very different political alignments that have emerged in America can marshal evidence in support of each issue on their distinct sociopolitical agendas.

Regarding "effective" parenting as a necessary preparation for success in school, it is quite clear by now that one should be very cautious about identifying effective parenting with kindly, understanding attitudes and practices that indulge the child. In so far as "effectiveness" has to do with educational achievement, ample data indicate that "good" students often come from demanding, rigid, and unreasoning homes! One might object at this point that parents have always known that home discipline and parental demands have something to do with a child's success in school and in life in general. They have applied all the methods available to them to socialize their children for what they think is appropriate behavior to this end. They have tried to be firm, shouted at them, cajoled them; they have applied "positive" as well as "negative" sanctions, to use Skinnerian terms, by withdrawing their allowance, by grounding them; and yes, they have even spanked them. In this, families have often resembled a battlefield. But what are parents to make of research that demonstrates that di-

sapproval tends to increase the likelihood that a child will show hostile behavior and that physical punishment increases the likelihood of social aggression? Moreover, what are parents to do when they are confronted by "experts" on child rearing with arguments that their customary methods are detrimental to their children and their future?

If it is already difficult for sophisticated researchers to sort out the many contradictory claims made, it certainly goes beyond the capacity of most parents to do so. In any event, the problematization of every family practice in the socialization of its young contributed in no small measure to a general public perception that the contemporary family was unable and unfit to carry out its important social task. It added fuel to the turmoil surrounding the "death of the family" debate flaunted by the ever-eager media from every newsstand. It also gave momentum to the rise and growth of the child care establishment conceived in a therapeutic mode—the legions of social workers, counselors, psychologists, and therapists that have become a part of every American school today. Intimating that schools and child care specialists know how to carry out the necessary socializing tasks and that families do not, that establishment transferred ever more of the traditional family functions to schools and child care specialists. The convenient alliance of therapists and educators that rapidly developed at this point soon began to confront the family as a massive hostile reality. All of these activities ultimately led to a diminution of the family's role and responsibility in the education of its children.

Together, these developments created havoc for the self-understanding of the family. Parents became increasingly uncertain about their child-rearing ability and their socializing practices; they lost self-confidence and became disoriented. As might have been expected, it was the child-centered middle-class family that became the principal captive of the educational-therapeutic complex, as a number of studies clearly demonstrate.[8] Anyone who has raised a child in the ghetto of America's suburbs can easily supplement academic findings with personal experience. The lower-class, inner-city family, on the other hand, tended to close

itself off against the massive intrusion into its life. To the bafflement of teachers and the many "friendly intruders" alike, these families developed into reluctant, commandeered consumers of those efforts and programs that went beyond the supply of direct material and financial aid. Parents and children felt disrespected, humiliated, and increasingly hostile toward all these efforts in their behalf.

The attack against the family's socializing and educational roles received an additional blow with the emergence of a variety of more overtly critical positions and radical movements in the late 1960s and early 1970s. Now it was no longer enough merely to uncover and illuminate the shortcomings of the family—and, by extension, those of the educational practices of American schools. Now the goals and values, the fundamental structure of modern Western society in general and of American society in particular became the primary issue. In other words, the problem was no longer a particular type of family—or educational system—held to be inadequate and malfunctioning; it was rather a "sick society," of which the "sick family" and an "ailing school" were integral parts. As the growing critique of Western industrial society sharpened into a critique of capitalism, the middle-class or bourgeois family and, by extension, a "bourgeois education" became primary objects of critical attention.

The policy positions emerging at this juncture focused on the fundamental reorganization of the larger structures of society. In the main they largely sought to bypass the family, just as they sought to bypass education when the failure to realize the increased expectations for education became obvious. Any attempt to reform or improve either was held to be futile as long as the system that had produced both remained in place.[9] The family policy proposals, like the education policy proposals, inspired by this vision sought to use the family and education as instruments for the fundamental reconstitution of Western capitalist society.

On the other hand, those critical policy positions that aimed at revolutionizing the institutions of the family and school concentrated on the transformation of the content as well as the style of socialization carried out within either institution. At issue here are the familiar bourgeois virtues that emphasize the acquisition of formal cognitive skills, that stress structure and discipline, and that seek to encourage achievement and success. Taken together, these virtues were thought to be "one-dimensional" deformations of what it means to be human. In a manner reminiscent of earlier criticisms of the estrangement of the school from the life of the working classes, it was now argued that schools that reflect the ethos of the dominant middle classes essentially serve to stifle and suppress the educational aspirations and achievement potential of lower-class children. Locked into the "cultural of poverty" of their families and ethnic groups, the children of America's poor were held to be neglected and forgotten by an ignorant and hostile school system. Experts, among whom the noted British scholar Basil Bernstein figured most prominently, proposed that if schools wished to be of use to the lower-class child, they would have to adapt to his particular mentality. The critique from within did not stop here. Inadvertently it became all-inclusive, a logical step, considering its revolutionary program. Family and school in capitalist society were declared to be destructive of all children, middle class as well as non-middle class. Powerful "saner" and "more human" countervisions of socialization and education soon became fashionable. The influential writings of A. S. Neill, particularly his book *Summerhill,* are perhaps the best-known, though by no means the only, all-inclusive critiques of the organization of personal life in capitalist society.

It is important to realize that the critical positions were verbalized in the main by a small coterie of intellectuals located in academe and in social policy institutions like the Carnegie Council. It gained momentum when the failure of the public schools became dramatically visible. As study after study was released and evidence

accumulated, it became increasingly evident that schools—no matter how hardworking and dedicated the teachers, no matter how adequate the physical facilities, no matter how well designed the curriculum, and no matter how much money spent to advance these aspects—failed to have substantial impact upon the performance and achievement of children. It became clear in particular that programs to bypass family disadvantages and to make a child's cultural background irrelevant, could not measure up to this task, and perhaps never would. It also became evident that the many attempts to reach this end had created havoc in the life of poor inner-city families—that is, precisely those people for whose benefit the interventionist programs had been developed in the first place. Targeted problems continued to persist, to multiply, and even to become magnified. The spreading dismay among many responsible educators over the failure of massive interventionist programs and attempts slowly gave way to what has been called a "post-reformist" stance of taking inventory and realistically rethinking the possibilities to reform American education. In this manner, the stage for rethinking the family's role in education had been set as well.

Taking stock of the realities that have emerged in what, in retrospect, amounted to a war of official society against the family's role in education, we today have the advantage of the larger view. The upheavals of the past decades can now be elucidated in a manner that escaped those who were actors in the events. We shall thus refrain from presenting a petty calculation of the costs of good intentions. In any event, the realities that have emerged stand in stark contrast to the beneficial rhetoric accompanying many of the efforts in behalf of children. Not only have many of the attempts to invest the therapeutically defined school with enormous tasks for which it seemed to be distinctly unsuited resulted in failure, but in the process of the transformation of their functions, schools have been diverted from their essential tasks. At the same time, efforts to take away from the family what is the family's have, in large measure, contributed to a dangerous weakening and, in some cases, an actual breakdown of the family. In the final analysis, we are

confronted with the paradox that schools, in attempting to bypass and supplant the family, have robbed themselves of their essential basis.

The inability of educators to accept the role of parents as an indispensable element in education may be the greatest obstacle to a more realistic assessment of what is possible and desirable. It has often been said that old dreams take long to die, particularly if material interests are vested in these dreams. The dream of equal opportunity for all Americans is a noble one. There is good evidence available today that many American parents have already taken steps to make equal educational opportunity more of a reality and less of a dream. Parents may go about it in different ways than educators and social planners, but they are not idle when it comes to the future of their children.

All through the war against the family, ordinary people continued to believe that the small, tightly knit, nuclear family unit, caring and mindful of children, was still the best guarantor of their children's future. They have struggled along unrecognized and largely unsupported. To be sure, the contemporary American family is no longer as stable and secure as it used to be. A considerable variety of arrangements—single parents, to-be-divorced parents, remarried, foster, and adoptive parents and grandparents—coexist with the more prevalent "typical" family of father and mother, well known to us. More often than not, these arrangements are dictated by necessity. All of these parents recognize that the student who fails in school often comes from a stressful home.[10] The normative value of the middle-class ethos is still accepted by the great majority of parents. In some cases, it has been reaccepted, though somewhat belatedly. The sizable number of American woman who support families on their own are no exception to this rule. Any researcher who cares to make an effort to ask "female heads of households" in the inner city about their aspirations for their children will be surprised by the degree of commitment to norms and standards associated with the old middle-class ethos.[11] Most parents agree on the value and the importance of their involvement in their children's education. Most of them regard schools as necessary, though inadequate. They also know that the real crisis in education lies in the abdication of parental responsibility. Different cultural, ethnic, and religious groups have different ways of coping with this essential task. Some try to establish greater control over what goes on in public schools; others may seek to take refuge in parochial and private educational institutions.

Parental influence on the education of a child in public schools can be more readily achieved in America's suburbs and small towns. Of late, American middle-class parents have become extraordinarily active when it comes to the educational advancement of their children. Looking after what they perceive to be in the best interests of their children, highly verbal middle-class parents, knowledgeable about their children's legal rights and skilled in using them to their advantage, have become the bane of many a small-sized school system. The battles of parents with school boards and administrators in small settings have by now taken on legendary proportions.[12]

Further evidence is beginning to accumulate on the progress of children in the public schools in America's inner cities. Black parents who believe that there is such a thing as a "good" school have begun to make enormous efforts to assure that their children can attend one.[13] The same evidence also shows that in the growing number of cases where parents have shifted their initial emphasis on racial balance to one on the quality of education and their ability to produce it, they have been strikingly successful in rehabilitating whole schools—and whole neighborhoods along with them.[14]

Other groups have turned to private schools that seem to be more adequately suited for the realization of their expectations for their children's education. The increased attractiveness of private schools to the affluent sector of America's cities and suburbs is a case in point.[15] Although parochial schools have recently encountered a number of problems (many flowing from demographic changes), none is

due to a decline in the belief in the importance of the middle-class ethos of parochial school—witness the attractiveness of parochial schools to non-Catholic inner-city minorities.[16] The mushrooming of Christian "alternative" schools, on the other hand, is propelled by more than just parental concern about the decline in learning. As Peter Skerry has cogently argued, these schools are based on the voluntarism that springs from deeply held religious beliefs. Their advocates protest the notion that a child is a mere creature of the state. These schools constitute about one-fifth of the total non-public school enrollment today and are largely composed of working- and lower-middle-class families. They are, perhaps, the most loyal adherents of the old middle-class ethos, which they perceive to be vital in the education of their children.[17]

Finally, there is the growing number of "survival" and "grass-roots" schools in the minority sector of American society. As the data gathered by the National Center for Neighborhood Enterprise suggest, these small independent schools—whose representatives first gathered in Washington, D.C., in 1983—claim to meet the academic and social needs of black, Hispanic, American Indian, and Asian American children, primarily in urban settings.[18] They all share the belief that they can do something better than the public schools. Each one of the roughly three hundred schools represented at the Washington meeting can point to a massive parental involvement as well as the development of strong academic curricula as their most distinctive features. Leery of public funding, they often struggle against enormous odds. But, as one participant observed, "that has never clouded the main issue of self-determination for our children."

There are clear signs that we are about to begin to form a better understanding of what aspects of schooling make a difference. At the same time, we are learning that those things that make a difference are the hardest to measure and manipulate. In *Fifteen Thousand Hours,* the British researcher Michael Rutter and his associates have provided us with some pointers.[19] Above all, they demonstrate beyond any doubt what many people have known for some time: schooling alone is just one of several factors in a

pupil's performance. "The child's own characteristics, his family, circumstances and home background, and his peer group also constitute substantial influences."[20] They emphasize the need for consistency between the values and practices of the home and those of the school. They show that discipline, standards, and the acceptance of norms originating in the family, when reinforced by a similar ethos in the school, make the best formula for an individual child's success.

 y the same token, we are about to learn that children continue to model their behavior on that of "significant" adults and that the influence of peer groups has perhaps been overestimated.[21] And a new breed of teachers and administrators on the local level is about to rediscover what an earlier generation of educators took for granted: a positive home environment that emphasizes parental understanding, parental control, and involvement is still the best precondition for a child's successful performance in school and life.

Amid the public dismay over the crisis in American education, there is reason to hope that the pattern of incremental change spearheaded by parents today in many small locales may eventually lead to necessary reforms. Admittedly, these efforts on the part of parents will be insufficient to be translated immediately and directly into a national ground swell. Lower-class parents will still have to learn how to become the best mediators for their children. They will still have to find the language and the method for exercising the responsibility they feel for their children. Those parents who already have started this trend may serve as an inspiration here.

The shared meanings of getting ahead and the vision of what is a good life in our pluralistic, open society are still firmly anchored in the social milieu of a family that, to a surprising degree, revolves around the old middle-class ethos. The vast majority of Americans, it would now seem, did not lose faith in the middle-class family and its ethos, but the American intellectual leadership did. And those who were confused and disheartened by the proliferation of attempts and programs that, perhaps inadvertently, weakened the family's role and responsibility in the socialization of children are beginning to realize that parents can and do make a difference in their children's prospects. Middle-American families—unfashionable, patriotic, industrious, and family-loving—may soon add the fourth R to education: The Repatriation of the School.

Footnotes

[1] See, e.g., the work of Peter Laslett, Anthony Wrigley, Alan Macfarlane, and Ferdinand Mount In England; Philippe Ariès, Jean-Louis Flandrin, and Emmanuel Le Rooy Ladurie in France; Lutz Berkner, Hans Meidick, Peter Liette, and Jürgen Schlumbohm in Germany; and Michael Mitterauer in Austria.

[2] This process has been brilliantly described by Philippe Ariès, *Centuries of Childhood: A Social History of Family Life* (New York: Knopf, 1962), and Peter Laslett, *The World We Have Lost* (New York: Scribner, 1965).

[3] Brigitte Berger and Peter Berger, *The War over the Family* (Garden City, N.Y.: Doubleday, 1983).

[4] Richard Coleman and Lee Rainwater, *Social Standing in America: New Dimensions of Class* (New York: Basic Books, 1978).

[5] See Diane Ravitch, *The Troubled Crusade: American Education, 1945-1980* (New York: Basic Books, 1983).

[6] James S. Coleman, *The Adolescent Society: The Social Life of the Teenager and Its Impact on Education* (Glencoe, Ill.: Free Press, 1961); Urie Bronfenbrenner, *Two Worlds of Childhood: U.S. and U.S.S.R.* (New York: Russell Sage, 1970).

[7] A good summary of the ambiguity of research can be found in Hope Jensen Leichter, ed., *The Family as Educator* (New York: Teachers College Press, 1974).

[8] See in particular John Seeley et al., *Crestwood Heights: A Study of the Culture of Suburban Life* (New York: Basic Books, 1956), which clearly demonstrates the middle-class family's relation to the schools.

[9] Examples of this type of attempt can be found in Christopher Jencks, *Inequality: A Reassessment of the Effects of Family and Schooling in America* (New York: Basic Books, 1972); Christopher Jencks et al., *Who Gets Ahead? The Determinants of Economic Success in America* (New York: Basic Books, 1979); Kenneth Keniston et al., *All Our Children: The American Family under Pressure* (New York: Harcourt Brace Jovanovich, 1977); Richard De Lone, *Small Futures: Children, Inequality, and the Limits of Liberal Reform* (New York: Harcourt Brace Jovanovich, 1979).

[10] The agreement on this point is wide among practitioners of child and youth care. Such divergent analysts as Ernest Boyer, Neil Postman, Robert Levine, Robert Hill, Andrew Billingsley, and Robert Coles have recently confirmed this premise.

[11] Robert Woodson of the National Center of Neighborhood Enterprise, Washington, D.C., has frequently brought together during the past few years inner-city women who are heads of household. The tapes and summaries of interviews are illuminating indeed. The materials that Robert Hill of the Bureau of Social Science Research, Washington, D.C., is currently collecting strongly support this claim as well.

[12] The school board meetings of the towns of Brookline, Newton, and Wellesley, Massachusetts, may serve as a typical reference here.

[13] J. S. Fuerst, "Report Card: Chicago's All-Black Schools," *Public Interest*, no. 64 (Summer 1981), pp. 79-91; Martin Kilson, "Black Social Classes and Intergenerational Poverty," ibid., pp. 58-78. See also the reports on George Washington Preparatory High School, in the Watts section of Los Angeles, as reported by Alfred S. Regnery at the Jan. 25, 1984, hearing of the Senate Committee on the Judiciary, Subcommittee on Juvenile Justice.

[14] In addition to the sources cited in note 13, see David L. Kirp, *Just Schools: The Idea of Racial Equality in American Education* (Berkeley: Univ. of California Press, 1982).

[15] James S. Coleman et al., *Public and Private Schools* (Washington, D.C.: NCES, 1981).

[16] See the various publications and research reports of Andrew Greeley for the National Opinion Research Center at the University of Chicago.

[17] Peter Skerry, "Christian Schools versus the I.R.S.," *Public Interest*, no. 61 (Fall 1980), pp. 18-41.

[18] National Center for Neighborhood Enterprise, Washington, D.C., Conference Report prepared by Joan Rafferty for the National Conference on Grass Roots Schools, 1983.

[19] Michael Rutter et al., *Fifteen Thousand Hours: Secondary Schools and Their Effects on Children* (Cambridge, Mass.: Harvard Univ. Press, 1979).

[20] Ibid., p. 168.

[21] See, e.g., reports on Peter L. Benson's (Search Institute, Minneapolis) research with 8,165 adolescents and 10,467 parents in 950 places, published by many daily papers around the country in Feb. 1984.

WHO
will teach the class of 2000 ?

An estimated 75,000 new elementary and junior high teachers begin their careers this month under unusual scrutiny. They're a generation of teachers who chose their profession while education was under fire. As they undertook teacher training, many of their colleges and universities were criticized for turning out low-caliber teachers. Some of their colleges scrambled to add last-minute requirements and test seniors' basic skills.

Even in states where the teacher shortage is acute, the new teachers are subject to political pressures and high public expectations. They'll be shaping teaching for decades to come, and they'll bear some of the responsibility for educating the kids who'll lead us all into the 21st century.

Who are these new teachers? What do they believe? What will they bring to their new profession? To find out, INSTRUCTOR surveyed more than 1,300 new elementary and junior high teachers as they completed work in 95 colleges and universities across America. Then INSTRUCTOR followed up with 25 in-depth telephone interviews, and a collective portrait emerged.

As you might expect, the new

This fall,* for the first time in more than a decade, large numbers of new teachers join elementary faculties. Who are they? What do they believe? Will they push for education reform? Instructor surveyed them to find out.

Mary Harbaugh

Mary Harbaugh is associate editor, *Instructor*.

teachers are mostly young women with bachelor's degrees. But a surprising one out of seven is over 30. One out of eight is a man, and nearly all expect to continue their educations.

One of the most remarkable and pervasive characteristics of the new teachers is their commitment to their profession. At a time when women—and men—have more career choices than ever before, the new teachers have chosen a

Editor's note: Fall, 1986.

teaching career for its own sake.

"When I first came into teaching, people tried to dissuade me from it," recalls Laura Shea, a new teacher from East Millinocket, Maine. "People kept saying, 'Are you *sure*?' Well, I *am* sure."

Mary Newton of Corona, California, is among several new teachers who are realizing a long-held dream. She began her education classes more than 10 years ago, but took time out to raise three children. Having finished classes last spring, Newton offers this assessment of how education majors have changed in 10 years. "I see people going into it because they really *want* to. I see people who are very committed. I see more seriousness. There's more of an interest in their profession, and I think that's exciting."

More than 90 percent of new teachers say they chose their profession because they love children and believe that teaching is important and honorable work. In telephone interviews, new teachers cited two additional reasons—the intellectual rewards of good teaching and a personal commitment to improving instruction. Fifty-two percent of new teachers expect to teach longer than 10 years, and some, like Nancy Sengstacken of Georgetown, South Carolina, hope to teach "forever."

The new teachers are remarkably open to new ideas. Their responses and comments show a fresh combination of traditional notions and bold thinking. Survey results also reveal a strong interest in reform.

A solid majority of new teachers say schooling would be improved by career ladders. Two-thirds support merit pay. That's twice the percentage of experienced teachers who support merit pay, according to a Gallup poll conducted last year.

A startling two out of five new teachers endorse the Reagan administration's controversial public/private school voucher

---

Ninety-two percent say they chose teaching because it's important and honorable work.

---

proposal and tuition tax credit plan, both ideas generally opposed by public-school leaders.

The new teachers believe strongly in values education, sex education, child abuse prevention, and substance abuse prevention. At the same time, two out of five support some form of school prayer, and two-thirds approve of corporal punishment in school under certain circumstances.

More than half say *all* teachers should be tested periodically, even though individuals acknowledge the difficulties of proper testing. Many have just passed a state-mandated test for new teachers themselves. "Because it's so hard to weed out incompetent teachers, we have kids growing up with holes in their education. We have got to change to help those kids," says Kari Dingler of Odessa, Texas. "I think we should

have competency tests for teachers. I'd be happy to take one."

Parallel to new teachers' interest in upgrading teaching standards is their commitment to tightening academic standards for students.

More than half believe teachers should be required to pass a competency test every few years.

Nearly three-fourths back raising minimum grade-level requirements, and more than half would end social promotion.

While social promotion may make sense for kids on the borderline, "I don't think it's fair to the kids to pass them if they're really far behind," explains Diane Beirne, an Iowan now in Florida. On this issue, new teachers agree with the general public, according to conclusions of a Gallup poll conducted last spring.

Of all the reform issues, teachers interviewed are most emphatic about slack standards at teacher colleges. "I found it easier than I thought it would be," relates Mary Lynn Miller of Seattle, Washington. "We were told a lot about how we should have high expectations of our students, how if we have them, our students will meet them. But I had teachers that didn't expect much of me. I found that kind of weird."

But others describe a whole series of improvements made in their colleges, mostly within the last year. "My college started a whole new program, which gives you a full year right in the classroom," notes Laura Shea. "There's been a positive turnaround."

Not only do new teachers endorse several specific reform proposals, but many applaud the overall effort to attempt improvements and seem

willing to ride out awkward adjustments. "They [reform leaders] are trying *hard*," notes Brenda Scott of Booneville, Mississippi. "There are some teachers who are fighting it. But when they get the kinks out of the programs, I think it will improve education."

Some new teachers feel a little overwhelmed by the number of parental responsibilities they're being asked to take on. Still, 41 percent support school prayer. "The kids aren't getting it at home anymore," explains Mary Newton. "There are kids out there that need it, they really do."

"If kids want to pray in school, that's terrific, if it's silent prayer that doesn't interfere with the rest

---

New teachers worry about student behavior and lack of parental and administrative support.

---

of education," says Brenda Loseke of Wichita, Kansas. "I am a Christian, but you can't force everyone to believe the same thing."

Lorraine Kozlowski of Chicago opposes prayer in public schools. "What we need is more values education. I think that's what most people who support prayer really want."

More than 80 percent of new teachers agree with Kozlowski about the desirability of values or character education in the classroom. This same interest in students' moral and ethical growth influences some attitudes about sex education. A full 86 percent of new teachers support sex education.

"I think that kids should have morality taught along with sex education," says Monica Hoffman of Eatonville, Washington. "I think responsibility is important. I think sometimes the morality is lacking. I think sometimes schools are afraid to get into morality."

"Sex education has become very necessary in a world where parents aren't around," explains Karen Coy, a New Mexican working in Kansas City.

The new teachers split evenly over whether elementary curriculum should address the threat of

Fifty-eight percent believe the American public is committed to improving public education.

nuclear war. Interviews reveal new teachers' concern is often not whether, but when and how, the topic should be taught. "It is important. Sometimes they try to teach them too much too young," observes Jennifer Ingram of Pensacola, Florida. "I don't think we should frighten children, and I think too often a lot on this topic does. But I do think children should have some understanding."

New teachers also have mixed feelings about the role of technology in the classroom, despite all the public attention to computers and videos. Computers have not won their broad support, although some who endorse specific uses do so heartily. Only a third feel prepared to teach computer skills. About half say they expect to teach computer skills rarely, if at all.

"Computers are important in today's world, but there's plenty of time to teach them after school or later on, in junior high," explains Lisa Anne Hecht of King's Park, New York. Computers shouldn't take time or resources away from more basic subjects, she adds.

Laura Walker of Boulder, Colorado, says, "If computers are

there, they should certainly be used. I think kids should be able to get acquainted with computers. But I don't think they should be a big part of the curriculum. I think they're pushing them too hard, too fast."

However, 53 percent of new teachers expect to use computer software at least occasionally. Slightly more new teachers say they'll use television at least occasionally. Videos and video equipment are most popular—72 percent expect to use them frequently or occasionally.

When asked about problems they anticipate in their first year of teaching, a few new teachers echo some of their more experienced colleagues. "I suppose I worry too much about reaching every single kid. There's probably no way you can reach every single kid, to change their lives," muses Monica Hoffman. "It's not a job you can go home and forget about."

More than half of new teachers worry about class size, lack of parental and administrative support, student behavior problems, lack of good texts and other materials, and too much paperwork. An immediate worry for some is money.

"My biggest challenge in the next few years, I guess, is to be financially secure," explains Lorraine Kozlowski, who will be starting at

The new teachers are supporters of sex education, substance abuse prevention, and character education.

$10,800 as eighth grade math and science teacher for a Chicago parochial school. "It's not too bad yet, because I'm young. It's as much as the school can afford. But the

Nearly three-quarters support raising minimum grade-level competency, and more than half would end social promotion.

working conditions are very good." She also plans to work a summer job.

Kozlowski is among the 17 percent of new teachers who expect to start at less than $12,500. Two of every five anticipate earning $12,500 to $15,000, while about a quarter expect to bring in $15,000 to $17,500. More than one in eight expect to earn more than $17,500 teaching their first year. Forty-four percent expect to earn extra income, like Kozlowski, outside teaching. Perhaps it's no surprise that more than 8 out of 10 new teachers say higher starting salaries would improve education.

Some new teachers feel unprepared to teach children requiring special attention. Almost half say they're not at all prepared to teach children with limited or no proficiency in English, and more than a third aren't prepared for educable mentally retarded children mainstreamed into their classrooms. Fifteen percent say they are unprepared for physically handicapped children, and 12 percent for learning disabled kids. While these groups of children make up a small percentage of students overall, their numbers are expected to grow in the years ahead, according to education analysts.

The new teachers are nearly unanimous in their belief that smaller class size and development of faculty/parent/student committees offer hope for improving in the quality of instruction.

How might such faculty/parent/student groups operate? During her student teaching, Juli Takenaka of Oakland, California, was involved in a program that brought parents, students, and teachers together after school to work with curriculum. Parents learned to appreciate some of the difficulties of teaching, children thrived under the attention of both parent and teacher, and the importance of schooling was brought home. "The results have been tremendous!" Takenaka notes.

The new teachers split almost evenly over whether the American public has a positive view of education, although 58 percent believe it is committed to improving schooling. But for many new teachers, their own commitment is enough right now. Overall, they're optimistic and eager to get to work, to take on the responsibilities of their new profession.

"I sense somehow there's going to be change," says Greg Cabrera of Riverside, California. "Maybe we're coming to an age of a more scientific approach to teaching. We're learning *how* to teach, and we're going to be teaching America for years. We're going to try."

This survey was conducted with the assistance of professors in 95 colleges of education, who distributed questionnaires to senior and graduate students majoring in preschool, elementary, or junior high education. A total of 1,313 questionnaires were completed by students and returned to INSTRUCTOR for tabulation. Percentages reported here have an average standard error of ±2 percent. Study conducted by International Media Futures, Inc./New York.

THE 18ᵀᴴ ANNUAL GALLUP POLL OF THE PUBLIC'S ATTITUDES TOWARD THE PUBLIC SCHOOLS

[handwritten: most important = drug use, 2nd = discipline (highest 16 of last 17)]

ALEC M. GALLUP

The annual Phi Delta Kappa/Gallup Poll of the Public's Attitudes Toward the Public Schools is a continuing source of reliable information concerning trends in opinion about significant school questions. For school officials, the poll is valuable in at least two ways: it alerts decision makers to overall public reaction to a variety of school programs and policies, and it serves as a national benchmark against which local attitudes can be measured.

Local officials are welcome to use questions asked in the PDK/Gallup surveys. The questions are not copyrighted. Moreover, no limits are placed on the use of information contained in these reports, beyond customary credit to the source and observance of the canons of accuracy and completeness of quotation.

Phi Delta Kappa's Dissemination Division, assisted by the Gallup Organization, is prepared to help school districts and other agencies survey local populations on education questions. For details about this service, write or telephone Neville Robertson, director of the Center for the Dissemination of Innovative Programs, Phi Delta Kappa, P. O. Box 789, Bloomington, IN 47402. The phone number is 812/339-1156.

Most Important Problems Facing Local Public Schools in 1986

For the first time in this survey's 18-year history, the U.S. public has identified drug use by students as the most important problem facing the public schools. More than half of our respondents mention either drugs (28%) or discipline (24%), which was rated most important in 16 of the 17 previous polls. (In 1971 "lack of proper financial support" was considered the most important problem.) Our best-educated respondents — those with college degrees — continue to perceive discipline rather than drugs as the schools' most important problem. The margin is substantial, 30% to 18%. Other differences in perception by population groups are shown in the second chart below.

The question:

What do you think are the biggest problems with which the public schools in this community must deal?

Support for Anti-Drug Measures In Local Schools

Survey respondents were asked to rate five measures for dealing with the drug problem in their local public schools. Nine in 10 support mandatory instruction in the dangers of drug abuse, roughly the same percentage who feel that education about the dangers of drug abuse should be a required course in the school curriculum (as reported in earlier studies). Eight in 10 favor the expulsion of students caught using drugs. Seven in 10 support using school funds to treat drug users, and the same proportion would permit school officials to search lockers when they suspect that drugs might be concealed in them. By a small majority (5-4), respondents even favor urinalysis to detect drug use.

Support for each measure is virtually the same for parents and nonparents of schoolchildren. However, young people (under 30), while they are more likely to favor use of school funds to treat drug users than are their elders, are substantially less likely to support two of the more stringent measures: locker searches and urinalysis. Nonwhites are somewhat more likely to favor locker searches and substantially more likely to favor urinalysis than are whites, but they are less likely to favor expulsion of drug users from school.

College-educated and upper-income respondents are somewhat more likely to favor use of school funds for treat-

From *Phi Delta Kappan*, September 1986, pp. 43-59. Reprinted by permission.

1. PERCEPTIONS OF EDUCATION IN AMERICA

	National Totals %	No Children In School %	Public School Parents %	Nonpublic School Parents %
Use of drugs	28	28	27	22
Lack of discipline	24	24	23	26
Lack of proper financial support	11	9	15	14
Poor curriculum/poor standards	8	7	10	11
Difficulty in getting good teachers	6	6	6	5
Moral standards/dress code	5	5	5	11
Drinking/alcoholism	5	4	5	8
Large schools/overcrowding	5	4	6	5
Teachers' lack of interest	4	4	6	7
Lack of respect for teachers/other students	4	4	4	3
Parents' lack of interest	4	3	5	4
Low teacher pay	3	2	4	3
Integration/busing	3	4	3	3
Crime/vandalism	3	3	3	1
Pupils' lack of interest/truancy	3	3	2	1
Problems with administration	2	2	3	5
Fighting	2	2	2	*
Mismanagement of funds/programs	1	1	1	3
Communication problems	1	1	1	3
Lack of needed teachers	1	1	1	2
Lack of proper facilities	1	1	1	2
Transportation	1	1	2	1
Teacher strikes	1	1	1	1
Too many schools/declining enrollment	1	1	1	*
Parents' involvement in school activities	1	1	1	*
There are no problems	2	2	4	3
Miscellaneous	6	6	4	6
Don't know	11	13	4	5

*Less than one-half of 1%.
(Figures add to more than 100% because of multiple answers.)

ing drug users than are their less-educated and less financially well-off counterparts.

The question:

This card lists various ways to deal with the problem of drugs in the public schools. As I read off each one of these plans, would you tell me whether you would favor or oppose its use in the public schools in your community?

	National Totals %	No Children In School %	Public School Parents %	Nonpublic School Parents %
Requiring instruction for all students in the dangers of drug abuse.				
Favor	90	90	91	92
Oppose	6	6	6	5
Don't know	4	4	3	3
Permitting expulsion of students who are caught using drugs in school buildings or on school grounds.				
Favor	78	77	81	82
Oppose	16	16	14	17
Don't know	6	7	5	1
Use of school funds to provide counseling and treatment for students who use drugs.				
Favor	69	68	70	83
Oppose	25	26	24	16
Don't know	6	6	6	1

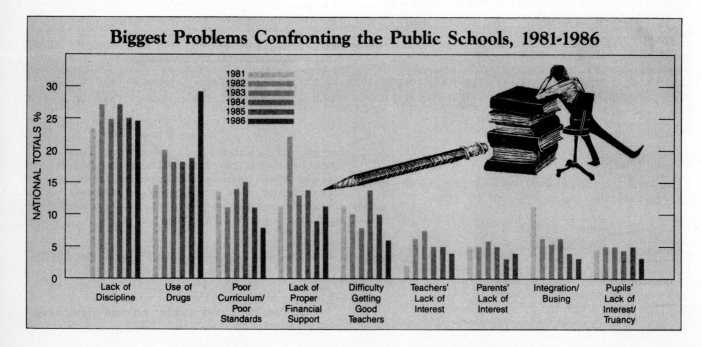

Biggest Problems Confronting the Public Schools, 1981-1986

	National Totals %	No Children In School %	Public School Parents %	Nonpublic School Parents %
Permitting teachers or school authorities to search lockers or personal property if they suspect drugs, without obtaining a court-issued search warrant.				
Favor	67	67	67	77
Oppose	28	28	30	22
Don't know	5	5	3	1
Testing students for drug use by urinalysis.				
Favor	49	49	49	49
Oppose	44	44	43	46
Don't know	7	7	8	5

Grading the Public Schools And Their Teachers

The 1986 survey indicates that the public schools are perceived as favorably as in 1984 and 1985, when they achieved their highest performance grades since 1976. Forty-one percent of Americans rate the public schools locally (in "this community") as either A or B.

Similarly, 28% of the public give the public schools, *nationally*, either an A or B — the highest grade since this measurement was initiated in 1981.

Teachers receive an A or B from almost half of the public (48%), a figure statistically equivalent to last year's 49%, which represented the highest rating recorded since the measurement was initiated in 1981.

Administrators are graded A or B by about four in 10 members of the public (42%), a somewhat lower figure than last year's record 48% but higher than the low point of 36% recorded at the beginning of the Eighties.

	1986 National Totals %	No Children In School %	Public School Parents %	Nonpublic School Parents %
A+B	41	36	55	40
A	11	8	18	11
B	30	28	37	29
C	28	27	29	29
D	11	11	11	16
FAIL	5	5	4	11
Don't know	15	21	1	4

National Ratings

The public's rating of the schools nationally has climbed steadily since the first measurement in 1981, from 20% A or B, recorded at that time, to the high point of 28% registered this year.

The question:

How about the public schools in the nation as a whole? What grade would you give the public schools nationally — A,B,C,D, or FAIL?

NATIONAL TOTALS	1986 %	1985 %	1984 %	1983 %	1982 %	1981 %
A+B	28	27	25	19	22	20
A	3	3	2	2	2	2
B	25	24	23	17	20	18
C	41	43	49	38	44	43
D	10	12	11	16	15	15
FAIL	5	3	4	6	4	6
Don't know	16	15	11	21	15	16

Rating the Schools on Success Characteristics

Good schools should have the following characteristics, according to a consensus of educational researchers.

A. The school's environment should be safe and orderly.

B. The school's principal should spend most of his or her time helping teachers improve their teaching.

C. School administrators and teachers should have high expectations of students and demand high achievement.

D. General agreement should exist among administrators, teachers, and parents about school goals.

E. Student progress toward school goals should be regularly measured and reported.

Public school parents were asked to judge how accurately each of the above statements describes the school their oldest child attends: very accurately, fairly accurately, not very accurately, or not at all accurately. The findings are encouraging to educators. About eight in 10 parents believe statements A and E apply very accurately or fairly accurately. About seven in 10 believe the same about statements C and D. About half believe statement B applies very accurately or fairly accurately.

Ironically, though many public school parents perceive drugs and discipline as major problems in the schools their children attend, the vast majority (85%) feel that these schools are either "very" or "fairly" safe and orderly.

The question:

This card lists some of the characteristics of good schools. As I read off each item by letter, would you tell me how accurately you feel it describes the school your oldest child attends — very accurately, fairly accurately, not very accurately, or not at all accurately?

	Combined Very Accurately/ Fairly Accurately %	Very Accurately %	Fairly Accurately %	Not Very Accurately %	Not at All Accurately %	Don't Know %
A. Safe, orderly school environment	84	40	44	10	2	4
E. Student progress measured, reported	80	41	39	9	5	6
C. Staff has high expectations, demands achievement	74	33	41	16	3	7
D. Staff, parents agree on school goals	70	31	39	14	6	10
B. Principal helps teachers	54	17	37	18	8	20

Ratings Given the Local Public Schools

	1986	1985	1984	1983	1982	1981	1980	1979	1978	1977	1976	1975	1974
A	11%	9%	10%	6%	8%	9%	10%	8%	9%	11%	13%	13%	18%
B	30%	34%	32%	25%	29%	27%	25%	26%	27%	26%	29%	30%	30%
C	28%	30%	35%	32%	33%	34%	29%	30%	30%	28%	28%	28%	21%
D	11%	10%	11%	13%	14%	13%	12%	11%	11%	11%	10%	9%	6%
FAIL	5%	4%		7%	5%	7%	6%	7%	8%	5%	6%	7%	5%
Don't Know	15%	13%	4% / 8%	17%	11%	10%	18%	18%	15%	19%	14%	13%	20%

The Goals of Education

Asked what they consider the chief reasons why people want their children to get an education, Americans tend to mention job- and finance-related reasons first. For example, about one-third (34%) cite job opportunities, 8% say to get a better-paying job, 4% say to obtain specialized training, and 9% say to achieve financial security.

Relatively few Americans mention preparation for life (23%), to acquire knowledge (10%), to become a better citizen (6%), to learn how to get along with others (4%), or to contribute to society (3%).

Furthermore, nonparents respond in virtually the same way as parents with children in the public schools.

The question:

People have different reasons why they want their children to get an education. What are the chief reasons that come to your mind?

	National Totals %	No Children In School %	Public School Parents %	Nonpublic School Parents %
Job opportunities/ better job	34	35	33	18
Preparation for life/ better life	23	22	25	33
Education is a necessity of life	12	12	12	10
More knowledge	10	10	10	11
Financial security/economic stability	9	8	11	13
To get a better-paying job	8	9	5	2
To become better citizens	6	6	6	5
For a successful life	5	4	7	6
To learn how to get along with people	4	4	3	1
For better/easier life than parents	4	2	7	3
Specialized training profession	4	3	4	9

	National Totals %	No Children In School %	Public School Parents %	Nonpublic School Parents %
Teaches person to think/learn/understand	3	3	3	8
To contribute to society	3	3	4	4
Personal development/ self-realization	3	3	4	3
To become self-sufficient (independence)	3	3	4	3
To learn basic skills/ fundamental learning skills	3	3	3	1
To develop the ability to deal with adult responsibilities	2	2	3	5
For happy/happier life	2	2	2	5
Creates opportunities/ opens doors	2	2	2	2
To develop an understanding and appreciation for culture	1	2	1	2
Helps keep children out of trouble	1	1	1	3
Social status	1	1	1	2
To develop self-discipline	1	1	1	1
To develop basic individual values	1	*	1	1
To develop critical thinking skills	1	1	*	1
Miscellaneous	2	2	1	3
Don't know	4	5	3	3

*Less than one-half of 1%.
(Figures add to more than 100% because of multiple answers.)

Attitudes Toward Federal, State, Local Influence on Public Education

This survey reveals that there is substantial support (57% to 17%) for more influence on public schools from local school boards, moderate support (45% to 32%) for more influence on the part of the state governments, and strong opposition to more federal influence on the way the public schools are run. The current 2-1 opposition to more federal influence (53% to 26%) is virtually the same as that recorded when the question was last asked in 1982, after the Reagan Administration took office.

Parents and nonparents have similar attitudes on these matters. Parents, however, are even more likely than nonparents to oppose increased federal influence. At the same time, they are somewhat more likely than nonparents to favor both increased influence by local school boards and by the state government.

Various population groups rather consistently support increased influence for local school boards, but some differences emerge on the question of increased control by state and federal government. Younger people and nonwhites are more likely than others to favor it. On the other hand, better-educated and higher-income segments of the population are more likely to favor less influence on the part of either the state governments or the federal government than are their less well-educated and less well-off counterparts.

The question on federal influence:

Thinking about the future, would you like the federal government in Washington to have more influence, or less influence, in determining the educational program of the local public schools?

NATIONAL TOTALS	1986 %	1982 %
More influence	26	28
Less influence	53	54
Same as now	12	10
Don't know	9	8

The question on state influence:

How about the state government? Would you like the state government to have more influence, or less influence, in determining the educational program of the local public schools?

	National Totals %	No Children In School %	Public School Parents %	Nonpublic School Parents %
More influence	45	46	45	35
Less influence	32	29	38	38
Same as now	16	16	13	20
Don't know	7	9	4	7

The question on local influence:

How about the local school board? Would you like the local school board to have more influence, or less influence, in determining the educational program of the local public schools?

	National Totals %	No Children In School %	Public School Parents %	Nonpublic School Parents %
More influence	57	56	61	55
Less influence	17	17	15	19
Same as now	17	16	19	19
Don't know	9	11	5	7

Financing the Public Schools

This survey reveals that 33% of Americans feel that the best way to finance the public schools is by means of state taxes. However, almost as many prefer federal taxes or local property taxes (24% in both instances).

It is instructive to relate what the public feels is the best source of funding for education — federal, state, or local taxes — to its views on which of the three divisions of government should have more influence on education policy. While the public disapproves of increased influence on the part of the federal government by a substantial margin, it is by no means opposed to accepting federal tax money.

The mild public preference for state taxes supports the revolution in school funding that began in the Seventies. Today, state sources generally yield more money for public schools than do local taxing units, though there are great variations among the states.

Despite the public's professed desire for better schools, resistance to increased local taxes for improving public education persists; only about one-third (37%) of Americans would be willing to pay more taxes should local school authorities say they are needed. This is roughly the same percentage as reported in these surveys over the past 15 years.

Resistance to increased taxes also surfaces when Americans are asked specifically whether they would favor or oppose increased property taxes or federal income taxes to improve public education. Only one-third would be willing to pay more property taxes, and only one-fourth would increase income taxes. In fact, as answers to our last finance question show, the only support for increases comes for taxes on alcohol and cigarettes and an increased percentage of the take from state lotteries, now held in 23 states.

The question on preferred ways of financing schools:

There is always a lot of discussion about the best way to finance the public schools. Which do you think is the best way to finance the public schools: by means of local property taxes, by state taxes, or by taxes from the federal government in Washington?

	National Totals %	No Children In School %	Public School Parents %	Nonpublic School Parents %
Local property taxes	24	22	28	22
State taxes	33	34	32	36
Taxes from federal government	24	23	28	22
Don't know	19	21	12	20

1. PERCEPTIONS OF EDUCATION IN AMERICA

The questions on knowledge of actual sources of public school support:

Now, where do you think most of the funds to finance the public schools come from: from local property taxes, from state taxes, or from the federal government in Washington? And what do you think is the second largest source?

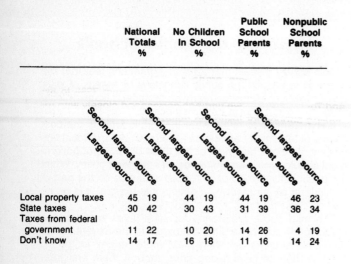

	National Totals %		No Children In School %		Public School Parents %		Nonpublic School Parents %	
	Largest source	Second largest source	Largest source	Second largest source	Largest source	Second largest source	Largest source	Second largest source
Local property taxes	45	19	44	19	44	19	46	23
State taxes	30	42	30	43	31	39	36	34
Taxes from federal government	11	22	10	20	14	26	4	19
Don't know	14	17	16	18	11	16	14	24

The question on voting to raise taxes for school support:

Suppose the local public schools said they needed much more money. As you feel at this time, would you vote to raise taxes for this purpose, or would you vote against raising taxes for this purpose?

	National Totals %	No Children In School %	Public School Parents %	Nonpublic School Parents %
For raise in taxes	37	34	45	38
Against raise in taxes	52	54	46	51
No opinion	11	12	9	11

Financial Support of the Public Schools

	Favor Raising Taxes %	Opposed to Raising Taxes %	Don't Know %
1986 survey	37	52	11
1985 survey	38	52	10
1984 survey	41	47	12
1983 survey	39	52	9
1981 survey	30	60	10
1972 survey	36	56	8
1971 survey	40	52	8
1970 survey	37	56	7
1969 survey	45	49	6

The question on preferred type of tax for school support:

Many states have recently passed school improvement legislation that requires additional financial expenditures. If your state needed to raise more money for the public schools, would you vote for or against the following proposals?

	National Totals %	No Children In School %	Public School Parents %	Nonpublic School Parents %
Increased alcoholic beverage taxes?				
Favor	79	78	82	79
Oppose	18	18	17	20
Don't know	3	4	1	1
Increasing the percentage of state lottery money that goes to support public schools in those states with a state lottery?				
Favor	78	77	81	69
Oppose	10	9	12	22
Don't know	12	14	7	9
Increased cigarette and tobacco taxes?				
Favor	74	74	74	79
Oppose	22	21	25	20
Don't know	4	5	1	1
Increased local property taxes?				
Favor	33	31	39	31
Oppose	60	61	56	63
Don't know	7	8	5	6
Increased gasoline taxes?				
Favor	28	28	29	29
Oppose	67	67	68	70
Don't know	5	5	3	1
Increased income taxes?				
Favor	27	25	31	26
Oppose	66	67	65	68
Don't know	7	8	4	6

Attitudes About AIDS

Two-thirds of the public would permit their children to attend school with a student who has AIDS. Perhaps surprisingly, the latest Gallup survey not only found an extraordinarily high level of public awareness of the disease (98%) but a very small proportion (6%) of the public who mistakenly believe that a person can contract AIDS merely by being in a public place with someone who has it.

The findings for this question only are based on telephone interviews with 1,004 adults, age 18 and older, conducted in scientifically selected localities across the U.S. during the period of 7-10 March 1986.

Only one-sixth (17%) of those who would *not* allow their children to attend classes with an AIDS victim believe that the disease can be transmitted by casual social contact, while 59% of this group voice the opposite opinion and 24% are undecided.

Although substantial majorities in all key population groups believe correctly that AIDS cannot be contracted by casual contact, this feeling is somewhat less prevalent — and uncertainty is more prevalent — among older, less-well-educated, and less-affluent people. Similarly, persons from these groups (which are highly interrelated) are less likely than their counterparts to say that they would permit their children to attend classes with a child who has AIDS.

This question was asked first: "Have you heard or read about the disease called AIDS — Acquired Immune Deficiency Syndrome?" Those who answered yes — an overwhelming 98% of the public — were then asked the following questions.

The first question:

Do you believe a person can get AIDS by being in a crowded place with someone who has it?

Casual Transmission of AIDS
(Based on aware group)

	Can Be Transmitted %	Cannot Be %	Not Sure %
NATIONAL TOTALS	6	81	13
Sex			
Men	7	79	14
Women	4	83	13
Race			
White	5	82	13
Nonwhite	10	79	11
Age			
18 - 29 years	8	86	6
30 - 49 years	5	86	9
50 and over	5	73	22
Education			
College graduates	2	91	7
College incomplete	5	87	8
High school graduates	5	82	13
High school incomplete	11	62	27
Region			
East	3	86	11
Midwest	6	81	13
South	6	77	17
West	6	83	11

The second question:

A 14-year-old Indiana boy who contracted AIDS through a contaminated blood transfusion was banned from attending school classes. After a county medical officer ruled that he posed no health threat to his classmates, he went back to school, but the parents of almost half of the students at his school kept their children home.

If you had children of this age, would you permit them to attend classes with a child who had AIDS, or not?

Permit Child to Attend School
With AIDS Victim?
(Based on aware group)

	Yes %	No %	Not Sure %
NATIONAL TOTALS	67	24	9
Sex			
Men	66	27	7
Women	67	22	11
Race			
White	67	24	9
Nonwhite	64	27	9
Age			
18 - 29 years	64	29	7
30 - 49 years	69	23	8
50 and over	65	23	12
Education			
College graduates	72	19	9
College incomplete	68	23	9
High school graduates	68	23	9
High school incomplete	57	35	8
Region			
East	64	27	9
Midwest	69	20	11
South	63	27	10
West	72	22	6

Support for Stricter Grade Promotion/ High School Graduation Requirements

To ascertain how the public feels about toughening requirements for grade promotion and for high school graduation, as has been recommended in national education reports, respondents were asked a series of questions. Those who supported stricter graduation requirements were asked whether they would do so if it meant that substantially fewer students would graduate. Finally, respondents were asked which of three proposals they preferred for dealing with those students who could not meet graduation requirements.

The survey reveals that Americans strongly favor stricter requirements for both grade promotion and high school graduation, and by virtually identical margins: 72% to 6% and 70% to 5%. These findings correspond closely with the public's support for testing to determine both grade promotion and high school graduation, as revealed in earlier surveys in this series.

The first question:

In your opinion, should promotion from grade to grade in the public schools be made more strict than it is now or less strict?

	National Totals %	No Children In School %	Public School Parents %	Nonpublic School Parents %
More strict	72	72	70	73
Less strict	6	5	7	6
Same as now	16	15	20	16
Don't know	6	8	3	5

The second question:

In your opinion, should the requirements for graduation from the public high schools be made more strict than they are now or less strict?

	National Totals %	No Children In School %	Public School Parents %	Nonpublic School Parents %
More strict	70	71	68	75
Less strict	5	5	7	*
Same as now	19	17	23	20
Don't know	6	7	2	5

*Less than one-half of 1%.

The third question:

Would you favor stricter requirements for high school graduation even if it meant that significantly fewer students would graduate than is now the case?

	National Totals %	No Children In School %	Public School Parents %	Nonpublic School Parents %
Yes	68	68	68	77
No	23	22	26	18
Don't know	9	10	6	5

1. PERCEPTIONS OF EDUCATION IN AMERICA

Groups most in favor of stricter standards for graduation are the college-educated, those in the highest-income households (i.e., $30,000 or over), and residents of the nation's largest cities (i.e., 1 million or more).

Among groups in the parent population, it is the college-educated and those whose children are above average academically who are most supportive of stricter requirements.

The final question in this series:

This card lists several ways to deal with those students who do not meet the requirements for public high school graduation. Which one of these plans would you prefer?

	National Totals %	No Children In School %	Public School Parents %	Nonpublic School Parents %
Have the high schools set up a remedial program for helping students who initially failed to meet the requirements for high school graduation to satisfy these requirements. This program would be supported by taxes.	45	44	45	53
Have high schools set up a remedial program for helping those students who initially failed to meet the requirements for high school graduation to satisfy these requirements. Students would be charged tuition to enter this program.	27	27	30	23
Have the high schools award more than one kind of diploma so that if a student cannot meet the requirements for a standard diploma, he or she would still be awarded a lesser diploma.	19	19	19	16
Don't know	9	10	6	8

Two of the proposals above involve remedial programs to help failing students to meet graduation requirements: one supported by taxes and the other paid for by student tuition. The third proposal calls for awarding a different diploma to those who do not meet the requirements of the standard diploma.

Note that almost three-quarters of Americans (72%) would opt for one of the two remedial programs. Support for the free, tax-supported proposal is preferred by a margin of almost 2-1 (45% to 27%) over the tuition proposal. Only one in five, however (19%), would choose proposal three, which would award a lesser degree to those who could not meet the requirements for the standard degree.

Attitudes toward the three proposals are virtually the same among parents of public school children and nonparents, as well as among the various groups in the total national population.

Support for National Testing

Not only have Americans consistently favored mandatory testing for grade promotion and high school graduation, but they continue overwhelmingly to support the concept of national tests to permit comparisons of the performance of students in various communities.

In the current survey almost eight in 10 members of the public favor the concept of national testing, roughly the same level of support found in three previous surveys, conducted over a 15-year period. Interestingly, parents are just as likely to favor national testing of student performance as are nonparents.

Support for national testing approaches eight in 10 in virtually every population segment of the national population, with the single exception of those persons in households with annual incomes of less than $10,000, where the percentage in favor of testing falls below seven in 10 (67%).

The question:

Would you like to see the students in the local schools given national tests so that their educational achievement could be compared with students in other communities?

	National Totals %	No Children In School %	Public School Parents %	Nonpublic School Parents %
Yes	77	76	78	82
No	16	15	19	17
Don't know	7	9	3	1

NATIONAL TOTALS			
1986 %	1983 %	1971 %	1970 %
Yes	77	75	70	75
No	16	17	21	16
No opinion	7	8	9	9

Teachers: Testing, Salaries, Shortages

Pressing issues involving teachers were investigated in the current survey: the public's attitudes toward teacher competency tests, attitudes toward teacher salary levels, and views on strategies for attracting teachers in shortage areas such as math, science, and technical and vocational subjects.

As shown in three previous education surveys, there is overwhelming, across-the-board support for teacher competency testing. In the current survey, more than eight Americans in 10 favor such tests (85%), almost the identical percentage supporting the idea in 1979.

Interestingly, the level of support for competency tests is virtually the same as that for tests to prove teachers' knowledge *before* they are awarded a teaching certificate, as reported in the annual education surveys in 1979 and again in 1981.

The public still feels that teacher salaries are too low, an attitude revealed on numerous past surveys. In the current survey, 49% of the respondents favor a teacher salary figure higher than the salary they think teachers actually receive. In contrast, only 14% feel that teachers should receive *less* than they are thought to make. Specifically, the public thinks that beginning teachers, on average, receive $16,500 (which is close to the actual national average), but think they *deserve* to make almost $5,000 more, or $21,000.

In your opinion, should experienced teachers be periodically required to pass a statewide basic competency test in their subject area or areas or not?

	National Totals %	No Children In School %	Public School Parents %	Nonpublic School Parents %
Yes, they should	85	84	87	87
No	11	11	11	13
Don't know	4	5	2	*

*Less than one-half of 1%.

The questions on teacher salaries:

This card lists various income categories. What do you think the annual salary should be for a beginning public school teacher in this community with a bachelor's degree and teaching certificate?

Now, what do you think the salary actually is in this community for a beginning teacher with a bachelor's degree and teaching certificate?

Salary Categories	What People Think Beginning Teachers Should Be Paid %	What People Think Beginning Teachers Are Actually Paid %
Less than $10,000	3	3
$10,000 - $11,999	4	7
$12,000 - $13,999	6	12
$14,000 - $15,999	13	15
$16,000 - $17,999	12	16
$18,000 - $19,999	16	11
$20,000 - $24,999	19	6
$25,000 - $29,999	8	3
$30,000 and over	6	2
Don't know	13	25

Average salary deserved: $21,300
Median salary deserved: $19,500

The chart below treats these data in another way:

	National Totals %	No Children In School %	Public School Parents %	Nonpublic School Parents %
Deserve higher salary than perceived as being paid	49	47	55	56
Deserve lower salary than perceived as being paid	14	14	15	8
Deserve same salary as perceived	10	9	10	13
Don't know	27	30	20	23

Population groups most likely to feel that teachers are underpaid are college graduates, those in the highest income category, younger people, and those living in the center cities. For example, among persons in the over-$40,000 annual income category, 69% feel that teachers are underpaid compared to only 9% who say the opposite. Comparable figures for college graduates are 67% to 7%; for persons

under 30, 58% to 16%; and for those living in the center cities, 57% to 14%.

There is one important regional difference: 44% of Western respondents think beginning teachers should be paid $20,000 or more. The comparable figure for the East is 29%, for the Midwest 31%, and for the South 31%.

When Should Children Begin School?

To find out what Americans consider the right age for children to start attending publicly supported schools, respondents to the 1986 survey were asked two sets of questions. The first set asked at which class level children should begin school, and since this would depend directly on the age of the child, the second set investigated the public's views on the appropriate starting age.

Specifically, respondents were asked whether tax-supported kindergarten should be made available to all parents who want it for their children. Then they were asked whether kindergarten should be made compulsory. The age questions sought to determine whether the public would favor or oppose starting school at age 4, a year earlier than is traditional, and, if this idea was rejected, what the public felt was the *right* age for children to begin school.

The findings reveal overwhelming support for making kindergarten available as a regular part of the public school system; eight in 10 respondents favor doing so. Almost as large a proportion (seven in 10) favor compulsory kindergarten.

On the other hand, the public opposes, by more than 2-1 (64% to 29%), having children start school at age 4. This finding reveals no attitude change since the early Seventies, when the same question was asked.

An important exception to the negative response to starting school at age 4 appears among nonwhites, however. A majority of nonwhites (55%) favor starting public school children at age 4; only about one-third (35%) oppose the idea.

The first question:

A proposal has been made to make kindergarten available for all those who wish it as part of the public school system. The program would be supported by taxes. Would you favor or oppose such a program in your school district?

	National Totals %	No Children In School %	Public School Parents %	Nonpublic School Parents %
Favor	80	77	86	78
Oppose	13	14	10	12
Don't know	7	9	4	10

The second question:

Some educators have proposed that kindergarten be made compulsory for all children before entering first grade. Would you favor or oppose such a program in your school district?

1. PERCEPTIONS OF EDUCATION IN AMERICA

	National Totals %	No Children In School %	Public School Parents %	Nonpublic School Parents %
Favor	71	68	80	80
Oppose	22	24	16	17
Don't know	7	8	4	3

The third question:

Some educators have proposed that young children start school a year earlier, at the age of 4. Does this sound like a good idea or not?

	National Totals %	No Children In School %	Public School Parents %	Nonpublic School Parents %
Yes, good idea	29	29	27	29
No	64	62	70	67
Don't know	7	9	3	4

	NATIONAL TOTALS		
	1986 %	1973 %	1972 %
Yes, good idea	29	30	30
No	64	64	64
Don't know	7	6	6

The final question:

At what age do you think children should start school?

	National Totals %	No Children In School %	Public School Parents %	Nonpublic School Parents %
4 years (or under)	29	29	27	29
5 years	41	40	44	42
6 years	18	18	20	23
7 years (or over)	2	1	2	*
No opinion	10	12	7	6

*Less than one-half of 1%.

The findings concerning what the public feels is the class level at which public school children should start school, cross-tabulated with the *age* at which they should begin, shows the following distribution of preferences:

	%
(Compulsory) Kindergarten at 5	34
(Compulsory) Kindergarten at 4	23
(Compulsory) Kindergarten at 6	10
(Compulsory) First grade at 6*	9
(Compulsory) First grade at 5	6
(Compulsory) First grade at 4	4
No opinion	14

*Most common arrangement.

Private and Parochial Schools

American attitudes toward the nation's nonpublic schools — i.e., both the parochial and the independent or private schools — were investigated in the 1986 survey in the following areas:

• the public's support of or opposition to the use of government tax funds to help the nation's parochial schools — and correspondingly to assist the private or independent schools;

• public support of or opposition to the adoption of the voucher system in this country;

• parents' interest in sending their children to private or parochial schools, if they had the necessary means; and

• parents' acceptance or rejection of a specific voucher proposal that would provide $600 a year to enroll their children in any private, parochial, or public school.

Survey findings reveal that the public is opposed to providing tax money to parochial schools at about the same level as in 1981 and even more than when the question was first asked in 1971. The public is even more negative about giving tax money to support private or independent schools. Only about one-quarter (27%) feel that the government should provide funds for the nation's private schools.

Analysis of responses to both questions in the current survey shows the following distribution:

	%
Favor tax money for *both* parochial and private schools	24
Favor tax money for parochial schools *only*	16
Favor tax money for private schools *only*	3
Favor tax money for *neither* parochial nor private schools	55
Don't know	2

Americans' support for the general concept of vouchers is roughly divided, pro and con, as has been the case on the several occasions that the issue has been investigated in this series. Public school parents are roughly divided (49% to 46%) about the desirability of sending their children to a private or parochial school, assuming they had the means to do so.

Response to the specific $600 voucher proposal is generally negative. Only one-quarter of parents (27%) would use the $600 voucher for a parochial or private school; i.e., about half of those say they would like to send their children to a nonpublic school. Although 6% say they would move their children from their current public school to another school, it would be a public institution. More than six in 10 (61%), however, would keep their children in the public school they now attend.

Support for Tax Assistance for Parochial Schools

About four in 10 respondents (42%) support the idea of giving tax money to parochial schools, compared to five in 10 who oppose it. This is about the same division that was reported in the 1981 survey.

The current findings reveal somewhat more opposition than when the question was first asked, in 1970, however. At that time the public *supported* use of tax funds for parochial schools by a slim 48% to 44% margin. Parents of public school children are even more opposed to the idea of giving tax money to parochial schools than are nonparents.

This opposition is shared by most major population groups; the only exception is people living in the East, the region with a heavy concentration of Catholics. In the East, a majority (55%) favors giving tax money to parochial schools, compared to the 35% who oppose the idea.

The question:

It has been proposed that some government tax money be used to help parochial (church-related) schools make ends meet. How do you feel about this? Do you favor or oppose giving some government tax money to help parochial schools?

	National Totals %	No Children In School %	Public School Parents %	Nonpublic School Parents %
Favor	42	42	40	57
Oppose	50	48	54	41
No opinion	8	10	6	2

NATIONAL TOTALS

	1986 %	1981 %	1970 %
Favor	42	40	48
Oppose	50	51	44
No opinion	8	9	8

Support for Tax Assistance to Private Schools

Two out of three Americans (65%) are opposed to giving tax money to the nation's private schools, and this proportion holds among parents of public school children as well as nonparents. This strong opposition permeates every segment of the population, including people living in the East, with its relatively high concentration of Catholics.

The question:

How do you feel about private schools? Do you favor or oppose giving some government tax money to help *private schools*?

	National Totals %	No Children In School %	Public School Parents %	Nonpublic School Parents %
Favor	27	26	26	48
Oppose	65	66	67	50
No opinion	8	8	7	2

Support for Vouchers

The same question about vouchers has been asked in this survey six times, beginning in 1970. Americans today support the voucher idea by a close 46% to 41% margin. This is a slight decline from its high point of approval in 1983, when the plan was favored by 51% of the public, while 38% opposed it.

Surprisingly, parents of public school children are only slightly more likely to favor the voucher system than are nonparents.

Although the public, collectively, approves of the voucher system by a narrow margin, majority support for its adoption emerges in certain population segments. Nonwhites favor adoption of the system by a wide margin (54% to 33%). Similarly, those under 30, Catholics, persons residing in the inner cities, and those who are dissatisfied with the performance of the public schools (i.e., give them a D or Failing grade) support the adoption of the voucher system by about a 5-3 margin.

The question:

In some nations the government allots a certain amount of money for each child for his education. The parents can send the child to any public, parochial, or private school they choose. This is called the "voucher system." Would you like to see such an idea adopted in this country?

	National Totals %	No Children In School %	Public School Parents %	Nonpublic School Parents %
Yes	46	44	51	64
No	41	41	41	28
No opinion	13	15	8	8

NATIONAL TOTALS

	1986 %	1985 %	1983 %	1981 %	1971 %	1970 %
Yes	46	45	51	43	38	43
No	41	40	38	41	44	46
No opinion	13	15	11	16	18	11

Research Procedure

The Sample. The sample used in this survey embraced a total of 1,552 adults (18 years of age and older). It is described as a modified probability sample of the U.S. population. Personal, in-home interviewing was conducted in all areas of the nation and in all types of communities. A description of the sample and sample design is available from Phi Delta Kappa.

Time of Interviewing. The fieldwork for this study was carried out during the period of 11-20 April 1986.

The Report. The heading "Nonpublic School Parents" includes parents of students who attend parochial schools and parents of students who attend private or independent schools.

Due allowance must be made for statistical variation, especially in the case of findings for groups consisting of relatively few respondents, e.g., nonpublic school parents.

The findings of this report apply only to the U.S. as a whole and not to individual communities. Local surveys, using the same questions, can be conducted to determine how local areas compare with the national norm.

Continuity and Change in Education

In every decade of the past century we have witnessed concern over the tension between the need for a sense of continuity in social traditions and the role of the nation's schools in providing that sense of continuity. This concern has been counterbalanced by an equally fervent awareness that continued change in the technological bases and economic structures of North American society places additional pressure for change in the content and manner of schooling. Continuity and change are twin forces in a historic polarity in dialogue over the purposes of education through the centuries. It may form a continuing dialogue as to the best directions educational systems might take in the future. The tension between the concepts of continuity and change and how these concepts are defined in each generation rests on the answers to the following questions. What is best about what has been thought and said and done that ought to remain in school curricula? What new developments in each generation must receive placement in formal curricular content? In each decade of the past one hundred years, these two questions have been reviewed and debated by British, Canadian, and American educators.

The 1980s have been no exception in terms of continuing dialogue among educational conservatives and liberal and radical interpreters of the nature and functions of continuity and change in schooling. What things should be retained in school curricula and what new skills and new bodies of knowledge ought to be added to educational studies? What humane interests should govern or at least be part of the formal education of all youth? What new scientific or technological content and skills must be implemented? This dilemma between continuity and change in the advancement of human knowledge bases and technological sophistication was essentially debated by Thomas Huxley, Matthew Arnold, and Herbert Spencer in the 1870s and 1880s.

As we have moved into the second half of the 1980s, we have had to face volatile economic realities in North America which have forced a search for new means to involve schooling in the preparation of the young for the demands of the times. The nationally prominent members of several commissions on the condition of formal education in North America have called on the nation's schools to establish a common academic curriculum. They have also called for a "computer and technological proficiency and for greater stress on the sciences, mathematics, and foreign languages in the schools." The full range of issues these commissions have embraced is taken up in Unit 3.

When the United States was the undisputed polit-ical leader of the world from 1945 to 1952, it was not necessary to deal with the very real challenge implied in the tension between continuity and change. Yet the displacement of hundreds of North American workers in recent years and the continued overdependence on the manufacturing and technological capabilities of Asian and European nations leads to one inevitable question: Should education in North America focus on educating youth to be functionally competitive in technological and scientific skills with their counterparts in Europe and Asia? The present curriculum has proven to be an ineffective and non-competitive mythic model for national educational development (witness the complete disutility in today's marketplace of the American general high school diploma). Should more time be spent examining how others educate their youth in comparison to the way the United States has chosen to do so? Does America wish to be an industrially and technologically independent force in the world or a dependent one?

In the late 1960s and early 1970s, the search for and development of alternative schools and alternative methods of educating persons in non-school environments dominated the literature in education. Intense dialogue continues regarding how to develop quality alternative learning experiences in the wake of recent reports on the state of schooling in America. Qualitative reconstruction of educational programming is a subject of great interest and debate in both public and private schools and among those interested in continued exploration of how to educate people in non-traditional educational environments. The search continues for a way to preserve the best and noblest of our traditions in education while creating more effective learning alternatives to serve the interests of those who desire a choice.

Current literature on continuity and change in education criticizes "outside experts" who seek to tell educators their own art. The resultant "fortress mentality" impedes the development of constructive dialogue among those who work in and out of formal educational settings. There are also those who severely criticize the manner in which school systems appear to follow so closely the needs of business and industry. They mistrust the motivations of the proposed innovations in schooling, while others defend a strong linkage between the development of high technology in industry and its rapid introduction into schooling. Parents seek a greater liasion with schools, industries, libraries, and museums. These various "publics" in and out of the profession must strive to reduce feelings of distrust in order to foster the ideal expressed so well by Matthew Arnold, that education should be "the best that has been thought and said." There is a place for the old and the new in education. Our youth deserve the best and most effective means of attaining mastery over what they try to learn.

The articles in this unit reflect the whole spectrum of the concerns outlined above. They all address some significant issues related to the problem of how to retain the best of what is known about effective schooling while providing reasonable choices as well. They deal with topics that, in one way or another, are concerned with the relationship between political and economic changes in society and change or continuity in the educational process. Although there is no unified North American consensus on either the aims of education or on the issue of change, most agree that it is necessary to seek ways to broaden the educational alternatives of persons in a rapidly changing high-tech society.

Looking Ahead: Challenge Questions

If it is true that there should be a common curriculum at the primary and middle grade levels, should there also be a common curriculum at the secondary level?

Whether public or private, should there be different types of North American secondary schools with different curricula and different instructional missions? What would be the relative advantages or disadvantages of such a policy?

What, if anything, can teachers in the public schools learn from teachers in private schools?

To what extent can schooling be restructured to most effectively emphasize academic achievement as well as intangible but important factors such as character and initiative?

Are there more political and economic pressures on educators than they can be reasonably expected to manage? Is this sort of pressure avoidable? If so, how? If not, why not?

What is a good school? What is your personal view of a sound balance between old and new in school curricula? What should be learned by everyone, and to what level of proficiency? What are your criteria for evaluating a school program?

Can schools become something other than what they are now? What are your reasons for your views?

What Can Schools Become?

What kinds of teaching and learning should we expect in the post-Pac-Man classroom? How can we use the computer revolution to free teachers from the laborious aspects of their job and enable them to concentrate on vitally important goals? Ms. Wassermann suggests some answers to these crucial questions.

Selma Wassermann

SELMA WASSERMANN is a professor of education at Simon Fraser University, Burnaby, B.C.

IN A MODERN office building in downtown Vancouver, the school of tomorrow recently opened. The Learning Store — a fully computerized, individualized classroom — provides unlimited machine time to students of all ages for remedial or enrichment work in such subjects as reading skills, spelling, basic arithmetic, algebra, and the like. The Learning Store is open seven days a week, from 8 a.m. to 10 p.m., and plans are being made for several neighborhood branches. The advertisement to come and learn is appealing:

> You set the speed at which you will learn!
> You really master your subject!
> You pick the time you want to come in.
> You learn on a "fast track" — no diversions, no delays.
> Your success is assured!

What does this mean for Norbert Finster, who teaches grade 6 at the Archive School down the street? Plenty.

In Finster's class, most of the learning time is concentrated in pencil-and-paper tasks that are dominated by the teacher.

In a one-hour language lesson, almost no one speaks except the teacher. A "thinking activity" consists of recall of single, correct answers from previously read materials. Throughout the school day, all activities flow from the teacher and are directed to the whole class. In spite of the variety of resource materials available in Finster's room, children's work is not displayed on the walls, nor is there any sign of art or pupil projects of any kind. If Finster's pupils are involved in curriculum experiences in any hands-on, three-dimensional ways, no evidence of such activity can be seen.

Finster's teaching shows little consideration for individual differences in learning style or in pacing — and little concern for individual interests or special talents. If curriculum is the "stuff of life" in the classroom, life here is withered, dry, gutless. John Goodlad's study of schools is captured in microcosm in this room.[1]

Given the alternative offered by the Learning Store — in which each learner sets his or her own pace in working toward mastery of course material; in which pupils always select content; in which every learner is assured success; in which teachers play diagnostic and facilitative roles, rather than controlling and judging ones; in which the initiative of the learners is cultivated rather than thwarted — the prospects for the survival of the Archive School and teachers like Norbert Finster are bleak. For, if mastery of content is the single, most important end of student learning, the Learning Store has Finster beat on every important criterion.

What Schools Are For

When Goodlad and his team of researchers asked parents and teachers about goals for schools and compared their responses with the goal statements provided by chief state school officers, they found "a very substantial agreement among the states" on the goals considered important. Parents, teachers, and state officials agreed that schools should emphasize academic goals, but they also believed that social, civic, vocational, and personal goals are of vital concern. "When it comes to education and schooling," Goodlad writes, "we Americans want it all. . . . We expect schools to teach the fundamentals, expose students to the world's knowledge, socialize them into our ways of governing and conducting economic affairs, develop their individual talents, and 'civilize them'. . . ."[2] Yet, despite what we say, schools have historically concentrated on academic goals. What's more, this concentration on academics usually intensifies in times of political or social unrest — a process that repeats itself with nauseating regularity about every 10 years. At such times, we typically demand that schools give us fewer frills, stricter discipline, longer hours, more homework, and more emphasis on "basic" skills. It should not come as a surprise that, in this era of unprecedented technological achievement, the social and political pressures on Norbert Finster push him in the direction of horse-and-buggy teaching.

From *Phi Delta Kappan*, June 1984, pp. 690-693. Reprinted by permission.

In previous years, Finster's pupils would have had little recourse but to wait out the shift to the next decade's educational panaceas. Today, they no longer have to wait. There is no waiting at the Learning Store. No waiting and no failing. Today's youngsters, who play computer games in the amusement arcades, who choose computer camps for holiday fun, and who ask for Apples for Christmas, will probably begin to put the same kind of pressure on mom as they do when whining for their favorite cereal in the supermarket. If the academic product, mastery of content, is to be our primary learning goal, then, by all means, let's go after it in style.

But what are the tradeoffs? What do our children stand to lose in the plush-carpeted corridors of the Learning Store? What might they become if they graduate with accumulated information and mastery of information access?

Every personal choice exacts a price. The Learning Store offers a stylish and effective route to the acquisition of information and the mastery of some fundamental skills, but it offers no means for helping students to use the acquired information and skills wisely. Chillingly absent from the individualized, self-paced, self-selected learning programs is any concern for the development of thinking abilities, for the development of moral and ethical behavior, for strengthening interpersonal skills. Absent, too, is any concern for the growth of the learner as a socially responsible, thoughtful, caring human being. Even amid the curricular banality of Finster's class, students learn to be together, to use their knowledge in interpersonal contexts — if only in the lunchroom and at recess.

It may appear that we now face an either/or choice — with each alternative having decided limitations. That is not the case. For I am suggesting that we begin to think about how to incorporate computer-based information and skills programs into our schools, thereby freeing the Finsters from the laborious information-dispensing functions of teaching and enabling them to concentrate on those other, vitally important learning goals that may be more important now than ever before in the history of education.

What Schools Can Become

In any vision of the future, all projections are deeply influenced by the ingrained values and beliefs of the visionary. In this report, I wish immediately to acknowledge my own biases, to make them explicit as the foundation on which my projections are built.

In my world of the future, I hope that people will be able to use knowledge wise-

What are the trade-offs? What do our children stand to lose in the plush-carpeted corridors of the Learning Store?

ly — that is, with concern for the future of humankind, not only in their rhetoric but in their day-to-day behavior. Naturally, I expect that schools and teachers will play a major role in bringing this about. Mine is a humanistic perspective, and perhaps an optimist's as well. In discussing *how* this might happen in classrooms, I have chosen to dwell on what I believe today's children need beyond mere information and skill in acquiring it, as well as on the role of the teacher. Though I treat these issues separately, this separation is only for convenience. In the day-to-day functioning of the classroom, teaching skills and curriculum are in constant, dynamic interaction.

Curriculum Experiences

In 1973, when Sylvia Ashton-Warner wrote her brilliant and perceptive study of today's children, she already noted that the 5-year-olds were "the advance guard of technology, with their long legs, proud faces and elongated bodies, the thrice great brains."[3] The children were beautiful — but somehow lacking. She called them "*mu*persons" — children who were "not eartheners at all" but "two-dimensional psychic mutations who lacked the third dimension of feeling." When Ashton-Warner tried to elicit from the children she studied their key vocabularies (those emotion-packed feeling words that come from deep within), the "*mu*children" instead asked for "outside" words, such as *puppy, helicopter, bike* — signaling that their inner worlds were already sealed over. Watching these children in action, she saw that they did not ask questions; they did not go outside to enjoy play; they did not come alive with curiosity.

Ashton-Warner asked, "Who will share his snack with Rocky?" A child-chorus responded, "Nobody."

Compassion and consideration for others had withered away. The sparkling, bright, and fanciful imagery of the children had flattened.

All of this was already evident a decade ago — even before the appearance of Pac-

Man and other computer games that are now found in more than two-thirds of the children's homes in Vancouver. Recently we introduced a water table into several first- and second-grade classrooms, and the children, sitting around it in small groups, spent most of an initial two-week period with their hands simply immersed in the water. Not playing. Not "experimenting" with the objects provided. Just "feeling" the water. Is this a signal of sensory deprivation of some kind?

The provision of curriculum experiences for the post-Pac-Man classroom should, I believe, reflect what is absent from the lives of children today and emphasize what is urgently needed to help them grow into three-dimensional human beings. Curriculum experiences should also focus on those dimensions of learning that computers are unable to provide effectively. The following list of suggestions is by no means exhaustive.

1. *The elevation and nurturing of children's feelings.* Bernard Berenson says that we all run away at the mention of the word *feelings* and that such avoidance behavior is a harbinger of increased alienation and truncated human growth.[4] Putting this condition at the top of my list, I realize, risks losing the interest of some readers. What the heck! If you're sailing on the *Titanic*, you might as well go first class.

We learn too early — often at great personal cost — to deny our feelings and to avoid dealing with them. Children whose primary playmate is Pac-Man are in grave danger of having insufficient opportunities to grow into feeling humans — the primary path to self-actualization. Is it too much to ask that the school curriculum now recognize the urgency of helping children to deal with their feelings in satisfying and socially acceptable ways?

2. *The promotion of interpersonal skills.* When many of us were growing up, our families' day-to-day lives brought us consistently into situations that required that we learn to live together humanly and humanely. We were called on to respond when Mrs. Green's husband lost his job, when Phyllis came down with scarlet fever, when Aunt Rachel broke her leg. Our life experiences thrust us into situations in which we learned to care for one another. We lived in neighborhoods, where people learned their humanity from participating in the drama of human life.

Today, our children's community is the two-dimensional plane of the TV screen, and their neighborhood is "Sesame Street" or Hazzard County. They are no longer participants, but observers, and observers not of life, but of pseudo-life. It is difficult to learn humanitarian concerns and high-level interpersonal functioning from the likes of "Soap" or from the models provided by such "heroes" as Johnny Carson and Trapper John. If children are to grow in their abilities to deal with other people, we may have to give this area of growth serious consideration in the classroom. Is it too much to ask that training in interpersonal skills be a component of the contemporary curriculum?

3. *The promotion of higher-order cognitive skills.* Everybody is for teaching students how to think. We all applaud it as one of the most important goals of schooling — in spite of the fact that so little of it goes on in today's classrooms. A third-grade teacher once told me that she was certainly in favor of teaching thinking, but how could she be expected to do that, when she had so much "curriculum to cover."

Perhaps now that much of the information-dispensing and skill-drilling functions of the teacher can be adequately carried out by effective computer programs, we can emphasize the development of children's problem-solving capabilities and the application of knowledge, information, and skills to more sophisticated and advanced problem-solving tasks. Is it too much to ask that the curriculum emphasize the higher-order cognitive skills that even our most colorful and imaginative computer programs cannot? Can we finally move teaching for thinking from our rhetoric into the life of our classrooms?

4. *The nurturing of creativity and imagination.* Creativity is one of the most highly valued of human qualities, according to Jacob Getzels and Philip Jackson.[5] According to Albert Einstein, creativity is far more consequential than knowledge in furthering the significant advances of humankind. For it is from rich and fertile imaginations, much more than from accumulated information, that such marvels as the geodesic dome, the theory of relativity, the 12-tone scale, the Fallingwater House at Bear Run, the first airplane, and *Finnegans Wake* spring to life. Once, playing with fantasy was one of the foremost activities of young children. If not in school, the world of make-believe was evident in sand-castle building, in stories of good guys and bad guys, in dress-up plays, in paper dolls, in doll houses, and in fire hats. Children learned to be dreamers, and in their dreams flourished the hopes and aspirations that shaped their lives. Of leaves they fashioned costumes; of dolls they made queens; of radio plays they made pretend worlds as real as any their parents knew.

Today's 5-year-old has fewer opportunities to experience fantasy. By the time she is 5, she has already spent about 5,000 hours of her playtime watching TV — almost 10% of her life. In kindergarten she may prefer "creative daydreaming" to coloring stenciled pumpkins orange, but the teacher informs her mother, "Don't wor-

ry. I'll knock that out of her and get her ready for first grade." With such limited opportunity to tap her creative imagination and with such a counterproductive set of forces already in motion, what kind of adult is she likely to become? And what kind of world is she likely to help create?

Ashton-Warner reminds us that, as we help to broaden a child's creative impulses, so do we help to diminish the destructive ones. Is it too much to ask that our curriculum permit — no, encourage and support and cultivate — the creative activities of children? Is it too much to ask that we put coloring books and stenciled Santa Clauses and cut-out Christmas trees behind us and bring to the classroom the primary tools of children's creative play — sand and water, finger paint, dress-up clothing, conversation, songs, daydreams, tears, quarrels, blocks, creative writing, clay, dolls, boats, chalk, paints, love, dancing? And not only to the primary grades, but throughout the school?

5. *The development of moral integrity.* When Louis Raths first introduced us to the idea of developing values as a part of the education of children, he cited the rapidly changing world, the increased evidence of violence and corruption, the shattering of our faith in family, church, and government as morally impeccable leaders, and the transitory nature of life, coupled with societal and personal dissembling and instability. Raths's major theme was the difficulty children face in growing up morally and ethically sound. If children learn ethical behavior from example, the examples surrounding them seemed to him, at best, shaky. Raths's book, *Values and Teaching*, was written in 1965 — almost 20 years ago. Have things grown worse since then? It's hard to say, but it is clear that they have not become a great deal better. It is increasingly rare for children to grow up today in the presence of many good and healthy examples of moral behavior.

It may be argued that schools are not places in which such learning is appropri-

> **C**urriculum experiences should focus on those dimensions of learning that computers are unable to provide effectively.

ate, that the development of values is best left to the home and the church. While I would not dispute the importance of these two institutions to the moral education of children, I would also point out that all decisions we make are value laden — from the simple, Whom shall I invite to this dinner party?, to the more complex, Who will get my vote? Whether we like it or not, there are moral dimensions to almost every area of the curriculum, from history to literature to art. Furthermore, with respect to science, George Pugh has pointed out that "to disregard the values issues in scientific decision making is to do so at our own peril."[6] Can we ask yet one more condition for the curriculum of the future, without causing it to collapse under the strain? Can we ask that the curriculum include the examination of values as they relate to decision making, so that children can analyze them and discuss them, as well as develop an awareness of the beliefs and attitudes that shape the decisions of their own lives?

The Role of the Teacher

How do all of these curriculum considerations influence the role of the teacher? What should teachers be called on to do, now that their information-dispensing function, which normally occupies more than 60% of their school time, can be substantially transferred to an electronic Miss Brooks? The following roles are as important as they are likely to remain beyond the capacity of any machine.

1. *The teacher as diagnostician.* Ever since we noticed that children were different, lo, these many moons ago, educators have been concerned with how these differences affect a child's learning capabilities. Even the most naive observer can hardly fail to notice the range of abilities, talents, individual difficulties, and learning styles that can be seen in any group of children. Sensitive teachers have long struggled with teaching strategies that attend to these individual differences. Yet pressure to cover the curriculum may have forced many teachers, who might have chosen to behave otherwise, to focus their efforts on whole-class instruction, treating all children as if they were the same.

The Learning Store offers each learner individual attention, coupled with a program designed to meet specific learning needs. The first step in designing such a program is diagnosis of those learning needs. Is it too much to ask that teachers do the same? Surely teachers can learn to diagnose individual learning needs through informed and intelligent observations and to use such data to teach individual children.

2. *The teacher as curriculum maker.* Some of us share the view that the curricu-

lum should be congruent with the total life experience of the child. It should reflect all parts of a child's life. When the curriculum is two-dimensional and flattened out, when it is cut up into bits and pieces, when it is boring, tedious, and banal, then we have small hope of competing successfully with our attractive electronic competitors. When the teacher can create a curriculum that is rich and purposeful and intense, when the curriculum is part of some coherent whole, when it provides for learning that makes sense in the lives of children, then we have a much greater chance of realizing those educational goals that extend beyond the acquisition of information.

It is long past time for teachers to exercise fully their professional function as curriculum makers. For too long this aspect of teaching has been left to the publishers, whose primary consideration is profit, not educational enrichment. A teacher-made curriculum could include an emphasis on helping students to grow as valuing and thinking people; it could allow students to share ideas, thoughts, and feelings with one another; it could allow for student choice, self-pacing, and individual learning styles. A teacher-made curriculum need not sacrifice content but could instead raise the level of content and wed content to process. This curriculum could insure that pupils become increasingly able to function as thoughtful, responsible individuals in a democratic society. A curriculum that fails to emphasize learning in groups and group-process skills, that avoids hands-on activities requiring manipulation of a variety of materials, and that gives inadequate time and attention to arts and crafts, to creative activities, and to higher-order problem-solving skills fails us today in the most critical ways imaginable.

3. *The teacher as facilitator.* When teachers find themselves freed from the

Whether we like it or not, there are moral dimensions to almost every area of the curriculum, from history to literature.

chains of telling, explaining, and showing how, what is left for them to say? Can we begin to conceive of teacher/student interactions that are responsive to pupils, that are something more than "talking at" pupils?

Study after study points to the importance of the facilitative role of teachers in promoting pupil learning.[7] Can teachers retrain themselves to respond to pupils' ideas with sensitive, intelligent questions aimed at raising the level of pupil thought?[8] Can teachers learn to respond empathically to pupils' feelings, modeling respect, regard, and genuineness?[9] Can teachers learn to listen to pupils and take their ideas seriously? Can teachers learn to respond in ways that preserve the dignity and self-respect of each learner?

This type of facilitative functioning implicitly requires that teachers abandon their traditional role as judge and jury in the grading of pupils' work. Can teachers learn to move beyond their value-laden statements about the worth of pupils, beyond ranking students by letters and numbers, to evaluation that emphasizes the diagnosis of learning needs and ways of meeting them?

If teachers can do all of this, the data suggest that such facilitative functioning will not only promote a healthier and mutually nourishing learning environment, but will also motivate pupils to learn.[10] When teachers learn to do these things, they will have the Learning Store outclassed, and we need no longer worry about the survival of schools.

I realize that this is a lot to ask of teachers — to include all of these dimensions of learning in their classrooms. But not a single aspect of what I have suggested here goes beyond the goals stated by parents, teachers, and state officials for the education of all children. The appearance of the Learning Store makes the need more urgent, but at the very same time, more accessible. For if teachers can be freed from the tedium of information-dispensing, of small-t teaching, day after blah-blahing day, they might just be ready to take on the more sophisticated functions of capital-T Teaching required by the post-Pac-Man classroom.

1. John I. Goodlad, *A Place Called School* (New York: McGraw-Hill, 1983), passim.

2. John I. Goodlad, "A Study of Schooling: Some Findings and Hypotheses," *Phi Delta Kappan*, March 1983, p. 468.

3. Sylvia Ashton-Warner, *Spearpoint: Teacher in America* (New York: Knopf, 1973), pp. 59-60.

4. Bernard Berenson, "New Directions in Teaching and Counseling," SITE Lecture Series, Simon Fraser University, July 1983.

5. Jacob Getzels and Philip Jackson, *Creativity and Intelligence* (New York: Wiley, 1962).

6. George Pugh, *The Biological Origins of Human Values* (New York: Basic Books, 1977).

7. David Aspy, *Kids Don't Learn from People They Don't Like* (Amherst, Mass.: Human Resource Development Press, 1977).

8. Selma Wassermann, *Put Some Thinking in Your Classroom* (San Diego: Coronado, 1978).

9. Robert Carkhuff, "Affective Education in the Age of Productivity," *Educational Leadership*, April 1982, pp. 484-88.

10. Aspy, *Kids Don't Learn. . . .*

Education And the Sony War

Joel Spring

JOEL SPRING is a professor in the College of Education, University of Cincinnati.

Until the federal government and state legislatures stop basing curricular changes on political and economic needs, the public schools will continue to be in a state of chaos, says Mr. Spring. As it is, the schools are captive to the profit motive of U.S. industry.

I N THE EARLY 1960s one would have been quickly branded a radical for arguing that the U.S. educational system was geared to meet the needs of international corporate competition. Times have certainly changed. The recent reports from federal, state, and private groups demanding an increase in academic standards in the public schools, particularly in science and mathematics, are unanimous in the contention that higher standards in the schools will help keep America competitive in foreign markets.[1]

It is important to ask why a ground swell of opinion supporting the idea that the public schools should be geared to meet the needs of high technology is cresting now. What has happened to the U.S. economy to cause educational concerns to shift from the problem of widespread unemployment that dominated the 1970s to a demand for increased academic requirements? The answer lies in the demographic changes of the last two decades and the response of U.S. business to those changes. The connection between changes in educational policy and industrial needs is direct.

The Seventies were years of declining growth in productivity, dwindling capital investment by U.S. industry, and relatively high unemployment, particularly among young workers. But there was no decrease in the demand for workers during this period. Instead, the high unemployment figures during the Seventies were caused by the large numbers of youths — members of the postwar baby boom — entering the labor market.[2] This flooding of the labor market caused wages to decline, particularly for entry-level occupations. In the 1970s and into the early 1980s young people in the U.S. have had a

difficult time finding employment at wages comparable to those of the previous decade.[3]

Because of these circumstances, government educational policy in the 1970s concentrated on the problem of youth unemployment. Career education and vocational education became major educational concerns of all levels of government. Federal policy was typified by the Youth Employment Act of 1977, which provided training and employment opportunities.[4] The response of the U.S. business community to a labor surplus and declining wages was to become more labor intensive and to decrease capital outlays.[5] For instance, a company might choose to increase production by adding a second or third shift, rather than by investing in new equipment.

These changes in labor use and capital investment led to the decline in the growth of productivity of U.S. industry. Productivity may be simply defined as the level of output divided by the amount of labor needed to produce it within a certain time. Under this definition, the increased use of labor naturally led to reduced growth in productivity. By 1977 the level of labor productivity in the U.S. was the same as it had been in 1960. On the other hand, Japan increased its labor productivity during the same period by approximately 255%.[6]

T HE TRENDS IN the early 1980s have been almost the exact opposite of those of the 1970s. With the passing of the baby boom, fewer youths are

now entering the labor market. One set of figures shows that the average number of new workers entering the labor force in the 1970s was approximately 2.5 million per year and that, by the late 1980s, this number will decline to approximately 1.5 million workers per year.[7] Another forecast estimates a 14% decline in the 1980s in the number of persons between 14 and 24 years old and a 20% decline in high school enrollments and graduates.[8] Col. George Bailey, former director of continuing education for the U.S. Army, argues that "during the next decade, the military, the colleges, and business and industry will all be competing for the same limited supply of people."[9]

The response of business and industry to the end of the baby boom has been twofold. On the one hand, employers are concerned about the decrease in the number of qualified employees for entry-level jobs. This dwindling pool of workers threatens to drive up wages. Thus business has been working with the schools to maximize the size of the labor pool by improving the education of those students who would have been marginally employable in the 1970s. This newfound interest in education is reflected in adopt-a-school programs, Jobs for America's Graduates, and local alliances between businesses and schools. It has also led to increased emphasis on career preparation in the schools themselves. In his study for the Carnegie Corporation, Michael Timpane details the extent of these new cooperative programs and argues that they have sprung up primarily in response to the growing shortage of entry-level workers.

From *Phi Delta Kappan*, April 1984, pp. 534-537. Reprinted by permission of the author and Phi Delta Kappan.

Meeting the short-term needs of U.S. business and industry does not necessarily result in economic benefits either to the economy or to the individual.

"For the first time in a generation," Timpane writes, "there will probably be, in several urban locations, an absolute shortage of labor supply for entry-level positions. Urban employers already report great difficulty in locating qualified employees for entry-level positions."[10]

On the other hand, the U.S. business community finds itself in difficulty because of delayed capital investments and declining productivity. Both business and political leaders have called for greater technological development to meet the growth of international competition. With regard to educational policy, this has meant a call for increased graduation requirements in mathematics, science, and other academic fields. Policy makers hope that these new graduates will lead U.S. industry to victory in the worldwide technological competition.

Both of these trends in educational policy are designed to provide U.S. business with an expanded pool of potential employees — and consequently a decline in wages. This will be particularly true if high unemployment continues to characterize the 1980s. If these two trends are successful, the market will be flooded with high school graduates with good work attitudes and minimum basic skills for entry-level positions and with highly qualified scientists and engineers.

Meeting the short-term needs of U.S. business and industry does not necessarily result in economic benefits either to the economy or to the individual. After all, the decision of business not to invest in new plants and equipment in the 1970s and instead to reap short-term profits is partly responsible for the present technological crisis. *The failure of the public schools did not cause the problem.* Indeed, it is hard to predict the social, political, and economic needs of the world that the first high school graduates to have completed 12 years of schooling under the present educational proposals will face in 1995.

In fact, if the schools continue to be geared to meet the changing needs of U.S. business, we can expect still another change in educational policy in the next decade to meet those changing desires. Thus the public school system becomes a captive of the profit motive of U.S. industry. And, let me emphasize again, this relationship guarantees neither an improved economy nor a higher standard of living for individuals. Indeed, such a close connection between education and industry might lead to *lower* wages, as different segments of the labor market are flooded by workers channeled there by the public school system. In effect, American business would be using the public school system to exploit the American worker.

EDUCATORS HAVE been quick to accept the demands that business makes on the schools because of the constant promise of more money for education. Over the last three decades U.S. educators have been willing to accept the extravagant claims that public schooling can win the Cold War, end poverty, and eliminate unemployment. Although all of these claims have been built on shaky premises, educators have seen them as ways of convincing the public of the worth of the schools and of the need for more money. In other words, extravagant claims about the power of public education provide an important means of public relations for public school educators.

The report of the National Commission on Excellence in Education is a case in point. It stresses both the importance of future investment in education and of an educational plan to meet the current needs of industry. The report argues that investment in public education is the key to solving the economic problems of the U.S. "If only to keep and improve on the slim competitive edge we still retain in world markets," the report urges, "we must rededicate ourselves to the reform of our educational system for the benefit of all. . . ." In language designed to frighten readers into shelling out more money for public education, the report states, "If an unfriendly foreign power had attempted to impose on America the mediocre educational performance that exists today, we might well have viewed it as an act of war."[11] The picture painted in *A Nation at Risk* is that of a tired giant losing a global trade war because of the failure of its public schools. The solution to the problems of international trade, according to the report, is the reform of public schooling.

In making these claims, the National Commission offered no evidence that public schooling can solve the problems of international trade and economic development. Indeed, the commissioners seem to have assumed that the economic problems of the U.S. are not being caused by problems in the economic system itself but by problems in the development of human capital. Again, they offered no proof. Ample proof is offered of the decline of public schools but not of the relationship of this decline to economic problems.

All the historical evidence from the last three decades of federal involvement in public schools suggests that public schooling is *not* the answer to social and economic problems. In the 1950s the public schools were called on to win the Cold War against the Soviet Union by providing more mathematicians and scientists. (The parallels between today's rhetoric and that of the 1950s should be noted.) In the 1950s the key to our technological race with the Soviet Union was believed to be the public schools. The National Defense Education Act was passed in 1958 to provide more funding for science, mathematics, and foreign language instruction. This legislation was very similar to several bills now pending in Congress. In addition, there was a fivefold increase in funding to the National Science Foundation to develop new curricula for the schools.[12]

What was the result of this federal involvement? There is no evidence that it won the military/technological war with the Soviet Union. In fact, all the evidence marshaled by the National Commission indicates that the public schools actually declined shortly after the National Defense Education Act was passed. Though it cannot be proved, there may even be a causal relationship between federal involvement and the academic decline of the schools.

In the 1960s Presidents Kennedy and Johnson called on the public schools to end poverty and improve the economic conditions of minority groups. The major piece of federal legislation in this "war on poverty" was the Elementary and Secondary Education Act of 1965. In the 1970s Presidents Nixon and Ford tried to solve the problems of unemployment by expanding career and vocational education programs. Despite all of these efforts to solve social and economic problems through public schooling, the U.S. still faces high unemployment and chronic poverty.

Now we face another demand: change the educational system to fit the national goal of increased technological development for improved international trade. The National Commission recommends that state and local requirements for high schools be changed to include, as a minimum, what the report calls the "five new basics." These new basics include four years of English, three years of mathematics, three years of science, three years of social studies, and one-half year of computer science.

The proposals of the National Commission parallel exactly what is happening as states try to improve their economic conditions by requiring more math and science courses as a means of attracting high-technology industries. As of May

47

1983 the Oregon state legislature was considering the establishment of a state high school for science and mathematics; Wyoming was considering scholarships for math and science teachers; New York was considering training programs and special scholarships for math and science teachers; and Connecticut was considering some form of loan program for math and science teachers. In all, 30 states were considering some form of special aid for math and science teaching. In addition, Congress was considering a $425 million math and science education bill.[13]

There is a certain irony in the fact that these proposals are designed to correct problems resulting from earlier proposals linking public goals with academic requirements. Most existing state-mandated academic standards are the products of some previous effort to achieve political, economic, or social goals. After its survey of trends in the high school curriculum, the National Commission concluded that "secondary school curricula have been homogenized, diluted, and diffused to the point that they no longer have a central purpose." But because the Commission does not analyze the causes for this diffuse curriculum, it travels down the same path that brought the schools to their present predicament.

Through the years the states and the federal government have continually added to and subtracted from the curriculum according to social, political, and economic needs. The public schools have been asked to solve problems ranging from driver safety to fighting communism. As Gene Maeroff writes, "Schools have been viewed by Congress primarily as instruments of social change. It is perhaps flattering to public education that it was awarded so pivotal a role in the perfecting of society, but the responsibility is a burden nonetheless."[14]

HAT THIS RUSH to save U.S. international trade means is that the public school curriculum is being biased toward yet another goal: namely, technological development. But is this the only problem faced by the United States? One could argue that the economic problems of the U.S. have been primarily political in origin. For instance, U.S. economic problems could be related to the high deficits and runaway inflation caused by the Vietnam war and the federal government's handling of the energy crisis of the 1970s. If this were true, then one might argue for more political education in the schools. But the point is that it is wrong to bias public school curricula in *any* one direction when there is no proof as to what are the most important social,

Educators have been quick to accept the demands that business makes on the schools because of the constant promise of more money for education.

economic, and political problems — much less their solutions.

This issue becomes clearer when one considers possible alternatives to raising academic requirements for secondary schools. Suppose America's problems stemmed from an inability of the population to think through important issues clearly. If this were true, why not have all secondary schools require three years of philosophy? Suppose the problem is the inability of the population to understand and act on political, social, and economic issues. One might then replace the meaningless hodgepodge of social studies courses with a requirement that all secondary students take three years of sociology, three years of economics, and three years of political science. Or suppose society has been ruined by too much technology and not enough appreciation of the arts and humanities. If this were true, why not require three years of music, three years of art, and three years of literature? All of these curricula could be defended in terms of some national need or purpose.

Until the federal government and the state legislatures stop making curriculum changes on the basis of social, political, and economic needs, the curriculum of the public schools will continue to be in a state of flux and chaos. The real question regarding the curriculum is, What knowledge is of most worth? In a democratic society, the answer to that central question should be given by individuals, not by governments. State legislatures must stop establishing academic requirements, and the federal government must stop trying to influence the curriculum to serve national policy objectives.

The recommendations of the National Commission offer no real hope for a reform that will cure the ills of U.S. education. All the problems addressed by the report have their origin in the present structure of public schooling. Merely changing academic requirements to suit the latest whim of the government — to serve some particular policy goal — will do nothing to alter that basic structure.

How long will the American public continue to believe extravagant claims

about the value of public schooling? How many more generations will accept the public relations strategy of public school educators, as they offer their product as a panacea for practically every social, political, or economic ill? How many more years will Congress and the state legislatures go along with the grandiose claims of the lobbyists for public education? Perhaps society will see through the current fog of rhetoric that envelops the recommendations of these new commissions; perhaps this time the public will realize that the public schools cannot solve such problems as the weakened position of the U.S. in international trade or the failure of the domestic economy. Indeed, we might even harbor the hope that someday the public schools will no longer be captives of the profit motive of U.S. industry and that the education of Americans will not be determined by the economic goals of business.

1. Three of the major reports are Education Commission of the States, *Action for Excellence: A Comprehensive Plan to Improve Our Nation's Schools* (Denver: ECS, 1983); Twentieth Century Fund Task Force on Federal Elementary and Secondary Education Policy, *Making the Grade* (New York: Twentieth Century Fund, 1983); and National Commission on Excellence in Education, *A Nation at Risk: The Imperative for Educational Reform* (Washington, D.C.: U.S. Government Printing Office, 1983).

2. See Daniel Quinn Mills, "Decisions About Employment in the 1980s: Overview and Underpinning," and Michael Wachter, "Economic Challenges Posed by Demographic Changes," in Eli Ginzberg et al., eds., *Work Decisions in the 1980s* (Boston: Auburn House, 1982).

3. "For example, while males 20 to 24 years old earned $73 for every $100 by prime-age males in 1955, they earned only $58 for every $100 in 1977," according to Wachter, p. 43.

4. For a discussion of the Youth Employment Act of 1977, see Joel Spring, *American Education*, 2nd ed. (New York: Longman, 1982), pp. 117-21.

5. "In fact, in the mid-1970s American manufacturing firms were cautious about capital investment, but relatively expansive about employment. . . . In the most telling comparison, American manufacturers and manufacturers in France, Japan, and Germany increased output between 1972 and 1978 by somewhat similar amounts. During the same period employment fell in France by 2.2%, in Japan by 4.7%, and in Germany by 12%; but in the United States, manufacturers increased employment by 615%," according to Mills, pp. 8-9.

6. Ibid., p. 5.

7. Wachter, pp. 35-42.

8. Michael Timpane, *Corporations and Public Education*, report distributed by Teachers College, Columbia University (New York: Carnegie Corporation, May 1982), pp. 8-9.

9. Quoted in Anne C. Lewis, "Washington Report: The Military Enters the Competition for Technically Trainable Graduates," *Phi Delta Kappan*, May 1983, p. 603.

10. Timpane, p. 8.

11. *A Nation at Risk*, p. 5.

12. A history of federal involvement in public schools after World War II can be found in Joel Spring, *The Sorting Machine* (New York: Longman, 1976).

13. "State Proposals to Bolster Math and Science Teaching," *Education Week*, 18 May 1983, pp. 14-16.

14. Gene Maeroff, *Don't Blame the Kids: The Trouble with America's Public Schools* (New York: McGraw-Hill, 1982), p. 8.

THE BEST PREP SCHOOL IN TOWN

JULIE BAUMGOLD

PRIVATE PRACTICE: *Prep for Prep teaches not only English, math, and science but confidence and discipline, a private-school mentality: Students must be prepared, teachers are counselors and friends.*

THE CHILDREN ARE USED TO it. They are used to the foundation ladies with their big leather pocketbooks and their sincere white faces sliding politely into their classrooms and scrunching down on those little desk chairs yet another time to watch them as they answer questions about the eccentricities of Thornton Wilder or hidden diseconomies while Gary Simons stands there hopefully.

The children are eleven years old and know what it's all about. They don't put on an act. They don't have to. Because they are gifted. Because they work desperately hard. Because they are part of Prep for Prep, one of the best and least-known private schools in New York, which Gary Simons runs. So now when the foundations come, the children barely look up, except at the teacher who is their way out of public schools and into the seventh grades of Brearley, Birch Wathen, Calhoun, Chapin, Collegiate, Dalton, Fieldston, Horace Mann, Night-

ingale-Bamford, Spence, Trinity, and twenty other schools that put aside scholarship places for them.

Prep for Prep takes place after hours at the Trinity School. About a dozen teachers—nineteen in the summer—come there from Chapin and Collegiate, from P.S. 107 and P.S. 383, for it is one of the few programs where both private- and public-school faculty cooperate. Students come there from the Grand Concourse, Park Place, Decatur Avenue. Sometimes, in the beginning, they don't know what a private school is, much less the differences among them. It is hard to get into Prep for Prep, and hard to stay in. Prep makes big demands on the character and intelligence of its students, on their parents and families.

Every year, Prep for Prep screens over 700 gifted students from minority groups and chooses about 100. They begin a fourteen-month program while they are still in public school, and then Prep helps place them in private schools. There it follows them, sending in advisers and

counselors to help and tutor them if necessary until college. For the first time this year, Prep graduates will enter universities like Princeton, Harvard, and Columbia. Prep for Prep costs about $4,500 for each student while he is in Prep and more for counseling later. The program, which has a budget this year of more than $735,000, is 95 percent privately funded by such groups as the Clark Foundation, the Edward John Noble Foundation, and the Esther A. and Joseph Klingenstein Fund.

The Prep children work full days in the summers before and after sixth grade, and during the academic year late Wednesday afternoons and all day Saturdays. There have been eight classes—they call them contingents—since it started, in 1978, with 25 students; it has grown to over 200 this summer. Prep is the main program of Broad Jump, a nonprofit organization that educates minority students, and Gary Simons is the executive director. It is independent of Trinity, but Dr. Robin Lester, the headmaster of Trinity, is a trustee and believes in it with all his heart and enthusiasm.

Prep for Prep is different from other such programs in that it takes students younger. It gives them crucial group support. It prepares them rigorously both academically and emotionally. It tries to provide what Robin Lester calls "the social comfort that a child must have," and it follows through with full-time counseling.

"What we ended up with is a model," says Lester, "one of the best middle schools in the country, and any of us might wonder if our middle schools work quite up to their mark."

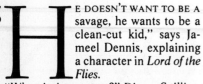

'HE DOESN'T WANT TO BE A savage, he wants to be a clean-cut kid," says Jameel Dennis, explaining a character in *Lord of the Flies*.

"What is innocence?" Diane Spillios, the head of the upper school at Chapin, asks her honors English class at Prep.

"Purity," says one.

"You don't have a bad conscience," says another.

" 'The darkness of man's heart'—what does that mean?" asks Spillios. The questions go on for the whole 50 minutes, the last period of this spring day, while outside the parents sit in the lobby like benched athletes, waiting for the quicksilver stars of their families, who are still too young to ride the subways alone.

"What is Wall Street?" asks Kathryn Bordonaro, who is teaching research skills. "What is the Latin root of 'corporation'?" This is the format of every class—all questions, to examine what they have read and push them beyond the material as they sit in a circle of fourteen. "Does this chapter remind you of something you learned today in history?" another teacher asks, because many of them know the curriculum of other classes and relate it.

"They are responsive and eager for anything you have to give," says Bruce Ravage, who teaches three periods of math after a full day at P.S. 107 in the East Bronx. "Here they let their defenses down. It makes it fun." "It's as close to perfect teaching as you can imagine," says Diane Spillios. "The big difference between Prep students and those in other independent schools where I've taught is their tremendous drive."

Prep for Prep gives courses in literature, math, writing, laboratory science, and American history. It teaches research skills, such as how to outline and write topic sentences, how to organize, take notes, highlight, make note cards, and use a library. It simulates a traditional school with homework, exams, and grades A to F. But beyond this, Prep

tries to build self-confidence and discipline, to develop a private-school mentality: Students must be prepared, teachers are counselors and friends, not just people to get away from when the bell rings. The Prep staff tries to prepare a child for the time when he returns to his neighborhood loaded with extra books and disappears inside, for the time when he gets called "Oreo" or "white boy" back home, or gets invited to a new friend's beach house that is bigger than his apartment building.

It's here in the classrooms at twilight that the visitor can see eight out of fourteen hands raised and waving like pendulums, hands tense with knowledge at the end of the regular school day. It is here in the summer session that a young Indian boy sits with his guidance group and a counselor as a personality problem of his is dissected. It is here that a gifted writer like twelve-year-old Daniel Baldwin, who is James Baldwin's nephew, reads an essay on the Freedom Riders: "I feel they had every reason in the world to defy the laws which held them in bondage, and separated them from society.... The freedom riders ... fought the white bats in the dark, gloomy cave of segregation!"

In the spring and summer months, it is especially hard for the children to get home after six, sometimes after eight, and have three and a half hours of homework and no street life in neighborhoods where it is so important. Michael Paniagua, now a Trinity junior, used to work until 2 A.M. on his Prep homework, with his sister typing for him, and admits he neglected his public-school work.

"I lost friends outside. I used to be the sports star of the block; now I'm never outside. They go places, and I'm not around," says Jameel Dennis, who lives on Sedgwick Avenue in the Bronx.

"I used to be really sporty," says Cylton Collymore Jr. "I'm a roomy person. I can't stay cooped up. Sometimes I walk through my block and everybody is outside."

Jameel and Cylton, Erica Terry, Jennifer Rosado, Daniel Baldwin, and Denise Burrell had stayed to talk about themselves and the program late one afternoon. They are all from Contingent VII and this fall will be entering their new schools. Daniel and Jameel will be going to Horace Mann, Cylton to Poly Prep, Erica to Dalton, Jennifer to Nightingale-Bamford, and Denise to Spence. As a group, they seem secure in their intelligence, almost excited by it, very well set in themselves. Like others in Prep for Prep, they have enormous self-possession, a winning poise, and a natural openness.

Jennifer, who wants to be a computer analyst and make $50,000 a year, says, "You can visit me at high-society par-

ties." Daniel wants to be a cartoonist and part-time poet; Jameel "a doctor in the surgical field"; Cylton is not sure—perhaps a pilot or a football player. Erica wants to be a lawyer or a newscaster, and Denise a journalist, because "my family tells me how nosy I am."

All of them say they have felt the burdens of the Prep work in addition to their public schools'. A few have wanted to quit. Erica speaks about pressure in her public school. Jameel says, "We finish fast, and the teacher says to the others, 'Why don't you finish as fast?' " "No one knew I was smart," says Denise. "I didn't flaunt it." "At least I fit into a group of people here," says Jennifer. "Brainiacs," says Daniel. Like other Preppers, they are bored with the repetitions of public-school work but were surprised when they first came to Prep and found others as intelligent. Sometimes, in their public schools, the Prep students have been the class clowns, sometimes the stars, sometimes the daydreamers, and sometimes just quiet and hidden until their scores were read. They all feel they will have friends when they go on to their new schools and are proud of having survived at Prep. "I don't know where I would be if I was a normal person," says Erica. "There wouldn't be much hope for the future."

"Prep for Prep becomes their lives," says Frankie Cruz, who has just graduated from Hotchkiss and is going to Princeton. "That's what I explain to all the new ones." This summer, he is running the advisory program of sixteen alumni who have come back to help. They talk about the new schools—they are models of what the others are working toward. Frankie and the others talk to the families, look over the work sheets, and know which students have to share rooms and baby-sit, whose parents help and push and whose can't understand as their children take on this new in-between identity, not black, not white—the identity of the gifted child who is at last working at his proper level alongside others who are equally gifted.

THERE ARE REASONS PREP FOR Prep has succeeded, why its students not only keep up but excel in their private schools, that go beyond the devotion of Simons and the teachers, beyond the dedication of Lester and other school heads and board members. The children are taken into the program at the right time—at an age when, as Simons says, "they have identity. At eleven or twelve, they realize, 'I am me, as apart from my family. Decisions can be made by me.' When they are younger, they can't make this commitment." They can travel then, and it is

ALUMNI HONORS: *Last year, former students at Prep for Prep included the outstanding junior at Trinity, a class speaker at Collegiate, and one of the class presidents of Nightingale-Bamford.*

then, in seventh grade, that they must confront the local junior highs.

"The minority child is harder to assess academically," says Simons. "At this age, they have the best chance both of doing well and having an impact on the community. Around ninth or tenth grade, there comes an awareness of race, a real stiffening and rigidity. It begins to happen when they start dating and when they realize the amount of money that they need to get by, what their place is in society."

Prep for Prep candidates must go through levels of screening. First, the public schools that cooperate recommend the program to more than 1,000 fifth-graders who have scored outstandingly on citywide reading tests. The schools realize by now that Prep works and that they can use it as a motivational tool. Students who are interested are then tested for three and a half hours. About a third of these candidates go on to the next level, which is an individual test and interviews with counselors and teachers to learn more about them and their family support. They write essays and take math placement tests. Sometimes, once taken in, they fail. About fifteen of the new students this summer will drop out or be voted out by the faculty, but only after extensive counseling and probationary periods and only when they are sure the child is being harmed or can't be reached. Then he is given exit counseling. "A child who is struggling here was used to being the best in his public school with little effort, and he may skimp here because he wants to return to the top," says Simons.

"The academic mortality rate of upper-middle-class kids in the 31 independent schools involved is larger than of the Prep for Prep students in the schools," says Lester, "because of the rigor of Prep's preparation. In our seventh grade, they hit the ground running . . . in the middle to upper end of the class." "When they enter, many are way ahead in study skills and coping with the volume and hard work," says Diane Spillios. Evelyn Halpert of Brearley finds it "the single most impressive and successful program of its kind." "It's an excellent program," says Patricia Redd Johnson, a director of admissions at Dalton. "They are two or three years above grade level. Generally, from Prep for Prep, their skills are excellent. The parents are

tremendously involved, and at Prep, minority students are respected. That's the key. Minority parents hover over their kids, and we hover over them as much as Prep does. Their egos are intact."

The outstanding junior at Trinity last year was Dwayne Davis from Prep. Many, like Frederica Miller, a Brearley eleventh-grader, go right into honors. Franklyn Arthur was her class president at Nightingale-Bamford. Sheldon Philp was chosen as class speaker in his first year at Collegiate. Marcella Goodridge is at the top of her class at Birch Wathen. The faculty chose Joseph Ayala as yearbook editor at Allen-Stevenson. Phillip Wong was first in his class in his very first term at Poly Prep.

Also, Prep for Prep follows through. Its paid counselors go from school to school, seeing the students, making sure their forms are filled out, checking their records, taking the temperature of their "social comfort," which influences their grades, and being "the people to lean on," as Frederica Miller says. The students already have a sense of community and support with their Prep friends.

Prep has its own excellent newspaper to celebrate their achievements, publish their speeches and writing, tell about their teachers and advisers. It has field trips and parties. A boy at Collegiate has his Prep friends at Dalton and Horace Mann, so "maybe he can't go on the ski trip, but he doesn't have to hang out on the corner," says Simons. "It makes it possible to have white friends and feel less vulnerable to the ordinary scorns and snubs of teenagers." If he goes to Riverdale, he goes with perhaps another friend from Prep and he knows the older Prep students who are already there. "It was hard to find a nice clique, since many had been there from the first grade," says Michael Paniagua of Trinity, "but I had three friends, and from there it spread."

'GARY SIMONS IS THE reason this has worked," says Robin Lester. "I have met a saint, and it is Simons. He is single-minded, he lacks perspective, but I suspect that's what saints do. He is crusty, but he helps us see the vision with him."

There was a day when Gary Simons was teaching at P.S. 140 in the Bronx when everything he had to do became very clear to him. As a boy, he had grown up in the Bronx, gone to J.H.S. 143, Bronx Science, and then upstate to Harpur College, where he saw a more personal way to learn. At P.S. 140, he taught the gifted sections, and it frustrated him that his students were trapped, facing the local junior highs. He took his four best students and worked out a separate curriculum for them. He found them willing to do enormous amounts of work. One of them was Frankie Cruz, who became a member of his first contingent at Prep.

"I was particularly indignant about what his experience had been, how he had been misevaluated and shifted around. We had an Easter party one day, and some of the students stayed and helped me to clean up. Frankie was sitting on a window ledge on top of some bookcases, and he was talking about the books we had read. We had kept quite a pace. There he was, this little boy with his baseball cap, and he said, 'I can't believe what I just did, how much we read.' He was naïve and self-congratulatory, and at that moment, it clicked—all these ideas I tried to put together. I knew then, dammit, it will fly, because there are so many kids like him who need to know what they can do."

As part of his fieldwork for his doctoral fellowship, Simons started Prep as a pilot project of Columbia University's Teachers College. Before this, he had gone around to the private schools to place certain students, and the results were mixed. They didn't have study skills or the experience of competing, and they felt isolated. So he designed Prep, which later became a project of Broad Jump, then run by Samuel Peabody, who stepped down in the third year of the program but remains as an active trustee. Like Robin Lester, Simons felt that students would learn best from each other, and enough serious minority students together would influence one another. Lester didn't have to divert any Trinity tuition money. He allowed Prep to use the classrooms at Trinity, the secretaries and Xeroxes. He believed in the progam right away, and his endorsement carried weight with the other school heads, says

Simons. Together, they insisted on the full fourteen months of preparation, though they knew that the corporations funding Prep were often impatient for results.

"There was no truancy in the first summer when the parents had to bring them," says Lester. (Now the summer students are bused in.) "We knew we had hit on something. There's a touch of the divine in these children and their families."

In their months at Prep and later, the students must go through many changes in the way they see themselves. First, at Prep they go from their public-school A's to their first C's. Then they go from being part of a racially similar group to the white world.

Prep starts preparing them for this in the first summer with a literature course with the theme of identity. They study *The Light in the Forest,* a novella by Conrad Richter about a white boy captured by Indians. What determines identity? Is it skin color or the culture you are raised in? They read *Dr. Jekyll and Mr. Hyde, The Man Who Would Be King, A Raisin in the Sun, I Remember Mama,* and Richard Wright's *Black Boy.* They read poems about skin color. They write their autobiographies. They have group guidance, during which, in front of their friends and a counselor, their work habits and any attitude problems are picked apart. Certain mechanisms that may have been crucial to their survival in public school are no longer acceptable—here they are bad habits. Some have survived the boredom of having things repeated in public school by tuning out. They have been taught by their parents to hit back and not be a victim. Or there's "snapping."

"You snap at people, at the way people look," a girl says to a boy in one guidance session.

"Snapping is virtually a social skill in the public schools, a kind of repartee, but it does not go well in other situations," says Simons.

"I keep hearing that you are unprepared in all your classes," Angel Martinez, the guidance counselor, says to another boy. They discuss why he is losing his work and what he should do: "Use a clipboard." "Folders, a stapler."

Martinez turns to a girl who is suddenly not doing well in history, and he asks how many note cards she has made for a project. The other students have made ten, twelve, fifteen.

"Three," says the girl. "The rest are at home." Home is a place where one child is autistic and another is dying of leukemia. The counselors had talked about her at lunch and felt she seemed solid enough to be able to take this now. "This first summer, we get them to be open,

then we talk about how to treat other people," says Simons.

They talk about what a rich person's home looks like, what to do if someone pushes ahead on a lunch line or says something nasty. "They tell you to be yourself. You may feel the sting of not having as much and wishing you did, but you are better in different ways," says Marcella Goodridge of Birch Wathen.

It is not just white voices teaching them. The alumni come back. There are black counselors like Sharon Spann and Bill Holmes, director of alumni activities. Holmes is from the South Bronx. Through ABC, another program to place minority-group students in private schools, he entered Collegiate and went on to Bowdoin College. The students learn from counselors like Angel Martinez and Michael Chung. Two of the four top administrators of Prep are black.

IN THE SECOND SUMMER, PREP GIVES a psychology course called "Invictus," named for the William Ernest Henley poem that ends, "I am the master of my fate: I am the captain of my soul." "Invictus" helps the students understand their own development and the influences on them of their peers, the media, and the culture. They talk about how their values are affected by different forces, what causes them to make certain decisions.

"With more awareness, they have more control about getting involved with drugs or being with people who are not serious about education, how to deal with money spent casually," says Simons."

When they enter their new schools, there are further problems with identity. "This involves a deeper questioning. Some say, 'Why me?,' some see it as an opportunity, and some say, 'What am I doing it for? How much must I give up of where I'm coming from?' But by the time they are seventeen, they have seen the dropouts at home, the fifteen-year-olds with babies, so it proceeds in stages," says Simons. "The ordinary adolescent problems with their parents are exacerbated by their going into a world their parents can't follow and sometimes do not comprehend." There are a few who cannot speak English and do not go to meetings, because they are uncomfortable. "Sometimes when the children leave a black environment," says Bill Holmes, "the parents see changes in terms of their voice, the way they dress, and their values that they don't like."

In the new schools, they share a school but not a whole way of life. It's hard to go to evening programs when they don't live in the neighborhood. Counselors like Sharon Spann say some parents don't

understand why the children have to stay late or why it's important for them to go to a friend's summer house. It may take them two and a half hours to get to school. There is one Brearley student from Queens who must take a bus, three subways, and another two buses. Spann sees all sorts of harrowing home problems. She says there's the perpetual problem of wanting. "They see a friend who goes to Spain for Christmas and has $200 in her wallet for shoes, and they want that Benetton sweater, that class trip to Boston that costs $150." Sometimes, she says, they feel burned out after Prep; sometimes they do not tell if they are not doing well.

Dwayne Davis described this double-identity problem in a speech he gave at Trinity: "[There are] two very familiar names to any black of a predominantly white school: 'Oreo' . . . and the standard 'white boy.' . . . When eventually you dress in argyles and loafers, you hear from your non-prep-school black peers: Who is Brooks Brothers? Why does your coat reach your knees, and why don't you have a leather bomber jacket? The desire to be accepted, . . . to adapt to the norm most profitable, results in the questioning of one's own character. . . . In the white stores, downtown, it is necessary to be twice as polite, well-groomed, and articulate simply to match up. . . . Most resentment, though, fades with the understanding of one's identity."

"One of our great fears is do our Trinity kids measure up to their standards of propriety and decency," says Lester.

Frankie Cruz has been through all the changes. He says he felt "comfortable" at P.S. 140. "I was close to home, and the whole family went there." He is the youngest of four children and learned English from his brother and sisters. His father is a dietary worker for a home for the aged, his mother a housewife. Simons recruited him for the first contingent at Prep, when things were still small and he felt like "a pioneer." After the first summer, he went right into Calhoun. He was athletic and had to organize himself. "I was very shy and quiet, and at Calhoun, I could just jump in. At home, the kids wondered why I carried so many books, but I managed to keep my friends." When he transferred to Hotchkiss, his family had to buy him luggage, ties, and jackets. He found it "rigorously demanding," and he was homesick, but he became Prep's first varsity-team captain and got into Williams, Wesleyan, and Dartmouth as well as Princeton.

"I want to be happy with what I have. To be a part of what I have and not feel I want more," he says.

'I HAVE, LIKE, A SPOTTED PAST," says Frederica Miller of Brearley, who was chosen to spend the first semester of this year at the Mountain School run by Milton Academy. "When I had a double work load, I was absent from Prep a lot. Finally Mr. Simons said, 'This is your last chance, Fred.'" "Prep worked hard with Frederica, helping her organize her home life and restructuring her work habits," says Simons. Sitting with her in the cafeteria at Brearley, it is easy to see how successfully she has made the transition, how well placed she is. She is a Brearley young woman all the way, and is very proud, finding her school "a really friendly place. It's hard, but in a relaxed way. Nobody tells you you have to do well, they just expect you to." She gets honors, though not high honors, because math and science drag her average down. "She is a remarkable girl, a credit to the program and Brearley," says headmistress Evelyn Halpert.

Frederica says she doesn't get jealous when she sees friends spend a lot of money on clothes—she thinks that's foolish—but it's hard sometimes when they go away. "I make the best of what I've got. No one flaunts at Brearley. You don't find people boasting, unless they want to get it in the neck."

Frederica came out of P.S. 163, where "some of the kids were really rowdy, and they didn't teach you all that great." She lives in what she calls an "average neighborhood, not exciting, not awful," and is the youngest of five brothers and sisters. Some of her neighborhood friends "have gone badly down," and most of her friends are now from Brearley. She was shy the first year, and her counselors and tutors helped.

"I've thought my future out. I had an idea of being a teacher, but I strayed away from that. I like journalism or psychology. I'll be out of grad school at 25, married at 30. I have strong opinions."

A new, larger contingent started at Prep last summer. New parents are sitting on the bench this fall. Simons says the next contingent's college acceptances will be even better than this year's. Lester talks about a Vietnamese student Trinity is taking after just one summer at Prep. "Just think what a child like this does for our school!" he says.

In a science lab, Elizabeth Walsh, a young teacher from Dalton, is about to demonstrate how to test for starches. The experiment begins. The students wrap their sneakers around the lab chairs. The questions start, the small hands go up and up, and, from the rear of the room, Gary Simons, with yet another visitor, watches and knows he is right.

A National Survey of Middle School Effectiveness

Data from 130 exemplary schools show that changing to middle school organization positively affects student achievement and personal development, learning climate, faculty morale, staff development, and parental and community involvement.

PAUL S. GEORGE AND LYNN L. OLDAKER

Paul S. George is professor of education, University of Florida, Gainesville, FL 32611. **Lynn L. Oldaker** is a teacher at Dryden Middle School, Juneau Public Schools, Box 210996, Auke Bay, AK 99821.

The middle school movement is one of the largest, most comprehensive efforts at educational reorganization in the history of American public schooling. Only the decades-long school consolidation process rivals it in terms of the number of school districts and students involved. Each year more districts open newly reorganized middle schools as alternatives to K-8, 7-9, 7-12, or other plans. Although decreasing enrollments have spurred a decline in the overall number of all types of middle level schools in the U.S., the number of identified middle schools continues to increase (NIE, 1983).

The lack of consistency used to evaluate the effectiveness of middle school programs—and the inconclusiveness of the available research—prompted us to conduct our own study in the fall of 1983. We invited central office staff members and school administrators in 34 states to supply data about the effects of implementing middle school programs in their districts.

Photographs courtesy of Fred Newton, North Middle School, Fort Campbell, Ky.

We developed a list of reputedly exemplary middle schools from schools identified by (1) the 1982 Study of Well-Disciplined Schools sponsored by Phi Delta Kappa, (2) the 1983 DOE National Secondary School Recognition Program, (3) a panel of ten persons recognized as experts in middle school education, and (4) several lists from books on middle school education. Of the schools we contacted, 130 (81 percent) responded.

To ascertain the degree to which the programs of these schools could be

North Middle School student Todd Meredith invites comments from classmates about their perceptions of his attitudes and behavior.

deemed effective for the education of early adolescents, we asked each respondent to supply detailed information about the extent to which the school conformed to certain guidelines. For instance,

● Ninety percent organized teachers and students into interdisciplinary teams, rather than self-contained and departmentalized instruction.

● Ninety-four percent used flexible scheduling during the school day, often with some kind of block schedule.

● Ninety-three percent included a home base period and teacher-advisor for each student.

● All of the respondents said their programs were designed with the nature of middle school students in mind.

● Ninety-nine percent focused curriculum on students' personal development and skills for continued learning, and a wide range of exploratory activities.

● All reported that administrators

and faculty members collaborated on decisions that shaped school policy.

These data indicate that the schools in this sample are characterized by the central components of the middle school philosophy. They are more than "middle" schools; they are schools that have achieved significant local, state, or national recognition by using a format that is relatively common.

Thus, our survey data apply most directly to other middle schools following that same format. We made no attempt to control or analyze data on the bases of socioeconomic status, school size, geographic location, or the influence of school leadership or talented instruction. Our conclusions are limited by the fact that we encouraged respondents to supply evidence regarding the positive effects of their middle school programs and not to stress negative aspects.

Student Achievement Rises
Our survey results dispute earlier

opinions that academic achievement is either unaffected or only modestly improved by a move to middle school organization. Sixty-two percent of the respondents described consistent academic improvement. An additional 28 percent supplied specific results demonstrating increased scores on state assessment tests, the California Achievement Test, the Iowa Test of Basic Skills, and similar tests. Eighty-five percent observed that teacher confidence in student abilities had increased, which, many suggested, led to higher expectations and greater student productivity. Other aspects of reorganized programs positively affecting student learning included coordination of skills and subjects by interdisciplinary teams as well as greater teacher awareness of pre-adolescent needs and abilities. Clearly, the experience of the most highly acclaimed middle schools is that academic achievement can be expected to improve following reorganization.

Discipline Problems Decrease
Reorganization improved discipline in almost every measurable manner. Tardiness and truancy decreased moderately or greatly according to a majority of respondents, as did school vandalism and theft. Approximately 80 percent noted a significant reduction in office referrals and suspensions, while close to 60 percent expelled fewer students after the transition. Almost 90 percent observed that teacher and staff confidence in managing disruptive students increased, diminishing involvement in discipline in many schools.

All the ancedotal evidence supported the positive effects of middle school programs on discipline. One-fourth of the respondents indicated that interdisciplinary team organization and grouping students in houses enabled teachers to develop consistent procedures for handling disruptions. Advisor-advisee programs and greater emphasis on school guidance improved communication and empathy between teachers and students, often defusing volatile emotions before they exploded in classroom confrontations. The cultivation of parental support in enforcing disciplinary actions greatly improved student behavior. Implementing highly structured discipline plans—such as Glasser's Reality Therapy and Canter's Assertive

"Advisor-advisee programs and greater emphasis on school guidance improved communication and empathy between teachers and students, often defusing volatile emotions before they exploded in classroom confrontations."

Discipline, which need teacher-teacher and teacher-administrator collaboration to be effective—was facilitated by staff development programs accompanying reorganization. Several respondents suggested that moving 9th graders to high schools left a group of younger adolescents more similar developmentally and generally less sophisticated and troublesome. When reoganization follows the pattern common to the schools administered by these respondents, educators and parents can expect a decrease in discipline problems.

Student Personal Development Is Enhanced

Certainly, one of the long-espoused goals of the middle school has been to focus on the unique nature and needs of young adolescents. Our results indicate that exemplary middle schools have been very successful in promoting student personal development. Over 80 percent of the respondents testified that student emotional health, creativity, and confidence in self-directed learning were positively affected by reorganization. Over 90 percent believed that student self-concept and social development also benefited.

Not a single respondent reported negative effects on student personal development. The success of team organization and teacher-based guidance in helping individuals develop closer peer relationships was cited repeatedly. Extracurricular and intramural athletic activities were open to all students and invited greater student participation, interaction, and competition. Awards for leadership, good citizenship, and cooperation in and out of classes enabled those who weren't honor roll students or star athletes to experience the important

satisfaction of peer recognition. Interdisciplinary teams, classroom guidance, and exploratory programs increased opportunities for student involvement and accomplishments, significantly improving student personal development.

Reorganization appeared to delay certain social pressures that seem to precipitate an undesirable sophistication in young people today. Schools can work with students before major growth spurts associated with puberty and help them adjust to new academic environments before problems develop. "No school-sponsored dances certainly delays the mating process!" quipped one respondent. Others conveyed strong parental support for their efforts to slow down preadolescent maturation.

Many respondents specifically attributed gains in student personal development to effective teacher guidance. A part of the original junior high concept, the classroom advisory group is making a strong comeback in reorganized middle schools. Although many respondents indicated that successful implementation was difficult, they praised its impact on helping students understand themselves and others during the trying time of early adolescence. When conceived and conducted with care, advisor-advisee programs appear gratifying to all involved.

School Learning Climate Turns Positive

Recent studies analyzing school effectiveness correlate learning climate with student behavior and achievement. Students who feel valued by teachers and view school as more than just a place to meet friends tend to show respect for their schools. The exemplary schools in this study developed programs that demonstrate persistent caring for students as young people and create a school environment to meet their special academic and personal needs. Predictably, respondents reported stronger school spirit since reorganization. Over 95 percent declared that students' attitudes toward school and feelings about teachers became moderately or strongly positive. Eighty-six percent witnessed greater student participation in special interest activities, while 75 percent noted better school attendance. Descriptions of student enthu-

siasm for involvement in school programs ran nearly five to one in favor of changes brought about by a move to middle school organization.

In discussions of reorganizing in schools from junior high to middle schools, educators and citizens often express concern about the proper role of interscholastic competition, cheerleading, and athletic awards. Proponents of such activities argue that their elimination will negatively affect school spirit; opponents stress that their inclusion in schools will exclude most students from participation and recognition, weakening school spirit. Our survey results indicate that when curriculums are designed to encourage greater student involvement in different ways, removal or significant modification of interscholastic sports programs does not diminish student pride and positive feelings. Failure to compensate for altering conventional athletic competition during reorganization, however, can be costly to school pride.

The majority of respondents identified new activities that effectively replaced traditional ones in generating student excitement and participation. Advisory groups and interdisciplinary team programs successfully stimulated student involvement, as did offering intramurals, clubs, exploratory classes, and awards for effort and excellence. Several schools retained interscholastic sports and cheerleading by restructuring them to include more students or by shifting responsibility for them to community agencies allowed to use school facilities after hours.

Faculty Morale Improves

Because of the complexities of our education system and frequent criticism by parents, politicians, and the press, many public school teachers exhibit alarmingly but understandably low morale. Not so in the nation's exemplary middle schools. An impressive 94 percent of the respondents described staff morale and rapport as either moderately or strongly positive following reorganization. Based on formal and informal observations, 93 percent concluded that a move to middle school organization favorably influenced staff attitudes toward change, and 82 percent noticed increased staff participation in special interest activities following the transition. Over half of the respondents cited lower teacher absenteeism and turnover, noting that some teachers fought transfers to other schools. All anecdotal comments but one praised the benefits to morale of implementating a middle school philosophy. Teachers voiced greater job satisfaction, and said that they worked more closely with one another and spent more leisure time together.

Such positive faculty morale did not magically appear when the middle schools opened their doors. Some faculty members lacked enthusiasm for reorganization and resisted change efforts. A noticeable number of secondary-trained teachers thought that some of the new things they were expected to do were unreasonable. As they enjoyed increased support on teams and more control over learning time, however, many skeptical teachers developed an appreciation for the appropriateness of middle school programs. Even those disillusioned with district policies and budgets, by a national clamor for educational reform, or with contract negotiations often conceded later that reorganization improved schooling and made their jobs more rewarding. One respondent's comment that it took ten years before his staff truly supported the middle school concept suggests that considerable patience may be a prerequisite for developing strong faculty morale. Other comments expressed concern about the life span of staff enthusiasm in middle schools, mentioning that some teachers could overextend themselves and lose interest within a few years if precautions were not taken.

Respondents reported that the interdisciplinary team organization component of the middle school program contributed greatly to staff morale. Previously isolated instructors became team members and developed the same sense of belonging and camaraderie they hoped to instill in their students. The flexibility in scheduling, which is inherent to team responsibility for a common group of students occupying generally the same area of the school, provided teachers with many options for instruction. Sharing knowledge of students and subjects increased their confidence and consistency.

Staff Development Is Effective

Reorganization to middle schools, according to respondents, provided am-

Photographs by Roger Easton, Chinook Middle School, Lacey, Washington

ple opportunities for teachers, principals, and district administrators to coordinate efforts to improve instruction and classroom management by requiring extensive staff development programs. Acknowledging that some teachers are more responsive to change than others and that staff members can occasionaly be worn down by too much inservice, administrators nonetheless noted greater staff development in designing and executing philosophy, curriculum, and objectives when they conducted staff development programs to facilitate reorganization. Inservice programs (characteristics of young adolescents, interdisciplinary teams, advisory-advisee groups) and educational improvement programs applicable to all grades (Effective Schooling, Instruction Theory Into Practice, Assertive Discipline, Reality Therapy) provided middle school staff with research findings and practices that can revitalize teaching and learning in these crucial grades. Most schools in the survey assessed teachers' needs and interests prior to, during, and after the transition; enlisted the aid of local universities and colleges when possible; encouraged individual and group attendance to state and national conferences about middle school education; and scheduled dozens of inservice workshops to improve instruction.

Parental Involvement and Support Strengthens

Survey respondents proudly described the positive parental involvement and support they experienced after reorganization to middle schools. They cited better attendance at open houses, conferences, and PTA meetings, as well as a greater propensity to volunteer as chaperones for field trips, dances, or other school socials; to help in libraries, cafeterias, and classrooms; to coach intramural athletics; and to teach minicourses in many of the exemplary middle schools. Administrators cultivated parental involvement during all stages of the transition, anticipating the potential value of their contributions and support. They took pains to explain why and how reorganization would improve schooling for their children and established communication channels that encouraged parents to ask questions and to make suggestions at any point in the reorganization process.

Administrators sought to capitalize on parental willingness to share responsibility for their children's education and were well rewarded for their efforts. One respondent boasted that parents told him, "You cannot change your program until my last child has gone through it!" and "My child likes school for the first time." Parents often voiced support for the middle school at board meetings and frequently voted to provide the money needed to maintain the level of educational services characteristic of exemplary middle schools.

Community Involvement and Coverage Is Favorable

Admitting that community concern for the cost of public education can spell financial trouble for reorganization programs—particularly those that require money to provide facilities and retrain staff—our respondents nonetheless reported favorable community support. Businesses, civic organizations, and community leaders resemble parents in their willingness to contribute to the schooling of middle level students. They attend and present assemblies, fund-raising events, and career awareness programs, thus generating and diffusing valuable support for the middle school throughout the community. People with and without children in the schools volunteer to cover classes, tutor exceptional students, and sponsor clubs, according to many administrators in our survey. "All we have to do is ask!" wrote one about his community's eagerness to help in the school. Other administrators related that although they would like to have even more community involvement and support, they were generally pleased with existing levels.

High School Staff Perceptions Moderate

In stark contrast to the strong vote of confidence given to middle school reorganization by parents, teachers, and surrounding communities, support wavered among high school staff. Barely half of the respondents from middle schools surveyed reported praise and approval from the upper grade teachers to whom they sent students. Most added that to earn support they had to overcome earlier suspicions and fears voiced by high school teachers who doubted the seriousness of middle school programs. Many acknowledged district emphasis on K-12 curriculum and articulation as very helpful in establishing positive reputations and relations with high schools. A few noted that reorganization inspired some high school teachers to improve their programs by implementing 9th grade interdisciplinary teams and by maintaining the close parent-teacher-student contact developed in the middle grades. Some re-

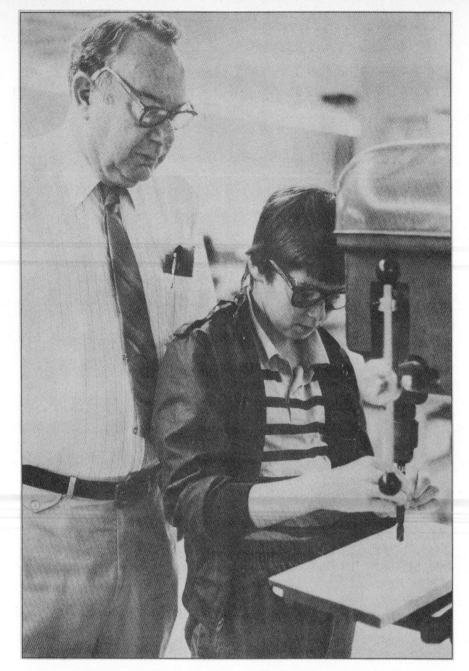

spondents indicated great pride when told by senior high staff that the middle schools must be doing something right since students were well prepared for their final school years. However, even this group who receive favorable support from their secondary counterparts expressed difficulty in pleasing high school personnel.

The other 46 percent of respondents reported criticism, fickle support, or apathy toward their programs on the part of the high school staff. Often high school teachers said that only those in the upper grades really teach and that it would be a step down to teach in middle school. The ab-

sence of ability grouping and interscholastic athletics was thought to disrupt high school programs, eliciting more negative comments. If reorganization moved 9th graders to high schools, contributed to overcrowding, or required a reallocation of funds previously designated for the high school, many high school instructors appeared to be quick to disregard any merit assigned to a program based on preadolescent needs. Many respondents suggested that schools at all levels should work hard to improve communication and cooperation. A few proposed reassigning district teachers to different buildings and

"Reorganization appeared to delay certain social pressures that seem to precipitate an undesirable sophistication in young people today."

grades more often and encouraging K-12 articulation to promote positive feelings among schools.

Dramatically Positive Results

The results of our survey indicate that highly successful middle schools have very similar programs, which tend to conform to the recommendations in the literature of middle level education in the last half century. Such programs are distinctly different from those common to elementary and high schools. When implemented in this way, the results are dramatically positive in terms of academic achievement, student behavior, school learning climate, faculty morale, and staff development.

Reference

National Institute of Education. *A Study of the Demography of Schools for Early Adolescents*. Washington, D.C.: U.S.D.O.E., Statistical Information Office, 1983.

[handwritten annotations:]
(1) outstanding principal
(2) high expectation for all
(3) orderly atmosphere
(4) regular testing
(5) emphasis on academic learning

Edmonds - schools where academic achievement seemed to be independent of social class
"Effective Schools"

A Good School

Diane Ravitch

Diane Ravitch, adjunct professor of history and education at Teachers College, Columbia University, is the author of, most recently, The Troubled Crusade: American Education, 1945-1980. *A collection of her essays,* The Schools We Deserve, *was published in the spring of 1985 by Basic Books.*

[handwritten annotation:]
learning as the major measurement of school quality

In the not distant past, when attitudes toward public education were strongly positive, it rarely occurred to anyone to seek out examples of "effective schools." The evident assumption was that most schools were good, and that the ineffectual school was an aberration. The first annual Gallup poll about public schools in 1969 showed a strikingly high regard for schools and the teaching profession; three out of four persons responded that they would like to see their children take up teaching as a career. The level of public esteem for the schools at that time was even more remarkable in light of the overwhelmingly negative tone of the popular literature on schools in the mid-1960s.

After a decade of strident attacks on the schools, a decade in which public confidence waned, a small number of educational writers and researchers started looking for examples of good schools. There had long been a tradition of writing about a particular school as a way of trumpeting certain values that the school embodied, but the climate of the times tended to define the "good school." In the Progressive Era, certain schools were singled out because of their anti-traditional features, such as their combination of work and play or their engagement in the social life of the surrounding community. In the 1960s, certain schools were lauded for their political activism or their success in "liberating" children from bourgeois values.

By the late 1970s and early 1980s, an "effective school" came to be identified with the characteristics set out in the writings of the late Ron Edmonds of the Harvard Graduate School of Education. Perhaps because Edmonds was black, he was able to assert values that would have sounded disturbingly traditional to the educational establishment if

voiced by a white. Edmonds identified schools where academic achievement seemed to be independent of pupils' social class, and he concluded that such schools had an outstanding principal, high expectations for all children, an orderly atmosphere, a regular testing program, and an emphasis on academic learning.

Edmonds's conclusions may have seemed like a series of commonplace observations to most people, but they were received as stunning insights in the arcane world of educational policy. (Outsiders are repeatedly astonished by what passes for revelation in the education field; for instance, one of the great discoveries of recent years—though still not universally accepted—is that student achievement may be positively related to something called "time on task." In other words, what one learns is determined in part by the time spent learning it.) Happily, Edmonds was not alone in his interest in learning as the major measurement of school quality. Other studies reinforced his view that student achievement could be raised by sound educational practices. To appreciate the importance of this change in orientation, one must recall the many years in which academic achievement was treated with disdain in comparison with non-academic goals.

Writing about a single school is also a good way for a writer to test his own educational ideals and to display them for public inspection. Now, in the interest of candor, I confess that I instinctually hew to John Dewey's admonition: "What the best and wisest parent wants for his own child, that must the community want for all of its children. Any other ideal for our schools is narrow and unlovely." The best and wisest parents, I expect, want their child to read

Reprinted from *THE AMERICAN SCHOLAR*, Volume 53, Number 4, Autumn, 1984. Copyright © 1984 by the author. Reprinted by permission of the publishers.

and write fluently; to speak articulately; to listen carefully; to learn to participate in the give-and-take of group discussion; to learn self-discipline and to develop the capacity for deferred gratification; to read and appreciate good literature; to have a strong knowledge of history, both of our own nation and of others; to appreciate the values of a free, democratic society; to understand science, mathematics, technology, and the natural world; to become engaged in the arts, both as a participant and as one capable of appreciating aesthetic excellence. I expect such parents would also want a good program of physical education and perhaps even competence in a foreign language. Presumably, these mythical best and wisest parents want their child to have some sense of possible occupation or profession, but it seems doubtful that they would want their child to use school time for vocational training, at least in the pre-collegiate years.

That our public schools have long operated on contrary assumptions should be obvious. The program I have described is usually called the academic track, and not more than 35 to 38 percent of American secondary students were recieving this kind of well-balanced preparation in the early 1980s. Acting not *in loco parentis* but on behalf of the state, educators have sorted children into vocational or general tracks, the former to prepare for a specific job, the latter being neither academic nor vocational. For reasons that are rooted largely in misplaced compassion—not in meanness or ignorance—our educational philosophy has dictated that academic learning is not for everyone; that it is too demanding for the average student; that its apparent inutility limits its value to the average student; that too much of it will cause students to drop out of high school in droves; and that such students should take courses that provide job skills, life skills, practical know-how, and immediate relevance to their own lives.

In public schools, curricular tracking has become a common practice. By tracking, I refer to the academic/vocational/general trichotomy, not to ability grouping. Ability grouping permits students to take different amounts of time to reach roughly similar goals; tracking offers students vastly different kinds of educational programs. The practice of tracking raises all sorts of questions: Who decides which students go into the academic track? At what ages does the tracking begin? To what extent is the decision to funnel a student into a non-academic track a response to his parents' occupations and social class? Should the public school—supported by taxes from all citizens—have the right to determine that some students will receive an education of high quality while others will get a denatured version?

To such questions, which go to the core of our democratic ideology, the defender of the present system might well respond: "Such naiveté! Dreams of perfection! In a perfect world, where all children have the same genetic and cultural inheritance, such a scheme of high-quality education for all might make sense. But in reality, children differ dramatically. Some come to school already knowing how to read, others can barely decipher words after six years of trying. Some are brilliant, others struggle to master the rudiments of learning. The smart ones are clearly college-bound and should have an academic curriculum. The others should have courses where the level of challenge is not too high, where they can have a feeling of success.

And more than subject matter, what the majority needs most is vocational training to get them ready for the workplace. That is what they want, and they should get it. Let us not forget that the great achievement of modern educational research has been the recognition that the curriculum must be adjusted to meet the differing needs of children."

For years, such views have represented the conventional wisdom in public education. The school that I have selected as an example of an effective school—the Edward R. Murrow High School of Brooklyn, New York—explicitly rejects these views. Its principal, Saul Bruckner, is a product of the public schools as well as a twenty-seven-year veteran of the New York City public school system. I learned a great deal by spending time in his school; I changed some of the ideas I brought with me. I am not sure that I agree with every practice and program in the school, but I deeply admire its tone and its high academic aspirations for all its pupils. I think what Bruckner is doing deserves attention, not because it is the only way or even the best way, but because it is one succesful way of wedding traditional goals with non-traditional means.

Murrow was opened in 1974 and officially designated an experimental school by the New York City Board of Education. Its 3,000 students are drawn from the borough of Brooklyn. Half of the students are white, and half are members of minority groups. One of the many unusual features of the school is that it treats all of its pupils as college-bound. No one is tracked into a vocational or "general" program. Yet the school is purposely composed of children with a broad range of abilities. By board of education mandate, at least 25 percent of Murrow's entering students read below grade level; no more than 25 percent read above grade level; and the remaining 50 percent read at grade level. There is no entrance examination, but competition for admission is vigorous; last year, there were some 9,500 applicants for 800 places in the entering class. Critics complain that special schools like Murrow "cream away" the best students from other public high schools, but about one-fourth of Murrow's enrollment consists of students from parochial and independent schools whose parents had previously rejected the public schools. Student morale is undoubtedly lifted by awareness of the difficulty of gaining entry into Murrow. The very process of applying makes every student a committed participant in his own education and eliminates the handful of unwilling students who otherwise make school life an ordeal for teachers and other students. Since Murrow has the luxury of not admitting those who have a well-established record of truancy, disruptive behavior, or criminal activity, it occasionally gets pilloried by detractors as "atypical," but the school may instead demonstrate that mixing those who want to learn with those who don't want to learn is no favor to either group.

Even though the students at Murrow represent a wide ability range, all are expected and required to take a strong academic program in order to graduate—that is, a minimum of five academic courses throughout the school year. The academically gifted take more than five, and there are advanced placement courses in every subject area. The New York City school system requires one year of a foreign language, but most students at Murrow take three or four (the school offers Spanish, French, Latin, Hebrew, and

Italian). Similarly, most students take more than the required two years of science and mathematics. Advanced science students may enroll in a sequence that includes six years of science; weak science students may take astronomy or horticulture instead of the rigorous course in physics. All must take at least four years of English, including a year of writing instruction, and three-and-a-half years of social studies. This level of academic engagement stands in stark contrast to the figures reported by national surveys. For example, only about 15 percent of American secondary students study *any* foreign language; only 6 percent of the nation's students finish a third year of foreign language study, but at Murrow at least 65 percent do. When compared to national enrollment rates in subjects like algebra, geometry, and the natural sciences, Murrow looks like a private school instead of a public school made up of a broad cross section of pupils.

The students who read two or more years below grade level receive intensive remedial instruction in reading and writing while still enrolled in regular courses. The school does not exclude average or below-average students from any of its uppper-level courses, as many schools do. Consequently, even advanced placement courses in English, social studies, mathematics, and science contain a diverse range of students, and occasionally teachers complain about students in their advanced placement class or the calculus class "who don't belong there." But the school's philosophy is that no student should be discouraged from taking on an academic challenge. Unlike many other public schools, Murrow does not practice grade inflation (20 percent of all its grades last year were "no credit," the equivalent of not passing the course) or social promotion (no one graduates until all of the academic requirements are met, and some students take longer than four years to finish).

The academic results of the Murrow program have been impressive. The annual dropout rate is only 4 percent, compared to a citywide rate of 11 percent. Daily attendance averages 88 percent, far above that of other urban high schools. Nearly 90 percent of its graduates continue either a four-year or a two-year college program. The school urges even those who intend to be secretaries to take a degree at a community college in order to enhance their occupational mobility later. The chairman of the social studies department, Mary Butz, explained to me on my first visit to the school, "The climate of the school is middle-class Jewish. These kids all believe that education will help them get ahead, move up into college and good jobs. They have bought the whole package. They believe in themselves, and they believe in us."

How can Murrow get away with its ambitious program? Well, for one thing, its students have been persuaded that Murrow is a very special school and that they are very special students. The school year and the day are organized somewhat differently than they are at a more traditional school. Instead of two semesters, there are four cycles of ten weeks each. The principal believes that the advantage of four ten-week courses is that students are encouraged to take risks, knowing that they won't be stuck for an entire year (or semester) with a bad choice. Instead of every subject meeting daily, the time is divided into four weekly meetings; this gives the students some blocks of optional time that they can use as they wish, either to study, do

homework, or socialize with friends. Unlike the students at most other schools, students at Murrow are permitted to cluster in the halls during their optional time, and affinity groups have claimed different territories (none based on race, however). "Over there are my theater groupies," says Bruckner. "And those kids are the science groupies." As we walk through the hall, he sees a Hispanic girl curled up on the tile floor, deeply engrossed in a paperback book. "What's that you're reading?" She holds up the book, and he reads: "Richard II." In the English "resource center" (like a study hall), a group of youngsters works together on a project. In an otherwise empty classroom, half-a-dozen boys are setting up a videotape camera, part of a project for their literature course, "Detective Story." In the computer center, two or three students share a single machine, figuring out problems together, teaching each other.

Murrow represents an ingenious answer to the question: How do you enlist students' interest in their education without giving them control of the curriculum? Murrow does it by setting high requirements for graduation, but the school permits students to meet those requirements by choosing among a carefully designed mix of required and elective courses. The required sophomore course in American literature, for example, focuses on textual analysis of major poems, novels, and plays. Whether required or elective, all academic courses include homework and writing exercises. The many ten-week elective courses have jazzy titles, but fairly traditional readings; for example, students in "Youth and Identity" read Salinger's *The Catcher in the Rye*, Carson McCullers's *A Member of the Wedding*, Paul Zindel's *The Pigman*, and Elie Wiesel's *Night*. Students in "Novel into Film" read *The Great Gatsby* and *Great Expectations*. Many electives are unabashedly classical, like the Shakespeare class that reads *Romeo and Juliet*, *Richard II*, and *Othello*, or the advanced placement course that reads the works of Milton, John Donne, Ben Jonson, Jane Austen, and other great English writers.

In reviewing the literary offerings available to Murrow students, I could not help but contrast them to my own public school education in Texas. Although it is customary to lament the decline of public education, I believe that Murrow is a far better school than my alma mater in Houston. The literature curriculum of San Jacinto High School was uniform and limited. I recall a year of British fiction that never moved beyond *Silas Marner* and *Julius Caesar*. I have no idea why this selection was inviolate for so long, especially since I believe that such books as *Pride and Prejudice* or *Emma* or *Great Expectations* are wonderfully appealing to adolescents, while few adolescents have the maturity to appreciate George Eliot's complex prose.

Wisely administered, electives enable a school to provide what I would call the illusion of choice. Students do, in fact, make choices, but "wisely administered" means that they should not be permitted to make bad choices, like junk courses without academic merit ("Bachelor Living" or "Personal Grooming"). The illusion of choice can be readily adapted to the English sequence because the traditional English I through English VIII (which I took in my four years of public education) can easily be rearranged and attractively packaged. Thus, a course called "The Woman Writer" appeals to the modern sensibility, but is a fine setting in which to teach the works of Jane Austen, George Eliot, and Charlotte Brontë, and "The Literature of Social

Protest" turns out to be a good marketing tool for the works of writers such as Orwell and Dickens.

Where the repackaging can work neatly for the English curriculum, it has proved to be nearly a disaster in the undisciplined realm of "social studies." This field—once dominated by history—is now rootless and very nearly formless. Among social studies educators, the phrase "chronological history" is frequently used as a term of derision. Even courses entitled "American History" are likely to eschew the traditional narrative of events, leaders, ideas, and institutions in favor of themes, topics, and trends. A significant portion of the Murrow social studies curriculum reflects the political and social fragmentation of the past generation, as well as the disorganization of the social studies as a field. There is a required course in American government, concentrating on political institutions, and a reqired course on American diplomatic history, presenting the history of America's foreign policy, but most other courses are either specialized excursions into some thematic "experience" (the word "history" is usually avoided) or overly broad, like "the global experience." While history is in retreat, psychology, economics, and law studies are thriving: a student, for example, may choose from among eight different psychology courses (for instance, Social Psychology, Abnormal Psychology, Developmental Psychology, the Psychology of Aging).

Despite my reservations, the social studies program at Murrow is far stronger than at most schools. For one thing, there are no contentless courses in "values clarification," "process skills," or "decision making"; second, while the catalogue contains the feminist "Herstory" and "The Black Experience," there is otherwise no further ethnic or group fragmentation of the curriculum. Perhaps most important, the department includes some gifted teachers, who have before them at all times the example of their principal, Saul Bruckner, himself a master teacher of American history. He is frequently in classrooms, observing, prodding, and instructing other members of the staff to enliven their presentations and teaching styles. Under his critical gaze, the course"Origins of Western Civilization" really is a treatment of Western civilization from ancient Rome to the Renaissance, and the "Isms" course turns out to be a history of eighteenth- and nineteenth-century Europe.

I ought to explain how I happened to learn about this school. I was involved in sponsoring a conference in Minneapolis in the spring of 1984, on behalf of the National Endowment for the Humanities, on improving the teaching of the humanities in the high schools. The opening speaker was a distinguished social historian, who discussed the problem of integrating ethnic diversity into the common culture. It has been my experience that public discussions of ethnicity, especially among educators, invariably are pervaded by a sanctimonious tone. Everyone speaks reverentially of the nobility and struggles of oppressed minority groups, and the air becomes heavy with guilt and piety.

During the coffee break, a young teacher grabbed me by the arm to tell me, in an unmistakably Brooklyn accent, that an American Indian woman—known in current bureaucratic language as a Native American person—had just assailed her in scatological language. "What?" I said. "What? How can this be?" "Well," she said, "this Indian woman asked me if she could use the bathroom, and I told

her that the bathroom was reserved for conference participants. So, she used the bathroom anyway. When she came out a few moments later, she jabbed her finger in my chest, called me by an odious term, and warned, 'White woman, don't mess with me anymore.' "

Her name card said, "Mary Butz, Edward R. Murrow High School, Brooklyn, New York." Charmed by her indifference to the demands of ethnic piety, I asked her to tell me about her school. She said, with what I later learned was characteristic candor, that it was the best school in New York City, because it had the best principal and "the greatest kids." I was startled, because over the years, I have met so many embittered teachers in the New York City school system, people who recall or have heard of the school system's reputation in another era, an era when the New York City public schools were widely recognized as pioneers and when their students were pressing hard for future greatness as literati or scientists.

Naturally, I wanted to see the best school in New York City, the best principal, and the greatest kids, particularly because I had been in so many high schools that seemed like armed camps and in so many subway cars at the end of the school day when high school students used their raw energy to intimidate everyone else. So not many days later, I trekked out to the Midwood section of Brooklyn to find an undistinguished, nearly windowless modern brick building, set in the midst of a pleasant middle-class neighborhood. An example of incredibly stupid planning, the Murrow building abuts elevated subway tracks (the noise of passing trains regularly disrupts classes) and has no surrounding campus, although the students are able to use another school's athletic field across the street.

As it happened, on the day that I arrived, Bruckner was teaching an advanced placement section of American history. There were about thirty youngsters in the class, and the question for the day was: "Was it moral for the U.S. to drop the atomic bomb on Japan?" Something inside me warned that I was in for a session of moralistic Truman-bashing, but I was wrong. The students (some of whom were Oriental) had read the textbook description of the war. When I entered, the class was discussing the incidence of cancer in Hiroshima and Nagasaki. Then Mr. Bruckner used an overhead projector to display contemporary news stories from the *New York Times* and the *Herald Tribune*. One headline told the human cost of caturing Okinawa: forty-five thousand American casualties, ninety thousand Japanese casualties. How many lives might be lost in an invasion of the mainland? A mimeographed handout discussed Japanese kamikaze raids and brutality toward American prisoners, which gave the students a flavor of Japanese and American wartime attitudes. A fair conclusion, which did not involve prejudice toward our Japanese adversaries, was that they would fight ferociously to the end. Lest anyone jump to the easy conclusion that the decision to drop the bomb was moral, the teacher also displayed comments by generals and revisionist historians who felt that dropping the bomb was not necessary to end the war.

The lesson was taught in a Socratic manner. Mr. Bruckner did not lecture. He asked questions and kept up a rapid-fire dialogue among the students. "Why?" "How do you know?" "What does this mean?" "Do you really think so ?" Sometimes he called on students who were desperately waving their arms, other times he solicited the views of those who were sitting quietly. By the time the class was finished, the students had covered a great deal of material about American foreign and domestic policies during World War II; they had argued heatedly; most of them had tried out different points of view, seeing the problem from different angles. It was a good lesson: it was well planned, utilizing a variety of materials and media; and the students were alert and responsive.

Bruckner's lesson was at odds with the usual characterization of American teaching. In the past year or two, most critics of the schools have complained about the quality of teaching. Educators like John Goodlad of UCLA and Theodore Sizer, a former headmaster of Andover Academy, have asserted that there is too much "teacher telling," too much student passivity, and little if any thought-provoking activity in the typical classroom. A major study prepared for the National Institute of Education a few years ago contended that teaching in American schools has remained unchanged—that is, boring and teacher-dominated—throughout the century. Well, I thought to myself, I have seen one great teacher; what happens in the other classrooms?

I visited many classrooms and observed teachers in every subject area. I saw some outstanding teaching, some passably good classes, and a few that failed, but in no instance did I see a teacher droning on to a class of bored students. The teaching style in the building was remarkably consistent, and every teacher used materials and experiences that were outside the textbook. In the best classes, the focus of the lesson was on the intellectual exchange sparked by the teacher and kept alive by student participation. In one literature class, the students debated O. Henry's use of language to establish the tone of a story; in a chemistry class, thirty-five students jointly figured out the answer to the question, "how does a battery operate?"

I later learned that Bruckner requires all his teachers to use what is called the "developmental lesson" or the "socialized recitation." If they do not know how to teach this way when they are assigned to Murrow, they are taught the method by their department chairman. At its best, it works magnificently: students listen, speak out, think, disagree with each other, change their minds, make judgments. For this method to work, two things are necessary: first, the teacher has to be well prepared, having planned out the lesson in advance with an "aim" or problem to be solved, with pivotal questions to provoke student discussion, and with materials (a political cartoon, a newspaper headline, a quotation from a participant or critic, or an excerpt from a book) to stimulate the new lines of inquiry; second, the students must bring something to the class in the way of reading or homework, so that they can respond to the teacher's questions with ideas and insights of their own. If the teacher does not prepare well and if the students are uninformed, the developmental lesson can dwindle into a vapid exchange of uninformed opinion, of less value than a traditional didactic lecture.

Bruckner's biggest problem is building a good teaching staff. Within the context of the public school bureaucracy, this requires consummate skill. When Bruckner opened Murrow in 1974, he was officially permitted to select only 35 percent of his staff. Because he was a veteran of "the system," he was able to play the teacher-selection game

like a Stradivarius, and he ended up with a staff in which about 70 percent of the teachers were of his choosing. He might encourage a skilled teacher to apply to join his staff, who would then not be counted as one of his "picks." Since the school opened in the midst of the city's fiscal crisis, Bruckner was able to hire many talented young teachers who had been laid off by other schools. Among the 30 percent or so that he did not choose were, inevitably, some lemons. It is possible, but not easy, to fire a probationary teacher (one who has taught for less than three years); it is nearly impossible to oust a tenured teacher. "A principal can't fire a teacher simply because he is boring or incompetent or even when you know that he treats the kids like dirt," Bruckner says. "He must be grossly negligent, persistently late for class, drunk in class, something like that."

What a principal can do, however, is lay off staff, but only in order of seniority. One principal, Bruckner says, wiped out most of his English department to get rid of a teacher with fifteen years of seniority; seven able young teachers were laid off in order to drop a bad senior teacher. Bruckner closed down his guidance department in order to remove the person assigned to Murrow. Eventually the Brooklyn superintendent for high schools ordered him to hire guidance counselors, and he continued to hire and lay off until he got the people he wanted. Usually it is easier to lay off personnel than to go through the procedure of ousting them. Not only is it time-consuming, but if the principal wins, the teacher is stripped of his license. It is akin to having a lawyer disbarred, with this exception: the teacher can get a licence in another area. For example, Bruckner had the licenses revoked from two probationary teachers, one who taught the handicapped (special education), another who taught social studies. Before long, both were reinstated. The ex-special education teacher had become an elementary teacher, and the ex-social studies teacher had moved into special education. "Well," Bruckner says with resignation, "I didn't get them out of the system, but I got them out of this school."

Bruckner speaks with passion about how the structure of public education contributes to the "infantilization" of teachers. "Teachers," he complains, "have little responsibility for the conditions of their working lives. We call teaching a profession, but if so, it is the only profession in which there is no opportunity for growth while remaining in the profession." The teacher has lost a great deal of authority to make decisions, not only to supervisors, but also to their own organizations and to federal, state, and local mandates. "For most of the important things in their day," Bruckner says, "teachers depend on someone else. Someone else assigns them a room, someone else gives them a daily schedule, someone else writes their lesson plan." Yet in the classroom they have total control, and no matter what the offcial course of study says, the teacher defines the curriculum every day. Outside the classroom, however, the teachers "are like students: they have very limited say over their lives, and that creates bitterness and hostility." To break through this "infantilization," Bruckner encourages teachers to design their own courses and to take more responsibility for school affairs. Perhaps the most promising innovation has sprung from the science department, where teachers visit one another's classrooms and discuss content and methodology; their professional critiques of one another take the place of an official observation by a supervisor. Bruckner hopes that other departments will follow suit: "Doctors observe each other practice and learn from one another; so do lawyers. Why shouldn't teachers?"

Like other big-city high schools in the 1980s, Murrow is constantly threatened by financial pressures. Average class size is now up to thirty-four in the city's high schools, the largest in many years. The library is funded at only one dollar per year per student; half of the library budget pays for the *New York Times* on microfilm and its index, leaving only $1,500 for books and magazine subscriptions. At today's prices, $1,500 does not buy much of either. In order to continue using a diversity of materials and media in the classroom, which is integral to the lively approach that Bruckner advocates, the school has heavy expenses for equipment, supplies, and repairs. Occasionally, he has traded in a teaching position (valued at $33,000) in order to maintain the school's Xerox machines, mimeograph machines, computers, overhead projectors, and audiovisual equipment.

The school has a climate that is relaxed and tension-free. Teachers and students alike know that they are in a good school, and this sense of being special contributes to high morale. Yet the tenuousness of the authority structure of a big school was revealed to me one morning when the principal was away at a conference mandated by the board of education. Word spread through the building that the police bomb squad had closed off part of the second and third floors, and it was true. Students milled in the corridors, elaborating on the rumor. An assistant principal announced on the public address system, "Everyone return to your classroom. There is no danger at the present moment." Since the police had sealed off a major portion of the building, most students had no classroom to return to. In the absence of sensible adult instruction, nearly half of the students went home. The surprising thing, Mary Butz observed, was not that so many left, but that so many stayed, because the bomb scare had effectively ended the school day.

Schools cannot function as they once did. Teachers cannot presume to have the respect of the students. They have to win it in the classroom. Many New York City school teachers have found it difficult to adjust to the loss of authority over the past generation and the change in the pupil demography from predominantly white to predominantly black and Hispanic. Some professionals in the New York City public schools labor with a sense of nostalgia for a lost golden age, a time when student motivation could be taken for granted and when teachers were respected figures in the community. This image of a lost golden age is a mixture of truth, misty memories, and

historical accident. The Great Depression was a time when many over-educated teachers entered the school system because there were no jobs in higher education or the professions; when there was an unusual number of second- and third-generation Jewish students who were eager to use their education to get ahead; and when the less-motivated students dropped out to work as elevator operators or messengers or in some other low-skill job.

Life was hard for most people during the Depression, but in many ways it was not as complicated for school people as it is today. Many of the children at Murrow, who come from a broad mix of racial, religious, and ethnic backgrounds, bear the scars of social dissolution. While trying to educate them, the school cannot ignore the family crises, the broken homes, the child abuse, the parental negligence that cuts across all socio-economic lines. In other urban schools, the wounds that families inflict on their children are far worse. Sometimes the best that a school can do is to provide a sympathetic adult who will listen.

Bruckner knows that the school competes for the child's attention with the pathology outside its doors, with the lure of television, drugs, sex, and the adolescent culture. He has not created a social service program; the school is not a social work agency. What he has tried to do is to make it a place where adolescents feel at home, a place that they might want to come to even if they didn't have to. He has done this, not by turning the school into a playing field with low hurdles, but by harnessing non-traditional means to traditional academic goals. The smart kids have no ceiling on their ambitions; they can go as far and as fast as their brains will take them. Not many public schools in the nation can match Murrow's advanced courses in science and mathematics. But this richness for the bright students is not achieved by pushing the average ones into nursing and automobile mechanics. All of them have available a strong basic curriculum and a diversity of learning opportunities that enable them to learn at their own pace, and all are accorded equal respect as students.

There are many different kinds of effective schools. Some of them, like Murrow's neighbor in Brooklyn, Midwood High School, are highly structured and traditional. Visiting Midwood is like stepping into a school in the early 1950s; it is quiet and orderly, and the students seem serious and purposeful. What effective schools have in common should be available to all American students: a strong academic curriculum, a principal with a vision and the courage to work for it, dedicated teachers, a commitment to learning, a mix of students from different backgrounds, and high expectations for all children.

The Struggle for Excellence: Striving for Higher Achievement

In the past three decades, criticism of schooling has made many North American educators dubious of the rhetoric of "blue ribbon" panels regarding excellence, however it is defined, and dubious as to the motivations of reform rhetoric. The goal of excellence is not controverted. Some of the suggestions for achieving it are controverted. Indeed, J. Myron Atkin is accurate when he refers to educators as "gun shy" of some of the new reform efforts. Before North American citizens can decide on what new changes to make in school curricula, they need to be made aware of the excellent aspects that already exist. In the dozens of individual, group, and commission reports on excellence, there is a disturbing and academically conservative and limiting commonality in the language of the reports. Most of the reports essentially say the same things, make the same recommendations, and avoid recommendations for basic structural changes in programming of North American elementary and secondary schools. Instead there is an almost unified appeal for a return to a basic curriculum.

Should excellence in schooling necessarily imply "sameness" in basic academic programming? Does an industrial high-tech social order have to diversify the types of educational programming it offers to its young? All other industrialized nations answer in the affirmative. Can it be that the United States, where individuality is purported to prevail, is the only industrialized nation where a common set of behavioral objectives is to be mastered by all of its young, whatever their unique gifts or burdens? For the United States, the answers to these questions hinge on whether a common basic academic program is necessary to meet foreign economic competition or basic domestic needs.

Part of what must be considered regarding excellence in education and the new reform rhetoric is whether or not more basic changes are needed in the content and purpose of elementary and secondary education than those recommended in the reports. Should excellence imply one thing, such as a common basic academic programming based on traditional classical curricula, or should excellence be multidimensional, with more than one meaning and different types of schools to deal with the different meanings of the concept? The reform reports have all failed to grapple honestly with this question. They also avoid dealing with the question of why other industrialized nations in Asia and Europe have always championed both traditional academic and technically oriented conceptions of excellence. The reform reports want changes in the present structure of schooling. Would they be willing to consider, or should they consider, basic changes in the structure of schooling itself? Calls for longer schools days and years and more homework are typical of scholastic bandaids on a seriously ill (and technologically "displaced") patient.

Where do teachers, school principals, teacher educators, and counselors fit into the construction of reform rhetoric? Why aren't their views as highly regarded as the opinions of others? What alternative structures should or should not be considered by the educational system? The essays in this unit were selected to provide penetrating insights into the issues at stake in the current debate over excellence. They require careful consideration.

This unit may be used in courses that deal primarily with the social context of schooling and the issues facing educators. The essays could relate to those parts of a course that highlight either curriculum issues or the history of education. They can also be discussed in conjunction with equality of educational opportunity discussed in Unit 6. The nation faces many problems as it strives for higher achievement. Popular concern regarding the subject makes the articles in this unit relevant to all discussions of the social context of education.

Looking Ahead: Challenge Questions

Examine the controversy surrounding how best to achieve excellence in education. What are the differences in the interests of members of "blue ribbon" commissions and the interests of teachers and school administrators? What might be the primary concerns of teachers when they consider the topic of educational reform?

What changes in society and its schools have created such intense interest in striving for excellence in education?

What can be learned from recent reports on the state of American education? What are your views on the recommendations being offered to improve the quality of schooling?

How could school curricula and instructional practices be modified to encourage excellence in teaching and learning?

What are the minimum academic standards that all high school graduates should have achieved?

What are the most significant issues to be addressed in the development and use of minimum competency testing?

Is there anything new in the struggle for excellence? What can be learned from the history of efforts to reform education?

Changing Our Thinking About Educational Change

J. Myron Atkin

J. Myron Atkin is Dean of the School of Education at Stanford University.

The education reform fervor triggered in early 1983 by the report of the National Commission on Excellence in Education, *A Nation at Risk*,[1] was greeted with trepidation by teachers and school administrators. Given its indictment of the quality of public education and its focus on the "rising tide of mediocrity" in the nation's schools, it was not clear whether the report was a prelude to educational improvement or the beginning of a new wave of attacks on schools and teachers. Judging from the polls, the public seemed to be in a mood to take constructive steps to improve the quality of public education, but teachers and school administrators had become gun-shy over a period of three decades as a result of previous reform efforts that assigned blame recklessly, raised expectations unrealistically, and led to legislative and other initiatives that sometimes had effects on teaching exactly the opposite of what had been intended.

As reports continued to be issued on the state of American secondary education in the months following *A Nation at Risk,* it became clear that an extraordinary phenomenon in the history of American education was taking place. Each new statement —Ernest Boyer's,[2] John Goodlad's,[3] Mortimer Adler's,[4] the College Board's,[5] the Twentieth Century Fund's,[6] the National Science Foundation's[7]—captured front-page attention, editorial comment (usually favorable), and even significant time on the television network evening news. Public interest in the quality of education clearly was deep. The mood for change was strong. It even began to appear that legislators were willing to appropriate more money for education if they could be convinced that the additional funds would produce higher quality.

The theme of the reports, taken as a group, was that the school curriculum had become soft, particularly for children with strong academic ability; that standards were poorly defined and low; that the quality of teachers seemed to be declining; that teacher education programs were weak; and that schools were not meeting the needs of business and industry as well as they should. Most of the recommendations for improving schools were couched in general terms, but the reports converged on the remedy that a common curriculum for all children should be reinstated and that clear goals and expectations for pupils in the subjects of English, history, science, and mathematics should be formulated. Teachers at the secondary school level should major in the subjects they were to teach. Some of the reports suggested that schools should be less preoccupied with training youngsters for specific occupations than with making sure they possess basic skills, especially in written communication.

The suggested educational reforms may not have seemed particularly startling, even if the public appetite for them was; but in addition to the extraordinary publicity attendant to release of the reports, the lineup of those who were pressing for change in the educational system was different and noteworthy. In the period immediately after the launching of Sputnik I, in 1957, those who exerted maximum influence on the tone and substance of education reform were university professors who were experts in the subjects taught in secondary and elementary schools. They provided the driving force and conceptual leadership for new programs in the teaching of biology, physics, mathematics, social science, and language. It was a major feature of the education reform scene ushered in in 1983 that for the first time in recent memory major business leaders were identifying education as a key national problem and priority. Chief executive officers of some of the country's major corporations began to involve themselves in coalitions to improve public education, giving of both their time and their influence. The country's productivity and trade position were seen as threatened, and the cure lay in part, the public was told, in producing a more efficient work force. The California Business Roundtable consisted of several-score corporation presidents (not their public affairs officers), who devoted significant energy and intelligence to learning about the state's educational problems and what might be done about them.

Just as significant, state-level politicians from coast to coast rediscovered the issue of education. Through most of the 1970s, education committees in the state capitols represented virtually the last choice for freshman legislators with verve and ambition. Governors, too, preferred to focus on social welfare programs, prisons, environmental issues, agriculture, and industrial expansion—anything, it seemed, but education. Before 1983, most politicians saw little advantage and considerable risk in emphasizing issues associated with educational improvement. Schools were being closed in every state because of the decline in the numbers of children. Money was tight. People feel passionately about their schools, particularly those who send their children to them, and politicians saw little to be gained by becoming associated with the unpopular decisions necessary to shrink a huge enterprise with a strong emotional foothold in virtually every community, while dealing with a powerful, large,and increasingly assertive union. Suddenly, it seemed in 1983, politicians were featuring education improvement in their major speeches and in their election platforms. Even those with national political aspirations, such as Gov. James Hunt of North Carolina, were asking to be judged on the basis of their records in education.

While the renewed interest in education seemed encouraging to many teachers and school administrators, there was still apprehension and skepticism. Would the nation hear once again that the problems in the schools are caused by teachers who are too child centered, or insufficiently informed about their subjects, or too preoccupied with raising their own salaries? Would there be a tendency to find scapegoats or to blame the victims? Just as much a cause of concern among informed school people, would there be initiatives by an awakening public that might actually impair the ability of schools to improve educational quality, however well motivated those initiatives might be? If so, it would not be the first time that the best of public intentions became associated with changes in schools that did not have the desired effects, and in fact were counterproductive. Educational change is tricky business. How does one balance the imperative of political will and the advantages of informed professional latitude? Which changes are best planned by state education departments and which by teachers and administrators in local districts? How does one best influence a "system" of about three million teachers who work for 16,000 different employers?

When Americans look for solutions to problems in the field of education, as in most areas of public concern,

they usually begin by examining the possibility of writing new laws. School codes—laws and accompanying regulations—now run to tens of thousands of pages in many states. Children do not read well? Pass a law that requires the demonstration of reading ability at a certain level before the child may be moved to the next grade or awarded a high school diploma. Concerned that handicapped children are not receiving instruction geared to their distinctive needs? Pass a law that requires an "individualized education plan" for each child; in addition, require that the plan be negotiated by the teacher with the parents to give those with the most at stake a chance to participate in the process. How better to assure accountability? Legislative responses to serious problems seem deeply satisfying. The laws often have a direct appeal and an apparently compelling logic. They are usually preceded by considerable study and debate. Those responsible for the initiatives work hard for them. The prime movers feel a sense of concrete accomplishment.

Examine the results of each piece of legislation designed to improve educational outcomes, however, and you begin to note results that do not always correspond to the intent of those who wrote the laws. With the passage of "minimum competency" laws, for example, test scores, at least for some children, go down, not up. Pass a law requiring an individualized education plan for each child, and service to handicapped children declines rather than expands. How come?

At one level, new laws are symbolic expressions of shifting public attention and priority. They reflect a new focus of public interest and sometimes crystallize consensus: we had better take the plight of handicapped children and their parents more seriously; our school system is not doing well enough for youngsters who need basic reading skills; non-English-speaking children need special attention. Insofar as such declarations represent a new resolve by the public to attend to a matter whose priority is elevated, little harm is done. Public schools are public institutions. Politics is an expression of the public will. Schools have always been subjected to intense political pressures. Howev-

er, when legislators move beyond an affirmation of intentions to frame laws governing specific educational practices, to be followed by regulations that prescribe the details of how teachers are to work with children and which tests are to be administered for which purpose, the results become unpredictable and often seemingly perverse. This is the situation in much of the United States today.

For example, with respect to the minimum competency legislation, the intention and the message to teachers and school administrators are clear enough. We have a large population of youngsters in school who are not learning basic skills associated with reading and computation. The situation is undesirable and perhaps intolerable. The law directs renewed attention to the educational needs of this population. Unless the examinations are passed, the child does not advance in the educational system or does not receive a diploma.

As intended, after such laws are introduced, reading scores do go up for youngsters who before the law was enacted did not possess the skills required to pass the examination. Children who did not read and compute are now reading and computing. But success is not that simple (though accomplishment is seldom acknowledged). It is noticed, too, that scores for the most able children begin to decline at the same time. What is happening?

Determining causality is always a difficult issue in understanding social phenomena, but it seems reasonable to conclude that without an increase in resources, which typically is the case when new demands to serve the educational needs of a large population of youngsters are imposed, the other children receive less time from teachers. Here is one way it happens: because of new test requirements, a school superintendent or a principal is expected to raise the skill levels of a significant number of youngsters in the school quickly, as many as 20 or 30 percent of the children in some instances. The administrator examines the resources available to meet the educational needs of all the youngsters in the school and decides to give priority to those policies that use available resources to serve the most children. The decision is made to close small classes and reassign their teachers. The principle seems reasonable, fair, uniform in applications, and easy to explain: concentrate the available teaching force in classes that enroll the largest number of children.

t turns out, however, that the large classes are the introductory courses in a subject or the remedial courses intended to teach the minimally required skills. The small classes are often those in advanced biology, or calculus, or the third year of a foreign language. The minimum competency movement, so reasonable in intent, seems to lower the educational accomplishments of a district's most able students because it deprives them of a chance to do advanced work, an outcome no one intended and few people predicted.

Minimum competency laws are passed at the state level. The Education of All Handicapped Children Act is a federal law. It is unusual for the federal government to become involved in matters of education. The Tenth Amendment to the Constitution reserves to the states those functions not explicitly assigned to the federal government, and education is not mentioned in the Constitution. In areas of clear federal responsibility, such as strengthening the national defense and assuring equal protection for all citizens, the Congress has a role. The Education of All Handicapped Children Act was passed in 1975. It flowed directly from principles that were enunciated in the 1960s and early 1970s as part of the civil rights movement. Handicapped children were seen in the minds of those who lobbied for them and of those in the Congress as a minority group, like blacks or Hispanics. They were entitled to the education received by everyone else. The law called for handicapped children to be put in the "least restrictive environment" in every school. This action led to the "mainstreaming" of handicapped children—that is, to their placement insofar as possible in regular, not special, cases.

In many instances such placements prove effective for the handicapped child, though not always. Many handicapping conditions require almost constant adult supervision. Mainstreaming has sometimes resulted in a reduction of service to the afflicted child. Putting that outcome aside, however, we can say that the placement of handicapped children in regular classrooms almost always requires a level of attention from the teacher that is disproportionate to the attention given other children. The regular teacher is often ill-prepared to work with youngsters who are mentally retarded, emotionally disturbed, orthopedically disabled, or visually impaired. The impulse to mainstream is humane. Often, though not always, it is in the best interest of the handicapped child. But there is a trade-off. The disproportionate amount of time that the teacher must work with handicapped youngsters is time taken from the other children.

Advocates of new social policy initiatives attempt to support their policy preferences with research whenever possible. When the new laws affecting the education of handicapped children were passed, there was indeed a considerable amount of education research indicating that the educational achievement of children with handicapping conditions was often improved by their being required to meet the standards held for other children, and in the same settings. However, about 90 percent of the studies that had been done on mainstreaming at that time addressed only the issue of how such a practice affects the children to be mainstreamed. Only a few studies gave any attention to the effect that such a practice has on the teacher or on the other children.[9]

In the same Education of All Handicapped Children Act, and as if to give another example of how laws about the details of teaching practice can be mischievous, the Congress incorporated a requirement that an "individualized education plan" be developed for each child, to be negotiated between teacher and parent. Such a plan was advocated by specialists in the education of handicapped children. Representatives and senators were also impressed by the effectiveness of such a practice in serving

the needs of handicapped children in many districts. It seemed to represent sound practice where it was used, and it provided an uncommon degree of accountability. Impressed, the legislators wrote the requirement into law.

Soon afterward, it was noticed that in order to develop the new plans for each child, teachers began to spend an increasing share of their time in conference with parents and in providing the written documentation that the law and subsequent regulation required. The written document —the individualized plan—became the instrument for monitoring compliance with the law. Administrators, parents, and the education auditors took the plans seriously. The result: teachers spent less time with the children. They were busier conferring with parents and keeping the written records that the law demanded. Since new teachers usually were not hired, direct service to handicapped children actually declined. To a degree, the preparation of the written document became a surrogate for personal service to youngsters.

Global definitions of educational problems tend to breed global solutions. Most legislators have a penchant for translating good ideas into legal requirements. It is the only tool at their disposal. They aren't stupid, of course, or mean. But the public expects them to act on problems, not necessarily with much thought about which problems are most amenable to legal redress and which to other methods.

Laws are blunt instruments. There is little understanding or appreciation of the fact that the provision of a personal service, such as teaching a child to understand the binomial theorem, often requires a degree of sensitivity and accommodation at the site where the service is provided that enables the person providing the service to adjust his or her approach depending on circumstances. Out of frustration with what we see as poor service, we attempt to assure at least a minimum level of accomplishment and accountability, but such attempts almost invariably lead to a standardization of practice. There frequently is some elevation in minimum accomplishment as a result, but there is usually a leveling down as well.

This argument is not meant to

minimize the importance of accountability on the part of teachers and school administrators. The issue, rather, is one of how to achieve a balance between the initiatives best taken by the public's elected representatives and those attempts at enhancing quality that are best left to the professionals who operate the system. The tension is not new in American education, but the momentum in recent years has been clearly in the direction of greater political assertiveness and reduced professional discretion.

To strike the most effective balance between politicians and teacher, it would be helpful to have a clearer picture of the kind of teacher the country wants. If teaching is something like plumbing, then it is appropriate for the public through various laws and codes to specify in considerable detail the standards to be applied in judging adequacy. Those who practice the craft must understand the requirements, but there is not much latitude associated with how an individual task is to be accomplished. If teaching third-grade arithmetic is like soldering a joint, then some individual discretion is required, as in any craft, but not much. The emphasis is on skill. On the other hand, if teaching mathematics requires that the teacher make adjustments based on the motivational level of different children in the class, on his or her understanding of the intellectual level at which different children are functioning, and on a comprehension of the subject matter sufficient to know which of the children's questions have intellectual mileage and which do not (and which should therefore dominate in classroom discussions), then considerable latitude is necessary at the level of classroom instruction. It makes little sense to try very much prescription of practice from afar.

Moving to a different issue associated with the current legally rooted strategies for educational change, we note that a partial result of the recent pattern of problem identification, leg-

islation, and regulation in education is that the public identifies one troublesome matter at a time, then directs virtually all attention to it. There is concern about gifted children and the space race in the late 1950s, and a massive attempt is made to improve the quality of the curriculum in science and mathematics. It turns out that the schools respond positively. America is first on the moon. High technology thrives. But the country does not seem to notice. In the time it takes to respond discernably to the identified problem, the public has shifted its attention to a different criticism of the schools, this time the distressing achievement levels of the poor. The nation and the schools redirect energy toward that population, again with success. Within a decade, test scores go up for those who used to do least well. But again the achievement does not seem to register with the public. Instead, there is a new outpouring of publicity about declining test sores for the brightest children and America's diminishing position in world trade. Priorities in education change with unpredictable frequency and intensity. The schools are told to work on one feature of the system with little understanding of what is as a result happening to others. And there is little acknowledgement of the volatile and impermanent nature of the public attention span.

One of the most troublesome aspects of the American inclination to change priorities quickly is that teachers become demoralized. As a group, those who staff the schools want to serve youngsters and please the public. Very few people enter the field because of the financial rewards or, these days, the job security. Teachers and school administrators are no more or no less conscientious than others. When the nation says it wants to train scientists and mathematicians, the schools respond; and they succeed. Similarly, monumental progress is made on teaching basic skills when the public sends the message to schools that this is the outcome it wants. However, when the accomplishments of the schools in response to each new declaration of urgency are ignored, discouragement sets in. It is understandable that priorities shift. They do in almost every enterprise. But, some-

how, in the field of education teachers seldom receive a message conveying a sense of appreciation for work that has been done well.

The argument advanced here is not that the country should diminish attempts to improve educational quality for a range of children in the schools through the political process. It should not diminish them. Rather, the intent is to question how such a goal is to be achieved without weakening the capacity of schools to provide education, and in particular without discouraging those who must play a major role in doing what the public wants. A possibly fatal flaw in attempts to improve programs primarily through legislative remedies is that expectations at the level of school and classroom are lowered for developing creative responses to problems. When it is reiterated in the various cycles of educational reform that problems and their resolution are universal and that legislators will develop the "solutions," the local inclination to be responsive is diminished. After a while, the expectation is created that problems will be solved primarily by somebody else.

For example, transcript analyses of California high school students reveal that there is considerable consistency in the courses taken by the top 20 percent of students. Putting aside the issue of what actually happens in Algebra I when the door is shut, the titles of the courses taken by the top-ability group are similar as one moves from one youngster to the next. They are probably guided in their choices by college requirements. Similarly, there is consistency in course titles for youngsters in the poorest achieving 20 percent. They probably know what courses they must take to prepare for the minimum competency examinations. However, there is little pattern in course taking for the middle 60 percent.

Are there too many electives? Are the youngsters preparing for a large number of different occupations? Is there a broad range of ability in the middle group? Is there considerable pressure from the community to offer a variety of courses? The "solution" to the "problem" of patternlessness depends in significant measure on the diagnosis. If the pattern reflects an outdated or no-longer-supported view about choice or a casual response to apparent interests, then a well-defined core curriculum may be indicated. On the other hand, if the population served is enormously varied and if the school has a community-supported approach to help different children reach clearly defensible goals, then a plan to institute a core program might be misdirected. Legislatures do not make these distinctions.

Another example: a school district is having great difficulty teaching youngsters in the first grade whose first language is not English. This problem indeed exists in thousands of school districts across the country. Assume that those who recognize and must deal with the issues understand the limitations of solely legislative remedies. What strategies for educational change make sense?

ne approach is to assemble experts: linguists, authorities on language acquisition, successful teachers, sociologists, psychologists, and others. Ask the group to develop a course of study based on the soundest research and most reasonable theories to teach English to six-year-old youngsters in American schools who speak it poorly and who were raised in a different tongue. Millions of dollars might be invested in course development by a determined nation. The task is then to "disseminate" the program devised by the experts to school districts around the country.

This method of curricular development and educational change was prevalent during the 1960s, when school programs were being modified at the urging of the National Science Foundation to develop a cadre of young people with strong education in science and mathematics. Outstanding scientists were assembled. They worked with teachers, psychologists, and other educational experts to prepare new courses. Although these efforts of the 1960s had many beneficial effects, the courses of study developed during that period were seldom used as designed. More traditional texts continued to predomi-

nate (though they began to include topics suggested by the reformers). Where the new texts were used as written, however, the programs rarely met the expectations of the developers. Physics texts, for example, were prepared to help children understand how scientific lines of argument are developed—that is, how scientists think about the issues they work on. The children were often expected to engage in independent inquiry so that they would begin to have firsthand experience with scientific thinking.

When the curriculum developers observed in classrooms where the new texts had been adopted, however, they were sometimes shocked by what they saw. Children were often taking turns reading from the new books. They would then be asked by the teacher to repeat what they had just read. The method of teaching was directly counter to the spirit intended by the course developers. Although books had been written to stimulate original inquiry, reading and occasional lecture, followed by recitation, were still the primary methods of instruction. Somehow the guiding impetus for the new courses did not seem to be captured by teachers, at least not by large numbers of them.

On the other hand, modern topics in science and mathematics were introduced as a result of the curricular reform movement. Texts became more accurate as well. Furthermore, teachers were motivated at a high level because outstanding scientists and mathematicians, by redirecting their own activities toward issues of precollege education, were underscoring the importance of secondary school teaching to the country. In addition, considerable amounts of money were devoted to new programs of in-service teacher education, often during the summer months, in which teachers were subsidized to learn about the new topics. There were thus many beneficial effects, but large-scale teaching in the spirit of the course developers was not one of them.

The implementation of new educational programs is a difficult and sensitive matter. Teachers vary enormously in their training, their interests, and their tastes. So do children. So do individual communities.

Different high schools have different expectations of their children and teachers that are complex and special —and uncomprehended in a policy-making body far from the school. A text-writing team has as much difficulty as a state legislature in designing courses and teaching approaches that they can expect to be instituted with fidelity.

Is there an approach to fostering educational change that holds more promise of success than those typically employed do, or are the current strategies for change in schools the only ones available? The answer is that there are indeed other methods, but they are relatively untried on a systematic basis, and there are weaknesses associated with them, too. To stay with the same example, if one wants to improve the teaching of English to youngsters in the first grade who speak it poorly and and for whom it is not the first language, it might at the outset be noted that because the problem is widespread in the United States there already are thousands of classrooms where teachers are wrestling with the issue. While there may not be a single, ideal approach in evidence anywhere, some teachers are clearly more effective than others. Furthermore, most observers would agree about which programs are best. One strategy for educational change that capitalizes upon rather than ignores the natural variation already existing within the system is to identify the teachers who do relatively well. What particular combination of teaching technique, site leadership, student population, community support, and school organization seems to be operating to have established a praiseworthy program? Instead of solely designing a completely new approach to the problem, those who want to improve schools might search as well for factors that seem responsible for existing high-quality programs. By analyzing their characteristics, one begins to understand how programs in other locations that seem similar in essential points like level of teachers' competence, demographics, and financial support might be improved. The main theme of this line of argument, of course, is the age-old admonition "Build on strength." Do not devote all energies to redressing weaknesses. An inclination to recognize and capitalize on strength is not only an acknowledgement of success that has arisen within the system; it also provides proven direction for educational change.

An approach broadly along the lines outlined here would place a greater premium than commonly exists on understanding the origins of current practice. Teachers and school administrators are no more capricious, stupid, or perverse than legislators, politicians, businessmen, or professors. As in every field, some are well motivated, some are more able, some are more intelligent than others; but, as a profession, teachers and school administrators strive as conscientiously as anyone else to meet the varying demands on their time and skills, probably more so because they are in the eye of the public continually. School boards, more than 16,000 of them across the country, are monitoring, setting policy, and providing direction. So are state departments of education. So are politicians. So are journalists. If a program for teaching reading, science, or mathematics exists in a school district, it has obviously met the usual impediments to innovation successfully. It becomes important, then, to understand how a new practice has taken root, how inertia was overcome, how competing interests have been accommodated, and how the resources were identified to establish the program. Instead of continual remediation, policymakers might begin to look at what's right and try to understand it.

The imagery employed here is that of biological evolution. Natural variation exists in a system as large as American education. Some of the variation is adaptive. The strategic task becomes one of finding out how the particular niche for the program was created and of reproducing or tailoring it to new settings.

Among the advantages of such an approach to educational change is the fact that the new school programs thus identified are credible to teachers and administrators. If practices exist, then those who currently teach

have reason to believe people already staffing the schools have the capacity to make improvements. Strategies for educational change that build on strength also have the advantage of raising the self-esteem of teachers, a significant goal in today's climate of criticism and crisis.

Strategies for changing schools are centered almost exclusively on the system of public education. More than independent schools, of course, public schools are regulated by and legally accountable to political bodies. Despite the extraordinary attention to the deficiencies of tax-supported education, there has been very little public interest in or movement toward non-public schools, at least so far. In 1976, 10.5 percent of the children in elementary and secondary schools were in non-public institutions, including parochial schools. That figure climbed to 10.9 percent in 1980. (In 1960, the figure was 13.3. percent.)[10]

It could be otherwise. In the national concern about and impatience with the educational system, one might expect attempts to seek an alternative. Such a possibility is highlighted by periodic attempts to introduce tuition tax credits and school voucher plans. Such initiatives may yet prevail. So far, however, despite the personal support given these two measures by the President of the United States, other politicians, business leaders, and the general public seem to be rejecting the private school option.

While there are many reasons for continued attention to the improvement of public education, and while it would be difficult to predict how long the emphasis will last, one explanatory factor may well be associated with our urgent search for national identity and purpose. Americans as a group have seemed disappointed with themselves through much of the 1960s and 1970s. There has been little celebration of accomplishment. As the country searches for institutions that have the potential to help establish a sense of nationhood, the schools stand out. There probably is a significant cultural memory that helps people appreciate the role of the public schools in helping to unify an extraordinarily varied population in the past. The common schools were an American invention of the nineteenth century. The public was persuaded that

they were created to pursue the common good. They are widely credited with helping an emerging people develop a sense of unity and purpose. There is an unarticulated hope, perhaps, that these institutions will be a major force once again in helping the country ascend to its next phase of accomplishment and pride.

Yet the potential of well-intended reform to cripple the system is real. In its impatience for change and in the national preoccupation with faults, the country runs the risk of weakening the very institutions it is trying to strengthen. Schools are more vulnerable than many people seem to think. If changes are imposed that lower morale or have other pronounced negative effects, even if unintended, the system is significantly damaged. It becomes a target for fresh criticism, and a downward spiral can be the result. For this reason, strategies for educational change should be examined with as much care and sensitivity as can be mustered—with a special eye on unintended side effects—even if such a posture means blunting some apparently irresistible reforms. Better to institute changes piecemeal and steadily than to risk large numbers of untested but mammoth perturbations to the system that as a result of unanticipated and undesirable consequences breed counterreaction and overcorrection. No system is infinitely resilient. It is time in American education to consider more conservative and realistic approaches to educational reform, even if they mean reassessment of the goals for public education and somewhat lowered expectations.

[1] National Commission on Excellence in Education, *A Nation at Risk: The Imperative for Educational Reform* (Washington, D.C.: Government Printing Office, 1983).
[2] Ernest L. Boyer, *High School: A Report on Secondary Education in America* (New York: Harper & Row, 1983).
[3] John I. Goodlad, *A Place Called School: Prospects for the Future* (New York: McGraw-Hill, 1983).
[4] Mortimer Jerome Adler, *The Paideia Proposal* (New York: Macmillan, 1982).
[5] College Entrance Examination Board, *Academic Preparation for College: What Students Need to Know and Be Able to Do* (New York: College Board, 1983).
[6] *Report of the Twentieth Century Fund Task Force on Federal Elementary and Secondary Education Policy* (New York: Twentieth Century Fund, 1983).
[7] National Science Board Commission on Precollege Education in Mathematics, Science and Technology, *Educating Americans for the 21st Century* (Washington, D.C.: Government Printing Office, 1983).
[8] Conrad Carlberg and Kenneth Kavale, "The Efficacy of Special versus Regular Class Placement for Exceptional Children: A Metaanalysis," *Journal of Special Education*, 14 (Fall 1980), pp. 295-309.

Sustaining the Momentum of State Education Reform: The Link Between Assessment And Financial Support

The crucial policy question is whether the reform movement will maintain its momentum, says Mr. Kirst. As the pace of new reforms slows over the next year, implementing, evaluating, and researching the cost-effectiveness of the various reforms becomes an urgent priority.

Michael W. Kirst

MICHAEL W. KIRST (Stanford University Chapter) is a professor of education at Stanford University and a member of the Kappan Board of Editorial Consultants. This article was taken from a paper prepared for the annual meeting of the Education Commission of the States, held in Philadelphia in July 1985. The research for this paper was supported by the National Institute of Education (Grant No. NIE-G-83-0003), but the analyses and conclusions do not necessarily reflect the views or the policies of that organization.

PUBLIC SCHOOL policy making is embedded in a complex societal matrix. It is not possible to consider the future of U.S. schools without examining the size and distribution of future populations, the future state of the economy and its ef-

fect on funds available for the schools, and the political context within which decisions will be made. The public school system is a "dependent variable" of larger social and economic forces.

These forces are sometimes cyclical.[1] For example, the launching of Sputnik I in 1957 triggered a series of policies that funneled resources into the training of gifted students, especially in science. In the mid-1960s President Johnson's War on Poverty produced a counter-trend: policies that redirected resources to the disadvantaged and the handicapped. In the 1980s concern about the economic position of the U.S. in world markets has focused public policy on higher academic standards and a more rigorous education for all students.

In addition to their cyclical tendencies, education policies are often determined by the actions of special interest groups outside of education. For example, Proposition 13 in California and spending caps in other states had their roots in the resentment of taxpayers about high property taxes and soaring inflation. Although the schools were affected deeply by these spending caps, they were only incidental targets.

In recent years, special interest groups within education have been less able than before to influence the directions taken by state education policy. The influence of these groups has been weakened not only by broad social forces and taxpayer groups, but by external authorities — including gover-

From *Phi Delta Kappan*, January 1986, pp. 341-345. Reprinted by permission of Phi Delta Kappan and the author.

In 1986 the pace of new reforms will slow significantly as fewer and fewer states and local districts enact omnibus bills.

nors, business leaders, and the courts — whose connections to education policy have traditionally been more distant.

In 1979 Walter Garms and I made some predictions about the demographic, fiscal, and political contexts of public education in the decade between 1980 and 1990. We predicted that expenditures on education would keep up with inflation but not show considerable real growth.[2] This was a more pessimistic scenario than the one we had witnessed during the preceding decade. Despite much discussion in the 1970s of declining enrollments and diminished public approval of education (as measured by the annual Gallup Poll of the Public's Attitudes Toward the Public Schools), that decade actually produced an after-inflation growth of $23 billion in total expenditures for education. Moreover, the ratio of pupils to instructional personnel dropped from 29:1 at the start of the 1970s to 20:1 at the end of that decade. Had this trend continued, the pupil/teacher ratio would have stood at 12:1 by the 1990s.

Between 1970 and 1980 state governments increased their total spending on education from $16.6 billion to $46.5 billion, an impressive 44.5% increase in real dollars. The state share of funding for education rose from 37% to almost 50%, while the local and federal shares declined.

All these positive fiscal trends occurred despite the fact that in the Seventies the education journals were focusing on the "management of decline." Falling enrollments and school closings during that period were painful, but hold-harmless fiscal distribution formulas cushioned the impact in most states. As the states focused on providing equity for the handicapped and the disadvan-

taged, there was a continuing trend toward state initiative in policy making and a narrowing of the zone in which local school authorities were free to make discretionary decisions.

Garms and I doubted that the growth in expenditures for education that had taken place during the 1970s would continue at the same pace during the 1980s. Our reasons included:

• *Demography.* Enrollment would drop in the high schools during the 1980s; even more important would be the rapid increase in the number of older voters, who tend to want lower property taxes. Only about one voter in five would have children attending public schools. The fastest-growing segment of the school population would be immigrants, who have a low rate of political participation. All these factors would make voters less likely to approve increases in property taxes.

• *Declines in commodity prices.* Declining oil prices seemed likely to hurt the southern and western states that rely on extraction taxes. Declines in farm prices would adversely affect the Midwest.

• *Public alienation.* The annual Gallup Polls showed a growing dissatisfaction with the performance of schools — a feeling that might translate into diminished political support.

• *Growing child-care needs.* The rate of participation in the labor force by women with school-age children had increased so rapidly that between 70% and 80% of mothers would be working by 1990. At the same time there was also rapid growth in the number of single-parent families. In our view, increased expenditures for child care would compete with government funding of the schools.

• *Federal budget priorities.* Federal policy favored defense, social security, and health programs. Federal spending was increasingly shifting from children to older people.

For these reasons, we felt that state governments would be the primary engines for real growth in school spending. Changing federal priorities made the federal government an unlikely source of new school funds, and the changing profile of local voters made significant increases in the local property tax unlikely.

I N THE EARLY 1980s, a pessimistic view of the funding prospects of education prevailed; real revenues for education (after inflation) de-

clined between 1980 and 1982. The U.S. suffered a recession that devastated many of its basic industries. However, in 1983 the fiscal and political picture for education changed drastically and unexpectedly. Education became the top priority in most states, as a wave of concern about academic excellence swept the nation. The underlying negative trends that Garms and I cited in 1979 were overwhelmed by a new willingness to fund "reforms" in the name of quality. Education was featured as a solution to the problems of economic stagnation at home and a shrinking share of markets abroad. More than 300 state commissions and many more local groups pushed for a new agenda for education. Per-pupil expenditures shot up by about 9% in real terms during 1983 and kept increasing faster than inflation during 1984 and 1985.[3]

In my view, the crucial policy question for the next five years is whether the reform movement will maintain its momentum. If it does, then expenditures for education will outstrip inflation, and the underlying negative trends will remain in the background. However, if the public and key policy makers perceive that education reform has failed or has not been properly implemented, then a less favorable future is likely.

The public must not see professional educators as having subverted the aims of the reformers. Consequently, implementing and evaluating these reforms should be a top priority for state policy makers and educational researchers. In 1986 the pace of new reforms will slow significantly as fewer and fewer states and local districts enact omnibus bills. Moreover, national economic growth is slowing dramatically, sparking tough competition for public funds. Therefore, researching the cost-effectiveness of the various education reforms becomes urgent, because not all of them can be expanded or even maintained.

Education policy has now passed through the "alarmed discovery" and "crisis activity" phases of the "issue-attention" cycle. Other reform movements, such as the movement to clean up the environment or the movement to revitalize the inner cities, have now degenerated into the subsequent policy phases of "disillusionment with results" and a "return to neglect."[4] In education the processes of implementation and adaptation, along with the elimination of unworkable reforms, have begun in earnest.

If education is not to go the way of the other reform movements and fall once again into neglect, these processes must work to the satisfaction of the public and of policy makers. For example, there is a widespread belief that teacher quality is crucial to increasing the academic attainment of students, but states are unsure what mix of reforms will work best to improve the teaching force. Few states can afford to fully fund the entire range of possible reforms. Consequently, the states are trying all kinds of interventions — including career ladders, higher base salaries, improved working conditions, sabbaticals, and forgivable loans — without a clear notion of which approaches will yield the best results.

Sustaining the reform movement becomes even more urgent when we consider that enrollment will grow by 2.1 million by 1990. Allan Odden estimates that a 5% real growth in total revenues will be required each year just to pay for this enrollment increase. He points out that the reforms recommended by the National Commission on Excellence in Education would require about a 20% increase in per-pupil expenditures. Yet only three of the reform states Odden studied have approached this level of increase.[5]

Since funding increases as large as 20% are unlikely, we must sort out which of the many possible state reforms should be expanded, which should be eliminated, and which should be left at their current funding level. This task will become even more pressing if a federal tax reform bill should end the deductibility of state and local taxes from the federal income tax. The elimination of such deductions would make it still more difficult to raise state and local taxes.

EVALUATING REFORMS

Although the reform movement has unquestionably had a positive effect on the setting of state education policy, politicians are already clamoring for results. And the reforms already in place do raise numerous unanswered questions. How does one assess omnibus bills, such as California's S.B. 813 with its 80 different reforms? Evaluators have focused on program evaluation, but these state reform packages are not programs. They are a welter of specific state interventions aimed at curriculum and instruction, and appropriate methodology for evaluating them is not well-developed.

Other urgent questions are raised by these state omnibus reforms. What is the proper balance between state and local control of education policy? Will bottom-up commitment at the school site reinforce top-down leadership at the state level or subvert it? Although most local districts are increasing the number of academic courses they offer, what will motivate students to enroll or be interested in these courses? Do some reforms, such as merit pay plans, outrun the present level of our technology? As science and mathematics enrollments increase (by about 20% between 1982 and 1984 in California high schools), who will teach these courses? And what will these reforms do to the dropout rate?

In the next five years, the major policy issues in education will focus on the problems, successes, and unanswered questions of state reform. We need to involve a variety of scholars and practitioners in helping to answer these numerous questions quickly. Fortunately, there is such diversity in the approaches to reform taken by the states and local districts that we have what amounts to a nationwide experiment to determine which approaches work best. For example, some states (Texas, Tennessee) have imposed a statewide career ladder, while others (Arizona) have relied on locally generated changes in career structures. An evaluation of all the policy issues raised by the state reforms between 1983 and 1985 will be very expensive. Only a few states, such as South Carolina and Tennessee, have earmarked significant money for indepth analyses of the impact of the reforms. It is ironic that, with so much riding on the public perception of these reforms, education is devoting so little of its resources to assessing their outcomes.

Several kinds and levels of evaluation might be appropriate for the complex and multipurpose state reform bills.

1. *Performance indicators.* Performance indicators are statewide numerical measures of trends in educational variables. In some cases these standardized state measures can be supplemented by locally devised indicators that vary in definition and concept depending on local conditions. Performance indicators pick up changes that are easily measured, but they can rarely penetrate behind the classroom door to measure such things as the content actually taught, teacher morale, or the type of intellectual tasks students are performing. Performance indicators are useful parts of a statewide assessment strategy, but if used alone they tend to overvalue what can be measured at the state level. Bill Honig, the state superintendent of schools in California, has created a system of statewide targets and individual school profiles for numerous uniform indicators, including changes in course-enrollment patterns, test scores, number of dropouts, and performance of college

> **P**oliticians are already clamoring for results. And the reforms already in place do raise numerous unanswered questions.

freshmen. These statewide indicators are supplemented by locally devised indicators in areas not easily measured at the state level, such as school climate, time spent on writing, and amount of homework.

2. *Overall studies of the financial impact of reforms.* Rather than carefully compare the cost of each reform, states have backed into allocating funds to the local districts according to the amount of uncommitted state revenue. Often money was provided through a state's basic finance formula, and the money was not tied to any specific reforms. Consequently, states need to know where the districts have spent the increased funding and whether some components of the reform effort have been over- or underfunded. For example, states need to know how much money was actually needed to institute state-mandated science courses or to create new approaches to local teacher evaluation. They also need to know which areas of the curriculum gained by the funding increases (usually math and science) and which areas lost (often home economics and industrial arts). States also need to know whether the reforms became more or less expensive as they became part of collective bargaining and whether local use of money var-

ied according to the prior spending level of a district.

In order for a reform to have any chance of working, some new resources must usually be provided. Cost analysis will help determine how much was spent in what areas, but it will not tell us anything about the results.

3. *Analysis of cost-effectiveness of various state interventions with the same specific objectives.* Henry Levin states the case for cost-effectiveness this way:

> [Cost-effectiveness] integrates the results of [program] costs in such a way that one can select the best educational results for any given costs, or [programs] that provide any given level of educational results for least cost. It is important to emphasize that both the cost and effectiveness aspects are important and must be integrated. Just as evaluators often consider only the effects of a particular alternative or intervention, administrators sometimes consider only costs. In both cases, the evaluation will be incomplete.[6]

Cost-effectiveness can provide important policy information, but it is limited to comparisons among programs with similar objectives. A possible example would be the use of loans, scholarships, or higher base salaries as a magnet to attract better-quality beginning teachers.

4. *Program evaluation.* Some states have created programs that can be evaluated as discrete activities, such as career ladders, preschool programs, or increases in the numbers of high school counselors. These programs can be evaluated by means of well-developed techniques of program evaluation that have been used to assess such programs as Title I.[7] As a first step, program evaluation can research what components of a program were actually implemented. It can then move to include costs, outcomes, and processes. A comparison of several programs with very similar objectives could constitute a study of their comparative cost-effectiveness.

Program evaluation cannot address well the interaction of several different state initiatives, however. Nor can it give us much insight into the cumulative impact of omnibus state reform activities.

5. *Impact of evaluation of several state interventions with the same general goal.* It is probably still premature to ask whether state reform is working in terms of student achievement. It is sen-

sible, however, to explore whether or not a reform has been implemented and, if so, whether its implementation is consistent with the broad objectives of state policy makers. Numerous state policies are directed toward the goal of increasing the "rigor" or "challenge" in the high school curriculum. The primary strategy is to increase the time students spend studying traditional academic subjects. Minimum state graduation requirements, tougher college entrance requirements, model state curricula, and the addition of science and social studies sections to statewide tests are some examples of policies designed to make secondary education more rigorous.

An example of an evaluation of this type of reform is a recent California study that examined changes in high school course offerings between 1982 and 1985. A sample of secondary schools was surveyed, and numbers of class sections in each departmental area were taken from teachers' master schedules. After adjusting for changes in enrollments, it became clear that substantially more sections of mathematics, science, and foreign languages were being offered, while the numbers of courses in home economics, industrial arts, and business were decreasing (see Figure 1). In science, the largest increase in offerings occurred in the physical sciences, apparently in response to the new graduation requirement of one year of physical science. All areas of mathematics increased, but computer science showed the largest increase

(91%), followed by more advanced math courses, such as calculus, geometry, analytic geometry, and trigonometry. Calculus and analytic geometry were offered 33% more often, while general math courses increased by only 11%.

The same study showed an even more substantial increase in the number of advanced placement course offerings. By 1984-85 the number of such courses offered in chemistry, physics, and European history had increased by 34%. In addition, new advanced placement courses were offered in computer science, foreign languages, art history, and music.

An obvious problem with these simple impact analyses is that there is no way to demonstrate cause-and-effect relationships. For instance, changes could be caused by local school board policies, by state interventions, or by other factors.[8] But if the direction of change is toward more academic coursework, state policy makers will be interested — even without a precise analysis of the unique state role or of the content covered in these courses.

6. *Studies of the cumulative effects of all state reforms in omnibus bills.* The total number of initiatives in many states makes it impossible to conceive of reform as a discrete program, such as Head Start, or a discrete policy, such as a civil rights mandate. Instead, reforms in South Carolina and Texas, for example, contain:

• *Broad, multiple targets.* Reform

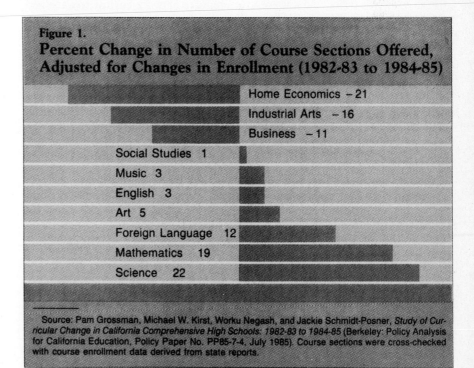

Figure 1.
Percent Change in Number of Course Sections Offered, Adjusted for Changes in Enrollment (1982-83 to 1984-85)

Home Economics – 21
Industrial Arts – 16
Business – 11
Social Studies 1
Music 3
English 3
Art 5
Foreign Language 12
Mathematics 19
Science 22

Source: Pam Grossman, Michael W. Kirst, Worku Negash, and Jackie Schmidt-Posner, *Study of Curricular Change in California Comprehensive High Schools: 1982-83 to 1984-85* (Berkeley: Policy Analysis for California Education, Policy Paper No. PP85-7-4, July 1985). Course sections were cross-checked with course enrollment data derived from state reports.

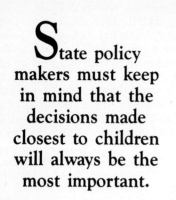

State policy makers must keep in mind that the decisions made closest to children will always be the most important.

packages seek to alter several components of school and district operations simultaneously.

• *Lack of programmatic articulation.* In several states many kinds of reform elements have been combined under a single statute. Education reform is a set of minimally related policies that will generate various responses at the local level. Given the nature of these state reforms, Michael Knapp and Marian Stearns argue that the evaluator should study the local system, not the state program. Specifically, they contend that school effects will:

derive from many small changes that cumulatively shift the climate for education, the perceived opportunities, the tenor of the curriculum. These shifts will be best detected by "taking the pulse" of the local educational system in ways that capture more than conventional indicators such as student test scores. . . .

The many pieces of the reform agenda compete with a buzzing universe at the school and district levels for the attention of educators. Collectively, the reforms will have their greatest impact if they: first, capture the attention of a critical mass of educators (and their relevant local constituencies); second, provide positive incentives for committing further energy to education (by current staff, as well as by new recruits); and third, generate hope for, and supportive imagery of, the schools among students, educators, and the public. Accordingly, evaluation research must document what is (and isn't) noticed at the local level, and determine the effects reform initiatives have on local motivation and morale (at the administrative, teacher, and student levels). In such reform movements the whole is greater, and far more important, than the parts. Those aspects of the local scene that reflect the whole — such as the commitment educators feel to re-

form goals — are consequently the most appropriate indicators of reform efforts.[9]

In short, local case studies and state-level interviews could be used to determine the level of commitment of local actors to the reform objectives and the adequacy of available resources to support local efforts.

In conducting this kind of evaluation, it is essential to differentiate initial from long-term impacts and to be aware of changes in local response over time. The initial effects will be evident in inputs and processes, such as changes in course enrollment patterns. Only after several years, however, should we expect significant changes in such areas as standardized testing. This type of research is extremely complex and expensive, and it takes a long time before even the initial results can be reported. It requires longitudinal, in-depth case studies of a sample of local schools within each state. Recent research on school effectiveness and school improvement shares some characteristics with investigating cumulative effects.

7. *Research that isolates cause-and-effect relationships.* State policy makers need to know whether there are identifiable cause-and-effect relationships between student achievement and such interventions as state-mandated curriculum alignment. Finding out will be difficult and expensive. How can we separate the effects of local policies from those of state policies when they either reinforce or work against one another? For instance, such innovations as career ladders may attract better-qualified candidates to the profession of teaching, while state-mandated, test-driven curriculum standards may repel the very same people.

Research on cause-and-effect relationships is probably best attempted in the later stages of assessing the reforms. First we should discover which programs have been implemented and whether a program has had any impact before we undertake sophisticated studies of cause and effect. There is no sense in researching cause and effect with respect to a program that never caught on with local educators.

Some experts contend that cause-and-effect or input/output studies are not appropriate for assessing state reforms.[10] The effects of social programs cannot be proved in the same way that one can prove a geometrical theorem or confirm a principle of physics. There are often multiple causes of educational change.[11]

The best evaluation of state reforms would assess implementation in various states and in local districts and schools within them. To focus first on implementation is crucial because what is delivered to children from state reforms varies greatly according to the specific local setting. Moreover, implementation is a multi-stage developmental process whereby local educators learn and adjust as they install the reforms.

As the education reform movement matures and bears fruit, state policy makers must keep in mind that the decisions made closest to children will always be the most important. Classroom teachers vary greatly in the ways in which they react to and adapt external, state-mandated reforms. And state-level leaders who wish to assess the impact of the reforms they have mandated must begin by assessing implementation at the local level. One cause may be crucial in a particular context, but another cause will be most salient in another local context. Certain state interventions may increase the probability that a local effect will occur, but they won't inevitably produce it.

1. For an elaboration of this point, see Michael W. Kirst and Walter I. Garms, "The Political Environment of School Finance Policy in the 1980s," in James W. Guthrie, ed., *School Finance Policies and Practices* (Cambridge, Mass.: Ballinger, 1980), pp. 47-78.
2. Ibid., p. 65.
3. See Allan Odden, "Education Finance 1985: Rising Tide or Steady Fiscal State?," *Educational Evaluation and Policy Analysis*, in press.
4. Anthony Downs, "Up and Down with Ecology: The Issue-Attention Cycle," *Public Interest*, Fall 1972, pp. 39-50.
5. The states were South Carolina, Tennessee, and Texas. See Allan Odden, "Sources of Funding for Education Reform," pp. 335-40, this *Kappan.*
6. Henry M. Levin, *Cost-Effectiveness: A Primer* (Beverly Hills, Calif.: Sage, 1983), p. 15.
7. Lee Cronbach et al., *Toward Reform of Program Evaluation* (San Francisco: Jossey-Bass, 1980).
8. Study conducted for Policy Analysis for California Education, by Pam Grossman, Michael Kirst, Jackie Posner, and Worku Negash, 1985.
9. Michael Knapp and Marian Stearns, "Improving System-Wide Performance: Evaluation Research and the State Education Reform Movement," in Joe Wholey, ed., *Towards Excellence: Roles for Evaluators* (Lexington, Mass.: Lexington Books, 1986). My discussion of the cumulative effects of reform is based entirely on this article.
10. Milbrey W. McLaughlin, *Implementation Realities and Evaluation Design* (Stanford, Calif.: Institute for Research on Educational Finance and Governance, Program Report No. 84-B1, 1984).
11. For a good overview of the difficulty of determining cause-and-effect relationships in educational research, see David R. Krathwohl, *Social and Behavioral Science Research* (San Francisco: Jossey-Bass, 1985), Ch. 9, pp. 211-28.

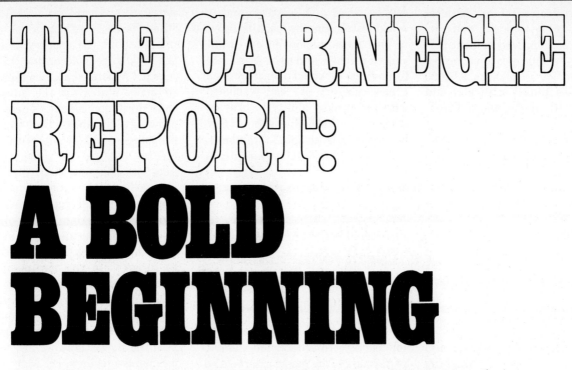

THE CARNEGIE REPORT:
A BOLD BEGINNING

A landmark report calls on teachers to take the lead in shaping their profession for the coming century

What if someone said to you, "You are responsible for setting national standards for yourself and fellow teachers. It is you who will decide how those entering your profession will be trained. You will now have the power—and the support services and staff necessary—to carry out your decisions about how students learn best"?

A new report, *A Nation Prepared: Teachers for the 21st Century,* by the Carnegie Forum on Education and the Economy, could make the scenario possible. The plan not only has political muscle behind it, but it also has the support of foundation money, teachers union chiefs, and corporate leaders.

The report makes a stirring argument for drastic *and* teacher-driven reforms. And it urges that the changes be made not because the quality of education has slipped or because we need to return to previous standards, but because we are now entering a knowledge-based economy dependent on people who can think, rather than perform rotely. Those entrusted with educating the citizens of the 21st century must be the ones to rebuild, not merely repair, the U.S. education system.

One of the Carnegie Report's most powerful recommendations calls for setting national standards for teachers through the establishment of a National Board. The National Board for Professional Teaching Standards would give practicing teachers—rather than state boards of education—primary responsibility for setting the standards of the teaching profession and determining who meets them. This board (eventually elected by those who become Board-certified) is expected to begin functioning next summer, and may begin issuing Teaching Certificates and Advanced Teaching Certificates within three years.

Certification of both new and experienced teachers by the National Board would be completely voluntary, but it is hoped that teachers would seek the credential over and above state licensure. Candidates would be assessed through techniques that would go far beyond multiple-choice examinations and that would rely in part on observations by highly trained teachers.

"Once the Board is in place, the profession will find itself, for the first time, in control of the definition of what it means to be a professional teacher. As the high standard set by the Board becomes widely known, public confidence in teachers will rise. Teachers, having set that standard, will have a considerable investment in maintaining and enforcing it. Certificates granted by the Board will lead to more career mobility and greater opportunities for advancement in the profession," the report says.

"The certificate will be an unambiguous statement that its holder is a highly qualified teacher. Certificate holders can expect to be eagerly sought by states and districts that pride themselves on the quality of their schools."

The certificates—along with level of responsibility, seniority, and contribution to improved student performance—should create pay ranges that could go as high as $39,000 (with a Teaching Certificate) and $46,000 (with an Advanced Teaching Certificate).

Another revolutionary proposal: States should abolish the under-

support staff and services, and it would restructure the teaching force to give more responsibility to advanced teachers and more assistance to novices. It would also introduce a new category of "lead teachers" with the proven ability to provide leadership in reshaping schools and helping colleagues uphold standards.

Districts should relate incentives

redesigning their profession. But "there is every reason to be optimistic about the country meeting the challenge," according to the report. "A strong base has been laid in many states for the advances that must come next. There is a growing awareness that further progress is unlikely without fundamental changes in structure. In fact, we suspect that dramatic change may be easier to achieve than incremental change, given the growing frustration with political gridlock and the increasing awareness that the biggest impediment to progress is the nature of the system itself."

A Nation Prepared raises many questions for teachers to consider: What about the role of principals? Will the suggestions on how to pay for changes really work? Many other questions will occur as the report is read in depth.

"We do not believe the educational system needs repairing; we believe it must be rebuilt to prepare our children for productive lives in the 21st century."

---

graduate degree in education and create a *new* Master in Teaching degree, involving intensive work in community schools, including an internship and residency. A similar recommendation has also been made by The Holmes Group of education-school deans and researchers, in another must-read report, *Tomorrow's Teachers*.

"The effect of greatly raising standards in the face of a (teacher) shortage would be electric. It would send a message to teachers and to young people deciding on a career that the country takes teachers and teaching seriously," according to the Carnegie Report. "But it must be done fairly. Dramatic improvements are not likely unless teachers clearly meet higher standards of preparation and skill, but it is unfair to those now in place to change the rules all at once."

Teachers, eventually meeting these high standards, would have much more authority in the running of schools. Schools would be restructured to provide a professional environment, freeing teachers to decide how best to meet state and local goals for children while still being held accountable for student progress.

The plan would provide more

for teachers to schoolwide student performance, the report asserts. And though it acknowledges the difficulty of establishing appropriate measures of student performance, it insists that teachers can help develop such measures.

A Nation Prepared also proposes mobilization of the nation's re-

sources to prepare minority youngsters for teaching careers.

States, corporations, colleges, community organizations, and others should work together to put in place a comprehensive program for pre-college education of minority youth—including both school and out-of-school programs.

Members of the Carnegie Forum are clear-eyed about what it takes to make such sweeping changes, especially if teachers don't perceive and adopt their essential role in

But the Carnegie Foundation has some experience with educational change and is not daunted. In the past 80 years, Carnegie has successfully introduced the basic concept

---

"Schools can only succeed if they operate on the principle that the essential resource is already inside the school: determined, intelligent, and capable teachers."

---

of high school academic credits, reorganized medical education in this country, played a major role in forming the Educational Testing Service, and helped in the expansion of higher education.

Another reason to look for progress on Carnegie recommendations: endorsement by task force members Mary Hatwood Futrell, president of the National Education Association, and Albert Shanker, president of the American Federation of Teachers.

THE CASE FOR CHANGE

An excerpt from the Carnegie Report

❝ People may wonder why 'lighthouse' schools, successful teaching projects, and leaders who innovate are not more widely imitated. Or, perhaps even more important, why these schools, projects, and leaders so often seem to flicker for a moment and then settle back to the routine. The answer is simple. Altruism and pride motivate those often unnoticed teachers who extend themselves to achieve much for their students and their schools. But the system's rewards do not go to those who produce the most achievement for the students and the greatest efficiency for the taxpayer. They go to those who play the game, stay out of controversy, and stand pat.

Consider the following. Teachers who routinely bring home students' papers and work on them late into the night are rewarded no differently from the teachers who do not. Administrators of districts with high administrative overhead suffer not at all in comparison to administrators who have figured out how to direct their resources to instructional services. Districts and schools that produce more learning in the same number of years have no reward at all. Special programs for the disadvantaged are often budgeted on the basis of children's poverty and skill levels. If the schools should succeed in raising their skills overmuch, the schools' reward would be the loss of the special funds. Continued receipt of the funds, of course, is in no way contingent on student progress. . . .

Schooling today is an overwhelmingly bureaucratic activity where, as one observer put it, 'Everyone has all of the brakes and no one has any of the motors.' It is unreasonable to hold teachers accountable for results when many of the important decisions about how students' needs are met are made by others.

To say all this is not to fault professional educators. It is to suggest that improved teacher performance and productivity await changes in the system within which they work. What is wanted is a system that does not have to depend so heavily on altruism, one that provides more rewards for superior performance and where there are real consequences for failure.

Such a system will not emerge from more extensive, more detailed, or more draconian measures. In recent years, some state legislatures, in their frustration with the perceived poor performance of the schools, have yielded to the temptation to specify in ever greater detail not only what educators are to accomplish, but how they are to go about it—the curriculum, texts, methods to be employed, and so on. The education code for some states is now printed in 10 or more volumes. To these commands are added the policies of school boards, the instructions of school district officials, and the wishes of parents. Though some would say that this weight of commands frees teachers and principals to do whatever they wish, the truth is otherwise.

It is this welter of rules that makes even worse the already heavily bureaucratic environment teachers must endure. Legislation cannot make teachers effective, nor can administrative bureaucracies in large districts. Both should seek to create conditions under which it is in the direct interest of teachers and principals to do everything possible to be effective and to help their colleagues be effective.

There are many ways to confront these issues. What is crucial is that a start be made, that the states, the schools, and teachers recognize the importance of properly structured incentives and develop policies that make it more likely that both performance and productivity will improve steadily. ❞

The next steps are up to teachers themselves. Here's what *A Nation Prepared* says directly to you: "What you think about these recommendations is important. Write to your associations and to policy leaders in your state. Talk about these ideas among your colleagues and with others in your community. Participate in local efforts to strengthen school programs, both as an individual and as a member of your association. Watch for the creation of the National Board. We especially invite you to act on the belief that teaching is a complex, difficult profession by seeking Board certification when it becomes available. After you become Board-certified, take advantage of your right to elect teacher representatives to the Board."

The two reports mentioned may be obtained as follows: For *A Nation Prepared: Teachers for the 21st Century,* send $9.95 to the Carnegie Forum on Education and the Economy, PO Box 157, Hyattsville, MD 20781. For *Tomorrow's Teachers: A Report of the Holmes Group,* send $6.50 to The Holmes Group, Inc., 501 Erickson Hall, East Lansing, MI 48824-1034.

Educational Ideals and Educational Practice: The Case of Minimum Competency Testing

Harvey Siegel

Michigan Technological University

Parents usually educate their children in such a manner that, however bad the world may be, they may adapt themselves to its present conditions. But, they ought to give them an education so much better than this, that a better condition of things may thereby be brought about in the future.

Immanuel Kant[1]

One could hardly be active in educational affairs these days and remain unaware of the minimum competency testing phenomenon. Minimum competency testing (henceforth MCT), our latest educational craze, is either being practiced or being contemplated in nearly every state of the union.[2] Like all educational movements, MCT has generated a storm of debate, and various criticisms and defenses of the practice can be heard: that it unfairly treats minority students; that it is a boon to educational efficiency and accountability; that establishing minumum competency mastery levels is arbitrary; and many more. There is one sort of consideration relevant to the assessment of MCT, however, that is conspicuously absent from public debate. That consideration is largely a philosophical one. Namely, is MCT compatible with our most defensible view of the aims of education? Is MCT consonant with our educational ideals? In particular, is the relation between MCT and the educational ideal of critical thinking a positive one?

In what follows, I hope to make a (brief) case for honoring the ideal of critical thinking and so for taking seriously the aim of developing students' critical thinking abilities. Then I will turn to an analysis of MCT, with an eye to answering the question: Is MCT helpful or harmful to our efforts to help students become critcal thinkers? Put more broadly, is MCT a justifiable educational practice, given our philosophically informed view of the aims of education? In arguing that it is not a justifiable practice, I hope to clarify the relationship between educational ideals and educa-

tional practices, and to expose the irrationality of pursuing practices which are incompatible with those ideals. My discussion will include: an articulation of the notion of critical thinking, and a defense of its status as a central educational ideal; a discussion of MCT, including a detailed analysis of the recent debate regarding MCT's alleged arbitrariness; an argument to the effect that, while MCT can avoid the charge of arbitrariness, it can do so only by exposing its gross inadequacy from the point of view of philosophically defensible educational ideals; and finally, some reflections regarding the relationship between educational ideals and educational practices. It is here that the general educational and curricular ramifications of the discussion concerning MCT, its alleged arbitrariness, and the ideal of critical thinking are drawn out. The general point made is that MCT, like all educational practices, must be conceived and conducted with an eye to philosophically defensible educational ideals; that MCT's failings are directly attributable to its inadequacy from the point of view of such ideals; and that educational policies and curricular designs which are conceived and implemented without regard for such ideals are bound to be inadequate, both philosophically and practically.

Critical Thinking As An Educational Ideal[3]

Generally speaking, a critical thinker is a person who is *appropriately moved by reasons*. Consequently, to be a critical thinker a person or student needs, first, to possess a variety of related reasoning skills. Such critical skills include those necessary for identifying and evaluating reasons. Relevant features of reasonable judgment—i.e., judgment grounded in reasons—include a grasp of *principles* (of various sorts) underlying the assessment of reasons.

From *Issues In Education*, Vol. 1, Nos. 2 and 3, 1983, pp. 154-170. Copyright 1983, American Educational Research Association, Washington, D.C.

Principled judgment is judgment which, at a minimum, is objective, impartial, and non-arbitrary. It is, moreover, judgment based on reasons or evidence of an appropriate kind and properly assessed. A critical thinker, then, is one whose judgment is governed by an appreciation of the cognitive force of reasons, and which is as such objective, impartial, non-arbitrary, and based on properly assessed evidence or reasons.

We can bring this characterization of the critical thinker down to earth a bit by thinking more concretely about the cognitive skills required for the execution of the just-described judgment. Most obviously, critical thinkers need to have facility in logic, for they must be able to assess the relation between claims and reasons brought forth in support of those claims. That is to say, critical thinkers must be able to assess arguments, and to pin down the connection for any given argument between the premises and conclusion of that argument.

I here use "logic" broadly to include both formal and informal logic, and it is perhaps appropriate to briefly discuss current controversy regarding the role of logic in critical thinking activity and pedagogy. In what is best seen as a reaction to the unhelpfulness of formal logic in evaluating typical examples of everyday reasoning, a new "informal logic movement" has sprung up. The defenders of informal logic often argue that formal logic is either absolutely irrelevant to, or positively harmful for, the student's ability to assess critically ordinary arguments; and therefore that formal logic should not be included in efforts to understand or teach critical thinking.[4] I would argue, to the contrary, that an adequate conception of critical thinking must include formal as well as informal logic. Formal logic can be seen as providing a paradigm of good argumentation. A deductively valid formal argument is as strong an argument as it is possible to have; the connection between the premises and conclusion of such an argument is as tight as any such connection can be. To put the point slightly differently, formal argumentation may profitably be seen as constituting an "ideal type" of argument, which (like ideal types in social science, or "ideal laws" like the ideal gas law in physical science) may not be typically, or ever actually encountered in everyday discourse, but which nevertheless are central to our theoretical understanding of argumentation. Since we want critical thinkers to have such understanding of argumentaion, formal logic is a necessary (though not necessarily a major) portion of an adequate critical thinking course or curriculum.

An additional reason for including formal logic in the critical thinking course is that critical thinking is largely concerned with the proper assessment of reasons, and formal logic provides an excellent source of clear reasons. For example, it is hard to imagine a more compelling reason for accepting the proposition "q" than the proposition "pvq. & p̄" ("p or q and not p"). Given the latter proposition, we have conclusive reason for accepting "q." In fact, propositions which deductively entail some other proposition seem to me to be the most compelling reasons for accepting that latter proposition there can be. Thus, exposure to formal logic seems desirable for the critical thinking course, for it illustrates well that fundamental property of "being a reason for."[5]

In addition to general facility in logic, a student must, for any given domain in which reasons play a role, have an understanding of the principles and methodological rules operative in that domain which determine the adequacy of reasons in that domain. For example, in science education it is insufficient simply to teach students our currently accepted theories and beliefs; for a student to be educated so as to be a critical thinker in matters scientific, the student must be brought to an understanding of the basis of our assessment of scientific claims: to an understanding of, for example, why a given experimental result supports theory T_1 but not T_2; why one objection to some scientific claim is crucial and devastating, another trivial and ineffective; and so on. The same point can be made with respect to other curriculum areas. In short, critical thinking requires a familiarity with and grasp of the nature of reasons and criteria for the assessment of reasons in the several domains of human activity in which reason plays a role, especially criteria governing the assessment of empirical evidence, as well as an understanding of "cross domain" or domain-neutral features of argument assessment proffered by logic.

In addition to the sort of skills and knowledge already mentioned, a critical thinker has as well a set of attitudes, habits of mind, dispositions, and character traits which may collectively be labeled the *critical attitude* or *critical spirit*. So, for example, a critical thinker would be capable not only of assessing the degree of support some piece of evidence provides for some claim, she must also be *disposed* to do so. Likewise, a critical thinker must possess a *willingness* to conform judgment to principle, an inclination to seek reasons, a character which rejects partiality and arbitrariness, and a commitment to objective judgment, even when such judgment is not in her self-interest. Moreover, one who possesses the critical spirit possesses habits of inquiry and assessment consonant with the considerations just sketched.

A noteworthy aspect of critical thinking is its explicit acknowledgment of the desirability of the student's self-sufficiency and autonomy. If we think it good that a student become a critical thinker, we must approve as well of the student's ability and tendency to consult her own independent judgment concerning matters of concern to her. Thus, the critical thinker must be autonomous; that is, free to judge and act independently of external constraint, on the basis of her own reasoned appraisal of the matter at hand. Relatedly, if we take the ideal of critical thinking seriously, we must endeavor to render the student self-sufficient and capable of determining (insofar as is possible) her own future. In this way we aim to bring the student quickly to the point in which she can join the adult community and be recognized as a fellow member of a community of equals. Critical thinking, in its open striving for the student's early achievement of autonomy and self-sufficiency, categorically rejects any educational plan which aims at the preparation of the student for some preconceived adult role or pre-established slot in some social arrangement. Rather, critical thinking aims at getting the student to be an active participant in the establishment of her own adult life, and of the social arrangements in which she is engaged. In this way critical thinking can be seen as an ideal with liberating and potentially revolutionary overtones. Critical thinking is not an enemy of the status quo as such, but it is an enemy of the *unjustifiable* status quo, and accordingly is a friend of all efforts aimed at the rational improvement of the status quo.[6]

3. THE STRUGGLE FOR EXCELLENCE

One might ask why we should take critical thinking seriously as an educational ideal. For one who takes the ideal seriously, this demand for justification must clearly be met. Elsewhere I have attempted to provide such justification in some detail;[7] consequently, I shall address myself to the question only briefly here. I believe there are three reasons (at least) for taking the ideal seriously. First, we are morally obligated to treat students (and everyone else) with respect. The Kantian principle of respect for persons requires that we treat students in a certain manner—one which honors students' demand for reasons and explanations, deals with students honestly, and recognizes the need to confront students' independent judgment. This manner of teaching, which might be called the *critical manner*, is morally required; it is also part and parcel of the ideal of critical thinking. So morality provides one powerful reason for operating our educational institutions in a way that accords with the critical thinking ideal. Second, we take as a practical educational aim the preparation of students for adult life. There are independent reasons for holding that such preparation involves the developing of students' self-sufficiency. This is a central component of critical thinking as well. The link between our general aim of preparing the student for adult life, which involves the development of the student's self-sufficiency, offers a second reason for taking the ideal seriously. Finally, if we accept the view that education is (at least in part) a matter of initiation into the central human traditions, and that to be initiated into those traditions is (in part) to learn the way in which reasons are assessed in those traditions, then critical thinking is an important educational ideal because it seeks to foster in students that knowledge and those dispositions and character traits conducive to the successful initiation of students into the rational traditions.

These three putative justifications for the ideal of critical thinking clearly stand in need of further analysis and argument. Nevertheless, I propose to leave the present discussion concerning the justification of critical thinking as it stands, so we may proceed to the consideration of our central concern, namely MCT. Our question becomes: Does MCT aid us in our efforts to help students to become critical thinkers? Is MCT compatible with the ideal of critical thinking? The following portion of this essay addresses these questions.

Minimum Competency Testing

MCT is a loosely defined set of educational practices which include the testing of students at various grade levels to determine the extent of their "mastery" of some set of "competencies." The specific competencies tested for vary from program to program, and are conceived of either as "school subject" (basic skill) competencies such as reading and mathematical computation, or as "life skill" (functional literacy) competencies such as balancing a checkbook or successfully answering an employment advertisement. The student is expected to demonstrate a certain specifiable level of mastery of the competency; if the student fails to so demonstrate, either retesting, remediation efforts, failure to be promoted to the next grade, failure to receive a high school diploma, or some combination of these is the result. The MCT movement is widely held to

be largely supported by politicians and the public at large rather than by educators,[8] and is generally held to be motivated both by an effort of state legislatures to wrest educational control from local school systems, and by the public's dismay at lowered standards and seeming abundance of high school graduates who are "functionally illiterate."[9] Arguments frequently given in support of MCT involve enhanced accountability, the need to stop the downward slide of test scores, and the need to provide students with the competencies necessary for functional participation in society.[10]

I will not attempt here any systematic review of the many arguments advanced in favor of or opposed to MCT. Rather, I will focus on one central consideration regarding the worth and justifiability of MCT that is related to the ideal of critical thinking; namely, the recent debate concerning the alleged arbitrariness of MCT. I hope that examination of this controversy will help us to arrive at a philosophically informed assessment of MCT. Particularly, my hope is that examination of the arbitrariness issue will clarify the relationship between MCT and the ideal of critical thinking.

The Arbitrariness of Standards

Perhaps the most philosophically pregnant dispute regarding MCT is that concerning MCT's alleged arbitrariness. Critics have repeatedly pointed out that a significant degree of arbitrariness is unavoidable in MCT, because there appears to be no non-arbitrary way of determining cut-off scores, or mastery levels, to differentiate those students who have attained minimum competency from those who have not. The most vocal of these critics, Gene V. Glass, states the position forcefully:

> I have read the writing of those who claim the ability to make the determination of mastery or competence in statistical or psychological ways. They can't. At least, they cannot determine "criterion levels" or standards other than arbitrarily.[11]

Glass argues that the difficulty of individual test items is largely ummonitored and typically fluctuates considerably,[12] and that cutoff scores are chosen more on the basis of the "tough" and "tendermindedness" of the test constructor than on any evidence that a particular cut-off score actually indicates mastery of the skill or subject matter being tested. In fact, Glass suggests that such a cut-off score is *in principle* unattainable, since there is no non-arbitrary way of establishing a point at which demonstrable non-mastery turns into demonstrable mastery:

> For most skills and performances, one can reasonably imagine a continuum stretching from "absence of the skill" to "conspicuous excellence." But it does not follow from the ability to recognize absence of the skill (e.g., This paraplegic can type zero words per minute at 0 percent accuracy) that one can recognize the highest level of skill below which the person will not be able to succeed (in life, at the next level of schooling, or in his chosen trade). What is the minimum level of skill required in this society to be a citizen, parent, carpenter, college professor, keypunch operator? Imagine that someone would dare to specify the highest level of reading performance below which no person could succeed in life as a parent. Counter-examples could be sup-

plied in abundance of persons whose reading performance is below the "minimal" level yet who are regarded as successful parents. And the situation is no different with a secretary or electrician—in case one wished to argue that minimal competence levels are possible for "training," if not for "education." What is the lowest level of proficiency at which a person can type and still be employed as a secretary? Nearly any typing rate above the trivial zero-point will admit exceptions; and if one were forced nonetheless to specify a minimal level, the rate of exceptions that was tolerable would be an arbitrary judgment.[13]

As this passage indicates, Glass holds that the arbitrariness endemic to MCT is so widespread, misleading, and potentially dangerous to students that MCT (and criterion-referenced testing generally) ought to be removed, root and branch, from the schools, and replaced with norm-referenced testing.

While Glass's case for the inherent arbitrariness of the standard setting required for MCT is powerfully made—and in fact, even his critics grant that in some sense he is right on that score—there are two difficulties with Glass's position. First, it is not clear that his suggestion regarding reliance on norm-referenced testing actually helps to avoid the arbitrariness problem. Glass's defense of norm-referenced testing is straightforward: Comparative judgments, or measurements of change of performance, are not arbitrary, or at least not as capriciously arbitrary as "absolute" judgments or measurements of criterion-referenced mastery:

> Perhaps the only criterion that is safe and convincing in education is change. Increases in cognitive performance are generally regarded as good, decreases as bad. Although one cannot make satisfactory judgments of performance (Is this level of reading performance good or masterful?), one can readily judge an improvement in performance as good and a decline as bad. My position on this matter is justified by appeal to a more general methodological question in evaluation. Is all meaningful evaluation comparative? Or do there exist absolute standards of value? I feel that in education there are virtually no absolute standards of value. "Goodness" and "badness" must be replaced by the essentially comparative concepts of "better" and "worse" . . . Absolute evaluation in education . . . has been capricious and authoritarian. On the other hand, the value judgments based on comparative evidence impress one as cogent and fair.[14]

Unfortunately, comparative evaluation does not so easily escape the charge of arbitrariness as Glass suggests. Granted that increase in cognitive performance is good, how much improvement is good enough to warrant, say, promotion from grade to grade, or graduation from high school? Surely zero-level change is insufficient; consequently here, just as in the case of criterion-referenced testing, a decision must be made, a point must be picked, which designates the minimum improvement necessary for promotion or graduation. And this decision appears to be as arbitrary as the decision concerning mastery levels Glass argues against so cogently. So the move to comparative education does not escape the charge of arbitrariness.[15]

The difficulty just noted concerns Glass's solution to the problem of the arbitrariness of MCT. A more serious difficulty with his position is one raised by several of his critics, most notably W. James Popham and Michael

Scriven, who claim that Glass's case for the arbitrariness of MCT is itself weak, and that MCT programs need not be as arbitrary as Glass claims. Popham notes that there are two senses of "arbitrary": judgmental and capricious; and argues that, while mastery levels are arbitrary in the first sense, they need not be arbitrary in the second, more pernicious sense:

> The cornerstone of Glass's attack on the setting of performance standards is his assertion that such standards are set arbitrarily. He uses the term in its most pejorative sense; that is, equating it with mindless and capricious action. But while it can be conceded that performance standards must be set *judgmentally*, it is patently incorrect to equate human judgment with arbitrariness in the negative sense.[16]

Popham claims that standard setting, while necessarily judgmental, need not be capriciously judgmental. This distinction is surely a reasonable one. But it does not in any way rebut Glass's indictment of the arbitrariness of MCT. For Glass is claiming not simply that standard-setting requires judgment, but that there will be no good reason for choosing one cut-off point over another. Let us distinguish between *grounded* judgment vs. capricious judgment, as Popham does. Then Glass's claim is that standard setting is always a matter of capricious, or ungrounded judgment. This is the thrust to Glass's criticisms of test item construction which fails to pay close attention to the difficulty of the item, and of setting cut-off scores according to whether or not the test constructor is "liberal" (e.g., 65 percent or 70 percent) or "tough-minded" (e.g., 90 percent).[17] Popham suggests that a grounded, non-capricious judgment of minumum competency standards can be had by educators—such judgments "can refer to the lowest level of proficiency *which they consider acceptable* for the situation at hand.[18] But, Glass must retort, on what basis is such consideration made? Is 90 percent proficiency considered acceptable because the educator is "tough-minded?" Is 70 percent considered acceptable because the educator in question is a "liberal guy"? Unless such considered judgments are grounded somehow, they are indeed capricious, and Popham's distinction between judgmental arbitrariness and capricious arbitrariness seems not to protect MCT from Glass's criticism.

Michael Scriven pushes the rebuttal of Glass's criticism of MCT further, by suggesting that judments concerning mastery levels can be grounded in empirical research. Scriven argues that *needs assessment* is the key which will provide the possibility of setting non-arbitrary standards of mastery:

> We can only set mastery levels—other than as a first approximation—in light of needs assessment, and typically a bi-level one that addresses both the needs of those being tested for the skills and so forth being tested, and the needs of certain clienteles (which may or may not include the testees) for the mastery test.[19]

Presumably Scriven has in mind something like this: To establish mastery levels for the successful automobile mechanic, one studies the needs of those clienteles in need of mechanics—e.g., frustrated automobile owners, dealership service managers, gas station operators, etc.—and the needs of aspiring mechanics. If it turns out, say, that the needs of various clienteles are for mechanics who can tune engines, troubleshoot and repair failures in the electrical system, and replace exhaust systems, then the needs of aspiring mechanics are those skills and abilities which would enable the student mechanic to satisfy those needs of the clienteles—e.g., to properly "read" the "scope" utilized for electronic tuneups, to follow with understanding the manufacturer's repair manual, to possess a good working knowlege of automobile electrical systems, to have a significant amount of manual dexterity with regard to screwdrivers, wrenches, ratchets, air compressors, and pneumatic hand tools, and so on. In this way, by tentatively setting up mastery standards, researching the efficacy of those standards, monitoring the needs of both students and clienteles, and adjusting standards in light of such research, nonarbitrary standards of mastery can be established.

There is much to be said for Scriven's realistic, common sense approach to the standard setting problem. Nevertheless, there is a crucial difficulty with it. For the needs assessment approach to standard setting for MCT to be successful, it must be the case that becoming educated is in the relevant respects like becoming a mechanic—that is, that in the former case as in the latter, research concerning needs assessment of students of the various clienteles of educational testing will turn up specifiable needs which, if met, would certify the student who met those needs as a well-educated or successfully educated person. However, as I will now attempt to show, such a parallel between specific occupations (like mechanic or typist) and education is dubious. Any philosophically defensible view of the aims of education—and especially, the view that critical thinking is an important educational aim—will preclude conceiving of education along the occupational training lines that the needs assessment approach assumes.

How do we determine what specific skills and abilities a student will need in the future, when the student's future is undetermined? Scriven writes:

> When you know how graduates need to perform on the job (the needs assessment) and you have a test you can use on pregraduates which has some predictive validity against job performance, you can set cutting scores (or bands).[20]

This makes sense only if we *do* know what job the student will need to perform well at. But while for technical training (e.g., auto mechanics school) we do know this, for the typical public school student we do not. Our ignorance on this point is not simply a matter of too little research, moreover. On the contrary, we do not seek to determine students' futures, for we typically regard that as in large part, if not solely, the prerogative of the student, and we recognize that, except for the rare student, the years of public education end far too quickly for such determination. Indeed, if we take seriously that component of the ideal of critical thinking which emphasizes the student's achievement of self-sufficiency and autonomy, we note that the student's future is essentialy always open. We educate so as to enable the student to *create* her future, not to submit to it. Unless education is to mean "training and socialization into predetermined adult roles and jobs," we cannot specify in advance what a student's future will be—and so, we cannot specify in advance the needs of students which testing will serve, nor the needs of the various clienteles of educational testing. For the job of life—the only job which all students must engage in—needs assessment seems a hopeless task. Education is not geared to any particular job performance; consequently, Scriven's needs assessment approach will not help our efforts to set standards for MCT, since it depends on identifying the job performance an educated person need pursue, and pushes too hard the weak analogy between becoming an educated person and becoming (say) a mechanic.

A Second Locus of Arbitrariness

There is, moreover, a related problem concerning the notions of "life skills" or "functional literacy" which bedevils most discussions of MCT. Thus far we have considered one charge of arbitrariness leveled at MCT, namely, the charge that, given specific skills or subject matter, setting mastery levels is arbitrary. There is another sort of arbitrariness to be considered as well, concerning the determination or constitution of those skills, abilities, and items of knowlege mastery which are necessary for the achievement of functional literacy. How do we determine what counts as functional literacy? Here is a second locus of arbitrariness, one not always sufficiently distinguished from the first. Schematically, the situation is as follows:

> *First level of arbitrariness*: given specified skills, etc., which constitute functional literacy, what constitutes mastery?
> *Second level arbitrariness*: what constitutes functional literacy? Which skills, etc., are to be specified?

Many critics of MCT have noted the arbitrariness of selecting the skills and abilities which are to constitute functional literacy or life skills. However, such arbitrariness is typically conflated with first level arbitrariness. Glass, for example, notes that:

> No one knows how well a person must read to succeed in life or what percent of the graduating class ought to be able to calculate compound interest payments.[21]

Here Glass runs together both first and second level arbitrariness. The first case, specifying how *well* a person must be able to read in order to "succeed in life," queries the *level* of reading skill necessary for mastery. This is first level arbitrariness. The second case, however, suggests that some members of the graduating class may succeed in life perfectly well, even though they are not able to calculate compound interest payments. Here what is being questioned is whether or not the ability to calculate compound interest payments is a part of functional literacy, or is a "life skill" *at all*. This is second level arbitrariness. For discussion of the arbitrariness of MCT to be conducted fruitfully, these two levels of arbitrariness must be distinguished and considered separately.

As argued earlier, Glass has provided a strong case for the unavoidability of first level arbitrariness. While that case is perhaps not conclusively made, it easily survives the criticism offered by Popham and Scriven.[22] Class has noted the problem of second level arbitrariness as well, but because he has failed adequately to distinguish the two levels, he has not offered any reason for taking second level arbitrariness to be either avoidable or unavoidable. Glass's arguments for the unavoidability of arbitrariness all speak to first level, standard setting arbitrariness. Scriven's suggestion for avoiding arbitrariness via needs assessment similarly founders on a confusion of the two levels of arbitrariness, for at best it offers a way to avoid first level arbitrariness in relatively narrow, job-related training programs, while failing to take into account both second level arbitrariness (Does being able to "perform on the job" make one functionally literate? Can one be trained for some specific occupation, unquestioningly accept that occupation as one's lot in life, and counted as one whose life is a "success"?) and the fact that becoming an educated person is in crucial respects very much unlike becoming a typist or mechanic, thus misconstruing the nature of the problem of avoiding first level arbitrariness. In order to settle the question, "is MCT unavoidably arbitrary?", then, we must specifically address the problem of second level arbitrariness, and inquire further into the notion of "functional literacy" (or "life skill").

The Notion of Functional Literacy

What constitutes functional literacy? Can we specify an acceptable conception of functional literacy? And how would such a conception be grounded? In his paper on curricular implications of MCT,[23] Harry Broudy notes that functional literacy can be defined narrowly, as "the ability to read utility bills and classified ads, to write a letter of application, do simple sums,"[24] or broadly as "being able to use language in all its forms to enlarge knowledge, clarify thought, enrich the imagination, and guide judgment."[25] The narrow definition offers at best a minimal conception of functional literacy; we may indeed doubt whether one whose skills and knowledge are limited to those specified by the narrow conception are either functional or literate. As Broudy argues, "Literacy itself presupposes more than mechanical mastery of the three R's . . . To be genuinely functional, literacy requires all strands of the curriculum."[26] Yet many proponents of MCT would reject the broad conception of functional literacy—as Popham notes, "The public is screaming for minimum warranties, not an enlightened conception of functional literacy."[27] Have we then unavoidable arbitrariness at the second level? Can we ground our judgments about the skills and knowledge a functionally literate person must possess?

I believe we can. Such judgements may, and indeed must, be grounded ultimately in a philosophical conception of the aims of education. What counts as functional, and as literate, depends on considerations concerning the powers, talents, and autonomy of well-educated persons. If, as suggested earlier, critical thinking is an important educational ideal, then the narrow conception of functional literacy will not do. If our educational aim is to get students to be critical thinkers, and if critical thinking involves much more than the narrow conception of functional literacy takes account of—which it does—then a student who is minimally competent must be a student who is at least minimally *critical*, not "functional" as narrowly construed. Insofar as MCT conceives of minimal competence in terms of narrow functional literacy, it is doomed to be an unjustifiable educational practice, since it would at best promote an educational scheme sorely lacking in attention to those aspects of a student's education that are crucial to the achievement of critical thinking.

It seems, then, that MCT is not unavoidably arbitrary.

While first level arbitrariness may be unavoidable, second level arbitrariness may be avoided by appealing to philosophical considerations concerning the aims of education and the skills, abilities, dispositions, and understandings of well-educated persons. This conclusion should provide little comfort to the proponents of MCT, however, for once we move to avoid second level arbitrariness we are immediately confronted by the huge disparity between the conception of education offered by the ideal of critical thinking, and that embodied in MCT programs. For the latter, education is a matter of getting students to master the mechanics of linguistic and computational skills, and some occupational skills sufficient for holding a place in the current economic order. For the former, education goes far beyond such considerations, by seeking to inculcate the skills, propensities, and habits of mind consonant with critical thinking, and the autonomy to control one's life and life-decisions. From the point of view of critical thinking, MCT is not arbitrary—it is rather colossally inadequate and indefensible—as educational practice, and as an embodiment of a serious conception of education.

Conclusion: Philosophical Ideals and Educational Practices

I have been arguing the MCT fails to deal seriously with or be informed by philosophical considerations concerning the aims of education and our conception of a well-educated person, and that, once these considerations are raised, MCT appears grossly inadequate as a central educational practice or focus. I have (briefly) defended the educational ideal of critical thinking, and claimed that MCT fails to measure up to that ideal, but I hope that the arguments presented have broader force. I surely do not claim to have settled the age-old question of the aims of education in favor of critical thinking. But I do claim that any defensible view of the aims of education would include features of critical thinking—skills of reasoning, appropriate habits of mind, autonomy, and self-sufficiency, for example—and that these features go far beyond the narrow conception of functional literacy tacitly adopted by MCT. Thus, MCT would be deficient from the point of view of *any* defensible view of the aims of education, not simply that of critical thinking. And, indeed, most of the criticisms of MCT offered above would stand independently of their connection with critical thinking.

There is a final, larger point to be made, which concerns the role of philosophical considerations in establishing educational polices and practices. There is a great tendency on the part of policy makers to shy away even from raising questions concerning the aims of education when considering policy alternatives. This tendency is no doubt related to the often-noted fondness for fads education regularly exhibits. Fads are frowned upon primarily because they are not serious or well-founded. Neither, I want to suggest, are educational practices (like MCT) which fail meaningfully to raise questions regarding their own aims. What is it that we are trying to accomplish in schools? What would the ideally educated student be like? Without at least tentative answers to such questions in hand, guiding educational practice, that practice is blind. Such questions demand careful philosophical reflection, and educational policy will remain ineffective and inconstant until it is guided

3. THE STRUGGLE FOR EXCELLENCE

by such considerations. Thus, educational practice and philosophical reflection are wed. Without the guidance of the latter, the former can only be folly.

Nowhere is this more clear than with regard to MCT. MCT, as I have argued, does not foster and is not compatible with critical thinking, or indeed with any defensible conception of the aims of education. To pursue MCT, unperturbed by the failure to match educational ideals with educational practice, is to condemn that practice to the eventual destiny of all educational fads: the dustbin of uninformed, ineffectual, unjustifiable, worthless, and failed educational endeavors.[28]

Footnotes

1. The Kant citation, from his *Education*, is taken from Maxine Greene, "Response to 'Competence and Excellence: The Search for An Egalitarian Standard, the Demand for a Universal Guarantee,' by Jenne K. Britell," in R.M. Jaeger and C.K. Tittle, eds., *Minimum Competency Achievement Testing* (Berkeley, CA: McCutchen Publishing Corp., 1980), 47.

2. Cris Pipho, "Minimum Competency Testing in 1978: A Look at State Standards," *Phi Delta Kappan* 59 (May 1978): 585-588.

3. Another, more detailed, attempt to explicate the ideal of critical thinking is made in my "Critical Thinking as An Educational Ideal," *The Educational Forum* 45 (November 1980): 7-23. The following discussion is partly based on that paper.

4. *See* the papers by Johnson & Blair, Kahane, Minkus and Scriven, in *Informal Logic*, ed. J. Anthony Blair and Ralph H. Johnson (Inverness, CA: Edgepress, 1980).

5. It has also been suggested, by Robert Binkley, that formal logic may help to develop what he calls "logical instinct," a trait he takes to be crucial to good thinking. *See* the paper by Binkley and also the paper by Woods, in Blair and Johnson.

6. These points are expanded on in Siegel, "Critical Thinking as An Educational Ideal," and in the writings of Israel Scheffler (on which I rely heavily) cited therein. Further ramifications of critical thinking for the curriculum and for teaching are spelled out in that former paper.

7. Siegel, 13-17.

8. *See* Pipho, 586.

9. Ibid., 586; *see* also Arthur E. Wise, "Minimum Competency Testing: Another Case of Hyper-Rationalization," *Phi Delta Kappan* 59 (May 1978): 596-598.

10. The educational literature on this point is voluminous. A good place to start is Pipho, and the articles collected in Jaeger and Tittle.

11. Gene V. Glass, "Standards and Criteria," *Journal of Educational Measurement* 15 (Winter 1978): 237-261; citation is from 237.

12. For examples, *see* Glass, 238-239.

13. Ibid., 250-251.

14. Ibid., 259.

15. Glass recognizes this problem, but does not offer any solution. Glass, 259-260. I am indebted to Judy Rule for helpful discussion on this point.

16. W. James Popham, "As Always, Provocative," *Journal of Education Measurement* (Englewood Cliffs, NJ: Prentice-Hall, 1978): 168.

17. Glass, 238-239; *see* also Gene V. Glass, "Minimum Competence and Incompetence in Florida," *Phi Delta Kappan* 59 (May 1978): 604.

18. Popham, 298 (emphasis in original). Popham contrasts this "lowest acceptable performance" conception of MCT with the conception Glass utilizes, namely a "requisite for the future" conception. But this distinction does not establish Popham's defense of MCT, because the arbitrariness charge Glass levels at MCT applies equally well to either of Popham's conceptions.

19. Michael Scriven, "How to Anchor Standards," *Journal of Educational Measurment* 15 (Winter 1978): 273-275; citation is from 274.

20. Ibid., 275.

21. Glass, "Minimum Competence and Incompetence in Florida," 603; *see* also Glass's discussion of "survival skills," 605.

22. How serious a problem first-level arbitrariness is remains open to debate. My own view is that first-level arbitrariness is not as serious as second-level arbitrariness, and that the latter can be avoided, although not in a way which strengthens the case for MCT; *see* below.

23. Harry Broudy, "Impact of Minimum Competency Testing on Curriculum," in Jaeger and Tittle, 108-117.

24. Ibid., 113.

25. Ibid., 115.

26. Ibid., 116.

27. W. James Popham, "Curriculum and Minimum Competency: A Reaction to the Remarks of H.S. Broudy," in Jaeger and Tittle, 122.

28. I am grateful to the students in my seminar on "Critical Thinking and MCT" at Northern Arizona University (Summer 1981) for insightful discussion of the topics here considered, to Sophie Haroutunian, and to the members of the California Association for Philosophy of Education for a lively and helpful discussion of an earlier draft. An early version of the present paper, entitled "Critical Literacy and Minimum Competency Testing," discusses other grounds for regarding MCT as inadequate from the point of view of critical thinking. These other grounds include MCT's reliance on testing, its tendency to reduce "maxima" to "minima,' ' and its conception of teachers as automata. That paper appears in E. Grossen, ed., *The 1983 Proceedings of the Far Western Philosophy of Education Society*, 46-64.

Huffing and Puffing And Blowing Schools Excellent

If we want real change in our classrooms, we must talk to teachers — maybe even listen to them, says Ms. Ohanian. For without teachers, real change will never happen.

Susan Ohanian

SUSAN OHANIAN, a third-grade teacher on leave of absence, is currently senior editor of Learning: The Magazine for Creative Teaching, *Springhouse, Pa.*

THE GOOD GRAY managers of the U.S., the fellows who gave us Wonder Bread, the Pinto, hormone-laden beef wrapped in Styrofoam, and *People* magazine — not to mention acid rain, the Kansas City Hyatt, $495 hammers, and political campaigns — are now loudly screaming that we teachers should mend our slothful ways and get back to excellence. I would invite the corporate leaders, the politicians, and the professorial consultants to climb down from their insular glass towers before casting any more stones of censure at, or even advice about, my lack of excellence in the classroom. Life in the Eighties is complicated. All of us are, in Thomas Hardy's words, "people distressed by events they did not cause." There is no reason for teachers alone to shoulder the blame.

The various commissions and task forces on educational excellence seem to exemplify one of those laws of human nature: you can tell what a community thinks of you by the committees you aren't asked to join. All of this education commission razzle-dazzle is nothing new; it constitutes just one more in a long, histrionic string of repudiations of teacher savvy and sensitivity. When national leaders decide that it's time to find out what's going on in the schools, they convene a panel of auto dealers and their fellow Rotarians. Individually, these folks are undoubtedly witty, astute, and kind to cats. Collectively, they produce a lot of bluster and blunder; their notions of reform are, at best, spongy. They say, in effect, "I'll huff and I'll puff and I'll blow your schoolhouse excellent."

Would that they could. But most schoolhouses are built of brick, and, though the people behind those brick walls may listen to a little corporate whistling in the dark, adding a course in computer literacy here and one in consumer math there, they remain impervious to real change, especially since no real change has been called for. If you want real change, you must talk to teachers, maybe even listen to them. For without teachers, real change will never happen.

I confess to feeling about most committees the way Lord Palmerston felt about delegations: they are "a noun of multitude, signifying many but not much." In line with this description, the multifarious state-of-education groups have employed the popular "ready, fire, aim" approach — relying not on the firsthand observations of teachers and students but on the collated reports of other report writers. I propose a national lottery for education consultants. Instead of listening to pronouncements from every state, county, block party, and gathering of the Moose, why not choose just one? We could then syndicate the banalities of this lone lucky consultant and be done with it.

As things now stand, the U.S. would be better served if these commissions and task forces developed a master plan for getting rid of Astroturf and saving the spotted bat, a species as endangered as the science teacher. The education community is ill-served by their unilateral advice pacts. One can't help but wonder why our corporate brethren don't go off and figure out how to run an airline or a steel mill. Not that we teachers wouldn't welcome them into our classrooms. I'm sure that any teacher in the land would extend an invitation to any member of the many commissions on excellence to come to the classroom and show him or her how to make efficient use of school time on the day before Halloween, during a snowstorm, on the morning after an X-rated movie on cable television, during the first half hour after a child vomits in class, or immediately after the school nurse checks the group for head lice.

I can glean a few crystal moments from my own years in the classroom, but I suspect that the pestiferous pedagognosticians will have a hard time fitting my treasured moments on their graphs of excellence: watching a scruffy, smelly, foulmouthed 16-year-old emerge from six months of solitary Scrabble-playing to write a letter to a dictionary publisher; seeing a deaf child understand a knock-

knock joke for the first time; sharing gravestone rubbings; judging an ice-cube-melting contest; publishing a 45-page student anthology of cat stories. I can almost claim that I never met a curriculum I didn't like — at some particular time, for some particular child. And that's my problem: all I can offer are particulars. When the one-size-fits-all, spray-and-use planners gather together, I run for cover. Any good teacher will tell you that a curriculum or an instructional approach can't be standardized and remain effective, even within a single classroom. There's always that child who needs something different.

In my first year of teaching, one of my ninth-graders refused to read *Silas Marner*. Wishing I had had the guts to refuse to teach that particular novel, I gave him a different book. I figured I had enough troubles without carrying the added weight of failing someone for saying no. In my more optimistic moments, I even hoped that this particular ninth-grader was exercising literary taste.

As I look back on that incident 18 long years ago, I marvel that I had the good sense to avoid that battle. It is fairly easy to see now that *Silas Marner* was not worth bloodshed or even tears, but I marvel that I sensed it then. The burdens of teaching are heavy; the joys, fleeting. Occasionally, good judgment and even excellence can be recognized in retrospect, but in the classroom you usually just hope that you can get through the day without having to apologize for anything.

We are ill-served by the present hardening of the categories, the separation of academic life into the real subjects and the frills. To hear some people tell it, a herd of basic skills escaped from the schoolhouse a few years back, apparently chased away by frivolous, fuzzy-headed electives. Now, if our economy, national security, and petrochemical lifestyle are to dominate, we need corporate help in corraling the wayward critters once again. Balderdash. All of this basic skills rumble-bumble is a smokescreen; whenever folks bring it up, check to see what they're selling. Mom, apple pie, two cars in every garage, and basic skills. Who could possibly be against such things?

People who talk about basic skills are expressing, of course, not a theory but a mood. Calling for a return to basic skills has the moral imperative of eating turnips; it is akin to the plaintive cry for law and order. Sure, we all want peace and quiet, a chicken in every microwave, and everybody reading at grade level. But these are weasel words, as easy to pin down as a whirling dervish.

Discussing absolute curriculums for high school is about as productive as talking about best diets or sharing theories on how to restrain proliferating zucchini. For all their technological pizzazz, our man-

The burdens of teaching are heavy; the joys, ephemeral. Occasionally, good judgment and even excellence can be recognized in retrospect.

darin advisors don't seem to understand that you simply do not educate children by the same methods employed to build rockets or harvest tomatoes.

I DROPPED OUT of high school English teaching (the first time) after just one year. Outside the school, students were terrorizing subway passengers, buying and selling dope, having babies. Inside, we gave departmental exams on Tennyson. Even when I did manage to figure out ways to supplement the curriculum, I had to sneak in early so that I could steal ditto paper and other supplies. Not to mention staying up until midnight weeping my way through 150 themes and my survival plans for the next day. In the ensuing two decades things have gotten not better, but steadily worse.

I wonder if concerned commission members and community leaders have any notion of just how debilitating it is for teachers, having figured out what to teach and even how to teach it, to then be forced to beg, borrow, and steal — and mostly do without — basic supplies. I wonder if the report writers have ever been in charge of a classroom for which it takes two weeks to secure enough chairs for the students. And even then the teacher has to fight hard to convince the janitor that leftover eighth-grade chairs simply won't do for fourth-graders. I know a lot of teachers who would cheerfully give up their copies of the reports on excellence for a ream of paper, a handful of #2 pencils, or a box of staples that fit the stapler.

As I look back over nearly two decades of teaching, I am rather amazed that my goal has remained constant since my second day: to help students believe not only that they have the skill to read but that they might actually *want* to read one day. My teaching career began midway through someone else's lesson plan, and I still have nightmares about that first day — that gruesome moment when I told the students to open the text to the next selection, "Hiawatha." I was out on the pavement that same afternoon, scouring bookstores for used paperbacks. I sensed that I

had to encourage students to read for their own information and pleasure, and I carefully watched their choices so that I could find out where to go next with them. When I could steal enough ditto paper, I typed up selections from some of my own favorites for us to read together. It may surprise those who are convinced that "excellence" must be imposed from above to know that the students' favorite literature was my laboriously typed excerpt from *The Once and Future King*. Interspersed with this rather eclectic curriculum was "real" school — the stuff of departmental exams and blue-ribbon commission recommendations.

Once, while I presented for my supervisor a required lesson on *Julius Caesar*, a belligerent girl (whose attendance had improved dramatically since the appearance of self-chosen books) steadfastly read her novel. My department chairman leaned over and whispered to her, "Don't you think you should put that book away and pay attention to the teacher?" "Who the hell are you?" demanded the girl. "If she wants me to put it away, let her tell me." She went back to her book, and I continued my performance. Later, it was hard to convince my boss that the girl's devotion to that book was an excellent moment for me, much more valid than my gyrations on *Julius Caesar*. Six weeks previously she had claimed that she "hated reading." Wasn't this progress? Do 100% of the students have to play the game? Her very presence in my class was a victory of sorts, and she was not, after all, painting her nails; she was reading.

Ten years later and hundreds of miles away, the students had changed but the official expectations had not. An investigator from the state education department complained because all my students were reading different books. He dismissed the fact that delinquents, dragged into our alternative program by truant officers and probation officers, were reading at least half an hour every day, with the query, "What major work do your sophomores read?" He was uncomfortable with and even hostile toward a classroom filled with Dick Francis, S.E. Hinton, Thomas Thompson, John McPhee, Edward Abbey, James Thurber, fix-it books, almanacs, sports and car magazines, and the *Daily News*. He was not placated by the fact that the *New York Times* was also in the room, as were copies of standard classics of literature. He wanted workbooks that focused on skills and 30 copies of *A Tale of Two Cities* or *Our Town*. We could have gotten away with Paul Zindel, if we'd had 30 copies. Experts on how schools should be run make it easier for teachers to pose clever comprehension questions about different drummers than to respect them.

STAN DROPPED OUT of high school the day he turned 16 because he "hated the damn bells, always making you stop what you're doing to go someplace else." Stan found a job as a carpenter's assistant in a Neighborhood Youth Corps program; by all accounts, he was clever, industrious, and dependable. That's what his boss told me, and I certainly found him to be all those things in the GED class the Corps required Stan to attend. He whizzed through all the GED sections except math. Although his common sense made him efficient at estimating, approximating, and making good guesses, Stan refused to learn the finer points of multiplication and long division.

It may be fitting and proper that a student who won't cooperate to the extent of learning long division should be denied any sort of high school seal of approval. But, if that is the way it's going to be, we should stop requiring such bureaucratic seals of approval for carpenters' assistants.

As Stan said when the Corps fired him for refusing to take any more classes in math, "All I ever wanted to do was work." If we are going to require college degrees for jobs that people once handled without an eighth-grade education, let us admit our reason: we are much more concerned with delaying entry into a glutted job market than with striving for excellence in education.

But the writers of reports on school reform don't know about Stan. Theirs is a too-narrow outlook on education — concerned with the dearth of foreign-language proficiency among incoming college freshmen, but not with the increasing numbers of young women who must drop out of school because they are pregnant or with the disaffected youths who neither need nor want a college-prep curriculum. I am disappointed that the commissions and task forces did not examine the lives of these students. But then, I'm prejudiced. I think that the needs of children should take precedence over the needs of Harvard and even over the needs of General Motors.

The reports on school reform imply that, if we teachers would just become more efficient and use class time more wisely, our students would score better on standardized tests, measure up to the Japanese in auto production, or whatever. What the writers of these reports fail to acknowledge is that in schooling, as in baseball, all moments are not of equal value. You have to put up with a lot of foul balls in the classroom.

Of *course* we need to evaluate teachers. But the current systems, which approach teacher evaluation with a meat inspector's outlook, are doomed to failure. Evaluating teachers is not like grading eggs or

If all teachers were paid a decent wage, maybe the notion of merit pay could be buried in the nearest landfill, with all the other deadly sludge.

beef. We need to encourage the proliferation of a variety of teaching styles, instead of setting up only two acceptable categories: Grade A and Grade B.

MAYBE IT IS TIME for a doctoral student or a governor's aide to examine the fact that teachers, by and large, are decidedly unenthusiastic about the idea of merit pay. We aren't scared off by so-called standards; we are distressed by the fact that teachers are once again being told how to do their job by people who have never done it. Merit pay will reward once again the politician and the showman among us. Expertise is too easy to fake. The Duke of Wellington once remarked that he liked the Order of the Garter because there was "no damned nonsense about merit" connected with it. If the state legislators and other politicians are so interested in rewarding merit, let them go first. If all teachers were paid a decent wage, maybe the notion of merit pay could be buried in the nearest landfill, along with all the other deadly sludge.

No one intimately involved in a classroom can appreciate the subtle interplays, the minute changes that take place among people in that setting — and, when things go very well, between a student and a text or an idea. So, when we are told to get ready for the lessons-by-appointment that are arranged every six months and duly noted in our personnel files, we go for the grand slam. Most of us can do this on schedule (and we have contracts stipulating that no one dare try an unscheduled visit), but lessons-by-appointment don't reveal tiddly-pom about our real strengths and weaknesses over the 180-day season. It always amazed me that students ham up such lessons as much as their teachers, cooperating in the production of show-and-tell tinsel for the benefit of visiting administrators. For 50 minutes twice a year, we all pretend that school is what everybody outside the classroom claims it should be. No student even asks to go to the bathroom.

After a while I stopped playing this game of gray-flannel excellence. I decided, "They want to evaluate me? Well, let them

see me in action" — which is often, to the unknowing eye, very close to inaction.

So my boss — the one who gets to lay down policy, write curriculum guidelines, and consult, no doubt, with important people from education commissions — sat in my classroom while three seventh-graders read joke books to one another, four students read notes I had written to them and wrote replies, two students quizzed each other for a social studies test in some other teacher's class, Charlie (left behind from the previous class) remained asleep, Sharon announced she was in love and got a pass to the library to find some poems honoring the event, Raymond picked up his novel where he had left off the day before, and Jack went through his daily litany about "not doing no friggin' work in this friggin' school." Interestingly, on another occasion, when I did perform a "show" lesson for an administrator, Jack played his role of model student. But since I wasn't faking it this time, neither did he.

A good teacher makes important decisions. Does Charlie need his sleep more than he needs reading? Do certain students need a review of social studies more than they need punctuation? A good teacher savors watching youngsters read joke books, when a few months earlier they refused to believe that books could ever be funny or worth sharing. A good teacher needles the obnoxious to get to work and encourages the light-hearted to view the library as a storehouse of infinite resources.

But after 10 minutes of this, my boss couldn't stand it any longer. She gathered up her agendas and her checklists and announced, "I'll come back when you are teaching." I noted that she'd been sitting across the table from Ron, who had gotten a good start on writing a poem. Three times he had called me over for help. I had nudged him to reexamine the sense of a metaphor, persuaded him to stop going for the easy rhyme, and helped him locate the thesaurus when he decided he needed a big word — one that "nobody else would know." I thought Ron's work nothing short of miraculous, but you won't find any record of these magic moments in my personnel file.

Even for the best of practitioners and observers, the teachable moment is fleeting; if you don't have a good eye, you are likely to miss it. Despite the claims of the mastery-learning crew and others of their ilk, teaching, like truth, is never pure and rarely simple. Too many expert witnesses mistake fluff and flutter for consequence. I figure that the only way to teach is well, and just how you do it is your own damn business. If my style doesn't fit on somebody else's checklist, too bad. We teachers must not be railroaded into pretending that we should be responsible for managing the timing and flow of education as efficiently and regularly as assembly-line workers produce toasters. We don't have to jump every time someone else rings a bell.

THE VARIOUS commission and task force reports released a flood of public sentiment for improving our schools — and a lot of cynicism in the faculty room. We knew what would happen. The flurry of public interest would soon be displaced by the next day's headline, and we teachers would be left with the nasty residue — the slush and slime of still more negative messages about how we do our jobs. The reports were so neat and precise, so self-confident in their delivery. And now here we sit in what has been portrayed as a very sloppy profession, never sure from one moment to the next that we are doing more good than harm. We are ill-served by cheap shots from the corporate and political remittance men and their consulting mercenaries whose words are akin to a nasty swarm of blood-sucking mosquitoes. Their bites may not kill, but they sure don't help us do our job.

I wish that the members of those commissions and task forces could realize how frustrating it is for us teachers to be pursued like horse thieves. There are so many witnesses for the prosecution on how we measure up in the classroom: the bus driver, the newspaper reporter, the mayor, the colleague across the hall. And now the professors and politicians are at it again. Teachers, it seems, are never acquitted. The best we can hope for is a hung jury.

Part of the problem is that we have no special skills, no secret rites all our own. Just about anybody can teach a lesson or two — perhaps even cope for a week or a month or a year. A few might even do it well. But the real test is to stick with teaching 10 years or more and *still* do it well, maybe even get better at it. Teaching, done well, can drive you crazy. I have taught for 18 years, 16 in the public schools, and I don't think I had one single comfortable day in the classroom. There is always that tension that you'll miss something important, fail to respond correctly to a student's unspoken need. Thirty years after the fact, my sister is still pained and even intimidated by an English teacher's red-penciled comment on her theme. I worry about how my students will remember me in 30 years. We don't teach a child for just one year; our message lingers for a lifetime. God knows, the temptation is always there to react badly to innumerable provocations: wacky kids, fetid curriculum guides, maggot-brained bureaucrats, sanctimonious reports on excellence.

I like to write about my crystal mo-

*E*ven for the best of practitioners and observers, the teachable moment is fleeting; if you don't have a good eye, you are likely to miss it.

ments in teaching. The savoring of these times is, I think, what keeps me going. But the call in the current wave of education reports for greater efficiency in the classroom helped me realize that my exuberant vignettes are misleading. Maybe some folks get the impression that I spent 16 years passing efficiently from one crystal moment to another.

Forget efficiency. Not enough attention is paid to the lag time in schools, the interminable length of some of those days. Thomas Boswell writes that a typical baseball game "is primarily dead time begging to be condensed. Any game that has more than a dozen key moments is one whale of a game." He might have been describing teaching — except that we have even more dead time. Any school *year* that has more than a dozen key moments is one whale of a year. Like baseball, teaching needs to develop a system for rewarding what Boswell describes as "a phlegmatic stability — a capacity to endure long aggravation and ignore many losses and embarrassments." Have any of the good consultants come up with a checklist to assess a teacher's response to embarrassment and aggravation?

There is, of course, an important difference between teaching and baseball: we teachers usually don't know when we've scored a run. Often we realize only months or years later that something we did might have been important, might have made a difference. Too often, we never know.

This fact was brought home to me a few years ago, when I was asked to write an article on discipline. I was singularly unenthusiastic. I don't know anything about discipline and don't care anything about discipline, I told myself. Only my disgust with all the wretched writing on the subject — plus my overweening desire to see my name in print — led me to agree to do the article. And then a fantastic thing began to happen: as I read other people's tomes on discipline, as I began to observe my own classroom routines and recall incidents from past years, fairly clear patterns began to emerge. Not only did I find that I have pretty strong convictions about discipline, but I decided that I had reacted rather well to some difficult circumstances in my own classrooms.

Thus my work as a writer helped me discover my craft as a teacher. But most teachers don't have this luxury. Ordinarily, teachers have neither the time nor the inclination to pause and reflect on what they do day after day, year after year. Maybe they're too tired from dodging missiles launched by the outside hordes. Certainly the system seems to be set up to keep teachers isolated, lonely, and defensive.

My own school district, for example, no longer lets anybody go out of town for professional purposes — not even if they pay their own expenses. No conventions, no seminars, no workshops, no chance to meet other professionals. I can't figure out if the people in charge keep us isolated more because they are scared we will *say* something or scared we will *hear* something. This is not to say that my district is not at the forefront of the excellence movement. Officials bought multiple copies of the report of the National Commission on Excellence in Education and offered them free to any teacher who would write a summary for the board of education. The pity is that we would have learned more about excellence had we been allowed to visit other classrooms right in our own buildings. But no one in charge believes that teachers can learn excellence from other teachers, especially not their own colleagues. Excellence is something that travels 'round the country first-class, on a 747. And if you can't afford first-class excellence, it will eventually be packaged and available by mail. But always, always, words about excellence in your classroom come from somewhere else.

ENOUGH OF THE phenomenology of excellence. Let's look at specifics. Our august advisors offer us fearful choices: four years of English or ignominy, more science and math or the collapse of the American dream. What the fellows spouting this doom fail to acknowledge is that it matters little if Johnny takes two years of English or six, if his teacher cannot do the job right. If ever an impossible task exists in this land, it is that of the high school English teacher.

To avoid being forced back into a high school English classroom, I fought local administrators, the union, and state certification officials. After 16 years of teaching and 48 graduate credits beyond my M.A. in English, I filled my summer with the dreaded course requirements for primary teachers rather than face "Horace's compromise." It is one thing to dream the impossible dream; it is quite another to be overrun by students and curriculum mandates. Until such time as union leaders or district administrators are willing to recognize and admit that merely mortal English teachers, given responsibility for 100-plus students, can do little more than herd the flock, I will find something else to do.

A lot of pompous words are circulating these days about something called scientific literacy, and something else is snowballing along under the name of computer literacy. Writers of the current wave of reports insist that requiring another year of science, another year of math, and a few months of computerese will somehow keep us in the forefront of the technological revolution, insuring a rising GNP, and so on. But does another year of the same old stuff really make sense? Most often, more of the same merely produces more of the same. The prestigious panels seem intent on fostering endurance, not excellence. They count minutes-on-task but ignore crucial questions of content.

Not to mention connections. If those panel members had bothered to talk to students, they would have uncovered a recurring complaint: nothing makes sense. Students don't see how given courses connect, either to their own lives or to other courses. I'm not talking about "relevance" — about teaching biographies of rock stars or cash-register math. I'm talking about showing students that learning can enrich their lives.

A rather rigid sequence of courses makes sense for a student who's headed for Harvard. Surely, however, such phenomena as the complex topics researched by winners of the national science competition and swelling enrollments in Advanced Placement classes attest to the availability of traditional academic challenges for those who are ready to accept them.

But what about the others? Do they really need to sit in more math classes, grinding out more solutions to problems on mortgage interest rates for homes they can no longer afford? Does algebra really teach these students to think? Does the inclined plane hold the secrets of the modern industrial state? I suspect that the number of people whose lives might be enriched by knowing about vectors or studying French is extremely small — smaller by far than the number whose lives might be enriched by listening to Vivaldi. Unfortunately, I did not notice any reports extolling the virtues of Vivaldi in our

High school should be a time of exploration, of trying on different hats — not a time of cramming oneself into a corporate mold.

schools. Art, music, and physical education (as contrasted with brute competition) have traditionally been given short shrift by our educational planners. Maybe this is because what students get out of an art class is less readily available to the scorekeepers. It's hard to know at a glance if national art appreciation is up or down by 1.43% in any given year.

I know that science is important. So are music and art and good books and skilled carpentry. Then what is this nonsense about getting rid of high school electives? Since when do U.S. students forfeit individual freedom when they enter the hallowed halls of high school?

I think of my own high school days, when my counselor kept reminding me that home economics was a requirement for graduation and I kept on signing up for music theory — even after they refused to give me any more "credit" for the course. Just before my senior year, my mother begged me to give in. "All they do in home ec is make white sauce," I complained. She pointed out that I didn't know how to make white sauce, but I took music theory for the fourth time anyway. I was corresponding with professors from across the U.S. on the theoretical necessity for the triple flat, and I could not be bothered with white sauce.

This story has two points. First, despite official requirements, I graduated on schedule. I doubt that most experts on education would have deemed my high school an excellent one, but the people in charge of my school — to their everlasting credit — knew when to look the other way. More important, they allowed me to pursue an interest that had no resale value. Even some of the professors of musicology with whom I was corresponding indicated that they thought it outrageous that a high school curriculum should deal with such esoterica. I didn't bother to explain that my teacher hadn't included triple sharps and triple flats in his lesson plans. In fact, he did not know that they existed. But he introduced me to music theory and honored my desire to travel narrow paths. When he couldn't answer my question about the triple flat, he suggested that I write the letters.

And that is where the important learning took place. I learned that it's okay for a person in charge to admit to not knowing everything; I learned that letters put the wisdom of the world in your mailbox; I learned that experts sometimes disagree. I also learned that the most satisfying learning comes when you do it simply because you want to. The course content doesn't matter. With teacher savvy, student cooperation, and a little luck, such excellence can occur in history class, in biology, in shop — anywhere.

High school should be a time of exploration, of trying on different hats — not a time of cramming oneself into a corporate mold. If Harvard wants its freshmen to have two or three or six years of a foreign language, that's fine. But it's not enough reason to make everyone else take two or three or six years of a foreign language too. The attitudes that students carry away with their diplomas are much more important than their SAT scores. If students can learn how to learn during their first 12 years of school, then anything is possible for them later on, and we teachers can feel that we have done our job. But if all that we give our students is more of the same — discrete facts disconnected from meaning or purpose — then we are in trouble.

We must be ever wary of wasting some youngster's life just because of a dubious notion that a rigorous, regimented curriculum will help restore to the U.S. a better balance of trade. As Nobel-Prize-winning economist Paul Samuelson once noted, man does not live by the GNP alone. At best, the recommendations of the commissions and task forces on school reform are hallucinatory; at worst, they are soul-destroying. Let us teachers not succumb to the temptation of asking what we can do for General Motors; let us continue to ask only what we can do for the children.

Morality and Values in Education

Spirited and fair dialogue concerning human affairs involves the give and take of incisive analytical deliberation. This is the best of traditional Western opinion in the manner in which moral dilemmas are resolved among just persons. Moral development was always one of the goals of education. From antiquity to the early twentieth century, the schools were never fully excused from the role. Moral standards are produced in all civilizations. It is usually one of the assigned responsibilities of schools to instruct students in certain standards of conduct which reflect certain core values cherished by those who sponsor schools. There are those today who would like to see North American schools abandon efforts at moral development, and there are others who strongly insist on such efforts. This unit will explore some of the different issues raised by efforts to teach moral decision making skills in schools.

Do the schools have a responsibility to inform students of shared civic values? There is renewed tension regarding this matter now. Democratic societies do not generally wish to see only indoctrination of common cherished values. Democratic countries have to help their citizens learn how to make moral decisions. Any attempt to teach ethical principles of human conduct must confront questions concerning how to do this in a just manner and what substantive moral values to include. Where a plurality of divergent moral systems coexist in a society, the schools must reflect a due regard for fair and compassionate approaches to the topic of moral education. Moral education of the young requires clarification as to what precisely constitutes morality. When advocates of competing moral standards demand that their views be represented in schools, the schools either have to find just, fair ways of doing this or reject the role of moral educator.

There has always been widespread interest in the subject of moral education. Since Socrates (and before), schools have been encouraged to teach certain civic values in order to develop more socially responsible citizens. However, civic education has taken many forms in the United States over the past ten decades. Several religious groups and secular organizations have called for the effective development of courses and curricula which

will teach elementary school, secondary school, and university students the basic skills needed to reason through ethical issues. They are still divided, however, over the type of curricula that would achieve such an educational ideal. There is also a stand-off between religious groups who would like to see their cherished core values taught in the schools and others who believe in the strictest possible separation of church and state in the public schools. But doesn't moral education involve much more than the issue of religion in tax-supported schools? Before the question of whether moral education belongs in public schools is resolved, a clearer understanding of what moral education means must be developed.

Although there is no overall agreement regarding how moral education should be approached in North America, there is an emerging consensus in the United States and Canada as to those civic values which the vast majority of citizens share, such as the belief in equality before the law, respect for life, the right to safety, the right to one's own convictions, and the value of participation as equals in society. Schools in all nations have always been called upon to encourage responsible student conduct and to teach those shared standards of civil duty which prevail in particular societies. American and Canadian schools have been called upon to do this since the seventeenth century. The issue cannot be avoided by schools, but it can be simplified by defining exactly what ethical principles all students should learn. Key issues include how to teach methods of ethical decision making in such a manner as to encourage virtuous and just behavior, and how it can be accomplished in pluralistic nations such as the United States and Canada in a manner in which students will retain their freedom to choose substantive standards of value. On the one hand, educators should not teach students merely superficial methods of choosing in the absense of any instruction as to what specific standards of virtue and moral behavior are available to them. On the other hand, educators must avoid indoctrinating students with their own values.

The essays in this unit represent a synthesis of some of the current rhetoric on how North American schools should perceive the very complex matter of moral education. The unit opens with a historical assessment of topic from a rather traditional perspective which is vigorously contested by several respondents. The balance of the unit develops around the major controversies surrounding the ethical and moral development of citizens in a free society.

This unit can be used in courses dealing with the historical or the philosophical foundations of education. The articles also relate well to issues confronting teachers, public pressures on schools, the rights of minorities, and the social responsibilities of schools.

Looking Ahead: Challenge Questions

Should local communities have total autonomy over the content of moral instruction in local schools as they did in the nineteenth century? What are the best lines of argument either for or against this?

What is moral education? What is your understanding of what it means? Why do so many people today wish to see some form of moral education in the schools?

What are some of the problems with the manner in which ethics and ethical decision-making skills have been taught in the schools? For what reasons is there continuing controversy regarding this topic?

What is civic education? How do states encourage civic education in the schools?

Should schools be involved in teaching people to reason about moral questions? Why or why not? If not, who should do it? Why?

What ethical principles should prevail in teaching about morals and ethics in schools?

What is the difference between indoctrination and instruction?

Should ethics be taught in the absense of studying different conceptions of virtue?

Is there a national consensus concerning what specific form of moral education should be taught in schools? Is such a consensus likely if it does not now exist?

What attitudes and skills are most appropriate for learning responsible approaches to moral decision making?

The Great Tradition in Education: Transmitting Moral Values

Edward A. Wynne

Edward A. Wynne is professor, College of Education, University of Illinois at Chicago Circle, Box 4348, Chicago, IL 60680.

America's public schools should restore proper emphasis on what has been the dominant concern of education throughout the ages.

Within the recent past, American education substantially disassociated itself from what may be called the great tradition in education: the deliberate transmission of moral values to students. Despite this separation, many education reforms are being considered or are under way to increase the academic demands made on students. These reforms can be generally helpful; however, unless they are sensitive to the implications of our break with the great tradition, their effect on student conduct and morality may be transitory or even harmful. To understand the significance of the great tradition, we must engage in a form of consciousness-raising by enriching our understanding of the past and by understanding the misperceptions that pervade contemporary education.

The transmission of moral values has been the dominant educational concern of most cultures throughout history. Most educational systems have been simultaneously concerned with the transmission of cognitive knowledge—skills, information, and techniques of intellectual analysis—but these admittedly important educational aims, have rarely been given priority over moral education. The current policies in American education that give secondary priority to transmitting morality represent a sharp fracture with the great tradition.

Our break with the past is especially significant in view of the increase since the early 1950s of youth disorder: suicide, homicide, and out-of-wedlock births. Patterns revealed by statistics coincide with popular conceptions about these behaviors. For instance, in 16 of the past 17 Gallup Polls on education, pupil discipline has been the most frequent criticism leveled against public schools. One may wonder if better discipline codes and more homework are adequate remedies for our current school problems, or whether these dysfunctions are more profound and should be treated with more sensitive and complex remedies. Although literacy and student diligence are unquestionably worthy of pursuit, they are only a part of the process of communicating serious morality. If we want to improve the ways we are now transmitting morality, it makes sense to recall the way morality was transmitted before youth disorder became such a distressing issue.

Some Definitions

The term "moral values" is ambiguous and requires some definition. It signifies the specific values that particular cultures generally hold in regard. Such values vary among cultures; during World War II, a Japanese who loved his homeland was likely to be hostile to Americans, and vice versa. Value conflicts along national or ethnic lines are common, although most cultures treat the characteristic we call "patriotism" as a moral value, and treat "treason" with opprobrium. Comparable patterns of value govern interpersonal relations in cultures: beliefs about proper family conduct or the nature of reciprocal relationships. Such beliefs are laden with strong moral components.

In sum, common "moral values" are the vital common beliefs that shape

"[The great tradition] assumed that most moral challenges arose in mundane situations, and that people were often prone to act improperly."

human relations in each culture. Often these values—as in the Ten Commandments—have what is popularly called a religious base. Whether their base is religious, traditional, or secular, however, such values are expected to be widely affirmed under most circumstances.

The term "educational systems" also is somewhat obscure. Contemporary Americans naturally think in terms of formal public or private schools and colleges. But for most history, and all prehistory, formal agencies were a minute part of children's and adolescents' education. In traditional cultures, education was largely transmitted by various formal and informal nonschool agencies: nuclear and extended families; religious institutions; "societies" for the young organized and monitored by adults. In addition, the complex incidental life of preindustrial rural and urban societies, and the demands of work in and out of the family socialized young persons into adult life. Many of these agencies still play important educational roles in contemporary America; nonetheless, in the modern period, the gradual replacement of such agencies by schools has been a strong trend.

Transmitting Moral Values

Whether the dominant educational system has been formal or informal, the transmission of moral values has persistently played a central role. This role has been necessary and universal for two reasons.

1. Human beings are uniquely adaptable animals and live in nearly all climates and in diverse cultural systems. But, as the anthropologist Yehudi Cohen (1964) put it, "No society allows for the random and promiscuous expression of emotions to just anyone. Rather, one may communicate those feelings, either verbally, physically, or materially, to certain people." Because our means of communicating emotions are socially specific, slow maturing young persons must be socialized gradually to the right—or moral—practices appropriate to their special environment.

2. Without effective moral formation, the human propensity for selfishness—or simply the advancement of self-interest—can destructively affect adult institutions. Thus, moral formation is necessary to cultivate our inherent, but moderate, propensity for disinterested sacrifice. The institutions of any persisting society must be organized to ensure that people's "unselfish genes" are adequately reinforced.

The general modes of moral formation have remained relatively stable throughout all cultures. To be sure, social class and sex-related differences have influenced the quantity and nature of moral formation delivered to the young; for instance, in many environments, limited resources have restricted the extent and intensity of the education provided to lower-class youths. Furthermore, the substance of the moral training transmitted to older youths has varied among cultures: according to Plato, Socrates was put to death because the Athenians disapproved of the moral training he was offering to Athenian young men. But such variations do not lessen the strength of the general model. Despite his affection for Socrates, Plato, in *The Republic* (circa 390 B.C.) emphasized the importance of constraining the learning influences on children and youths, to ensure appropriate moral outcomes.

Although secular and church-related educators have disputed the *means* of moral formation since the nineteenth century both, until comparatively recently, have agreed on their programs' behavioral *ends*. Children should be moral: honest, diligent, obedient, and patriotic. Thus, after the American Revolution, deists and secularists such as Thomas Jefferson and John Adams felt democracy would fail unless citizens acquired an unusually high degree of self-discipline and public spiritedness. They termed this medley of values "republican virtue." After

the revolution, many of the original 13 states framed constitutions with provisions such as "... no government can be preserved to any people, but by a firm adherence to justice, moderation, temperance, frugality, and virtue."[1] The founders believed that popular education would be a means of developing such precious traits. As the social historians David J. and Sheila Rothman have written, "The business of schools [in our early history] was not reading and writing but citizenship, not education but social control." The term "social control" may have a pejorative sound to our modern ears, but it simply and correctly means that schools were concerned with affecting conduct, rather than transmitting information or affecting states of mind.

Characteristics of the Great Tradition

Although issues in moral formation posed some conflicts in traditional societies, there were great areas of congruence around the great tradition of transmitting moral values. Documents generated in historical societies as well as ethnographic studies of many ancient and primitive cultures reveal through anecdote and insight the principles that characterize the tradition. Since the principles are too often ignored in contemporary education, we should consider them in some detail.

● *The tradition was concerned with good habits of conduct as contrasted with moral concepts or moral rationales.* Thus, the tradition emphasized visible courtesy and deference. In the moral mandate, "Honor thy father and mother," the act of *honoring* can be seen. It is easier to observe people *honoring* their parents than *loving* them. Loving, a state of mind, usually must be inferred.

● *The tradition focused on day-to-day moral issues: telling the truth in the face of evident temptation, being polite, or obeying legitimate authority.* It assumed that most moral challenges arose in mundane situations, and that people were often prone to act improperly.

● *The great tradition assumed that no single agency in society had the sole responsibility for moral education.* The varieties of moral problems confronting adults and youths were innumerable. Thus, youths had to be taught to practice morality in many

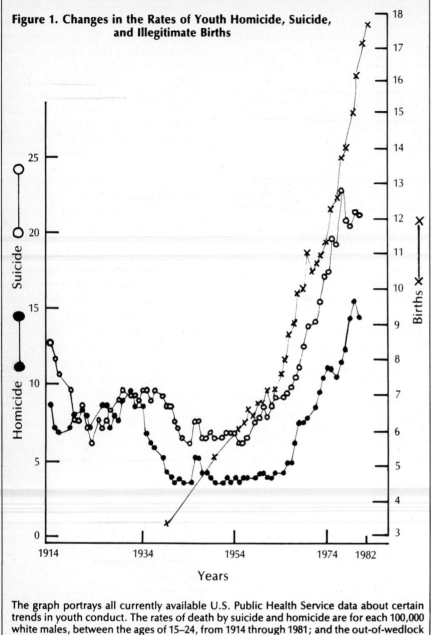

Figure 1. Changes in the Rates of Youth Homicide, Suicide, and Illegitimate Births

The graph portrays all currently available U.S. Public Health Service data about certain trends in youth conduct. The rates of death by suicide and homicide are for each 100,000 white males, between the ages of 15–24, from 1914 through 1981; and the out-of-wedlock births are for each 1,000 unmarried white females, between the ages of 15–19, from 1940 through 1982. There are no comparable statistics from earlier periods. However, the remarkable recent increases, plus the general tendency for each such disorder to be associated with the spread of urbanization, support the contention that the current rates are at the highest point in American history since 1607.

were to be aggressively punished, as punishment not only suppressed bad examples, but also corrected particular wrongdoers. The tradition also developed concepts such as "scandal," a public, immoral act that also lowered the prestige of a person or institution. Conversely, since secret immoral acts were less likely to confuse or misdirect innocent persons, they received less disapproval.

• *The tradition was not hostile to the intellectual analysis of moral problems.* Adults recognized that life occasionally generates moral dilemmas. In the Jewish religious tradition, learned men were expected to analyze and debate Talmudic moral issues. Other cultures have displayed similar patterns. But such analyses typically relied on a strong foundation of habit-oriented, mundane moral instruction and practice. Instruction in exegetical analysis commenced only after the selected neophyte had undergone long periods of testing, memorized large portions of semididactic classics, and displayed appropriate deference to exegetical experts.

• *The great tradition assumed that the most important and complex moral values were transmitted through persistent and intimate person-to-person interaction.* In many cases, adult mentors were assigned to develop close and significant relationships with particular youths. The youths might serve as apprentices to such persons, or the mentors might accept significant responsibilities for a young relative. In either case, constructive moral shaping required a comparatively high level of engagement.

• *The tradition usually treated "learners," who were sometimes students, as members of vital groups, such as teams, classes, or clubs.* These groups were important reference points for communicating values, among them group loyalty, and the diverse incidents of group life provided occasions for object lessons. The emphasis on collective life contrasts sharply with the individualism that pervades contemporary American education, and which is often mistaken for "humanism."

• *The tradition had a pessimistic opinion about the perfectibility of human beings, and about the feasibility or value of breaking with previous socialization patterns.* The tradition did not contend that whatever "is" is

environments. One agency, for example, the nuclear family or the neighborhood, might be deficient, so considerable redundancy was needed. In other words, there could be no neutrality about educating the young in morality: youth-serving agencies were either actively promoral or indifferent.

• *The tradition assumed that moral conduct, especially of the young, needed persistent and pervasive reinforcement.* To advance this end, literature, proverbs, legends, drama, ritual, and

folk tales were used for cautionary purposes. Systems of symbolic and real rewards were developed and sustained: schools used ribbons, awards, and other signs of moral merit; noneducational agencies used praise and criticism as well as many symbolic forms of recognition.

• *The tradition saw an important relationship between the advancement of moral learning and the suppression of wrong conduct.* Wrong acts, especially in the presence of the young,

"It is ridiculous to believe children are capable of objectively assessing most of the beliefs and values they must absorb as effective adults."

necessarily right, but it did assume that the persistence of certain conduct over hundreds of years suggested that careful deliberation should precede any modification or rejection.

As schooling spread, the tendency was to present the formal curriculum in a manner consistent with the tradition, and thus to focus on the transmission of correct habits and values. We should not assume that the interjection of moral concern was necessarily cumbersome. The famous *McGuffey's Reader* series featured stories and essays by substantial writers, such as Walter Scott and Charles Dickens. The literary quality of such writings was appropriate to the age of the student. Significantly, both the materials and their authors supported the development of certain desired traits.

Character Education

The most recent efflorescence of the great tradition in America can be found in the "character education" movement in our public schools between 1880 and about 1930. That movement attempted to make public schools more efficient transmitters of appropriate moral values.

The efforts to foster character education assumed schools had to operate from a purely secular basis, which posed special challenges for moral formation. Whereas some earlier education reformers had semisecular sympathies, in previous eras their impact had been tempered by the proreligious forces concurrently affecting schools. Before 1900, for example, probably 15–25 percent of American elementary and secondary school pupils attended either private or public schools that were explicitly religious; another 25–50 percent attended public schools that were tacitly religious. For example, they used readings from the *King James Bible*.

The character education movement articulated numerous traditional moral aims: promptness, truthfulness, courtesy, and obedience. The move-

ment strove to develop elementary and secondary school programs to foster such conduct. It emphasized techniques such as appropriately structured materials in history and literature; school clubs and other extracurricular activities; rigorous pupil discipline codes; and daily flag salutes and frequent assemblies. Many relatively elaborate character education plans were designed and disseminated to schools and school districts. Often the plans were adopted through the mandate of state legislatures or state boards of education. Some modern authorities, such as James Q. Wilson (1973), have perceived a strong relationship between the character education movement and the relatively high levels of youth order in America during the nineteenth century.

An Unfavorable Evaluation

From the first, the supporters of character education emphasized rational organization and research. Despite such attempts, much of the research was superficial. Nonetheless, the research persisted because of the importance attributed to character, and gradually its quality improved. During the mid-1920s, researchers led by Hugh Hartschorne and Mark A. May concluded that the relationship between pupil good conduct and the application of formal character education approach was slight. Good conduct appeared to be relatively situation-specific: a person might routinely act correctly in one situation and incorrectly in another slightly different one. A person could cheat on exams, for example, but not steal money from the class fund. This situational specificity meant that good character was not a unified trait that could be cultivated by any single approach.

Despite this research, character education was never formally abandoned. Few educators or researchers have ever said publicly that schools should *not* be concerned with the morality or character of their pupils. Indeed, recent research and statistical reanalysis of earlier data has contended that Hartschorne and May's findings were excessively negative. Still, their research was a turning point in the relationship between American public education and the great tradition of moral values. Before the research many schools were fully concerned

with carrying forward that tradition, and the intellectual forces affecting schools were in sympathy with such efforts. Even after the 1930s, many schools still reflexively maintained their former commitment to moral formation; the prevailing intellectual climate among researchers and academics, however, was indifferent or hostile to such efforts. Gradually, a disjunction arose between what some educators and many parents thought was appropriate (and what some of them applied), and what was favored by a smaller, more formally trained group of experts.

Ironically, the research findings of Hartschorne and May did not refute conflict with the major intellectual themes of the great tradition. The tradition emphasized that moral formation was complex. To be effective, it had to be incremental, diverse, pervasive, persistent, and rigorous. Essentially, it relied on probalistic principles: the more frequent and more diverse techniques applied, the more likely that more youths would be properly formed; but even if all techniques were applied, some youths would be "missed." Given such principles, it logically follows that the measured long-term effect of any limited program of "moral instruction" would be minute.

The Hartschorne and May findings demonstrated that American expectations for character education were unrealistic, a proposition not inconsistent with expectations we seem to have for *any* education technique. This does not mean that education's effects are inconsequential, but that Americans often approach education from a semi-utopian perspective. We have trouble realizing that many things happen slowly, and that not all problems are solvable.

New Approaches to Moral Instruction

During the 1930s, 1940s, and 1950s, there was little intellectual or research concern with moral formation in America. Schools continued to be engaged in moral instruction, both deliberately or incidentally, but the in-school process relied on momentum stimulated by earlier perspectives. In other words, moral instruction went on, but without substantial intellectual underpinning.

4. MORALITY AND VALUES IN EDUCATION

Since the 1960s, a number of different—perhaps more scientific—approaches to moral instruction have evolved. Many of these approaches have been described by the term "moral education." Among these have been values clarification, identified with Louis L. Raths and Sidney B. Simon, and the moral development approach identified with Lawrence Kohlberg and his colleagues. Despite the variations among contemporary approaches, almost all the more recent techniques have had certain common elements. Their developers were not school teachers, ministers, or education administrators, but college professors who sought to emphasize the scientific base for their efforts. But, most important, the approaches disavowed the great tradition's persistent concern with affecting conduct. The moral dilemmas used in some exercises were highly abstract and probably would never arise in real life. Their aim was to cause students to feel or reason in particular ways rather than to practice right conduct immediately.

The developers of the new systems were conscious of Hartschorne and May's research. They recognized the difficulty of shaping conduct and presumably felt that shaping patterns of reasoning was more feasible. Furthermore, many of the moral education approaches were designed as curriculum materials that could be taught through lectures and class discussion. Such designs facilitated their adoption by teachers and schools. Had the approaches aimed to pervasively affect pupil day-to-day conduct, they would have been more difficult to disseminate. Finally, both the researchers and the proponents of the new approaches felt it was morally unjustifiable to apply the vital pressures needed to actually shape pupils' conduct, feeling such pressures would constitute "indoctrination." On the other hand, methods of moral reasoning apparently might be taught as routine school subjects with the tacit consent of the pupils involved.

The anti-indoctrination stance central to the new approaches invites amplification. Obviously, the great tradition regarded the issue of indoctrination as a specious question. Proponents of the great tradition say, "Of course indoctrination happens. It is ridiculous to believe children are capable of objectively assessing most of the beliefs and values they must absorb to be effective adults. They must learn a certain body of 'doctrine' to function on a day-to-day basis in society. There is good and bad doctrine, and thus things must be weighed and assessed. But such assessment is largely the responsibility of parents and other appropriate adults."

It is hard to articulate fairly the position of the anti-indoctrinators. Although they are against indoctrination, they provide no clear answer as to how children are given many real choices in a relatively immutable world necessarily maintained by adults. The anti-indoctrinators also do not say what adults are to do when children's value choices and resulting potential conduct are clearly harmful to them or others. After all, punishments for bad value choices are, in effect, forms of indoctrination. And the idea of presenting pupils with any particular approach to moral education in a school is inherently indoctrinative: the pupils are not allowed to refuse to come to school, or to hear seriously the pros and cons articulated by sympathetic spokespersons (or critics) for moral education or to freely choose among various approaches to them. Providing such choices is antithetical to the operation of any school.

To consider another perspective, the secular nature of the typical public school obviously indoctrinates pupils against practicing religion in that environment, although most religions contend that some religious practices of a public nature are inextricably related to day-to-day life. This "reality" of separating religion and public education is understandable. However, it is disingenuous to call this policy nonindoctrinative. Thus, it is specious to talk about student choices. The point is that, *on the whole, school is and should and must be inherently indoctrinative.* The only significant questions are: Will the indoctrination be overt or covert, and what will be indoctrinated?

The great tradition has never died. Many administrators and teachers in public and private schools have continued practices consistent with its principles. Given the increased support from academics and intellectuals, and the concrete recommendations presented in Walberg's and my article which follows, these principles deserve widespread professional support.

[1]The Virginia Constitution.

References

Cohen, Y. *The Transition from Childhood to Adolescence.* Chicago: Aldine, 1964.

Hartschorne, H., and May, M. A. *Studies in Deceit, Studies in Service and Self-Control,* and *Studies in the Organization of Character.* New York: Macmillan, 1928, 1929, 1930.

Klapp, O. *The Collective Search for Identity.* New York: Holt, Rinehart, and Winston, 1969.

Meyers, E. *Education in the Perspective of History.* New York: Harper & Row, 1960.

Rothman, D. J., and Rothman, S. M. *Sources of American Social Tradition.* New York: Basic, 1975.

Wilkinson, R. *Governing Elites.* New York: Oxford University Press, 1969.

Wilson, J. Q. "Crime and American Culture." *The Public Interest* 70 (Winter 1973): 22–48.

Wynne, E. A. *Looking at Schools.* Lexington, MA.: Heath/Lexington, 1980.

Yulish, S. M. *The Search for a Civic Religion.* Lanham, Md.: University Press of America, 1980.

Note: partial support for the research underlying this article was received from NIE Grant No. G-83–0012.

Moral Education in the United States

FRANKLIN PARKER

Franklin Parker was Benedum Professor of Education, West Virginia University, Morgantown. In the fall of 1986, he became Distinguished Professor, Center for Excellence in Education, Northern Arizona University, Flagstaff.

AMERICA began as a country in search of religious freedom. Religion for salvation and good behavior, begun in colonial schools, lasted in modified form well into the nineteenth century. Fear of a single dominant religion led to adoption of the First Amendment to the United States Constitution, separating church and state. Yet Horace Mann and other public school founders favored and promoted the general Protestant moral ethic that pervaded American schools.

In a college curriculum dominated by Latin classics, theology, and some mathematics, the moral philosophy course taught by the president to seniors was the unifying capstone, stressing character in those soon-to-be leaders. This moral philosophy course, which had originated in the medieval university's seven liberal arts, was the incubator of subjects soon to spring from it and replace it: the social, natural, and physical sciences.

Many changes led to the lessening of this strong moralistic atmosphere, particularly by the 1890s, a decade historians say marked the nation's shift from rural-agrarian simplicity to urban-industrial complexity. Sectarian religious battles, fueled in part by new immigrants' religious beliefs or lack of them, tended to reduce religion-based ethics in lower and higher schools.

Science, with its reliance on testable facts, began to raise questions about and challenge ethical beliefs and value judgments. The moral philosophy course faded and higher education's unit was fragmented under the onslaught of new subjects, electives, subject-department dominance, and undergraduate and graduate specialization.

What declined was idealism, introspection, intuition, unity, and undergraduate ethical and moral concerns. Scholars in new subjects, wanting to imitate science, embraced its methods and tried to make new discoveries and so enhance their reputations. With the coming of Freudian and behavioristic psychology, psychological adjustment tended to replace ethical choice.

Curriculum unity and the ethical and moral atmosphere it fostered also declined in the lower schools, swamped at the turn of the century by numbers, duties, and courses. The restructuring of schooling into elementary, junior high, and senior high schools may have helped house students better and hold mass enrollments, but by isolating younger from older students, it lessened older children's ethical influence.

Besides restructuring, a new philosophy of adjustment entered public schools—pragmatic, progressive, experimental, child-centered, activity-oriented. Its spokesman was John Dewey; observers did not at first grasp that his concern was to integrate and reconcile what educationally had always been kept separate: interest *and* effort, school *and* society, individualism *and* the group, the child *and* the curriculum.

Progressive methods added to the new tasks imposed on public schools, which were already Americanizing immigrants' children, socializing the young, caring for their health, and equipping them for work. The progressive movement also changed course content. Civics and American history gave way to broader-based social studies, and some criticized progressive education for fostering broader social ethics at the expense of individual ethics. Inevitably weakened was the ethical content of the old courses and the moral atmosphere of the old schools.

The Great Depression led higher educators to try to recapture the ethical unity of the old moral philosophy course by reviving the liberal arts. World War II also shocked educators into a renewed search for curriculum unity and moral uplift. Then Sputnik, in 1957, shocked Americans into vast curriculum revision for bright students; the academic scene was tilted toward the gifted, isolating the average and below-average student.

Cracks had already appeared in that student generation, and writers and artists, such as J. D. Salinger and James Dean, had already tried to mirror the somber mood of troubled youth. This modern anxiety came to a boil in the social turmoil of the 1960s and early 1970s—civil rights, freedom riders, free speech, student protests, Vietnam, Watergate, women's liberation, the energy crunch—all aggravated by the recession and job losses of the early 1980s. These dislocations, plus rising crime and drug use, showed a discontent, anger, and drive for

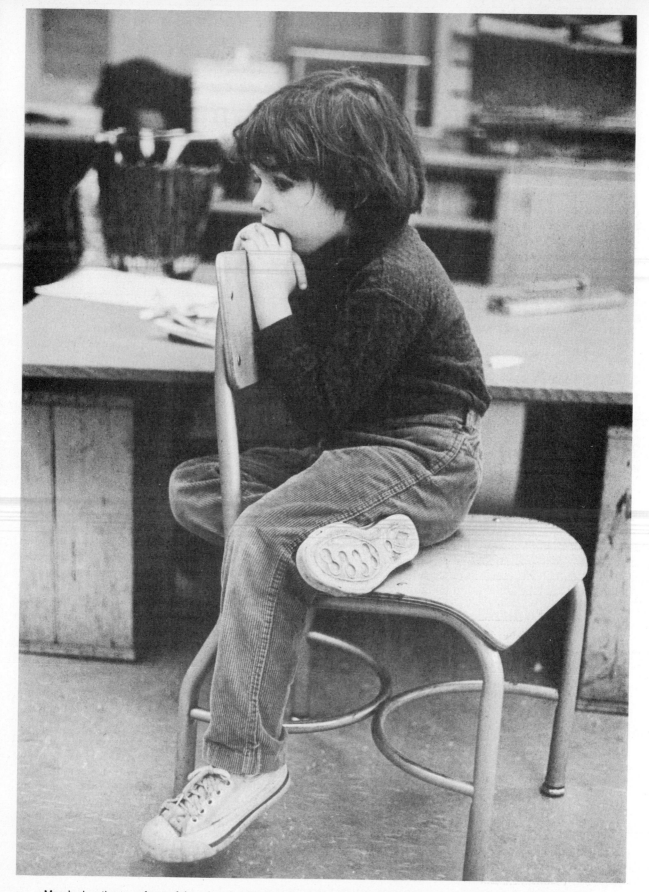

Moral education as a facet of the educational program in American schools, has, over the years, been eroded by First Amendment decisions, social dislocation, and the redefinition of traditional family values. Today the school system is at a crossroads and has an opportunity to play an increasing role in America's moral foundation. This child is faced with a system that may or may not allow him to develop a positive set of values.

self-destruction that are still incomprehensible. Violent acts are television events shown daily, and a 1983 study reported American drug use as the highest in any industrialized nation.

To rising crime and drug use add a 50 percent divorce rate. Add the pain, anger, guilt, and confusion of child custody fights and property division. Add the new crime of child snatching by divorced parents. Add the many one-parent homes, latchkey children, runaway children, etc. One is hard put to explain the profound and sudden shift in American mores and to account for the drive for self-destruction among so many young Americans, though some have tried: The pollster Daniel Yankelovich, for example, has argued that the trauma of national limitations in the era of the 1973 oil embargo, coming after the affluence of the 1960s and early 1970s, has put us in a new stage, seeking community, commitment, and connectedness, and has restored ethical and moral anchors.

Signs of New Life

An overview of the moral education revival in lower schools includes:

1. Released time (since 1913) sent public school children to nearby churches and synagogues for religious instruction or offered such instruction near or in public schools. In 1947, two million children were so taught. In 1948, the Supreme Court declared such instruction unconstitutional when given on school grounds during school time (in 1952 it approved such instruction *off* school grounds). Released time has since dwindled because of First Amendment challenges.

2. Prayer in public schools was also declared unconstitutional by the Supreme Court (in 1961); despite challenges, the ruling seems likely to stand.

3. Humanistic education (since the early 1960s), including affective learning, emphasized concern for others and valuing human relations, and stressed feeling, sympathy, altruism, helpfulness. Humanistic education has a growing literature but few formal programs.

4. With values clarification, the idea is to clarify dilemmas from a subjective point of view, choose from alternatives, and act on that choice; it is said to be popular in classrooms and successful in book sales. However, values clarification has also been called superficial, ineffective, and possibly dangerous because of its public disclosures, subjectivity, and moral relativism.

5. Moral development or moral reasoning has a large following, literature, measuring scales, curricular programs, and prestigious leaders, such as Jean Piaget and Lawrence Kohlberg.

The California legislature and state board of education a few years ago did recommend moral education for kindergarten through grade 12. Yet one surveyor of California public high schools found that nearly half of the high schools did not have a moral education syllabus, course, or program; 80 percent of high schools did not have a list of moral education materials available for their teachers; and over 80 percent of schools reported very little school district urging for moral education. The investigator pointed out correctly that moral education must first be taught to future teachers before it can be effective in schools and that, as yet, California teacher education institutions have shown little interest in it.

6. Private Christian academies spread rapidly in the last decade. They emphasize religion, morality, and basic skills. Many were begun to circumvent racial integration. Though many have small enrollments and do not survive, they reflect a strong national concern for moral education and are backed by the new evangelical Right and by President Reagan.

College Ethics Courses

But it is in higher education that ethics courses have really grown. A 1977-78 survey by the Hastings Center, in New York, shows that out of 2,270 higher education catalogs, 623 list 2,757 ethics courses. Fifty percent of these courses were applied ethics: bioethics, business ethics, secretarial ethics, legal ethics, medical ethics, etc. The surveyors estimate that up to 12,000 courses are now offered in United States undergraduate colleges; that most of them began in the last 10 years; and that most of them tend to be interdisciplinary, elective, and oriented to such specific issues as euthanasia, bribery, atomic power, and the reporting of misdeeds.

The survey identified these concerns: the qualifications of ethics teachers; what department should administer ethics courses; disputes over course goals, methods, and content, and student evaluation; and whether ethics should be a course on its own or part of other courses. Surveyors found ethics teachers feeling somewhat isolated from their colleagues and fearful that the ethics phenomenon is a fad rather than something of lasting interest.

Do Soviet schools teach moral values any better than we do? Their moral education ideas were pioneered by Anton S. Makarenko, who, from 1920, successfully salvaged war-orphaned delinquents by appealing to their group spirit, cooperativeness, and loyalties. Attitudes are shaped by exhortation, banners, posters, textbooks, teachers, and quotations from Lenin, Makarenko, and others. Children are exposed to exemplary models of revolutionary heroes, workers, peasants, soldiers—all showing courage, effort, and victory in adversity. Soviet youth groups are well organized, staffed, and financed. The Soviets use open indoctrination, a method most Americans abhor. While comparable statistics may not be available, observers say that Soviet crime, juvenile delinquency, alcoholism, divorce, and other evidence of immorality are not negligible.

Change and dislocation have been the pattern of our time. Consequently, blows have fallen on family, home, marriage, children, church, state, school, and nation. Yet each persists and is resilient. School especially needs to be a place set aside to transmit and improve the culture. If, as most Americans believe, moral education and ethics courses have healing power, if they help our better natures and highest hopes, then we ought to support and nurture them.

Ethics Without Virtue

Moral Education in America

CHRISTINA HOFF SOMMERS

Christina Hoff Sommers, assistant professor of philosophy at Clark University, is the editor of an anthology, Vice and Virtue in Everyday Life *(Harcourt Brace Jovanovich).*

What do students in our nation's schools do all day? Most of them are clearly not spending their time reading the classics, learning math, or studying the physical sciences. It is likely that, along with photography workshops, keeping journals, and perhaps learning about computers, students spend part of their day in moral education classes. But these classes are not, as one might expect, designed to acquaint students with the Western moral tradition. Professional theorists in schools of education have found that tradition wanting and have devised an alternative, one they have marketed in public schools with notable success.

A reform of moral education is not a task to be undertaken lightly. The sincerity and personal integrity of the theorist-reformers is not at issue, but their qualifications as moral educators is a legitimate subject of concern. The leaders of reform do not worry about credentials. They are convinced that traditional middle-class morality is at best useless and at worst pernicious, and they have confidence in the new morality that is to replace the old and in the novel techniques to be applied to this end. In 1970 Theodore Sizer, then dean of the Harvard School of Education, co-edited with his wife Nancy a book entitled *Moral Education.* The preface set the tone by condemning the morality of "the Christian gentleman," "the American prairie," the Mc-Guffey *Reader,* and the hypocrisy of teachers who tolerate a grading system that is "the terror of the young." According to the Sizers, all of the authors in the anthology agree that "the 'old morality' can and should be scrapped."

The movement to reform moral education has its seat in the most prestigious institutions of education. Its theories are seldom contested, and its practice is spreading. Students who have received the new moral instruction have been turning up in freshman college classes in increasing numbers. While giving college ethics courses during the past six years, I have become convinced that the need for a critical appraisal of the claims and assumptions of the movement is urgent. My experience is that the students who received the new teaching have been ill served by their mentors.

One gains some idea of the new moral educators from the terminology they use. Courses in ethics are called "values clarification" or "cognitive moral development"; teachers are "values processors," "values facilitators," or "reflective-active listeners"; lessons in moral reasoning are "sensitivity modules"; volunteer work in the community is an "action module"; and teachers "dialogue" with students to help them discover their own systems of values. In these dialogues the teacher avoids discussing "old bags of virtues," such as wisdom, courage, compassion, and "proper" behavior, because any attempt to instill these would be to indoctrinate the student. Some leaders of the new reform movement advise teachers that effective moral education cannot take place in the "authoritarian" atmosphere of the average American high school. The teacher ought to democratize the classroom, turning it into a "just community" where the student and teacher have an equal say. Furthermore, the student who takes a normative ethics course in college will likely encounter a professor who also has a principled aversion to the inculcation of moral precepts and who will confine classroom discussion to such issues of social concern as the Karen Ann Quinlan case, recombinant DNA research, or the moral responsibilities of corporations.

The result is a system of moral education that is silent about virtue.

The teaching of virtue is not viewed as a legitimate aim of a moral curriculum, but there is no dearth of alternative approaches. From the time the values education movement began in the late nineteen sixties, its theorists have produced an enormous number of articles, books, films, manuals, and doctoral dissertations; there are now journals, advanced degree programs, and entire institutes dedicated exclusively to moral pedagogy; and for the past several years, teachers, counselors, and education specialists have been attending conferences, seminars, workshops, and retreats to improve their skills in values-processing. At present, two opposing ideologies dominate moral education: the values clarification movement, whose best-known proponent is Sidney Simon of the University of Massachusetts School of Education; and the cognitive moral development movement, whose chief spokesman is Lawrence Kohlberg, a professor of psychology and education, and director of the Center for Moral Education at Harvard.

Values clarification, according to Sidney Simon, is "based on the premise that none of us has the 'right' set of values to pass on to other people's children." Its methods are meant to help students to get at "their own feelings, their own ideas, their own beliefs, so that the choices and decisions they make are conscious and deliberate, based on their own value system." The success of the values clarification movement has been phenomenal. In 1975 a study from the Hoover Institute referred to "hundreds perhaps thousands of school programs that employ the clarification methodology" and reported that ten states have officially adopted values clarification as a model for their moral education programs. Proponents of values clarification consider it inappropriate for a teacher to encourage students, however subtly or indirectly, to adopt the values of the teacher or the community. In their book, *Readings in Values Clarification*, Simon and his colleague Howard Kirschenbaum write:

We call this approach "moralizing," although it has also been known as inculcation, imposition, indoctrination, and in its most extreme form brainwashing. Moralizing is the direct or indirect transfer of a set of values from one person or group to another person or group.

The student of values clarification is taught awareness of his preferences and his right to their satisfaction in a democratic society. To help students discover what it is that they genuinely value, they are asked to respond to questionnaires called "strategies." Some typical questions are: Which animal would you rather be: an ant, a beaver, or a donkey? Which season do you like best? Do you prefer hiking, swimming, or watching television? In one strategy called "Values Geography," the student is helped to discover his geographical preferences; other lessons solicit his reaction to seat belts, messy handwriting, hiking, wall-to-wall carpeting, cheating, abortion, hit-and-run drivers, and a mother who severely beats a two-year-old child.

Western literature and history are two traditional alienating influences that the values clarification movement is on guard against. Simon has written that he has ceased to find meaning "in the history of war or the structure of a sonnet, and more meaning in the search to find value in life." He and his colleagues believe that exposure to one's cultural heritage is not likely to be morally beneficial to the "average student."

Because values are complex and because man's thoughts and accomplishments are both abundant and complicated, it is difficult to recommend that the average student rely on this approach. It takes substantial mental stamina and ability and much time and energy to travel this road. While the study of our cultural heritage can be defended on other grounds, we would not expect it to be sufficient for value education.

The values clarification theorist does not believe that moral sensibility and social conscience are, in significant measure, learned by reading and discussing the classics. Instead Simon speaks of the precious legacy we can leave to "generations of young people if we teach them to set their priorities and rank order the marvelous items in life's cafeteria."

As a college teacher coping with the motley ideologies of high school graduates, I find this alarming. Young people today, many of whom are in a complete moral stupor, need to be shown that there is an important distinction between moral and nonmoral decisions. Values clarification blurs the distinction. Children are queried about their views on homemade Christmas gifts, people who wear wigs, and whether or not they approve of abortion or would turn in a hit-and-run driver as if no significant differences existed among these issues.

It is not surprising that teachers trained in neutrality and the principled avoidance of "moralizing" sometimes find themselves in bizarre classroom situations. In a junior high school in Newton, Massachusetts, a teacher put on the blackboard a poster of a Hell's Angel wearing a swastika. The students were asked to react. "He's honest, anyway. He's living out his own feelings," answered one. "He's not fooling," said another. When the students seemed to react favorably to the Hell's Angel, the teacher ventured to suggest that "an alienated person might not be happy."

The following conversation took place between a values clarification teacher and her students:

STUDENT: Does this mean that we can decide for ourselves whether to be honest on tests here?

TEACHER: No, that means that you can decide on the value. I personally value honesty; and although you may choose to be dishonest, I shall insist that we be honest in our tests. In other areas of your life, you may have more freedom to be dishonest.

AND ANOTHER TEACHER: My class deals with morality and right and wrong quite a bit. I don't expect them all to agree with me; each has to satisfy himself according to his own conviction, as long as he is sincere, and thinks he is pursuing what is right. I often discuss cheating this way, but I always get defeated because they will argue that cheating is all right. After you accept the idea that kids have the right to build a position with logical arguments, you have to accept what they come up with.

The student has values; the values clarification teacher is merely "facilitating" the student's access to them. Thus, no values are taught. The emphasis is on *learning how*, not on *learning that*. The student does not learn *that* acts of stealing are wrong; he learns how to respond to such acts.

The values clarification course is, in this sense, contentless. As if to make up for this, it is methodologically rich. It is to be expected that an advocate of values clarification emphasizes method over content in other areas of education, and indeed he does. Many handbooks, strategies, board games, and kits have been developed to help teachers adapt the methods of values clarification to such subjects as English, history, science, math, and even home economics and Spanish. Values clarification guides for girl scout troops and Sunday school classes are also available, as well as manuals to assist parents in clarifying values at the dinner table.

Simon and his colleagues explain that it is useless and anachronistic to teach the student at a "facts level." In a history lesson on the Constitution, for example, the teacher is advised not to waste too much time on such questions as where and when the Constitution was drawn up. Undue attention should also not be given to the "concepts level," where, for example, the teacher discusses the moral origins of the Bill of Rights. When the learning of subject matter is unavoidable, Simon and his colleagues recommend that it be lifted to a higher and more urgent level where students are asked "you-centered" questions, such as, "What rights do you have in your family?" Or, "Many student governments are really token governments controlled by the 'mother country,' i.e., the administration. Is this true in your school? What can you do about it?" And, "When was the last time you signed a petition?"

The classical moral tradition will not be revived by the practitioners of values clarification. Indeed, it is, in their eyes, an alien tradition that is insensitive to the needs and rights of the contemporary student.

II

Lawrence Kohlberg, the leader of the second major movement in moral education, shares with values clarification educators a low opinion of traditional morality. In his contribution to Theodore and Nancy Sizer's anthology, *Moral Education*, he writes, "Far from knowing whether it can be taught, I have no idea what virtue really is." Kohlberg's disclaimer is not a Socratic confession of ignorance; he considers the teaching of traditional virtues to be at best a waste of time and at worst coercive. Like Sidney Simon, he, too, uses the language of conspiracy to characterize the American educational system. He refers often to the "hidden curriculum" and insists that the teacher must not be "an agent of the state, the church, or the social system, [but] rather... a free moral agent dealing with children who are free moral agents." Kohlberg cites as an example of covert indoctrination a teacher who yelled at some boys for not returning their books to the proper place. "The teacher would have been surprised to know that her concerns with classroom management defined for her children what she and her school thought were basic values, or that she was engaged in indoctrination." Kohlberg and his disciples are currently busy transforming some of the best school systems in the country into "just communities" where no such indoctrination takes place.

Kohlberg's authority derives from his cognitive developmental approach to moral education. Following John Dewey, Kohlberg distinguishes three main stages of moral development (each of which is partitioned into a higher and lower stage, making six in all). The first stage is called the premoral or preconventional reward/punishment level. In the second stage morals are conventional but unreflective. In the third stage moral principles are autonomously chosen on rational grounds. Kohlberg's research applies Piaget's idea that the child possesses certain cognitive structures that come successively into play as the child develops. According to Kohlberg, the latent structures are a cross-cultural fact of cognitive psychology. Kohlberg's more specific thesis on the unfolding of the child's innate moral propensities has received a great deal of deserved attention. The literature on Kohlberg is controversial, and it is far too early to say whether his ideas are sound enough for eventual use in the classroom. Kohlberg himself has urged and already put into practice pedagogical applications of his ideas.

From the assumption of innateness, it is but a short step to the belief that the appropriate external circumstances will promote the full moral development of the child. It then becomes the job of the educator to provide those circumstances "facilitating" the child to his moral maturity. The innate structures are essentially contentless, and Kohlberg and his followers do not think it is the job of the moral educator to develop a virtuous person by supplying the content—that is, the traditional virtues. To do that would be, in Kohlberg's contemptuous phrase, to impose on the child an "old bag of virtues." Kohlberg and his associate Moshe Blatt remark in the *Journal of Moral Education*:

Moral education is best conceived as a natural process of dialogue among peers, rather than as a process of didactic instruction or preaching. The teacher and the curriculum are best conceived as facilitators of this dialogue.

If moral education is to be a dialogue among peers, the relation between teacher and student must be radically transformed. Fully prepared to accept these consequences, Kohlberg, in 1974, founded the Cluster School in Cambridge, Massachusetts. It consisted of thirty students, six teachers, dozens of consultants, and Kohlberg—all of whom had an equal voice in running the school. According to Kohlberg, "The only way school can help graduating students become persons who can make society a just community is to let them try experimentally to make the school themselves." As he soon learned, these student-citizens were forever stealing from one another and using drugs during school hours. These transgressions provoked a long series of democratically conducted "town meetings" that to an outsider look very much like EST encounter groups. The students were frequently taken on retreats (Kohlberg and his associates share with the values clarification people a penchant for retreats), where many of them broke the rules against sex and drugs. This provoked more democratic confrontations where, Kohlberg was proud to report, it was usually decided that for the sake of the group the students would police one another on subsequent retreats and turn in the names of the transgressors. Commenting on the rash of thefts at the Cluster School, Kohlberg said, "At the moment there is clearly a norm in the Cluster School of maintaining trust around property issues. But there is uncertainty about whether the norm has [fully] developed." Since the Cluster School lasted only five years, this uncertainty will never be resolved.

In turning to the just communities, Kohlberg has consciously abandoned his earlier goal of developing individual students to the highest stages of moral development. The most he now hopes for is development to stage four, where students learn to respect the new just social order. His reasons are revealing. In 1980 in an anthology edited by Ralph Mosher, *Moral Education: A First Generation of Research and Development*, Kohlberg writes, "Perhaps all stage six persons of the 1960's had been wiped out, perhaps they had regressed, or maybe it was all my imagination in the first place."

The Cluster School has been the subject of a great many articles and doctoral theses. Careers have been advanced just by praising it. In Mosher's anthology one critic writes about the school:

Cluster School . . . in my judgment, is a unique secondary school environment, characterized by a respect and caring for persons and a determination to make the governance structure one in which students can experience the roles necessary for full participation in democracy.

From these remarks—and similar ones by others who visited Cluster School—you would never guess that the school was in shambles and just about to close. The school was racially divided; drugs, sex, and theft were rampant; and Kohlberg was fighting bitterly with the teachers. Here was a school —with thirty students and six exceptionally trained and dedicated teachers—that by any objective standard must be counted a failure. Yet in American professional education nothing succeeds like failure. Having scored their failure at the Cluster School, the Kohlbergians have put their ideas to work in more established schools. (For example, they now exercise a significant influence in such diverse public school systems as Pittsburgh, Pennsylvania; Salt Lake City, Utah; Scarsdale, New York; and Brookline, Massachusetts.)

Brookline High School in Massachusetts

provides a particularly sad example of the way the new ideologies can penetrate a fine high school. The school administration has been taken over by Kohlbergians who, with the help of federal funds, are trying to turn it into a "just community." To this end the governance of the school has been given over to the entire school community—students, teachers, administrators, secretaries, and janitorial staff. To make the process work smoothly, not all students are invited to the weekly "town meetings," just their representatives. But, because many of the two thousand or so students are indifferent, many student representatives are self-appointed. And a big problem is that most of the teachers do not attend (nor, of course, do tired secretaries and maintenance workers).

I attended one meeting with thirty students, five teachers, two student visitors from Scarsdale who are working with Kohlberg and studying the Brookline program in hopes of using it in New York, and two observers from the Carnegie-Mellon Foundation, who were there to investigate the possibility of making a film about the Brookline experiment for public television. The kids who participated in the meeting were charming and articulate, and the Carnegie-Mellon people were clearly pleased, and they will make their film. Like many educational experts who admire the Brookline town meetings, these observers are probably unaware that many of the teachers feel harassed and manipulated by the Kohlberg administration. So far, the participants in the town meetings—who are mostly teenagers exercising more power than they will ever be granted in college or graduate school—have voted to rescind a rule against Walkman radios on campus, to prohibit homework assignments for vacation periods, to disallow surprise quizzes, and they have instituted a procedure for bringing teachers who give tests or assignments that are too demanding before a "Fairness Committee." One teacher told me that the students had never asked for the powers they now enjoy. According to the teacher, the school authorities handed these powers over to students "for their own good." Just communities are Kohlberg's answer to the oppression exercised by established authority. Evidently, Kohlberg sees no need to question his assumption that established authority is intrinsically suspect. In any event, it is ironic that now, when teachers with authority are so rare, educational theorists like Kohlberg are proposing that authority itself is the evil to be combated.

Ralph Mosher, a Harvard-trained Kohlbergian, is the chief educational consultant to the Brookline High School. In his anthology he writes the following about the standards that had been in place:

Moral education, all the more powerful because it is "hidden," is embedded in the tacit values of the curriculum and the school. For example, the most worthy/valued student in Brookline High School is the one who achieves early admission to Harvard on a full scholarship. How few can accomplish this is obvious. Yet teachers, counselors, and parents put great, albeit subtle, pressure on the many to do likewise.... What the research [in moral education] has attempted to do is to make some schooling more just.

Mosher's attitude is instructive. Ideals, it seems, are not goals to aim for. They must be attainable by the majority of students. If any goals are set up, they must be ones to which most students can realistically aspire. For Mosher, vigilance against superimposing a hidden agenda with elitist bias is the order of the day.

Kohlberg's ideas have taken hold in the better schools, where one can still find a fair number of parents who can afford to hold attitudes against elitism. Should the public schools of Brookline, Cambridge, or Scarsdale fail to provide the education necessary for admission to the best colleges, those parents have recourse to some fine private schools in the neighborhood. In the meantime they can indulge the unexceptionable concept of a just community, whose egalitarian character is welcomed by those who find themselves uncomfortably well-fixed, particularly after the radical views they held in the halcyon sixties.

The values clarification and cognitive development reformers are well aware that they are riding a wave of public concern about the need for an effective system of moral education. Thus Mosher writes:

[A] high proportion of Americans (four of five in recent Gallup Polls) support moral education in the public schools. What the respondents mean by moral education is, of course, moot. Probably the teaching of virtues such as honesty, respect for adults, moderation in the use of alcohol/drugs, sexual restraint and so on.... Educators would have to exceed Caesar's wife not to capitalize on an idea whose time appeared to have come.

This last remark about capitalizing on the parent's desire for higher moral standards is disarmingly cynical. Naturally the public wants its "old bag of virtues," but educational theorists such as Mosher are convinced that giving the public what it wants is ineffective and unjust. The traditional moralists have failed (witness Watergate), so now it's their turn. Mosher's attitude to the benighted parents is condescending. No doubt for Mosher and Kohlberg, the morally confident leaders of the reform movement, theirs is the right kind of elitism.

The deprecation of moralizing common to values clarification and cognitive development theory has been effective even in those schools where the reforms have not yet penetrated. Increasingly nowadays, few teachers have the temerity to praise any middle-class virtues. The exception is the virtue of tolerance. But, when tolerance is the sole virtue, students' capacity for moral indignation, so important for moral development, is severely inhibited. The result is moral passivity and confusion and a shift of moral focus from the individual to society.

III

The student entering college today shows the effects of an educational system that has kept its distance from the traditional virtues. Unencumbered by the "old bag of virtues," the student arrives toting a ragbag of another stripe whose contents may be roughly itemized as follows: psychological egoism (the belief that the primary motive for action is selfishness), moral relativism (the doctrine that what is praiseworthy or contemptible is a matter of cultural conditioning), and radical tolerance (the doctrine that to be culturally and socially aware is to understand and excuse the putative wrongdoer). Another item in the bag is the conviction that the seat of moral responsibility is found in society and its institutions, not in individuals.

The half-baked relativism of the college student tends to undermine his common sense. In a term paper that is far from atypical, one of my students wrote that Jonathan Swift's "modest proposal" for solving the problem of hunger in Ireland by harvesting Irish babies for food was "good for Swift's society, but not for ours." All too often one comes up against a grotesquely distorted perspective that common sense has little power to set right. In one discussion in my introductory philosophy class, several students were convinced that the death of one person and the death of ten thousand is equally bad. When a sophomore was asked whether she saw Nagasaki as the moral equivalent of a traffic accident, she replied, "From a moral point of view, yes." Teachers of moral philosophy who are not themselves moral agnostics trade such stories for dark amusement. But it appears that teachers in other disciplines are also struck by the moral perversity of their students. Richard M. Hunt, a professor of government at Harvard University, gave a course on the Holocaust to one hundred Harvard undergraduates. In the course he was disturbed to find that a majority of students adopted the view that the rise of Hitler and the Nazis was inevitable, that no one could have resisted it, and that in the end no one was responsible for what happened. Hunt's teaching assistant remarked to him, "You know, I think if some of our students were sitting as judges at the Nuremberg trials, they would probably acquit—or at least pardon—most of the Nazi defendants." Professor Hunt has dubbed his students' forgiving attitude toward the past "no-fault history."

It is fair to say that many college students are thoroughly confused about morality. What they sorely need are some straightforward courses in moral philosophy and a sound and unabashed introduction to the Western moral tradition—something they may never have had before. But few teachers will use that tradition as a source of moral instruction: the fear of indoctrination is even stronger in the colleges than it is at primary and secondary schools. In a recent study of the teaching of ethics prepared by the Hastings Center, a well-respected institute for the study of ethical questions, the authors write:

A major concern about the teaching of ethics has been whether and to what extent it is appropriate to teach courses on ethics in a pluralistic society, and whether it is possible to teach such courses without engaging in unacceptable indoctrination.

And elsewhere in the same report:

No teacher of ethics can assume that he or she has a solid grasp on the nature of morality as to pretend to know what finally counts as good moral conduct. No society can assume that it has any better grasp of what so counts as to empower teachers to propagate it in colleges and universities. Perhaps most importantly, the premise of higher education is that students are at an age where they have to begin coming to their own conclusions and shaping their own view of the world.

It would, however, be altogether incorrect to say that the colleges are ignoring moral instruction. The spread of moral agnosticism has been accompanied by an extraordinary increase in courses of applied ethics. Philosophy departments, isolated and marginal for many years, are now attracting unprecedented numbers of students to their courses in medical ethics, business ethics, ethics for everyday life, ethics for engineers, nurses, social workers, and lawyers. Today there are dozens of journals and conferences, hundreds of books and articles, and—according to the Hastings Center—eleven thousand college courses in applied ethics.

The new interest in applied ethics is itself a

phenomenon to be welcomed. Public discussions of controversial issues will surely benefit from the contributions of philosophers, and the literature of applied ethics should be read by anyone who seeks a responsible understanding of topical issues. In reading the anthologies of applied ethics, a student encounters arguments of philosophers who take strong stands on important social questions. These arguments often shake a student's confidence in moral relativism. Nevertheless, the literature of applied ethics, like the literature of values clarification and cognitive moral development, has little or nothing to say about matters of individual virtue. The resurgence of moral education in the college thus reinforces the shift away from personal morals to an almost exclusive preoccupation with the morality of institutional policies. After all, most students are not likely to be involved personally in administering the death penalty or selecting candidates for kidney dialysis; and, since most will never do recombinant DNA research, or even have abortions, the purpose of the courses in applied ethics is to teach students how to form responsible opinions on questions of social policy. A strong ethical curriculum is a good thing, but a curriculum of ethics without virtue is a cause for concern.

The applied ethics movement in the universities started in the late nineteen sixties when philosophers became interested once again in normative ethics. Between 1940 and 1968 ethics had been theoretical and methodologically self-conscious, to the relative neglect of practical ethics. A large number of philosophers emerged from the sixties eager to contribute to national moral debates. But like Simon, Kohlberg, and their followers, these philosophers were suspicious and distrustful of moralizing and deeply averse to indoctrination. It is no small feat to launch a powerful and influential movement in normative ethics without recourse to the language of vice and virtue and a strong notion of personal responsibility, but that is exactly what is being attempted. The new university moralists, uncomfortable and ideologically at odds with the discredited middle-class ethic, are making their reform movement succeed by addressing themselves, not to the vices and virtues of individuals, but to the moral character of our nation's institutions. Take a look at almost any text used today in college ethics courses—for example, *Ethics for Modern Life*, edited by R. Abelson and M. Friquegnon, *Today's Moral Problems*, edited by R. Wasserstrom, or *Moral Problems* by J. Rachels—and you will find that almost all of the articles consist of philosophical evaluations of the conduct and poli-

cies of schools, hospitals, courts, corporations, and the United States government.

Inevitably the student forms the idea that applying ethics to modern life is mainly a question of learning how to be for or against social and institutional policies. Appropriately enough, many of the articles sound like briefs written for a judge or legislator. In that sort of ethical climate, a student soon loses sight of himself as a moral agent and begins to see himself as a moral spectator or a protojurist. This is not to deny that many of the issues have an immediate personal dimension. They do, but the primary emphasis is not on what one is to do as a person but on what one is to believe as a member of society—in other words, on ideology and doctrine rather than on personal responsibility and practical decency.

The move to issue-oriented courses is hailed as a move back to the days when moral instruction played a significant role in education. Nothing could be further from the truth. Where Aristotle, Aquinas, Mill, and Kant are telling us how to behave, the contemporary university moralist is concerned with what we are to advocate, vote for, protest against, and endorse. Michael Walzer has compared the applied ethics movement to the scholarly activities of the Greek Academicians, the Talmudists, and the medieval Casuists. The comparison is inept, for those earlier moralists were working in a tradition in which it was assumed that the practical end of all moral theory was the virtuous individual. The ancient sophist, with his expertise in rhetoric and politics, is a more convincing analogue to the teachers of issue-oriented ethics, who find little time for the history of ethical theory with its traditional emphasis on the good and virtuous life. One may therefore be wary of the widespread enthusiasm for the "exciting new developments" in the teaching of ethics. Especially misleading is the frequent observation that the revival of interest in practical ethics is a great advance over the earlier preoccupation with evaluative language (meta-ethics). Admittedly the preoccupation with meta-ethics that characterized the teaching of ethics a decade ago left the student undernourished by neglecting normative ethics. But, in all fairness, neither students nor teachers were under any illusion that meta-ethics was the whole of ethics. Today the student is learning that normative ethics is primarily social policy. This being so, moral action should be politically directed; the individual's task is to bring the right civic institutions (the true moral agents) into place. The student tacitly assumes that ethics is not a daily affair, that it is a matter for specialists, and that its practical benefits are deferred until the time of institutional reform.

The result of identifying normative ethics with public policy is justification for and reinforcement of moral passivity in the student. Even problems that call for large-scale political solutions have their immediate private dimension, but a student trained in a practical ethics that has avoided or de-emphasized individual responsibility is simply unprepared for any demand that is not politically or ideologically formulated. The student is placed in the undemanding role of the indignant moral spectator who needs not face the comparatively minor corruptions in his own life.

How, finally, is one to account for the ethics-without-virtue phenomenon? A fully adequate answer is beyond me, but clearly there is a great deal more to the story than the national disenchantment with a system of education that "failed to prevent" moral lapses such as Watergate. A historian of ideas would probably take us back to romantics like Rousseau and to realists like Marx. George Steiner has written of this theme in Rousseau:

In the Rousseauist mythology of conduct, a man could commit a crime either because his education had not taught him how to distinguish good and evil, or because he had been corrupted by society. Responsibility lay with his school or environment for evil cannot be native to the soul. And because the individual is not wholly responsible he cannot be wholly damned.

The values clarification theorists can find little to disagree with in this description.

For social-minded reformers, justice is the principal virtue, and social policy is where ethics is really "at." The assumption is that there is an implicit conflict between the just society and the repressive morality of its undemocratic predecessors. An extreme version of this theme is presented in a little book edited by Trotsky, *Their Morals and Ours*, with it searing attack on the "conservative banalities of bourgeois morality." For Trotsky, of course, social reform requires revolution, but his indictment of the hypocrisies and "brutalities" of "their morals" must sound familiar to the Kohlbergians. The fate of those societies that have actually succeeded in replacing personal morality with social policy is the going price for ignoring the admonition of Max Weber: "He who seeks salvation of the soul—of his own and others—should not seek it along the avenue of politics."

An essay on contemporary trends in moral education would be incomplete without mention of the Moral Majority. I have refrained from discussing this movement partly because it receives a great deal of public attention compared to the relative neglect of the movements inspired by the New England professors of education. But I suspect another reason for my silence is my own dismay that at this moment the Moral Majority constitutes the only vocal and self-confident alternative to the ethics-without-virtue movement.

Reopening the Books on Ethics: The Role of Education in a Free Society

Educational institutions at all levels must reestablish effective programs of moral and civic education.

John A. Howard

Dr. Howard is President of the Rockford Institute in Illinois, a nonprofit study center which focuses on the purposes, functions, and interdependence of all the major institutions of society. This article is reprinted with permission from *On Freedom: Essays from the Frankfurt Conference,* published by Devin-Adair Publishers, 6 North Water Street, Greenwich, Connecticut 06830. The essays in the book were presented at a Rockford Institute-sponsored conference entitled, "For Your Freedom, and Ours," held in West Germany, November 1982.

Edmund Burke, in his "Letter to the Sheriffs of the City of Bristol," addressed the central paradox of liberty, the inherent and never wholly reconcilable conflict between private judgment, which makes freedom a blessed estate, and the individual's responsibility to the community, which makes freedom a prickly burden. "The *extreme* of liberty," Burke asserted, "(which is its abstract perfection, but its real fault) obtains nowhere, nor ought to obtain anywhere.... Liberty must be limited to be possessed."[1] The relentless tension between the human impulse to pursue one's own course and the necessity to

modify one's conduct according to the needs of the group has challenged generations of philosophers and precipitated the collapse of powerful governments. This polarity must be dealt with in every organized endeavor—in commerce, industry, medicine, jurisprudence, and in the family. There is no immunity from it even for artistic creation, which by common consent demands for its fulfillment the utmost in independent judgment. Listen to the editors of the highly regarded *Saturday Review of Literature* in their denunciation of an award which the United States Library of Congress bestowed upon Ezra Pound for his *Pisan Cantos:*

> While one must divorce politics from art, it is quite another matter to use the word "politics" as a substitute for values. We do not believe, in short, that art has nothing to do with values. We do not believe that what a poet says is necessarily of lesser importance than the way he says it. We do not believe that a poet can shatter ethics and values and still be a good poet. We do not believe that poetry can convert words into maggots that eat at human dignity and still be good poetry.[2]

This editorial, I believe, speaks directly to the issue in question. The problem is certainly not how to prevent an Ezra Pound or anyone else from writing whatever seems important to him. The question, rather, is what shall the community prize and praise, what shall be the values and ideals and standards which shape the life of the society, and how shall worthy ideals and values be perpetuated. The editors of the *Saturday Review* were insisting that those who hold major responsibilities in the realm of public beliefs are inexcusably delinquent if they contribute to the destruction of standards of civilized conduct. The editors understood the importance of Burke's assertion that liberty must be limited to be possessed.

Parts dominated the whole

It has been 33 years since the *Saturday Review's* criticism of the award committee created a heated controversy. During this last third of a century, there have been very few voices of intellectual or cultural prominence asserting and defending the interests of the entire society. In fact, this has been an era in which the parts have been granted virtually unquestioned dominance over the whole. The large debates have been about which of the competing interest groups shall prevail, not whether the common

From *American Education,* October 1984, pp. 6-11. From ON FREEDOM: ESSAYS FROM THE FRANKFURT CONFERENCE. Reprinted by permission from the Devin Adair Publishers. Copyright © 1984 by the Rockford Institute.

welfare would be served or injured by the outcome of an issue.

During the campus turmoil of the 1960s the statements, silences, actions, and inactions of the leaders of American colleges and universities illustrated and underscored this change away from a concern for the whole society to smaller parochial concerns. The open and sometimes violent assault by the student radicals upon the values and traditions and operating principles of the free society was of a much larger magnitude than the mere awarding of the literary prize to Mr. Pound. Almost no university president spoke out forcefully about the interests of the society which were then under attack. The *rational* public debate which did take place about the meaning and resolution of the campus convulsions seldom extended beyond a discussion of the nature and obligations of academic freedom. Academic freedom, to be sure, is a matter of basic importance, but one must ask: Is academic freedom more important than other principles of community life, more important than order, rationality and lawfulness?

Academic autonomy proclaimed

When the campus turmoil had run its course, an altogether new set of assumptions had come to prevail in much of American higher education. One of those new principles seems to be that if academic freedom is not superior to all other considerations, at least no other public claims can be permitted to encroach upon the definition and application of academic freedom. Academic autonomy had been proclaimed. Although the ideas which crystallized in this new stance had been gaining support through many decades, the open assertion of the university's independence from the prevailing norms of the society marked a fundamental change from the concepts which had previously guided the course of American education.

The contrast between the old educational philosophy and the new one was brought into sharp focus by a report issued in 1979 by the Hastings Center in New York. In an analysis entitled "The Teaching of Ethics in the Undergraduate Curriculum 1876–1976," the author, Douglas Sloan, wrote:

> Throughout most of the nineteenth century the most important course in the college curriculum was moral philosophy, taught usually by the college president and required of all senior students....
>
> The full significance and centrality of moral philosophy in the nineteenth-century college curriculum can only be understood in the light of the assumption held by American leaders that no nation could survive, let alone prosper, without some common moral and social values....
>
> The entire college experience was meant above all to be an experience in character development and the moral life.[3]

The question is ... what shall the community prize and praise, what shall be the values and ideals and standards which shape the life of the society....

Moral development was also the dominant concern in the schools as well as the colleges of that era. The McGuffey Readers, filled with little tales of moral elevation, were the common classroom sustenance of generations of Americans.

Education's role rejected

Let us consider briefly some of the factors which contributed to the rejection of education's role as the guardian and tutor of public morals and ethics. One was the growing acceptance among faculty members of various new theories and philosophies, among them scientific naturalism, moral relativism, and subjectivity. More and more scholars had come to believe that the eternal verities had been proven false, or at least suspect, or were even barricades on the path to the total fulfillment of human nature. The rapidity with which ancient scientific certitudes yielded to new discoveries encouraged an analogy that ancient moral certitudes were equally vulnerable.

You will recognize this concept of a precise and demanding role for education was not an aberration that sprang up only in America, perhaps from puritanical New Englanders or from untutored frontiersmen. Rather, it was the American version of a long heritage of political and social theory deeply rooted in classical philosophy. During the 19th century, the United States was not alone in the prominence it gave to moral and ethical education. François Guizot, who successfully led the debate in the French Parliament to establish a national system of secondary education and then was named Minister of Education to implement that legislation, was above all a moralist. Earlier he had founded the first French pedagogical journal, *Les Annales de L'Éducation*, stressing in one editorial after another the necessity to imbue children with the principles of noble conduct.

Matthew Arnold, the English poet, but also an Oxford professor and for 35 years an inspector of British elementary schools, was chosen to head a delegation sent to France to try to discover why the French system of education seemed significantly more effective than the British one. Throughout that investigation, everywhere he went, Arnold encountered praise for Guizot and the priorities he had established. Matthew Arnold's own definition of education was "learning and propagating the best that has been thought and said in this world."

Codes achieve group objectives

At the risk of belaboring the obvious, let us go to the next step and remind ourselves of the critical relationship between moral and ethical training and the well-being of the free society. For a nation as for every other group, be it family, athletic team, committee, or business enterprise, there must be some means by which the actions of the participants can be coordinated to achieve the objectives of the group. In the totalitarian society, decisions are made by the central authority as to what the citizens will do and will not do, and those decisions are enforced by terrorism, brainwashing, false imprisonment, and all the other techniques of tyranny. In the free society, the characteristic means of cooperation is the voluntary observance of informal codes of conduct. They include courtesy, honor, sportsmanship, lawfulness, integrity, professional ethics, marital fidelity, respect for private property, providing a good day's work for a good day's pay, and countless other informal norms.

A second factor was a dramatic change in the qualifications of the people chosen as the leaders of American academic institutions. In the United States, prior to World War II, the college or university president characteristically took a major part in shaping the curriculum and guiding the educational program. Presidents Woodrow Wilson of Princeton, Robert Maynard Hutchins of Chicago, and James Bryan Conant of Harvard were not simply dynamic leaders of their universities, they were also commanding voices in the public discussion of educational philosophy. One is hard put to identify even one counterpart of those men today. In the last few decades the academic leaders seem to have been chosen for their skills in mediating conflicts, raising money, and managing complex organizations. The purposes of education languish in the councils of academic power; the agendas are almost totally devoted to the mechanics of financing and delivering education.

One other factor in the fundamental change in the concept of the relationship between education and society deserves comment. During the last forty years, the volume and cost of research conducted on the campuses has increased phenomenally. The salaries and the benefits now offered by universities in the competition to lure eminent research scholars to their premises have put the recruitment of renowned researchers almost on a par with that of professional football stars. In 1962, Harvard's President Pusey was moved to issue a formal report about the consequences of the massive research funds that had been flowing to the campuses from the government. Among other concerns, he noted that programs in science had grown rapidly in contrast to programs in all other fields of study and that the number of faculty appointments primarily devoted to research had grown out of all proportion to appointments for classroom teaching, which earlier had been the raison d'être of the university, so that decisions about many aspects of the university were affected by the large voting block of research-minded professors.

Is academic freedom more important than other principles of community life, more important than order, rationality, and lawfulness?

As the research function was catapulted into prominence, the principles which govern research activity tended to prevail in those instances where they were in conflict with the previous assumptions of the academic community. By its nature, research must be uninhibited. It makes no sense to encourage a scholar to study a topic and tell him there are three aspects of it that are forbidden. All possibilities must be open to him if he is to perform his work thoroughly. By logical extension, it is judged inappropriate to impose limitations on the political, social, and even moral sympathies and affiliations of faculty members. From the research point of view, enthusiasts of violent revolution, partisans of sexual liberation, and advocates of any bizarre religious cult should be as eligible for a professorship as anyone else, provided they have the proper scholarly credentials. This research pressure against normative judgments reenforced the growing acceptance of moral relativism by the teaching faculty at a time when the academic leadership had already become little inclined to concern itself with such matters as the content and the character of the educational program and the impact that the educational program has upon the values, beliefs, and priorities of the students.

Traditional standards dismantled

By the middle of the 1960s the faculty support for any normative stance on the part of the university had dwindled to the point that when the student militants made their demands, in many places the whole structure of policies and regulations through which traditional standards of conduct had been prescribed by the university was rapidly dismantled. On some campuses, the transformation not only involved the abdication of authority for all out-of-class aspects of the student's experience, but went so far as the sharing of authority with students for curricular planning, the performance rating of faculty members, the selection of the university president, and even membership on the Board of Trustees.

The consequences of this upheaval in the university's view of its relationship to the students can only be fully comprehended in the light of a clear understanding of the justification for the educational philosophy which had been abandoned. Douglas Sloan noted in the passage already cited that the American leaders of the 19th century believed that no nation could survive, let alone prosper, without common moral and social values. These earlier leaders perceived that the schooling in every country serves as the primary instrument by which the society imbues each new generation with a commitment to the ideals, the mores, and the institutions which characterize that particular kind of society and make it viable. It is not a question of simply imparting information about the *patria*, but rather of acculturating and indoctrinating the young as partisans of their homeland, carefully preparing them to accept and fulfill their responsibilities and obligations as citizens.

The general observance of such standards of behavior contributes to an amicable and productive community. When people behave in a civilized fashion, it is easy to get along together. A large-scale rejection of these informal standards eats away at the fabric of good will and mutual trust which more than anything else makes life in the free society a friendly and agreeable circumstance, in contrast to the state of permanent suspicion and fear which characterize the tyranny. If citizens increasingly disregard the informal civilized norms, all the systems and institutions of the society begin to operate less effectively; and when irresponsible conduct becomes widespread, the government is called on to pass more and more laws to regulate citizen behavior, so that the free society is converted into a system of government coercion. The breakdown of the informal codes of conduct is the precursor of the conversion of the free society to a controlled society.

Civilized behavior is learned behavior

Despite the flights of enthusiasm of philosophers and theorists asserting the contrary, history makes it clear that the human being, left to his own devices, is not likely to behave in a manner that promotes the well-being of the community. The definition of a savage is, after all, a person who does his own thing. Civilized behavior is learned behavior. We do ourselves a great disservice if we persist in believing the contrary. The apologists for the current non-normative stance of the universities insist that if students are exposed to various and contradictory views of mankind, and of the good society and the good life, their intelligence will lead them to wise or at least tolerable decisions about how they lead their own lives.

The response to that attitude of detached indifference about values was set forth by Gordon Chalmers in one of the very important works of educational philosophy to appear in the United States since 1950. Dr. Chalmers' book was entitled, significantly, *The Republic and the Person*. He wrote:

> The late William Allan Neilson, speaking at the 1940 Commencement of Kenyon College, told the graduates that his generation of university professors and presidents had been guilty of wrapping the young in romantic cotton wool.... Speaking of the aim and temper of college education, President Neilson quoted from *The City of Man* ... the opinion of numerous intellectual leaders that the liberalism they had taught and promoted in the Twenties and Thirties was in important particulars established not on ethical fact, but on sentiment. It was, said the author of that volume, a "disintegrated liberalism." They stated that the illusions of the

---

American leaders of the 19th century believed that no nation could survive, let alone prosper, without common moral and social values.

> Thirties had produced a timidity and lack of conviction in many Americans concerning the true character of the Nazis and their threat to democracy. One may add that they also produced a romanticized notion of the true nature of Communism. This sentimentalism was directly traceable to the ethical ignorance of persons thought to be learned. Many of these later admitted that the university world had persuaded the young that evil itself, extensive and malignant, does not exist.[4]

"The ethical ignorance of persons thought to be learned" is a hazard of no small consequences when it is prevalent in the academic community. Let us return again to the dominant non-normative orthodoxy of the universities. The process of education presupposes that knowledge has something to teach ignorance, experience something to teach inexperience, and informed judgment something to teach raw judgment.

In the sciences, these suppositions still hold firm. The student is not subjected to a great range of conflicting views about gravity, genetics, and thermodynamics. He is provided with what is judged by the professor to be the most accurate and advanced understanding of the subject available. In science, a body of accumulated knowledge still has authority. However, in the more universally demanding realm of ethics and human values, ignorance, inexperience, and raw judgment have been proclaimed the equivalent of trained expertise. Each student is encouraged to arrive at his own conclusions. This is a rejection of the nature and meaning of education, and one which the free society may not be able to withstand.

Education for responsible citizenship

It is an easy thing to be critical of imperfect human beings and imperfect institutions. The more useful and more difficult role of the analyst is to offer some guidelines for better accomplishing the desired objectives. What we have asserted is a principle of the free society—the necessity for the educational system to prepare the young for responsible citizenship. The determination of what shall be the subject matter that attends to that principle is a complex and hazardous undertaking. There can be no single blueprint that serves all free societies equally well or even all communities in one society because, as Edmund Burke observed in the letter cited earlier, "social and civil freedom, like all other things in common life, are variously mixed and modified, enjoyed in very diffferent degrees, and shaped into an infinite diversity of forms, according to the temper and circumstances of every community."[5]

The point of departure in designing a citizenship-training program needs to be the identification of principles of the free society that are vital to the community well-being. Let us touch on three illustrations that might qualify for that designation:

1. The principle of the rule of law. Each citizen needs to understand that chaos results when each person decides for himself which laws he will obey and which he will disregard. Each citizen must be brought to a recognition that the lawlessness of one individual harms all individuals. The ignorance of, or perhaps indifference to, this principle is approaching universality in the United States. There seems to be no recognition that when an individual takes up an illegal habit, for example the use of illegal drugs, the level of his concern for abiding by all other laws is automatically decreased.

2. The principle of orderly change. An enduring society must have provision for attending to new circumstances and new requirements. The free society does so through its legislative bodies at all levels of government. It is therefore important that the voters select as legislators individuals of integrity, objectivity, and breadth of understanding who can accurately anticipate the probable consequences of the laws they enact, choosing a careful course that balances the proper interests of the citizens variously affected by the legislation. The degree to which this principle has faded from public consciousness in any free society can be measured by the character of the incumbent legislators. I must confess that integrity, objectivity, and broad knowledge do not come immediately to mind when one thinks of the members of the United States Congress. One hopes that other free nations are faring better in this regard.

3. The principles of justice. It is essential for the citizens to understand that the processes by which the free society mediates and adjudicates conflicts are dependent for their effectiveness on facts, objectivity, and rationality. When one

party to an issue distorts the truth or asserts lies, or tries to stir up fear or hatred against the other party, not only is the just resolution of the conflict jeopardized, but a process of the utmost importance to the free society is compromised. We are now seeing the institutionalization of the antithesis of this principle in the argumentation of public issues. Emotions and partial truths tend to dominate in the argumentation of difficult questions, the nuclear freeze being a current example.

It will be recognized that each civic principle identifies a pattern of behavior which must prevail and therefore must be instilled in the hearts and minds of the citizens, the three principles we have cited pointing variously to the necessity for lawfulness, truthfulness, a respect for the rights of others, and the intelligent fulfillment of one's voting privilege. Moral education is the automatic partner of and the necessary complement to citizenship education. While there will be some principles on which curriculum planners may readily reach an agreement, the difficult part of arriving at a full agenda for civic and moral education is how to deal with subjects on which there is strong disagreement. In this respect, the experience of the United States offers guidance.

Benefits of decentralized control

Until quite recently in America, the primary authority for the governance of education was decentralized. It was the responsibility of each local school board and each board of trustees of a college or university to determine the educational purposes and priorities that would prevail in the program under its jurisdiction. The benefits of decentralized control were many and substantial. In the first place, there was a wholesome diversity of policies, programs, and techniques which not only well served the pluralistic nature of the nation, but also led to wide experimentation in the improvement of educational

programs. In the second place, a great many citizens, and especially the parents of students, were able to involve themselves in the deliberations about the educational program because they had direct access to the people of their own community who controlled the policy decisions of the schools. Furthermore, if the decisions made by the school policymakers did not satisfy the people, they could take action to elect different policymakers. Those who governed the educational program had to be responsible to the parents of the students. And finally, when the primary determinant in educational policies is the central government, as is now the case in the United States, any effort to address such matters as moral and civic education is reduced to the lowest common denominator of agreement. And in the present state of our culture, that means virtual oblivion. One is inclined to believe that what is gained by the decentralization of educational responsiblity is greater than what is lost through an absence of national standards and uniform priorities.

Well, what have we said here? First, that every free society must find ways to deal with the conflict between the desires of the individual and the obligations he must accept as a member of the community. Second, that the process of formal schooling is the mechanism by which the society assures that the common interests are protected and that this is done by training the young people to understand their own nation, to adopt its ideals, and to abide by its requirements. Third, that one of the absolutely fundamental requirements of the free society is the acceptance by the citizens of many informal codes of conduct, those standards of behavior constituting the means by which the free society addresses that tension between the individual and the group. Fourth, that whereas the schools and colleges in the United States and some other nations formerly transmitted the ideals and the informal codes of conduct quite effectively through granting a high priority to character education and citizenship education, that activity has largely been discontinued. One observer has phrased this change as a shift from education to learning. And here, I wish to pick up a loose end. In mentioning the conflict between the principles governing research and those governing education, I should have observed that there is no reason why those two functions cannot be conducted on the same premises with productive interaction so long as the distinguishing principles of each are recognized and appropriately safeguarded. Fifth, we have commented upon the processes of determining what should comprise the agenda of character education and citizenship education, with the principles of the free society constituting the absolute base for that determination.

The educational system has largely disassociated itself from one of its functions, a function that is critically important to the strength and survival of a free society. We have, in the United States, produced several generations of cultural orphans, people who have little knowledge and even less appreciation of their heritage of freedom, or the struggles and sacrifices which produced it. By failing to impart to our citizens a passionate devotion to their freedom and an understanding of their obligations as free citizens, we have inadvertently engaged in a kind of unilateral intellectual disarmament which could well prove more devastating to the cause of liberty than would the voluntary destruction of our defense arsenals.

I suggest that there is no task of such importance for the schools and colleges, and few tasks of such importance for free governments, as the reconstitution of effective programs of moral and civic education.

NOTES

[1] Edmund Burke, Published Letter, May 16, 1777, cited in Peter J. Stanlis, ed., *Edmund Burke, On Conciliation With The Colonies and Other Papers* (Lunenberg, Vermont: The Stinebour Press, 1975), p. 255.
[2] *Saturday Review of Literature*, "A Reply to Mr. Evans," July 2, 1949, 32:22, cited in Gordon Keith Chalmers, *The Republic and the Person* (Chicago: Henry Regnery Company, 1952), p. 25.
[3] Douglas Sloan, "The Teaching of Ethics in the American Undergraduate Curriculum 1876-1976," Hastings Center Report (Hastings-on-Hudson, New York, December 1979), pp. 21-23.
[4] Chalmers, op. cit., pp. 3,4.
[5] Burke, idem.

Discipline Problems in the Schools

Probably nothing creates more anxiety for pre-service teachers than the issue of behavioral problems in public schools. Professors in teacher education programs must devote considerable time to the discussion of strategies for ethical behvioral management plans for use in public schools. While the need for dialogue about controlling classes is unfortunate, it is a very real dimension of public schooling. Findings from federal research projects indicate that serious discipline problems still exist in schools today. The lead article of this unit details some of that research. Few problems influence the morale of teachers more than the issue of managing student behavior in the elementary and secondary schools. School discipline involves many moral, legal, and ethical questions. It is a highly value-laden topic on which there is a great diversity of opinion over what techniques of behavior management are effective and desirable. The essays in this unit repond to some of the concerns of in-service as well as pre-service teachers on this issue.

Teachers' core ethical principles come into play in their efforts to decide what constitutes both defensible and desirable standards of teacher-student relations. As in medicine, realistic preventive techniques and humane but clear principles of procedure in dealing with issues seem to be effective approaches toward good student behavior. Teachers need to realize that before they control behavior they must identify what students behaviors they desire in their classrooms. They need to reflect as well on what emotional tone and what ethical principles are implied by their own behaviors. In order to optimize their chances for achieving the classroom learning atmosphere they wish to have, teachers must strive for emotional balance within themselves; they must learn to be accurate observers; they

must learn the skills involved in hearing and/or seeing clearly what goes on in their classrooms; and they must build just, fair strategies of intervention for constructing the conditions for students to learn self-control and behavior management. A good teacher is a good model of courtesy, respect, tact, and discretion. Children learn from how they see other persons behave as well as from how they are told to behave.

Recent studies point out some effective preventive measures to minimize the incidence of serious discipline problems in the classroom. Researchers examine why disobedience and disrespect toward teachers are common in some settings but rare in others. They explore ways to reduce the level of hostility, violence, and disobedience in the more troubled school settings. Experts study teacher behaviors that may trigger or encourage disobedience. Some suggest that teachers would be able to control student behavior more effectively and humanely if they had more control over conditions and situations that often incite or anger students. In the interest of creating genuine and humane conditions for learning, educators are engaged in a critical reexamination of all dimensions of this issue. These dimensions cross socioeconomic lines throughout the country; it is not just an urban issue.

Teachers are demanding the respect to which they believe all working people are entitled. They want safety, peace, security, a sense of pride, and the opportunity to practice their art in environments where that effort is appreciated. Nothing less than this is satisfactory. Nothing less should be. The National Education Association (NEA) and the American Federation of Teachers (AFT) are calling for public support of teachers in order to improve the quality of teaching and learning in the schools. Teachers

Unit 5

must be treated with respect. This would indeed be a major turning point in American education. It is a goal worth seeking.

This unit can be used in conjunction with several sectors of basic foundations courses. The selections can be related to classroom management issues, teacher leadership skills, the legal foundations of education, and the rights and responsibilities of teachers and students. In addition, the articles could also be discussed in portions of the course involving curriculum and instruction or individualized approaches to testing. The unit falls between the units on moral education and equality of opportunity because it can be directly related to either or both of them.

Looking Ahead: Challenge Questions

What reliable information is available on the extent and severity of school discipline problems in North America? What sources contain such information?

What are some of the best means for preventing or minimizing serious misbehavior in school settings?

What types of punishment are defensible in teaching?

What ethical issues may be raised in the management of student behavior in school settings? What specific authority should a teacher have?

What are some of the best techniques for helping someone to learn self-control?

What civil rights do students have? Do public schools have fewer rights for controlling student behavior problems than do private schools? Why or why not?

Do any coercive approaches to behavioral management in schools work better than noncoercive ones?

Does corporal punishment have a place in disciplining students? Give reasons for being for or against it.

What are the rights of a teacher in managing student behavior?

Research Evidence of A School Discipline Problem

Illustration by Joe LaMantia

Keith Baker

KEITH BAKER is a social science analyst in the Office of the Deputy Undersecretary for Planning, Budget, and Evaluation in the U.S. Department of Education. He helped prepare the Cabinet Council Report, Disorder in Our Public Schools, *and the congressional testimony that provided material for this article.*

Research indicates that the discipline problem in U.S. public schools is severe enough that it should concern educators, says Mr. Baker. The education community must face the problem squarely and take steps to improve conditions in the schools.

IF WE ARE TO improve discipline in our schools, we must first agree that a problem exists. Considerable research evidence indicates that the discipline problem in U.S. public schools is severe enough that it should concern educators for a number of reasons.

Crime and violence in the schools merit attention because they are socially undesirable. In a statistical sense, murder in the schools is not a big problem, because it does not happen very often. In a moral sense, however, even one murder is unacceptable. Crime and violence of any kind in the schools must always be a concern of educators. Even where the school crime rate is zero, educators must make sure it stays that way.

Schools in which the crime rate is high probably experience high rates of other, less serious discipline problems as well. Therefore, we can probably use the findings of studies of school crime to help us solve other discipline problems. For example, one of the major conclusions to emerge from the most extensive study of school crime and violence yet conducted is that school safety depends on clearly stated and fairly enforced rules of behavior. That is generally good advice, and its value is not limited to crime prevention.

Finally, educators must be concerned about the lack of discipline in the schools because an educational environment depends on good discipline. A study of inner-city schools in London used data collected over a number of years to show that, when children move from primary school (ages 5 to 11) to secondary school, their behavior and achievement are affected by school characteristics.[1] Students who transferred from behaviorally "bad" elementary schools to "good" secondary schools became good students and vice versa.

The relationship between good behavior and academic performance is shown in Table 1, which displays data from a nationally representative sample of 30,000 high school sophomores. For all types of misbehavior, there was a clear association between poor grades and misbehavior. For example, a student whose grades were mostly D's was nine times as likely as a student whose grades were mostly A's to have had trouble with the law, 24 times less likely to have done homework assignments, and about three times more likely to have cut classes.[2]

Drug abuse and drinking, which must also be numbered among a school's discipline problems, both have a debilitating effect on learning and are generally illegal — at least for young people. A reviewer of the literature on adolescent drug abuse concluded that problem drinking among teenagers is generally related to poor school performance, participation in antisocial activities, and lack of supervision.[3] A study of 367 high school students found that regular consumption of alcohol was associated with lower grades.[4]

A good climate for learning is a climate with good discipline. Fundamental to improving the quality of the schools is the maintenance of a degree of civil behavior sufficient to allow educational improvements to have a chance to succeed.

THE EXTENT OF THE PROBLEM

Eight years ago, the National Institute of Education (NIE) surveyed a nationally representative sample of principals, teachers, and students in secondary schools on the extent of criminal activity in U.S. schools.[5] Because many crimes are not reported to the police, a survey of the population of potential victims of crime provides better statistics on the scope of the problem than do court records or records

of police arrests. In fact, the NIE study, commonly referred to as the "Safe School Study," found that only about one in every 58 crimes that occurred in the schools was reported to the police.

According to the Safe School Study, the scope of criminal activity *each month* in America's secondary schools in 1976 was as follows:

- 282,000 students were physically attacked;
- 112,000 students were robbed through force, weapons, or threat;
- 2.4 million students had their personal property stolen;
- 800,000 students stayed home from school because they were afraid to attend;
- 6,000 teachers were robbed;
- 1,000 teachers were assaulted seriously enough to require medical attention;
- 125,000 teachers were threatened with physical harm;
- more than 125,000 teachers encountered at least one situation in which they were afraid to confront misbehaving students;
- one out of two teachers was on the receiving end of an insult or obscene gesture;
- 2,400 fires were set in schools;
- 13,000 thefts of school property occurred;
- 24,000 incidents of vandalism occurred; and
- 42,000 cases of damage to school property occurred.

These figures reflect what happened during a *typical* month in U.S. secondary schools. Over the course of the 1976 school year, there was more than one theft for every secondary school student and teacher in the United States.

Students as victims. As the NIE study showed, students are the most frequent victims of crime in the schools. In addition to the obvious undesirability of being

a victim of a crime, the crime rate in schools has an indirect, but perhaps even more serious, effect on students: crime in school teaches students to fear school.

A study of 1,200 families in Philadelphia found that 27% of the adolescents feared school grounds, 28% feared school hallways, and 22% feared their classrooms.[6] In a study of the Dade County, Florida, public schools, one-fifth of the secondary public school students said that their ability to learn in the classroom was adversely affected by fear of other students.[7]

A detailed analysis of data from the Safe School Study found that in 1976 there were about 3.7 million fearful students in public high schools.[8] Almost 800,000 secondary students (8%) reported staying home from school for at least one day a month because they were afraid to go to school. Students who were afraid received lower grades and were more likely to rate themselves below average in reading ability. These students viewed schools as hostile places offering little promise of academic reward or personal safety. They

> Educators must be concerned about the lack of discipline in the schools because an educational environment depends on good discipline.

Table 1. Grades and Behavior of a Sample Of High School Sophomores

Type of Misbehavior	Grades			
	Mostly A's	Mostly B's	Mostly C's	Mostly D's
Average days absent per semester	2.28	2.99	4.20	7.87
Average days late per semester	2.05	3.12	4.41	6.44
Percentage of sample not doing assigned homework	1.10	2.73	6.27	24.72
Percentage of sample who cut a class during the school year	28.73	43.39	58.15	67.21
Percentage of sample who have been in serious trouble with the law	1.62	2.93	7.37	14.06

*Source: Thomas DiPrete, Chandra Muller, and Nora Shaeffer, *Discipline and Order in American High Schools* (Washington, D.C.: National Center for Education Statistics, 1981).

were more likely than nonfearful students to think that teachers were unable to maintain order or to hold students' interest. Apprehensive students were more likely to dislike their schools, their teachers, and their fellow students. The authors of the study pointed out that fear among students reduces their ability to concentrate on schoolwork, creates an atmosphere of hostility and mistrust in school, undermines morale, and teaches that the staff is not in control — that "student disorder is more powerful than the adult call for order."

The Safe School Study found that students from minority groups were generally much more likely to be victims of crime than were white students. Consistent with this finding, in 1982 the Gallup Poll found that members of minority groups were more concerned about school crime than whites were. While 68% of white respondents thought that the discipline problem in the schools was very serious or fairly serious, 81% of nonwhite respondents believed this to be the case.[9]

Students can victimize themselves, too. Alcohol and drug abuse are examples of so-called victimless crimes, in which the victim is the perpetrator. Students' abuse of alcohol and drugs is widespread. As the Third Special Report to the U.S. Congress on Alcohol and Health noted:

A national survey of students in grades 7 through 12 found 74% of the teenagers were drinkers . . . [and] nearly 19% of the students were problem drinkers — 23% of the boys and 15% of the girls.

Approximately two-thirds of high school seniors report ever having used any illicit drug — 60% marijuana, 39% an illicit drug other than marijuana. Six in 10 have used marijuana at least once; one in two use it daily.[10]

Teachers as victims. For many teachers, school has become a hazardous environment and a place to fear. Many teachers face situations in which self-preservation, not teaching, becomes their major concern. For example, a teacher in New Orleans watched while two boys threw a smaller student off a second-floor balcony. The teacher chose not to intervene, lest she, too, be attacked. Other teachers are not so lucky. In Los Angeles, high school girls who were angry about their grades tossed lighted matches into their teacher's hair, setting it on fire. Subsequently, the teacher suffered an emotional collapse.

But criminal acts are only part of the problem that confronts teachers daily in their classrooms. Generally uncivil behavior by students is one of the major causes of teacher burnout. In one survey, 58% of the teachers polled reported that "individual students who continually mis-

Table 2. Number of Teachers Who Would Not Go into Teaching Again, by Experience with Discipline Problems	
Discipline Problem	Number of Teachers Who Would Not Go into Teaching Again for Every 100 Who Would
Had students with six or more chronic behavior problems	146
Misbehavior interfered with teaching to a great extent	183
School's disciplinary policy not clear	132
School's disciplinary policy not strict enough	131
Personal property damaged or stolen	192
Attacked by a student	184

Source: National Education Association, *Teacher Opinion Poll* (Washington, D.C.: NEA, 1980).

behave" are the primary cause of job-related stress.[11]

Teacher burnout is a major problem in U.S. schools. More than 90% of 1,282 teachers surveyed in one study had experienced feelings of burnout, and 85% of 7,000 teachers surveyed in another study felt that there were chronic health problems related to teaching. Nearly half (40%) of the teachers responding said that they took prescription drugs to treat job-related illness. In another study of 5,000 Chicago teachers, more than half reported having had some job-related illness.[12]

The stress of teaching led one psychiatrist to compare teaching to war, calling teacher burnout a type of "combat neurosis." In another study, Alfred Bloch and Ruth Bloch reported having treated 575 teachers psychiatrically over a seven-year span.[13] All the treated teachers shared two characteristics: they reported that school was an extremely stressful environment and that violence at school was out of control.

Job-related stress drives teachers out of teaching. *Learning* magazine surveyed more than 1,000 teachers, almost one-quarter of whom said that they were planning to leave teaching because of burnout.[14] The National Education Association (NEA) asked active teachers if they would go into teaching again if they had the chance to begin anew.[15] Table 2 shows that teachers who would not go into teaching again were much more likely to have experienced discipline problems than were teachers who would go into teaching again.

Elementary school teachers in the NEA poll reported just as much on-the-job stress as did high school teachers. This finding raises an important point that is often overlooked in the public debate over the lack of discipline in the schools: the

problem is not confined to urban high schools. In fact, the NEA teacher poll found that elementary school teachers generally reported *more* interference with their teaching from student misbehavior than did high school teachers. Half of all elementary school teachers in the U.S. reported that student misbehavior interfered with their teaching to a moderate or great extent. Very few (7.7%) elementary teachers reported having no problems with student misbehavior.

Of course, there are obvious differences in the types of misbehavior encountered in the high schools and in the elementary schools. High school teachers are more likely to encounter criminal acts. However, an impromptu game of tag in a second-grade classroom can more seriously disrupt learning for an entire class than a single act of violence on the school grounds.

The NEA poll suggests that student misbehavior interferes more with teaching in the elementary schools than in the high schools. Yet more serious misbehavior — especially criminal acts — occurs in the secondary schools.

Is this a contradiction? Probably not. In many high school classrooms teachers and students have worked out a compromise, a tacit understanding that allows them to coexist in a state of truce. The teacher "agrees" to let troublesome students sit in the back of the room, read comic books, and ignore the lesson. In return, these students tacitly agree not to disrupt the class — at least not too often. The teacher then addresses the lesson only to those students who want to pay attention and ignores the others.

Elementary school teachers do not do this. They are more likely to insist that all students pay attention to the lesson. Consequently, elementary teachers face a

Criminal acts are only part of the problem. Generally uncivil behavior by students is one of the major causes of teacher burnout.

more persistent battle with disruptive students.

Taxpayers as victims. Although teachers and students are the most direct victims of classroom disorder, taxpayers are also victimized. The Safe School Study found that each month there were 2,400 acts of arson, 13,000 thefts of school property, 24,000 incidents of vandalism, and 42,000 cases of damage to school property. The National Parent/Teacher Association (PTA) has observed that the annual cost of vandalism — probably in excess of $600 million — exceeds the nation's total spending for textbooks.[16]

TRENDS OVER TIME

As I pointed out above, the most comprehensive data on the extent of school crime come from the Safe School Study and were collected in 1976. Since then, many schools have undertaken programs to reduce school crime and to improve discipline. What has happened during the past eight years?

Deciding whether the problem is getting better or worse is difficult because so few trend data exist. Here I will review two kinds of data: 1) trend data from those few areas for which such data exist and 2) the most recently available data, which, though not nationally representative, provide a picture of the current situation in various parts of the U.S.

Oliver Moles analyzed two sets of data that permit national trends to be established over several years.[17] Using the NEA teacher poll, Moles examined teachers who were victims of assault and property damage between 1972 and 1983 and teachers who were victims of theft between 1978 and 1983. He reported that there were more attacks on teachers during the period from 1979 through 1983 than in the period from 1972 to 1978. Property damage held more or less constant during the same period, except for peaks in 1972

and 1979. Except for a peak in 1979, theft held fairly constant.

Moles used the Department of Justice's crime victimization surveys to study crimes against students and argued that these surveys do not give accurate estimates of the *level* of school crime. However, they can be used to assess trends, since the bias in the data should be the same each year. The crime victimization surveys contain data from 1973 through 1980 on both completed and attempted assaults, thefts, and robberies. Moles concluded that completed assaults rose between 1973 and 1978, dipped in 1979, and then returned to the 1978 level. Attempted assaults were stable over the eight-year period. Theft, the crime most frequently reported by students, declined steadily over the period. The number of reported robberies in several years was too small to permit meaningful analysis.

A comparison of data from 1976 with Moles's data from 1980 shows that assaults on teachers increased by 59% and theft of teachers' property increased by 46%. Completed assaults against students rose by 13%, but attempted assaults declined by 17%. Completed thefts against students dropped by 60%, and attempted thefts fell by 43%.

Another source of information on the changing pattern of school discipline problems is a question from the NEA teacher poll that asked the extent to which teachers find that student misbehavior interferes with their ability to teach. From 1980 through 1983 this question was asked in the same way. The results, displayed in Table 3, suggest some decline in the proportion of teachers complaining of moderate to great interference and a corresponding increase in the proportion of teachers saying that student misbehavior interfered with their teaching to a small extent. The proportion of teachers who reported no behavior problems remained roughly constant at about 10% of all teachers.

From these studies, what can we conclude about the trends in discipline prob-

lems since 1976? The picture is confusing. There have been increases in the incidence of some crimes — most notably crimes against teachers — and declines in the incidence of other crimes — most notably thefts against students.

On balance, the data suggest a slight overall improvement. However, it must also be noted that considerable year-to-year variations exist in many of these statistics and that, with the exception of thefts against students from 1973 to 1980, there are no clear-cut trends. On the one hand, it is encouraging to see any indication of improvement. On the other hand, it is discouraging to see that the improvement is so small, especially in light of the extensive efforts of many schools to cope with the problem.

A second way to update the data from the Safe School Study is to examine the most recent data available from school districts and states to see if they are currently experiencing problems. In 1983 the *Detroit Free Press* conducted a survey of teachers across Michigan and found that, during the last school year, 46% of all teachers in the state had been threatened with violence — including 23% who had been threatened by parents of their students.[18] One out of five teachers (19%) had been hit by a student, while 3% had been hit by an intruder and 3% had been hit by a parent. Two out of three teachers said that unmotivated and undisciplined students were a serious problem in their classrooms. One middle school teacher included a can of Mace among her basic teaching supplies.

A study of California schools over a five-month period in 1981 found 100,000 incidents of violence, with an average of 24 teachers and 215 students assaulted every day. Property damage during the five months was $10 million.[19]

The National School Boards Association reported on a 1983 study of crime in seven school districts across the U.S.[20] More than 10% of the students in four of the seven districts admitted breaking windows in school buildings. From 6.6% to

Table 3. Extent to Which Student Misbehavior Interferes with Teaching

Degree of Interference	1979 %	1980 %	1981 %	1982 %	1983 %
Great	16.8	20.9	23.2	17.0	14.5
Moderate	23.1	32.9	28.9	29.8	30.4
Small	33.9	37.7	37.5	42.9	46.0
None	26.2*	8.5	10.4	10.2	9.1
N	1,768	1,731	1,257	1,310	1,467

*In 1979 this response category was "little, if at all."
Source: National Education Association, *Teacher Opinion Poll* (Washington, D.C.: NEA, 1979, 1980, 1981, 1982, 1983).

> Teachers who function as baby sitters or police officers are not teaching. Students whose teachers do not teach cannot learn.

21.7% of the students in the districts admitted stealing from other students' desks. The proportion of students in each district who reported that they had been victims of such thefts ranged from a low of 42.6% to a high of 72.2%. Between 5.5% and 19.5% of the students reported being victims of physical attacks. A total of 16.4% of the teachers in the seven districts reported that students verbally abused them and swore at them. In one city, 80% of the teachers reported being the victims of verbal abuse.

Boston established a Safe Schools Commission that interviewed 495 high school students from four Boston high schools and found a "disturbingly large amount of victimization"[21] — including the fact that 38% of all Boston high school students had been victims of robbery, assault, or larceny during the previous school year and that incidents occurred at the rate of 63 per 100 students. This is one of the few studies to have differentiated victimization rates (the number of victims during some specified period) from rates of incidence (the number of crimes committed). The difference between the two shows that a large proportion of victims were victimized more than once.

Half of the students reported racial harassment. More than one in four students (28%) said that they were fearful at school on occasion, and 36% said that they avoided some places at school from fear for their personal safety. Twenty-eight percent of Boston high school students admitted carrying weapons to school.

Another study for the Boston Safe Schools Commission surveyed a representative sample of 874 Boston public school teachers and found that half of them had been victimized at least once on school property during the previous year; 11.6% had been victimized five or more times.[22] One out of three Boston teachers (32%) claimed to be afraid or extremely

afraid while at school. Theft and vandalism were considered to be very widespread by 19% of the teachers, and 12% said that drug use was very widespread.

For the 1982-83 school year, the Los Angeles Unified School District reported 13,154 violations of the law (down 4% from the year before) and property losses totaling $5,824,784 (down 11% from the year before).[23]

Nationally, the 1983 NEA teacher poll reported that during the preceding school year 28% of all teachers had personal property stolen or damaged at school. During the same period, 4.2% had been attacked by students.

To repeat an important point, crime statistics are the best available data, but they represent only part of the problem. Noncriminal misbehavior probably has a far more serious negative impact on the educational process. In the 1983 NEA teacher poll, very few teachers (less than 10%) reported *no* deleterious effects on their teaching from student misbehavior. By contrast, 14.5% reported that misbehavior interfered with their ability to teach to a great extent, 30.4% reported moderate problems, and 46% reported interference to a small extent.

In Boston, 28% of the teachers thought discipline was a very severe or an extremely severe problem in their schools; this figure includes 17% of elementary teachers and 36% of middle school teachers.[24] Thirty percent of the Boston teachers thought that persistent disruption of classes was very widespread, and 23% said that verbal abuse was very widespread. Elementary and high school teachers classified 8% of their students as severe discipline problems, while middle school teachers reported that 15% of their students were severe discipline problems. More than half of the teachers (53%) disagreed or strongly disagreed with the statement that "student troublemakers are kept in line."

From this brief rundown of studies that can be used to update the findings of the Safe School Study, we can conclude that lack of discipline continues to be a

serious problem in U.S. schools. Even if there has been some modest improvement since 1976, the current level of discipline problems — especially the level of disruptive behavior in the classroom — is a major problem for public education.

LEARNING IS THE MOST IMPORTANT VICTIM

From an educational perspective, the most important victim of student misbehavior is learning. Students in a drunken or drugged stupor cannot learn. Fighting students cannot learn. Students playing tag or being generally boisterous in the classroom cannot learn. Imagine what happens to the time spent on learning tasks when teachers spend between 30% and 80% of their time addressing discipline problems.[25]

In most cases, the educational consequences of student misbehavior go beyond the effects on the individual misbehaving student. When a third-grade teacher has to interrupt a reading lesson to stop an impromptu game of tag involving only two students, the education of the entire class suffers. When teacher burnout resulting from the stress of coping with ill-mannered students reduces a teacher's classroom effectiveness or drives a good teacher out of teaching, every one of that teacher's students suffers. When crime and violence create an atmosphere of fear and hostility at school, the efficiency of the education of all students is impaired. Teachers who function as baby sitters or police officers are not teaching. Students whose teachers do not teach cannot learn.

In the study of Boston teachers, teachers were asked their opinion of students. Teachers who had been victims of violence were much more likely than nonvictims to have negative attitudes toward *all* students in their classrooms. Victimized teachers were more likely to think that their students had severe behavior problems, were underachievers, or had minor behavior problems. Victimized teachers thought their students were less interested in school, less likely to have high ability,

Table 4. Percentage of Students Inclined Toward Unethical Behavior, by Victimization by School Crime

If You Could Get Away with It, Would You:	Attack		Robbery	
	Victims	Nonvictims	Victims	Nonvictims
Cheat on a test?	23	19	25	19
Spray-paint school walls?	10	4	11	4
Take money from other students?	9	4	9	4
Skip school?	28	24	27	24

Source: National Institute of Education, *Violent Schools, Safe Schools: The Safe School Study Report to the Congress, Vol. 1* (Washington, D.C.: NIE, 1978).

and more likely to have low ability. The research literature has demonstrated that teachers' expectations of students are related to students' performance. Therefore, victimizing a teacher may indirectly affect the learning of all of that teacher's students.

Children also learn from the misbehavior of others. They learn that authority cannot or will not protect them. They learn to be afraid of school. They learn that adults fear children. They learn that crime does indeed pay, as every day they see other students who rob, steal, talk back, fight, or refuse to do homework — yet are not punished. In such a climate, it should not be surprising that ethical standards of students suffer. The Safe School Study showed that victims of attacks or robberies in high schools were more inclined toward unethical behavior than were nonvictims (Table 4).

THE SCHOOLS' RESPONSE

The data reviewed above and the continuing public concern over school discipline suggest that the response of the schools to the discipline problem has been inadequate. This conclusion is supported by other data. For example, in the 1982 NEA teacher poll, three out of five teachers who had been physically attacked by students felt that the response of school officials was inadequate. In almost half of the cases, no significant disciplinary action was taken.

In addition to surveying students and teachers to determine the actual incidence of crime in schools, the Safe School Study also asked principals about the existence of crime in the schools. The contrast between the views of students and teachers and the views of principals is sobering. While teachers and students reported being victims of more than three million crimes a month, 75% of the principals claimed that crime was either not a problem or only a small problem in their schools. Principals acknowledged only 157,000 crimes and said that two-thirds of these were never reported to the police. In Boston, 57% of the teachers disagreed or strongly disagreed that their principals were effective disciplinarians, 53% disagreed or strongly disagreed that student troublemakers were kept in line, and 43% felt that the school board was not at all responsive to teachers' concerns about their safety. Among elementary school teachers, 59% thought that suspensions were not used often enough.[26]

When students who commit *criminal* acts go unpunished, the merely unruly or disorderly students know that they have even less to fear. School administrators should pay heed to the National PTA's recommendation: "Students should be

punished by the law when they are involved in assaults or violence."[27]

Why are school officials so reluctant to face the discipline problem? First, principals may be motivated to ignore or play down the problem out of fear of appearing incompetent and unable to control their schools. Before the problem can be solved, however, school officials must admit that it exists.

Second, many schools have failed to establish even minimal procedures for dealing with the discipline problem. In many cases, school officials do not know what is happening. Corrective action cannot begin until school officials know the extent and nature of the problem.

Third, many disciplinary actions are ineffective because they are inappropriate. For example, in one school, 45% of all suspensions were for tardiness or skipping classes. It seems obvious that suspending a student who has clearly indicated that he or she does not wish to attend school is more a reward than a punishment. In such cases, a Saturday detention might be more effective than a three-day suspension. Take another example. Many schools still use corporal punishment, though some research indicates that corporal punishment is relatively ineffective.[28] Schools must find more creative solutions to the discipline problem.

Fourth, a number of recent court decisions may have had a chilling effect on the willingness of school officials to enforce disciplinary standards.[29] It is not clear from the literature whether or not school officials have actually been hampered in their enforcement efforts by the actions of the courts or whether some school officials fail to act because they believe the courts have blocked them from acting. In any case, too many of them fail to act.

Fifth, laws and regulations have unintended consequences. To some degree, laws restricting the age at which students can leave school only exacerbate the problem of school discipline. Young people who are kept in school against their will probably create more discipline problems than other students. The U.S. Office for Civil Rights collects information on suspensions and expulsions and analyzes it for patterns of discrimination. Requiring disciplinary actions to be reported may also discourage school officials from taking action against misbehaving minority students (whose victims are also likely to be minority students). As a result, minority students may inadvertently become the victims of violation of their right to a safe school.

The American Association of School Administrators listed the following reasons for administrators and teachers to be reluctant to report crimes in school.[30] The list for administrators includes:

- to avoid bad publicity;
- to avoid blame;
- to avoid litigation;
- because they find some offenses too trivial to report;
- because they prefer to take care of the problems themselves;
- because they suspect that the police and the courts will not work with them; and
- to avoid appearing ineffective.

The list for teachers includes:
- to avoid blame;
- to avoid legal action;
- from fear of retaliation;
- because they are not sure who was to blame; and
- to avoid stigmatizing young people as criminals.

School crime and disorder pose major challenges to America's schools. An effective school system must maintain a level of civil behavior sufficient to allow learning to take place. The available evidence, though not complete, suggests that in far too many of our schools uncivil and even criminal behavior disrupts the learning process.

Although many schools have taken steps to improve their disciplinary climate, one continuing cause of the persistence of discipline problems remains: the failure of many educators and administrators to face the problem squarely, to recognize its importance, and to take steps to improve conditions in the schools.

1. Michael Rutter et al., *Fifteen Thousand Hours: Secondary Schools and Their Effects on Children* (Cambridge, Mass.: Harvard University Press, 1979).
2. Thomas DiPrete, Chandra Muller, and Nora Shaeffer, *Discipline and Order in American High Schools* (Washington, D.C.: National Center for Education Statistics, 1981).
3. M. T. Schmidt and L. D. Hankoff, "Adolescent Alcohol Abuse and Its Prevention," *Public Health Review*, vol. 8, 1979, pp. 107-53.
4. T. Bradley, "High School Drinking Habits Among Illinois Students," *Journal of Alcohol and Drug Abuse Education*, vol. 28, 1982, pp. 59-65.
5. National Institute of Education, *Violent Schools, Safe Schools: The Safe School Study Report to the Congress, Vol. 1* (Washington, D.C.: NIE, 1978).
6. Michael Lalli and Leonard D. Savitz, "The Fear of Crime in the School Enterprise and Its Consequences," *Education and Urban Society*, vol. 8, 1976.
7. Dade County Public Schools, *Experiences of Teachers and Students with Disruptive Behavior in the Dade Public Schools* (Miami, Fla.: Dade County Public Schools, 1976).
8. Ivor Wayne and Robert J. Rubel, "Student Fear in Secondary Schools," *Urban Review*, vol. 14, 1982, pp. 197-237.
9. George H. Gallup, "The 14th Annual Gallup Poll of the Public's Attitudes Toward the Public Schools," *Phi Delta Kappan*, September 1982, pp. 37-50.
10. Ernest P. Noble, ed., *Third Special Report to the U.S. Congress on Alcohol and Health* (Rockville, Md.: National Institute of Alcohol Abuse and Alcoholism, 1978).
11. Fred Feitler and Edward Tokar, "Getting a Handle on Teacher Stress," *Educational Leadership*, March 1982, pp. 456-57.

5. DISCIPLINE PROBLEMS IN THE SCHOOLS

12. R. C. Newell, "Learning to Survive in the Classroom," *American Teacher*, February 1981.

13. Alfred M. Bloch, "Combat Neurosis in Inner-City Schools," *American Journal of Psychiatry*, vol. 135, 1978, pp. 1189-92; and Alfred M. Bloch and Ruth Bloch, "Teachers: A New Endangered Species," in Robert Rubel and Keith Baker, eds., *Violence and Crime in Schools* (Lexington, Mass.: D. C. Heath, 1980), pp. 81-90.

14. "Readers Report on the Tragedy of Burnout," *Learning*, April 1979, pp. 76-77.

15. National Education Association, *Teacher Opinion Poll* (Washington, D.C.: NEA, 1980, 1982, 1983).

16. James McPartland and Edward McDill, eds., *Violence in Schools* (Lexington, Mass.: D. C. Heath, 1977).

17. Oliver C. Moles, "Trends in Interpersonal Crimes in Schools," paper presented at the annual meeting of the American Educational Research Association, Montreal, April 1983.

18. Glen Macnow, "Violence Casts Pall over Teachers' Lives," *Detroit Free Press*, 19 September 1983, p. 1-A.

19. Kimberly Sawyer, "The Right to Safe Schools: A Newly Recognized Inalienable Right," *Pacific Law Journal*, vol. 14, 1983, pp. 1309-41.

20. National School Boards Association, *Toward Better and Safer Schools* (Alexandria, Va.: NSBA, 1984).

21. James S. Fox, *Violence, Victimization, and Discipline in Four Boston Public High Schools* (Boston: Safe Schools Commission, 1983).

22. Karen S. Seashore, *Boston Teachers' Views About Problems of Violence and Discipline in the Public Schools* (Boston: Safe Schools Commission, 1983).

23. Los Angeles Unified School District, *Statistical Digest (1982-83)* (Los Angeles: Office of Administrative Services, Security Section, n.d.).

24. Seashore, *Boston Teachers' Views.* . . .

25. Debbie Walsh, quoted in, "Our Schools Come to Order," *American Teacher*, November 1983, p. 14.

26. Seashore, *Boston Teachers' Views.* . . .

27. McPartland and McDill, *Violence in Schools*, p. 104.

28. J. H. Meier, "Corporal Punishment in the Schools," *Childhood Education*, vol. 58, 1982, pp. 235-37; and Irwin A. Hyman et al., "Discipline in the High School: Organizational Factors and Roles for the School Psychologist," *School Psychology Review*, vol. 11, 1982, pp. 409-16.

29. Julius Menacker, "The Supreme Court Smorgasbord of Educational Policy Choices," *Planning and Changing*, vol. 13, 1982, pp. 92-103; William Hazard, "Court Intervention in Pupil Discipline," *American Behavioral Scientist*, vol. 23, 1979, pp. 169-205; Edward A. Wynne, "What Are the Courts Doing to Our Children?," *Public Interest*, Summer 1981, pp. 3-18; and Larry Eberlein, "The Teacher in the Courtroom: New Role Expectations?," *Clearing House*, vol. 53, 1980, pp. 287-91.

30. American Association of School Administrators, *Reporting: Violence, Vandalism, and Other Incidents in Schools* (Arlington, Va.: AASA, 1981).

Good, Old-Fashioned Discipline: The Politics Of Punitiveness

Irwin A. Hyman and John D'Alessandro

IRWIN A. HYMAN (Temple University Chapter) is director of the National Center for the Study of Corporal Punishment and Alternatives in the Schools and a professor of school psychology at Temple University, Philadelphia, where JOHN D'ALESSANDRO is a doctoral student in school psychology. This article is based in part on Congressional testimony given by the authors.

Millions of schoolchildren each year are subjected to physical punishment, suspension, and expulsion. The authors call for an end to outmoded notions of the desirability of corporal punishment as a primary pedagogical strategy.

Illustration by Mark Braught

IN THE ANNUAL Gallup Poll of the Public's Attitudes Toward the Public Schools, respondents consistently rank discipline as the major problem plaguing U.S. education. The attention given by the mass media to this finding each year is a mixed blessing, illuminating

From *Phi Delta Kappan*, September 1984, pp. 39-45. Reprinted by permission of the authors and Phi Delta Kappan.

5. DISCIPLINE PROBLEMS IN THE SCHOOLS

a national concern but also engendering a harmful overreaction. Politicians, the media, and special interest groups — all of whom benefit from the myth that U.S. schools are in chaos — foster a "get tough" response. Thus encouraged, the public calls on school leaders and legislators to resolve the discipline problem with a haste that precludes careful planning, execution, and evaluation of potential solutions. Indeed, as Robert Rubel has noted, "school systems across the country find themselves attempting to respond in rational ways to irrational stimuli."[1]

Violence and lack of discipline are both historical and contemporary realities in the schools. But the sensational treatment of these problems in the media today encourages continual political warfare between liberals and conservatives over issues of freedom and control. In other words, the political struggles over school discipline spring from ideological differences (which, in turn, tend to foster inaccurate assessments of the nature and extent of the problem).

The Reagan Administration has established school discipline as a major campaign issue. In March 1984 the Administration also established (through a noncompetitive grant) a National School Safety Center, designed to orchestrate and promote an avowedly right-wing approach to school discipline. We intend in this article to critically analyze the Administration's policies with regard to discipline in the schools. We will attempt to present a rational, data-based view of this highly politicized issue, but in some instances we will have to fight fire with fire and engage in political rhetoric.

THE BAUER REPORT

The current focus on discipline in the schools began on 8 December 1983 when President Reagan, speaking in Indianapolis, suggested that we solve the problems of U.S. education, without spending more money, simply by a return to "good, old-fashioned discipline." His comment, and a barrage of later press releases and speeches, took their substance from a report issued by the Working Group on School Violence/Discipline of Reagan's Cabinet Council on Human Resources. The report originally bore the title, "Chaos in the Classroom: Enemy of American Education," an indication of its general tenor. The unsigned report is generally credited to Gary Bauer, deputy undersecretary of education, who has been its chief spokesperson.

The Bauer Report suggests that problems of discipline really began when students gained the protection of due process against arbitrary actions by school officials. The report asserts that the exten-

A realistic assessment of available data indicates that the hands of school administrators are not tied by due process.

sion of constitutional rights to students has tied the hands of school administrators who must deal with troublemakers — and has thereby increased substantially the number of episodes of classroom disruption and violence. To rectify the current imbalance in power between school officials and students, the report proposes that the Department of Justice file friend-of-the-court briefs to increase the authority of administrators and teachers and to discourage the filing of suits related to discipline.

However, a realistic assessment of available data indicates that the hands of school administrators are *not* tied by due process or by other constitutional considerations. Indeed, it is difficult to reconcile the image of powerless school administrators that the Bauer Report projects with the number of suspensions, expulsions, and pushouts that take place in U.S. schools each year. Education Department figures show that only 72.8% of all students who started high school with the class of 1982 actually graduated; by contrast, 77.2% of the class of 1972 received diplomas. In inner-city high schools, the figures are more dramatic. For example, most inner-city high schools in New Jersey lose more than half of each class prior to graduation.

Meanwhile, the Bauer Report attempts to elicit support for its position from minority groups by pointing out that minority students are most often the victims of school violence. Although this is true, minority students are also punished by school officials more frequently and more severely than white students. In a study of 56 schools, for example, Gary Gottfredson found that 31% of black males had been suspended at least once during the term just past — a rate double that of white males. Black males also received corporal punishment far more often than their white counterparts.[2]

The Bauer Report is a series of disjointed statements, skewed statistics, and questionable assumptions that clearly reflect right-wing ideology. The conclu-

sions of the document mislead the uninformed reader, who could hardly be expected to guess the next step in the Administration's hidden agenda: the establishment of a national center. Before exploring the real purpose of the Bauer Report, however, let us turn to the statistics around which the ideological battle lines are drawn.

THE DATA ON SCHOOL CRIME

Valid interpretation of the data on school crime is difficult. All crime is underreported for a variety of reasons, which range from lack of faith in the system to fear of spiraling insurance premiums. Hence, any change in the procedures for reporting a crime will be accompanied by a corresponding change — which may be more apparent than real — in the number of reported offenses. Thus an increase in school crime can be validly inferred only if the reporting procedures have been held constant.

The Bauer Report fails to take methodological changes into account. For example, the report cites a National Education Association (NEA) poll that shows a 53% increase in the number of incidents of school violence directed at teachers between 1977 and 1983. But the NEA revised its poll questions twice during that interval to make them more inclusive. These revisions make it impossible to determine whether violence directed against teachers actually increased — or perhaps even decreased — between 1977 and 1983.

The establishment of security offices in many schools, a movement that began in earnest during the late Sixties, may likewise have stepped up the reporting of school crimes. There are two reasons for this. First, heavy-handed security measures tend to provoke, rather than to deter, certain kinds of crimes.[3] Second, security officers have a vested interest in reporting crimes, the raison d'être for their jobs. By contrast, school principals, who had typically been responsible for the reporting of school crimes prior to the creation of the security offices, have a vested interest in drawing attention away from the extent of such problems in their buildings.

Valid comparisons of school violence from one year to another are further hampered by the vagaries of classifying offenses. In preparation for testifying before Congress, we examined the records of 40 reported assaults on teachers in an urban school district. These incidents, considered the 40 most serious by district officials, ranged from throwing candy at a teacher to a bona fide physical attack. The difficulty of extracting valid meaning from such data highlights our concern about the Bauer Report, which draws conclusions regarding crime rates over time. In actuality, crime rates may vary in a district simply because of a change in a school's chief disciplinarian; differing definitions of offenses can also cause crime rates to fluctuate across districts.

Interpreting the data on school crime is also hampered by other problems. It is incorrect to assume, for example, that offenders and victims form mutually exclusive groups. Nor can school crime be understood in isolation from the neighborhoods in which it occurs.[4] *The Safe School Study* stressed that a community's crime rate — which correlates strongly with its rates of unemployment, family disruption, and poverty — best predicts the level of school violence in that community. Secretary of Education Terrel Bell supports this position, although Undersecretary Bauer has contradicted it, claiming that poverty is no excuse for misbehavior.

Conventional wisdom holds that students commit most of the violent acts in the schools, but one study challenges even that basic assumption. Using data from the 1974-75 National Crime Survey, Jackson Toby found that most violent crimes in the schools had been committed by intruders. For example, he estimated that 100% of teacher rapes and 94% of student rapes in the 26 cities included in that survey were committed by "stranger intruders."[5] A return to "good, old-fashioned discipline" would do little to reduce the problem of intruders in the schools.

Given the complexity of the problem of school crime and the difficulties of interpreting the data, what can be validly deduced? From an analysis of the research on school crime, Oliver Moles, a staff member with the National Institute of Education, concluded that the data contradict the popular notion that school crime is progressively increasing.[6] Most other researchers who have studied school crime have echoed his opinion.[7]

Meanwhile, how has the Reagan Administration recommended that we solve the complex problem of school crime? Through "good, old-fashioned discipline." This remedy evokes an earlier time when schools were invariably peaceful and children unquestioningly obeyed teachers and other authorities — a utopia that never existed.

GOOD, OLD-FASHIONED DISCIPLINE

An extensive review of U.S. history shows colonial schools to have been coercive and repressive. Children were taught by repetitive drill, and corporal punishment was the primary method of discipline. Nor were the students alone in finding their schools oppressive; newspapers carried numerous advertisements between 1750 and 1770 that offered rewards for the

"**G**ood, old-fashioned discipline" was bad for both teachers and students in the good old days, and it remains so today.

location and return of runaway teachers.[8] The literature of this period contains few allusions to serious violence by students — perhaps because so many youngsters were excluded from schooling altogether.

As education became more widespread in the 19th century, so did school violence. The schools of that time were still woefully inadequate with regard to physical facilities, teaching methods, and disciplinary practices. Rote drill continued to be the most common teaching method; the schools were also characterized by strict adherence to rigid rules and by training for reflexive obedience through the pervasive use of corporal punishment.

"Good, old-fashioned discipline" was bad for both teachers and students in the good old days, and it remains so today. Moreover, despite President Reagan's contentions to the contrary, "good, old-fashioned discipline" is alive and well in contemporary American classrooms. Millions of schoolchildren each year are subjected to physical punishment, suspension, or expulsion.

An ongoing series of studies by the National Center for the Study of Corporal Punishment and Alternatives in the Schools (NCSCPAS) reveals that large numbers of American students are regularly paddled — especially in the Southeast, where corporal punishment is strongly defended.[9] The national press has covered incidents in which students have been struck with such items as doubled-over belts, lacrosse sticks, jai alai sticks, baseball bats, arrows, electrical cords, bamboo rods, rubber hoses, hammers, and wooden drawer dividers. Some teachers have used cattle prods and similar devices to administer electric shocks to children. Other youngsters have been kicked, choked, or punched — forced to eat cigarettes or to have their faces smeared with hot sauce. One Chicago principal used a pocketknife to drill a hole in a pupil's fingernail.

Such extreme incidents are rare, but they reveal this society's acceptance of

pain as a legitimate pedagogical technique. Indeed, teachers and administrators have frequently been exonerated of abusive actions toward schoolchildren that would have been judged illegal had these educators used the same approaches to discipline their own children. Meanwhile, research has shown that oppressive responses to students' disruptive behaviors scarcely ever yield effective solutions.[10] Yet the Reagan Administration seems resolutely committed to a philosophy of punitiveness.

The President himself commended Joseph Clark, a New Jersey high school principal who expelled 10% of his students during his first week on the job. Other politicians and reporters for the media quickly joined Reagan in making Clark a folk hero. Yet Clark's tenure as principal has been marked by a strict approach to discipline that has yielded a 50% dropout/pushout rate. On "The Phil Donahue Show," Clark credited his techniques with doubling the minimum competency test scores of his 3,000 students in just six months. He also asserted that schools are no places for thugs, punks, and hooligans.

Clark's public utterances strike a responsive chord with the American public. But what happens to the 50% of Clark's students who have dropped out or been pushed out of school between grades 8 and 12 in an urban community with high youth unemployment? Has his repressive approach to discipline solved the problem or merely made it worse? We deplore the endorsement of this kind of solution.

DISCIPLINE IN A DEMOCRACY

Americans tend to turn reflexively to punishment as a solution for behavioral problems. Indeed, most Americans view *punishment* and *discipline* as synonymous.

But discipline in a democracy should spring from internal controls, not from fear of punishment. Effective disciplinary techniques in a democracy also incorporate respect for the rights of individuals. In schools that use such disciplinary techniques, the students perceive their teachers and administrators as fair and just. Successful approaches to discipline in the schools enhance individuals' self-esteem and encourage cooperation. Although necessary at times, punishment in such schools is used rationally — not merely to humiliate and alienate students. To establish an effective disciplinary program, school officials must first understand the motives for student misbehavior.

Our statements above suggest that successful disciplinary programs bring the *process* of democracy into the schools.

Unfortunately, however, too many people confuse democracy in education with permissiveness. This misunderstanding gives critics an easy label with which to attack those who propose such an approach to discipline.

Neither educators nor the lay public can examine the issues of discipline and punishment objectively. Discipline is something we have all experienced from birth. It comes from parents, religious leaders, teachers, employers, and, increasingly, from community and governmental agencies. No wonder we have difficulty being objective. Yet recent research reveals that our own disciplinary practices depend more on the manner in which we ourselves were disciplined as children than on any other consideration.[11]

In addition, disciplinary practices are slow to change because of ignorance of the causes of student misbehavior. Disciplinary problems in a school can be caused by many things, among them: 1) inadequate parenting, 2) ineffective teacher training, 3) poor school organization, 4) inadequate administrative leadership, 5) inappropriate curricula, 6) the overuse of suspensions and other punishments, 7) inborn traits of individual students (such as neurological impairments) that may interact with certain environments to cause severe behavioral or learning disorders, 8) poor self-esteem and frustration with learning, 9) overexposure to violence through television and the other mass media, 10) racism, 11) lack of employment opportunities, 12) peer pressures, 13) overcrowding, and 14) specific social, political, and bureaucratic factors that ignore the needs of the young.

PROMOTING EFFECTIVE DISCIPLINE

There are many remedies to disciplinary problems, and no single approach will be universally successful. But our handling of disciplinary problems in the schools can be improved in many ways. As we proceed with this effort, here are a few things that we ought to consider.

Improving the data base. To make the research on discipline more useful, we must establish clear descriptions of misbehavior and of punishment. For example, NCSCPAS staff members are currently developing a school-based, computerized, uniform reporting system,[12] from which administrators and teachers can retrieve data on given children, teachers, types of offenses, and so on. This system, which provides important feedback, can be used to monitor and redirect efforts aimed at the prevention of disciplinary problems.

Improving schools. The best way to improve school discipline is to improve school climate. However, many facets of school climate are easily measured but

> **R**esearch shows that school vandalism is dramatically reduced when students view their schools positively as places of learning.

hard to change. To be effective, improvement efforts require the support, understanding, and commitment of the school board, the district administrators, the building administrators, the teaching staff, and the support staff.

Improving school staffs. Few U.S. educators have received formal training in the theory, research, and practice of school discipline. The vast majority of U.S. educators will require inservice training to help them link theory and practice effectively.

Our approach to such training assumes that teachers have differing predispositions toward discipline and that, for many reasons, children respond differently to any given disciplinary technique.[13] This training approach also assumes that teachers will change when they discern a discrepancy between how they believe they should handle discipline and how they actually do handle it. To make participating teachers aware of such discrepancies, outside observers pay a series of visits to their classrooms. The teachers also complete questionnaires and consent to have videotapes made of their teaching. Group work with other teachers, consultations with school psychologists, self-exploration activities, and the reading of selected resource materials also encourage teacher participants to change their disciplinary methods.

Systemwide change is difficult, but individual principals have great latitude. *The Safe School Study* clearly indicates that building administrators set the disciplinary tone for their schools.[14] Moreover, effective administrators do not espouse "good, old-fashioned discipline." Indeed, most data indicate that punitive administrators merely cause students to suppress their anger and hostility until the inevitable moment when it erupts against people and property. Research also shows that school vandalism is dramatically reduced when students view their schools positively as places of learning. By fostering an appropriate climate for learning, each principal has the power to help his or her students view their school in this light.

In recent years, many administrators have turned instead to discipline codes, although there is scanty empirical evidence that such devices are effective over time. Dolores Lally, in what appears to be the first data-based study of discipline codes, found that disciplinarians most frequently evaluated their schools' codes as effective if they had played a major role in developing them.[15] Although discipline codes may be helpful, they are not panaceas. Too often administrators use them rigidly, without regard for extenuating circumstances. We need more research to identify the strengths and weaknesses of such codes.

We do know that most of the principals who seek consultations on discipline are individuals who are willing to experiment with new ideas. Unfortunately, it is much harder to convince many other principals and teachers of the need for positive approaches to discipline.

Improving teacher training. Staff members at the NCSCPAS have conducted exhaustive studies of programs for training teachers to discipline their students effectively.[16] The approaches they have examined have included behavior modification, transactional analysis, reality therapy, teacher effectiveness training, social literacy, Adlerian approaches, and training in human relations. In addition to analyzing each program separately, the NCSCPAS staff members looked for common features.

Their analyses showed that most of the training programs focus on seven general techniques with which teachers can motivate students and deal with disciplinary problems: 1) providing feedback to students about their behaviors, feelings, and ideas; 2) using diagnostic strategies to better understand students and student/teacher interactions; 3) modifying the classroom climate; 4) applying techniques of behavior modification; 5) using democratic procedures for solving classroom problems; 6) expressing emotions appropriately; and 7) using therapeutic approaches to behavioral problems. Other research by NCSCPAS suggests a need for more individualization in the training of teachers.

Other considerations. In addition to the general remedies we have just discussed, educators can employ a number of specific measures to improve school discipline. Prevention is a prime example. At first glance, prevention seems expensive and difficult to implement, but it is cost-effective in the long run. For example, potential delinquents who are identified early and whose families receive appropriate counseling cost society less than their counterparts who actually become delinquents.

Other effective strategies to promote

good discipline include well-planned alternative school programs, in-school suspensions (though inadequate funding often makes this tactic more punishing for teachers than for students), and automatic calling machines that relay recorded messages to parents of truant children. Time-out is a helpful punishment technique, if it is not overused. In cases of theft or vandalism, schools have used restitution programs successfully. Peer and cross-age counseling have proven helpful to youngsters with behavioral problems. Special after-school programs have benefited latchkey children. (Indeed, after-school recreation programs and other youth activities are simple but effective ways to structure the leisure time of *all* children.) Some schools have found that they need well-trained security personnel and judicious safety measures. Last but not least, caring, enthusiastic, and masterful teachers go a long way toward preventing serious discipline problems from arising in the first place.

THE POINTS we have made above, and other research data as well, have been systematically distorted, inadequately presented, or totally ignored by the Reagan Administration. The Bauer Report and the call for "good, old-fashioned discipline" appear to have been intended solely to woo votes from alarmed citizens, to curry favor with teachers and administrators who favor a get-tough stance, and to set the scene for the establishment of the National School Safety Center.

Despite President Reagan's rhetoric against the use of federal funds to improve discipline in U.S. schools, his Administration awarded a noncompetitive grant of $4.5 million to Pepperdine University in March 1984 to create the National School Safety Center. The Democrats were quick to attack this move. The 23 May 1984 issue of *Education Week* listed some of the concerns of Democratic members of the House and Senate subcommittees. These included: 1) suspicions of political patronage, because of the long and friendly association of Edwin Meese III and George Nicholson, director of the Center, with Pepperdine University; 2) the lack of consultation with recognized experts on school discipline; 3) the political (rather than educational or scientific) orientation of the Center staff; and 4) the possible use of the Center to undermine Section 1983 of the Civil Rights Act of 1964.

The source of funding for the Center is another concern. The funding is part of $15.7 million in noncompetitive grants awarded by Alfred Regnery, director of the Office of Juvenile Justice and Delin-

There are many models of effective school discipline from which schools can choose; they should be matched to the needs of schools.

quency Prevention (OJJDP). Regnery, son of ultraconservative publisher Henry Regnery and a frequent seminar presenter with Moral Majority leader Jerry Falwell, believes that the OJJDP has focused too much effort on prevention and rehabilitation.[17] His views on this matter are under attack by most professionals in the field.

Meanwhile, the Human Resources Subcommittee of the House Education and Labor Committee has reported the existence of a secret Justice Department memorandum alluding to the Civil Rights Act of 1964. Informed sources report that the memorandum — written by Roger Clegg, assistant attorney general for legal policy — suggests that the emphasis of the Center on safer schools could be used to undermine Section 1983 of the Civil Rights Act, which enables students and parents to sue school officials for civil rights violations. The implications are chilling, since the Civil Rights Act is much broader. Repeal or weakening of this Act would deny the right it provides for *any* citizen to sue *any* public official for a civil rights violation.

From the Bauer Report and from the stance of most of those individuals who have been involved in funding and staffing the Center, it appears that the Center will focus on injecting right-wing ideology into the schools. This would be a clear reversal of the trend in the Seventies to increase the constitutional rights of students, especially the right of due process in cases involving discipline. The following information regarding the establishment of the Center supports this contention.[18]

• Pepperdine University is widely perceived as a conservative liberal arts college with a "Christian" orientation. It offers no programs in juvenile justice and has on its faculty no recognized experts on school discipline or school safety.

• Pepperdine does not usually seek federal funds and has never overseen a federal research project. In fact, Nicholson asked Pepperdine to accept the Center grant so that he could organize the Center

300 miles away, in Sacramento, where he and many of his staff members live.

• President Reagan and Meese, a long-time political ally of Nicholson, are both annual contributors to the university of at least $1,000.

• Bill Treanor, executive director of the National Youth Work Alliance, testified during a Senate hearing in March 1984 that the Justice Department had discontinued the National School Resource Network, an organization serving essentially the same function as the new Center. Treanor called the whole affair "a rip-off."

• A. L. Carlisle, who heads the National Steering Committee of State Juvenile Justice Advisory Groups, publicly stated that she had never heard of George Nicholson before his appointment as Center director. She also stated that the National School Safety Center is unnecessary and that the money could have been better spent to fully fund the apparently successful projects on the prevention of school violence that were cut off when Regnery became administrator of the OJJDP.

• Many fear that any potential contributions of the Center will be compromised by the fact that Nicholson and his staff lack background in school discipline. Although unknown nationally, Nicholson has had a stormy political career in California. Law enforcement officials identify him with the extreme right because of his "law-and-order" pronouncements as executive director of the California District Attorneys Association. He reinforced this image in his role as deputy district attorney in Alameda County, California, a position previously held by Meese, who later became his close political ally. An audit of the California District Attorneys Association under Nicholson's leadership caused a furor that ended in his return of funds that he claimed to have received through a computer error and that he had used to cover personal expenses. The association also returned a substantial additional sum to the state after Nicholson left his position as executive director. During his three years with the California Justice Department, Nicholson overspent his budget by approximately 100%. When he ran for the post of state attorney general, his past indiscretions were well-publicized. These included the improper use of official state stationery and facilities to promote conservative political causes. Nicholson's flamboyance and zeal earned him only weak support from some elements of the conservative establishment, which probably contributed to his election loss. His image was not enhanced when the California Bar Association frustrated his bid for a judgeship by rating him unqualified.

5. DISCIPLINE PROBLEMS IN THE SCHOOLS

THE STRIDENCY of our attack on the Center, its political context, and its director may seem one-sided. However, in our opinion, the infusion of an extreme political ideology into an area of education that sorely needs objectivity justifies this kind of response. Educators and educational researchers can choose to ignore a bad situation or to enter the political fray. We believe that entering the fray is crucial when educational issues are taken out of the realm of reason.

The awarding of a large, noncompetitive grant to fund the Center was clearly a mistake. There are many other approaches to improving school discipline. For example, the expanding knowledge base requires rational examination and translation into practice. We already know of many models of effective school discipline from which schools can choose.[19] Optimally, these models should be matched to the needs of specific schools; thus we should develop guidelines to help individual schools evaluate the models and select appropriate ones. Moreover, as communities and schools change, so must our approaches to discipline change.

Meanwhile, we should develop a national pool of experts on discipline, who will train at least one staff member in each participating school. For such training, we suggest that the schools choose teams that include both a high-level administrator with organizational clout and a school psychologist, social worker, or counselor who understands the developmental, social, and emotional facets of misbehavior.

Most important, we can improve discipline in the schools by improving the general quality of education. This approach will not be cheap. But we believe that it will prove less expensive than dealing with citizens who have been pushed out of an inflexible educational system to become unemployable adults.

We exhort the Reagan Administration and other policy makers to reflect objectively on what we already know about discipline. From such reflection will surely come a disavowal of outmoded notions about the desirability of punishment as a primary pedagogical strategy.

We can improve discipline in the schools by improving the general quality of education. This approach will not be cheap.

1. Robert Rubel, *The Unruly School* (Lexington, Mass.: Lexington Books, 1977), p. 10.
2. Gary Gottfredson, "School Discipline," testimony before the Subcommittee on Elementary, Secondary, and Vocational Education of the Committee on Education and Labor, U.S. House of Representatives, 23 January 1984.
3. G. Roy Mayer, Tom Butterworth, Mary Nafpaktitis, and Beth Sulzer-Azaroff, "Preventing School Vandalism and Improving Discipline: A Three-Year Study," *Journal of Applied Behavior Analysis*, Winter 1983, pp. 355-69.
4. Joan McDermott, "Crime in the School and in the Community: Offenders, Victims, and Fearful Youths," *Crime and Delinquency*, April 1983, pp. 270-82.
5. Jackson Toby, "Violence in School," in Michael Tonry and Norval Morris, eds., *Crime and Justice: An Annual Review of Research, Vol. 4* (Chicago: University of Chicago Press, 1983).
6. Oliver Moles, *Trends in Interpersonal Crimes in School* (Washington, D.C.: National Institute of Education, 1983).
7. Irwin Hyman and John D'Alessandro, "School Discipline in America," testimony before the Subcommittee on Elementary, Secondary, and Vocational Education of the Committee on Education and Labor, U.S. House of Representatives, 24 January 1984.
8. Joan Newman and Graeme Newman, "Crime and Punishment in the Schooling Process: A Historical Analysis," in Keith Baker and Robert J. Rubel, eds., *Violence and Crime in the Schools* (Lexington, Mass.: D.C. Heath, 1980). See also Ellwood P. Cubberly, *The History of Education* (Boston: Houghton Mifflin, 1920).
9. Jacqueline Clarke, Rebecca Liberman-Lascoe, and Irwin Hyman, "Corporal Punishment in the Schools as Reported in Nationwide Newspapers," *Children and Youth Services*, vol. 4, 1982, pp. 47-56; Jacqueline Clarke, Richard Erdlen, and Irwin Hyman, "Analysis of Recent Corporal Punishment Cases Reported in National Newspapers," paper presented at the annual convention of the National Association of School Psychologists, Philadelphia, 20 April 1984; and Irwin Hyman and James Wise, *Corporal Punishment in American Education* (Philadelphia: Temple University Press, 1979).
10. Daniel Duke, "The Etiology of Student Misbehavior and the Depersonalization of Blame," *Review of Educational Research*, vol. 48, 1978, pp. 415-37; Irwin Hyman and David Bogacki, "Legal and Ethical Issues in the Discipline of Emotionally Disturbed Children," in Marvin Fine, ed., *Systematic Intervention with Emotionally Disturbed Children* (Jamaica, N.Y.: SP Medical & Scientific Books, 1984); Irwin Hyman, Dennis Flanagan, and Kathleen Smith, "Discipline in the Schools," in Cecil Reynolds and Terry Gutkin, eds., *A Handbook for the Practice of School Psychology* (New York: John Wiley & Sons, 1982); Irwin Hyman, "Corporal Punishment: America's Officially Sanctioned Form of Child Abuse," in Gertrude Williams and John Money, eds., *Traumatic Abuse and Neglect of Children at Home* (Baltimore: Johns Hopkins University Press, 1980); idem, "Democracy, Mental Health, and Achievement: A Modern Educational Mythology," *Annual Yearbook* (n.p.: New Jersey Association of Secondary School Teachers, 1970); and idem, "Some Effects of Teaching Style on Pupil Behavior" (Doctoral dissertation, Rutgers University, 1964).
11. Naomi Lennox, "Teachers' Use of Corporal Punishment as a Function of Modeling" (Doctoral dissertation, Temple University, 1983); and Beth Sofer, "Psychologists' Attitudes Toward Corporal Punishment" (Doctoral dissertation, Temple University, 1983).
12. Gary Berkowitz, Irwin Hyman, and Dolores Lally, "The Development of a Schoolwide Computerized Uniform Reporting System," paper presented at the annual convention of the National Association of School Psychologists, Philadelphia, 20 April 1984.
13. Mariann Pokalo and Irwin Hyman, "The Teacher Improvement Model for Organization Development," paper presented at the annual convention of the National Association of School Psychologists, Detroit, 24 March 1983.
14. National Institute of Education, *Violent Schools, Safe Schools: The Safe School Study Report to the Congress, Vol. 1* (Washington, D.C.: U.S. Department of Health, Education, and Welfare, 1977).
15. Dolores Lally, "Administrators' Perceptions of the Effectiveness of Discipline Codes in New Jersey High Schools" (Doctoral dissertation, Temple University, 1982).
16. Irwin Hyman and Dolores Lally, "The Effectiveness of Staff Development Programs to Improve School Discipline," *Urban Review*, vol. 14, 1982, pp. 181-96.
17. See, for example, Susan Cunningham, "Discretionary Justice: The Furor over Juvenile Research Funds," *American Psychological Association Monitor*, July 1984, pp. 1, 14; and Larry Bush, "Fat Grants and Sleazy Politics: Reagan's Porn Paranoia," *Playboy*, August 1984, pp. 51-52.
18. Information on George Nicholson has been obtained, in large part, from a series of newspaper articles in the *Sacramento Bee*, written primarily by Claire Cooper.
19. Numerous models to prevent school violence are described in documents published by such groups as the National Institute of Education, the Justice Department, the Phi Delta Kappa Commission on Discipline, the Center for Social Organization of Schools at Johns Hopkins University, the National Alliance for Safe Schools, and the National Center for the Study of Corporal Punishment and Alternatives in the Schools. ⃞

Discipline Is Not the Problem:
Control Theory in the Classroom

WILLIAM GLASSER

William Glasser, author of Control Therapy in the Classroom *(Harper and Row, New York City), is President, Institute for Reality Therapy, Canoga Park, California.*

$\mathcal{I}$F we want students to be motivated to work hard in school and to follow rules, we must discard the stimulus-response theory of human behavior on which all education is based (the idea that the behavior of all living creatures is their best response to some external event that impinges on them) and turn to a new psychology—control theory, which explains that living people are motivated from within themselves and that what happens outside of us is never the cause of anything we do.

Basic to control theory is the concept that our genes instruct us to attempt to survive, to love and belong, and to struggle for power, fun, and freedom. If what is offered in school is not seen by students as related to one or more of these built-in needs, they will struggle against, and/or withdraw from, any or all of a curriculum that is not satisfying.

Without expanding existing resources, we can use this theory to begin to make some lasting improvements in our schools. We can stop trying to motivate students with externally imposed programs and face the control theory fact that the only thing we can teach them is that working hard and following rules will get them what they want.

If students experience a school program that convinces them that this teaching is valid, they will work hard and follow rules. In practice, all hard-working, disciplined students have managed to learn this whether they have been taught it or not. But, because we do not teach this way, and depend almost totally on reward and punishment which do not work, most students do not learn this vital lesson. Because our society provides no acceptable alternative to school, students, who have nowhere else to go, suffer years of frustration and become in-school dropouts—discouraging to teachers and destructive to themselves.

The only way we can motivate students in schools is to teach them that school is a place where, to a reasonable extent, their basic genetic instructions or needs can be satisfied. It is not difficult to persuade college students that they will be more financially secure with a degree in business. But is it hard to convince tenth-graders they will starve unless they buckle down and learn. To motivate students, schools must concern themselves less with security and survival and more with the ever-pressing psychological needs for friendship, freedom, fun, and power.

Accepting Facts

Lack of discipline is not the problem; the problem is our unwillingness to accept the biologic fact that we cannot be externally motivated to act in the interest of anyone except ourselves. Even when we are altruistic to the point of self-sacrifice, we are satisfying the genetic instruction to love. We may seem to sacrifice ourselves, but we are, in fact, satisfying ourselves at the same time.

We must offer students an education which they can see will satisfy both their immediate and future needs. Because humans have lan-guage, we have a sense of the future and are willing to work now for what we believe will satisfy us later. When we are very young, we do not know what will satisfy us later, but good parents begin to teach us this immediately. When we get to school, good teaching should continue this future-oriented process while not neglecting our need for present satisfaction.

Before any school can begin to make the changes that would make the curriculum congruent with control theory, teachers and administrators need to take the time and effort to learn this new theory and to appreciate how different it is from stimulus-response theory. To learn control theory, you must practice it in your own life. It cannot be learned or used unless you become familiar with it on a daily basis. What you discover as you practice it and discard the nonhuman stimulus-response theory is that you quickly gain greater control of your own life. In particular, you will discover that your important personal relationships improve as you get along better with friends and family.

As this happens, you begin to appreciate its power, and you are motivated to begin to use it in your profession. Control theory must come into a school not as an outside program but from those in the school who have learned it and realize its worth. These people can explain it to others and encourage them to learn it enough to put it to work in their school. Significant progress takes place when a whole faculty of a school begins to get involved.

Any school can provide warmth and human care. To the extent that it does, there are immediate payoffs.

From *The Education Digest*, May 1986, pp. 36-39. Condensed from: Glasser, W. (1985), "Discipline has never been the problem and isn't the problem now." *Theory Into Practice*, 24, 241-246. Copyright 1985 College Education, The Ohio State University.

Warmth and care are done *with* students, not to or for them. They can be made available through any interaction but can also be formalized by giving students opportunities such as classroom discussions to share their ideas with teachers and classmates. If students reject warmth and care, they believe it is not sincere. But if we keep offering it, the power of the genetic instructions will eventually assert itself, and students will make an effort to learn what is offered.

Young people find it most difficult to satisfy their need for power because they do not easily grasp that the subject matter itself is power. Too many schools emphasize grades more than the power inherent in a good education. Students fail to experience the strength that is gained when knowledge is shared and communicated. Rarely is creative thinking, the most powerful of all human behaviors, encouraged in school. Rote learning offers little power unless the student is taught and accepts that some rote is necessary to lay the foundation for thought and creativity. Where rote is valued for itself, students feel frustrated and powerless.

Community Work

Schools should be in close contact with communities so that students can put some of what they learn into practice through school-supervised work, both paid and volunteer. Students should have a chance to work in their community beginning around age 10 and continuing until graduation. It is an intoxicating experience, and even a small amount goes a long way in satisfying the need for power. This need, when frustrated, causes many students to turn to alcohol and other drugs to dull the pain of its frustration.

Even a faculty well aware of the importance of freedom may find itself in the hypocritical position of advocating, in history courses, what students fail to experience in school. Few students want complete freedom; they see it as threatening to their security. The freedom which is most important to us is the freedom to make some choices about what we do. If, as too often happens in school, we are told we don't have a choice, this need is severely frustrated. If schools could figure out a way to give students more choices, most students would not complain about lacking freedom in school.

For example, students could be allowed to choose which teacher they want, what to study, where to sit in class, and what to do on the playground. Since tests are intimidating but necessary, students could be given the chance to take more open-book and take-home tests. They could be given the option of makeup tests on their own time if they are not satisfied with a test result and want to improve their grade. From the standpoint of maintaining order, students asked to offer rules to the administration will obey those rules more.

Since we are inherently competitive—winning is among the most effective ways to satisfy our need for power—more effort should be made toward implementing team competitions in academic areas. This would supplement the athletic, art, drama, and music competitions that are held now. Team competitions are better than individual ones because they put less pressure on any one student, and, when a team loses, the group provides belonging and support. Individual losses can be too frustrating for all but the strongest of young students. Since we live in a teamwork society, this is good preparation for life.

Schools should endeavor to persuade every student to participate on both an academic and a nonacademic team, but no one should be forced. If such activities are need-fulfilling, students will eventually get involved. The need for power is the hardest need for young people to satisfy, and these competitive programs would go a long way toward filling this void.

Rewarding Process

A school that operates by control theory should not (and likely would not) listen to outside suggestions as to what should be done. Teachers who hope to find a cookbook for how to teach successfully will never find it. If control theory becomes part of their lives, they will use it to figure out what they believe will provide satisfying opportunities for their students. It is a rewarding process for both faculty and students to be involved in figuring out how to satisfy the needs of everyone. Teachers as well as students must find school a satisfying place.

I recently had a chance to discuss with a high school faculty the problem of what to do when students deliberately skip class. They were concerned that their "three cuts and you're out" policy was not working well. Excluded students were just wasting their time in what are misnamed "study" halls, at the same time complaining bitterly, "How can I get an education if I am not allowed into class?"

I suggested that any inflexible policy is difficult to work to everyone's satisfaction and that perhaps they might provide a general education course at no credit to replace the dead time of study hall. In it, any teacher or invited community member could teach anything that might be of more value than wasting time in study hall. It could be an ongoing, nongraded, noncredit educational experience. After some period of time, students who applied themselves could petition to get back to the class from which they had been excluded. This would give them some control over their lives. Control theory states that the worst behaviors we see are chosen by people who have lost control.

Control theory is long overdue. If it were applied, students would need fewer special programs, and long-term discipline programs would decline. The spinoffs would include greater teacher satisfaction and greater community involvement and acceptance. If we continue to follow the dead end of stimulus-response psychology and focus on the symptom rather than the cause, our schools will never be significantly better or more "disciplined" than they are now.

Help for the hot-tempered kid

How to encourage children to recognize their boiling points

Michael Petti

Michael Petti is school psychologist for Woodbridge Township, New Jersey's largest suburban school district.

At the water fountain fifth grader Scott punches Carlos in the stomach because Carlos cut in front of his buddy Eric. Meanwhile in the lunchroom third grader Paula screams out a few choice words because the aide reminded her to remain seated while eating.

Temper flare-ups like these occur unexpectedly and at any time at school. Often, teachers are forced to use external control at the time, leaving the lesson—how to control a temper—left unlearned.

There are certain daily strategies that can be used to help students to learn self-control. And if a quick-tempered student, such as Scott, is helped to deal with his anger, it is certainly an important lesson for him as well as his future acquaintances.

Show a child it is possible to change. Some children believe that being a hothead is part of their nature. Take Paula, for instance, who thinks she is "just like Mom" in that they both tend to blow off steam easily. Just as you can convince pupils that they are able to learn, you can convince someone like this child that she can change her explosive behavior. Pep talks and rap sessions are useful tools. In an academic sense,

you probably use this technique all the time. When a student is stuck on a new math concept, you remind him or her that just three weeks earlier, he or she was unable to do one-digit multiplication and now has mastered the technique. Then you tell him or her that in all probability, he or she will be able to do the two-digit multiplication easily three weeks from now. With Paula, you can cite previous examples of her success with self-control: "Paula, I know you can control your temper. Yesterday, you did not explode when James accidentally knocked over your books."

In calm situations remind a pupil, such as Paula, that all people get mad and want to explode with anger. The difference, however, is that they don't. In a quiet and friendly moment with Paula, point out how someone else in the class, perhaps her best friend, Becca, was able to control her temper when she couldn't find her sneakers for gym class. Here, too, you can remind Paula that losing control will not solve the problem. Her friend did not yell or curse because things did not go exactly as planned. Instead, Becca looked under her desk, checked her locker, and finally noticed her sneakers under her book bag. You might ask Paula how long it might have taken Becca to find the lost sneakers if she had wasted her time by flying into a rage.

Discourage pupils from thinking they are Judge Wapner of "People's Court." This strategy applies to Scott, a child quick to correct an injustice. When he thought Carlos cut in front of Eric, he felt justified in punching Carlos for "punishment." You can tell Judge Scott that people who drive cars do not make rash judgments about, or retaliations for, the actions of other drivers. Even if the other driver was obviously wrong, responsible adults don't pull up at the next stoplight and curse him or her out. In a calm atmosphere, explain to Scott that he will always be agitated if he feels he has to correct everyone and everything that he perceives as wrong in this world.

Another student, Jay, needs a little help, too. What starts out as a little discussion about which toy company makes the best transformers turns into a nasty argument. Sensing that he is losing, Jay calls the other student's mother a foul name.

When both students have calmed down, point out to them that they both may be right to a degree. While one toy is more graphic and may be the better of the two artistically, the other toy might convert more easily into a robot, thereby being the better of the two toys mechanically.

Explain that a person can lose a dispute without losing self-respect. Tell Jay that by "going off the wall," he is throwing his self-respect right out the window. Adults and children

do not admire sore losers. Suggest to Jay that he back away from arguments. Explain that some people can never be won over. Throughout the year, you might need to build up his self-esteem by having him be your helper. In this way, he can still feel good about himself, even when he has lost an argument.

The next strategy could apply to George, the boy whom Jay has argued with. *Discourage kids like George from talking down to others.* Some people, such as Jay, may lash out if they are backed into a corner. George can be discouraged from this behavior through role reversal. Through the use of play or a puppet show, you can imitate his one-upmanship and let him take the part of the student being talked down to. George will then have an idea of how his remarks make others feel.

Try to get a student to understand someone else's feelings. For instance, Jane yells at her peers when they do not play exactly by her rules. Pretend to be Jane playing a game with another student. Every time she makes a mistake in the game, complain and say that she's doing it all wrong. Afterwards, ask her how she feels about

---

> ## "Some kids think of themselves as Judge Wapner. They're quick to punish perceived injustices."

---

being picked on. Then explain to the child that she does not make her friends feel very good when she constantly tells them how to play. People do not like it when someone is always trying to be the boss.

Get the student to ask for clarifications before confronting another person angrily. Because Meagan often misinterprets comments, she's often on the defensive and miffed with people. Just as students can learn to memorize their multiplication tables,

students like Meagan can learn to memorize and repeat verbatim in many situations: "I think you are saying. . . ." The intent is for the child to make a sincere effort to find out what the other person really means.

Discourage students from being jealous. When Shinita breaks Amy's crayons because Amy receives a better grade on her spelling paper, she is probably envious. Explain to Shinita that she is only putting herself down when she acts jealous. Help her to see herself in a better light by reviewing her past accomplishments. List them on a special index card for her to keep.

Help children to recognize their own boiling point. When Scott feels dumped on, he becomes tense. Paula may feel her temple throbbing, and Shinita may feel a sudden burst of energy. Discuss with the students how they feel right before they explode with anger. Once they are able to recognize clues that their bodies are sending them, they may be able to learn how to remain calm. Suggest thinking about something else—a favorite TV show, a fun activity. Slowly counting to 10 might help.

Teach the child to recognize the boiling point of others. If someone is getting angry, students should learn to hold off arguing with him or her. Kids can jot down all possible tip-offs that a certain person may be getting mad (a red face, tapping a pencil).

Encourage students to talk over concerns when both parties are calm. Discourage kids from bottling up annoying things to the point that they become preoccupied with them and then display a burst of anger. Have them practice assertive responses to neutral situations that include talking to others about petty matters.

Karen has learned how to do this. When her teacher praises Karen's friends but not Karen for the castle built for social studies, she feels hurt and angry. Instead of showing her teacher how furious she is, Karen remembers that the teacher she had last year encouraged her to discuss her concerns. Karen then calmly and courteously explains that she also worked on the project.

Help the pupil see the public image

that he or she presents when incensed. You do not need video equipment. A mirror will be very effective. You might also want to have a tape recorder handy. When the dust has settled in a day or two, replay the ranting and raving. If a child sees or hears the spectacle that he or she makes, he or she may finally realize how intense his or her anger becomes.

Teach students to release pent-up anger and frustrations. Suggest that they engage in a physical activity, such as bike riding, bouncing a ball, or running, to work off anger. Another way to ease tension is to discuss the matter with a close friend.

Get the student to ask: "Is this really worth getting upset about?" Present hypothetical situations and have the student judge whether the matter is worth getting angry over. If he or she feels that it is, ask why. Are there other solutions to the situation that would not involve getting hot under the collar? If students become defensive or their minds are blank, remind them that the goal of this exercise is to use their imaginations.

Just as it is difficult for a dieter to give up certain foods, it is hard for some people to stop being hotheads. *Encourage kids to give themselves a pat on the back for any incident wherein they were able to successfully control their tempers.*

Learning to defuse a short temper takes practice and there will be setbacks. Progress is not as evident as when a student is able to master a list of spelling words in a week. *When a student demonstrates control as a result of your help and encouragement, give yourself a pat on the back.* This strategy will help *you* from losing your cool later when new situations heat up.

Equal Opportunity and American Education

What constitutes the civil rights of students and teachers in schools has been a question often raised before state and federal courts. The equal treatment of students under national constitutional guidelines is of great importance. Decisions made by the courts on issues affecting the lives of students and teachers concern the study of religion in schools, prayer and scripture reading in schools, the racial desegregation of schools, bilingual education, and academic freedom for teachers and students. The federal judiciary in the United States has established important precedents in all of the above areas. In both Canada and the United States, there is great importance attached to the development of workable opportunity structures in national educational systems. The interpretation of what these opportunity structures are has evolved over many years, and the evolution of lines of argument in the courts on these matters continues.

The just balance of the equity interests of citizens of democratic societies is based on the belief that in any free society a plurality of interests must be protected. In addition, so must the dignity and opportunity of each individual citizen to optimize his or her possibilities as a human being. The unjust limitation of freedom of expression or the limitation of an opportunity to attain an adequate education are not tolerable possibilities in any democracy.

Few matters are more basic to the maintenance of democratic social institutions than the establishment of just principles for guiding the education of the young. From preschool to post-graduate school fellowships, issues of equality must be considered by those who seek an education. The vast and complex cultural pluralism that people enjoy in North America is a priceless treasure and the source of the need for guarantees under the law for equality in education.

Americans have witnessed one of the greatest struggles for equality before the law in all of human history. That struggle is well known to educators, especially. More than thirty years ago, the Supreme Court of the United States gave the first of what was to be a long chain of decisions affecting majority-minority relations in American schools. The famous 1954 decision of the United States Supreme Court in *Brown vs. Board of Education of Topeka*, expanded the equity agenda for education to include equality of educational opportunity for women, linguistic minorities, cultural minorities, the aged, and the defenseless. This struggle to achieve the full implementation of the American constitutional promise to equality of opportunity in the field of education has been a triumphant testimony to the possibility of social justice under the law. Future generations of Americans and other free peoples will forever look with awe at the struggle for civil rights in American schools from 1954 to the closing years of the present century. Rarely have free peoples asserted their rights under the law as forcefully and effectively as the American people have on the question of equality of educational opportunity.

Determined to uphold constitutional promises, and inspired by the knowledge that significant progress has been made on this issue, the closing years of this century can be approached with renewed hope and confidence. A vast body of research and opinion on this issue has evolved from the many federal court decisions since 1954. Problems of equity in the schools have been well documented and the nation is developing increased sophistication and effectiveness in the development of solutions to these problems. The desegregation of American schools has been forcefully initiated over the nation, and progress is continuing in majority-minority relations in the schools. It is not only the cultural minorities who have benefited from the federal school desegregation cases, however. Affirmative action in employment and admission to professional schools, the students' rights issue, and the rights of women and the aged have been based on the same constitutional arguments and precedents established in the major school desegregation cases and the Civil Rights Act of 1964. Likewise, the rights of linguistic minorities to learn the English language in public schools have been based on these same constitutional principles. Every American has benefited either directly or indirectly from this triumph of constitutional law over racist tradition.

The essays in this unit provide solid background on these matters. The first article reviews major United States Supreme Court cases involving religion, prayer, and Bible reading in schools, the recent precedents regarding tuition tax credits, school desegregation, and academic freedom. The second article reviews the historical development of American education in the thirty-three years since *Brown vs. Board of Education of Topeka* (the first school desegregation case). The third article is an excellent summary of research studies on the long-term effects of school desegregation on the students who participate in the desegregation process. The next article by Cynthia Gorney is very informative about the education of linguistic minorities and the controversy over bilingual education. Myra and David Sadkers' article on sexism in the classroom of the 1980s points to the unfinished work yet to be done in dealing with "gender" issues in schools.

The selections can be related to many of the major themes in undergraduate courses for preservice teachers. The profession of teaching is subject to significant pressures from many different kinds of equity interest groups in the United States. These articles relate not only to the general issue of equality of opportunity in the field of education, but to specific human rights which form the very basis for the struggle for social justice in the schools.

Looking Ahead: Challenge Questions

What have been the most important legal precedents affecting freedom of belief in American schools?

What were the constitutional precedents for the school desegregation cases?

What academic freedoms should every teacher and student have?

What are the issues in the controversy over bilingual education?

What are the remaining "gender issues" facing North American schools?

The Courts and Education

Thomas R. Ascik

Thomas R. Ascik, a lawyer and former teacher, is a Senior Research Assistant in the Law and Public Management Division of the National Institute of Education, U.S. Department of Education.

The Supreme Court said in 1960 that "the vigilant protection of constitutional freedoms is nowhere more vital than in the community of American schools."[1] Starting with the cases of *Everson v. Board of Education* (1947) and *Brown v. Board of Education* (1954), and continuing with one precedent-shattering case after another, the Supreme Court has applied the concept of constitutional rights to nearly every aspect of American education. Although the United States has been flooded by studies and reports severely critical of the nation's public schools,[2] the historic changes in education wrought by the Supreme Court over the past four decades have hardly been mentioned.

Most critical are those rulings in which the Supreme Court has applied the Constitution to education without prior precedent. These have particularly affected public aid to nonpublic schools, prayer and spiritual values in public schools, racial segregation, and teacher and student rights. In these four areas, the Court, on its own initiative, has broken with the rest and established comprehensive national educational policies.

PUBLIC AID TO NONPUBLIC SCHOOLS

The authority of any branch of the federal government to intervene in state public policies regarding religion traditionally has been governed by the doctrine of the 1833 case of *Barron v. Baltimore.*[3] In this case, concerning city damage to private property, Chief Justice John Marshall, speaking for a unanimous Supreme Court, ruled that the Court had no jurisdiction over the case because the Bill of Rights placed no restrictions on the actions of city or state governments. The framers of the Bill of Rights had not "intended them to be limitations on the powers of the state governments,"[4] explained Marshall.

In the 1920s and 1930s, however, the Court abandoned *Barron v. Baltimore* and began developing perhaps the most important judicial doctrine of this century: the "incorporation" of the Bill of Rights into the Fourteenth Amendment. That amendment, ratified in 1868, made federal citizenship preeminent over state citizenship and declared in its most important parts that "no state shall...deprive any person of life, liberty, or prosperity, without due process of law; nor deny to any person within its jurisdiction the equal protection of the laws."

By incorporating the various rights guaranteed by the Bill of Rights into these Fourteenth Amendment guarantees, the Court gave itself power to overturn state law dealing with almost all areas covered by the ten amendments of the Bill of Rights.

The Court ruled in the 1947 case of *Everson v. Board of Education,*[5] for instance, that the First Amendment's clause prohibiting laws "respecting an establishment of religion" was binding on the states. In this most important Supreme Court education case, except for *Brown v. Board of Education* (1954), the Court was construing the Establishment Clause for the first time. At stake was the constitutionality of a New Jersey statute requiring local school boards to provide free transportation, along established routes, to children attending nonprofit, private (including religiously affiliated) schools.

More significant than the specific ruling in the case was the Court's construction of the First Amendment's Establishment Clause. Declared the Court:

The "establishment of religion" clause of the First Amendment means at least this: Neither a state nor the Federal Government can set up a church. Neither can it pass laws which aid one religion,

From *The World & I*, March 1986, pp. 661-675. Reprinted by permission of the Heritage Foundation.

aid all religions, or prefer one religion over another. Neither can it force nor influence a person to go to or to remain away from a church against his will or force him to profess a belief or disbelief in any religion. No person can be punished for entertaining or professing religious beliefs or disbeliefs, for church attendance or nonattendance. No tax in any amount, large or small, can be levied to support any religious activities or institutions, whatever they may be called, or whatever form they may adopt to teach or practice religion. Neither a state nor the Federal Government can, openly or secretly, participate in the affairs of any religious organizations or groups and vice versa. In the words of Jefferson, the clause against establishment of religion by law was intended to erect "a wall of separation between Church and State.''... That Amendment requires the state to be neutral in its relations with groups of religious believers and nonbelievers.[6]

Until this declaration, the most widely held view of the meaning of the Establishment Clause was that it prohibited government preference of one religion over another. When the Supreme Court concluded that states cannot "pass laws which aid one religion, aid all religions, or prefer one religion over another," it introduced for the first time the notion that the Establishment Clause forbade not only government preference of one religion over another but also government preference of religion over non-religion.

ore than twenty years passed before the Court heard its next significant case concerning government aid to religious schools, *Board of Education v. Allen*.[7] In *Allen*, the Court examined a challenge to a New York statute that required local school boards to purchase textbooks (in secular subjects only) and loan them, without charge, to all children enrolled in grades seven through

twelve of public or private schools. The books were not limited to those actually in use in the public schools but could include those "designated for use" in the public schools or otherwise approved by the local board of education.

The Court applied *Everson* to the case and decided that the provision of textbooks, like transportation, was permissible means to the accomplishment of the legitimate state objective of secular education of all children. Religious schools participated in the public interest because "they pursue two goals, religious instruction and secular education.''[8] Parochial schools, the Court said, "are performing, in addition to their sectarian function, the task of secular education.''[9] This was the birth of the "secular-sectarian" distinction that has defined religious schools as partly serving the public good (the secular subjects in the curriculum) and partly not (religious instruction).

Various cases followed that further defined the principles laid down in *Everson*, including a case dealing with the question of reimbursement to nonpublic schools for their expenditures on teachers of secular subjects and secular institutional materials (*Lemon v. Kurtzman* [1971][10]). In *Lemon*, the Court ruled the reimbursements unconstitutional because of the danger a teacher under religious control could pose to the separation of the religious from the secular. In *Committee for Public Education and Liberty v. Nyquist* (1973),[11] maintenance and repair grants to nonpublic schools were judged to have the primary effect of advancing religion because the buildings maintained and repaired were not restricted to secular purposes. Also in this case, tuition reimbursements and tuition tax deductions were rejected by the Court as being effectively indistinguishable from aid to the schools themselves: "The effect of the aid is unmistakably to provide desired financial support for nonpublic sectarian institutions.''[12] Furthermore, said the Court, states could not "encourage or reward"[13] parents for sending their children to religious schools because this advances religion. Finally, the plan failed the "politically divisive" test because it had the "grave potential" of stimulating "continuing political strife over religion.''[14]

Separate strong dissents were filed by Chief Justice Warren Burger and by Justices William Rehnquist and Byron White. Burger thought that there was a definitive difference between government aid to individuals and direct aid to religious institutions. He wrote: "The private individual makes the decision that may indirectly benefit church-sponsored schools; to that extent the state involvement with religion is substantially attenuated.''[15] Rehnquist argued that, if the Court could uphold the constitutionality of exempting churches from taxation, then it should similarly uphold the constitutionality of exempting parents from taxation for certain educational expenses. White contended that the Court was ruling as unconstitutional schemes that had "any effect"[16] of advancing religion, whereas the test was properly one of "primary effect.''

The Thirty-Years War between the Supreme Court and those states seeking to give public aid to their private schools may have ended with the Supreme Court's 1983 decision in *Mueller v. Allen*.[17] In an opinion written by Justice Rehnquist, a majority of the Court upheld a Minnesota law allowing a deduction on state income taxes for tuition, textbooks, and transportation expenses incurred in the education of students in elementary or secondary schools—public or nonpublic.

Rehnquist decided that the deduction had a secular purpose of "ensuring that the state's citizenry is well-educated"[18] regardless of the type of schools attended. Minnesota also had "a strong public interest"[19] in assuring the survival of religious and non-religious private schools because such schools relieve the public schools of the financial burden of educating a certain percentage of the youth population and because private schools provide "a wholesome competition"[20] for public schools. Furthermore, the primary effect of the law was not the advancement of religion, Rehnquist concluded, in the most important part of his opinion.

Minnesota's plan was distinguished from the tax deductions in *Nyquist* because "the deduction is available for educational expenses incurred by all parents, including those whose children attend public schools and those whose children attend nonsectarian private schools or sectarian private schools."[21] Rehnquist cited the Court's 1981 decision in the *Widmar v. Vincent*[22] ruling that if a state university makes its facilities available for use by student groups, it must allow student religious groups to use the facilities on an equal basis. In keeping with the *Widmar* decision, Minnesota was here providing benefits on an equal basis to a "broad spectrum of citizens,"[23] and this nondiscriminatory breadth was "an important index of secular effect."[24]

Having thus distinguished *Nyquist*, the Court was then able to say that there is a significant difference, in terms of the Establishment Clause, between providing aid to parents and providing it directly to schools despite the reality that "financial assistance provided to parents ultimately has an economic effect comparable to that of aid given directly to the schools attended by their children."[25] Religious schools received public funds "only as a result of numerous, private choices of individual parents of school-age children,"[26] and this exercise of parental choice caused the financial benefits flowing to religious schools to be much "attentuated."[27]

Implications

The *Mueller* decision and the *Widmar* decision requiring state universities to give "equal access" to student religious groups may signal an emerging Supreme Court view of the relationship of church to state and a possible end to the struggle between the states and the Court over public aid for nonpublic education. In *Mueller*, the Court accepted the principle that parents whose children attended religious schools could receive benefits so long as public school parents were equally eligible for benefits. This principle, allowing a state to accommodate its citizens with religious purposes on an equal basis with those pursuing secular purposes, received strong bipartisan support in Congress in 1984. By significant majorities, both Houses passed the

"equal access" bill requiring elementary and secondary schools to allow student religious clubs to use their facilities on an equal basis with other student clubs. This was nothing more than the extension of *Widmar* to elementary and secondary schools.

In the United States, religion has always been the major motivation for the formation and continuation of private schools. Without the *Everson* doctrine, therefore, there would be many more U.S. private schools.

SPIRITUAL VALUES IN PUBLIC SCHOOLS

The Supreme Court addressed prayer in schools in the 1962 case of *Engle v. Vital*,[28] a constitutional challenge to the mandated daily recitation of a nondenominational prayer in a New York State school district that said:

> Almighty God, we acknowledge our dependence upon Thee, and we beg Thy blessings upon us, our parents, our teachers, and our country.

The prayer had been carefully crafted in consultation with a wide range of Jewish and Christian leaders and officially recommended (in 1951 and 1955) to the state's school districts by the New York State Board of Regents as part of its "Statement on Moral and Spritual Training in the Schools." In the lower state courts and the New York Court of Appeals (the highest court of New York), the constitutional challenge to the prayer had been rejected with the caveat that no student could be compelled to recite the prayer. Twenty-three other states joined New York in its petition to have the Supreme Court uphold the constitutionality of the prayer. This, however, the Court did not do.

In what might have been unique for such an important case, Justice Hugo Black, writing for the Court, referred to no previous Supreme Court decision as precedent. Instead, he explained the decision by means of an essay on the history of the separation of church and state. Significantly, almost all of the history considered was preconstitutional—the history of religion in England and the writings of various men, especially Madison

and Jefferson, at the time of the ratification of the Constitution and of the Bill of Rights. Justice Potter Stewart, the sole dissenter, argued that the case brought the Free Exercise Clause into consideration in two ways.[29] First, the lack of compulsion meant that the state was not interfering with the free exercise of anyone's religion. Second, the children who wanted to pray were denied the free exercise of their religion, Stewart contended, and they were denied the "opportunity of sharing the spiritual heritage of our Nation."[30] History is relevant, Stewart argued, but not "the history of an established church in sixteenth century England or in eighteenth century America."[31] Instead, the relevant history was the "history of the religious traditions of our people, reflected in countless practices of the institutions and officials of our government."[32]

A year later in the companion cases of *Abington v. Schempp* and *Murray v. Curlett*,[33] the Court struck down state laws requiring the reading of the Bible in public schools. In *Schempp*, the Unitarian plaintiffs challenged a Pennsylvania state law, passed in 1949, requiring the reading of ten verses from the Bible, without comment or interpretation, in the public schools at the beginning of each day. Upon written request, parents could excuse their children from the readings. The plaintiffs had bypassed the Pennsylvania Supreme Court and sued in federal district court, where the law was struck down in a decision based primarily on the *Everson* decision.

In *Murray*, militant atheist Madlyn Murray and her son challenged a 50-year-old rule of the Baltimore School Board requiring the reading of the Lord's Prayer each day in the city's public schools. As in Pennsylvania, parents could excuse their children from the practice. Murray did not request that her son be excused but brought the suit claiming that the rule violated religious liberty by "placing a premium on belief as against nonbelief."[34] The Maryland Supreme Court appealed to the U.S. Supreme Court, and eighteen other states joined Maryland's defense of its customs.

The Supreme Court ruled in favor of Murray. *Engle* and especially *Everson* formed the basis of the decision.

The Court quoted the *Everson* statement that neither the states nor the federal government "can pass laws which aid one religion, aid all religions, or prefer one religion over another." Once more the Supreme Court was ruling that the influence of religion must be absolutely segregated from the affairs of state. Finally, the Court invented a test for the establishment of religion: a law is constitutional only if it has "a secular legislative purpose and a primary effect that neither advances nor inhibits religion."[35] According to these principles, the practices in these cases were unconstitutional because they were indisputably exercises of which both purpose and effect were religious. The Court denied that its decision advanced what amounted to a religion of secularism but gave no reason for its denial.

n *Epperson v. Arkansas* (1968),[36] the Supreme Court added a new wrinkle to its judicial attitude toward religion: a law may be unconstitutional, stated the Court, if the legislative motive for passing the law was religious. Since 1928, an Arkansas law prohibited the teaching of evolution in its public schools. The law had never been enforced. In 1965, however, a high school biology teacher, confronted with newly adopted biology textbooks that taught evolution, maintained that she was caught between opposing duties and sued to have the law declared void. In a two-sentence opinion, the Arkansas Supreme Court turned back the challenge by concluding that the law was a "valid exercise of the state's power to specify the curriculum in its public schools."[37]

In addition to the question of religious influence in public schools, at least four other profound issues were involved here: the content of the school curriculum, the authority of states over their public schools, the authority and ability of the federal judiciary to prescribe or proscribe parts of the curriculum, and the growing legal movement to have the federal courts promulgate some First

Amendment-based rights of academic freedom. In its resolution of the *Epperson* case, the Supreme Court confined itself to two rationales. The first and more important rationale for the decision was the principle of the *Everson*, *Engle*, and *Schempp* cases. There was no relationship between church and state, the Court said; instead there was a wall. Such a statute clearly violated the "purpose" of the *Schempp* two-part test. The purpose of the statute was clearly religious, and the state did not have the right to make its decisions about school curricula "based upon reasons that violate the First Amendment."[38] In its strongest statement yet about the *Everson* neutrality principle, the Court emphasized that government must treat religion and nonreligion equally, for "the First Amendment mandates government neutrality between religion and religion, and between religion and nonreligion."[39]

As its second rationale, the Court quoted the statement in *Shelton v. Tucker*, that "the vigilant protection of constitutional freedoms is nowhere more vital than in the community of American schools," and the statement in *Keyishian v. Board of Regents* that the First Amendment will not tolerate "a pall of orthodoxy over the classroom."

Through *Epperson v. Arkansas*, the Court brought the results of constitutional litigation affecting higher education to elementary and secondary schools. To Arkansas's claim that it had constitutional power over its public schools, the Supreme Court declared that the Bill of Rights is applicable everywhere, and constitutional powers are not superior to constitutional rights. Said the Court: "Fundamental values of freedom of speech and inquiry and of belief"[40] are at stake here. Quoting *Keyishian*, "It is much too late to argue that the State may impose upon the teachers in its schools any conditions that it chooses, however restrictive they may be of constitutional guarantees."[41] With this concern for the academic freedom (free speech) of teachers, the Court invented independent rights for teachers to control the curriculum of public schools.

Implications

No court has ever doubted the au-

thority of the states to prescribe moral and spiritual instruction in their public schools. The New York State Board of Regents was exercising that authority when it composed the prayer that became the issue in *Engle*. Today there is a growing consensus that more character training is needed in public schools. Historically, almost all systematic codes of Western morality or developed notions of character have been based on religion.

The effect of these Supreme Court decisions has been to prevent religion from influencing the education of those attending public schools. These decisions have forced those who believe that education cannot be separated from religion and who cannot afford private schools to attend institutions whose governing values are antagonistic to their own. In his concurrence in *Epperson*, Justice Black strongly implied that, if the wall of separation meant that nonreligion may influence the curriculum of public schools but religion may not, then the wall might very well be interfering with the free exercise of religion of some of those in attendance. This is, of course, a step beyond governmental neutrality between religion and nonreligion. Under governmental neutrality, the schools are merely indifferent to the values of religious people.

If any statement about the relationship of religion to education is itself a religious statement, then public education that does not discriminate against anyone is impossible under a system of absolute separation of church and state. The only alternative is the opportunity for individuals to exempt themselves at those times when the values presented or implied are antagonistic to their own. But the Court has rejected this principle of voluntariness. So the dilemma grows.

In his dissent in *Schempp*, Justice Stewart said government and religion must necessarily interact. Until *Everson*, they had at least been interacting throughout American history without any of the persecution that the court said it was trying to prevent with the *Engle* decision. In fact, it was *Everson* that launched an unprecedented era of church-state conflict in the U.S., chiefly in the context of education. American history before *Everson* dealt with interaction; since *Everson* it has been the history of conflict. It may be that neutrality is impossible.

DESEGREGATION

An abundance of writing has traced the development of the Supreme Court's doctrine regarding the desegregation of public schools. Three questions place the controversy in perspective: (1) When did the Supreme Court decide that desegregation was incompatible with the American tradition of neighborhood schools? (2) How did the Court come to endorse busing as a remedy for segregation? (3) What has been the attitude of the Court toward education—teaching and learning—in the midst of the desegregation issue?

The fundamental ruling in *Brown v. Board of Education (Brown I)*,[42] the most important education case and probably the most important Supreme Court ruling except for *Marbury v. Madison* (1801), was that school systems are forbidden intentionally to segregate the races by law or practice. Yet the Court's basis for this ruling and the full meaning of the ruling have been enigmatic and the cause of much disagreement. Legally, the Court addressed two questions: Does the Constitution forbid segregation; and, if it does, how can the Court get past its own 1896 ruling in *Plessy v. Ferguson*[43] that as long as public policy treated the races "equally," it could require them to be "separate?"

ddressing the "separate but equal" doctrine of *Plessy*, the Court was faced with a situation in which there were "findings...that the Negro and white schools involved have been equalized, or are being equalized, with respect to buildings, curricula, qualifications and salaries of teachers, and other 'tangible' factors."[44] With no deprivation of equality in measurable educational factors, the Court decided to consider whether there was equality of "intangible" factors. It decided that there was not and that the definitive inequality was the separateness itself.

The effect on blacks of racial segregation was "a feeling of inferiority as to their status in the community that may affect their hearts and minds in a way unlikely ever to be undone."[45] In its now-famous Footnote Eleven, the Court justified this psychological interpretation and inaugurated a new area of American law by citing the research of various social scientists. "Separate educational facilities are inherently unequal,"[46] the Court concluded. Thus, with this combination of the "separate" with the "equal," the Court effectively overturned *Plessy* in *Brown I* by declaring that modern social science had proved that separate equality was impossible in education.

In reaching this momentous decision, the Court did not address the enormous problem of how to require the dismantling of dual school systems until the following year in the second installment of the same case, *Brown II*.[47] Here, the Court refrained from attempting to declare a universal remedy applicable to every discriminating school system, but concluded, instead, that "because of their proximity to local conditions and the possible need for further hearings, the courts that originally heard those cases can best"[48] fashion specific remedies and, in each case, decide upon the best means to "effectuate a transition to a racially nondiscriminatory school system."[49] This was the beginning of the now commonplace judicial supervision of school systems.

Because the Court in *Brown II* put the burden on school authorities, federal district courts in the South spent the next thirteen years ruling on the constitutionality of various schemes that these authorities fashioned to carry out the mandate of *Brown I*. Only a few cases of significance reached the Supreme Court over this period. In truth, *Brown II* was not much more specific than *Brown I*. Until the Supreme Court's decision in *Green v. New Kent County* (1968), neither the lower federal courts nor the school systems knew whether the *Brown* mandate contained a prescription as well as a proscription.

In *Green v. New Kent County*, the Supreme Court announced that it was going to demand more than simply dropping laws requiring segregation. The case concerned the school board of the Virginia county of New Kent, a

county with complete racial segregation between its only two schools, which initiated a "freedom-of-choice" plan whereby black and white students could choose which school they wanted to attend. Students not exercising this choice were reassigned to the school they had attended the previous year.

The effect of this plan was to offer to every student, black or white, the opportunity to attend either school, the traditionally all-black school or the traditionally all-white school, while not disturbing the segregated status quo if few or no students made the choice. This plan presented the Court with the question whether its *Brown* decision required the changing of the old laws requiring segregation, that is, de jure segregation, or the changing of the results of the old laws, that is, de facto segregation.

The school board, in effect, was asking the Court to rule on this distinction between de jure and de facto segregation. In reply, the Court said that it had already done so in *Brown II*: "The Board attempts to cast the issue in its broadest form by arguing that its 'freedom-of-choice' plan may be faulted only by reading the Fourteenth Amendment as universally requiring 'compulsory integration,' a reading it insists the wording of the Amendment will not support. But that argument ignores the thrust of *Brown II*."[50] This "thrust" was the requirement of the "abolition of the system of segregation and its effects,"[51] the Court explained.

The Court here was introducing the notion that segregation had continuing legal effects after the policy of segregation itself was ended. In telling the New Kent School Board that it was not merely freedom or lack of coercion but a certain social result that it was seeking, the Court said that the continuing effects of segregation (what one may have thought was an aspect of de facto segregation) were part of de jure segregation. In other words, it maintained that it was very unlikely that there could be legally acceptable de facto segregation in any district that had a history of de jure segregation. A plan was to be measured by its "effectiveness...in achieving desegregation."[52] Eliminating segregation was not enough; desegregation must be achieved.

After *Green*, it was only logical for

the Court to endorse busing and racial balance in *Swann v. Charlotte-Mecklenburg Board of Education* (1971).[53] If the prime evidence of the continuing efforts of a defunct policy of segregation was, as the Court said in *Green*, schools that remained heavily one race, and if a legally enforceable freedom to transfer was ineffective in achieving the redistribution of the two races, then the races must be specifically reassigned to achieve that goal. In *Swann* the Court endorsed three means of reassigning students: racial balances and quotas, busing, and the redrawing of school attendance zones. The Court's rationale for the acceptability of all three was the same: They all worked—that is, they were indisputably "effective" in achieving racial redistribution. *Swann* was the specific application of *Green*.

In summary, the *Brown* decision declared that the problem was that the races were legally required to be separate—not the inequality of facilities, curricula, or staff between black and white schools. The Court ruled that separation was itself an inequality (a psychological inequality) and was unconstitutional. In *Green*, the Court found that the continuing effect of segregation was the continuing separation of the races, and this finding was used to justify race-conscious student reassignment in *Swann*.

n *Milliken v. Bradley* (1977) (*Milliken II*),[54] however, the Court concluded what, on its face, seemed to be a contradiction not only of *Green* but also of *Brown*. The main issue of the case was "the question whether federal courts can order remedial education programs as part of a school desegregation decree."[55]

In *Milliken II*, the defendant Detroit school system charged that the district court's remedy of requiring the system to undertake the retraining of teachers and provide remedial reading and testing and counseling services to black children was not based on the nature of the constitutional violation; and that "the Court's decree must be limited to remedying unlawful pupil assignments."[56] In rejecting this argument, the Court answered that a federal court's power to fashion remedies was "broad and flexible."[57]

What the Court really did in *Milliken II* was extend the "continuing effects" of *Green* and while doing away with the "separation" basis for *Brown* and *Green*. "Discriminatory student assignment policies can themselves manifest and breed other inequalities built into a dual system based on racial discrimination....Pupil assignment also does not automatically remedy the impact of previous, unlawful educational isolation,"[58] the Court concluded. For the first time, the Court was saying that there was a justifiable "impact" of racial separation beyond the separation itself.

Implications

In many cities where the question of busing has become moot because blacks have come to comprise the majority of the enrollment, the courts are more interested today in educational remedies than in busing and other remedies of mandatory student reassignment. This often becomes quite detailed, with the judge prescribing not only specific remedial programs but also the books to be used in such programs. Thus judges have taken over educational duties.

The *Brown* decision, the Civil Rights Act of 1964, the Voting Rights Act, and other laws have helped to change black political impotence to power. The full participation of blacks in government policy making may allow judges to permit the revival of local control of schools. If the courts are convinced that there are no impediments to black equality of political opportunity, they may be willing to give back control of the schools to communities, parents, and educators. This would allow the courts to avoid the problem of judicial prescription of the school curriculum. And it may be a necessity for the educational and social welfare of the children.

Contemporary research in education suggests that community and parent involvement and a shared sense of purpose are central to an effective school.[59] A federal district court recently endorsed these conclusions in the desegregation case involving the school system of Norfolk, Virginia. Faced with the obvious failure of busing,[60] the dubious status of the "self-image" social psychology incorporated into *Brown*,[61] and the difficulties of judicial supervision of the curriculum, the courts may have to turn to other means to guarantee equality of educational opportunity for all children.

THE RIGHTS OF TEACHERS AND STUDENTS

The first important case applying the constitutional principle of free speech to the field of education was *Shelton v. Tucker* (1960).[62] One of the most important First Amendment cases, it was decided by a narrow five to four margin. An Arkansas statute required prospective teachers at public schools or colleges to disclose every organization to which he or she had belonged or contributed regularly in the preceding five years. Some teachers who refused to do so, challenged the statute as a deprivation of their "rights to personal association, and academic liberty, protected by the Due Process Clause of the Fourteenth Amendment from invasion by state action."[63]

In overruling the Arkansas Supreme Court, which had upheld the statute, The Supreme Court said that this case differed from that group of First Amendment cases[64] in which the Court had invalidated state statutes because the statutes did not really serve a legitimate governmental purpose. Here, there was "no question of the relevance of a State's inquiry into the fitness and competence of its teachers."[65] Nevertheless, without any discussion at all, the Court immediately reached two definitive conclusions:

1. It declared that teachers had "a right of free association, a right closely allied to freedom of speech and a right which, like free speech, lies at the foundation of a free society."[66]

2. Rather than consider the issue of the permissible qualifications that a state may place on public employment, or the question of the uniqueness of teachers as public employees, the Court asserted that a constitutionally protected "personal freedom"[67] of teachers was at stake here. At stake were "freedom of speech....freedom of inquiry....free-

dom of association....the free spirit of teachers....the free play of the spirit....the free[dom] to inquire, to study, and to evaluate."[68] Consequently, "the vigilant protection of constitutional freedoms is nowhere more vital than in the community of American schools."[69] This last statement and the two conclusions upon which it is based have presaged most of the substance of other key cases.

The Court found that a teacher could have many associations that would have no bearing upon the teacher's competence or fitness. Therefore, "The statute's comprehensive interference with associational freedom goes far beyond what might be justified in the exercise of the State's legitimate inquiry into the fitness and competency of its teachers."[70] The four dissenters all joined two separate dissents written by Justices John Harlan and Felix Frankfurter. Their similar arguments had two main points. First, there was no evidence that the information collected had ever been abused or used in a discriminatory manner. Secondly, this was a reasonable and not excessive way for the state to exercise its conceded right to inquire into the fitness of its teachers.

That a major change had been effected in the attitude of the federal judiciary to the situation of teachers in government-operated schools was made evident in *Keyishian v. Board of Regents of New York* (1967).[71] In *Keyishian* the Court overturned the same New York "loyalty oath" law that it had sustained fifteen years earlier in *Adler v. Board of Education*.[72] The law excluded anyone from public employment who advocated the overthrow of the government by force or violence. Pursuant to the law, the Board of Regents of the state university system had required university employees to certify that they were not members of the Communist party or, if they were, that they had communicated the fact to the president of the university. Keyishian and three other faculty members refused to certify themselves and challenged the constitutionality of the law and its application.

In *Adler*, the Court had turned back such a challenge and declared:

A teacher works in a sensitive area in a classroom. There he shapes the attitude of young minds toward the society in which they live. In this, the state has a vital concern. It must preserve the integrity of the schools. That the school authorities have the right and the duty to screen the officials, teachers, and employees as to their fitness to maintain the integrity of the schools as a part of ordered society, cannot be doubted.[73]

But in *Keyishian*, the Court decided that the New York law was unconstitutional. Declared the Court:

There can be no doubt of the legitimacy of New York's interest in protecting its education system from subversion. But "even though the governmental purpose be legitimate and substantial, that purpose cannot be pursued by means that broadly stifle fundamental personal liberties when the end can be more narrowly achieved." *Shelton v. Tucker*...."The vigilant protection of constitutional freedoms is nowhere more vital than in the community of American schools." *Shelton v. Tucker*."[74]

In *Adler*, the Court had said that teachers "may work for the school system upon the reasonable terms laid down by the proper authorities of New York. If they do not choose to work on such terms, they are at liberty to retain their beliefs and association and go elsewhere."[75] But throughout the *Keyishian* opinion, the Court cited numerous cases that it had decided in the area of the First Amendment since 1952. What had happened between 1952 and 1967 was that the reach of the First Amendment had been dramatically extended by the Court.

In the 1968 case of *Pickering v. Board of Education*,[76] the *Shelton* and *Keyishian* rationales for freedom of association for teachers were applied by the Supreme Court to freedom of speech for teachers. A county board of education in Illinois had dismissed a teacher, after a public hearing, for publishing a letter in a newspaper criticizing the board's performance in the area of school finance. The board found that numerous statements in the letter were false and that the publication of the statements unjustifiably impugned the board and the school administration.

The Supreme Court found that the teacher's right to free speech prevented his dismissal:

To the extent that the Illinois Supreme Court's opinion may be read to suggest that teachers may constitutionally be compelled to relinquish the First Amendment rights they would otherwise enjoy as citizens to comment on matters of public interest in connection with the operation of the public schools in which they work, it proceeds on a premise that has been unequivocally rejected in numerous prior decisons of this Court....*Shelton v. Tucker*....*Keyishian v. Board of Regents*...."The theory that public employment which may be denied altogether may be subjected to any conditions, regardless of how unreasonable, has been uniformly rejected." *Keyishian v. Board of Regents*....the threat of dismissal from public employment is nonetheless a potent means of inhibiting speech.[77]

In *Tinker v. Des Moines* (1969),[78] the rights established in *Shelton* and *Keyishian* were extended to students:

First Amendment rights, applied in light of the special characteristics of the school environment, are available to teachers and students. It can hardly be argued that either students or teachers shed their constitutional rights to freedom of speech or expression at the schoolhouse gate.[79]

The case stemmed from the deliberate defiance of a school system's rule prohibiting the wearing of armbands —in this instance protesting the Vietnam War. "Our problem," the Court said, "lies in the area where students in the exercise of First Amendment rights collide with the rules of the school authorities."[80] Wearing of armbands was akin to "pure speech" and implicated "direct, primary First Amendment rights."[81] The students' expression of their political views by wearing armbands had caused no disorder or disturbance in the schools, had not interfered with schools' work, and had not intruded upon the rights of other students. Furthermore, the mere fear of a disturbance was not reason enough to justify this curtailment of speech, the Court decided, because "our Constitution says we must take this risk."[82] With this ruling, the Court established a new presumption in American education. "In the absence of a specific showing of constitutionally valid reasons to regulate their speech, students are entitled to freedom of expression of their views."[83]

In a scorching dissent, Justice Black, a lifelong First Amendment advocate, asserted that the Court had launched a "new revolutionary era of permissiveness in this country fostered by the judiciary"[84] by arrogating to itself "rather than to the State's elected officals charged with running the schools, the decision as to which school disciplinary regulations are 'reasonable'."[85] Although he did not explicitly deny that students have free speech rights, Black may have argued so in effect, writing: "Nor are public school students sent to the schools at public expense to broadcast political or any other views to educate and inform the public...taxpayers send children to school on the premise that at their age they need to learn, not teach."[86]

With its decision, the Court reversed what had been the unquestioned social agreement that school authorities were to be obeyed always and that only in the rarest and most extraordinary cases, where a student had been seriously wronged, could a redress of grievances be pursued. Now, with regard to speech in schools, the reasons for student obedience must be demonstrable beforehand.

Implications

The issue of the *Brown* case was student assignment; in *Everson* and its progeny, the Supreme Court was intervening to prevent religion from influencing education. In both areas, the Court rearranged traditional ways of doing things in American education. However, when it applied the constitutional principles of freedom of speech and freedom of association to education, the Court added to the educational enterprise. To the business of teaching and learning were added "direct, primary First Amendment rights" of teachers and students, that is to say, personal liberties, independent of educational purposes but applied to education, enforceable in a court of law.

Schools have a purpose other than that for which they were established, the Supreme Court has said. This purpose is often called "academic freedom," and as the Supreme Court has outlined, it is protected by courts even when not desired by those who founded, and continue to fund, the public schools. For students, it means that they have a legally enforceable right to do other things than learn at school. And for teachers, it means that they have a legally enforceable right to be employed at schools, regardless of whether the school authorities want them there, and a legally enforceable right to say things other than what the school hired them to say. These rights, especially with the powerful presumptions that they carry with them, have fundamentally altered the school board-teacher and teacher-student relationships.

[1] *Shelton v. Tucker* 364 U.S. 479 at 487 (1960).
[2] Mortimer Adler, *The Paideia Proposal*; U.S. Department of Education, *A Nation at Risk*; Ernest L. Boyer, *A Report on Secondary Education in America*; Twentieth Century Fund, *Report of the Twentieth Century Fund Task Force on Federal Elementary and Secondary Education Policy*; John Goodlad, *A Place Called School: Prospects for the Future*.
[3] 7 Pet. 243.
[4] This Just Compensation Clause prohibits the federal government from condemning anyone's property without paying him a just compensation for his loss at 249.
[5] 330 U.S. 1.
[6] *Ibid*. at 15-16.
[7] 392 U.S. 236.
[8] *Ibid*. at 243.
[9] *Ibid*. at 248.
[10] 403 U.S. 602 (1971)—together with *Early v. DiCenso*.
[11] 413 U.S. 756.
[12] *Ibid*. at 783.
[13] *Ibid*. at 791.
[14] *Ibid*. at 795.
[15] *Ibid*. at 802.
[16] *Ibid*. at 823.
[17] 103 S. Ct. 3062.
[18] *Ibid*. at 3067.
[19] *Ibid*.
[20] *Ibid*., quoting Justice Powell in *Wolman v. Walter*, 433 U.S. 229 (1977) at 262.
[21] *Ibid*. at 3068.
[22] 454 U.S. 263.
[23] *Mueller* at 3069.
[24] *Ibid*. at 3068.
[25] *Ibid*. at 3069.
[26] *Ibid*.
[27] *Ibid*.
[28] 370 U.S. 421.
[29] *Ibid*. at 430.
[30] *Ibid*. at 445.
[31] *Ibid*. at 446.
[32] *Ibid*.
[33] 374 U.S. 203.
[34] *Ibid*. at 212.
[35] *Ibid*. at 222.
[36] 393 U.S. 97.
[37] 242 Ark. 922, 416 S.W. 2d 322 (1967).
[38] *Epperson* at 107.
[39] *Ibid*. at 104.
[40] *Ibid*.
[41] *Ibid*. at 107.
[42] 347 U.S. 483.
[43] 163 U.S. 537.
[44] *Brown* at 493.
[45] *Ibid*. at 492.
[46] *Ibid*. at 494.
[47] 349 U.S. 294 (1955).
[48] 391 U.S. 563.
[49] *Ibid*. at 568, 574.
[50] 393 U.S. 503.
[51] *Ibid*. at 506.
[52] *Ibid*. at 339.
[53] 402 U.S. 1.
[54] 433 U.S. 267.
[55] *Ibid*. at 279.
[56] *Ibid*. at 270.
[57] *Ibid*. at 281.
[58] *Ibid*. at 283, 287-88.
[59] See: Thomas Ascik, "Looking at Some Research on What Makes An Effective School," in *Blueprint for Educational Reform*, The Free Congress Foundation, Summer 1984. Also, inter alia: Richard Murnane, "Interpreting the Evidence on School Effectiveness," *Teachers College Record*, Fall 1981; Thomas Corcoran and Barbara Hansen, "The Quest for Excellence: Making Public Schools More Effective," The New Jersey School Boards Association, 1983; Gilbert Austin, "Exemplary Schools and the Search for Effectiveness," *Educational Leadership*, October 1979; and Edgar Epps, "Towards Effective Desegregated Schools," paper commissioned by the National Institute of Education, 1983.
[60] David Armor, "The Evidence on Busing," *The Public Interest*, 28, 1972; and James Coleman, "Recent Trends in School Integration," *Educational Researcher*, July-August 1975; Dennis Cuddy, "The Problem of Forced Busing and a Possible Solution," *Phi Delta Kappan*, September 1984.
[61] "School Desegregation, The Social Science Role," *American Psychologist*, 38, 8, August 1983; Walter G. Stephan, "Blacks and Brown: The Effects of School Desegregation on Black Students," *School Desegregation and Black Achievement*, National Institute of Education, 1984.
[62] 364 U.S. 484.
[63] *Ibid*. at 485.
[64] E.g., *NAACP v. Alabama*, 357 U.S. 449 (1958).
[65] *Shelton* at 485.
[66] *Ibid*. at 486.
[67] *Ibid*.
[68] *Ibid*. at 487.
[69] *Ibid*.
[70] *Ibid*. at 490.
[71] 385 U.S. 589.
342 U.S. 485.
Ibid. at 493.
Keyishian at 602-03.
Adler at 492.
Keyishian at 605-06.
[77] *Ibid*. at 300.
[78] *Ibid*.
[79] *Green* at 437.
[80] *Ibid*. at 440.
[81] *Ibid*. at 507.
[82] *Ibid*. at 508.
[83] *Ibid*. at 509.
[84] *Ibid*. at 511.
[85] *Ibid*. at 518.

School Desegregation Since *Brown:*

A 30-Year Perspective

"Thirty years after Brown *saw Federal disinvestment in public schooling, a retreat from equality, and a return to pre-*Brown *'separate but equal' programs and facilities."*

Franklin Parker

Dr. Parker, Associate Education Editor of USA Today, *is Distinguished Professor, Center for Excellence in Education, Northern Arizona University, Flagstaff.*

"**T**ERRIBLE. A disaster!" is how a northern, urban, white friend of mine described school desegregation 30 years after the 1954 landmark decision in *Brown v. Board of Education of Topeka.*

"We are well rid of it [segregation]," wrote James Kilpatrick, a conservative Southern writer and one-time segregation-ist in the Morgantown, W. Va., *Dominion Post* on May 16, 1984. "An oppressed people gained but . . . jurisprudence lost." Supreme Court justices saw segregation as immoral and decided it was unconstitutional. Later misguided decisions, Kilpatrick held, led the Court to amend, rather than interpret, the Constitution. Such decisions and Federally imposed school redistricting and busing drove whites into suburbs and caused far worse urban resegregation. The 14th Amendment and constitutional intent were thrown into the trash heap. "For this arrogant usurpation of power they cannot be forgiven," he wrote, citing as evidence *The Burden of Brown,* a major study by historian Raymond Wolters. Before examining Wolters' critical findings, one can note positive statements made about *Brown* 30 years later:

"The chain of events triggered by *Brown* changed the daily operation of the nation's schools," wrote Hope Aldrich in *Education Week,* June 6, 1984. It "gave impetus to the most far-reaching civil rights movement in the United States since . . . Reconstruction.''

"*Brown* . . . stands as a national confession of error,'' editorialized *The New York Times* on May 17, 1984. ''It propelled the modern civil rights movement. . . It reaffirmed the American spirit of equality and rekindled hope of peaceful transformation. It is a living monument, a cause for celebration.''

"The Supreme Court in *Brown* established a legal precedent that led to the end of state-sponsored racial apartheid,'' wrote University of Oregon Law School Dean Derrick Bell in *The Christian Science Monitor,* May 17, 1984. ''Encouraged by the Court's stirring words, blacks threw off the stifling veil of racial humiliation and began a national freedom self-help effort that continues to the present time.''

Wolters' *The Burden of Brown* asserts that the Court's unanimous decision reversing the "separate but equal'' *Plessy v. Ferguson* (1896) interpretation was right. It was also right to declare state-imposed racially segregated schools unconstitutional. Where the Court erred was in calling for *more* than state action to correct state error, in repeating scholars' opinions that blacks in segregated schools suffered damage in inferiority feelings and in lower educational attainment. Some critics think that repeating emotional language went beyond the Court's role in interpreting the Constitution. Court language stated: "Separate educational facilities are inherently unequal and generate a feeling of inferiority as to the [blacks'] status in the community that may affect their hearts and minds in a way unlikely ever to be undone.''

Wolters infers that unjudicial language encouraged further constitutional abuse. *Brown* 1 (1954) called desegregation unconstitutional, while *Brown* 2 (1955) called for desegregation with all deliberate speed, but listed no deadlines. Public consensus led Congress to enact the 1964 Civil Rights Act, Section 407 of which authorized the U.S. Attorney General to initiate school desegregation action.

Many school boards' "freedom of choice'' desegregation plans relied on local persuasion, which often translated into holding the *status quo.* Some time after the freedom of choice plan in New Kent County, Va., 85% of blacks remained in all-black schools. In oral argument, Chief Justice Earl Warren asked the school board lawyer, "Isn't the new result of freedom of choice that while they took down the fence, they put booby traps in place of it?'' Justice Thurgood Marshall asked, "Assuming a Negro parent wants to send his child to the . . . previously white school and his employer said, 'I suggest you do not do it,' would that be freedom of choice?''

In *Green v. New Kent County* (1968), the Supreme Court voided freedom of choice, called it a continuation of segregation, and required statistical evidence of integration. After *Green,* Federal judges set quantitative desegregation standards school boards had to meet.

To states' righters and strict Constitution constructionists, the Court's shift from desegregation to Federal enforcement amended, not interpreted, the Constitution. In *Brown* (1954), the Court held that the Constitution is color *blind*; in *Green* (1968), it held that the Constitution is color *conscious.* Wolters noted, "After *Green,* desegregation no longer meant assignment without regard to race; it meant assignment according to race to produce greater racial mixing.'' He continued: "Sensing the possibility of achieving social balance by judicial decree, liberals endorsed the concept of government by an unelected judicial elite. . . .'' Urban whites found this social engineering and judicial reconstruction distasteful. They retreated to suburbs and private schools. They joined the conservative coalition which has since curbed court-ordered busing and redistricting.

Wolters believes public education suffered from liberal court orders, from progressive educators linked to Federal programs, and from irresponsible urban rioters. Segregation was wrong in mid-20th-century America, he says, but the Constitution suffered when judges presumed to make social policy. Reform belongs to elected representatives, not to unelected judges.

To balance Wolters' negative view, Rosemary C. Salomone, a professor of education law at Harvard University, writing in *Education Week* on Aug. 22, 1984, pointed to *Brown*'s wider influence. Southern opposition did turn to compliance. Pres. Lyndon Johnson and Congress did translate *Brown* into a national agenda. Witness Title VI of the 1964 Civil Rights Act, which prohibited discrimination in Federally funded programs. Note Title I of the 1965 Elementary and Secondary Education Act (ESEA), which provided unprecedented aid to remedial programs for the disadvantaged. *Brown* also helped universalize and particularize equality. Witness PL 94-142 for the handicapped. Note Title IX of the 1972 Education Amendments Act for women.

A loss of support

These benefits, Salomone noted, lost support in the conservative aftermath of the 1974 OPEC oil crisis, gas lines, awareness of limited resources, stagflation, and the economic threat from Japan's cars and Korea's steel. Equality became suspect; it was expensive and trod on majority toes. Proof lay in the North's massive resistance to mandatory busing.

California's Proposition 13 heralded a taxpayer rebellion. Education of the handicapped was seen as diverting scarce local and state funds. Bilingual education retreated under hard-hat emphasis on "speaking American.'' Withholding Federal school funds for civil rights noncompliance made Federal assistance "coercion'' to many Americans.

Economic retrenchment and conservative renewal helped Pres. Reagan pursue limited government, less Federal spending, and a return to state-initiated programs. Since then, critics charge, we have had block grants, civil rights deregulation, a halt to court-ordered busing, and pressures for tuition tax relief and school prayer. Thirty years after *Brown* saw Federal disinvestment in public schooling, a retreat from equality, and a return to pre-*Brown* "separate but equal'' programs and facilities.

Advocates of *A Nation at Risk* and other 1983 critical school reports link decades of civil rights changes with the decline of educational excellence. They doubt that we can be equal and excellent, too.

Some see a backlash against educational excellence by those who must implement it. Concerns are how to get the needed large funds, how to achieve high standards for all, what to do with those who fail, how to raise teacher quality, and how to maintain public pressure for better schools. That pressure is already dissipating, pointed out *New York Times* education writer Fred M. Hechinger on Oct. 31, 1984. As a major 1984 campaign issue, education took a back seat to deficits, star wars, and personalities.

Brown's influence now seems to some less than its 1954 promise. Nevertheless, Federal programs did work and were beneficial, as the facts show, but the public does not perceive. ESEA Title I remedial programs did raise reading and math achievement scores. ESEA Title VII's bilingual programs did reduce Hispanic drop-out rates. Title IX of the 1972 Education Amendments Act did increase women's participation in school athletics. Projects Headstart and Follow Through succeeded.

We may still be too close to judge the *Brown* revolution. Longer perspective will confirm that Gunnar Myrdal correctly noted the contradiction between justice for all and mistreatment of blacks, that the NAACP rightly pursued school desegregation cases to the highest court in the land, that Howard Law School Dean Charles Hamilton Houston taught winning legal strategies to Thurgood Marshall and other black lawyers, and that Earl Warren nobly led a brave Court to knock down school segregation's walls. *Brown* remains a landmark against centuries of injustice.

A Long-Term View of School Desegregation: Some Recent Studies of Graduates as Adults

School desegregation is not simply another education reform; it also reforms the socialization function of schools. The authors present evidence that school desegregation leads to desegregation in several areas of adult life.

Jomills Henry Braddock II, Robert L. Crain, and James M. McPartland

Photo by David Sutton

JOMILLS HENRY BRADDOCK II and ROBERT L. CRAIN are principal research scientists and co-directors of the Education and Work Program, Center for Social Organization of Schools, Johns Hopkins University, Baltimore. JAMES M. McPARTLAND is co-director of the Center.

> *The case for or against desegregation should not be argued in terms of academic achievement. If we want a segregated society, we should have segregated schools. If we want a desegregated society, we should have desegregated schools.[1]*

IN 1984, THE 30th anniversary of *Brown* v. *Board of Education*, it is important to keep in mind this elegantly blunt statement by Christopher Jencks. Social scientists and educators are mistaken, if they assume that the only point — or even the main point — of the *Brown* decision was to insure that black students are given equal opportunities to learn the basic skills. Schools have a broader mission than that. Writing for the Supreme Court in *Brown*, Chief Justice Earl Warren noted:

> Today, education is perhaps the most important function of state and local governments. . . . It is the very foundation of good citizenship . . . . [I]t is a

From *Phi Delta Kappan,* December 1984, pp. 259-264. Reprinted by permission of the author and Phi Delta Kappan.

Racial segregation gives birth to and nurtures a form of avoidance learning that helps to maintain the separation of blacks and whites.

principal instrument in awakening the child to cultural values, in preparing him for later professional training, and in helping him to adjust normally to his environment. In these days it is doubtful that any child may reasonably be expected to succeed in life if he is denied the opportunity of an education.[2]

Warren's view is widely shared by both scholars and policy makers. A major goal of public education in the U.S. has always been to facilitate the assimilation of minorities; indeed, school desegregation may be the most significant example of a national policy using educational reform to achieve this end.

Yet the debate over the merits of school desegregation has virtually ignored the goal of assimilation, focusing instead on such narrow issues as whether achievement test scores rise or fall after desegregation. The evidence suggests that the test scores of minority students rise after desegregation, but this outcome is not the real test of the value of desegregating the schools. The real test is whether desegregation enables minorities to join other Americans in becoming well-educated, economically successful, and socially well-adjusted adults.

Clearly, we cannot evaluate school desegregation as if it were simply another educational innovation, akin to "new" math or to an innovative technique of individualizing reading instruction. Schools do more than teach academic skills; they also socialize the young for membership in adult society. School desegregation is not simply an educational reform; it also reforms the socialization function of the schools. For this reason, U.S. society cannot avoid the pain of decisions about school desegregation simply by improving the quality of segregated schools. Desegregation puts majorities and minorities together so that they can learn to coexist with one another, not so that they can learn to read.

Data from our work at the Center for Social Organization of Schools and from the research of a few colleagues elsewhere

suggest that school desegregation is leading to desegregation in several areas of adult life. Table 1 lists the relevant studies. These studies, which have typically followed large groups of students through school and into adulthood, are few in number because of their high cost.

WITHOUT EXCEPTION, the studies listed in Table 1 show that desegregation of schools leads to desegregation in later life — in college, in social situations, and on the job. One of the most dysfunctional aspects of racial segregation is its tendency to become self-perpetuating. Racial segregation gives birth to and nurtures a form of avoidance learning that helps to maintain the separation of blacks and whites.[3]

Prior to the *Brown* decision, blacks were educated in a dual school system that offered them putatively inferior training, especially in the South. When schools in the South began to desegregate, blacks were legally entitled to attend formerly all-white elementary and secondary schools. However, in part because of anticipated hostility from whites and in part because of the belief that prior differences in educational preparation might place them at a competitive disadvantage in desegregated schools, many blacks in the South were ambivalent about and reluctant to take full advantage of this hard-won educational opportunity.

For this reason, the Supreme Court ruled that "freedom of choice" — that is, offering blacks the opportunity to leave segregated schools for desegregated ones — is unconstitutional. The Court recognized that a century of segregation had created enormous social inertia that would, given the opportunity, maintain segregated schools far into the future.

Just as blacks who grew up in segregated schools are reluctant to send their children to desegregated schools, so they are also reluctant to place themselves in desegregated adult settings. As contact theory would predict, blacks have learned to avoid and to withdraw from interracial situations that might cause them pain or indignity. Even though the situation has changed, and the pain and indignity have lessened or disappeared altogether, many blacks remain reluctant to test the new arrangements.

Thus, as we have already pointed out, historic patterns of de jure and de facto segregation have generated a social inertia that sustains blacks' isolation from major social institutions. And this long-standing isolation of blacks has perpetuated patterns of avoidance learning and social behavior among whites that cause them to resist desegregation in the schools and in other social settings. Desegregation of elementary and secondary schools would help the U.S. to replace a self-perpetuating cycle of segregation with a self-perpetuating cycle of desegregation.

The first two research studies listed in Table 1 found that minority students who have been educated in desegregated elementary and secondary schools are more likely than their counterparts from segregated schools to attend predominantly white colleges and universities.[4] Blacks who have attended segregated schools in the South tend to perpetuate their segregation by enrolling in traditionally black four-year colleges. Blacks who have attended segregated schools in the North are more likely than their counterparts from desegregated schools to enroll in predominantly black community colleges located in urban areas.

The third study listed in Table 1 found that both blacks and whites who have attended desegregated schools are more likely than their counterparts from segre-

Photos by David Sutton

gated schools to be working in desegregated settings.[5] The fourth study, by Robert Crain and Carol Weisman, used data collected in the 1960s by the U.S. Commission on Civil Rights; this study showed that blacks educated in desegregated schools are more likely than those educated in segregated ones to have white social contacts and to live in integrated neighborhoods.[6] The fifth study listed in Table 1 showed that blacks from desegregated schools are more likely than their counterparts from segregated schools to work in desegregated settings.[7]

The sixth and seventh studies listed in Table 1 found that blacks who have attended desegregated schools are more likely to work in desegregated settings, more likely to live in racially mixed neighborhoods, and more likely to have cross-racial friendships.[8] (The seventh study, conducted by Robert Crain and funded by the National Institute of Education, was a 15-year follow-up evaluation of an experimental desegregation program in Hartford, Connecticut.)

The eighth study in Table 1, also conducted by Crain, showed that a national sample of employers gives preference in hiring to black graduates of desegregated high schools.[9] And the last two studies in Table 1, which looked at entire communities, showed that those cities with desegregated schools are also more likely to have integrated neighborhoods.[10]

THE STUDIES IN Table 1 show strong and consistent effects: members of minority groups who have been educated in segregated schools will generally move into segregated niches in adult society. If they have had no childhood experience with whites, members of minority groups will tend to avoid dealing with whites as adults. Sometimes they practice avoidance because they expect rejection. But this avoidance may also be explained by the fact that they have had no chance to develop effective ways of interacting and coping with whites; moreover, they have lacked opportunities in competitive situations to test their abilities against those of whites. We think it is likely, too, that the same mechanism that produces prejudice among whites from segregated backgrounds will produce prejudice among blacks who have had no contact with whites.

It seems intuitively obvious that, among blacks, the social and psychological barriers to seeking or sustaining memberships in desegregated groups should be greater for those individuals who unrealistically expect hostile reactions from whites, who have little confidence that they can function successfully in interracial situations, or who have trouble dealing with the strains that may accompany interpersonal contacts across racial lines. And indeed, Crain found, in his study of participants in the Hartford desegregation program, that minority males who had graduated from segregated schools perceived more racism, both in college and in business settings, than did males who had graduated from desegregated schools.[11] If childhood experiences in desegregated settings help blacks to break down these social and psychological barriers, the logical outcome would seem to be less avoidance or withdrawal from integrated situations in adulthood.

School desegregation also changes the attitudes and behavior of whites, by reducing racial stereotypes and removing whites' fears of hostile reactions in interracial settings. Using data on racial attitudes derived from national surveys, Richard Scott and James McPartland found that attending desegregated schools improves the attitudes of both blacks and whites toward future interracial situations.[12]

Similarly, mainstream institutions respond to school desegregation by providing more opportunities for blacks to associate with whites. Cities that have desegregated schools develop a larger quantity of desegregated housing than do cities with segregated school systems. Corporations

Table 1. Summary of

Study	Data	Independent Variable
Braddock (1980)	Survey in 1972 of black students attending four colleges in Florida (N = 253)	High school racial composition
Braddock and McPartland (1982)	Black subsample of the National Longitudinal Study (NLS) High School Class of 1972 (N = 3,119)	Elementary/secondary school racial composition
Braddock, McPartland, and Trent (1984)	Black and white subsamples of the NLS Class of 1972 merged with survey data from their 1976 and 1979 employers (blacks = 1,518; whites = 1,957)	High school and college racial composition
Crain and Weisman (1972)	Survey in 1966 of blacks living in North and West (N = 1,651)	Elementary/secondary school racial composition
Braddock and McPartland (1983)	Two-year follow-up of black subsample of NLS 1980-81 Youth Cohort (N = 1,074)	High school racial composition
Green (1981; 1982)	Ten-year follow-up of 1971 black college freshmen surveyed by American Council on Education (N = 1,400)	High school and college racial composition
Crain (1984a)	Survey in 1982 of Project Concern participants (N = 660)	Elementary/secondary school racial composition
Crain (1984b)	Survey of employers of NLS respondents (N = 4,080)	Inner-city school vs. suburban school
Pearce (1980)	14 communities	Change in school segregation indices
Pearce, Crain, and Farley (1984)	25 large cities	Change in school segregation indices

also react more positively to black applicants who come to them from desegregated schools. Thus, even if the attitudes and behaviors of minority and majority students did not change, school desegregation would still make white-controlled institutions more open to members of minority groups, thereby creating greater opportunities for adult desegregation.

Nowhere is this result more apparent than in the two studies of the impact of schools on local housing markets.[13] We tend to think of schools simply as educational settings, but they are also major employers and respected social institutions in their communities. As such, the schools exert a powerful influence on local real estate values, and the choice of a school site is one of the most powerful city-planning tools available to local government. Cities that locate their schools and assign students to them in a manner that promotes segregation will find that they are also segregating their housing market.

AN OLD ARGUMENT, which has recently resurfaced, suggests that separate-but-equal is as good for the society as integrated-and-equal. Where the schools are concerned, at least, that argument is wrong.

Segregation in elementary and secondary schools leads to segregation in adult life — which inevitably means inequality of opportunity with regard to higher education, employment, and housing. If they wish to attend college, for example, high school graduates who are members of minority groups often have no choice but to attend a predominantly white institution. But if they have been ill-prepared by their elementary and secondary schools to cope with whites, they have been ill-prepared to cope with higher education.

Meanwhile, high school and college

Recent Research Evidence on the Effects of Desegregation

Dependent Variable	Control Variables	Findings
Racial composition of college	Socioeconomic status, sex, high school grades, college costs and reputation, financial aid, and proximity to college	Black students from majority-white high schools are more likely to enroll at majority-white four-year colleges.
Racial composition of college	Socioeconomic status, sex, high school grades and test scores, region, and proximity to college	Black students from majority-white elementary/secondary schools are more likely to enroll in and persist at majority-white two- and four-year colleges.
Racial composition of employing firm	Sex, age, public vs. private employment, educational attainment, region, and community racial composition	Blacks and whites from desegregated elementary/secondary schools are more likely to work in desegregated firms; blacks from predominantly white colleges are also more likely to work in desegregated firms.
Interracial contact, neighborhood racial composition, racial composition of occupation	Socioeconomic status, age, sex, region of birth	Blacks from desegregated elementary/secondary schools are more likely to have white social contacts, live in integrated neighborhoods.
Racial composition of co-worker groups and attitudes toward white supervisors and white co-workers	Sex, age, public vs. private employment, job status, and community racial composition	Northern blacks from majority-white high schools are more likely to have white co-workers. In the South, this relationship is also positive but confounded with community racial composition. Desegregated blacks evaluate white co-workers and supervisors more positively than do segregated blacks.
Racial composition of co-worker and friendship groups	Sex, high school grades, college major, etc.	Black adults who graduated from majority-white high schools or majority-white colleges and who grew up in majority-white neighborhoods are more likely to have white work associates and friends.
Interracial contact and neighborhood racial composition	Socioeconomic status, age, and test scores	Blacks who attend desegregated schools are more likely to move into integrated neighborhoods and to have a greater number of white friends.
Employment decisions about applicants	Race, age, sex, education, and how applicant came to firm	Employers give preference to blacks from desegregated (i.e., suburban) schools.
Change in degree of desegregation in housing and in marketing policies in housing	Communities matched by size, region, racial composition	Communities with a communitywide school desegregation plan have more integration in housing and less "racial steering" by the real estate industry.
Change in housing segregation indices	City size, racial composition, previous level of segregation	Central cities where schools are desegregated have more desegregation in housing.

graduates who are members of minority groups must deal with an employment market dominated by white-owned institutions. If they lack the credentials that

Members of minority groups who have been educated in segregated schools will generally move into segregated niches in adult society.

impress white personnel directors, these graduates are not likely to receive job offers. Moreover, researchers have found that blacks from segregated schools who have white supervisors in the workplace have more negative feelings about those supervisors than do blacks from desegregated schools.[14] Thus blacks educated in segregated schools are probably less likely to keep their jobs with white employers and to earn promotions.

Finally, in today's economy, the major portion of the average family's net worth is tied up in the family home. But those blacks who reside in the inner city have purchased homes characterized by declining property values, and they suffer serious economic losses as a consequence.

The perpetuation of segregation from childhood into adulthood might not be economically and socially harmful to minorities in a society in which minority-owned institutions provided ample opportunities for economic and social success. But U.S. society does not provide such opportunities. Therefore, segregation is harmful, because most minority-group members must find their ways into desegregated institutions if they are to achieve success as adults.

SOME OF THE STUDIES we have completed lend support to this statement. For example, a 1981 study by Jomills Braddock and Marvin Dawkins showed that blacks educated in desegregated high schools made better grades both in historically black colleges and in predominantly white ones.[15] Similarly, Robert Crain, Rita Mahard, and Ruth Narot found in 1983 that black males educated in segregated junior high schools in the South had much lower test scores as students in desegregated high schools than did black males educated in desegregated junior high schools in the South.[16]

By the same token, a 1978 study by Crain and Mahard showed that in the

North, which has very few predominantly black four-year colleges, blacks educated in desegregated elementary and secondary schools are more likely than blacks in the South to graduate from college.[17] This seems to be the case partly because blacks in the North are more likely to choose to attend a four-year college, partly because

they make higher grades there, and partly because they are less willing to drop out. Braddock and McPartland reported similar findings in 1982.[18] And Kenneth Green, in his analysis of data on black college freshmen collected by the American Council on Education, found that blacks from desegregated schools tended to make higher grades in college and to have higher college graduation rates than blacks from segregated schools.[19]

We are also beginning to accumulate some evidence that black graduates of desegregated schools have better employment opportunities than do their counterparts from segregated schools. In a study done nearly 20 years ago, Crain and Weisman found that black males from desegre-

We have considerable evidence that school desegregation is a necessary step to insure quality of economic opportunity to minorities in the U.S.

gated schools had better jobs and higher incomes than their peers from segregated schools.[20] Analyses by Braddock,[21] Braddock and McPartland,[22] Mickey Burnim,[23] and Harold Brown and David Ford,[24] using four different samples of data, all showed that black graduates of predominantly white colleges and universities enjoyed some degree of income advantage over their counterparts who had graduated from predominantly black institutions. If we combine these findings with those of Crain, from his study of employer stereotypes of blacks from segregated schools,[25] and with those of Diana Pearce in 1980 and of Pearce, Crain, and Reynolds Farley in 1984 on housing opportunities in cities that have desegregated schools,[26] we have considerable evidence that school desegregation is a necessary step to insure equality of economic opportunity to minorities in U.S. society.

Additional research remains to be done, however. We need more studies of how whites relate to blacks as a result of their own segregated or desegregated schooling. Nor is there yet a good study, using up-to-date data, to replicate the Crain and Weisman finding that black graduates of desegregated elementary and secondary schools enjoy higher incomes than their counterparts from segregated schools.

Nonetheless, the evidence already in hand tells us that the initial conception of the impact of school desegregation, as expressed in 1954 in the *Brown* decision, has been borne out. The schools are the place in which a society socializes its next generation of citizens. The research findings that we have presented here suggest that the U.S. cannot afford segregated schools, if this nation is genuinely committed to providing equality of opportunity to every citizen.

1. Christopher Jencks et al., *Inequality* (New York: Basic Books, 1972), p. 106.

2. *Brown* v. *Board of Education*, 347 U.S. 483 (1954).

3. Thomas Pettigrew, "Continuing Barriers to Desegregated Education in the South," *Sociology of Education*, Winter 1965, pp. 99-111.

4. Jomills Henry Braddock II, "The Perpetuation of Segregation Across Levels of Education: A Behavioral Assessment of the Contact-Hypothesis," *Sociology of Education*, July 1980, pp. 178-86; and Jomills Henry Braddock II and James M. McPartland, "Assessing School Desegregation Effects: New Directions in Research," in Ronald Corwin, ed., *Research in Sociology of Education and Socialization, Vol. 3* (Greenwich, Conn.: JAI, 1982), pp. 259-82.

5. Jomills Henry Braddock II, James M. McPartland, and William Trent, "Desegregated Schools and Desegregated Work Environments," paper presented at the annual meeting of the American Educational Research Association, New Orleans, 1984.

6. Robert L. Crain and Carol Weisman, *Discrimination, Personality, and Achievement* (New York: Seminar Press, 1972). See also U.S. Commission on Civil Rights, *Racial Isolation in the Public Schools, Vols. I and II* (Washington, D.C.: U.S. Government Printing Office, 1967).

7. Jomills Henry Braddock II and James M. McPartland, *More Evidence on Social-Psychological Processes That Perpetuate Minority Segregation: The Relationship of School Desegregation and Employment Segregation*, Report No. 338 (Baltimore: Center for Social Organization of Schools, Johns Hopkins University, 1983).

8. Kenneth Green, "Integration and Attainment: Preliminary Results from a National Longitudinal Study of the Impact of School Desegregation," paper presented at the annual meeting of the American Educational Research Association, Los Angeles, 1981; idem, "The Impact of Neighborhood and Secondary School Integration on Educational Achievement and Occupational Attainment of College-Bound Blacks" (Doctoral dissertation, University of California-Los Angeles, 1982); and Robert L. Crain, "Desegregated Schools and the Non-Academic Side of College Survival,"

9. Robert L. Crain, *The Quality of American High School Graduates: What Personnel Officers Say and Do About It*, Report No. 354 (Baltimore: Center for Social Organization of Schools, Johns Hopkins University, 1984).

10. Diana Pearce, *Breaking Down the Barriers: New Evidence on the Impact of Metropolitan School Desegregation on Housing Patterns* (Washington, D.C.: National Institute of Education, 1980); and Diana Pearce, Robert L. Crain, and Reynolds Farley, "Lessons Not Lost: The Effect of School Desegregation on the Rate of Residential Desegregation in Large Central Cities," paper presented at the annual meeting of the American Educational Research Association, New Orleans, 1984.

11. Crain, "Desegregated Schools . . . ."

12. Richard Scott and James M. McPartland, "Desegregation as National Policy: Correlates of Racial Attitudes," *American Educational Research Journal*, vol. 19, 1982, pp. 397-414.

13. Pearce, *Breaking Down the Barriers . . .*; and Pearce, Crain, and Farley, "Lessons Not Lost . . . ."

14. Braddock and McPartland, *More Evidence on Social-Psychological Processes . . . .*

15. Jomills Henry Braddock II and Marvin Dawkins, "Predicting Black Achievement in Higher Education," *Journal of Negro Education*, vol. 50, 1981, pp. 319-27.

16. Robert L. Crain, Rita Mahard, and Ruth Narot, *Making Desegregation Work* (Cambridge, Mass.: Ballinger, 1983).

17. Robert L. Crain and Rita Mahard, "School Racial Composition and Black College Attendance and Achievement Test Performance," *Sociology of Education*, vol. 51, 1978, pp. 81-101.

18. Braddock and McPartland, "Assessing School Desegregation Effects . . . ."

19. Green, "The Impact of Neighborhood and Secondary School Integration. . . ."

20. Crain and Weisman, *Discrimination, Personality, and Achievement.*

21. Jomills Henry Braddock II, "College Race and Black Occupational Attainment," paper presented at the annual meeting of the American Sociological Association, Detroit, 1983.

22. Jomills Henry Braddock II and James M. McPartland, "Some Costs and Benefits for Black College Students of Enrollment at Predominantly White Institutions," in Michael Nettles and Robert Thoeny, eds., *Qualitative Dimensions of Desegregation in Higher Education* (San Francisco: Jossey-Bass, forthcoming).

23. Mickey Burnim, "The Earnings Effect of Black Matriculation in Predominantly White Colleges," *Industrial and Labor Relations Review*, vol. 33, 1980, pp. 518-24.

24. Harold Brown and David Ford, "An Exploratory Analysis of Discrimination in the Employment of Black MBA Graduates," *Journal of Applied Psychology*, vol. 62, 1977, pp. 50-56.

25. Crain, "The Quality of American High School Graduates . . . ."

26. Pearce, *Breaking Down the Barriers . . .*; and Pearce, Crain, and Farley, "Lessons Not Lost . . . ."

The Bilingual Education Battle

Cynthia Gorney
Washington Post Staff Writer

They were a mystery to Barbara Ruel, these exuberant Spanish-speaking children in Redwood City, Calif., whose faces went empty every time she opened a reader and began to write English vocabulary on the blackboard. Even the most recent of the Central American immigrants understood some English, and Ruel was a veteran reading teacher, but every word she gave them seemed gone by the next week. They would stare at their readers, and Ruel could see them struggling, as though the shapes had blurred before them.

What was she doing wrong?

Then in 1976, intrigued by a controversial idea that was gaining momentum among a few teachers, Ruel decided to try something so different that she was not certain the school administration would even allow it. Working in secret, she and her Spanish-speaking aide sat down together and wrote an entire first-grade reading primer in Spanish.

Ten words a week, Ruel told the aide—two characters, a boy and a girl, admiring spring. *Mariposa.* Butterfly. *El pajaro vuele.* The bird flies. Ruel ran the pages off on the school mimeograph, the aide watched the door to make sure no one was coming, and with no advance warning Ruel presented her Spanish-speaking first-graders one day with a small stapled volume written entirely in their own language.

All at once, Ruel says now, she had a roomful of voracious readers. She had children who ran to her at the end of each day to ask what stories or new sentences they might take home that night. "We could not keep up with them," she said recently. "I thought, 'God, it's fabulous, it's just fabulous.' They started to read like normal first-graders read."

And as Barbara Ruel sat back in the nearly deserted lunchroom at Hoover Elementary and remembered those children, a single glimpse through the open classroom doors nearby might have hinted at the breadth of the change in the decade since Ruel stapled together her primers. The school district's hard-bound Spanish readers lay in fat stacks on the bookshelves, wall-length dual alphabet charts displayed the Spanish *ll* and *ch*, and a bright construction-paper leprechaun smoked a pipe under the large bulletin board letters that identified him: *El Duende.*

Ten years ago, spurred by a Supreme Court decision arguably as significant for non-English-speaking students as *Brown v. Board of Education* was for black students, the U.S. Office of Education began an effort of which the premise was unprecedented in American education. The scope was massive, affecting school districts from southern Florida to the Alaskan bush. Although their drive did not carry the force of law, the officials, wielding educational research and the Supreme Court ruling, declared that in the American public school system, every non-English-speaking child below high school age had a right to be taught in his own language—to learn basic subjects from a bilingual teacher so the child might develop self-confidence, sharpen his thinking skills and keep from falling behind in school while he was mastering English.

It was called "bilingual education," and the clamor it raised was tremendous, from the legislative battles to the heated school board meetings to the teachers who stopped speaking to each other in faculty lunchrooms. In the modern history of this nation's public schools, nothing except racial desegregation has so thoroughly entangled the classroom

From *The Washington Post National Weekly Edition*, July 29, 1985, pp. 6-10. © The Washington Post.

with intense feelings about ethnicity, politics and the meaning of becoming an American.

And although the outcry has quieted since the the early 1980s, the dilemmas of bilingual education have not. If you set out this year on a random tour of American classrooms, you would find, amid teachers still deeply divided about the idea, half a million children enrolled in widely varying programs that their schools classify as bilingual education—an effort that is costing local school boards and the federal government about $500 million a year.

You would find young Boston Haitians learning culture in Creole, and Mississippi Indians learning to read in Choctaw, and children of Michigan immigrants learning history in Albanian and Arabic. You would find math workbooks in Spanish, Italian reading primers, Chinese vocabulary cards, Navajo storybooks, an Earth sciences text in Lao, a U.S. history text in Vietnamese, and color and shape charts written in the Filipino dialect Tagalog.

In Houston or San Francisco, you would visit classrooms that take another approach, in which non-English-speaking students are immersed in English as a Second Language courses—they hear and read nothing but English.

You would visit a Spanish bilingual class whose teacher speaks no Spanish; a bilingual Cambodian class whose teacher speaks no Khmer; a bilingual Chinese class whose teacher has no intention of learning Chinese and believes most dual-language education has no place in the taxpayer-funded schools of an English-speaking society.

You would visit Oakland, where on March 1, nine years after state officials began requiring bilingual education for children who speak another language more fluently than they speak English, the California State Education Code finally caught up with Franklin Elementary School.

Spurred by an Oakland parents' lawsuit demanding improved bilingual classes citywide, a judge ordered the city's schools into compliance with the state guidelines that map out the largest bilingual education effort in the nation. In California, if an elementary school has one grade with at least 10 limited-English students from a particular language group, the school has to offer a bilingual class just for them.

Inside Franklin, which sits in the midst of inexpensive rental housing that attracts new immigrants, 14 languages are spoken in the course of a normal school day. According to state regulations, the school was supposed to offer bilingual classes in Cantonese, Spanish, Vietnamese, Lao, Khmer and the Ethiopian language Tigrinya.

Priscilla McClendon, a fifth-grade teacher who jokes that she finds challenge aplenty in just mastering English, was assigned a group of fourth- and fifth-grade Cambodians and told to promise in writing that she would learn Khmer.

Francesca Ferrari was assigned a collection of first- to third-grade Ethiopians and told to promise in writing that she would learn Tigrinya. Since state law requires at least one-third of the children in a bilingual class to be native English speakers, she got some of those, too—eight black American children and one Hispanic girl whose mother had just pulled her out of a Spanish bilingual class because she thought her daughter wasn't learning enough English.

Pat Eimerl lost her Cambodian-Vietnamese-Ethiopian-Thai-Hispanic sixth grade, which on the books had been labeled a Cambodian bilingual class, since Eimerl had earlier promised in writing to learn Khmer. Her new students, all of whom filed in one afternoon carrying the contents of their former desks, are Cantonese-speaking Vietnamese. Eimerl was told to promise she would learn Cantonese, since this was now supposed to be a Chinese bilingual class, but for weeks she refused to sign the promise.

"See, with Cambodian I'm safe, because there aren't any classes," Eimerl said, referring to language classes for teachers. She was so angry her voice shook, "But there are Chinese classes. I've got three kids. I'm 40 years old. I'm not about to go try to learn Chinese."

A Disappointing Decade

When federal officials began the push for bilingual education, grand hopes and promising research armed them against their critics. High school dropout rates for Hispanics were far higher than those for white students, they observed; here, they argued, was a possible remedy. Theory and their own convictions convinced them that students who learned at least part-time in their native language had a much better chance in the schools: They would keep up academically, they would maintain their self-esteem, and they might in the end become literate and articulate in two languages.

A decade later, much of the whole enterprise has dismayed both its longtime critics and some of the people who most ardently believe in bilingual education. National Hispanic high school dropout rates, although not reliably monitored, are as high as ever: just under 40 percent, according to estimates by the Washington-based National Hispanic Policy Development Project. Teachers from San Francisco to Providence can be heard complaining that bilingual classes hold students back or keep them away from English. A U.S. Department of Education study, published in 1983 to vehement criticism from many bilingual educators, found "no consistent evidence" that dual-language instruction improved students' academic progress.

And bilingual advocates say schools are slapping the "bilingual" label on classes that have almost nothing to do with dual-language teaching. They also say that because some states don't require bilingual education and some schools ignore their own state requirements, more than three-quarters of the limited-English-speaking children in this country are receiving no dual-language instruction at all.

"What's going on in 90 percent of the classrooms in this country is a joke in respect to what bilingual education ought to be," says Duane Campbell, a Spanish-English bilingual teacher who now works in the bilingual teacher training program at California State University at Sacramento. "And if you're going to tell me that doesn't work, I'll agree with you. It doesn't work."

The term "bilingual education" covers such vast territory—gifted teachers and dreadful teachers, imaginative new workshops and rote learning in overcrowded classrooms—that it defies the kind of generalizations people seem to want when such a controversial idea is proposed as public policy. So complex is the argument that critics and advocates cannot even agree on how many children in this country come to school with what the jargon calls "limited English proficiency;" the estimates range from 1.5 million to 3.5 million.

But a look at the problems in this massive undertaking, the business of helping immigrant schoolchildren in their own language, might begin at Franklin Elementary, or Franklin Year-Round, as the school is officially named: Its side-by-side buildings now hold children in a schedule that has eliminated the summer break. Down the long hallways, the bulletin boards all a-color with spring tulips and construction paper Humpty-Dumptys, doorways frame bright classrooms crowded desk to desk with the children of the new immigration. *Phumpuang Phaisan, Khadijah Muhammed, Phonevil Pomsouvanh, Kai-Phong Mack, Alejandro Esparza.* The names, in careful block lettering, fill pink and green class lists on the desk of Franklin's harried bilingual coordinator, and next to each name the numerical code for the language the child brought to school: Khmer, Tigrinya, Lao, Cantonese, Spanish.

"If you figure just the amount of time, money and education disruption . . . the fact that English speakers have zero rights . . . this has been costly as hell," says Martha Muller, the coordinator who for the last three months has been shuffling and reshuffling names into lists that will comply with California state education laws. "The law is not meant for this kind of school. It is meant for a nice, neat, orderly, Spanish-English population, or a Chinese-English population, or something. But it's not meant for a multilanguage school."

"Now that we're in compliance, it's just as ridiculous as when we were out of compliance," says Michael Phillips, who teaches his combined fourth- and fifth-grade class in both English and the Vietnamese he learned in preparation for a year's military assignment in Vietnam. "So all my English-speaking kids have to sit there and wait while I'm translating for the Vietnamese. Now who's being served there?"

As chaotic as it is at this school, with nearly every morning bringing new immigrants to the front office to enroll their children, bilingual education at Franklin is in some of the same trouble that has plagued schools across the country for the past decade. It begins with California state law—a law, similar to those in some of the 22 states that mandate or permit bilingual classes, that lays out the number of speakers of any single language that is supposed to trigger a bilingual class.

It was violations of that requirement, among many other complaints, that moved a group of Oakland parents last fall to bring what turned into a bitterly argued lawsuit that accused the city school board of causing "irreparable injury" to thousands of students by failing to offer them bilingual classes. The documentation listed Franklin as one of the worst offenders: The school was missing teachers or aides in five languages, including Lao and Tigrinya. How does a school find candidates for a job like that?

School officials actually interviewed a few people, Franklin principal Jay Cleckner says, although lawyers for the parents' group insisted Oakland had done far too little recruiting and hiring. But almost nobody qualified as an American classroom teacher, Cleckner says. And if a few spoke English well enough to work as classroom aides, he says, he could not keep them in part-time jobs that paid about $5 an hour and offered no benefits. "I have interviewed for aides and for teachers, people who are very qualified," Clecker says. "But they can go back to work for four times what I can pay them, and I tell them, 'Go. Take care of yourself.' "

Where Do You Find a Teacher Who Speaks Hmong?

The national shortage of qualified teachers has for some years been one of bilingual education's major problems. There is not a single Khmer- or Hmong-speaking credentialed teacher in California, which has the nation's highest numbers of refugees from Cambodia and the part of Laos that was home to the Hmong people. Even qualified teachers who speak fluent Spanish are in short supply in many states; when Houston bilingual administrator Delia Pompa was presented this year with the revised Texas mandates for bilingual education through fifth grade, she calculated that even with extensive recruiting and $1,500 bonuses for the mostly Spanish-speaking dual-language teachers, conventional teaching patterns were going to leave the district short 400 teachers qualified to work in two languages.

"Before, when Hispanics went to college, they went into teaching," says Pompa, who plans to accommodate the short-

age by classroom rearrangements such as teacher pairing. "Hispanics are starting to go into other professions . . . Teaching, and education in general, is going through a low period. Teaching isn't looked at as a real respected profession. You're looking at a lot of problems."

Hardly anybody seriously expects schoolteachers such as the ones at Franklin to learn Khmer or Lao in their spare time. But one of the ways many areas have adapted to the shortage is by asking teachers to sign up for courses in languages that seem more manageable to learn. In California, state figures show that fully half the "bilingual" teachers are regular teachers who have pledged to learn dual-language teaching methods and become fluent in a second language (usually Spanish, but occasionally English) while a bilingual aide helps them with the children.

That leads to a whole new set of problems. How well those teachers are actually learning both the language and the complicated business of dual-language teaching varies from school to school, particularly since many principals are dubious about the idea to begin with. One elementary school will house an after-hours class for teachers who are genuinely committed to learning Spanish, and usually doing so on their own time. A second will sign up "bilingual" teachers who plainly have little interest in ever learning more than a few words of the language. Even when they do try, bilingual advocates sometimes wonder what comes of their efforts: A Hispanic attorney tells of the newly trained Texas teacher who stood before a parents' group and began, "*Damas y caballos*," which is a salutation of sorts; it means "Ladies and horses."

And the proceedings inside the dual-language class are only as effective as the teacher who runs it. In visits this spring to more than 20 bilingual classrooms, a reporter watched one bilingual teacher review long division in English scarcely intelligible through his Spanish accent, and another teacher who spoke no Spanish and left all the Spanish business to an aide she clearly distrusted: "I don't even think she's graduated from high school," the teacher confided.

Here were teachers translating right through history and arithmetic lessons, despite linguists' warnings that simultaneous translation is the least effective bilingual teaching method because it lets the student listen to the language he knows best. Here were teachers frustrated by school systems that hurried children into full-time English so fast that, as the teachers saw it, some of the point of bilingual education was being lost—the idea that children's English work will be stronger and more confident if they are allowed to develop fully and work in their own language at least part time for more than a year or two.

Here were teachers so tired of the whole bilingual effort—of juggling multiple two-language reading groups, battling supervisors and watching children's confusion when a school offered them dual-language classes at one grade but then abruptly not at another—that the teachers had finally bailed out. "You go crazy—that's why a lot of bilingual teachers go out of the program, because they can't handle it," says Erlinda Griffin, a quadrilingual Filipina who left bilingual teaching seven years ago for a school supervisory job in the central California farm city of Fresno. Griffin believes bilingual education theory, and she has seen programs that seem to her to use it successfully. "But unfortunately, they were in the minority—there were so few of them."

And here, too, were teachers, nearly all of them monolingual English speakers, convinced that the bilingual classes they had seen were in large part misguided efforts that held a lot of children back. An Arizona teacher remembered Geme, her Navajo student who had sat through five years of bilingual classes before somebody realized the boy was having trouble because he had spoken scarcely a word of Navajo before he came to school. A suburban San Francisco teacher remembered Spanish-speaking children who never seemed to make the promised transition into English. A Rhode Island counselor remembered the Puerto Rican boy, bewildered by his referral to bilingual classes, who told the counselor in flawless English that he had grown up and gone to school in Lawrence, Mass.

"This is the stuff that goes on all the time," the counselor said. "I think a lot of kids are kept in those programs simply to build up the numbers and justify the programs. We've got kids in those programs who are fluent in English."

Remedial Instruction vs. Linguistic Enrichment

If anybody does belong in bilingual classes, who is it? Some states reserve bilingual classes for children who speak Spanish or some other language, prompting complaints about ethnic and linguistic segregation. California requires them whenever possible to be in classes with native English speakers so the children won't be segregated and will have role models to help them learn the language.

But that doesn't satisfy everybody either. Because most bilingual classes are designed as remedial programs, aimed at moving children into English as rapidly as possible, English-speaking parents have often been disappointed when they allow their children into bilingual classes in the hope that they will learn Spanish. And in towns such as Fillmore, a heavily Hispanic southern California farming community where the expansion of bilingual classes set off an angry Anglo protest this spring, English-speaking parents say their children waste time in a class taught partly in another language.

"Who's going to meet *my* daughter's needs?" demands Judy Collins, a Fillmore parent whose husband recently proposed a controversial city council-adopted resolution making English the "official language" of Fillmore. "The amount of time that teacher is speaking Spanish is time that my child is not getting English instruction," Collins says.

Complaints like these have complicated the response to a generally unenthusiastic 1983 bilingual-education report by two U.S. Department of Education researchers. At the request of a White House policy review group, the researchers examined several hundred studies on bilingual education, many of which concluded that the classes had improved students' academic performance, and found only 39 to be "methodologically acceptable." After analyzing those 39 studies, the researchers reported bilingual education producing only mixed results.

"Sometimes kids did better," says Department of Education analyst Keith Baker, the report's coauthor. "Sometimes it had no effect. And sometimes it had negative effects."

Baker and his partner, who have been criticized for their own methodology, suggested in the report that although limited-English-speaking children clearly needed some special attention, education officials might rethink their reliance on classes using native languages—that full-time intensive English programs, for example, might be more effective in some cases.

Would Franklin Elementary's Francesca Ferrari, facing her tiny Ellis Island of a classroom earlier this year, have done any of her students a greater service by using their own language?

"This I do not know," she says. "I do not know what I really think about bilingual education."

When the Oakland parents' lawsuit was settled in May, with school officials committing themselves to a considerable expansion of the bilingual staff, the central office finally found some qualified teachers' aides for Franklin; a Tigrinya-speaking Ethiopian man now helps in Ferrari's classroom for 80 minutes a day. And she welcomes his presence, she says. He makes things easier for her. In June they were working on *sq* words, and Ferrari did not have to go into contortions or bring lemons into class to explain *squirt* and *squint* and *squid*.

These are ideas the children would have grasped without translation, Ferrari says. Demonstrations, in her experience, are sometimes even more vivid than translation. But she is happy to have the aide anyway—"grateful," Ferrari says. "I think it's a sense of security for the children to have him there, I really do."

Her class no longer includes the Spanish-speaking child; it is now all Ethiopian and native English-speaking children, and in March, as a welcoming gesture, Ferrari put up an Ethiopian market poster and wrote the Tigrinya words for "How are you?" in big bright letters on a poster she taped to the classroom door: *Camilla ha.*

Some weeks later, in discreet messages conveyed through the principal's office, Ferrari was told that this had distressed the Ethiopian families. Parents of all but three of her Ethiopian students indicated on signed forms that they wished their children taught exclusively in English, so Ferrari need no longer abide by her implausible promise to learn Tigrinya.

"They don't want their culture brought in," Ferrari says. "They feel they can take care of that at home." She took the poster down and pulled *Camilla ha* off the classroom door.

Immersion: An Aid or a Threat to Bilingual Education?

In a San Francisco classroom bright with wall decorations, a line of raggedly cut paper pandas stretched overhead, Liana Szeto sat cross-legged on the floor and explained the morning game to the children around her. She would start with five plastic cubes and a milk carton with the top cut off, and they were to close their eyes while she hid some of the cubes under the milk carton. Then they could count the remaining cubes and figure out how many she had hidden.

Szeto suggested Sparky might make the next guess.

Jesse (Sparky) Manger, a small blond boy in standard-issue kindergarten blue jeans and sneakers, squeezed his eyes shut and covered them with his hands. "Sparky," Szeto said, *"Gu yahp bihn yauh gei do go?"*

Just as she had all morning—just as she does for every full school day in a class made up of white children, black children, Chinese-American children and a Chinese-Hispanic child—Szeto was speaking straight Cantonese.

Sparky, whisking his hands away and gazing at the single cube left atop the milk carton, contemplated her question: Yes, he could guess how many she had left inside. *"Sei,"* he said. Szeto lifted the carton and clapped her hands in approval. Four, of course, was right.

Szeto, a 27-year-old Hong Kong immigrant who coaxes and performs her way through each day with a vigor that is almost exhausting to watch, speaks excellent English; she learned it in Hong Kong schools and in the junior high schools she attended when her family arrived in San Francisco. But many of her students don't realize she speaks any English. From the first day of school last September, confronted with 24 kindergarten children who by and large spoke not a word of Cantonese, Szeto has never used English in her classroom. She uses posters, gestures, games, songs, repetition, theatrics, picture books, field trips and anything else she imagines might help her teach, but whenever she speaks—from "Please take out your pencils" to "Let's tell the story of the five foolish fishermen!"—she speaks in Cantonese.

And Sparky Manger's mother Judy, an airline ticket agent who has cringed at most Americans' inability to manage other languages, is delighted. "With China becoming a world power, in his lifetime, it's really going to be beneficial for him to learn Chinese," she says. "I thought he was going to come home and say, 'Mom, what have you done to me?' And he's never once said anything to me about that. He loves it . . . Now he tells me his name is Jesse Wong sometimes."

There is a label in educationalese for the work Szeto is doing with these children, all of whom were sent to West Portal School because their parents wanted to experiment with a teaching method now being tried in at least 18 public school districts around the country. It is called language immersion, and although the methods vary, the principle is the same: English-speaking children, principally from homes where nothing but English is spoken, spend part or all of their days in classes conducted entirely in another language.

In Baton Rouge, La., fourth-graders last month were discussing the tax system, studying the Louisiana government and answering written test questions about layers of the atmosphere—all in French. In Culver City, Calif., fifth-graders were working long-division problems and reading aloud stories about construction workers and shy cats—all in Spanish.

There is Spanish immersion in Tulsa, French immersion in Montgomery County, Md., German immersion in Milwaukee and Cincinnati. San Francisco school officials, already immersing students in Spanish and Cantonese, are thinking of adding Mandarin.

And although some of the programs, like San Francisco's, are too new for any serious evaluation, many administrators have reported results comparable to those out of Canada, where for 20 years public schools have been offering French immersion that University of Southern California linguistics professor Stephen D. Krashen has written "may be the most successful program ever recorded in the professional language-teaching literature."

In the vast new array of efforts at teaching in two languages, no approach has been so carefully monitored, so widely praised for its effectiveness—and, in one of the more complicated ironies of this whole controversial field, so disturbing to advocates of the more familiar theories of bilingual education, which insist that a child should learn to read and think first in his native language.

The vision of these immersion classes, of American-born children learning math and reading from teachers who never address them in English, has prompted opponents of public bilingual education to ask the obvious question: If you can drop an English-speaking child into a special all-Spanish classroom and get him working and thinking in Spanish with no damage to his psyche or test scores, why can't you do the same thing in reverse? Isn't this a natural way to accustom Spanish speakers to English without having to teach them reading and basic skills in Spanish?

School districts in several states already are trying special all-English programs for Spanish-speakers, and the federal government, in U.S. Department of Education reports and in increased availability of special funds, has troubled bilingual-education advocates by showing considerable interest in the idea. And the heat this argument has generated—some teachers and language experts use words like "a crock" and "a crime" to describe the practice of immersing Spanish-speakers into special all-English classes—is part of the national debate about America's attitude toward non-English languages, about the role of language in an immigrant society, about the ties between language and the human spirit.

'If I Can Speak Spanish, I Can Do Anything'

It was show-and-tell time in an afternoon kindergarten and first-grade class in Culver City's El Rincon School, just outside Los Angeles. Irma Wright, her black hair curled and a carnation pinned to her lapel, summoned around her a noisy collection of children and announced who would begin.

"Tu no eres primera," she admonished a small blond girl who had clamored to be first. *"Cheryl es primera."*

The child nodded, resigned to the primacy of Cheryl, and said in English, "Can I be second?"

Thus it went, the children—nearly every one of them from an English-speaking home—looking entirely unconcerned that their teacher spoke to them only in rapid, native Spanish. Cheryl showed off a stuffed gray bear that she said belonged to her mother, and Wright asked, *"Quien le dio eso a tu madre?"* Nobody had given it to her mother, Cheryl answered. "She saw it and she got it in a store."

"Que tiene este oso en la nariz?" Wright asked, wondering what was appliqued on the bear's nose. The children knew a heart when they saw one: *"Un corazon!"* they cried.

Irma Wright, a Hispanic woman who grew up in El Paso, has been teaching the kindergarten immersion class since 1971, when the Culver City schools opened the first U.S. version of the program that was generating so much interest in Canada. A school outside Montreal, now in its 20th year, had set off the whole experiment when a group of English-speaking parents asked for a dramatic and effective way to teach their children French; by last year, according to an article in the Canadian magazine Language and Society, 115,000 Canadian children were studying in one of the French immersion programs now offered in every province.

Culver City administrators, under the supervision of linguists at the University of California at Los Angeles, followed almost precisely the Quebec model: no English at all for the first two years (although the children are free to speak English, and the teacher must be bilingual so that she or he can understand and answer); an hour a day of English reading and language arts in second and third grades; and then a steady increase of English teaching time, until by the fifth grade students are doing more than a third of their classwork in English. "When they leave the elementary school, they are functionally bilingual," says Eugene Ziff, the principal at El Rincon. "They can understand, read, write and speak Spanish in a functional manner, and they have done this without losing any of their basic skills in English."

As he has done for dozens of uncertain parents, Ziff pulls out the mimeographed sheet listing El Rincon's most recent scores on the California Test of Basic Skills, which is administered in both English and Spanish to students in the immersion classes. In 1983 the sixth-grade students were testing out at eighth-grade level on English vocabulary and comprehension. Language mechanics and expression, math concepts and computation—all showed above-average scores, and in the case of language expression, far above average. Only English spelling fell slightly short.

As for their Spanish skills, the Spanish reading test scores are not quite up to averages for native language speakers, but a visit to Mary Nabours' fourth- and fifth-grade classroom, for example, is startling: Children with names like Jennifer Feingold and Pentti Monkkonen read easily from their Spanish texts, or talk in Spanish about characters in the story they have just finished, or work in longhand on their definitions.

Their accents range from good to nearly native; Nabours, who is American but lived in Mexico while studying Spanish, speaks with almost no trace of an American accent. They discuss words like *supongo,* suppose, and *interes,* as in bank interest, and if their grammar is often not quite right, they plow cheerfully through what they are trying to say. A lively red-haired girl, asked to escort a visitor to the kindergarten, is asked in Spanish whether she found the two languages difficult to manage, and she says in slightly ungrammatical but entirely unselfconscious Spanish, "No, because I'm used to it."

"They don't have any trouble getting across what they want to say," Nabours says. "The program encourages creativity in a certain way, but the main thing it encourages—this is my opinion; I can't prove it, but I feel it in every cell in my body—is this feeling of, 'I can' . . . . 'If I can speak Spanish, I can do anything. I can do math. I can do science. I can do anything.' "

So why shouldn't it work in reverse? Why shouldn't Spanish speakers learn English the same way? To answer that, teachers like Nabours believe, you must think about English and Spanish and the social roles they play here. The linguists who designed immersion programs like Culver City's have insisted the programs be used only for children who speak English, children who will go straight into an English middle school, children whose families have sought out the second language and who will never, as long as they live in North America, risk losing the language they grew up with.

One six-school program in San Diego is using the Culver City model on both English and Spanish speakers, immersing them all into Spanish and then gradually working English into half the school day, but its goal is the same as Culver City's—to encourage bilingualism, and to celebrate the learning and reading of two languages rather than one.

That very notion, the idea that schools should promote bilingualism and should have advanced classes in both languages, has been thoroughly attacked during public debates over dual-language education for Hispanics. There is still a strong feeling among many teachers and parents' groups that American schools ought to be teaching in English, that offering special classes for bilingual children amounts to catering to certain ethnic groups.

When Spanish speakers are immersed in English, as several Texas school districts are doing in a state-sponsored pilot program, no one imagines that they will gradually have Spanish worked back in to take over half their school day. The point is simply to teach them English, using techniques that have worked for Anglophones in places like Culver City: Speak nothing but English to the children, but let them use Spanish when they wish; use vocabulary and phrasing aimed at children just learning the language; fill the gaps with posters and pantomime and things the children can touch.

English as a Second Language, Houston-Style

Teacher Rachel Echavarry smiles as she traverses the rows of quiet children, holding up small picture cards and waiting for each response.

"Jesus, what's this?"

"It's a cat."

"What's this?"

"It's a cow."

"Where is the cow?" Hesitation.

Then, tentatively: "The cow—is in—the barn."

There is nothing unique about a class like this; it is standard English as a Second Language (ESL) teaching, offered as part of many public schools' bilingual programs. The difference, at Gregory-Lincoln Education Center in Houston and the other Texas schools trying similar approaches, is that Jesus and his classmates are immersed in English all day. They are never supposed to hear Spanish from their teachers. Indeed, many of

From Chinatown to The Supreme Court

SAN FRANCISCO—Even as Edward Steinman pushed his lawsuit, working his way through the courts with an argument that would help spread bilingual education through the American public school system, his aunts invoked the memory of his late father—the child of immigrants from Russia, speaking nothing but Yiddish, who was thrown into American public schools and made to learn English on his own.

And the elder Steinman did learn English, fluently enough to spend his life as a journalist. "I think there are many, like my father, who did it without bilingual education," Steinman says. "But the studies show there are hundreds of thousands of people who without bilingual education are not going to learn English."

Steinman was barely out of law school, a long-haired 25-year-old working in 1970 out of a cramped basement office in San Francisco's Chinatown. Some of his Chinese clients would come to him for other reasons, then end up complaining that their children were not following what went on in school, like the woman who visited him to talk about a problem with her landlord. Then, as Steinman remembers it, she hesitantly began answering his questions about her 6-year-old son.

The boy, Steinman says she told him, spoke only Chinese. The teachers spoke only English. The woman's name was Kam Wai Lau, and within a year the name of her son, Kinney, led the long list of plaintiffs in a lawsuit that eventually reached the U.S. Supreme Court. Confronted with evidence that fewer than half of San Francisco's Chinese-speaking students were receiving any language help, the court declared that schools must offer language-minority children some special attention. And that attention, a federal panel concluded in 1975 in a controversial set of guidelines, was to be dual-language education. Although bilingual education was not a new idea, this was different because the government was demanding it.

As for the young Lau, who now goes by the name of Kenny and is a 21-year-old part-time computer programming student at San Francisco's City College, the whole case is a memory so dim that he had to be reminded in an interview who Steinman was. "I think the only reason I lost out is because I was lazy—that's all there is to it," he says. "It's nothing to do with understanding what an instructor's saying."

Might Chinese language instruction have helped him do better in school?

"I don't know," he says. "Well, maybe—yeah, it might have made a difference—let's say if I didn't understand something, maybe I could hear a different version of it in Chinese. I don't know. Never happened to me."

—Cynthia Gorney

the teachers at Gregory-Lincoln do not speak Spanish or any of the Indochinese languages that nearly a quarter of the students arrive with; instead, in Saturday workshops and in-class training, they have studied ESL teaching techniques.

How well it works—whether these Texas children are having an easier time learning English while keeping up in their other classes—is still in some dispute.

"Thank God for the English immersion," says Linda Hunter, a fourth-grade teacher now in her 10th year at Gregory-Lincoln, which used to offer an hour a day of Spanish-language instruction. Her colleague Sherilyn Kozodoy, a third-grade teacher whose class includes two Spanish-speaking children, agrees. "I had students in [my former school] who had been going to the bilingual classes for three or four years and still had difficulty with the English language," Kozodoy says. "They learn it much more slowly."

Some teachers are similarly enthusiastic in Texas cities such as McAllen, which has attracted national attention for its English immersion pilot; and in Virginia's Fairfax County, which for seven years has insisted on intensive English instead of dual-language instruction. But preliminary Texas data indicate so far that the immersion classes there, experimentally begun four years ago in cities that also offered bilingual programs, are producing English test scores no higher than those from the bilingual classes, and there are misgivings about the experiment even among some administrators in charge of it.

"I had one teacher start crying and saying, 'Look, I can't do this, it's not fair to the kids,'" says Pompa, Houston's bilingual education administrator. "There were others, to be perfectly fair, who thought it was a good option . . . . I'll be honest. I would prefer a dual language program, because I don't know what kind of cognitive deficits [the immersion children] are going to have four or five years later. And I think there are going to be some."

Wallace Lambert, the social psychologist and language expert who developed the first French immersion programs in Quebec, has argued for more than a decade that to use these techniques on language-minority children is, as he wrote in a 1984 California Department of Education volume, "not only wrong but dangerous." The danger, he argues, lies in what he calls "subtractive bilingualism"—the elimination in school of the language the child first used to think, to conceive ideas and accept who he is.

"We are not removing their language from school," counters Sally Clyburn, acting instructional supervisor for the Houston schools. "We are removing the language from instruction . . . the students *are* using their native language. They can be seen walking to the school cafeteria, to and from the playground, using their native language."

"The child is basically being told, 'Your language is not worth anything,'" says William Prather, who teaches in Spanish to English speakers at Rock Creek Elementary School's Spanish immersion program in Chevy Chase, Md., and who thinks the approach is entirely wrong for non-English speakers. Teachers like Prather and Mary Nabours believe a child whose language is kept out of the classroom will probably lose much of it, if his is not the language of society at large, and that public schools do children a great disservice that way.

The argument over language immersion is not really about the merits of the few programs now trying in some formal and monitored way to place non-English speaking children in special all-English classes. There are not very many of those programs—most are either small experiments or are aimed at children like the Indochinese, who often have no bilingual teachers available—and it is highly unlikely that in the near future they could replace bilingual classes. Federal funds that can be used for special English immersion programs are limited to less than 10 percent of the $139 million budgeted for bilingual education this year.

The battle over that funding was fierce, though, with bilingual education critics wanting much more of the budgeted money to be available to English immersion-type experiments. Bilingual education advocates fought back, some of them declaring that these special immersion classes were simply a convoluted path back to the days when schools openly sent Spanish and Chinese-speaking children to fend for themselves in standard all-English classes—the kind of approach the Supreme Court prohibited 11 years ago.

So the argument is really about the value and meaning of native language in a child's schooling, and that makes it much bigger and more complicated than the proceedings inside a few public school classrooms.

"I think the issue becomes an emotional issue, and people stop looking at what kids need, and what works for kids," says Houston's Delia Pompa. "It becomes in some ways a threat, and sometimes 'I-made-it-why-can't-they,' and sometimes people bring political baggage and emotional baggage to it. I think sometimes people miss the point."

Sexism in the Schoolroom of the '80s

THINGS HAVEN'T CHANGED.
BOYS STILL GET MORE ATTENTION, ENCOURAGEMENT
AND AIRTIME THAN GIRLS DO.

MYRA AND DAVID SADKER

Myra and David Sadker are professors of education at American University, Washington, D.C.

If a boy calls out in class, he gets teacher attention, especially intellectual attention. If a girl calls out in class, she is told to raise her hand before speaking. Teachers praise boys more than girls, give boys more academic help and are more likely to accept boys' comments during classroom discussions. These are only a few examples of how teachers favor boys. Through this advantage boys increase their chances for better education and possibly higher pay and quicker promotions. Although many believe that classroom sexism disappeared in the early '70s, it hasn't.

Education is not a spectator sport. Numerous researchers, most recently John Goodlad, former dean of education at the University of California at Los Angeles and author of *A Place Called School*, have shown that when students participate in classroom discussion they hold more positive attitudes toward school, and that positive attitudes enhance learning. It is no coincidence that girls are more passive in the classroom and score lower than boys on SAT's.

Most teachers claim that girls participate and are called on in class as often as boys. But a three-year study we recently completed found that this is not true; vocally, boys clearly dominate the classroom. When we showed teachers and administrators a film of a classroom discussion and asked who was talking more, the teachers overwhelmingly said the girls were. But in reality, the boys in the film were out-talking the girls at a ratio of three to one. Even educators who are active in feminist issues were unable to spot the sex bias until they counted and coded who was talking and who was just watching. Stereotypes of garrulous and gossipy women are so strong that teachers fail to see this communi-cations gender gap even when it is right before their eyes.

Field researchers in our study observed students in more than a hundred fourth-, sixth- and eighth-grade classes in four states and the District of Columbia. The teachers and students were male and female, black and white, from urban, suburban and rural communities. Half of the classrooms covered language arts and English—subjects in which girls traditionally have excelled; the other half covered math and science—traditionally male domains.

We found that at all grade levels, in all communities and in all subject areas, boys dominated classroom communication. They participated in more interactions than girls did and their participation became greater as the year went on.

Our research contradicted the traditional assumption that girls dominate classroom discussion in reading while boys are dominant in math. We found that whether the subject was language arts and English or math and science, boys got more than their fair share of teacher attention.

Some critics claim that if teachers talk more to male students, it is simply because boys are more assertive in grabbing their attention—a classic case of the squeaky wheel getting the educational oil. In fact, our research shows that boys are more assertive in the classroom. While girls sit patiently with their hands raised, boys literally grab teacher attention. They are eight times more likely than girls to call out answers. However, male assertiveness is not the whole answer.

Teachers behave differently, depending on whether boys or girls call out answers during discussions. When boys call out comments without raising their hands, teachers accept their answers. However, when girls call out, teachers reprimand this "inappropriate" behavior with messages such as, "In this class we don't shout out answers, we raise our hands." The message is subtle but powerful: Boys should be academically assertive and grab teacher attention; girls should act like ladies and keep quiet.

Teachers in our study revealed an interaction pattern that we called a "mind sex." After calling on a student, they tended to keep calling on students of the same sex. While this pattern applied to both sexes, it was far more pronounced among boys and allowed them more than their fair share of airtime.

It may be that when teachers call on someone, they continue thinking of that sex. Another explanation may be found in the seating patterns of elementary, secondary and even postsecondary classrooms. In approximately half of the classrooms in our study, male and female students sat in separate parts of the room. Sometimes the teacher created this segregation, but more often, the students segregated themselves. A teacher's tendency to interact with same-sex students may be a simple matter of where each sex sits. For example, a teacher calls on a female student, looks around the same area and then continues questioning the students around this girl, all of whom are female. When the teacher refocuses to a section of the classroom where boys are seated, boys receive the series of questions. And because

WHILE GIRLS SIT PATIENTLY WITH THEIR HANDS RAISED, BOYS LITERALLY GRAB TEACHER ATTENTION.

boys are more assertive, the teacher may interact with their section longer.

Girls are often shortchanged in quality as well as in quantity of teacher attention. In 1975 psychologists Lisa Serbin and K. Daniel O'Leary, then at the State University of New York at Stony Brook, studied classroom interaction at the preschool level and found that teachers gave boys more attention, praised them more often and were at least twice as likely to have extended conversations with them. Serbin and O'Leary also found that teachers were twice as likely to give male students detailed instructions on how to do things for themselves. With female students, teachers were more likely to do it for them instead. The result was that boys learned to become independent, girls learned to become dependent.

Instructors at the other end of the educational spectrum also exhibit this same "let me do it for you" behavior toward female students. Constantina Safilios-Rothschild, a sociologist with the Population Council in New York, studied sex desegregation at the Coast Guard Academy and found that the instructors were giving detailed instructions on how to accomplish tasks to male students, but were doing the jobs and operating the equipment for the female students.

Years of experience have shown that the best way to learn something is to do it yourself; classroom chivalry is not only misplaced, it is detrimental. It is also important to give students specific and direct feedback about the quality of their work and answers. During classroom discussion, teachers in our study reacted to boys' answers with dynamic, precise and effective re-

sponses, while they often gave girls bland and diffuse reactions.

Teachers' reactions were classified in four categories: praise ("Good answer"); criticism ("That answer is wrong"); help and remediation ("Try again—but check your long division"); or acceptance without any evaluation or assistance ("OK" "Uh-huh").

Despite caricatures of school as a harsh and punitive place, fewer than 5 percent of the teachers' reactions were criticisms, even of the mildest sort. But praise didn't happen often either; it made up slightly more than 10 percent of teachers' reactions. More than 50 percent of teachers' responses fell into the "OK" category.

Teachers distributed these four reactions differently among boys than among girls. Here are some of the typical patterns.

Teacher: "What's the capital of Maryland? Joel?"
Joel: "Baltimore."
Teacher: "What's the largest city in Maryland, Joel?"
Joel: "Baltimore."
Teacher: "That's good. But Baltimore isn't the capital. The capital is also the location of the U.S. Naval Academy. Joel, do you want to try again?"
Joel: "Annapolis."
Teacher: "Excellent. Anne, what's the capital of Maine?"
Anne: "Portland."
Teacher: "Judy, do you want to try?"
Judy: "Augusta."
Teacher: "OK."

In this snapshot of a classroom discussion, Joel was told when his answer was wrong (criticism); was helped to discover the correct answer (remediation); and was praised when he offered the correct response. When Anne was wrong, the teacher, rather than staying with her, moved to Judy, who received only simple acceptance for her correct answer. Joel received the more specific teacher reaction and benefited from a longer, more precise and intense educational interaction.

Too often, girls remain in the dark about the quality of their answers. Teachers rarely tell them if their answers are excellent, need to be improved or are just plain wrong. Unfortunately, acceptance, the imprecise response packing the least educational punch, gets the most equitable sex distribution in classrooms. Active students receiving precise feedback are more likely to achieve academically. And they are more likely to be boys. Consider the following:

☐ Although girls start school ahead of boys in reading and basic computation, by the time they graduate from high school, boys have higher SAT scores in both areas.

☐ By high school, some girls become less committed to careers, although their grades and achievement-test scores may be as good as boys'. Many girls' interests turn to marriage or stereotypically female jobs. Part of the reason may be that some women feel that men disapprove of their using their intelligence.

☐ Girls are less likely to take math and science courses and to participate in special or gifted programs in these subjects, even if they have a talent for them. They are also more likely to believe that they are incapable of pursuing math and science in college and to avoid the subjects.

☐ Girls are more likely to attribute failure to internal factors, such as ability, rather than to external factors, such as luck.

The sexist communication game is played at work, as well as at school. As reported in numerous studies it goes like this:

☐ Men speak more often and frequently interrupt women.

☐ Listeners recall more from male speakers than from female speakers, even when both use a similar speaking style and cover identical content.

☐ Women participate less actively in conversation. They do more smiling and gazing; they are more often the passive bystanders in professional and social conversations among peers.

☐ Women often transform declarative statements into tentative comments. This is accomplished by using qualifiers ("kind of " or "I guess") and by adding tag questions ("This is a good movie, isn't it?"). These tentative patterns weaken impact and signal a lack of power and influence.

Sexist treatment in the classroom encourages formation of patterns such as these, which give men more dominance and power than women in the working world. But there is a light at the end of the educational tunnel. Classroom biases are not etched in stone, and training can eliminate these patterns. Sixty teachers in our study received four days of training to establish equity in classroom interactions. These trained teachers succeeded in eliminating classroom bias. Although our training focused on equality, it improved overall teaching effectiveness as well. Classes taught by these trained teachers had a higher level of intellectual discussion and contained more effective and precise teacher responses for all students.

There is an urgent need to remove sexism from the classroom and give women the same educational encouragement and support that men receive. When women are treated equally in the classroom, they will be more likely to achieve equality in the workplace.

Serving Special Needs and Individualizing Instruction

We are all human beings sharing the same universe and the common hertiage of our species, and yet, marvelously, we are each exceptional in some way. We each have special gifts, and we each have special limitations. The ancient Greeks believed every person could be educated to the optimum extent in order to perfect his or her excellent qualities as a person. To a certain extent, we can also be educated to compensate for disabilities. Children are born into many special circumstances and different social atmospheres. Some must struggle to survive and fight to maintain their sense of dignity and self-worth. What constitutes the most "appropriate" learning atmosphere for each student has become a serious legal and moral question in recent years.

All individuals are special, unique human beings who have different levels of abilities and needs in certain areas. Often these special needs or abilities are called exceptionalities. Exceptionalities of certain kinds, whether they be physical or cognitive (mental), sometimes require special intervention or treatment skills. The Education of All Handicapped Children Act of 1975 (PL 94-142) was passed by Congress to address the special needs of handicapped learners by placing them in least restrictive learning environments. However, exceptionality does not just refer to handicaps. Gifted persons are exceptional too, and their least restrictive learning environments can indeed call for special intervention strategies. Herein lies one of the dilemmas of special education as a sector of teacher education. There are many special and exceptional students, and they all need carefully worked out strategies for optimizing their chances for a quality education. In addition to diagnosed exceptionalities, children sometimes develop special needs for carefully individualized attention from their teachers due to injuries or mistreatment. The nation's schools are called upon to address a range of special needs that is so vast the schools are financially and professionally stressed to their limits.

Since the passage of Public Law 94-142, there has been increased sensitivity to the educational requirements of exceptional children and youth. What might be a liberating classroom learning climate for one student may be a stifling and boring one for another student. In addition,

major changes in national life-styles have led to special nontraditional life circumstances for many youth. Some who have two parents who work and others who live with only one parent find themselves among the new generation of "latchkey" kids. Perhaps special after-school activities should be provided for such children.

Helping children adjust to the demands of school and providing them with opportunities for fulfilling their own unique learning potential challenges the talents of any teacher. Mainstreaming is the educational policy response to the federal legislation passed in 1975 to aid handicapped students by placing them in individually prescribed, least restrictive learning environments. However, there is a big gap between the hopes and expectations for mainstreaming and the policy realities of efforts to implement it. The attempt to develop individualized diagnostic and teaching strategies that classroom teachers can use with their students is part of the national effort to respond constructively to the needs of exceptional children. As a result, the tension created by trying to attain equality and quality in schools is raising new educational issues. Some of these issues are concerned with how to provide enriched learning experiences for gifted students while providing least restrictive learning environments for cognitively (intellectually) handicapped students. Other issues relate to the demands placed on teachers' time and the difficulties involved in the total effort to individualize instructional programs for students. There are shortages of resources for both diagnosis and treatment.

The unit opens with an account of the serious problems encountered in correctly implementing the educational approaches to mainstreaming. "Legal" compliance is not the same as "educational" compliance. Many school districts achieve legal compliance with mainstreaming but at the expense of the intent of the federal and state laws which were passed to guarantee the rights of exceptional children. Ritty and Frost summarize what teachers and other school staff can do to assist children and youth living in single-parent families. The Johnsons survey student-student interaction in classrooms. They focus on cooperative as opposed to competitive approaches to classroom learning. The unit also contains an essay on child abuse and neglect. The article explains how teachers and others can identify and help children who are being mistreated or neglected in their home settings. The authors offer clear definitions of child abuse and neglect and include several good sources of information. Finally, there is a brief article on how to identify and assist students who are abusing drugs.

Each year this anthology addresses some professional concerns that are usually not included in traditional textbooks on curriculum and instruction but are issues of real interest to all teachers. Over the years, the selections in this unit have not always fallen under the typical definitions of social foundations of education, or methods of teaching, or curriculum and instruction. However, some of the articles are directly related to curriculum and instructions of social foundations of education or methods of teaching or curriculum and instruction. However, some

The selections in this unit work well with courses about the methods of teaching curriculum and instruction, the equity agenda, equality of opportunity, and the general social foundations of education.

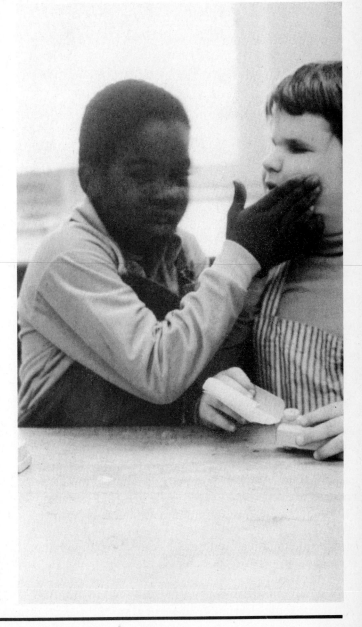

Looking Ahead: Challenge Questions

How could a mainstreaming program in a school be "legal" but not "educational"?

What is meant by "least restrictive" placement? What would be an example of such placement for children with various handicaps? What might such a placement be for a "gifted" exceptional child?

What can school systems and teachers do to assist students living in single-parent homes?

How can "latchkey kids" be helped?

What can teachers do to identify child abuse and neglect? How can abused or neglected children be helped?

Are the professional situations of elementary and secondary teachers different when it comes to individualizing instruction? If so, in what specific ways? If not, why not?

What is meant by individualization? How can it be accomplished?

"Appropriate" School Programs:

Legal vs. Educational Approaches

Steven Carlson
Steven Carlson teaches in the Department of Educational
Psychology in the Special Education Program at Rutgers
University.

*Progress toward a greater
degree of independent
functioning should be as
apparent outside of the special
class as it is inside.*

With the passage of Public Law 94-142, the
Education for All Handicapped Children Act,
disabled children and youth were guaranteed a
free, appropriate public education. Unfortunately, a
legally appropriate education may be very different
from an *educationally* appropriate education. I hope
to explain the important difference between them.
Parents need to understand both the legal and the
educational issues. While all parents are not going
to be legal experts, all parents can evaluate the
quality and educational appropriateness of
programs for disabled children and youth, with the
help of some clear guidelines.

The Legal Definition of Appropriateness

The courts have struggled with the meaning of
appropriateness and a legal definition has slowly
emerged. This legal definition currently rests on
three "legs."

The first leg examines how well proper
procedures were followed in protecting the rights of
children and parents. The law requires that
• Notification of parents about the evaluation and
  placement of their children in special education.
• Parental permission before these actions can be
  taken.
• Parental participation in initial decisions and in
  any subsequent changes in a child's program.
• Specific guidelines for evaluation and specific
  means for appeal.
A legally appropriate program is, according to this
first leg, one in which these parental rights have
been respected.

The second "leg" investigates the degree to
which the recommended program of services and
studies was followed. If the recommendations of
the multidisciplinary team, to which the parent has
agreed, are followed, the program may be
considered legally appropriate. For example, the
recommendation is for two hours of physical
therapy each week. Legally, the question is: Has
the recommendation been followed or not? How

closely the recommendation must be followed has not yet been legally determined.

The final "leg" of this legal triad examines the actual progress a student makes in school. Movement through school grades is considered the final confirmation of the legal appropriateness of the program.

It may be legal, but is it educationally appropriate?

While these three areas of legal concern provide some assurance of attention to the educational problems faced by disabled children and youth, they fail to address the issue very much on the mind of most parents: *educational effectiveness*. It is possible for a child to be properly evaluated, properly placed, and progress through the grades, yet learn less than might be hoped or expected. For example, grade progress may be due to lowered standards and teacher expectations rather than to increased quality of teaching or level of student learning.

Standards for Educationally Appropriate Special Programs

The issue of quality must be addressed by parents and concerned educators. At the present time, educational appropriateness is itself not a legal issue. The following guidelines are provided to assist concerned parents and educators to evaluate program appropriateness *where quality of learning is the central concern*. These guidelines are general in nature and care must be taken to remember that they are suggestions, not legal requirements.

Uniqueness

To be educationally appropriate, a program should be a new and unique learning experience. This means that whatever the reason for placing a child in special education, the services provided should differ from those which were previously provided. The greater the similarity between regular and special programs, the weaker the case for educational appropriateness. Repeating, in a different classroom, what has already been shown not to work makes little sense. Additionally, if special programs are not truly unique, it is possible that the negative consequences of labeling and/or removing a child from a less restrictive setting will outweigh the positive benefits of the special program. Recent research makes it quite clear that special education sometimes fails to be truly different.

Parents can help guard against this possibility by understanding the purpose of student evaluation and by raising questions during the Individual Education Program (IEP) meeting. One part of this evaluation is to determine whether a student is eligible for special education services; another part is to determine what should be taught and the best way to teach it. This second part of the evaluation process determines the potential effectiveness of instruction. Educational evaluation should uncover what specific skills must be learned as well as the adequacy of teaching techniques and materials used in the past. Parents can ask evaluators to discuss what was done in the past, what is being recommended for the future, the differences between these approaches, and the reasons why current suggestions will be more effective.

A child's IEP should specifically state *what* to teach and *how* to teach. Moreover, practices previously shown to be ineffective should be discontinued and those with promise should be the focus of future instruction. Often, a child's IEP describes the special education curriculum but provides neither the parent nor the teacher with the most important information: the way that the curriculum will be translated into learning.

Recent research makes it quite clear that special education sometimes fails to be truly different.

Long Range Benefit

An educationally appropriate program is one in which instructional goals and objectives lead toward the long range goal of independence. If a child differs from his or her peers to such an extent that a special program of studies is necessary, emphasis should be placed on reducing the size of this difference. It is important for school planning teams and parents to anticipate future school and life demands. This means that a good program will strive to alter the child's impaired approach to learning, social functioning, or dealing with his or her environment.

For example, a child is placed in a special program due to an emotional or behavioral disability. Success in the regular classroom, in the social environment of the school, or in future adult life may depend upon the child behaving in a more acceptable way. Instructional emphasis, therefore, should be on behavioral change. If the special setting serves only to control the behavior and to teach traditional skills, the child's underlying problem will not be addressed or solved. In this case, the child will not be able to function well in non-special settings in the future. The standard of long range independence is equally true for programs for children with learning, physical, and sensory disabilities.

Parents might ask school planning teams whether they have considered future requirements for independent functioning, and how proposed instruction can be expected to reduce the need for future special services. Hopefully, parents will feel free to raise such concerns and to work with school personnel to assure that they are addressed. Once instruction begins, progress toward a greater degree of independent functioning should be as apparent outside of the special class as it is inside. Additional effort should be made to make sure that children, even those who succeed in special classrooms, can apply this learning in other school and life situations.

Attention to the long range benefit of special education is very important. Parents and teachers who are primarily concerned with academic performance must remember that a diploma is of little value to a student who is unprepared to function independently in life, to find employment at the level of his or her true potential, or to take advantage of academic or technical training beyond high school.

High Expectations

An educationally appropriate program is one where expectations for student performance are high. Learning activities and requirements for independence should be challenging. The lives of disabled children and youth are often filled with frustrations and failures. As a result, teachers and parents frequently strive to reduce the probability, or even possibility, of failure. Although such attitudes and practices are well intended, all too often they result in an unnecessary lowering of standards and expectations.

It has long been known that, whenever possible, children will live up or down to the expectations held for them by teachers and parents. This is the main reason for maintaining reasonable yet challenging expectations. Hesitating to challenge children may result in increased dependence since the teacher or parent must do for the child what the child could be taught to do for him or herself. It is important to remember that these children, many of whom lag behind their peers in some significant way, will not "catch up" by going even more slowly, being asked to do less, and having more provided for them. It may well be that disabled children need to work harder than their non-disabled peers. It may also be that teachers and/or parents who lower their expectations may be

making it harder for disabled children to adjust to the consequences of their disabilities.

One sign of a program with high expectations is often the confidence of the special teacher that "with hard work we can do it."

Classroom instruction should generally be intensive and briskly paced with little time wasted in nonproductive discussion or fun activities that have marginal instructional value. A teacher with high expectations will find ways to make challenging and productive learning activities enjoyable.

When it is necessary to lower performance standards, instruction should be designed to help children attain standards that are ever more demanding. Whether special materials are used or regular materials are modified, children can still be taught how to cope with the idea of "standards." Future employers are not likely to modify the workplace or alter work materials. Once out of school, the child will be expected to meet many, if not all, the same demands as his or her peers.

An educationally appropriate, quality program is one which addresses this harsh reality, which maintains high performance standards, and which helps children and youth learn to meet the expectations which will be imposed on them throughout life.

Instruction is Powerful

An educationally appropriate program is one where the special teacher uses those techniques and principles which have proven to lead to greater student progress. There is a great deal of research with both disabled and non-disabled children which assesses the effectiveness of various teaching styles. Since teachers make choices about their teaching techniques, they should choose those that work best.

Although independent seat work has an important place in teaching and learning, it should comprise only a portion of a child's learning time. The teacher can constantly call upon students to answer questions and demonstrate developing skills. When errors are made. children should receive immediate and specific feedback on the nature of their error, including direct instruction about how to avoid such errors in the future.

Children can be engaged in learning a high percentage of time. Then, there is little "down time" spent waiting for the teacher or locating materials. Lessons should move quickly, activities should be varied, and positive comments should be offered to show students that their efforts are both valuable and valued. Time should be spent reviewing previously learned skills so that important information is not forgotten. Learning activities should be challenging and designed so that, with effort, the student can be successful.

Disabled children have more to lose than their peers if the initial approach to instruction is wrong and left uncorrected throughout the school year.

Moving Toward Goals

In an educationally appropriate program, instruction either leads toward specific goals or general change. Disabled children often present teachers with complex instructional problems which must be solved. It is unreasonable to believe that any teacher can be 100% successful in helping children if the goals which have been established are truly challenging.

It is not unreasonable, however, to expect teachers to be aware of a child's progress toward goal attainment. When students are initially placed in special education programs, information collected during the evaluation serves as the basis for educated guesses about what the child needs to learn and how the child will learn best. As with any guess, error is a possibility.

Disabled children have more to lose than their peers if the initial approach to instruction is wrong and left uncorrected throughout the school year. Not only should highly specific performance information be routinely collected, but this data should be used to modify instruction if the child's progress slowed or stalled.

If progress is less than desired, a program may still be appropriate if the teacher is using information about a student's performance to discard techniques that do not work, and substitute other techniques, gradually finding the necessary formula for maximizing student progress. Many people believe that it is this fine tuning which distinguishes special from traditional education.

Parents can ask to review specific information on their child's progress. Examples would be asking about the percentage of words read correctly and incorrectly at the start of instruction and at the present time, or how much the independent mobility of a physically disabled child has changed from week to week.

Specific information about how a child learns is far more useful for fine tuning instruction than test scores. In most cases, even testing experts would maintain that scores, especially those which express grade level performance, are relatively useless for purposes of instruction. If progress is limited, parents should ask the teacher to explain how instruction has been changed to lead toward progress in the future.

Teacher Training

In an educationally appropriate program, teaching is done by individuals who have formal training or recognized expertise. Few would disagree that a teacher should know how to teach the skills and behaviors which are called for in a child's IEP. In elementary school resource rooms, or part day programs, where basic skill instruction (reading, spelling, etc.) is often the emphasis, teacher training is generally adequate because these skills are a standard of special education training.

Self-contained, or full day classroom programs, require teachers to teach not only essential basic skills, but such subjects as science, health, and social studies. It is quite possible that the special education teachers who deliver such instruction have received little or no training in how to do so. If they do teach such material, they may not be effective. Even worse, if they feel unprepared to teach a certain subject, they may fail to teach it at all.

This deficiency may also exist in the secondary grades when a special educator either tutors a student in a particular area or actually provides all the instruction and academic credit in subjects like government, biology, or history. Even when teachers are trained, they should be familiar with a variety of approaches and materials, capable of analyzing errors and providing proper correction, and able to teach students the reasoning which leads to the correct answer.

Parents must feel free to ask the planning team whether any standard material is not part of the program, why it is omitted, and whether the child's teacher has had training in the areas selected as learning goals. No teacher can be expected to be expert in everything. Quality programs may require students to receive instruction from more than one special educator or be creative in modifying other standard practices.

Consistency of Goals and Instruction

An educationally appropriate program is one where instruction and classroom activities always correspond to the child's IEP. Legal guidelines require that IEP goals be taught but say little about how consistent the plan and the practice must be. It is unreasonable to expect that pre-defined goals will be attained if they are not being emphasized in instruction. Ideally, there should be few instances where instruction is not directly related to these goals.

Parents can try to visit their child's classroom occasionally and, at a convenient time, discuss with the teacher what is being taught and its relationship to the IEP goals. It is not uncommon for teachers to discover that children have more pressing needs than those formally documented on the IEP. It is important, however, that parents and team members be consulted before significant changes are made. Occasionally, teachers claim that they are unaware of what goals specific children are expected to meet. In these cases, appropriateness is questionable, and parents need to take an active interest in the content of instruction.

Conclusion

Providing educationally appropriate, quality programs to disabled children is a relatively new phenomenon in education. It must be assumed that this undertaking, like any other important and complex new effort, will have problems. When quality of instruction is the immediate concern, there appears to be little help available from the courts. The surest way to improve quality appears to be true cooperation between parents and educators.

Such cooperation may take time and effort to develop. It is important to recognize that all parties are interested in the well-being of the child. Differences are often not in values but in approach. The guidelines which I have offered are intended as a general yardstick for parents and educators to evaluate program appropriateness from the perspective of quality. I hope they will lead toward improvements in the education of disabled children by helping all parties to recognize that real change takes time and depends upon mutual respect and trust.

Single-parent families: How can schools help?

J. Michael Ritty and Martha B. Frost

J. Michael Ritty, Ph.D., works in elementary and reading education in the Center for Teacher Education and Educational Services at the State University of New York at Plattsburgh.

Martha B. Frost, Ed.D., is assistant professor in the Center for Human Resources at the State University of New York at Plattsburgh. Ritty and Frost co-direct "The Schools and Single-Parent Families Project" at Plattsburgh.

Today's family bears little resemblance to the family of yesterday, with its working dad, stay-at-home mom, three children, dog and cat. One change is the number of single-parent families, which has increased by more than 70 percent in the last decade to one in four families. Already female-headed households are increasing 10 times as quickly as two-parent families, according to U.S. Census Bureau figures.

In fact, the nuclear family, that is, two parents and children, showed a decline during this same period. This is the same family most of us grew up in and expected to head when we became adults. If these trends continue, two-parent families could be a minority in a few generations.

Presently 14 million children are part of single-parent families, and the Census Bureau estimates that this number will increase by 1 million children *every year*. How are these children doing emotionally, academically, socially—with only one live-in parent? Are they coping well?

A recent study by the NAESP reports that children in single-parent families are at a disadvantage academically when compared with children in two-parent families. Single parents and educators question these findings. But the reality is that many teachers and principals do not recognize the needs of single-parent families or do not know how to deal with this problem in the classroom.

The following questions and answers attempt to illuminate the role that schools need to play in reaching out to help single parents and their children.

Why does our educational system ignore the needs of children from single-parent families?

Schools sometimes resist acknowledging new family structures for a number of reasons:

● The legal issues surrounding custody;

● The desire to protect the student's and family's privacy;

● A feeling of treating all families equally means treating them as if they were all alike;

● An underlying fear that to acknowledge divorce and remarriage openly in policies and procedures will somehow withdraw support for the "ideal" family;

● The budget constraints that make it hard for schools to meet the changing needs of the family.

Other reasons include the fact that many teachers and administrators are afraid to deal with the issue because it is sensitive and controversial.

Should parents notify the school principal in the case of a separation or divorce?

A parent plays an important role in the school life of the child. Every parent must work with the school to help develop the best educational atmosphere for the child. For their child's sake, during a separation or divorce, parents should make the school aware of any changes that occur in the family.

In the case of a death, families usually find notifying the school a normal part of the process. But we usually don't see divorce as a natural part of life, and so it is not as openly discussed. When the school is notified in case of death, school personnel are often helpful and show an awareness of the child's behavior, activities and feelings. In the case of a divorce, parents often do not communicate the stressful changes that are occurring within the family.

The parents, both custodial and noncustodial, still have the rights and responsibilities of parenthood. Parents should be very careful to keep any of their own arguments out of the school system. They should try to work on a friendly basis with the school on matters concerning their children.

What are the effects of separation and divorce on children?

In a five-year study of 60 families of divorce, children viewed their parents' separation and divorce as extraordinarily stressful. Fewer than 10 percent were relieved by the divorce decision despite considerable exposure to intense marital conflict or physical violence between their parents. The stress a child suffers during and after his or her parents' divorce ranks closely to the trauma of losing a parent through death.

Typically children may be flooded with feelings they cannot fully understand or articulate. These include anger at being caught in a situation they cannot change, guilt from feeling they may have somehow contributed to the breakup, and sadness over the loss of the parent who no longer lives with the family.

In school, a child's behavior and ability to perform is affected if he or she is under great stress—whatever the cause. A student may not reveal any personal information directly, but teachers should watch for indirect signs, many of which indicate stress. These signs can include inattention, absentmindedness, behavioral problems, and withdrawal in the classroom.

How can a teacher help a child who is under stress because of a family breakup?

The teacher is often the most stable element in the life of a child whose parents are undergoing a separation or divorce. The trauma the child may be experiencing at home can be offset by the stability provided by the classroom teacher.

Teachers must be made aware of children whose parents are going through a separation or divorce. They need to be aware of the child's feelings and notice the child's behavior and activities. This does not mean changing activities for the child or giving special privileges. However, teachers do need to understand the changes or difficulties that the child may be going through.

Divorce is often very difficult to talk about. The teacher should not sympathize with the child or take sides on the issue, however. The important thing for a teacher to do when a child is going through a crisis is to empathize, be supportive and help the child better understand the situation.

How does a separation or divorce affect children's schoolwork?

Unfortunately, some children find it difficult to deal with their parents' divorce and perform poorly in school. These children especially need the help of teachers and other school personnel. Some children's grades and school work may drop initially. Usually within a year, however, they are back to the level they were performing at prior

to the separation or divorce. Some children actually improve in academic ability after a separation or divorce. For many children, this may be the first time in a long while that there is freedom from noise, arguing, or other turmoil that may have affected the family.

In every case we have to look at the children as individuals.

What kind of programs are available to help schools, parents, and children?

Few programs now exist. The programs we developed at the Schools and Single-Parent Families Project focus on helping school personnel, parents, and students understand the difficulties that single-parent families are facing.

In general, such programs should help participants communicate better, understand the problems of individuals within the group, and work on solutions that will work within their own school system. For example, all participants should be informed of legal, moral, and emotional difficulties that single-parent families face.

School personnel need to realize what goes on within the single-parent family. Teachers must look at the curriculum to make it responsive to the needs of the single parent and children. They must examine their behavior and realize that certain behavior by the teacher or activities in the classroom inadvertently may upset some children. The school personnel must identify and deal with those elements in a curriculum that could be considered problems.

Parents must understand their own feelings and the behavior that is occurring within their changing family. They must discuss how feelings and behavior affect the relationships among children, parents, and the school. Finally they must take positive steps to help themselves and their local school district.

Children need to know that it is all right to have mixed-up feelings when a change is taking place in the family. Students need to be willing to share their experiences with each other so that they feel that they are not the only ones who are hurting. And they must learn to take an active role in their own schooling.

Finally school personnel, parents, and students must share their ideas, their concerns, their needs. They must open the lines of communication as a means of better understanding everyone involved.

CHECKING IN:
An Alternative for Latchkey Kids

Judy McKnight
and Betsy Shelsby

Judy McKnight is supervisor and Betsy Shelsby director of the Family Day Care Check-In Project, Fairfax County Office for Children, Fairfax, Virginia.

Photos: Dick Swartz

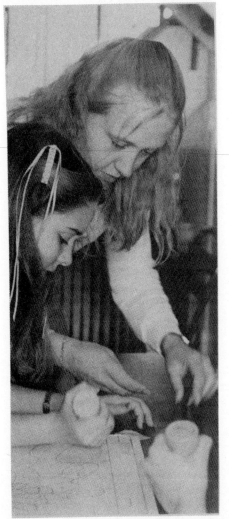

The summer before his 6th-grade year, 11-year-old Jason and his family moved from Toledo, Ohio to Reston, Virginia. Jason's grandmother came along to care for him and his younger brother and to help them get settled in their new school while their mother started a new job. When their grandmother left, Jason and his brother went to a family day care provider who cared for school-age children before and after school.

This arrangement worked well for Jason's younger brother, but not for Jason. Because the other children in the home were much younger, Jason had no one his own age to play with. Spending all afternoon in the family day care home was restricting. He didn't like to go there. After several weeks, Jason and his mother agreed that he could go home alone after school.

In Ohio, Jason had often taken care of himself and his brother after school. He had lived in his Toledo neighborhood for five years, had many friends and knew the neighbors. His aunt lived three blocks away, and his grandmother regularly came over to be with her grandchildren. But being at home alone in Reston was different. By the time the school year began, Jason had made only a few friends. His mother had met only one neighbor. Jason was apprehensive about being in the house alone, and he was lonely. Jason's mother knew she needed to look for an alternative.

Twelve-year-old Anne has lived in Reston for 11 years. When her 7th-grade school year began, Anne, like many of her friends—and like some seven million children, ages six to 13, across the country*—was on her own after school. Anne and her friends spent their after-school hours visiting with each other and hanging around a nearby shopping center. As far as Anne was concerned, it was a good arrangement. She enjoyed being with her friends, and if she wanted to, she could go home and be alone. But Anne admitted that she went home only when there was nothing else to do.

Anne's after-school routines did not suit her mother, however. When she came home from work, she often found Anne bored and unhappy. Chores and homework were frequently not done. Anne's mother was concerned that Anne had too much "bumming around" time. She realized that her daughter needed more structure.

What had started off as a concern became a problem when Anne began missing school. Frequent absences and incompleted work alerted teachers and school administrators to the problem. A phone call to her mother clarified the situation for everyone: "Bumming around" was no longer only an after-school activity for Anne; it had become a way to spend the school day. Something had to be done.

Although Jason and Anne might not have considered their situations similiar, both of their mothers faced the same dilemma. They both worked; they both had children who needed some kind of after-school

Reprinted from *Children Today*, May/June 1984, pp. 23-25. Published by the Office of Human Development Services, Department of Health and Human Services six times a year.

Anne displays her stained glass work—a popular art project. On the preceding page, Barbara helps Kristen with her stained glass project.

dom and responsibility. Although the contracts are between parents, providers and agencies, day care plans are discussed during conferences involving parents, providers, agency representatives and children. At this time children talk about what responsibilities they feel they are ready to assume; parents outline what freedoms they feel comfortable giving; and providers and agency representatives explain and clarify system policies and procedures.

Each child's day care plan is different, based on the needs, interests and routines discussed and decided upon during the conferences. For example, one plan might allow a 12-year-old to go home after school and check in by phone with the provider, proceed to soccer practice and then go to her provider's home and wait for her mother to pick her up after work. Another plan might call for an 11-year-old to have a snack with his provider right after school, play with friends at a neighborhood playground and return to the provider's home at 4:30 to do homework.

The Reston Children's Center Senior Satellite Program was exactly what Anne's and Jason's mothers needed for their children. Anne had attended Reston Children's Center as a preschooler and in elementary school, and her mother had heard about the Senior Satellite Program last fall. At that time, though, she hadn't thought Anne needed it. Five months later, she knew Anne did.

Jason's mother found out about the program from the family day care provider who cares for her youngest son. She discussed Jason's dilemma with a center worker, and when a senior satellite provider in her neighborhood had a vacancy, the center notified her. She enrolled Jason immediately.

Their provider, Barbara, cares for Jason, Anne and two other children. One of these children, 9-year-old Kristen, is enrolled in the center's regular family day care program for younger school-age children. She spends all of her after-school hours at Barbara's house. Would she like to be part of the senior program one day? Kristen isn't sure. She likes being with Barbara and she doesn't know how she would feel about being at home alone.

For Kristen and the other children,

support and supervision; they both had children who had been in self-care and who considered themselves capable of taking care of themselves. In addition, neither child wanted to be associated with a traditional child care situation, and neither parent wanted to have to force her child to enroll in a traditional program. But was there an alternative? Reston Children's Center, a cooperative preschool and day care center in the community, offered one.

In 1982, the Fairfax County Office for Children (OFC) in Fairfax, Virginia received a grant from the Administration for Children, Youth and Families, OHDS, to design and test a family day care check-in program for pre-adolescent children. The Reston Children's Center was one of two non-profit organizations in the county to receive start-up funds to pilot test the program during the 1983-84 school year. Throughout the school year, OFC has provided consultation and technical assistance to the Reston Center's Senior Satellite Program and to the KIDS Check-in Club of Springfield, Virginia, the other site, which is operated by the

Potomac Area Camp Fire Council. Together, the programs serve about 30 children, primarily between the ages of 11 and 13. At present, parents pay $1.00 an hour to participate.

The check-in programs are designed to provide flexible care and supervision for older elementary and junior high school children, who are assigned to a trained, neighborhood-based family day care provider. With parental permission, children can spend time in their own homes, visit friends, play in their neighborhoods or attend after-school and community activities. Under a special contract, parents designate exactly how much freedom and responsibility they want their children to have. The same contract also defines the role that the providers play in the supervision and care of children and the responsibilities parents assume when they enroll their children in a check-in program.

For children and parents, the use of contracts has a particular advantage: It requires parents and children to sit down and develop day care plans that address both parental concerns about safety and supervision and young adolescent desires for free-

Barbara is not just a provider—she is a counselor, confidante and friend. Her low-keyed manner and sincere interest in the well-being and concerns of the children in her care make her an effective, popular caregiver.

The afternoon routine at Barbara's house is a study in meeting each child's needs. Usually, all four children come directly to her house after school. After greeting them with a snack, she listens with interest to "what happened" at school today. As they sit around the table, the children discuss their day, answer each other's and Barbara's questions and tease each other—not unlike siblings.

After snack, the children do homework, play with Barbara's husband's computer, or just talk and play games together. Barbara often plans craft projects for them. "We don't have to do the projects," Kristen points out, "but we usually do. They're fun." Anne agrees. "The things we make here you can take home and use for something," she says. "They come out looking nice."

Barbara also takes the children places. They plan their outings together. Swimming, ice skating, roller skating and going to a local playground are among their favorite activities. But from Barbara's point of view, the most important thing she does is listen. "The children feel comfortable with me," she says. "They talk freely about things that are happening at school and with their friends. They share thoughts and feelings that are immediate—that would get lost if the children had to wait until 6:00 or 7:00 when their parents get home."

Jason has his mother's permission to spend time in his own home and to play with friends in the neighborhood, but he usually spends a lot of time at Barbara's house. He likes her and he likes the atmosphere in her home. And even though he is the only boy, a shy smile revealed the pleasure he derives from his special role in this group of females. When Jason leaves to go about his own approved business, he always calls Barbara when he arrives at his destination and he checks in with her hourly.

During Anne's first two weeks in the satellite program, she was required to spend all of her time at Barbara's house. During the third week, she was allowed to spend some time with her friends. Now she reports to Barbara's house three days a week and goes home for two. Anne likes Barbara, and she likes being at her house. She is relaxed there; she banters freely with the other children, and she feels accepted. Barbara and the other children provide Anne with companionship, a sense of belonging and a way to structure her after-school hours.

The after-school day care needs of upper elementary and junior high children are different from those of younger school-age children. When parents aren't available, children need guidance, supervision, an adult to turn to, and a variety of interesting activities that they can do alone or as part of a group. As children grow older, they simply need these supports in different degrees. As their individual interests develop, children need more flexibility and more opportunities to create and choose their own activities. As they become more responsible and more capable of doing for themselves, they need less intense supervision. By early adolescence, children have developed their own interests and are capable, to a large degree, of self-care. However, when parents are not accessible or available, they still need to have a responsible adult available.

Reston Children's Center meets these unique needs for Jason, Anne and the 14 other children who are enrolled in the Senior Satellite Program during its 10-month pilot period. Jason's mother looks forward to the program continuing into the summer and plans to use it again next year. Anne's mother echoes her satisfaction. "It's the kind of service that should be available for everyone," she says. "We all need someone to turn to and to depend on. I used to get real restless from 3:00 on. Anne would call, but I felt stranded because I was so far away."

Both pilot sites will continue the after-school program beyond the grant period, and the Potomac Area Camp Fire Council also plans to replicate the KIDS Check-in Club in a Maryland location.

We hope that the family day care check-in program will serve as a model for other organizations and communities interested in providing a special and much-needed service: flexible care and supervision for children who are almost—but not quite—ready to go it alone for several hours a day.

*U.S. Department of Labor, Women's Bureau, *Employers and Child Care: Establishing Services Through the Workplace*, Pamphlet No. 23, Washington, D.C., Aug. 1982.

Student-Student Interaction:
Ignored but Powerful

Roger T. Johnson
David W. Johnson

Roger T. Johnson and David W. Johnson are Professors, Cooperative Learning Center, University of Minnesota, Minneapolis, Minnesota.

Cooperative learning is a powerful instructional technique that prospective teachers must learn in order to appropriately foster the interpersonal and academic growth of students. Paradoxically, although cooperative learning evidences the greatest potential for engendering student learning, it is used no more than 20% of the time in most American classrooms. In this article, the Johnsons review the research that has been conducted on the three possible goals structures used by teachers (cooperative, competitive and individualistic) and discuss the implications of these findings for changing teacher preparation practices.

How students perceive each other and interact with one another in the classroom is a neglected aspect of instruction. In preservice and inservice teacher training, much time is devoted to helping teachers structure interactions between students and content (i.e., textbooks and curriculum packages) and between teachers and students. How students should interact with one another, however, is relatively ignored. In many cases, peer influences have been viewed by teachers as encouraging off-task, disruptive behavior in the classroom. Teachers have been encouraged to think that good classrooms are ones where students work quietly and alone. Students, on the other hand, tend to perceive school as a competitive enterprise, a place where it is important that one do better than others. This perception, already in place for

many students when they enter, grows as they progress through school (Johnson and Johnson, 1975). The extensive research on student-student interaction, however, strongly supports structuring the classroom to facilitate students' working cooperatively, talking things through with one another, and supporting one another's learning (Deutsch, 1962; Johnson and Johnson, 1983; Sharan, 1980; Slavin, 1977).

Student-student interaction should not be ignored or left to chance. The classroom is first and foremost a scene where a teacher and 25 or more students interact with one another over extensive periods of time. When a situation exists in which teachers perceive one interaction pattern and students another, and both patterns are opposite of the direction indicated by the research, then that situation needs to be changed. The places to begin that change are teacher education and inservice programs. How teachers guide students to interact with one another during instruction will influence the way students learn, the attitudes they form about the subject matter and the instructor, and the perceptions they have about themselves and others.

Definitions

There are three basic ways students can interact with each other as they learn. They can compete to see who is "best"; they can work individualistically toward a set goal without needing to pay attention to the efforts of other students; or they can work cooperatively, exhibiting concern about each other's learning as well as their own. The study of cooperative, competitive, and individualistic situations stems from a well-formulated theory developed by Morton Deutsch in the late 1940s.

Deutsch, in his extension of Lewin's theory of motivation, conceptualized three possible goal structures: cooperative,

From *Journal of Teacher Education*, July/August 1985, pp. 22-26. Reprinted by permission of the American Association of Colleges for Teacher Education.

competitive, and individualistic. He defined a *cooperative* interaction pattern as one in which the goals of separate individuals are linked together so that there is a positive correlation among their goal attainments. An individual in this goal structure can achieve his or her mutual goal only if the other participants achieve their mutual goals. Thus a person seeks an outcome that is beneficial to all those with whom he or she is cooperatively linked.

In a *competitive* situation the goals of the separate individuals are linked so that there is a negative correlation among their goal attainments. An individual can attain his or her goal only if the other participants cannot achieve their goals. Thus a person seeks an outcome that is personally beneficial but that is detrimental to the others with whom he or she is linked.

Finally, in an *individualistic* situation there is no correlation among the goal attainments of the participants. Whether an individual accomplishes his or her goal has no influence on whether other individuals accomplish their goals. Thus a person seeks an outcome that is personally beneficial, ignoring as irrelevant the goal achievement efforts of other individuals in the situation.

In the late 1960s the authors began efforts to contribute to the theory of student-student interaction by (a) extending Deutsch's theory to instructional situations and the classroom; (b) reviewing and systematizing the existing research on the three interaction patterns; (c) conducting a program of research to extend cooperative theory and practice; and (d) translating the research findings into a set of concrete teaching strategies for teachers.

Research Summary

Extensive research exists on student-student interaction. We have examined over a thousand studies dating back to the late 1800s. Besides overall reviews of the research (Deutsch, 1962; Johnson and Johnson, 1983; Sharan, 1980; Slavin, 1977), the authors have completed two meta-analyses: one evaluating the effects of cooperative, competitive, and individualistic interactions on achievement (Johnson, Maruyama, Johnson, Nelson, and Skon, 1981), and another examining the effects of the different interaction patterns on acceptance of differences in peers (Johnson, Johnson, DeWeerdt, Lyons, and Zaidman, 1983). These data suggest:

1. Cooperative learning experiences tend to promote more learning than do competitive or individualistic learning experiences. This suggestion was overwhelmingly indicated by the results of a meta-analysis we conducted analyzing 122 studies from 1924 to 1981 for the purpose of examining the research on student-student interaction patterns and achievement (Johnson et al., 1981). Although this finding remained constant over a range of age groups, subject areas, and learning activities, the gap in achievement favoring cooperation widens when the learning tasks are more difficult (i.e., problem solving, divergent thinking, decision making, conceptual learning). When achievement and student-student interaction are examined by ability level, the lower one-third of the students appear to be the big gainers in the cooperative settings. The middle and upper third of the students maintain a smaller but consistent advantage in the cooperative setting. Our speculation is that the need to talk about information and ideas rather than just think about them is one of the variables contributing to higher achievement. In addition to basic achievement, retention of information and the development of specific strategies

are enhanced for all students by the cooperative interaction (Armstrong et al., 1981; Garibaldi, 1979; Humphreys, Johnson and Johnson, 1982; Johnson and Johnson, 1980, 1982, 1984; Johnson, Johnson, Johnson, and Anderson, 1976; Johnson, Johnson, Roy, and Zaidman, 1985; Johnson, Johnson, and Scott, 1978; Johnson, Johnson, and Skon, 1979; Johnson, Johnson, Tiffany, and Zaidman, 1983; Johnson, Skon, and Johnson, 1980; R. Johnson, Bjorkland, and Krotee, 1984; R. Johnson and Johnson, 1979; R. Johnson, Johnson, DeWeerdt et al., 1983; R. Johnson, Johnson, and Tauer, 1979; Lowry and Johnson, 1981; Martino and Johnson, 1979; Skon et al., 1981; Smith et al., 1981, 1982).

2. Cooperative learning experiences compared to competitive and individualistic ones tend to promote higher motivation to learn, especially intrinsic motivation (Garibaldi, 1979; Gunderson and Johnson, 1980; Johnson, Johnson, and Skon, 1979; Johnson and Johnson, 1979; Lowry and Johnson, 1981; Smith et al., 1981; Wheeler and Ryan, 1973). Students who are urged on by their peers tend to be more motivated than students who have peers competing against them. It is a bit more surprising to see the students in cooperative settings move toward intrinsic motivation, paying more attention to the group's success and less to extrinsic rewards. We are examining the effects of group success as there seems to be more strength in a group celebration of success than in most individual celebrations.

3. Cooperative learning experiences, compared with competitive and individualistic ones, tend to produce more positive attitudes toward the instructional experiences and the instructors (Johnson and Johnson, 1983). This positiveness is a consistent finding in the research that compares student-student interaction patterns.

4. Cooperative learning experiences are linked with higher levels of self-esteem and healthier processes for deriving conclusions about one's self-worth than are competitive or individualistic ones (Johnson and Johnson, 1983).

5. Cooperative learning experiences, compared to competitive and individualistic ones, have been found to result in stronger perceptions that other students care about how much one learns, and that other students want to provide assistance (Johnson and Johnson, 1983). Further, a meta-analysis on the impact of the different student-student interaction patterns on interpersonal attraction among heterogeneous and homogeneous samples of students revealed that cooperative learning experiences promote greater acceptance of differences and interpersonal attraction among students from different ethnic backgrounds, and among handicapped and nonhandicapped students (Johnson et al., 1983). Putting students in cooperative contact who might not ordinarily seek such interactions and having them work cooperatively moves students beyond initial prejudices toward other students to multidimensional views of one another. Furthermore, such experiences allow them to deal with each other as fellow students rather than as stereotypes (Johnson and Johnson, 1980).

Many more learning outcomes are positively influenced by having students work together cooperatively (Johnson and Johnson, 1983). With all the data that are available, it is surprising that practice in classrooms is not more consistent with research findings. Current estimates of the use of small group learning would indicate that students in American schools are working together only 7% to 20% of the time (Johnson and Johnson, 1976; Walberg, 1982). It is also likely that much of this small group interaction would not qualify as cooperative under the Deutsch definition. The teacher needs to be able to monitor groups, to intervene to teach appropriate behaviors, and to provide time for students to process their interactions on instructional tasks. The teaching of collaborative skills includes communication, leadership, trust, and conflict resolution skills.

Our position is not that all learning should be structured to be cooperative. Indeed, in spite of the research support for cooperative interaction, students also need to learn how to compete appropriately and work individualistically. To give students flexibility and additional skills, an ideal classroom would evidence all three interaction patterns, carefully orchestrated by the teacher to build a cooperative umbrella over the class with competitive and individualistic experiences included under it.

Implications for Teacher Education

Cooperative learning groups have become a major instructional tool of many teachers in this country and in other countries (Johnson et al., 1984), but, regrettably, they are not found in most teacher education programs. At least two themes for teacher education programs emerge from the research on student-student interaction.

First, the strategies for structuring each of these interactions in the classroom (cooperative, competitive, and individualistic) should be taught to teachers so that every lesson plan provides specific information for students about the desired interaction during the session. Special emphasis needs to be placed on the cooperative goal structure because it has been relatively neglected and is the most powerful of the three for learning. Strategies for structuring appropriate interaction among students are detailed in *Circles of Learning* (Johnson, Johnson, Holubec and Roy, 1984) and *Learning Together and Alone* (Johnson and Johnson, 1975).

There are five basic aspects of cooperative learning to look for in a classroom:

1. Students are sitting close to each other, talking through the instructional material, for the most part in small (two or three member), heterogeneous groups.

2. There is a strong sense of positive interdependence among group members. The feeling of "sink or swim together" is usually structured in a number of ways in each lesson including a clear, mutual group goal; a group reward (i.e., bonus points for each member on the basis of the group's performance); perhaps different coordinated roles for group members; perhaps a jigsaw of the materials or a single paper for the group.

3. There is a strong sense of individual accountability, a conviction in the group that each group member needs to know the material and be able to explain it rationally. The instructor, moving among the groups as they work, posing a question to a randomly selected group member reminds groups that it is not appropriate to "hitchhike" or to allow any "hitchhiking" in the group.

4. The instructor is monitoring the work of the groups, sometimes using a systematic observation technique to get data on how well the group members are interacting with one another and how well they are progressing on the instructional tasks.

5. There is time provided for the groups to evaluate their success on the instructional tasks and the interaction that took place in the group. In many classrooms there is a sheet that needs to be carefully completed and handed in as part of the instructional work.

In the preservice program at the University of Minnesota for Elementary School Teaching, the concept of appropriate student-student interaction is introduced in the first course students take, and the strategies of how to structure appropriate student-student interaction are taught during methods courses and practiced in school-based, microteaching experiences. A similar pattern is followed for many of the secondary teaching majors as well.

A second theme for teacher education programs that emerges from the research on student-student interaction is that cooperation should be modeled by instructors in education classes. Cooperation is just as powerful for adult learning as it is for younger students. Teacher educators who master the strategies for structuring appropriate interactions among students and who can structure cooperative relationships within their classes, are modeling the strategies being taught and benefiting their classes consistent with the outcomes highlighted in the research.

There are three levels of modeling cooperation in the teacher education program: informal use, structured work groups, and long-term base groups. Informal use of cooperation includes planned time during lectures to have students turn to the person next to them and interact regarding some aspect of the instructional material. If a teacher interrupts a lecture every twelve to fifteen minutes with a question or problem that the students deal with in pairs, students have to take a more active part in the learning. In addition, the rehearsal during this "pair time" tends to increase the number of students who are willing to take part in a larger discussion afterwards. This technique works well with large lecture classes. Another informal technique that has been effective is the Focus Trio where students in threesomes are given a question at the beginning of class with three or four minutes to predict a solution or response. At the end of the lecture, film, or discussion, the threesomes are asked to process on paper the material or ideas in a specific way. Just asking students to reach agreement on what the three most important things were in class can be an engaging exercise and will change the way they listen in class.

Formal work groups are structured for lab sessions, problem-solving or decision-making groups, or to deal with specific information. They tend to be structured to be heterogeneous by the instructor and would follow the procedures outlined in *Circles of Learning* (Johnson et al., 1984). They are usually set up for a short time period and produce a single group product, or a set of answers.

The Base Group is a long-term group that usually lasts throughout the quarter or semester whose members provide support for one another, sometimes take quizzes together, have a joint project of some kind, and process the material being dealt with in the class. For example, most of our graduate classes begin with participants, predominantly teachers, coming in after school and moving immediately into Base Groups set up during the first session. They congratulate each other on living through the week and then share with each other what they have done toward the assignments for the class. Often they will process relevant experiences from their classrooms and bring books and dittoed material to share. After approximately ten minutes, class starts, but in a much different atmosphere than if we were to start class without the Base Group interaction.

Modeling the cooperative structure in the teacher education program in a careful way not only gives students a deeper understanding of the strategies, but also makes a statement about building bridges from research to practice. In addition, the more practice in working cooperatively that prospective teachers have, the more developed their own collaborative skills will be. Students who are most reluctant to work cooperatively may be the ones who need the most practice. Teaching education students to be more effective in linking with other professionals, in talking through problems together, and in co-planning and processing their teaching should pay dividends in a school setting where teachers work as part of a total staff.

Summary

Teacher education programs can prepare teachers to structure appropriate student-student interactions in classes. The orchestration of appropriate cooperative, competitive, and individualistic goal structures should be part of every teacher's repertoire so that he or she can select the interaction pattern that best suits an anticipated instructional sequence. Students should know before they start a lesson what the appropriate interaction is.

The research indicates that cooperation should be the dominant interaction pattern in the classroom and researchers cite advantages of a predominantly cooperative setting over a predominantly competitive or individualistic setting. In a cooperative setting it is reasonable to expect increased achievement, more positive attitudes, a climate for acceptance of differences, and a positive effect on many other learning outcomes.

Specific strategies for setting up appropriate interaction among students in a classroom have been identified that can be mastered by teachers and modeled by teacher educators. Cooperation should not stop at the student level. Teachers who have experienced cooperation and have some skill in structuring it and in helping students to become more adept at cooperating are more likely to be skillful themselves in linking with other staff members to make schools a more productive place to work.

━━━━━━━━━━━ References ━━━━━━━━━━━

Armstrong, B., Johnson, D. W., & Balow, B. (1981). Effects of cooperative versus individualistic learning experiences on interpersonal attraction between learning-disabled and normal-progress elementary school students. *Contemporary Educational Psychology, 6,* 102-109.

Deutsch, M. (1962). Cooperation and trust: Some theoretical notes. In M. R. Jones (Ed.), *Nebraska symposium on motivation* (pp. 275-319). Lincoln: University of Nebraska Press.

Garibaldi, A. (1979). The effective contributions of cooperative and group goal structures. *Journal of Educational Psychology, 71,* 788-795.

Gunderson, B., & Johnson, D. W. (1980). Building positive attitudes by using cooperative learning groups. *Foreign Language Annals, 13,* 39-46.

Humphreys, B., Johnson, R., & Johnson, D. (1982). Effects of cooperative, competitive, and individualistic learning on students' achievement in science class. *Journal of Research in Science Teaching, 19,* 351-356.

Johnson, D. W., & Johnson, R. (1975). *Learning together and alone: Cooperation, competition and individualization.* Englewood Cliffs, NJ: Prentice-Hall.

Johnson, D. W., & Johnson, R. (1976). Students' perceptions of and preferences for cooperative and competitive learning experiences. *Perceptual and Motor Skills, 42,* 989-990.

Johnson, D. W., & Johnson, R. (1979). Conflict in the classroom: Controversy and learning. *Review of Educational Research, 49,* 51-70.

Johnson, R., Johnson, D. W., & Tauer, M. (1979). The effects of cooperative, competitive, and individualistic goal structures on students' attitudes and achievement. *Journal of Psychology, 102,* 191-198.

Johnson, D. W., & Johnson, R. (1980). Integrating handicapped students into the mainstream. *Exceptional Children, 46,* 89-98.

Johnson, D. W., & Johnson, R. (1982). Effects of cooperative and individualistic instruction on handicapped and non-handicapped students. *Journal of Social Psychology, 118,* 257-268.

Johnson, D. W., & Johnson, R. (1983). The socialization and achievement crisis: Are cooperative learning experiences the solution? In L. Bickman (Ed.), *Applied social psychology annual 4.* Beverly Hills, CA: Sage Publications.

Johnson, D. W., Johnson, R., & Maruyama, G. (1983). Interdependence and interpersonal attraction among heterogeneous and homogeneous individuals: A theoretical formulation and a meta-analysis of the research. *Review of Educational Research, 53,* 5-54.

Johnson, D. W., & Johnson, R. (1984). Building acceptance of differences between handicapped and nonhandicapped students: The effects of cooperative and individualistic problems. *Journal of Social Psychology, 122,* 257-267.

Johnson, D. W., Johnson, R. T., Holubec, E., & Roy, P. (1984). *Circles of learning: Cooperation in the classroom.* Alexandria, VA: Association for Supervision and Curriculum Development.

Johnson, D. W., Johnson, R., Johnson, J., & Anderson, D. (1976). The effects of cooperative vs. individualized instruction on student prosocial behavior, attitudes toward learning, and achievement. *Journal of Educational Psychology, 68,* 446-452.

Johnson, D. W., Johnson, R., Roy, P., & Zaidman, B. (1985). *Oral interaction in cooperative learning groups: Speaking, listening, and the nature of statements made by high-, medium-, and low-achieving students.* Manuscript submitted for publication.

Johnson, D. W., Johnson, R., & Scott, L. (1978). The effects of cooperative and individualized instruction on student attitudes and achievement. *Journal of Social Psychology, 104,* 207-216.

Johnson, D. W., Johnson, R., & Skon, L. (1979). Student achievement on different types of tasks under cooperative, competitive, and individualistic conditions. *Contemporary Educational Psychology, 4,* 99-106.

Johnson, D. W., Johnson, R., Tiffany, M., & Zaidman, B. (1983). Are low-achievers disliked in a cooperative situation? A test of rival theories in a mixed ethnic situation. *Contemporary Educational Psychology, 8,* 189-200.

Johnson, D. W., Maruyama, G., Johnson, R., Nelson, D., & Skon, L. (1981). The effects of cooperative, competitive, and individualistic goal structures on achievement: A meta-analysis. *Psychological Bulletin, 89,* 47-62.

Johnson, D. W., Skon, L., & Johnson, R. (1980). The effects of cooperative, competitive, and individualistic goal structures on student achievement on different types of tasks. *American Educational Research Journal, 17,* 83-93.

Johnson, R., Bjorkland, R., & Krotee, M. (1984). The effects of cooperative, competitive and individualistic student interaction patterns on achievement and attitudes of the golf skill of putting. *The Research Quarterly for Exercise and Sport, 55* (2), 38-43.

Johnson, R., & Johnson, D. W. (1979). Type of task and student achievement and attitudes in interpersonal cooperation, competition, and individualization. *Journal of Social Psychology, 108,* 37-48.

Johnson, R., Johnson, D. W., DeWeerdt, N., Lyons, V., & Zaidman, B. (1983). Integrating severely adaptively handicapped seventh-grade students into constructive relationships with nonhandicapped peers in science class. *American Journal of Mental Deficiency, 87,* 611-618.

Lowry, N., & Johnson, D. W. (1981). The effects of controversy on students' motivation and learning. *Journal of Social Psychology, 115,* 31-43.

Martino, L., & Johnson, D. W. (1979). Cooperative and individualistic experiences among disabled and normal children. *Journal of Social Psychology, 107,* 177-183.

Sharan, S. (1980). Cooperative learning in small groups: Recent methods and effects on achievement, attitudes and ethnic relations. *Review of Educational Research, 50,* 241-271.

Skon, L., Johnson, D. W., & Johnson, R. (1981). Cooperative peer interaction versus individualistic efforts: Effects on the acquisition of cognitive reasoning strategies. *Journal of Educational Psychology, 73,* 83-92.

Slavin, R. (1977). Classroom reward structure: Analytical and practical review. *Review of Educational Research, 47,* 633-650.

Smith, K., Johnson, D. W., & Johnson, R. (1981). Can conflict be constructive? Controversy versus concurrence seeking in learning groups. *Journal of Educational Psychology, 73,* 651-663.

Walberg, H. (1982). *Educational and scientific literacy.* University of Illinois, mimeographed report.

Wheeler, R., & Ryan, F. (1973). Effects of cooperative and competitive environments on the attitudes and achievement of elementary school students engaged in social studies inquiry activities. *Journal of Educational Psychology, 65,* 402-407.

Child Abuse and Neglect

Prevention and Reporting

Barbara J. Meddin
Anita L. Rosen

Barbara J. Meddin, Ph.D., is a child protection specialist and human services consultant in Carbondale, Illinois.

Anita L. Rosen, Ph.D., is a private consultant in Silver Spring, Maryland.

Each year nearly 1.2 million children in the United States are reported to be abused or neglected. Even more alarming is the possibility that more than 2 million other cases are not reported to the agencies whose responsibility it is to protect children from further abuse (U.S. Department of Health and Human Services, 1981).

Most of these situations are treatable, however, and a great deal of harm to children is preventable (Kempe & Helfer, 1972). Because teachers are often the only adults who regularly see the child outside of the immediate family, teachers are often the first to observe children who have been or are at risk for abuse and/or neglect (McCaffrey & Tewey, 1978).

Teachers of young children are an essential part of the professional team that can prevent abuse and neglect. What steps can you as a teacher take to be alert to potential abuse or neglect? If indeed you believe a child has been harmed or is at risk of harm, how should it be reported?

What is child abuse and/or neglect?

Child abuse and/or neglect is any action or inaction that results in the harm or potential risk of harm to a child. Includes

- physical abuse (cuts, welts, bruises, burns);
- sexual abuse (molestation, exploitation, intercourse);
- physical neglect (medical or educational neglect, and inadequate supervision, food, clothing, or shelter);
- emotional abuse (actions that result in significant harm to the child's intellectual, emotional, or social development or functioning); and
- emotional neglect (inaction by the adult to meet the child's needs for nurture and support).

Reprinted by permission from *Young Children*, Vol. 41, No. 4 (May 1986), pp. 26-30. Copyright © 1984, National Association for the Education of Young Children, 1834 Connecticut Ave., N.W., Washington, DC 20009.

7. SERVING SPECIAL NEEDS AND INDIVIDUALIZING INSTRUCTION

Every state mandates that *suspected* cases of child abuse be reported by professionals such as teachers (Education Commission of the States, 1976). In Illinois, for example, professionals who do not report are subject to loss of their license to practice the profession. Those who report suspected cases are protected by law from any personal or civil liability growing out of that report (Illinois Public Law, 1979).

Teachers are not expected to know for sure whether a child has been harmed as a result of abuse and/or neglect. It is up to the child welfare or child protection agency to confirm the existence of abuse or neglect. Neither is the teacher expected to take custody of the child. The child protection agency or the police decide what action needs to be taken to protect the child.

Only about 13% of all child abuse reports are made by teachers or other school personnel (The American Humane Association, 1983). It appears that teachers are reluctant to report suspected cases, especially when physical neglect or emotional abuse and neglect are involved. Some teachers may feel they should not interfere with family relationships or childrearing techniques, and thus do not report cases where children are at risk (Underhill, 1974). However, it is both a legal and ethical responsibility for teachers to combine their knowledge of child development and their observation skills to identify children in need of protection.

Indicators of abuse and neglect

Physical manifestations, child or adult behaviors, and environmental situations may indicate a child has or may be at risk of abuse or neglect. The factors that most often can be observed by teachers will be discussed here.

Child characteristics

Many of the characteristics described here occur in contexts other than abusive situations. Rarely does the presence or absence of a single factor signal child abuse. A pattern of these factors and behaviors will more likely indicate harm or risk to the child.

Teachers of young children often observe bruises or wounds on children that are in various stages of healing. This indicates the injuries occurred at different times, and may have been inflicted on a regular basis. Physical abuse can be suspected, for example, if injuries appear a day or so after a holiday or long weekend (bruises take a day to show up). Injuries that occur on multiple planes of the body or that leave a mark that looks like a hand or tool should also be considered nonaccidental.

Children naturally use their hands to protect themselves. Usually when a child falls, the hands go out to stop the fall and protect the face. Children's hands, knees, or foreheads are usually injured when they attempt to break their fall. If children report their injuries were caused by a fall, but the injuries do not include these areas, you should be suspicious.

When children fall, they also are most likely to fall on one side or plane of the body. Therefore, multiple injuries, such as a head injury coupled with a bruise to the ribs or buttocks, should be considered suspicious because more than one plane of the body is involved.

For example, a first grade teacher noticed that a child in her class returned from the Christmas holiday with bruises on the right side of her face and on the back of her left arm.

Although the child said she had fallen, the teacher contacted the state child welfare agency. The child's mother initially contended the girl had been roughhousing with her brothers. Further investigation revealed that she had been hit twice by her grandfather who had been visiting and allegedly could not tolerate the girl's loud noises.

Burns often leave clues as to their origin. Oval burns may be caused by a cigarette. Stocking or doughnut-shaped burns may indicate that the child was put into a hot substance. Any burn that leaves an imprint of an item, such as an electric stove burner on a child's hand, may indicate that the injury was not accidental. The natural response of children is to withdraw when a body part comes in contact with a hot object; thus only a small section of skin is usually burned if the burn is accidental.

School-age children who come to school early and leave late may be indicating they have a reason not to go home. Likewise, young children who say they have been harmed should be believed. Rarely do children make up reports of abuse.

Older children may also discuss harmful events with classmates. Help children feel comfortable enough to confide in you because of your shared concern for a child. Susan, age 8, told a friend she had been molested by her father. The classmate confided in the teacher, who made a report. Susan had indeed been molested. Through counseling for the family, the molestation was stopped.

Children who take food from others may be suffering from neglect. One agency investigated a case where a preschool child constantly took food from other children's lunches. The child was receiving one-half of a peanut butter sandwich a day at home and needed the additional food for survival.

Another common sign of neglect is children who come to school inappropriately dressed for the weather. The child who wears sandals in the winter or who doesn't wear a coat on a cold snowy day meets the definition of neglect and can be seen as at risk of harm.

Young children cannot be expected to sit still for long periods. However, some children who have trouble sitting may be experiencing discomfort in their genital areas as a result of sexual abuse. Children whose knowledge of the sexual act is much more sophisticated than that of peers or for their level of development may also be indicating they have been sexually abused. For example, a child might engage in inappropriate sex play with dolls or with other children in the dramatic play area or at recess.

Radical behavior changes in children, or regressive behavior, should be viewed as a possible indicator of abuse or neglect. For example, children who suddenly become extremely hostile or withdrawn should be considered to be possible victims of abuse or neglect. Regression often indicates that children are attempting to protect themselves or to cope with the situation. Typical of such a behavior change might be the 5-year-old child who develops toileting problems. Likewise, the child who strives to do everything exactly right, or fears doing anything wrong, may be trying to avoid incurring the anger of adults.

Another behavior that is a possible clue to abuse or neglect is the child who always stays in the background of activities. This child usually watches intently to see what adults are doing—possibly to keep out of the way of adults in order to prevent being harmed.

Children who are abused frequently expect such abuse

184

from all adults. Do you know children who cower when you lift your hand in the air? Are there children in your group who hide broken crayons rather than asking for tape to repair them? Discussion, stories written by the children, drawings, or sharing time may also reveal episodes of abuse and neglect.

It is important to stress that teachers should be alert to a *pattern* of characteristics and behaviors that indicate child abuse or neglect.

Watch for a *pattern* of characteristics and behaviors that indicate child abuse or neglect.

Indicators of child abuse

Child

- bruises or wounds in various stages of healing
- injuries on two or more planes of the body
- injuries reported to be caused by falling but which do not include hands, knees, or forehead
- oval, immersion, doughnut-shaped, or imprint burns
- reluctance to leave school
- inappropriate dress for the weather
- discomfort when sitting
- sophisticated sexual knowledge or play
- radical behavior changes or regressive behavior
- child withdraws or watches adults
- child seems to expect abuse
- revealing discussion, stories, or drawings

Adult

- unrealistic expectations for child
- reliance on child to meet social or emotional needs
- lack of basic childrearing knowledge or skills
- substance abuse

Stress

- positive or negative changes—moving, new baby, unemployment, divorce

---

Adult characteristics

Parent (or other prime caregiver) behavior may also give clues that children are at risk of harm. Most preschool program staff see parents twice a day, and occasionally during parent conferences or home visits as well. Teachers of primary-age children have fewer occasions to observe parents, but can still be aware of parent behaviors through responses to notes, questionnaires, or phone calls.

There are a number of indicators of an adult's inability or unwillingness to care for and protect children. The parent who has unrealistic expectations for the child can be seen as placing the child at risk. For example, a parent may believe a 6-month-old child can be toilet trained, or that a 5-year-old

should be able to read, or that an 8-year-old should always act like a lady.

Adults who look to their children to meet some of their own social or emotional needs can also be seen as a high-risk parent. The teenager who keeps her baby to have someone to love her is likely to be very disappointed!

Whenever possible, observe the parent and child interacting with one another. Parents who lack basic childrearing knowledge or skills place children at risk. For instance, a parent who doesn't know about nutrition or health care, or who has a serious physical illness, may be unable to adequately care for a child. Parents who are substance abusers—either drugs or alcohol—place their children at risk. Because most parents don't deliberately harm their children, all the parents with these types of problems need support to help them function in healthier ways with their children.

At the same time, when teachers observe parenting styles, they must be aware of and sensitive to social and cultural differences. Child protection services are not designed to impose middle-class parenting standards on everyone, but are aimed at insuring a *minimum* standard of care for all children so they are free from harm.

While none of the above factors automatically indicate child abuse, the presence of any of them, along with other clues or patterns of suspected abuse, may indicate harm or potential harm for children.

Stress in the environment

Adult stress can often be the cause of one-time or chronic harm to children. Therefore, whenever a family is under stress, the likelihood that abuse or neglect may occur is increased. The source of stress can be either positive or negative—a move, the birth of a new baby, unemployment, death, inadequate housing, divorce. Any stressor can affect parents' ability to care for their children and to maintain their own self-control.

Once again, however, stress should be considered as just one indicator that may produce a potentially dangerous situation for children.

Preventing abuse and neglect

Teachers of young children have many opportunities to aid in the prevention of child abuse and neglect. Certainly each teacher is a role model for parents. Many of your actions, such as your way of greeting children when they return from an illness or vacation, your methods for handling misbehavior, and your expectations for children, can help parents see positive ways to guide children.

For teachers who are not in contact with children's parents every day, it is more difficult to serve as a role model. However, you can talk with parents often by phone, hold discussion groups about common concerns such as discipline or early reading, and encourage parents to visit your classroom.

Once you are familiar with the clues that indicate children and families may be at risk, you can spot potential problems early. If a family is going to move, for example, you can talk with them about how to make a more comfortable transition for their children into their new school (Jalongo, 1985).

If you sense a potential danger to the child, you can help the family link up with appropriate supports, such as counseling services or material assistance, before their need becomes overwhelming and children are harmed.

What happens when a report is made?

In most states, one child welfare agency receives and investigates reports of suspected child abuse or neglect. The main purpose of the agency is to protect children from harm or from further harm, not to punish parents. These agencies work on the assumption that the best context for childrearing is in the child's own home (Kadushin, 1978).

Program directors and principals should offer in-service training to teachers to keep them abreast of the state's reporting law, the specific practices of the state child welfare agency, and the school's policy and procedures. Familiarity with the procedure, and the implicit support for reporting suspected abuse, can help teachers to follow through with their responsibility.

Filing a report of suspected child abuse begins a process through which the child welfare agency determines whether or not the child has actually been harmed or is at risk of harm from abuse or neglect. When harm has occurred, then the agency works to protect the child and help the family protect the child. The emphasis is always on treatment, not punishment. Teachers are an important part of a multidisciplinary team to help prevent and treat victims of abuse and neglect.

While teachers may hesitate to report suspected cases of abuse or neglect for fear of straining the parent-teacher relationship, that fear is often unfounded (Jirsa, 1981). Most parents love their children and are concerned about their welfare. Abuse and neglect rarely occur as a result of deliberate intent to harm a child. Rather, it occurs when a parent temporarily lacks control or judgment, or lacks the knowledge or resources to adequately care for the child. After their initial and appropriate anger at the intervention of the agency, most parents feel a sense of relief that the problems has been identified, and they are usually very willing to work toward a solution.

Teachers are role models for parents.

When abuse or neglect is a reality, children will not necessarily be removed from their parents. The agency will strive to take the appropriate action to protect the child at home in the short run, while working with the parents to solve the problem for the future. All services are aimed at enhancing the parents' ability to care for and protect their children.

Before calling your local child protection agency, review the policy and procedures established for your program or school. These policies may help you determine when it is best to report, may support you in making the report, and may stipulate channels for reporting. The report should always be made in accordance with those policies and procedures, and should be done factually and without emotion.

Depending upon the state, a report is made either to a central or a local field office of the child welfare agency. That agency must begin its investigation by contact with the child, the child's family, and the alleged perpetrator of the harm. This contact is usually initiated within 24 hours, but can begin immediately if it appears the child is currently in danger.

While the family will not be told who initiated action, the agency may ask for your name, address, and phone number when you make the report. This identification is necessary in case the agency needs to get back to you for further information.

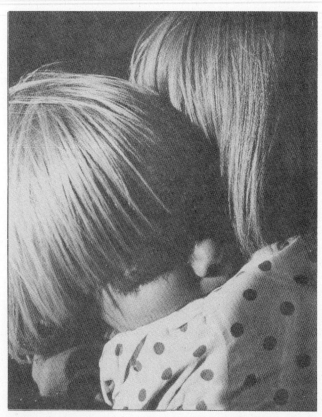

All services are aimed at enhancing the parents' ability to care for and protect their children.

In cases where only the potential for abuse or neglect exists, the link with the child welfare agency can provide parents with the resources or referrals needed to create a more effective home environment.

Like teachers, child welfare professionals' first allegiance is to the child. Teachers of young children are in a unique position to both report and help prevent child abuse and neglect through their daily contact with children and families.

When in doubt, report. Only then can we all work together to intervene on behalf of the child, work toward solutions, and enhance the quality of life for children and families.

References

American Humane Association. (1983). *Highlights of official child neglect and abuse reporting.* Denver, CO: Author.

Education Commission of the States. (1976, March). *A comparison of the states' child abuse statutes* (Report No. 84). Denver, CO: Author.

Kempe, H., & Helfer, R. (Eds.). (1972). *Helping the battered child and his family.* Philadelphia: Lippincott.

Jalongo, M. R. (1985, September). When young children move. *Young Children, 40*(6), 51–57.

Jirsa, J. (1981). Planning a child abuse referral system. *Social Work in Education, 3*(2), p. 10.

Kadushin, A. (1978). *Child welfare strategy in the coming years.* Washington, DC: National Association of Social Workers.

Illinois Public Law. (1979, November). *The abused and neglected child reporting act* (Public Act 81-1077).

McCaffrey, M., & Tewey, S. (1978, October). Preparing educators to participate in the community response to child abuse and neglect. *Exceptional Children, 45*(2), p. 115.

Underhill, E. (1974). The strange silence of teachers, doctors, and social workers in the face of cruelty to children. *International Child Welfare Review,* (21), 16–21.

U.S. Department of Health and Human Services. (1981). *Study findings: National study of the incidence and severity of child abuse and neglect.* Washington, DC: Superintendent of Documents.

The authors wish to thank Leigh Bartlett of the Department of Community Services in Perth, Australia for her help in developing case examples provided here.

Kids and Drugs:

Why, When and What Can We Do About It

**Coryl LaRue Jones and
Catherine S. Bell-Bolek**

Coryl LaRue Jones, Ph.D., is a Research Psychologist and Catherine S. Bell-Bolek is Chief, Prevention Research Branch, Division of Clinical Research, National Institute on Drug Abuse.

A 5-year decline in drug use among American high school seniors stalled in 1985. That year, according to figures from an annual national survey conducted by the Institute for Social Research, University of Michigan, 61 percent of the students surveyed reported trying an illicit drug at some time—and 40 percent used a drug other than marijuana.[1]

Although the 1985 levels are half of what they were in their peak years in the 1970s, they are higher than 1984. Only the use of LSD, methaqualone and the amphetamines (second to marijuana as the largest class of illicitly used substances) continued to decline, while the levels of use of cocaine, PCP and opiates other than heroin, which had been declining, increased in 1985. Cocaine had been tried by 17 percent of the students in 1985 as compared to 10 percent in 1976. It is interesting to note that while nearly 80 percent of seniors acknowledged the harmful effects of using cocaine, only 34 percent saw much risk in experimenting with it. More than 70 percent saw harm in using marijuana (up from 43 percent in 1983), and almost 60 percent listed potential harm as their reason for quitting.

Although nationally only five percent of seniors had tried PCP, its

From *Children Today*, May/June 1986, pp. 5-10. Reprinted by permission of the authors.

. . . prevention efforts need to explore what drug use means to teenagers. . . and to respond to the values of adolescents. . .

use increased in epidemic proportions in certain cities (for example, Washington, D.C., Los Angeles and Detroit). Because of the sense of omnipotent power associated with PCP use and its low manufacturing cost, this regionalized pattern of use may spread among disadvantaged urban youth.

Despite age factors affecting legality of use, alcohol and cigarettes are defined as licit drugs. Five percent of high school seniors reported daily use of alcohol, and 39 percent reported participating in heavy party drinking (five or more drinks in a row). One in five seniors is a daily smoker. While this rate is lower than the peak year of 1977, it indicates an increase from 1984. Other tragedies are that experimentation with tobacco is occurring at increasingly younger ages and that young people are increasing their use of smokeless tobacco.

The question of how to prevent drug abuse can best be answered if we can understand something about why an individual begins to experiment with drugs and when such activities are likely to take place.

Gateway Theory and Gateway Drugs

According to the gateway theory developed by Denise Kandel, a predictable sequence of use of specific drugs exists: legal substances (first tobacco, then beer and wine and progressing to hard liquor), then the illegal drugs (marijuana, then other illicit drugs). Both Kandel and Richard Jessor report that adoles-

cents rarely proceed directly from the "gateway drugs" (tobacco, beer and wine) to illicit drugs such as heroin and cocaine without the intermediate steps of using hard liquor and marijuana.

Of course, this sequence of drug use is not absolute. In some communities, inhalants are the first drugs used by children, particularly children in ethnic minority groups. In addition, some adolescents will try a drug, then stop using it.

Lee Robins noted that persons who initiated drug use very early (under age 15) or late (after age 24) were those who tended to develop the most dysfunctional drug use patterns. Underlying psychiatric problems were associated with early and late onset of drug use. From her research with young children in Washington, D.C., Patricia Bush would add a preliminary stage: salience of use of substances in the home—meaning involvement of the child in lighting cigarettes, serving drinks and taking medicines without supervision.

The findings discussed here and in the following section are reported in a recent monograph, *The Etiology of Drug Abuse: Implications for Prevention,* published by the National Institute on Drug Abuse.[2]

Why and When

The peak years for initiating and using drugs are between the ages of 14 and 21. The fact that experimentation with and limited use of tobacco, alcohol and marijuana take place predominantly in social situations, with solitary use relatively rare, suggests that in the majority of cases, drug abuse is a function of the adolescent's social interaction and experimentation with lifestyle.

The mobility of adolescents brings exposure to new associates, and the egocentricity of young people makes them feel invulnerable—until they try to stop use. With rare exception, the psychopharmacological factors associated with compulsive drug use are hidden for a while and develop after increased, prolonged and regular patterns of drug use. After a regular pattern of use is established, in the case of drugs with an addictive potential, the physiological reinforcing properties and fear of withdrawal appear to contribute to the adolescent's maintaining a regular pattern of use independent of social context. The social context then becomes servant to the acquisition of drugs.

The "I can stop whenever I want to" syndrome appears to dominate adolescent thinking, regardless of warnings from parents and teachers. From a developmental point of view, adolescents wish to make decisions for themselves. In the early stages of experimental use, they also perceive certain social and feeling states as benefits. Even the most moralistic and rigid of preadoles-

> *. . . drug abuse is a function of the adolescent's social interaction and experimentation with lifestyle.*

cents (actually, most preadolescents fit this pattern) can be vulnerable when they begin to personalize their own value systems through testing the values of others.

Within this framework, factors that increase the likelihood of initiating drug experimentation include coming from a home in which parents, older siblings or other family members smoke, drink or use drugs; living with a family that tolerates drug use or believes it is harmless or an expected aspect of adolescent behavior; and having friends who use drugs or approve of their use. Other factors include the child's need to explore developing feelings and to search for something to make him or her feel good about life.

The glamorous portrayal of drug and alcohol use in the media also contributes to experimentation. Even the identification of drug taking as a severe risk provides a fascination for the risk-taking adolescent. For some adolescents, risk is not a deterrent but a challenge.

Biological vulnerability to dysfunctional drug use is a major possibility, as research evidence is indicating with regard to alcoholism.

Disciplinary tactics used by adults can also be a factor in influencing a young person's drug use. Diana Baumrind reports that children of parents who use authoritative, in contrast to authoritarian or permissive, discipline techniques are more inclined to be rational abstainers from drug use.

Differences in the values and aspirations of young people also influence their risk of drug abuse. A desire for independence based on achievement is one of the strongest protective factors against drug abuse and to cessation of drug use after experimentation. Youths who are aware and knowledgeable about the health, social and legal consequences of drug abuse and who care about their health and future tend to be less likely to experiment with drugs unless they have psychological problems.

Substance users differ from nonusers in their social behaviors. Nonusers report more involvement with extracurricular activities, such as sports, clubs and part-time jobs, while drug users tend to be more involved in sexual activity, truancy, delinquency and hyperaggressive and rebellious behaviors and to have poor relationships with others. Which problem behavior precedes another is an open question.

Jessor believes in the existence of a syndrome of health-compromising behaviors, which he calls problem behavior, and which include drug abuse, early sexual activity, truancy and delinquency. This problem behavior theory leads intervention experts to suggest that prevention efforts should focus on the underlying determinants of these problem be-

haviors rather than on drug abuse as an isolated behavior.

Baumrind takes a different stance. She believes that risk taking is a normal developmental attribute of adolescence, a part of the process that begins when the child risks taking his or her first step, and that labeling a child delinquent for such behavior may result in a self-fulfilling prophecy. She warns that since adolescence is a time of individuation, coercive approaches that frustrate attempts to gain independence may stimulate rebellion and increase, rather than decrease, drug use.

Because risk taking is a component of human development leading, hopefully, toward mastery and higher levels of development, the dilemma for drug abuse prevention approaches is how to support the positive aspects of exploration while simultaneously reducing or eliminating life-endangering risk taking involving drugs. Just because drugs are ubiquitous in our society, one cannot assume that drug use is an expected outcome of adolescent experimentation with lifestyle.

In reviewing intervention programs for adolescents, David Murray and Cheryl Perry state that drug use meets certain personal and social needs of adolescents and that prevention efforts need to explore what drug use means to teenagers so that alternatives can be developed by the adolescents to meet their own needs.

Adolescence is recognized as a time of great physical and emotional

> *Disciplinary tactics used by adults can also be a factor in influencing a young person's drug use.*

change—a time when a person has to learn to cope with pain, as a poet or teenager might put it. Experimentation with a wide range of behaviors and lifestyles is typical, as is a great concern for body image and the physiologic changes taking place. This narcissism is both a potential cause of drug abuse and a clue to designing potential prevention programs—programs that help adolescents come to understand themselves. We can capitalize on this by using approaches that help them realize that other kids have the same mixed-up feelings and concerns about the changes they must face and let them know that their drug use may make them unattractive or unpleasant to be around. It is also important for them to learn about the discipline and deprivations that their sports, rock and movie idols experience to achieve their status, in contrast to how some of them live after they have achieved acclaim.

School-Based Prevention Programs

Some of these principles have been incorporated in school-based substance abuse prevention programs. In 1984, when the National Institute on Drug Abuse reviewed research on such programs,[3] six basic approaches were identified: drug abuse education and affective education as educational modes; alternative programs; psychosocial approaches (resistance strategies referred to as "social inoculation") and personal and social skills train-

ing; and cognitive-developmental training, which focuses on physiological reactions to smoking experimentation and user perceptions. (This latter approach is fairly new and results are not yet available.) These prevention programs were conducted primarily in junior high schools and focused on the use of tobacco.

The drug education programs of the 1970s only disseminated information, usually "fear arousal messages," and were particularly unsuccessful. They lacked credibility, and results indicated increases in the level of drug use by program participants. Affective educational programs designed to meet the children's social and emotional needs and to train them in decision-making skills (values clarification, analysis of consequences of behavioral choices and identification of alternative behaviors) did not provide them with specific skills to resist pro-drug pressures. Research indicated little or no effect on levels of drug abuse. These findings suggest that traditional educational approaches were too narrow in focus.

The same fate was true of alternative programs, which did not focus on drugs per se but on community projects intended to reduce alienation and to provide young people with opportunities for recreation, socialization and informal education. Such programs had little or no

effect on actual levels of drug use, although the programs provided other benefits to participants.

The psychosocial approaches provide a better conceptual framework. These interventions, while all school based, differ in who delivers the message (a classmate, older peer, teacher), the methods of teaching specific techniques for resisting social pressures (role play, modeling) and the use of social contracts (commitments not to use drugs). Some programs emphasize the development of general coping skills, some are substance specific and others are presented within the context of comprehensive school health programs.

Those that teach techniques to resist pressures to use drugs—the "Say No" strategy, among others—are frequently called social inoculation programs, a term which can be misleading because it implies that one "shot" will provide lasting immunity. Research suggests that booster sessions and other types of reinforcement are necessary. Evaluation of the social inoculation and social skills training programs to prevent drug abuse produced similar results: They reduced onset of drug use at statistically significant levels, but in many cases results were confounded by methodological and analytical problems.

Points To Keep In Mind

In intervention research, children are at varying stages of develop-

A desire for independence based on achievement is one of the strongest protective factors against drug abuse. . .

ment—for cognitive and psychosocial reasons, they may not be able to comprehend or apply health or drug messages to their own lives. They are also at varying stages of autonomy affecting drug use—in their use of medicines, the presence of alcohol, tobacco and other drugs in the home and the influences and availability of psychoactive substances in the community and at school. We need to learn how to communicate with children at these various stages and according to their individual needs. For example, Patricia Bush reports that children tend to develop their attitudes and beliefs about medicines and abusable substances by the time they are 10 years old. This is rarely reflected in strategies used in drug abuse prevention programs. Health promotion research is beginning to provide models for prevention programs. From such research, we have learned that any approach that ignores the child's developmental stage of comprehension—and the fact that the child's comprehension of health information may lag behind other cognitive areas—will not be productive.

Prevention programs also need to respond to the values of adolescents: independence versus slavish adherence to peer pressure as it replaces parental authority; health and attractive body image when children are vulnerable to fears about the rapid changes in their bodies and moods; and natural highs from physical and mental experiences that support the development of competence, skill and ma-

turation. One should always question interventions—whether for prevention or treatment—in which developmentally regressive demands are placed on young people with drug abuse problems, as this runs contrary to the adolescent's developmental needs to develop critical judgment and independence.

Drug abuse prevention and intervention studies outside the school are rare. Interventions oriented toward families tend to select participants based on their having at least one parent or sibling with drug-related problems. Little research has been done regarding other potentially high risk youth, such as infants exposed to drugs in utero, children in high risk family environments or who exhibit developmental difficulties, single teenage mothers and their children, school dropouts and unemployed youth. These populations include a high proportion of minority youth. Special prevention efforts targeted on persons with predisposing genetic, biologic and developmental risk factors are also needed.

A prejudice also exists based on social class. Research to prevent mental health and substance abuse problems among low socioeconomic populations targets such areas as environmental influences, family man-

agement, failures in parenting and failure of the child to develop along a maturational trajectory leading to competence and economic stability. However, families of higher socioeconomic status can also face these same problems, and research on these families should not neglect the family and focus on adolescent peer groups without asking why a child may select certain friends and influences while rejecting others.

Training children regarding the use of abusable substances is a sensitive issue. Children in families with a member who abuses alcohol tend to dislike alcohol because of the effects they experience. Such children do not initiate use early, yet they later tend to develop dysfunctional use patterns when their adult lives become stressful. Children in families who are introduced to moderate alcohol use initiate use early, frequently in the presence of their parents, and tend not to develop dysfunctional use patterns. One implication we need to know more about is the degree to which families with moderate use patterns train their children to develop self-regulatory habits regarding alcohol use and help them avoid the problems associated with alcohol consumption or drug use.

Parents have looked to the media, to law enforcement and to other people's children for the cause of and solution to drug problems. However, the findings are consistent: The family's pattern of alcohol and drug use, together with parental

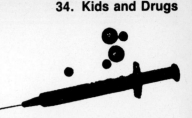

> *The family may prove to be the most enduring point of prevention or intervention.*

child care practices, are significant influences leading young people into acceptance of drug use in their environment. The important impact of the parents is on the development of the child's personality, which in turn influences the child's choice of friends.

The family may prove to be the most enduring point of prevention or intervention. Peer influences, as hazardous as they can prove to be in adolescence, are focused on the adolescent's short-term rather than long-term goals, which means that school-based programs are important, but not a comprehensive solution. We must use all avenues to help our children develop the ability to think about the future, to help them seek a future worth having. We can do this by helping them develop skills and perceptions that give them hope, competence, independence and a good feeling about themselves, for without these, drugs provide a very enticing way to feel good, if only for a moment.

[1] L.D. Johnson, P.O. O'Malley and J.G. Bachman, *Use of Licit and Illicit Drugs by America's High School Students 1975-84,* National Institute on Drug Abuse, DHHS Pub. No. (ADM) 85-1394, Washington, D.C., U.S. Government Printing Office, 1985.

[2] C.L. Jones and R.J. Battjes (Eds.), *Etiology of Drug Abuse: Implications for Prevention,* NIDA Research Monograph No. 56, DHHS Pub. No. (ADM) 85-1335, Washington, D.C., U.S. Government Printing Office, 1985.

[3] C.S. Bell and R.J. Battjes (Eds.), *Prevention Research: Deterring Drug Abuse Among Children and Adolescents,* NIDA Research Monograph No. 63, DHHS Pub. No. (ADM) 85-1334, Washington, D.C., U.S. Government Printing Office, 1985.

The Profession of Teaching Today

The American Association of Colleges for Teacher Education (AACTE) has called for and is implementing planning arrangements for the national certification of teachers. The National Education Association (NEA) and the American Federation of Teachers (AFT) have entered into dialogue over this matter. AACTE seems to be rallying for the medical model of national board certification in what would amount to the various teaching "specialties" for which persons would seek certification as teachers. The Carnegie Forum on Education has published *A Nation Prepared: Teachers for the 21st Century* which calls for similar recommendations for the reform of teacher education. The Carnegie Forum on Education has powerful bipartisan economic and political support. In addition, the Holmes Group of deans, as well as other leaders in teacher education, has issued its own extensive report on reform of teacher education. The Holmes Group report, entitled *Tomorrow's Teachers*, has made recommendations for changing and improving the relationships between teacher education institutions and the elementary and secondary schools of the nation. All in all, almost thirty national reports relating in one way or another to dramatic change in North American teacher education have been published since 1983. Never before have there been such comprehensive and intensive reform recommendations for teacher education on this continent.

Though major changes have occurred in teacher education over the past fifteen years, recent developments indicate that even greater change can be expected in the next few years. The nation's teachers are confronting new proposals each year which directly affect their morale and security.

Difficult teaching conditions, created to a large extent by phenomena such as mainstreaming and competency testing, are intensifying pressures on teachers. They are being asked to do and know more while they receive less assistance in meeting the demands of nontraditional so-cial and testing pressures in their classrooms.

In addition, teachers are deeply affected by economic frustrations caused by the fact that their real wages and purchasing power have declined in recent years. The President's Commission Report and others have called for higher pay and career ladders for teachers, as well as for merit pay to attract more academically talented young people into the profession. But, so far, little has been done by either the national or the state legislatures to fund such efforts, and most local communities are unable to do so.

How does a nation achieve a dramatic qualitative advance in the field of education if it is unwilling to pay for it? Blaming most of the problems in education on teacher incompetence is like blaming the victim. Several ways to improve the quality of teaching include the funding of in-service education for teachers, revising the funding of education so that teachers can earn wages adequate to their level of professional preparation, and implementing a way to demonstrate teacher competency in the profession.

According to the Rand Corporation and other research groups, critical shortages of teachers already exist in mathematics, the sciences, foreign languages, and in the education of children of linguistic minorities. Shortages are expected to develop in most, if not all, areas of teaching in the next ten years. Children will always need well-educated and competent teachers. However, the profession may not be able to provide them unless more academically talented people can be attracted to the field.

To give hope to the profession and to build both its competence and its self-confidence, teachers must be motivated to an even greater effort for professional growth. Teachers need support. Simply criticizing them and refusing to alter those social and economic conditions which affect the quality of their work will not solve national problems in education. Nor will it lead to excellence at the elementary or secondary school levels. There is no free lunch in educational reform. Not only must teachers work to improve the public's image of and confidence in them, but the public must confront its own misunderstanding of the level of commitment required to achieve excellence. If the American and Canadian peoples want quality schools, the working conditions and the means of funding elementary and secondary schooling must be examined by national, state, and provincial legislatures with wisdom, foresight, and compassion.

Children cannot learn if they feel that no one believes in their ability to learn. The quality of teachers will not improve if they are not appreciated or respected. Teachers need to know that the public cares and respects them enough to fund their professional improvement and to recognize them for the important force they are in the life of the nation.

The articles in this unit consider the quality of education and the status of the teaching profession today.

Looking Ahead: Challenge Questions

List what you think are the five most important issues confronting the teaching profession today (with number one being the most important and number five the least important). What criteria did you use in ranking the issues? What is your position on each of them?

Does teaching have some problems that other professions don't seem to have? If so, what are they? What can be done about them?

What seem to be the major issues affecting teacher morale?

What are the best reasons for a person to choose a career in teaching?

What are the most critical social pressures on teachers? Why are teachers sometimes used as scapegoats?

What are the problems with some of the solutions offered for meeting the anticipated shortages of teachers? What are examples of "stir-and-serve" approaches to teacher education?

THE MAKING OF A PROFESSION

ALBERT SHANKER

Albert Shanker is president of the American Federation of Teachers. This article is based on a speech delivered to the Representative Assembly of the New York State United Teachers on April 27, 1985.

I HAVE spent more than thirty years arguing for unionism and collective bargaining, for better salaries and working conditions for teachers. We cannot abandon these goals — far from it — but today I am convinced that unless we go beyond collective bargaining to the achievement of true teacher professionalism, we will fail in our major objectives: to preserve public education in the United States and to improve the status of teachers economically, socially, and politically.

It is unusual for me to be advocating professionalism. My experience with the way the word *professional* is used in schools has not been good. There was the long battle of "professional" versus "unionist," the idea that it was unprofessional for teachers to work to improve their salaries and conditions through effective organizing, militant struggle, and political action. That battle we've largely won. There was also the way the word *professional* was used so often to beat teachers down. A few examples from my early teaching experience will explain why I haven't liked the term very much.

I can remember my first exposure to it as a teacher. I started teaching in a very tough elementary school. I had great doubts as to whether I would make it, and after a couple of weeks, the door was opened and the assistant principal stood there. I remember thinking, "Thank God, help is coming." I kept motioning him in, but he continued to stand there, sort of pointing at something, for what seemed like a very long time but was probably only thirty seconds. Finally he said to me, "Mr. Shanker, there are a couple of pieces of paper on the floor over there. It is very unsightly and very *unprofessional.*" Then he left.

Soon thereafter I went to my first faculty conference. In those days, not many men taught in elementary schools; there was only one other male teacher in that school. At the faculty conference, the organizational chart of the school was distributed, including a schedule of duties — who had hall patrol, lunch patrol, and so forth, including "snow patrol." Snow patrol, by tradition, was assigned to the male teacher. On snow days, he gave up his lunch period and walked around outside the building, warning kids not to throw snowballs at each other. Sure enough, Mr. Jones and Mr. Shanker were now assigned to snow patrol. Mr. Jones raised his hand and was called on by the principal. The teacher said, "Now that there are two men on the faculty to handle snow patrol, would it be okay to rotate — you know, the first day of snow he goes, and the next day I go?" The principal frowned at him and replied, "Mr. Jones, that is very *unprofessional.* First of all, it is unprofessional because the duty schedule has already been mimeographed, as you see. Secondly, I am surprised that you aren't concerned that one child might throw a snowball at another and hit him in the eye, with permanent damage. It's very unprofessional of you." So that was my second run-in with this new and unusual use of *professional* and *unprofessional.*

I have also distrusted the word professional because of how it was, and is, used so often to force teachers to obey orders that go against their sense of sound educational practice. Professionalism, in this Orwellian sense, is not a standard but a threat: Do this, don't say that, or else.

In spite of this unfortunate history, we should not be forced to abandon a perfectly good word because others have misused it.

I mean professional in its more rigorous, classical sense. A professional is a person who is an expert, and by virtue of that expertise is permitted to operate fairly

From *American Educator,* Vol. 9, No. 3, Fall 1985, pp. 10-17, 46, 48. © American Federation of Teachers, 1985.

independently, to make decisions, to exercise discretion, to be free of most direct supervision. No one stands over a surgeon at the operating table with directions to cut a little to the left or to the right. The surgeon is trusted to make appropriate medical decisions, and because of that trust and the expertise involved is generally very well compensated.

Unfortunately, professionalism for teachers is still not a question of the right or wrong thing to do but, rather, of who has the power to tell whom what to do. Teachers are still a long way from being members of a profession, as many of us and the larger society understand that word.

I BELIEVE that the realization of authentic professionalism for teachers will require a second revolution in American public education, one that builds upon the revolution we in the AFT made a quarter of a century ago when we pioneered collective bargaining for teachers. Collective bargaining has been a very powerful instrument. Through it we have increased teachers' salaries, limited class size, removed some of the more onerous nonteaching chores, established an impartial procedure for the resolution of grievances, given teachers a powerful political voice in their communities and in the country, and much more. Surely we cannot abandon it; if teacher salaries have slipped in recent years in relation to those of other occupations, think of how much more they would have slipped without that collective strength. Teachers need and must jealously guard the right to bargain collectively. And, yet, we have not been able to achieve all that we had hoped for through the bargaining process, and it is now time to go beyond it to something additional and quite different.

We learned early on that the negotiation process would not meet all of our needs. In New York City — and I daresay everywhere that a union represents teachers — we would go through a long process of listening to our members, usually at lunch and afterschool meetings. We collected bargaining "demands," the items teachers wanted, often as many as seven hundred or eight hundred. While some of these dealt with salary, class size, and similar issues, many more had to do with professional matters, the items different groups of teachers — math teachers, English teachers, physical education teachers, and others — wanted that would make their professional lives more satisfying.

Collecting the demands was one thing, getting them addressed, another. We went to the bargaining table under the assumption that boards of education would resist the salary demands but be open to a discussion of ways to reorganize the schools so that teachers and children would be happier and more productive. But quite the opposite was the case. Typically, the school board said: "You're a union. We'll be happy to talk with you about the salaries and working conditions teachers want. But we will not talk to you about anything that's good for children, because you weren't elected to represent the children. Professional issues are not subject to negotiation."

And so there we were. Teachers had gone from being weak and unorganized to being strong, unionized employees with considerable power. But many of the issues we wanted to deal with could not be taken up at the negotiating table. Substantial improvements were made, but they fell short of creating the professional workplace that our members wanted then and want today.

If we are to achieve that professionalism, we have to take a step beyond collective bargaining — not to abandon it, but to build on it, to develop new processes, new institutions, new procedures that will bring us what teachers want in addition to what we get from collective bargaining: status, dignity, a voice in professional matters, the compensation of a professional. The question for us is: How do we get there, how do we achieve professional status, responsibility, and salaries for teachers?

A MERICAN WORK and American workers have changed dramatically in the last thirty years or so, as those of us who served on the AFL-CIO Committee on the Evolution of Work learned in the course of our research. If I had asked my parents, "Why are you working?" they would have thought I was crazy. The only reason they were working was to feed and clothe and shelter the family. It never dawned on them to think of a job primarily in terms of pride or satisfaction. Today, however, the answers pollsters get when they ask the question are quite different. The first response is not "because I have to earn a living." Instead, people say something like this: "because I'm able to express various interests that I have through my job"; "because I get satisfaction"; "because I am respected on the job"; "because I'm allowed to do my work the way I think best, and I do it very well, and I like that."

Moreover, when the pollsters went further and asked what workers thought of the boss, the answers were even more surprising. The expectation was that there would be a fair amount of hostility expressed. On the contrary, roughly 70 pecent of all employees in the United States say that their boss is good to work for, helpful when presented with problems. They like working at their jobs. They think well of unions — but only for the worker down the block who has a rotten boss, not for themselves. They believe unions create adversarial relationships that bring rigid rules in their wake. Before you know it, says the typical worker, I won't be able to exercise the judgment that I now exercise; the rules will infringe upon my ability to do my job well, and I won't get the same amount of satisfaction from it.

So, more and more frequently in the industrial world, workers — and they are educated workers these days — are being treated with dignity and respect. But not in the educational workplace — and not teachers. Teachers are not accorded the trust and confidence that are becoming routine in the modern factory; our schools are the last bastions of the rigid nineteenth-century industrial hierarchy. Two recent efforts at major overhaul, one in education, the other in the automobile industry, are worth comparing.

As the education reform reports were being issued, the California Business Roundtable, composed of the chief executive officers of the eighty or so largest corporations in that state, persuaded the legislature and the governor to enact major new education law. The state came up with $2.7 billion in new money for education over a two-year period, badly needed in the wake of

No one stands over a surgeon at the operating table with directions to cut a little to the left or to the right.

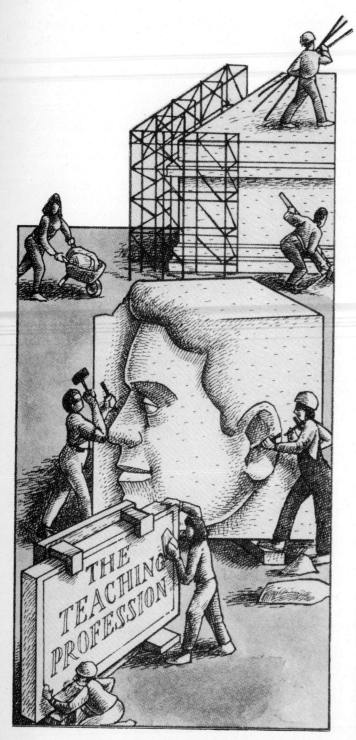

Proposition 13 — but also with a piece of legislation 150 pages long that prescribed for teachers what textbooks to use, how many hours students should be instructed in this subject and that subject, virtually everything that teachers were expected to do. There is no other occupation that is regulated in this way by state legislatures, and California is by no means unique. The Regents Action Plan in New York and the Part 100 Regulations designed to implement it suffer from the same apparent lack of confidence in teachers, as do similar plans in other states. (Some of this, of course, probably stems from the thinking that anyone willing to work for the typically low salary paid to today's teacher bears careful watching!) The hazard of this approach, aside from the demoralization it creates within the ranks of existing teachers, is that no bright, young, self-directed college graduate will want to become a teacher, to enter a field in which there is little opportunity to exercise judgment or to make professional decisions.

The American auto industry, on the other hand, has learned a valuable lesson from its Japanese competitors. Instead of supervising workers to death, rewarding the good ones and firing the bad ones — and later recalling the automobile lemons that this poor procedure manufactures — Japan treats its workers differently. It accords them lifetime job security and involves each and every one of them in constantly trying to make the *system* of production better. The result is that the Japanese, carefully consulting those who actually do the work, have discovered how to make the product right to begin with, which is far less expensive than the recall/remake process that American cars have gone through.

A COUPLE of years ago, Myron Tribus, director of the Center for Advanced Engineering Study at M.I.T., wrote an article entitled "Deming's Way" about the ideas of W. Edwards Deming, the father of Japanese quality control. It appeared in the Spring 1983 issue of *New Management*, published by the Graduate School of Business Administration at the University of Southern California. The Deming manager, Tribus wrote, "believes that he and the workers have a natural division of labor: They are responsible for doing the work *within the system*, and he is responsible for *improving the system*. He realizes that the potentials for improving the system are never ending, so he does not call upon consultants to teach him how to design the 'best' system. He knows that doesn't exist. Any system can be continuously improved. And the only people who really know where the potentials for improvement lie are the workers themselves. . . .

"Under 'Deming's Way,'" Tribus continued, "the manager understands that he needs the workers not only to do work but to improve the system. Thus he will not regard them simply as flesh and bone robots, but as thinking, creative human beings."

American industry is catching on. There is a true story about a Ford small truck plant that was so bad it was about to go out of business. But before closing it down, Ford decided to try the Japanese method. It would ask each worker what was wrong, how the procedure and the product could be improved. For example, one of the managers approached a worker who was working in a pit. He had a fairly heavy tool; and every fifteen or twenty seconds or so as a new truck came above him on the assembly line, he would pull the trigger on the tool and tighten a bolt. The manager came up to him, and the conversation went something like this:

Manager: "Look, this place is going to close down soon unless we improve. So you've got nothing to lose, and I'm asking all the workers here about things that go wrong. Tell me honestly, Jack, when you try to tighten these bolts, do you ever miss?"

Jack: "Yes."

Manager: "How often do you miss?"

Jack: "Well, about every six minutes or so I don't tighten one of the bolts."

Manager: "Why is that?"

Jack: "Well, it's a very hard job. You have to keep looking up all day and holding the tool, and I get a crick in my neck. And every once in a while, I get a muscle spasm and my head jerks away so that I can't look up; and when the spasm has passed, so has the truck, and I haven't tightened the bolt. I feel bad about it, but there's nothing I can do."

Manager: "Do you have any ideas about what we can do?"

Jack: "Yes. I've been thinking about this for a long time. There are really two things you can do. One is to put a little pedal under my foot so that every time I feel a crick in my neck I press the pedal and the assembly line will stop for a second; and as soon as I shake off the crick, I would tighten the bolt. Of course, it would mean that every six minutes or so the assembly line would stop for a couple of seconds, but you would get all the bolts tightened. And the other thing is — could you have me standing on top of the truck holding this tool down, because that would be a lot easier and a lot more natural than looking up and holding the tool up?"

That's what the Ford management did in that plant. It went around to all the workers and sought their ideas about solving problems. And then Ford redid the entire plant in accordance with the wishes of the employees. The result was that the plant became the best in the entire Ford Motor Company anywhere in the country. It's a classic case.

HOW MUCH of that happens in schools? When a decision is made to change anything about the organization of a school, the curriculum, the materials, or anything else, that decision is made by legislatures, state education departments, school boards, superintendents, principals. And as long as those who govern schools keep making this same mistake in thinking — that all they have to do is have supervisors watching the teachers to see who's good and who's bad and reward some and punish others — they're going to keep having the failures and the "lemons" who are "recalled" for remediation and dropout prevention. The only thing that's going to turn the schools around is to start turning the decision making as to what works and what doesn't work over to the people who are actually doing the work and know what's happening in classrooms.

The major struggle in education over the next period will be to attract and retain good teachers; and unless there is this kind of change, we will lose it. Even if we

The major struggle in education over the next period will be to attract and retain good teachers; and unless there is fundamental change, we will lose it.

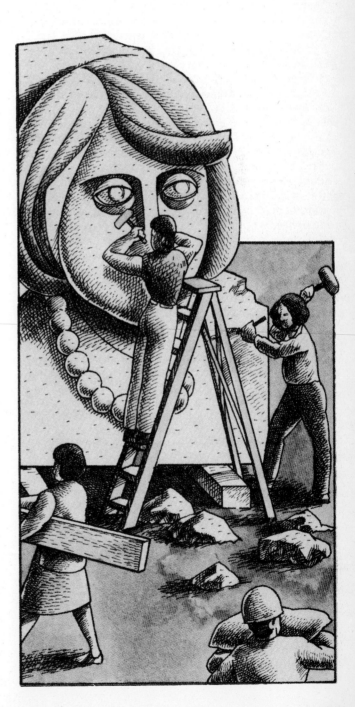

were to get better salaries and some improvement in working conditions, intelligent, well-educated people today, people who have other options, will not work for long in a traditional type of factory. The future of education depends very heavily on making teaching a profession and giving teachers a modicum of control over their environment.

WHAT DOES it mean to have a profession, to be a professional?

First, you cannot have a profession without high standards. Standards for entering teaching today are not very high, nor are they perceived as being high. College professors will steer the brighter students away from careers in teaching because they're "too smart for that." One of the reasons we are not getting our share of such students is because they don't want to go into an occupation that reputedly anybody can get into, where the rites of passage are perceived as easy, undemanding, and where the job itself is often a way station on the road to something else. If I were the president of the American Federation of Ex-Teachers, I would have a much larger constituency. There are more ex-teachers than teachers — sometimes it seems that everyone out there, everyone I encounter when I walk down the street or check into an airport or do a television interview is an ex-teacher. Why is that? How many ex-surgeons are there? How many people go through the trouble of becoming an actuary and then decide to do something else? As was the case with other occupations on the way toward professionalization, raising the standard of entry will attract many of the higher-caliber young people who are gravitating toward other careers. Indeed, there is beginning evidence that in states that have increased entry standards for teachers, more people with more solid academic credentials have applied to teach than in previous years. High standards would also mean an end to the practice of certifying any warm body to teach on an "emergency" or "provisional" basis. It's not tolerated in any other field and should not be in teaching.

Second, there is no profession without a knowledge base. I have not suggested that we should take the power away from school boards and superintendents and principals because we're teachers and we want more power; that isn't it at all. We ought to have the power to make educational decisions because we *know more* — more about what is right and wrong to do in the education of children, more about what distinguishes a good textbook from a poor one, more about a wide range of issues in education. Some of this knowledge base we do possess, some we don't yet and ought to develop. Raising standards requires expanding the knowledge base and demonstrating that we have it.

Third, there is no profession without a well-established, formal set of collegial or peer relationships. While there is a great amount of satisfaction in working with children, unless classroom time is supplemented by the different rewards, learning experiences, and self-regulation that come from a relationship with colleagues, it leads to extreme isolation and drives many out of the classroom and the profession. The current structure makes such collegiality virtually impossible.

Professional self-regulation is dependent upon a well-developed peer structure. Doctors do not have an absolute right to do anything they want. No doctor is going to say to you: "Well, any other doctor would give you the following pills and that would take care of the problem, but I don't like that — it's boring — so I'm going to give you something different and see what happens." Doctors don't behave that way. They act in accordance with a knowledge base and in accordance with what their peers expect on the basis of that knowledge.

Fourth, there is no profession unless the practitioners are seen as acting in the interest of their clients. Here we have a problem. At one time we were viewed as quite powerless, given flowers for our lapels on Teacher Recognition Day, patted on the head. Then along came this adversarial procedure known as collective bargaining. The pendulum has swung, and virtually no one now views teachers as being pattable on the head — the pooch barks, and even bites. We tend to be viewed today as though we are acting only in our own self-interest, wanting better salaries and smaller classes so our lives can be made easier. (The public rarely considers that what we want may be good for children.) That image is standing in the way of our achieving professional status, for not only must we act on behalf of our clients, we also must be perceived as acting that way.

WE HAVE a decision to make. We can continue working away only at collective bargaining. But if that is our decision, I predict that in ten or fifteen years we will find that we have largely been on a treadmill. In good years, we will make some gains; and in bad years, we will have to work very hard just to stand still. Right now there is low pay, linked to low standards, linked to an absence of trust; because supervisors and the public believe that you can't trust people who are willing to work for so little and have been brought in on low standards. All this leads to an excess of supervision and to generally low prestige.

On a national basis that's where teachers are in mid-1985. This situation has to be changed. Teachers must be viewed as professionals, as experts whose judgment can be counted on, as a group that acts on behalf of its clients and takes responsibility for the quality and performance of its own ranks.

There are some steps that ought to be taken to achieve these goals. Some of them teachers can take themselves, others will require policy action. The ideas I will list are not exhaustive, but they are a beginning. Some of these proposals are in a very formative stage. They do not represent official policy of our organization. I offer them as ideas for discussion and debate, revision and enlargement.

1. A National Teacher Examination

Last January, I proposed that there be a rigorous, national, entry-level examination for teaching, similar to those for the bar and for medicine. This would not be a government examination. Rather, it would be devised initially by a commission composed of outstanding people in education and perhaps similarly qualified people in other professions who have had some experience in administering professional examinations. Ultimately, there would be a national Teacher Professional Practices Board, composed of the practitioners themselves, to update and administer the exam; but at the beginning, it would be useful to have well-known experts, so that the examination would get wide publicity that would increase the pressure on states and local districts to require it for certification.

The exam would consist of three parts. First, there would be a stiff test of subject matter knowledge that would require candidates to think and to write and to organize their thoughts and be able to persuade. The second part, probably given on a different day, would test knowledge of pedagogy, educational issues, the ability to apply educational principles to different student developmental needs and learning styles. The third part of the examination would be a supervised internship program of from one to three years in which teachers would actually be evaluated on the basis of how well they work with students and with their colleagues. This careful induction process also would be invaluable to beginning teachers and would stand in sharp contrast to the sink-or-swim atmosphere into which they are now thrown.

With the exception of "A Nation at Risk," nothing in education in the past five or six years has gotten as much attention and editorial support as my proposal of a demanding national examination. But aside from having touched a sensitive public nerve, the idea is getting support because we have put ourselves and our union on the line on behalf of it. In my speech to the National Press Club, I said that within a few years after the establishment of such an examination, the American Federation of Teachers would refuse to accept into membership any newly hired teacher who had not passed the exam. I was signalling the public that we, the teachers, care about the quality of teachers, that we care about what happens in schools, that we are even prepared to make an organizational sacrifice in terms of not recruiting into membership or collecting the dues of people who do not meet high, professional standards.

2. Expanding Choices for Parents, Students, and Teachers

Second, I believe that we in the teacher union movement ought to support the greatest possible choice among public schools for parents, students, and teachers. Offering parents and students more options is not the same thing as conferring legal rights or instituting some sort of voucher system. In fact, the more public school choices we offer parents and students, the better are our arguments against destructive schemes like tuition tax credits and vouchers. And surely a competition among public schools, where everyone competes under the same ground rules, is a lot healthier than a private versus public competition, which is inherently unequal and unfair because the rules don't apply to all.

The current system of placing kids in school on the basis of geography is one that was designed a long time ago, when most people who sent their children to school were not educated and wouldn't have been able to make an informed decision about a school; parents

looked up to teachers and accepted the authority of government. But times have changed, and much of the public is just as well educated as teachers, some more educated. The day of automatic agreement that one's child will attend such and such school is over; parents shop for public schools when they move to a different community, and many will seek nonpublic alternatives if what they regard as a decent public school is not available to them. Students who drop out or attend high school only sporadically may be telling us not necessarily that they don't want school at all but that they don't want the particular school they're going to. Attendance is much higher and dropout rates are much lower in those public schools — vocational and option academic high schools — that students themselves have chosen.

Increased public school choice also relates to the idea that a professional must be seen to be acting in the interests of the client. Most clients *choose* the professionals they see — a doctor, a lawyer, an accountant. Children are the only clients who are perceived as the captives of the professionals who deal with them. Expanding public school choice — within schools, among schools in a district, among districts — would therefore go a long way toward getting rid of the notion that children or parents are captives and would also enable teachers to develop distinctive programs and a wider range of educational styles.

Teachers also need and deserve another kind of choice. Teaching may be the only occupation in this country in which, if you move voluntarily from one place to another, you have to suffer for it because almost invariably the new district will not credit more than a fraction of your prior experience toward salary. You may also lose pension credit. Teaching is the only occupation you have to leave in order to improve your lot. One of the elements of widening choice in public schools, therefore, ought to be freedom for teachers to move around without penalty. Just as we ought not to lose students to private schools because of lack of sufficient choice in public education, we ought not to lose teachers to other jobs because they have no real mobility in teaching. (Of course, in failing to grant full credit for prior public school experience, school districts also prevent themselves from competing for talented teachers from other districts. I don't know of any business that could stay open very long if it denied itself the opportunity to compete for talent.)

3. A Professional Teacher Board

One of the things we might do to bring about the needed revolution does not require local, state, or national legislation. We could create — perhaps first through a coalition of locals, then regionally within a state and eventually even on a statewide basis — a "Professional Teacher Board." It would be made up of outstanding teachers, selected through a process that we would develop. The board would be independent, even though initially appointed by the union, in the same sense that the Supreme Court of the United States is independent even though the justices are appointed by presidents — and most presidents have been surprised by the actions of their appointees.

The purposes of this professional board would be many. Let me suggest a few:

• Like other professional boards, it would develop standards and an ethical code for teachers. It would, for example, administer the national examination on a state level. It could inspect the practice of out-of-license teaching, which usually is inimical to the idea of high subject area qualifications determined by examination. It could determine that, beyond ascertaining that the truth has been fairly reached, a union does not have the obligation of defending a teacher against discharge based on immoral or criminal conduct.

• The board could handle various types of complaints from parents. For example, is a teacher propagandizing for a particular point of view rather than teaching the various sides of a controversial political issue objectively — that is, teaching students to think? To what extent, in such cases, is academic freedom infringed upon?

• The board could set up procedures to evaluate textbooks and other instructional materials. Textbook selection is a national disgrace. Textbooks are selected by school boards who have little knowledge of what to look for. Teachers who have studied the new knowledge base about textbooks (and others who will) should be able to stand up before a school board or other body and demonstrate what's right and what's wrong about a textbook from a highly authoritative standpoint, much as a doctor or lawyer might explain the fine points of a case to a group of laymen. This kind of knowledge is power. Its demonstration would earn for teachers the kind of professional respect that precedes professional empowerment.

• Finally, like all other professional boards, the professional teacher board should be prepared to play an honest part when the question of incompetence is raised. If a teacher is brought up on charges of incompetence, the board ought to select three outstanding teachers from somewhere else in the state to observe the teacher so accused and issue an independent report that evaluates the judgment of the principal or other supervisor. Of course, in order for this procedure to work, the three teachers have to be absolutely independent, the only direction from the union being that they're on jury duty as professional jurors and are to call it as they see it as teachers and as professionals.

What I am talking about is a process of peer appeal. The teacher would still have the right to a hearing panel and to go to court. But I see four possible scenarios that might be played out:

(1) both the teacher and the supervisor agree in writing that the decision of the teacher review panel is binding;

(2) the teacher agrees but the principal refuses, in which case the refusal of the principal to allow a trio of outstanding teachers to review the decision should be taken into account by any existing panel of law;

(3) the principal agrees but the teacher refuses, in which case that refusal ought also to be taken into account by the existing panel of law; and

(4) both parties refuse, in which case existing procedures are followed without the intervention of the teacher review panel.

I am not proposing an abandonment of due process. Due process means that the decision of the supervisor is subject to outside review. I am suggesting that outstanding professionals from within teaching but from outside the immediate situation are just as equipped as — indeed, probably more so than — a panel of outside lawyers or other citizens to do an honest and professional job.

This could, of course, be the most controversial function of the teacher professional board, but we do not have the right to be called professionals — and we will never convince the public that we are — unless we are prepared honestly to decide what constitutes competence in our profession and what constitutes incompetence and apply those definitions to ourselves and our colleagues.

4. A Different Kind of Career Ladder

I'm not opposed to a career ladder in principle, but most of the proposals I've seen are merely devices to give a handful of people more money than others. Many, perhaps most, are a kind of cover-up for merit pay. There are ways, however, of creating a meaningful career ladder. For example, since the training of teachers is at least in part the responsibility of colleges and universities, why not give the teachers who train newcomers during an internship period official employment status and rank on the faculties of area institutions of higher education that offer teacher training programs?

This would have a number of immediate benefits. First, the teacher trainers would receive additional compensation, some of which would come from the college or university. Trainers could serve for a limited period and be replaced with outstanding others, so there would be an opportunity for many to be part of such a program. Second, there would be an automatic change in the image and status of such teachers and undoubtedly some positive spillover in the public mind to elementary and secondary teachers in general. Third, one of the most valid criticisms of colleges of teacher education is that courses are given by many people who have never themselves taught in elementary and secondary schools but, rather, are scholars and theorists. Clearly we still need the theorists and the researchers, but such faculties ought to be leavened by those who have had considerable classroom experience and continue to practice in the classroom.

Certification by independent boards would eliminate the possibility of favoritism.

There is no reason to limit university employment status to classroom teachers who train other teachers. Teachers who are engaged in textbook evaluation or curriculum design might also give the university courses that teach newcomers how to do this. Legions of doctors and lawyers both practice their profession and teach in the institutions that train their future colleagues. It is a major mark of a true profession.

How would teachers qualify for higher rank within the profession? One approach would be to have national education specialty boards examine and certify teachers in their subject or specialty areas on a voluntary basis. Those going through the extra training, testing, and evaluation would be considered specialists and would receive more pay. In math, for example, interested groups could come together to establish requirements for becoming a board-certified math teacher. This would be similar to medical specialty boards that certify physicians who choose to undertake additional training and tests in a medical specialty beyond general practice.

This approach, which was first proposed by educational consultant Myron Lieberman in a piece published in 1959 in *Phi Delta Kappan* magazine and which is being updated for publication this October, would avoid the pitfalls associated with traditional merit pay schemes. Certification by independent boards would eliminate the possibility of favoritism by principals, superintendents, and school boards. In addition, since there would be no arbitrary limit on the number of teachers who could qualify for certification, it would not lead to the competition and demoralization associated with plans that decide ahead of time that only 5 percent, 10 percent, or 15 percent of teachers can be considered meritorious.

Since the certification would be nationally portable, it would also give teachers more career flexibility.

5. Restructuring the Delivery of Education

I am convinced that unless there is a wholesale restructuring of the way in which educational services are delivered, teaching will not become a genuine profession and schools will not be able to meet the needs of all students for an excellent education.

There are 2 million public school teachers in the United States. Half of them will retire and be replaced in the next decade. At the same time, there is going to be a talent shortage in this country; and given the increased demand for talent by new and revamped industries and by other agencies of government, there is very little chance that public education will get enough high-caliber career teachers. The demographics are against us.

So are the economics. We know that vastly increased teacher salaries will be needed to recruit and retain good teachers. Suppose we gave each teacher a 50 percent increase. That would still not make us a very well-paid profession, but, with pensions, taxes, and other costs, it would total approximately $30 billion. Title I at its highest point was about $3.5 billion, so there is no likelihood at all of giving 2 million teachers a 50 percent raise.

So we are not going to get either the talent or the money to replace a million teachers soon and another million some years later. What do we do? Part of the

answer is to consider what it is that teachers do and whether part of it can be accomplished in some other ways, freeing teachers to do what *only* they can, the genuine, professional tasks. This would mean a smaller number of *career* teachers earning genuinely professional salaries, say, double the current rate. Let me suggest some parts of a structure to accomplish this:

● Career teachers would be assisted by substantial numbers of very bright college graduates who come into teaching for a variety of reasons — to repay a college loan, meet a scholarship commitment, fulfill some personal idealism in the same way people went into the Peace Corps — but who do not intend to stay more than five years or so. A good deal of the normal classroom work would be turned over to these very bright and idealistic "transients" who would not be regarded as career teachers, who would not have quite the same rites of passage into the profession (but would, nevertheless, have to demonstrate smarts and skills), who would be trained by the career teachers and work under their guidance and mentorship — and who could, of course, should they ultimately want to, pursue a path to the level of career teacher.

Career teachers would be engaged not mainly in lecturing students but in actively coaching students, teaching thinking skills, stimulating creativity, working with students on rewriting papers, helping students learn to reason, argue and persuade. They would have far fewer students and be able to spend an appropriate amount of time with each. In addition, the career teachers would train the novice teachers, evaluate textbooks, select other materials, design curricula, serve on the professional practice boards that set and monitor the standards for the profession, be part of university faculties and engage in a variety of other activities both with students and with their colleagues.

● We need to use the new technology to do what it can do best, so that teachers will have the time to do what they do best. Three of the major education reports in the wake of "A Nation at Risk" dealt with what actually goes on in classrooms, those by Ernest Boyer, Theodore Sizer, and John Goodlad. Enormously sympathetic to teachers, they nevertheless were extremely critical of how teachers teach. They found that most teachers spend an inordinate amount of their teaching time, up to 85 percent, lecturing, with very little exchange with students. And, of course, since most teachers' lecture styles are not as entertaining as the previous evening's television fare, the attention span of the students (or even adults, for that matter) is not very long. Now, some of what teachers are lecturing about today can be dealt with much more effectively with the new technology. A well-produced half-hour videocassette on how the Eskimos live in Alaska is likely to communicate memorable information much better than any lecture, and in a medium that has already grabbed today's students from infancy on. The technology is here. Either we will seize it and use it to our advantage — to free teachers for what it is they can do uniquely, professionally — or it will be imposed on us in some unthinking attempt to replace some teachers without improving the work lives, status, or salaries of the others.

Why shouldn't teachers be given the flexibility to teach from their strengths?

● There is much more we could do to restructure schools and create a profession. Why shouldn't teachers be given the flexibility to teach from their strengths? Some elementary school teachers have a particular bent for math, others would prefer to focus on the teaching of reading skills. Why shouldn't teachers be able to trade off with their colleagues, not only in different subjects but in different aspects of the same subject? Some teachers have a particular knack for teaching writing, while others are especially talented in stimulating an appreciation of poetry — why must both kinds be English teachers who do everything? Doctors and lawyers don't have difficulty in recommending colleagues with different strengths.

● Another major change would be to restructure our school calender into shorter time units, perhaps terms no longer than six or even three weeks, in which less material and fewer concepts are fully taught. This would give teachers and students a better opportunity to zero in on anything gone amiss. The longer the wait, the harder it is to tell what's wrong — and waiting a year makes such analysis untimely and correction harder. That's why some students drop farther and farther behind. If we empowered teachers to improve the system — like Deming's managers — they might consider using time in much more varied ways, moving youngsters along at their own pace. The rigid school year encourages youngsters (and sometimes teachers) to follow the Scarlet O'Hara path — "I'll think about it tomorrow." After all, missing a few days in September or October doesn't seem very important when the reckoning doesn't come until June; but often by December, a child is too far behind to catch up, and the syndrome of failure sets in. Creative thinking on the shape of the school year is long overdue.

THERE ARE undoubtedly many other good ideas for our schools, and classroom teachers, if they have the opportunity, will come up with some of the best. But change is overdue. I am convinced that we will not attract the best and the brightest who are graduating today if teachers continue to be treated as they currently are, as workers in an old-fashioned factory who may not exercise judgment and discretion, who are supervised and directed by everyone from the state legislature to the school principal. Our schools are organized today exactly the way they were a century ago. Managers of other institutions are finding different and better ways to operate for these different times, but school administrators continue to cling to the factory model. For our part, we can continue, through collective bargaining, to make some incremental changes in salaries, in the size of classes, and in some other areas. But if that's all we do, we are likely to draw into teaching ever lower segments of the talent pool, with disastrous results for us, for our students, for public education, and for the country. In order to turn the situation around, we have to take a number of serious steps such as those I've discussed.

Many of us will ask how — even whether — these changes will be accepted by our members. They are huge and revolutionary. But this is not the first time we've had a vision of what needed to be done. How many thought a quarter of a century ago that more than half a million teachers would join a union? We did. How many thought that government bodies would sit at the table and deal with us as equals? Or allow a dispute between the "sovereign" government and public "servants" to be argued on the merits and decided by outside impartial arbitrators? We who lead teachers were once only a handful of believers with a vision, but we accomplished what most thought impossible. Now we have the same goals but a new vision. Now we must make a second revolution.

On Stir-and-Serve Recipes for Teaching

Photos by David B. Sutton

Freeze-dried, ready-made teachers aren't the answer to the problems that face the teaching profession, says Ms. Ohanian. Children need real teachers, and real teachers must be trained.

Susan Ohanian

SUSAN OHANIAN, a third-grade teacher on leave of absence, is currently a senior editor for Learning: The Magazine for Creative Teaching.

THE NOTION that just about any Joe Blow can walk in off the street and take over a classroom is gaining ground. It makes me nervous. No, more than that: it infuriates me. We should squash once and for all the idea that schools can be adequately staffed by 32 bookkeepers and a plumber. The right teacher-proof curriculum is not sufficient; children need real teachers, and real teachers must be trained.

Nor am I charmed by the idea of signing up out-of-work computer programmers and retired professors to teach math and science. The mass media like to scoff that current certification requirements would keep Albert Einstein from teaching in the public schools. That news is not all bad. Is there any evidence that Einstein worked particularly well with young children? A Nobel Prize does not guarantee excellence in the classroom.

From *Phi Delta Kappan*, June 1985, pp. 696-701. Reprinted by permission of the author and Phi Delta Kappan.

205

We demand from our professors materials with immediate applicability. We are indignant when they try instead to offer ideas to grow on.

Having sat through more stupid education courses than I wish to recall, I am not altogether comfortable defending schools of education. But I suspect that the blame for worthless courses lies as much with the teachers who take them as with the professors who teach them. As a group, we teachers are intransigently anti-intellectual. We demand from our professors carry-out formulae, materials with the immediate applicability of scratch-and-sniff stickers. We are indignant when they try instead to offer ideas to grow on, seeds that we have to nurture in our own gardens.

We teachers frequently complain that education courses do not prepare us for the rigorous, confusing work ahead — that they do not show us how to run our classrooms. We refuse to admit that no course or manual can give us all the help we crave. We should not expect professors to set up our classroom systems, as though each of us were heading out to operate a fast-food franchise. There is no instant, stir-and-serve recipe for running a classroom.

Too often, teachers judge the success of education courses by the weight of the materials they cart away — cute cutouts or "story starters," all ready for immediate use. One popular journal for teachers promises 100 new ideas in every issue. "You can use them on Monday" is the promise. No one gets rich admitting that genuinely good ideas are hard to come by.

I understand only too well this yearning for the tangible, the usable. We are, after all, members of a profession ruled by pragmatism. People who sit in judgment on us don't ask about our students, "Are they happy? Are they creative? Are they helpful, sensitive, loving? Will they want to read a book next year?" Instead, these people demand, "What are their test scores?" — as if those numbers, though they passeth understanding, will somehow prove that we're doing a good job.

DURING MY FIRST 12 years of teaching I was desperate for new ideas, constantly foraging for schemes with which to engage the children. My frenetic activity was

due, in part, to the fact that I was given a different teaching assignment every two years. I figured, "Different children require different methods, different materials." So I would race off to the library or to the arts-and-crafts store. I'd buy another filing cabinet and join another book club for teachers.

But even when I settled in with the same assignment for a six-year stretch, my frenzy did not abate. My classroom became a veritable curriculum warehouse, stuffed with every innovative whiz-bang gizmo I could buy, borrow, or invent. I spent hundreds of hours reading, constructing, laminating. My husband gave up reminding me that I had promised to put the cut-and-paste factory in our living

room out of business, once I figured out what to teach. When I wasn't inventing projects, I was taking courses: cardboard carpentry, architectural awareness, science process, Cuisenaire rods, Chinese art, test construction and evaluation, curriculum development, and so on. I even took two courses in the computer language, BASIC. (I thought maybe I'd missed the point in the first course, so I took another — just to be sure.)

I didn't take those courses on whim, any more than I invented curriculum because I had nothing better to do. I chose my courses deliberately, trying to inform my work as a reading teacher. Although I now look back on much of my frenzied search for methods and media as rather

It is possible to have an inborn talent for teaching, but those teachers who endure and triumph are made — rigorously trained — and not born.

naive, I don't see it as time wasted. I learned a lot. Mostly I learned to simplify. And then to simplify some more.

But the path to simplicity is littered with complexities. And I suspect that it is hard to figure out how to simplify our lives if we haven't cluttered them in the first place. Sure, we teachers clutter up our classrooms with too much claptrap. The fribble is often alluring at first, and it is hard to recognize that the more gadgets we rely on, the poorer we are — at home as well as at school.

People probably always yearn for gadgets, especially if they haven't had much chance to fool around with them. A university research project makes this point rather nicely. The researcher decided to investigate the effects of computer-assisted instruction in English-as-a-second-language (ESL) classes. He set up a computer-taught group and a control group. Both were instructed in ESL for one year. And guess which group had the more positive attitude about computer-assisted instruction at the end of that year? The youngsters who *didn't* get to use the computers.

Not surprisingly, we teachers are compulsive pack rats. Fearing the vagaries of future school budgets, we hoard construction paper until it is old and brittle and unusable. We worry that we may need that paper more next year than we need it today. Have you ever known a teacher who could throw away a set of ditto masters? Or half a game of Scrabble? For years I had a gross of tiny, child-proof, left-handed scissors. Child-proof scissors are a horror in the first place. Those designed for left-handers are beyond description. Why did I keep them? Hey, they were mine, weren't they?

Most of us never use 80% of the materials jammed into our classrooms, but we cling to them "just in case." Because our job is hectic, pressured, stressful, we seldom have a reflective moment to clear our minds, let alone our cupboards. Maybe every teacher should change schools every three years and be allowed to take along only what he or she can carry. However, I must add to this suggestion my own statement of full disclosure: the last time I changed classrooms, after 13 years in the district, it took six strong men and a truck to transfer my belongings. And that was *after* I had filled two dumpsters.

The good professors must stop yielding to our acquisitive pressures; they must refuse to hand out their 100 — or even 10 — snazzy new ideas for the well-stocked classroom. They must offer fewer methods, fewer recipes. We teachers need *less* practicality, not more. We need to have our lives informed by Tolstoy, Jane Addams, Suzanne Langer, Rudolf Arnheim, and their ilk — not by folks who promise the keys to classroom control and creative bulletin boards, along with 100 steps to reading success.

We need a sense of purpose from our professors, not a timetable. Better that they show us a way to find our own ways than that they hand out their own detailed maps of the territory. A map isn't of much use to people who don't know where they're headed. The only way to become familiar with the terrain is to explore a little. I nominate the professors to scout ahead, chart the waters, post the quicksand. I know that I still have to climb my own mountain, but I would welcome scholarly advice about the climbing conditions.

CRITICS OF schools of education insist that prospective teachers would profit more from observing good teachers at work than from taking impractical courses on pedagogy. Maybe so. But what are those novices going to see? Is one observation as good as another? After all, a person can look at "Guernica" and not see it, listen to the "Eroica" and not hear it. E.H. Gombrich says that every observation we make is the result of the questions we ask. And where do novices get the questions? How can they ask intelligent questions without knowing something about the subject? Can anyone really *see* a classroom without some theoretical, historical, developmental savvy?

No one enters a classroom as a *tabula rasa*, of course. We all know something about schools because we have, for better or for worse, been there. We know how schools are supposed to be. At least, we think we do. So we judge schools, as we judge anything, with a notion — or schema — of reality in our heads. Most of us don't just look *at* something; we look *for* something, because we have a hypothesis, a hidden agenda. We observe and evaluate with our minds, our memories, our experiences, our linguistic habits. Obviously, the more we know, the more we see.

But teachers cannot walk into classrooms and simply teach what they know. First, they don't know enough. Second, even this seemingly restrictive world — constrained by bells, desks, and textbooks — contains a rich stock of themes from which teachers must choose their own motifs. They must be flexible and inventive enough to modify the schema they carried into their classrooms.

I was one of those people almost literally picked up off a street corner and allowed to teach in New York City under an emergency credential. I walked into the middle of someone else's lesson plan, and, though it didn't take me 10 minutes to realize that a round-robin reading of "Paul Revere's Ride" was not going to work, it took me quite a while to come up with something much better.

All I could manage at first was to teach as I had been taught. But as I learned more about the students and about ways to get around the assigned curriculum, a more ideal classroom began to emerge in my head. It remains a shadowy image — one I glimpse and even touch occasionally, but one I have long since stopped trying to file neatly in my planbook. That's okay. The bird seen through the window is more provocative than the one in the cage.

Teaching, like art, is born of a schema. That's why we need the professors with their satchels of theory, as well as our own observations and practice. Those who hope to be effective teachers must recognize that teaching is a craft of careful artifice; the profession requires more than a spontaneous overflow of good intentions or the simple cataloguing and distribution of information. It is possible, I suppose, to have an inborn talent for teaching, but I am sure that those teachers who endure and triumph are *made* — rigorously trained — and not born.

Much of the training must be self-initiated. People who have some nagging notion of the ideal classroom tickling their psyches probably look more for patterns that appeal than for practices that are guaranteed to produce higher standardized test scores. Such teachers probably have a capacity for ambiguity; they look for snippets of familiarity but do not insist on sameness. Such teachers have a greater need for aesthetic and psychological satisfaction than for a neat and tidy cupboard. But they also have a willingness to practice the craft, to try out new brushstrokes, to discard dried-out palettes.

Most of us, children and adults alike, have a strong need to make sense of the disparate elements in our lives, to bring them together, to find patterns, to make meaning. This desire for meaning is so strong that some teachers, tired and defeated by the system, rely on ritual to get them through the day, the week, the year. External order and ritual are the only things they have left to give. And these things usually satisfy the casual observer, who believes that teachers who provide clean and orderly classrooms are providing enough.

This is one reason I want the professors in on the act — out of their ivory towers and into our dusty school corridors. Maybe well-informed people, good observers who are not bogged down by school minutiae, could convince us that a tidy desk is far from enough. The professors need to promote the search for a different order, a subtler pattern — one that lies not in behavioral checklists but rather, to use Chia Yi's words, in constant "combining, scattering, waning, waxing."

I T WAS MY OWN search for pattern that led me to try using science as a way to inform, enhance, and give order to my work as a reading teacher. The children and I were far too familiar with the rituals of remedial reading for those routines to fall much short of torture. I've never understood why students who have trouble with a certain system of decoding should be made to rehearse that system over and over again. A few times over the course of a few years, maybe. But surely there comes a time to try a different approach. Reading had already been ruined for my students by the time they came to me. I needed to see how they approached pedagogic puzzlement, and such puzzlement would never occur if I persisted in making them circle blends on worksheets. That's why I learned how to mess around in science.

Tell a poor reader that it's time to read, and watch the impenetrable curtain of defeat and despair descend. So my students and I spent our time on science. All year. We made cottage cheese, explored surface tension, built bridges, figured out optical illusions. And not once did my students associate experiment cards, books on the theory of sound, or my insistence that observations be recorded in writing with the onerous task that they knew reading to be. Children told me that my room was a good place. Too bad, they added, that I wasn't a real teacher.

That reading room, where children were busily measuring, making — and reading — received full parental support and had its moment in the limelight. There were a lot of visitors. The teachers among them invariably asked, "How did you get this job?" Clearly, they intended to apply for one like it.

Get the job? Only in the first year of my teaching career was I ever handed a

No job of any value can be given out, like a box of chalk. We get the jobs we deserve. Maybe that's why so many teachers are disappointed.

job. Ever after, I've made my own. No job of any value can be given out, like a box of chalk. We get the jobs we deserve. Maybe that's why so many teachers are disappointed. They believe all those promises that someone else can do the thinking for them.

I held seven different jobs in my school district, and I earned the right to love every one of them. That's not to say that I didn't have plenty of moments of anger, frustration, rage. But I also experienced deep satisfaction.

Because my seven jobs required some pretty dramatic shifts in grade level, people were always asking me, "Where is it better — high school or the primary grades?" It's a question I have never been able to answer, mainly because the more grade levels I taught, the more similarities I saw. Sure, high school dropouts enrolled in an alternative program are harder to tune in to the beauty of a poem than are seventh-graders. Third-graders cry more, talk more; seventh-graders scale more heights and sink into deeper pits. But a common thread runs throughout, and it was that thread I clung to.

Maybe I see this sameness because my teaching is dominated less by skill than by idea — the secret, elusive form. I have a hard time reading other people's prescriptions, let alone writing my own. I always figure that, if you can get the idea right, the specific skill will come. Teaching is too personal, even too metaphysical, to be charted like the daily temperature. Teaching is like a Chinese lyric painting, not a bus schedule.

We need to look very closely at just who is calling for "the upgrading of teacher skills," lest this turn out to be the clarion call of those folks with something to sell. The world does not come to us in neat little packages. Even if we could identify just what a *skill* is, does *more* definitely denote *better*? What profiteth a child whose teacher has gathered up an immense pile of pishposh? We must take care, lest the examiners who claim they

can dissect and label the educational process leave us holding a bag of gizzards.

We teachers must recognize that we do not need the behaviorist-competency thugs to chart our course. For us, reality is a feeling state, details of daily routine fade, and what remains is atmosphere, tone, emotion. The ages and the talents of the children become irrelevant. What counts is attitude and endeavor. That's why, even when we try, we often can't pass on a terrific lesson plan to a friend; we probably can't even save it for ourselves to use again next year. It's virtually impossible to teach the same lesson twice.

I'M AFRAID that all of this sounds rather dim, maybe even dubious. But this is where the professors might step in. There are so many outrageous examples of bad pedagogy that it's easy to overlook the good — easy, but not excusable. The professors need to shape up their own schools of education first — getting rid of Papercutting 306, even if it's the most profitable course in the summer school catalogue. Then they need to get out in the field to work with student teachers, principals, and children.

Is it outrageous to think that the professors might even pop into the class-

Teaching is too personal, too metaphysical, to be charted like the temperature. Teaching is like a Chinese lyric painting, not a bus schedule.

But aspiring teachers have a responsibility, too. They must heed the advice of Confucius:

> If a man won't try, I will not teach him; if a man makes no effort, I will not help him. I show one corner, and if a man cannot find the other three, I am not going to repeat myself.

We teachers must stop asking the education professors for the whole house. I know plenty of teachers who are disappointed, indignant, and eventually destroyed by the fact that nobody has handed them all four corners. But the best we can expect from any program of courses or training is the jagged edge of one corner. Then it is up to us to read the research and to collaborate with the children to find the other three corners. And, because teaching must be a renewable contract, if we don't keep seeking new understanding, we'll find that the corners we thought we knew very well will keep slipping away. There are constant, subtle shifts in the schoolroom. One can never be sure of knowing the floorplan forever and ever.

In trying to renew my faith in myself as a teacher, I find little help in the "how to" books, those nasty little tomes that define learning in 87 steps. I like to think of learning as a wave that washes over the learner, rather than as a series of incremental hurdles to be pre- and posttested. I reject *How to Teach Reading in 100 Lessons*, relying instead on *The Mustard Seed Garden Manual of Painting*, which advises that "neither complexity in itself nor simplicity is enough" — nor dexterity alone nor conscientiousness. "To be without method is worse."

What can we do? What is the solution? In painting, there is an answer: "Study 10,000 volumes and walk 10,000 miles." One more thing is required of teachers. We must also work with 10,000 children.

rooms of veteran teachers now and then? Wouldn't it be something if their research occasionally involved real children and real teachers (and if they had to face bells, mandated tests, bake sales, and field trips to mess up their carefully laid plans), instead of four children in a lab staffed by 63 graduate students? That's probably a scary thought for some professors.

I know of one school of education that relegates the observation and direction of student teachers to the local school district. The district, in turn, passes this responsibility on to an administrator who has never taught. In such a situation, pedagogy gets turned upside down and inside out. The outcome is empty platitudes, not effective classroom practice. The student teacher, who is paying for expert training, is being defrauded. The children are being cheated. The system is stupid and immoral. We need teacher trainers who know educational theory and who are savvy about children. Those professors who won't help us should be replaced by ones who will.

Teachers aim at turning loose the mind's eyes

*Challenging students to reason with images
instead of words, to think sideways and
upside down, schools now teach imagination*

Doug Stewart

*Doug Stewart is a freelance writer in Ipswich,
Massachusetts, who specializes in scientific subjects.*

Jim Rymarcsuk, decked out in a purple bow tie and bright red boots, trudges across the linoleum floor of a classroom at Stanford University, dragging a large inner tube behind him. The inner tube provides air pressure for a plastic slide whistle attached to his right ankle. Rymarcsuk, a 20-year-old mechanical engineering major, pauses every few seconds to balance on his left foot, which enables him to operate the whistle's slide by raising and lowering his right. His classmates on the sidelines give him a round of applause after he labors through "Mary Had a Little Lamb."

Rymarcsuk and his fellow students are enrolled in Mechanical Engineering 101, "Visual Thinking," and I'm on hand to see them demonstrate their projects. The assignment has been to design a pair of shoes that plays a musical composition as you walk ten or more feet in them, a task that Rymarcsuk has interpreted rather loosely. The project description passed out to students began, "Ever wonder why most people play music with their hands but dance with their feet? What would it be like the other way around?"

That upside-down point of view is at the heart of ME 101 and a growing number of other visual-thinking courses around the country. If these courses had a

motto, it would be, "Make the familiar strange." The goal in each case is to free the eyes and the mind from stereotypes and taboos and to see surroundings in new ways, make connections between unlikely elements, and sketch, tinker and imagine until ideas emerge.

"We'd rather see a spectacular, innovative failure than a tightly developed successful one," says David Haygood, one of ME 101's instructors this year and an ardent believer in the unexpected. He notes that the course is popular with everyone, not just engineers. "You should be willing to pop around in different directions, even ones that aren't very good," he says. "Without that, there's no poof, no aha!, no magic."

Before settling on his air-powered slide whistle, Jim Rymarcsuk cruised the local junk stores for several days (the projects have a $20 ceiling), looking at familiar objects and trying to imagine new uses for them. At the outset, the instructors encouraged the class to make lists of ways that instruments could be played (plucked, squeezed, shaken, popped) and ways of moving (crutches, skateboards, pogo sticks), then look for ways to link them. As the demonstration proceeds, most of the students get into the freewheeling, easy-on-the-criticism spirit of the assignment, although most of the music that they generate is, to put it charitably, atonal.

For the project, "shoe" is defined as a device or assembly connected to the leg below the knee. One young man wears a motley pair of bowling shoes with the fronts torn off, the better to articulate trumpet-style keys with his toes. A young woman inches intently across the room, eyes on the floor, as pieces of her mysterious and inoperable machine drop off behind her—some kind of ski tow, by the looks of it. Haygood cheerfully calls out, "Ten feet! Ten feet!" to cut short the less successful walks.

What is being taught here is not hard-core engineering but something more intangible: imagination. The course is the brainchild of Bob McKim, who wrote the basic text for ME 101, a book called *Experiences in Visual Thinking*. McKim is a design professor at Stanford, and an informal, easily amused man who himself likes to fiddle with scissors, tape and pieces of shirt cardboard. "Back in the early Sixties here, I was teaching students how to design new products," he recalls. "I noticed that many of our students had trouble generating new ideas. They'd say, literally, 'I don't have any imagination.' What they'd been rewarded for in school was to manipulate words and numbers and pick single answers on multiple-choice quizzes." They were, McKim decided, visual illiterates.

He began teaching basic sketching skills to his students. He soon realized the students had trouble not only drawing but seeing. They took the objects around them for granted, looking closely enough only to give them labels like "table" and "door" and stopping there. (Quick—without looking, draw your telephone on a piece of paper, letters and numbers in place. It should be easy. You've looked at it thousands of times, haven't you?) One of the exercises McKim recommends is looking around a room and grouping objects by color (rediture) or texture (smoothiture), rather than function (furniture). Viewed in this way, he says, the shapes, colors and patterns of one's surroundings begin to emerge from what he calls the shadow of familiarity.

"Visual thinking breaks you out of the mindset of language, which keeps you stuck in a certain way of seeing and expressing the world," McKim says. He makes clear he doesn't expect people to do all their thinking in images. Words, logic and numbers are indispensable, he says, especially in refining and testing an idea. Rather, images provide a rich, expressive medium for thought that complements analytical reasoning and offers quicker, more unexpected jumps and connections.

"We don't really know what thinking is all about," McKim says. "It takes place below the threshold of consciousness. All we know are the results of it. With visual thinking, the results are images."

To McKim, imagery is more than what your eyes see and your hand sketches. There is also inner imagery, what you see with your eyes closed. One's ability to picture imaginary scenes can be strengthened with practice, he believes. His book is filled with exercises in imagining. Stop reading, for example, shut your eyes, and imagine an apple. What did you see? Most people will summon up a featureless red apple, perhaps even a vague, black-and-white apple. Now, imagine you're actually holding a crisp, ripe apple. Feel its weight, its waxy skin, its coolness. Feel for bruises. Play with its stem. Now imagine biting into the apple. Hear the crunch. Smell and taste its juice. Who wouldn't conjure up a more realistic, three-dimensional apple the second time around?

Exercises like this, McKim says, make us think more vividly. When problems are imagined in such a tangible, seeable way, solutions come to mind with more force, more variety and more detail. "As designers here, we're trying to design things that don't exist, not sketch things we see," McKim tells me, "so we need to use inner imagery and make our sketches from that."

Across the continent at the Massachusetts Institute of Technology, Woodie Flowers teaches a similar class —ME 2.70, Introduction to Design. Flowers, a Louisiana native with large, sleepy eyes and a twangy voice, readily admits his course is "McKimish." Here, however, as befits MIT's more hard-edged image, students visualize bricks as well as apples.

"The first time the students meet in the lab, we have an easy contest to break the ice," Flowers says, perched on a high stool in his Cambridge office. "We might pass around a brick and say, 'Feel it, remember it.' Then we give everyone some computer cards and say, 'Build a tower at least two card-lengths high that can support the brick.'" The winner, Flowers says, is the student with the lowest-cost tower, cost being determined by the total number of cards, folds and staples used. To prevent the students from doing too much testing and not enough visualizing, the brick remains off limits until each structure is completed.

Such little games are a precursor to a much bigger drama, a two-night trial by fire in which the course's 200-odd students pit their final projects against one another. Using identical kits of ingredients—cardboard tubing, string, parts of Venetian blinds, electric motors—the students build devices designed to perform some specified task such as putting a round peg in a square hole. Each device must carry out its job in 20 seconds while a competing student's device tries to do likewise from the opposite end of a lab table.

This year's contest is called "The Harvest." The battleground is a four-by-six-foot table with model hills, valleys and occasional obstacles. Clogging the landscape are 300 Ping-Pong balls. The machines' function is to gather the balls as quickly as possible.

Squeezing into the auditorium a half-hour before the start of the first night's competition, I'm barely able to find a seat. Boisterous undergraduates with cameras and noisemakers soon pack the aisles and line the walls. As the elimination rounds proceed, an impressive variety of rickety-looking machines do battle with the Ping-Pong balls and each other—bulldozers, sweepers, scoops, rakes, paddlewheels and assorted hybrids. One device rolls forward and slips a wide spatula under a mass of balls. The spatula slowly rises and the balls roll back over the device's inclined roof and into the home gutter. A number of machines, including the eventual winner, are low, square tractors that drive over a group of balls, then pull them back using one-way, comblike fingers along the front end.

The ambience in the hall is a far cry from the mellow mood at Stanford. After one machine refuses to budge and its opponent tips over at the other end, flailing helplessly like a wounded praying mantis, the referees call a double loss and the crowd roars its approval.

The Stanford and MIT courses may differ in character, but they share a common goal: to spur students to come up with new ideas. In both cases, the variety and volume of drawings in a student's idea log, or visual notebook, count toward the course grade at least as much as the performance of the student's final device. "If all the projects look alike, then it's a bad contest," Flowers tells me later.

One of the habits that Flowers and his instructors try to discourage is a single-minded infatuation with one particular idea. Author and lecturer Edward de Bono has called this habit "vertical" thinking, akin to digging a hole in one place and, not finding what you're after, digging deeper and deeper. Using "lateral" thinking, on the other hand, you climb out and try digging new holes here and there.

The hands-down crowd favorite in this year's contest, something dubbed the Spinmobile, is a product of lateral thinking. Its inventor, junior Annabelle Kim, has taken the course's ethic to heart, and the Spinmobile is the result of her third trip back to the drawing board in the past month. Torque problems and friction torpedoed her first two ideas, a double-ended bulldozer and a two-armed flinger/gatherer. "With my second idea, I could have messed around, cut springs in half and so forth, but I only had two nights to go at that point," she explains to me later, "so I just switched my plans and tried to build something really basic."

That something is an ingenious two-wheeled box with short, flexible arms attached at two corners diagonally across from each other. The wheels spin in opposite directions, the box twirls comically, and the two curved arms beat a spectacular barrage of Ping-Pong balls back toward the gutter. Other than its wheels and its motor, the Spinmobile has no moving parts. To standing ovations in round after round, it annihilates tractors and rakes, losing only in the semi-final round—a moral victory for lateral thinking.

Consumer goods for an imaginary planet

Despite their different styles, Bob McKim's course and Woodie Flowers' course share a common ancestry as well as a common purpose. The spiritual father of both was an engineering professor named John Arnold. Arnold ran a program in creative engineering at MIT in the 1950s before leaving to start up the design program at Stanford. Arnold wasn't a self-proclaimed visual thinker, but he was an enthusiastic advocate of yanking students out of the familiar and forcing them into the strange. To this end, Arnold announced the discovery of an imaginary planet called Arcturus IV (there is a real star named Arcturus), where the gravity was 11 times greater than Earth's, the crops grew upside down, and the inhabitants had three eyes and fragile bones.

Students were asked to design consumer goods for this world. Arcturan power tools, for example, ended up being cable-driven, their motors on the ground; a conventional drill weighing four pounds on Earth would have weighed 44 on Arcturus IV, too heavy for a native's delicate arm to support. Other students designed egg-shaped cars and stereo viewers for three-eyed heads. In both his classes and his seminars for visiting engineers, Arnold avoided criticizing even the craziest-sounding suggestions. "It's easier to tone down a wild idea," he told *Life* magazine in 1955, "than to tone up a dull one." His students went on to design new products for such companies as General Motors, Corning Glass and General Electric.

Arnold's idea of using outer space as a way to cut students off Earthly stereotypes was picked up and embellished by Ed Zagorski, a professor of industrial design at the University of Illinois at Urbana-Champaign. In 1961, following NASA's first manned flight, Zagorski dreamed up what has become a classic design problem in engineering schools around the country: the egg drop. The idea was to simulate suborbital flight, substituting a raw egg for Alan Shepard. Students built containers that could be launched 200 feet into the air by a truck-spring catapult and deposited in the campus reflecting pool—without breaking the egg inside. One student cushioned his egg in a container stuffed with peat moss and gelatin, then used a firecracker to pop open a parachute in midflight. Once the capsule was safely afloat, an aspirin tablet holding apart two electrical contacts dissolved, and a tiny electric motor powered the craft ashore.

"Now that was pizzazz," Zagorski recalls. Zagorski doesn't look like a grand old man of creative industrial design. At 63, he's as athletic as a 40-year-old, as imaginative as a child of five. He still teaches what he calls fun and games to first-year industrial design majors.

Zagorski stresses ideas, not technique. He recently asked a class to make something that answered the question: What is a million? One student spent several days popping popcorn, then filled a 32-cubic-foot box with it. Another read a poem on eternity by James Joyce. "It did feel like an eternity," Zagorski admits. A third built a cardboard cube 18 inches on a side with the tips of four corners cut away to reveal clear plastic containers of sewing pins. To complete the illusion, a cinderblock hidden at the cube's center gave the box the proper heft. "To get students to create something original," Zagorski says, "you've got to force them out of the familiar."

A flurry of books and courses have extended visual thinking beyond the classroom, popularizing the idea of left-brain, right-brain duality—the left side said to be verbal and analytical, the right side intuitive and visual. The phrase, "making the familiar strange," in fact, was coined by a business consultant, an impatient, gravel-voiced man named William Gordon. As head of SES Associates in Cambridge, Massachusetts, Gordon runs seminars that teach business people to be more creative by making connections between seemingly unrelated images. "The basis of creativity has always been a new connection," he says. "To make connections would take hours using words. Your subconscious has to use pictures."

Gordon believes that an inventor's flash of insight is actually a connection drawn between two images. This process, he says, can be studied and practiced instead of being left to chance. The process is illustrated by one of his inventions, Pringle's potato chips. When a potato chip manufacturer came to him with a problem—how to ship their product in a more cost-effective way—Gordon and his colleagues tried to think of natural analogies. Someone recommended raking leaves: how bulky they were when dry, but how neatly they layered and stacked when moist and all one shape. This led to the answer—making chips of uniform size and shape, so they could be stacked in cans.

There are a number of other business-consulting firms that preach the virtues of visual thinking, and one of the most successful is Synectics Inc., headed by Gordon's former partner, George Prince. Its seminars have helped General Electric improve their dishwashers, assisted NASA in coming up with thermometers for astronauts, and guided Colgate-Palmolive staff members in designing new tennis shoes.

To generate new ideas, Prince, like Gordon, encourages those who attend his seminars to think visually, conjuring up mental pictures and letting them lead rapidly to new visual associations. To help people keep track of their thoughts, the conference room walls in Synectics' earth-toned Cambridge headquarters are lined with two-by-three-foot sketch pads, and jars of felt-tipped colored markers are everywhere.

"What I like," says Prince, a soft-spoken, avuncular man in his 60s, "is to take an accident and make it a process." Sometimes during a seminar Prince smears a bottle's worth of ketchup on a piece of newsprint, then hangs the sheet on a wall and asks everyone in the room to write down what they see. These imaginings are then slowly read aloud as the group continues to write. "Some excursions are more productive than others," says Prince, "but once you get a group going, almost anything works."

The shock of seeing George Prince smear ketchup on a piece of paper, often with his foot, is no doubt heightened by the plush surroundings. At Boston's Charlestown High School, on the other hand, a little spilled ketchup would be unlikely to draw much attention. There, in a sticky-floored classroom overlooking a boarded-up housing project, design teacher Bruce McIntosh (above) is borrowing the techniques of visual thinking to stimulate the imaginations of inner-city high school children.

"If you tell students to build a chair out of cardboard," says McIntosh, "they all build things with flat surfaces and four legs. So you don't say 'chair,' you say 'sitting machine.'" To forestall the usual knee-jerk objection that cardboard isn't for sitting, McIntosh and fellow teacher Robin Graves lead up to the project in a roundabout way. First, they have each student support a ruler an inch above a desk using a piece of paper. Then three rulers. "You get a kid who realizes he can hold four books up with just a piece of paper, and it just blows him away," McIntosh says.

McIntosh, an exuberant, nonstop talker, is an expert at envisioning strange uses for familiar things. Where most people see junk, he sees exciting raw material for his class—perforated sheets of plastic, multicolored foam pads, heavy-duty cardboard tubing. "We're making amazing stuff out of things people have already thrown away," he says. His inverted perspective is clearly rubbing off on his students: on a back wall is a collage depicting a dancing Ricardo Montalban with an oversize digital watch for a belt, two bare arms for legs, and a sneaker for a cigar. Somehow the composition works perfectly.

McIntosh and Graves worry that by the high school years a child's natural willingness to imagine and invent is fading, replaced by a desire to avoid mistakes and find the right answer. "Younger kids have a lot more flexibility," McIntosh says. "They don't know that something won't work, or that they can't draw, or that dogs can't fly."

To back up this last claim, McIntosh refers me to a book that Edward de Bono once published containing children's drawings of dog-exercising machines: remote-control airplanes carrying long leashes; treadmills with films of rabbits projected at one end; magnetic bones that are shot from catapults and return like boomerangs, the dog presumably racing back and forth underneath. De Bono wrote, "Children are not really searching for the best way of doing something. . . . It is enough if the ideas fit together."

Young children do indeed seem to have active visual

imaginations, and with practice, children might be able to hang on to this ability to experience the world visually, instead of losing their visual skills as they develop verbal ones. That, at any rate, is what a 29-year-old Stanford graduate student and confirmed visual thinker named Scott Kim believes. Kim is the author of *Inversions*, a book filled with words that can be flipped or rotated and still say the same thing—or something significantly different. Its cover, for example, reads "Inversions" right side up and "Scott Kim" upside down.

"A lot of my biggest fans are five and six years old, just when they're learning to read," Kim tells me over breakfast one morning at a café near the Stanford campus. To children that age, Kim points out, a letter is still a shape, not a label, so even the familiar is probably a trifle strange. Kim has written an activity guide for schools called "Thinking Upside Down" that shows children how to try their own inversions, and he has put together a software tutorial for making inversions with a computer.

Like many other visual thinkers, Kim wouldn't leave home without a sketch pad. While we talk, he sketches constantly, jotting down words surrounded by boxes, arrows and dotted lines. When he has trouble expressing himself to me, he frowns, waves both hands in the air between us, palms flat as though he were erasing a blackboard, and then starts again.

"The way I understand something is to reinvent it," Kim says. "I put myself in the inventor's shoes. The thing I want to understand now is computers." Kim's own PhD work focuses on how people might interact with computers using pictures instead of words. Kim is excited about computers like the Macintosh that let people choose pictorial commands and make free-hand drawings using a hand-held electronic mouse. "Words are dominant over pictures in academic and serious circles because they're easier to produce," he says, "but computers like the Mac are changing that. To me, computers are the answer to getting visual thinking recognized."

Perhaps creative people have always recognized it, and the rest of us are only now beginning to notice. I recall asking Stanford's Bob McKim how he went about dreaming up his own inventions, most of them highly technical medical devices. "I set myself up for having accidents," he told me. Everyone has accidents, he pointed out, but visual thinkers don't just run off and get a mop. They study the result. "An architect friend of mine was once making a cardboard model of a seaside home," McKim said. "By accident, he knocked the model over so it rested partly on its roof." As a result, somewhere in the vicinity of Monterey, California, there is a homeowner who probably loves the way his beach house looks but who has no idea that it's actually upside down.

PROFILE OF AN EFFECTIVE TEACHER

A WELL-KNOWN RESEARCHER TRACES THE ONGOING
HUNT FOR THE GOOD TEACHER. AFTER MORE THAN
40 YEARS, WE HAVE SOME IDEA ABOUT WHAT
TEACHER BEHAVIORS LEAD TO EFFECTIVENESS IN
THE CLASSROOM. NOW IT'S TIME TO GET THE
WORD OUT.

Donald R. Cruickshank

*DONALD R. CRUICKSHANK is professor
of teacher education at The Ohio State
University, Columbus. His research has
supported development of teacher education
curriculum and instructional materials
including simulation laboratories and
reflective teaching manuals.*

Short of the search for the Holy
Grail, there hardly has been a
human quest more persistently and
doggedly pursued than the hunt for the
"good" teacher.

In order to make objective
recommendations to school boards
about hiring, tenure and reward, or
dismissal, principals, supervisory
personnel and school superintendents
need to know which teachers are good
teachers. Absence of clear criteria by
which to judge effectiveness prevents
accurate assessment and often leads to
teacher dismissals and subsequent court
cases. In addition, when adults ask,
"Are our children with a first-rate
professional?" public school personnel
need to be ready with an answer that is
based on informed appraisal of teacher
performance.

Teacher educators need information
about teacher effectiveness to give
direction to the development of more

objective admission and exit criteria
and to help determine curriculum
needs.

Research Methodology and Findings

Inquiry of teacher effectiveness can
be thought about as occurring in two
eras—the first prior to 1960, the
second, since.

The First Era

Methodology. According to Ellena,
Stevenson and Webb, studies of
teacher effectiveness began about 1900,
peaked in 1928-32, and then
maintained a relatively high plateau
until the Fifties.[1] These studies could
be characterized as a search for teacher
traits or characteristics that described
and permitted identification of "good"
teaching. In parallel with the testing
movement of the times, teacher
evaluation and rating devices that were
generated often contained personality
factors assumed by educational
experts, and sometimes pupils, to be
desirable attributes of members of the
teaching force. Could several raters,
who usually were school administrators
or supervisors, agree on the merit of a
given teacher? Could good teachers be

separated from poor teachers on the
basis of the items on the rating scales?

In 1961, Barr synthesized numerous
items on such rating scales into 15:
buoyancy, consideration,
cooperativeness, dependability,
emotional stability, ethicalness,
expressiveness, flexibility, forcefulness,
judgement, mental alertness,
objectivity, personal magnetism,
physical drive, and scholarliness.[2] In
addition to searching for important
teacher personality-like traits,
researchers also looked at intelligence,
sex, marital status, voice/speech,
cultural background, interests,
appearance, educational background,
knowledge of subject matter,
knowledge of professional education,
and scholastic achievement and the
relationship of these characteristics to
administrator or supervisor ratings. A
smaller number of studies began to
explore relationships among these
variables and pupil achievement or
desired changes in pupil behavior.

It is important to note that there
were problems encountered in the
conduct of research using rating scale
and raters, and with the use of pupil
gain as a criterion measure.

With regard to rating scales, the
problems were legion.[3] It was obvious
that items on the scales were
subjectively derived, not necessarily

From *Educational Horizons,* Winter 1985, pp. 90-92. Reprinted by permission of Phi Lamda Theta.

agreed upon, and frequently vague in meaning. In addition, because the raters tended to be school administrators and supervisors, it was difficult, if not impossible, to eliminate personal bias. Therefore, teachers participating in early studies frequently were judged on defective criteria by unreliable raters.

Shortcomings associated with studies using pupil gain as a criterion measure included obtaining agreement on the kind of pupil gain desirable; selecting or developing an instrument to measure attainment of that goal; and separating out the effects of current teaching from the effects of former teachers, parents, siblings, television, etc.

Findings. Researchers, who sought to determine who were good teachers and to differentiate between good and poor teachers on the basis of rater agreement on the items, provided unimpressive results.

First, two or more raters simultaneously observing the same teacher often disagreed on the quality of the teaching.[4] In the second instance, teachers judged a priori to be good could not be separated from poor teachers on the basis of the rating scale items.[5] Finally, low correlations were found between pupil gain criteria and other criteria.[6] Some of the conclusions drawn around 1960 from the early studies are listed here:

- People cannot be expected to be in close agreement when they evaluate teaching.[7]
- Traits or characteristics, taken by themselves, cannot be used to predict teaching effectiveness. Nor have researchers been successful in combining the traits in such a way as to produce a useful index.[8]
- Few, if any, facts are now deemed established about teacher effectiveness and many former findings have been repudiated. It is not an exaggeration to say that we do not know today how to select, train for, encourage, or evaluate teacher effectiveness.[9]

The Second Era

Fortunately the hunt for the good teacher took a different trail at the onset of the Sixties as a result of 1) the emergence of models to guide inquiry on teaching, and 2) the appearance of more objective classroom observation instruments. Persons contributing prominently to the new era were Mitzel, Biddle, and Flanders.

Models. Mitzel contributed substantially to models of inquiry. In his chapter in the *Encyclopedia of*

"IN ORDER TO MAKE OBJECTIVE RECOMMENDATIONS TO SCHOOL BOARDS ABOUT HIRING, TENURE AND REWARD, OR DISMISSAL, PRINCIPALS, SUPERVISORY PERSONNEL AND SCHOOL SUPERINTENDENTS NEED TO KNOW WHICH TEACHERS ARE GOOD TEACHERS."

Educational Research, he proposed that teaching effectiveness criteria could be classified according to "product, process, or presage."[10]

Product is defined as a change in student behavior. *Process* includes both teacher and student behaviors—rapport, teacher clarity, student attentiveness—that have mediating effects on product variables. *Presage* is considered to be a teacher characteristic such as intelligence, industry, adaptability, GPA in college, success in student teaching.

Presumably, presage affects process and process affects product. Mitzel helped us to recognize that the goal of teaching is pupil learning rather than superordinate ratings and that who the teacher is and what the teacher does in the classroom, a dimension overlooked in the early era, may contribute in some linear way to that goal.

Biddle, like Mitzel, was interested in establishing relationships between classroom behavior and teacher effects.[11] He suggested that teacher effectiveness criteria could be classified according to seven variables: teacher formative experiences, teacher properties, teacher behaviors, immediate effects (pupil responses), classroom situations, school and community contexts, and long-term consequences such as pupil gain.

Later, Biddle seemed to join Mitzel's ideas with his own in "a model for the study of classroom teaching," which seems to make the whole business visual and perhaps understandable.[12] (See figure 1.)

From these early models, educators began to see that the study of teaching and teacher effectiveness is a complex activity, and that most of the variables and their relationships had not been adequately or properly studied.

Observation instruments. The appearance of classroom observation instruments for the systematic analysis of teaching supplanted teacher rating scales and changed the focus of attention from teacher traits and characteristics to teacher classroom

behavior, more significant to pupil learning.

Flanders was among dozens of scholars who began to create instruments by which teacher behavior could be observed and recorded. He noted and compared the resultant patterns of teacher behavior with pupil gain to see if they were related or unrelated.[13] His was the most frequently used instrument. It permitted observation of teachers' use of "verbal influence," defined as "teacher talk" and "pupil talk," in a variety of classroom situations.

Given one of the models for research on teaching and one or more observational instruments, the new era researcher could study life in classrooms and either describe it, look for associations, or manipulate classroom variables by way of experiments. It could be said that the new era provided both better illumination of what could and should be studied and some requisite instrumentation. It also shifted focus from administrator or supervisor ratings to pupil learning.

Findings of the second era. Armed with a presage-process-product teacher effectiveness model and classroom observation instruments, a new cohort of hunters took to the field.[14]

The modern era of research on teacher effectiveness was given both visibility and momentum in 1971 when Rosenshine and Furst reported some seemingly impressive results based on a review of 50 process-product studies.[15] The studies attempted to identify relationships between process variables (teacher behaviors) and pupil gain (product variables). In 1975, the National Institute of Education (NIE) held a conference at which federally supported research on elementary teacher effectiveness was reported.[16] Throughout the 1970s and into the early 1980s the studies continued.

At this writing, Brophy and Good provide the most recent literature review.[17] They describe "major programs (sets of studies) of process-

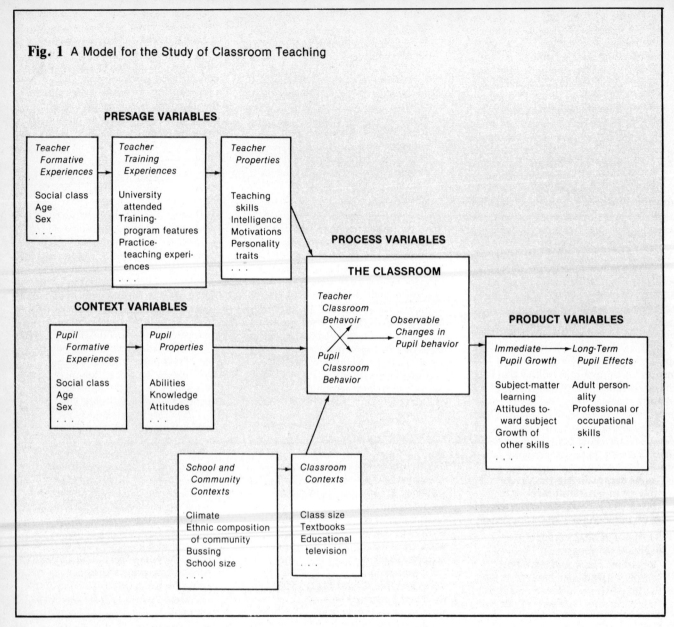

Fig. 1 A Model for the Study of Classroom Teaching

product research'' presenting the following studies and findings.

1. The Canterbury Studies of elementary science teaching:
- Content coverage is more important than particular teacher behaviors.
- Younger students need to participate overtly.
- Questions should be asked one at a time, be clear and at an appropriate cognitive level.
- Enthusiastic reactions from teachers are motivating.
- Reviewing and summarizing lesson parts are helpful.

2. Flanders:
- Teacher talk is positively associated with pupil achievement and attitude.
- Indirectness, praise, acceptance of pupil ideas are positively associated with pupil attitudes and achievement.
- Restrictiveness and negative authority tend to be negatively related to pupil attitudes.
- Flexibility is correlated positively with pupil attitude and achievement.

3. Soar and Soar's studies of elementary teaching:
- Regarding classroom emotional climate, neutral climates are at least as supportive of achievement as are warm climates. Negative climates appear dysfunctional.
- Regarding teacher management or control, students learn more in classrooms where teachers establish limits on pupil freedom and choice, physical movement and disruption, and where teachers talk more and control pupils' task behavior.

4. Stalling's Follow-Through Evaluation Study supports:
- Student opportunity to learn the required content;
- A recitation pattern of teacher questioning;
- Pupils spending most of their time being instructed by teachers or working independently under close teacher supervision.

5. Stalling's California Early Childhood Education Study supports:
- Spending more time on academic tasks;
- Teachers actively instructing in small groups;
- Giving more instruction, asking more academic questions;
- Providing more feedback.

6. *Stalling's Teaching Basic Skills (reading) in Secondary Schools Study supports:*
- Quantity of instruction;
- Reviewing or discussing assignments;
- Having students read aloud;
- Praising success;
- Providing support and corrective feedback.

Negative correlates found were: 1) teachers not interacting with students; 2) too much teacher time spent organizing rather than instructing; 3) providing students choices of activities; 4) students working independently; and 5) outside intrusions and social interaction.

7. *Brophy and Evertson in the Texas Teacher Effectiveness Study found that elementary teachers who produce greatest achievement are:*
- Task oriented;
- Businesslike;
- Interact with students mostly within a teacher-student relationship;
- Spend most time on academic activities;
- Are persistent;
- Confident;
- Spend minimal time in transitions and;
- Insure that students participate about equally.

Conversely, teachers producing the least achievement were more concerned with affect than cognition or disliked their students and concentrated on authority and discipline.

8. *In the Junior High Study (grades seven and eight), Evertson, Brophy and others studied English and mathematics classes.* In the former, the results seem to support greater achievement where teacher praise was relatively frequent during class discussion and where serious misbehavior was uncommon. Pupil attitudes were most favorable when the teacher was perceived as nice and the class enjoyable but undemanding. In mathematics classes, the more successful teachers taught more "actively," spending more time lecturing, demonstrating, or leading recitation or discussion. When they gave seatwork, it was more likely to be

assisted and monitored. Instruction was whole class, for the most part, and movement was at a brisk pace. Teachers explained thoroughly and were "withit."

9. *Brophy and Evertson in the First Grade Reading Group Study reported greater achievement gains where:*
- More time was spent in reading groups and less time with misbehavior;
- Transitions were shorter;
- The teacher sat so as to be able to monitor the class while teaching a reading group;
- Lessons had overviews;
- Phonetics were used to introduce new words;
- Pupils frequently had opportunities to read and to answer questions;
- Questions were addressed to individual learners in order;
- Incorrect answers were followed by reteaching and;
- Praise was specific.

10. *Good and Grouws looked for correlates of pupil achievement in fourth-grade arithmetic and found that higher achieving teachers:*
- Had better managed classes;
- Spent less time in transitions;
- Moved at a brisker pace;
- Covered more content;
- Instructed more clearly;
- Asked fewer questions that yielded incorrect answers;
- Retaught;
- Monitored seatwork and provided feedback;
- Their students called out more answers, asked more questions, and initiated more academic contracts.

11. *The Beginning Teacher Evaluation Study (BTES), a series of studies of second- and fifth-grade classes seems to suggest that achievement occurs in classes where teachers:*
- Are well-organized;
- Maximize time devoted to instruction;
- Minimize time spent on preparation, procedures, or discipline;
- Spend most time actively instructing and monitoring seatwork.

Achievement also was associated with

the amount of time pupils were exposed to academic content, the percentage of time they actually spent engaged in academic activities, and the degree to which they were able to respond successfully. Combining these concepts, BTES coined the term "academic learning time" or the time pupils actually spend engaged in academic tasks that can be performed with high success. Further, pupil achievement was associated with accurate diagnosis and prescription of learning needs and learning tasks, frequent provision of immediate feedback, an emphasis on academic rather than affective goals, and pupil academic responsibility and cooperation.

12. *The Stanford Studies found pupil achievement related to teachers:*
- Using an overview or analogy to introduce material;
- Reviewing, repeating;
- Praising or repeating pupil answers;
- Being patient in waiting for responses;
- Integrating the responses into the lesson;
- Making clear presentations;
- Providing feedback to student responses and improving responses that are incomplete or incorrect;
- Using lower order questions.

13. *The Vagueness studies (often inappropriately referred to as "clarity" studies) report that teacher use of vague terms, mazes and discontinuity, or adding more content, impedes pupil achievement.*

14. *Brophy and Good also report additional variables gleaned from the work of individual investigators that relate to achievement:*
- Opportunity to learn the content of the test;
- Time on task that is teacher supervised;
- Selection of appropriate goals of instruction;
- Involving students in organizing and planning;
- Giving clear direction;
- Listening to students;
- Good monitoring;
- Active instruction;
- Teacher clarity;
- Order and control;
- Use of structuring and "organizers" to help students learn;
- Appropriate "wait time."

A Summative Profile

At the risk of comparing apples and oranges, for indeed the studies reviewed and reported here focused on many different grade levels, content areas, pupil characteristics and teaching outcomes, I will condense the above disparate findings, and others not noted here due to space limitations, on teacher effects in the hope of offering some standards for improvement.

Findings for *classroom organization* seem to support the teacher playing a central, dominant classroom role but involving students in planning and organizing, having a structured curriculum, setting high goals and communicating them to students, working mostly with the whole class and less often with supervised small groups, providing independent work that is interesting and worthwhile, and minimizing "busy work."

Findings for *didactic teaching* support the teacher's persistence in seeking high goals, putting the daily schedule on the chalkboard, providing extensive content coverage, providing learning activities at an appropriate level of difficulty, differentiating instruction between high and low socioeconomic students, teaching systematically step by step, providing adequate opportunity to learn criterion material, providing structure and structuring comments, maintaining a brisk lesson pace, using questions suitable to the lesson's cognitive level, requiring public and overt student participation, providing adequate "wait time," accepting and using student ideas, providing immediate individual feedback, shaping student responses so they are correct, maintaining task involvement, monitoring individual progress, using distributed and successful practice, praising judiciously, using little criticism, individualizing, reviewing, summarizing, providing teaching variety, and maintaining a classroom absent of negative emotional climate. Further, effective teachers involve all students, limit student choices, hold students responsible for their work, attend to students equitably and capitalize on unexpected student wants.

Findings for *classroom management* suggest that the teacher set and maintain clear rules and consistently apply them using positive reinforcement, limit student physical freedom, monitor student behavior, hold students responsible for their behavior, direct students upon completion of their work, minimize transition time, deal with misbehavior quickly, negotiate student compliance and demonstrate "withitness," smoothness, momentum, ability to overlap, challenge, variety, and grouping alerting.

Findings for teachers would seem to indicate that they need to be well-organized, efficient, task oriented,

"IT WAS OBVIOUS THAT ITEMS ON THE SCALES WERE SUBJECTIVELY DERIVED, NOT NECESSARILY AGREED UPON, AND FREQUENTLY VAGUE IN MEANING."

knowledgeable, verbally fluent, aware of student developmental levels, clear, enthusiastic, self-confident, confident of student abilities, hold high expectations, be friendly and warm, encouraging and supportive, attentive, accepting, and tolerant.

As a whole, and acknowledging the many caveats reported elsewhere by researchers and reviewers,[18] the new data base is more substantial than that of the first era of research on teaching. It is hoped that it will complement, if not supplant, knowledge presently used in teacher evaluation, selection, and preservice curriculum.

Already, efforts are being made to bring the results of the new teacher effects research to the attention of special audiences. The Association for Supervision and Curriculum Develpment has produced two related books for its members.[19] The American Association of Colleges for Teacher Education published *Essential Knowledge for Beginning Educators*.[20] The State of Florida has attempted to use the results to design a teacher observation-evaluation system,[21] and at this writing, The National Institute of Education is conducting competition for federal funds to implement the results in teacher education programs.

The second era of research clearly provides some substantial evidence about who is a good teacher. This research can serve the needs and purposes of the many stakeholders in education. Results of this most recent hunt indicate that some teachers make more of a difference than do others and that the behaviors of effective teachers can be and to some extent have been found. A major problem remaining is to get the news out and to use it in ways that will cause teaching and learning to prosper.

1. W. Ellena, M. Stevenson, and H. Webb, *Who's a Good Teacher* (Washington, D. C.: American Association of School Administrators, Department of Classroom Teachers of the National Education Association, National School Boards Association, 1961).

2. A. Barr, et al., "Wisconsin Studies of the Measurement and Prediction of Teacher Effectiveness," *The Journal of Experimental Education* 30 (1961): 135.

3. D. Cruickshank, "The Effects of Frustration and Characterization on Teacher Ratings" (Doctoral diss., University of Rochester, 1963).

4. Barr, et al., "Wisconsin Studies," 141.

5. Ibid., ii,143.

6. Ibid., 140.

7. R. Howsam, *Who's a Good Teacher: Problems and Progress in Teacher Evaluation* (Burlingame, CA: California School Boards Association and the California Teachers Association, 1960), 11.

8. Ibid., 26.

9. B. Biddle and W. Ellena, *Contemporary Research on Teacher Effectiveness* (New York: Holt, Rinehart and Winston, Inc., 1964), vi.

10. H. Mitzel, "Teacher Effectiveness," in *Encyclopedia of Educational Research*, ed. C. Harris (New York: Macmillan, 1960), 1481-1485.

11. Biddle and Ellena, *Contemporary Research*.

12. M. Dunkin and B. Biddle, *A Study of Teaching* (New York: Holt, Rinehart and Winston, 1974).

13. N. Flanders, *Interaction Analysis in the Classroom: A Manual for Observers* (Ann Arbor, MI: University of Michigan, 1960).

14. J. Brophy, "Teacher Behavior and Its Effects," *Journal of Educational Psychology*, 71 (1979): 733-750; J. Brophy and T. Good, "Teacher Behavior and Student Achievement," in *Handbook of Research on Teaching*, ed. M. Wittrock (New York: Macmillan, 1985); D. Cruickshank, "Synthesis of Selected Recent Research on Teacher Effects," *Journal of Teacher Education* 27 (1976): 57-60; Dunkin and Biddle, *A Study of Teaching*; N. Gage, *The Scientific Basis of the Art of Teaching* (New York: Teachers College Press, Columbia University, 1978); N. Gage, "What Do We Know about Teaching Effectiveness?" *Phi Delta Kappan* 66 (1984): 87-93; T. Good, "Classroom Research: A Decade of Progress" (Paper presented at the meeting of the American Educational Research Association, Montreal, Canada, April 1983); T. Good, "Teacher Effectiveness in the Elementary School," *Journal of Teacher Education* 30 (1979): 52-64; D. Medley, *Teacher Competence and Teaching Effectiveness* (Washington, D. C.: The American Association of Colleges for Teacher Education, 1977); D. Medley, "Teacher Effectiveness," in *Encyclopedia of Educational Research*, ed. H. Mitzel (New York: Free Press, 1982), 1894-1903; B. Rosenshine and D. Berliner, "Academic Engaged Time," *British Journal of Teacher Education* 4 (1978): 3-16; R. S. Soar and R. M. Soar, "An Attempt to Identify Measures of Teacher Affectiveness from Four Studies," *Journal of Teacher Education* 27 (1976): 261-267; and H. Walberg, "Synthesis of Research on

"RESULTS . . . INDICATE THAT SOME
TEACHERS MAKE MORE OF A DIFFERENCE
THAN DO OTHERS AND THAT THE
BEHAVIORS OF EFFECTIVE TEACHERS
CAN BE AND TO SOME EXTENT
HAVE BEEN FOUND."

fostered research especially on the most promising findings.

16. Cruickshank, "Synthesis."

17. Brophy and Good, "Teacher Behavior."

18. Ibid.

19. P. Hosford, ed., *Using What We Know About Teaching* (Alexandria, VA: Association for Supervision and Curriculum Development, 1984); T. Levin and R. Long, *Effective Instruction* (Alexandria, VA: Association for Supervision and Curriculum Development, 1981).

20. D. Smith, ed., *Essential Knowledge for Beginning Educators* (Washington, D. C.: American Association of Colleges for Teacher Education, 1983).

21. Coalition for the Development of a Performance Evaluation System, *Domains of the Florida Performance Measurement System* (Tallahassee, FL: Office of Teacher Education, Certification and Inservice Staff Development, 1983).

Teaching," in *Handbook of Research on Teaching*, ed. M. Wittrock (New York: Macmillan, 1985).
15. B. Rosenshine, *Teaching Behaviors and Student Achievement* (London: National Foundation for Educational Research, 1971); and

B. Rosenshine and N. Furst, "Research on Teacher Performance Criteria," in *Research in Teacher Education*, ed., B. O. Smith (Englewood Cliffs, NJ: Prentice-Hall, 1967). This review was severely but probably somewhat fairly criticized by some. However, its impact cannot be denied as it

A Look to the Future

The late 1980s are alive with the spirit of change in North American education. The future of education will be affected by the recommendations of such groups as the American Association of Colleges for Teacher Education (AACTE), The Rand Corporation, The Carnegie Forum on Education, The Holmes Group, the National Academy of Education, and similar scholarly research and development groups. The tidal wave of recommendations will produce basic changes in how teachers are educated, in how their career opportunities will be structured, and in how elementary and secondary schools will be structured.

The future is bright for education, provided a sufficient amount of national resources can be created or redirected to achieve the goals of the almost thirty formal group reports calling for reform. While many of the signals from the national commission reports are clear, some of the signals from state legislatures for revised state certification standards are ambiguous at best. Other state legislatures and teacher certification agencies are determined to support the many recent proposed reforms in teacher education and the conduct of schooling.

Given the tenor of all the reports and dialogue about increasing rates of technological development and social change in the nation, great changes in education can be expected as well. The future of education will be affected by many factors, such as the shifting social demographics of the population served by North American schools, and the revolution in the information sciences. The emergence of user friendly software and the massive rate of growth in the popular use of personal computers ensures that schools of the future will rely on and use more and more of the new information technologies which facilitate high degrees of individualization in classrooms. In addition, major changes may be developing in how people become teachers and in the organizational structure of the profession itself.

The future of any system depends on the outcome of its past and present. The future of education will be determined by the current criticisms and proposals for change growing out of what is a significant dialectical debate. The focus of the debate concerns what constitutes a just, national response to human needs in a period of technological change. The reshaping of curricula at the elementary and secondary school levels as well as the reshaping of teacher education curricula will reflect the outcome of this debate. The history of technological change in all human societies since the beginning of industrial development in the late eighteenth century has clearly demonstrated that major advances in technological development and major breakthroughs in the basic sciences lead to more rapid rates of social change. Society is on the verge of discoveries which will lead to the creation of whole new technologies in the dawning years of the twenty-first century—hardly more than a dozen years from now. All of the social, economic, and educational institutions on earth will be affected by these scientific breakthroughs. A basic issue is not whether the schools can remain aloof from the needs of industry or the economic demands of society, but how to develop a just, humane, and compassionate expression of the noblest ideals of free persons in the face of inevitable technological and economic change. Another concern is how to let go of predetermined visions of the future which limit our possibilities as a free people. The schools, of course, will be called upon to face these issues. There is a need for the most enlightened, insightful, and compassionate teachers ever educated by North American universities in order to prepare the youth of the future in a manner which will humanize the high-tech world in which they will live.

All of the articles included in this unit touch on some of the issues raised above. They can be related to any discussions on the aims of education, the future of education, or curriculum development. They also reflect highly divergent perspectives in philosophy of education.

Looking Ahead: Challenge Questions

What might be the shape of school curriculum by the year 2000?

What changes in society are most likely to affect educational change?

How can information about population demographics, potential discoveries in the basic sciences, and the rate and direction of technological change in Canada and the United States assist in planning for the educational future? What planning strategies are needed?

How can curriculum development today prepare students to work in an uncertain future? What knowledge bases are most important? What skills are most important?

Is a national consensus on educational values possible?

Based on all of the commission reports of recent years, is it possible to identify any clear directions in which teacher education in North America is headed?

Marvin J. Cetron, Barbara Soriano, and Margaret Gayle

Schools of the Future

Education Approaches the Twenty-First Century

Surviving the current crisis in education requires major reforms. Schools must stay open longer, pay teachers better, and open their doors to a different kind of student—the adult worker in need of retraining.

Nearly 30 reports issued by commissions, task forces, and individuals have made it clear to the American people that their nation will be "at risk" unless they pay attention to their schools.

Most of these reports emphasize the need to better prepare students for entering college. Yet three-fourths of U.S. kids don't graduate from college.

A major responsibility of schools in the future will be to prepare students to enter a rapidly changing job market. If the United States is to continue to compete in the worldwide marketplace, American workers will need to be more highly trained than at present. This means a greater emphasis on high-tech vocational education will be needed—an issue most educational reformers have ignored.

Schools will be responsible for preparing students who are adaptable and able to respond quickly to the changing requirements of new technologies. In the near future, workers' jobs will change dramatically every 5 to 10 years. Schools will train both youth and adults; adult workers will need re-education and retraining whenever business and industry update their operations. In the future, workers will be displaced frequently and will be moving constantly from one occupation to another. They will need periodic retraining because each new job will be different from the previous one.

Schools of the Future

By 1990, most adults will be working a 32-hour week. During the time that they are not at work, many will be preparing for their next job. While the adult workweek is getting shorter, the student schoolweek will be getting longer.

Not only will the normal academic day be longer for children, but the buildings themselves will be open a minimum of 12 hours a day. Schools will be providing services to the community, to business, and to young students who will use the recreation facilities, computer labs, and job simulation stations—modules that combine computers, videodiscs, and instrumentation to duplicate job-work environments.

Many schools may be open 24 hours a day. They will be training centers for adults from 4 p.m. to midnight; some will also serve business through their computer and communication facilities from midnight until the next morning when young students arrive again.

Individual communities may conduct classes that include both adults and high-school students. But if for some reason this combination is unsuccessful, the groups can separate and work independently. In some communities, adults might take over portions of school buildings that have been closed because of declining school enrollments.

At present, most schools are in session for approximately 180 days a year. A number of the reform reports recommend an increase to 210 days a year or 240 days to match schools abroad, but many people have objected. Funds have not been available; some students and teachers feel they do not have the mental energy for a longer year; and families want free time to make summer plans. Also, school buildings generally are not air-conditioned.

Schools in the 1990s, however, increasingly will extend the time that buildings are in service. Air conditioning and modifications in the size and structure of classrooms will accommodate the changing purposes of school programs.

Some students will have the option of accelerating their progress through the school year in order to graduate and enter college or the job market earlier. Others may spend time at school in the summer to enrich their academic backgrounds through telecommunications coursework with another school district, state, or country.

Adults may find summer months a good time to train for a new phase of their careers. The core academic year will lengthen to 210 days, but students will not necessarily be in the school building at all times during this period.

Factors Affecting the Future of Schools

A number of current trends will affect work and schools in the twenty-first century:

• Minority populations will become the majority in most grade schools in the nation's large and middle-sized school districts.

• Computers will be available to students in prosperous districts on a 1:4 ratio. (The United States spent a total of $1 billion on textbooks in its entire 200-year history. In the next five to six years alone, the nation will spend $1 billion on computer-assisted education. Only one-third of this will be bought by and for schools; the remaining two-thirds will be provided by wealthier parents for their own children, thus creating an educational inequity far more debilitating than physical segregation. Society must do something to provide access to computers for all children.)

• Federal grants will provide a major portion of the funding for job training and equipment (including computers) in poor school districts.

• Total employment will rise by 17% to 25% as the workweek declines to 32 hours by 1990 and to 20-25 hours by 2000.

• Women, particularly married women, will enter the work force at a faster rate than any other group within the population.

• More businesses will be involved in schools, including apprenticeship training.

• Older citizens (over 55) increasingly will become students in public schools, job-training programs, and community source programs.

• A core, nine-month program will be offered in elementary and high schools, shifting electives to later in the lengthened day and to summer sessions.

• Teachers' salaries on an annual basis will be raised to within 10% of parity with other professionals requiring college degrees.

—Marvin J. Cetron, Barbara Soriano, and Margaret Gayle

Good-Bye, Little Red Schoolhouse?

Interactive cable television and computer communication links with the school may allow school districts to close down costly old buildings even if enrollments are increasing. As the workweek shortens from 32 hours a week in 1990 to 20-25 hours a week in the year 2000, families will want to make plans for the periods children would previously have been in school. Students will be able to time their study hours to fit these family schedules.

Computers will be used for the drill and practice of skills introduced by the teacher; they will also be used for helping students explore creative and problem-solving situations. Today's educational software, however, rarely does either job very well.

Teachers will effect some of the

biggest changes in educational software. Their experience with computers in the classrooms during the late 1980s will give them insight into the ways such software will need to change. The teachers who are particularly good at making modifications may even leave the classroom and launch their own software-writing businesses.

Planning Individualized Education

Many teachers will operate in teaching teams, which will be able to use frequently updated information on their students to design individual education plans (IEPs). IEPs are simply plans for instruction. Each student will have a plan tailored to his or her own background, interests, and skills.

The IEPs in today's schools list skills in reading or math, for example, and suggest how the teacher should test the student to see if the skills have been mastered. IEPs in the future will also recommend whether students should learn each skill in a small or a large group, independently, one-on-one with a teacher, or a combination of these formats. They will suggest which senses the student should use more frequently to develop them further—for example, visual (reading books or computer screens) rather than aural (listening to tapes).

Once the quality of educational software improves, schools will be able to teach and drill students in basic skills more efficiently and also increase the percentage of students achieving certain minimum competencies.

Students who work relatively well without a great deal of supervision will be assigned to teachers who work well with large groups. Often, lessons will be introduced and skills developed through teacher-managed computer systems. Teachers will be responsible for setting up the instructional schedules, reviewing progress with the students, and seeing that students have opportunities to participate in a broad range of learning situations: problem-solving groups; independent information-gathering activities in the school or the community; music, art, or drama activities led by professionals from these disciplines; or computer-based drill routines.

For students who need to work in small groups, teachers skilled in handling and coordinating small-group experiences will move these students from teacher-student interaction to student-student interaction. Students will teach each other, not because the teacher does not have time and is trying to find a way to keep these student teams busy but because effective learning can take place in these teams.

Teachers will be assigned students based on the kind of teaching they do best. Students will be assigned to groups based on the way they learn best, according to what learning researchers feel they need to be successful. Students will not be assigned by grade level but by the developmental level they have reached in each area. Neither teachers nor parents will be concerned with pupil-teacher ratios.

No More Pencils, No More Books?

As software improves, computers will begin to replace some kinds of textbooks; they already can replace drillbooks. Software can be tailored to meet individual student needs and can be updated more quickly and inexpensively than textbooks. The writing and computing deficiencies that national educational reform groups have noted among today's students may often be remedied by simple practice—something computers do tirelessly.

Computers themselves could even provide income for the school: Parents might come to school to learn how to use computers in their businesses, and companies could use school computer facilities to run their data at night. And computers can be linked with videodiscs or with equipment that simulates the job environment.

Computers linked with video-discs will provide sight, sound,

Adults may make up a large proportion of the future "student body" as they come back to classrooms to learn high-tech skills. To accommodate them, schools will be open longer—at night and during summers.

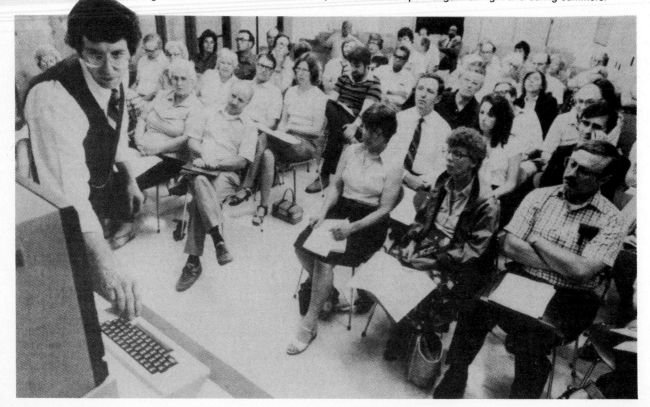

and movement. Some lessons in history, language, politics, psychology, math, word problems, and music, art, or dance could be taught or reinforced from one video-disc. Software, written by a member of a teaching team, will program sequences of visual images from a disc. The computer program will stop and start the disc every so often to ask the student questions.

Widespread use of computer-linked equipment will not be a major feature of schools until the twenty-first century, but certain schools will use computers in this way long before 1995. Computer simulations of certain job procedures have been used to train employees for 10 years in certain industries. Because sophisticated workplace simulation equipment is expensive, it will probably be placed only in regional centers where students will be sent for short periods of time to study and live in supervised dormitories attached to the public school system. Finally, individual high schools will begin to offer simulation as a means of job training.

Teachers and Business

Before the mid-1990s, teachers will receive higher pay—raised to at least 90% of comparable professionals' salaries. The current, popular concept of merit pay is not as relevant as the concept of pay equity, or parity. Teachers are the lowest paid of all professionals. In 40 out of the 50 states, a starting garbage collector earns more money than a starting teacher. Something must be done now.

Funding required to raise teachers' salaries will come in large part from businesses contracting with schools to retrain their workers; from private individuals studying skills for their next jobs; from selling computer time, day-care, and geriatric services to the community; and from other ways of using school buildings more efficiently.

As business becomes more closely connected with schools, it is possible that skilled teachers will join private business in even greater numbers than they do today. Teachers may choose to con-

Future Students

Students of the twenty-first century will probably include toddlers, children, youth, adults, and older citizens. A typical school district may provide learning experiences and training for students ages 3 to 21 and for adults ages 21 to 80-plus.

Students could have many options within the extended framework of the day and year:

• Attending school seven hours a day and 210 days or more a year, depending on their needs and ability to handle tasks.

• Selecting a variety of programs, both required and elec-

tive, in academic, vocational, or enrichment programs.

• Working from an interactive computer/videodisc learning station at home or school.

• Working on a job and going to school.

• Doing apprenticeships with master teachers.

• Having opportunities for expanded time in a science laboratory, music class, art class, or vocational class.

• Having opportunities to be tutored individually or in small groups.

—Marvin J. Cetron, Barbara Soriano,
and Margaret Gayle

tinue their careers as trainers of employees for private businesses. Many times, however, businesses will find that teachers are valuable employees in other respects. Some of the services that teachers will be able to sell to businesses include communication skills, performance evaluation skills, group management abilities, and information management skills.

Schools that wish to keep their most skilled teachers will probably offer flexible work schedules so that teachers can participate in both worlds and will not be forced to make a choice. In this way, schools will not passively let businesses raid their personnel.

All Students Will Train for Jobs

Training for the job world does not keep people from going to college. One indication is that, from 1974 to 1979, part-time college enrollment increased by 25.8%. More students are now prolonging the period between when they graduate from high school and when they enter college. Some of that delay is caused by the fact that federal loans

and grants for college students have declined dramatically.

As schools provide more resources for teaching adults, they will be able to offer job training based on jobs that are actually available, not those that are becoming obsolete.

From the eighth grade on, many students may actually be placed in different businesses that use the skills they are learning. If businesses that might provide a wide range of experience are not immediately available to the school, students will be able to travel to a learning center staffed with instructors and containing the latest equipment suited to students' career fields.

In either location, students will have their work supervised and graded by employers' standards. A trainer will watch them at the work site or via television hookup. The trainer will be able to talk with the student. After this experience at the work site, students will return to the school to have their performance reviewed. The school will then judge whether the students

Future Teachers

It may not be necessary for all of a school's staff to be trained in education. Educators will be part of the career team and will be able to provide the guidance necessary to assure that experts from fields outside of education will present their materials effectively.

The educator of the future will have extensive experience with such topics as brain development chemistry, learning environment alternatives, cognitive and psychosomatic evaluation, and affective development.

The traditional teaching job will be divided into parts. After good computer-managed courseware has been installed in schools, the information gathered on teachers' performance in a variety of situations will determine which jobs will go to which teachers. School systems will encourage this specialization be-

cause they may make money from selling various services to business interests—or teachers may work part time and sell the services themselves. Some of the new jobs may be:

• Learning diagnostician.
• Information gatherer for software programs.
• Courseware writer.
• Curriculum designer.
• Mental-health diagnostician.
• Evaluator of learning performances.
• Evaluator of social skills.
• Small-group learning facilitator.
• Large-group learning facilitator.
• Media-instruction producer.
• Home-based instruction designer.
• Home-based instruction monitor.

—Marvin J. Cetron, Barbara Soriano, and Margaret Gayle

need additional attention, practice at a simulator, or study.

Taking the last two years of high school for job preparation does not mean that the advanced-course needs of students bound for college must be put aside. Schools will, however, be forced to become more effective in teaching English, mathematics, history, and science courses before the tenth grade. Students who plan to enter professions requiring intermediate or advanced skills in foreign languages, science, or math could sample jobs in related fields while studying those subjects.

Vocational education will no longer be a narrow field of study. Rather than the quickly legislated, quickly funded, inadequate remedy for a stalled economy that it has been in the past, vocational education will prepare students for careers of challenges and changes—not just for a first job.

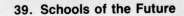

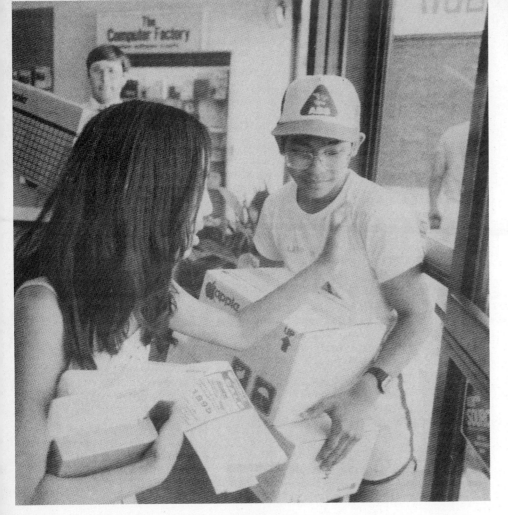

Family purchases computer and software, enabling children to do much school work at home. Computer and communications technologies will allow some school districts to close down costly facilities despite increasing enrollments.

We can forecast a basically positive, progressive future for America's schools based on current international and national economic and social trends. These trends could change direction, however, thereby altering our predictions.

But nothing will alter these forecasts as greatly as inaction. If America's citizens ignore these warnings about their educational and industrial future, the nation's economic stability and preeminence will be jeopardized.

Marvin J. Cetron is president of Forecasting International, Ltd., 1001 N. Highland Street, Arlington, Virginia 22210. He is author of the best-seller *Encounters with the Future* (McGraw-Hill, 1982, 308 pages, paperback, $5.95) and *Jobs of the Future* (McGraw-Hill, 1984, 258 pages, $15.95).

Barbara Soriano is a Washington-based consultant and can be reached at Forecasting International, Ltd.

Margaret Gayle is an associate director of vocational education with the North Carolina State Department of Public Instruction, Raleigh, North Carolina 27611.

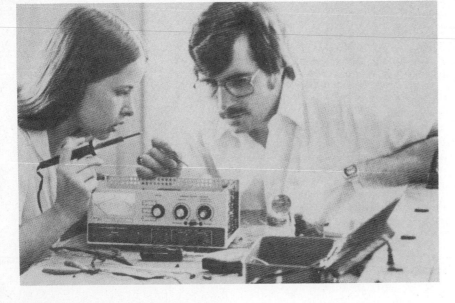

Students learn computer maintenance and electronics fabrication. High-tech vocational education will become a vital component of schools' curricula, say authors Cetron, Soriano, and Gayle.

The EDUCATION OF CHILDREN

Brad Edmondson

Brad Edmondson is assistant editor of
American Demographics.

Most parents see "a good education" as the surest way to transform their babies into successful adults. Because children embody so many parental hopes, the nation's schools are a leading indicator of society's goals for the next generation.

Since World War II, educational goals have shifted repeatedly with public opinion. The GI Bill in the 1940s, Sputnik-related science programs in the 1950s, and the "free schools" movement in the 1960s reflected prevailing conceptions of what was desirable for society. Today the educational system's function is, as Senator Gary Hart put it, to be "our first line of national economic defense" from foreign competition and a spur to economic growth.

Over the last 40 years, American education has become big business. Between 1945 and 1975, the percentage of GNP spent on all schools, kindergarten through college, rose from 2 percent to 7.7 percent. That share fell to an estimated 6.7 percent by 1984, due in part to declining numbers of school-aged children. Yet expenditures for all schools rose from $119 billion in 1975 to an estimated $245 billion in 1984.

Schools are a national priority, but they are also a national scapegoat. The Presidential report *A Nation At Risk*, released in 1983, warned of a "rising tide of mediocrity" in education which threatened America's very survival. Today, educational excellence is an often-discussed but little-understood goal. Public frustration with the schools is evidence of the gap between our ideal images on the one hand, and educational realities on the other.

What are these realities in 1986? What population trends will shape the agenda for schools in the next decade?

First, growth in the number of children aged 6 to 13 will increase the demands on the nation's elementary schools, while continuing declines in the 14-to-17 age group will reduce enrollment in high schools. However, because of migration, local and regional differences in population growth will be significant. Some school districts already are experiencing the same overcrowded classrooms and teacher shortages they faced 20 years ago, while others continue to lose students.

Regional variations in minority enrollment will be even more pronounced, as southern, western, and urban schools continue assimilating a wave of first-generation Hispanic and Asian immigrant children. In 1970, minorities were 21 percent of total enrollment in public elementary and secondary schools; in 1982, they were 27 percent.

A smaller proportion of households are raising children today than in the 1970s, and a growing number of upper-income families are choosing to send their children to private schools. Meanwhile, large families are concentrated increasingly among low-income groups. Childless families, and those who send their children to private schools, may be asked to subsidize an increasing share of public education through property taxes.

THE BRAINY BABY

According to *American Demographics* projections,* there will be little change in the number of preschoolers over the next decade. The 3.7 million births of 1985 should rise slightly until 1990, then fall to 3.5 million by 1995. The number of pre-schoolers aged 1 to 5 should rise from 17.8 million in 1985 to 18.5 million in 1990, then fall to 18 million by 1995.

The slowing growth among pre-schoolers will reflect the end of the childbearing years for older baby boomers, whose offspring are now swelling elementary school enroll-ment today. Educators will be ad-justing to the bulge and bust of baby-boomer babies for the next 20 years.

The baby boom's echo is louder in the Sunbelt, however. The number of children under age 5 grew by 9 percent nationally between 1980 and 1984, but they grew 11 percent in the South, 17 percent in the West, 5 percent in the Northeast, and 2 percent in the Midwest. According to the Washington, D.C.-based fore-casting firm Woods & Poole Eco-nomics, the total U.S. population will increase by 12 percent between 1985 and 1995, but the Northeast will grow only 3 percent while the Midwest gains 6 percent, the South 16 percent, and the West 21 percent.

Growth in the number of children may be even more concentrated than these projections imply: The Na-tional Planning Association predicts that from 1980 to 2000, five states—California, Florida, Texas, Arizona, and North Carolina—will account for 73 percent of the national gain in children under age 14. School administrators in some districts will be unaware of en-rollment changes, while others will have to cope with growth rivaling the peak of the baby boom.

Today's infants and preschoolers are the focus of a trend emphasizing

earlier and more comprehensive ed-ucational programs. Baby-boom parents are the best educated in American history; one in four men and one in five women have a college degree. Today's well-educated par-ents are causing a boom in edu-cational products for preschoolers.

Working mothers are also affecting demand for preschooler educational programs, particularly day care. In 1970, only one-fourth of married mothers with children aged one or younger were in the labor force and one-third of those with children younger than age 6 were working. In 1985, the participation rates were 49 and 54 percent respectively. Over 70 percent of employed mothers work full-time; even when the youngest

child is under age 3, 65 percent of working mothers have full-time jobs.

AN EARLY START

When parents need someone to look after their preschooler, family and friends are the overwhelming choice, but the use of group day-care centers is increasing. "We don't really need to do much market research because we've spent all our time trying to catch up with demand," said Ann Muscari, director of corporate com-munication for Kinder-Care Learning Centers, Inc. Kinder-Care opened its first day-care center in 1968 and its 1,000th last August. "Our perception is that many more parents would pay for day care if a reasonably priced center was available," Muscari said.

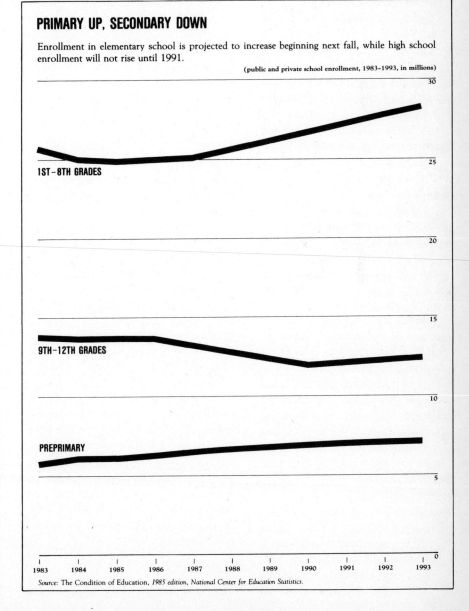

PRIMARY UP, SECONDARY DOWN

Enrollment in elementary school is projected to increase beginning next fall, while high school enrollment will not rise until 1991.

(public and private school enrollment, 1983-1993, in millions)

Source: The Condition of Education, *1985 edition, National Center for Education Statistics.*

9. A LOOK TO THE FUTURE

How does Kinder-Care choose new sites for day care? "Frequently towns will contact us and invite us to build— they assure us of the demand," Muscari said. "We also have a staff of scouts who look at the demographics of local areas, including the number of working families, income and education levels, and so on." In 1985, Kinder-Care focused on building its centers in the West, Midwest and Mid-Atlantic states.

The company's promotional brochure aims at working parents who feel that "the hours they are away from their child can be the longest hours of the day." The brochure emphasizes safety, a "loving atmosphere," and educational programs tailored to each preschool year of age. Kinder-Care also offers special activities such as Klubmates, an after-school program for the 6-to-12-year-olds; Kinder-Camp, a summer program for preschoolers; and Kindustry, a network of business-sponsored centers.

Working families are also fueling growth in nursery schools and full-day kindergarten programs. The National Center for Education Statistics (NCES) estimated 5.7 million children aged 3 to 6 were in preprimary programs in 1983, a 33 percent increase since 1970. The NCES predicts that enrollment will increase 25 percent to 7.1 million in 1993, despite slow growth in the number of preschoolers.

According to the Census Bureau, 20 percent of all kindergartners were in full-day programs in 1973, increasing to 33 percent in 1983. "The rate still is increasing rapidly," said Dr. Leslie Williams, a preprimary enrollment specialist at Columbia Teachers College. "We expect that full-day kindergarten will become the majority of programs in the next three to four years."

All 14 public schools in Stamford, Connecticut have offered full-day kindergarten since 1980. "Our kindergarten enrollment went up 8 percent when we switched to full-day," said John Davidson, a research associate for the school district. "It

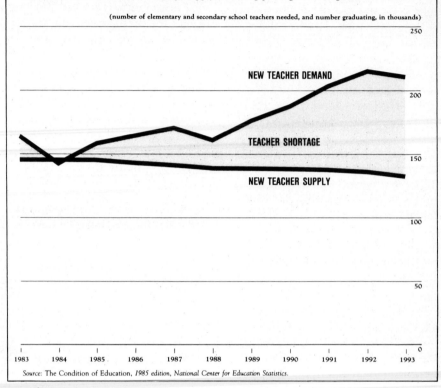

EDUCATION AND NUTRITION ARE THE SELLING POINTS IN THE KID'S MARKET TODAY.

SUPPLY AND DEMAND, 1983–1993

The demand for teachers now outstrips supply, and the gap will grow through 1993.

(number of elementary and secondary school teachers needed, and number graduating, in thousands)

NEW TEACHER DEMAND

TEACHER SHORTAGE

NEW TEACHER SUPPLY

Source: The Condition of Education, 1985 edition, National Center for Education Statistics.

was obviously something the public wanted."

Davidson said that Stamford went full-day for three reasons: first, because administrators believed that it would improve the education of preschoolers; second, because an increasing number of kindergarteners had attended half-day nursery school programs, "and we wanted to keep them moving forward;" and third, to compete with private schools. "Stamford is not a typical town," Davidson said. "It only has 100,000 residents, but it's the third-largest corporate center in the U.S. We have a lot of families making over $100,000, a lot of poor families, and very few middle-class people." To staunch the flow of affluent children from public schools, Davidson said, Stamford must enhance its programs continuously.

SELLING POINTS

The buzzword for working parents is

"quality time." This translates into purchases of educational toys, books, and computer software, so that the parent becomes a teacher and the child a perpetual student. "Education and nutrition are the two hot selling points in the kids' market today," said Marvin Schoenwald, a children's market researcher. "If you can convince parents that it's got educational or nutritional value, you've got it made."

Quality time has been a boon to sales of children's books. According to the Association of American Publishers, sales of juvenile hardbound and paperbound books, designed for children aged 2 to 17, jumped 21 percent between 1982 and 1984. Although the industry does not break out sales figures for the 2-to-6 age group, *The New York Times* has reported that preschoolers' books enjoyed $80 to $90 million in sales in 1984, up 20 percent from 1983, and that 1985 figures are

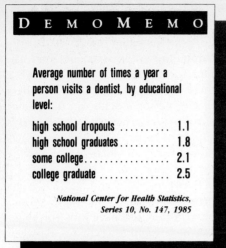

D E M O M E M O

Average number of times a year a person visits a dentist, by educational level:

high school dropouts 1.1
high school graduates 1.8
some college 2.1
college graduate 2.5

National Center for Health Statistics, Series 10, No. 147, 1985

expected to be 15 percent higher.

"I think children can benefit from being around books from the moment of birth," said Marilyn Hollinshead, president of the Association of Booksellers for Children and the owner of Pittsburgh's Pinocchio Bookstore. Workbooks are strong sellers: A new line from Random House uses sound, specially treated paper and a light pen to teach children shapes, letters and colors. When the child touches the pen to the page, a speaker implanted in the book emits a tone to indicate correct and incorrect answers.

Educating children from birth may or may not pay off, but there is evidence that educating parents from birth does work. Last October, the Missouri Department of Elementary and Secondary Education announced the results of a three-year study of 380 families with newborns. Beginning during pregnancy and continuing for three years, parents were given regular training in subjects as varied as child development, detecting sickness, and how to discipline infants without punishing them. By age 3, the children in the study showed mental and linguistic growth far exceeding that of other children.

Gymboree, a chain of "integrative play" centers, has enjoyed rapid growth by catering to the educational demands of parents. The company uses theories of sensory integration, neurological organization, and psychomotor development to organize a series of activities for parents and their children aged 3 months through 4 years. Founded in 1976, Gymboree now operates 230 centers in 29 states and Canada and plans to open 100 new centers a year, according to public affairs vice president Karen Anderson.

Anderson said that the typical Gymboree mother is older, well-educated, and raising her first child. Ninety-two percent of Gymboree's customers are aged 26 or older, and 57 percent are aged 30 or older; two-thirds of the women are college graduates, and over half have family incomes of $40,000 or more. "We appeal to educated people who believe in the concept of shaping a

D E M O M E M O

Percent of 1982 high school graduates who earned an A average in courses, by subject:

English 17%
math 17%
science 19%
business 22%
arts 45%

National Center for Education Statistics, 1985

child's development," she said. "These are the same people who believe in preschool programs, Montessori education, and Lamaze classes. They're trendsetters, and the rest of the country will follow them."

THE SUPPLIERS

Even in a growing area, economic and political factors are at least as important as demographics in determining the demand for education-related products. Public schools are not businesses; they are local institutions controlled by boards of elected officials whose actions are unpredictable.

Yet there was one clear trend in most school districts during the last decade: cost-cutting. State-supported education became more basic as art, music, sports and remedial programs were cut to reduce taxes. An increasing number of parents are now taking up the slack by purchasing supplementary educational products and programs for their children, and the businesses serving American education are happy to oblige them.

Last year, privately held Encyclopedia Britannica, Inc. acquired the American Learning Corporation, creators of The Reading Game, an after-school "prescriptive" reading center which tests and then tutors a student two times a week for $25 per hour. The company has been renamed Britannica Learning Corporation (BLC), and although remedial programs are still its main emphasis, speed reading and supplementary programs now have been added, and adult test preparation, math drills, and science programs are on the drawing board. According to president Stanley Frank, BLC plans to add one center per week until 500 Reading Games are operating across the country.

"We did a lot of research before we decided to get into this field," Frank said. "We decided that many schools were encountering limited financial resources, and they were being forced to cut the supplementary programs we would provide. Also, more parents now seem willing to pay for supplementary education programs."

Britannica isn't alone in recognizing

D E M O M E M O

Percent of handicapped students in regular classes, by type of handicap:

learning disability 78%
mentally retarded 29%
deaf 38%
deaf and blind 9%

National Center for Education Statistics, 1985

9. A LOOK TO THE FUTURE

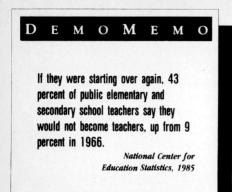

the opportunity; Kinder-Care recently acquired Sylvan Learning Corporation, a rapidly growing remedial reading and math program. With over 200 centers nationwide, Sylvan calls itself "the McDonald's of education."

Communications director Lisa Scattaregia said that Sylvan recently completed two consumer studies. The first classified customers using VISION, a geodemographic cluster analysis program from National Decision Systems, while the second used focus groups of parents with children at Sylvan to explore attitudes toward supplementary and remedial education. The research helps new franchise owners get started, she said, while providing company executives with a "dimensional customer profile."

Publishing giant Houghton Mifflin relies on research to stay on top of the education market, according to Claudia Regan, assistant communications director for their schoolbook division. "Our greatest strength has always been at the elementary level," Regan said. "In the last few years, the elementary divisions have been developing new programs and software to hit the market just as the numbers start growing. We're also using longer-range plans to get our secondary programs ready for the 1990s, when the high schools will turn around."

Mead Products Company watches fashion trends and demographics when it designs tablets, spiral notebooks and organizers, according to marketing services manager Paul McClain. "You have to have quality

for the parents, but popular culture affects us as much as anything," he said. "Our products have to maintain a contemporary look to appeal to high school students, for example, while putting a licensed character on a notebook often increases its appeal for younger people. We acquired the rights to Garfield the Cat recently, and we're very happy about it."

The Mead Corporation is a leading producer of forest products and a marketer of over 3,000 stationery and office supply items, but school supplies are its original product. This year, McClain says, Mead is catering to parents by releasing a durable line of school supplies and special yellow-tinted paper designed to reduce eye strain, while courting fashion-conscious kids with such items as hologram-cover notebooks, color-coordinated portfolios, and, of course, licensed characters like Garfield.

Demographic growth doesn't mean much to the Blue Bird Body Company, the nation's leading manufacturer of school buses. Charles Bartlett, vice president for marketing, says that the privately owned company's sales peaked at about 30,000 buses five years ago and have declined to 26,000 or 27,000 this year. "There are many reasons," he said. "First, the districts don't have as much money. Many of them used to replace a bus after eight years, but now they'll let it go until it can't be fixed any longer. If it's a growing district, they might go to split sessions, which means that the bus works harder, or they might increase the minimum distance where they start picking up kids."

NO MORE GLUT

Now that elementary school enrollments are rising again, teachers' fortunes are improving. The NCES predicts that elementary enrollment should increase from 27.1 million in 1985 to 30.9 million in 1992.*

In 1970, this country had a teacher

* Secondary enrollment should continue to decline until 1990. At 16.8 million today, secondary enrollment should be at 15.5 million in 1992.

glut. As a result, teacher salaries fell an average of 15 percent in real dollars through the last decade, dampening college students' enthusiasm for teaching careers. By 1983, there was a shortage of 4,000 teachers in the nation's schools. As school enrollment grows and the nation's supply of experienced teachers grows older, the U.S. faces a nationwide teacher shortage.

Between 1983 and 1987, NCES projections show that there should be 108 new teaching jobs for every 100 new teaching graduates. Between 1988 and 1992, there should be 126 new jobs awaiting every 100 graduates. Current shortages are most pronounced in western schools, in central cities, and in large school districts; the specializations most in demand are bilingual education, special education, computer sciences, art, music, and remedial education, and teacher shortages are also predicted for science and math.

Elementary education is now a buyer's market. In response, 27 states have recently passed laws boosting teacher salaries, 25 states have begun or are planning career ladder programs which reward teacher performance and knowledge of subject matter with a "master teacher" designation and higher pay, teacher strikes are declining in number, and there is a nationwide hunt for teachers.

PRIVATE CHOICES

In a democratic society, educational policy is set by the voting public. But in recent years, an increasing number of families are voting with their checkbooks by sending their children to private schools. Public schools still educate nine out of every ten American children, but they are losing increasing numbers of white, affluent children whose families pay the greatest share of school taxes.

During the 1970s, while public school enrollment was falling, private enrollment rose slightly. Between 1980 and 1984, public enrollment fell 5 percent while private enrollment rose 7 percent. Only 5 percent of children with family incomes of $25,000 or less go to private school, while 20 percent of children with family incomes of $50,000 or more attend private school.

The trend toward parental purchases of preprimary educational programs has an ominous cast for public schools as well. "We may be witnessing the birth of a tradition," writes educational analyst Emily Feistritzer.* "We have more families

* C. Emily Feistritzer, "A New Baby Boomlet Hits The Schools," The Washington Post, June 16, 1985, p. C1.

in which both parents work. They are becoming accustomed to paying tuition to send their children to private schools. The tuition becomes part of their household budget. Are they likely to take their children out of private schools when they reach the first grade? From the little data we have, the answer appears to be probably not."

"We're acutely aware of the competition we face from private schools," said Stamford's John Davidson. "The public demands quality when they purchase something, and it doesn't really matter if they pay for it with taxes or tuition."

The public consistently opposes raising taxes for local schools, according to the Gallup poll. In 1985, school tax increases were opposed by 52 percent of Americans, and approved by only 38 percent.

Gallup results also show that there are significant differences in what the public wants from the schools and what teachers want. When asked to state the goals of American education, the public said that teaching children "to speak and write correctly" was most important, while teachers said that "developing good work habits" came first. The public's second choice, "to develop standards of what is right and wrong," was rated tenth by teachers.

When asked to name the biggest problems facing local public schools, the public has consistently named "lack of discipline" first since 1969. But teachers rate "lack of discipline" fourth and "parents' lack of interest and support" first, by a wide margin.

Schools are reflections of society. "By its very nature, education is a forecast," writes educator Diane Ravitch,* "for in deciding what children should learn, we are making a statement about what they will need to know in the future."

* Diane Ravitch, The Schools We Deserve, New York: Basic Books, 1985, p. 297.

CURRICULUM IN THE YEAR 2000: TENSIONS AND POSSIBILITIES

Michael W. Apple

MICHAEL W. APPLE is professor of curriculum and instruction and educational policy studies at the University of Wisconsin, Madison. He has written extensively on the relationship between curriculum and society. Among his books are Ideology and Curriculum *(1979) and* Education and Power *(1982). He thanks Shigeru Asanuma, Esteban De La Torre, David Hursh, Ki Seok Kim, Dan Liston, Yolanda Rojas, and Leslie Rothaus for their important contributions to this article.*

Predictions of the future, even in the best of times, are hazardous. So many unforeseen variables and unexpected circumstances can influence outcomes. If this is so in the best of times, it will be even more the case in the next few decades, for these are certainly not the best of times. Thus all of my claims in this article should be preceded by a single word: *if.*

Much of what I am predicting about U.S. education in general and the curriculum in particular depends on political and economic factors. For example, I am not very optimistic about the future for urban school districts. I see the curriculum in urban schools becoming more dated and less flexible in the next 10 to 20 years. I arrive at this prediction from a sense — backed by a decent amount of evidence — that our economy will continue to sputter, if not to stall, in the foreseeable future, thereby creating a serious dilemma for the hard-working teachers and administrators in numerous school districts across the U.S.[1] However, there are also hopeful signs, especially in attempts — even in the face of serious financial difficulties — to keep necessary programs alive and to make curricular content more representative and honestly reflective of a significant portion of the U.S. population.

Basically, though, I see the next two decades as a time of increasing conflict in curriculum. School programs will reflect the splintering of common interests and the polarization of the larger society, trends largely caused by pressures and conflicts over which the schools have little control. A significant amount of the blame will also lie in curricular decisions made as long ago as the early Sixties or as recently as today.

Before going further, I must review some important social and economic facts. It is unfortunate but true that 80% of the benefits of current social policies go to the top 20% of the population. Moreover, the gap between the haves and the have-nots is widening, due in part to the severe economic problems that the U.S. is now experiencing.[2] To their credit, most Americans feel uncomfortable about this situation. But this general discomfort will not prevent many interest groups from arguing that it is not "our" responsibility to alter economic disparities. Nor will it prevent economic inequities from creating serious tensions in U.S. education. If anything, the state of the economy and contradictory attitudes toward it will exacerbate the problems that educators now face. In the next two decades, the curriculum will reflect many of these tensions in the larger society. This should not surprise us. Only rarely has curricular content *not* reflected what is happening outside the school.[3]

I will focus here on three interrelated areas: the content of the curriculum, its form (or how it is organized), and the process of decision making that shapes it. Only by considering all three factors can we understand the forces, building today, that will set limits on and create possibilities for the curriculum in the year 2000.

One major issue that is brewing now and will continue to grow is the debate about "basics." This is not a simple problem. There are many competing conceptions of what everyone should be taught, of what knowledge will be the most valuable to students and to the society. The current controversy over bilingual programs in elementary schools and contemporary proposals to "upgrade" content and to reduce electives in the secondary schools are cases in point. Defining the basics will prove to be one of the most difficult issues that the schools will face, because schools will serve as arenas in which various groups will do battle for their differing conceptions of what the society should value.

It is clear, for instance, that the content of the curriculum has become a major political issue. The activism of conservative and extremist groups has increased measurably. This activism will continue to grow, feeding on past successes that result in increased funding. Mel and Norma Gabler of Longview, Texas, are prime examples; they speak for a larger movement that spends considerable time denouncing textbooks that are "unpatriotic," that reject "absolute values" and "free enterprise," that emphasize too strongly the contributions of minority groups, and so on. Armed with the notion that God is on their side, they are likely to scrutinize an ever-broader swath of curricular content, intent on purging it of any taint of "un-Americanism" and "secular humanism." The increase in book banning and the evolution/creation controversy document the growing willingness of such groups to enter into debates over what should be taught in the schools. Thus educators will have to give more attention to justifying *why* they teach what they do. And this task will be increasingly difficult, because teacher-training institutions are moving toward greater stress on *how* to teach, not on providing justifications for and skills in arguing about *why* educators teach particular information, skills, and attitudes. Unless this trend is reversed, teachers and administrators will be hard pressed to defend curricular decisions against well-organized and well-funded attacks.

Tension between business and organized labor will also manifest itself in conflict over curricular content. On the one hand, we are currently witnessing the emergence of industry as a powerful pressure group that seeks to influence education. Businesses across the U.S. have established departments whose goals are to distribute curricular materials to schools, to convince textbook publishers to tout the benefits of free enterprise, to lobby state legislators, and to provide summer internships for teachers that will help them develop a more positive perspective on business. I see no sign that this type of pressure will abate.[4] On the other hand, labor unions have begun to stress the importance of labor education. A movement is growing to teach labor history and to encourage students to examine critically the problems of the U.S. economy and the imbalance in economic planning. These conflicting goals — to teach content that will produce citizens who will meet the needs of industry and simultaneously to examine critically industrial models and power and the putative lack of concern of big business with the needs of workers — will create a good deal of friction over what should be taught.

This friction will be heightened by the growing cooperation between state departments of education and the business community. In times of economic difficulty, when tax revenues are lower and jobs are hard to find, it is not unusual for school programs to become more closely aligned to the needs of business. We can expect to see more emphasis on teaching job-related skills and on disciplining students according to the norms that guide the workplace. This shift will be difficult to accomplish, because the U.S. job market is clearly changing. New skills rapidly become obsolete, and new jobs are not being created quickly enough.[5] Furthermore, many individuals will object to this closer relationship between the schools and industry, arguing that business generally has its own profits, not the common good, at heart. Thus one more conflict over curriculum will arise.

These two "political" issues — defining the basics and determining the proper relationship of the school to business and to labor — will not be the only ones to surface. The basics will also be expanded to include academic areas that now seem to receive less attention than they deserve. Clearly, there will be attempts, largely positive, to strengthen the teaching of mathematics and science. Several states are already preparing to mandate more science and mathematics courses for high school graduation and the retraining of teachers at state expense, in an effort to reverse the current shortage of qualified math and science teachers. This increased emphasis on mathematics and science will be accompanied by a greater focus on computers in all areas of the curriculum, but especially in math and science. We must be exceptionally cautious and avoid jumping on yet another technological bandwagon. There is no quick fix for the difficult problems we face. Without higher salaries and greater prestige to attract and keep well-trained teachers in these curricular areas, the prospects for success are mixed.

An unfortunate trend will accompany this increased emphasis on mathematics, science, and technology: increased differentiation of the curriculum. Schools will try to identify "gifted" students much earlier. We will see a return to tracking systems and more ability grouping than is currently in evidence. When large amounts of financial, material, and human resources are available, such differentiation may make it easier for teachers and support personnel to meet individual needs by working intensively with students, taking each to the limit of his or her capabilities. But in a time of fiscal crisis, such resources will not be readily available; in such a time, the reinstitution of differentiated curricula and tracking systems will often have the opposite effect: to ratify the low socioeconomic position of many children.[6]

The fiscal crisis will have other profound effects. Since less money will mean fewer teachers and support services, we will see an accompanying steady decline in curricular alternatives as well. There will simply be fewer programs and options.

Moreover, fiscal constraints will hinder the replacement of existing instructional materials (which provide the foundation for nearly all curricula); the average age of textbooks used in the schools will increase and perhaps even double. This trend will be most evident in large urban areas, because they will suffer disproportionate declines in tax revenues and in state and federal support. As a result, the gap in the quality of curricular offerings and instructional materials will broaden between cities and their more affluent suburbs. Thus curricular content will differ by race and social class.

As I have already noted, we must consider curricular content, form, and the process of decision making simultaneously. There is no guarantee that President Reagan's New Federalism will go beyond rhetoric, but evidence suggests that decision making will shift to the state level. Oddly, this shift — though aimed at increasing the responsiveness of state authorities to local districts — will actually decrease curricular diversity. As decision-making power coalesces at the state level, publishers will tailor their textbooks increasingly to the values of those states that encourage statewide textbook adoptions — generally through reimbursements to local school districts for some portion of the cost if they select their instructional materials from an approved list. For publishers, getting materials placed on such lists is quite important, since it nearly guarantees high sales and profits. Given this economic fact, states such as Texas and California, which have state textbook adoption policies, will have disproportionate power to determine which textbooks and resources will be available throughout the U.S. Hence we will see even greater standardization of the curriculum. The curriculum will become "safer," less controversial, less likely to alienate any powerful interest group.

I have argued that curricular content will become both a political football and more homogenized (due to economic pressures on publishers and political and economic pressures on local and state education authorities). A third trend will also become apparent: The form or organization of the curriculum will become increasingly technical and management-oriented. And this will have a serious impact on teachers.

A fundamental change in the curriculum of the American school began in the early 1960s, especially at the elementary level. Sputnik inspired fear that the teaching of mathematics and science lacked sufficient rigor and that the academic disciplines were not central enough in the curriculum; in response, the U.S. government funded a large number of projects that focused on producing new curricular materials. A significant proportion of these materials turned out to be "teacher-proof." They specified everything that a teacher had to know, say, and do. Often, they even specified acceptable student responses. This approach — to specify *everything* and leave nothing to chance — was tacitly sexist, since it seemed to assume that elementary school teachers (most of whom were women) could not cope on their own with sophisticated mathematics and science.[7] To insure that these materials would be purchased and used, the government reimbursed school systems for the bulk of their costs.

Although many of these new materials were not used in the ways that their developers had envisioned,[8] they did signal an important modification in the curriculum — one that we will be living with for years to come. The curriculum became less a locally planned program and more a series of commercial "systems" (in reading, mathematics, and so on). These systems integrated diagnostic and achievement tests, teacher and student activities, and teaching materials. Such integration has its strengths, of course. It does make possible more efficient planning, for example. But its weaknesses may prove to outweigh its strengths.

What we have actually seen is the *de-skilling* of our teaching force. Since so much of the curriculum is now conceived outside the schools, teachers often are asked to do little more than to execute someone else's goals and plans and to carry out someone else's suggested activities. A trend that has had a long history in industry — the separation of conception from execution — is now apparent as well in U.S. classrooms.[9]

This trend will have important consequences. When individuals cease to plan and control their own work, the skills essential to these tasks atrophy and are forgotten. Skills that teachers have built up over decades of hard work — setting curricular goals, establishing content, designing lessons and instructional strategies, individualizing instruction from an intimate knowledge of each student's desires and needs, and so on — are lost. In the process, the very things that make teaching a professional activity — the control of one's expertise and time — are also dissipated. There is no better formula for alienation and burnout than the loss of control of the job. Hence, the tendency of the curriculum to become totally standardized and systematized, totally focused on competencies measured by tests, and largely dependent on predesigned commercial materials may have consequences that are exactly the opposite of what we intend. Instead of professional teachers who care about what they do and why they do it, we may have only alienated executors of someone else's plans. Given the kinds of materials that now dominate many classrooms in such curricular areas as mathematics and reading, this danger seems likely to increase over time.

The economics of this process of de-skilling is worth noting. In essence, we have established a capital-intensive curriculum in our classrooms. Simply to keep the program going, a large amount of money must be set aside for the ongoing purchase of consumable materials. School districts may soon find themselves burdened with expensive "white elephants," as school budgets are reduced and money is no longer available to purchase the requisite workbooks, tests, worksheets, revised editions of "modules," and so

forth. School districts will then have to turn to their own staffs to create materials that are less expensive and more responsive to their students' needs — only to find that the necessary skills for doing this have been lost. This will be a very real predicament.

At the same time that teachers are being de-skilled, however, they are gaining greater control over which curricular materials and textbooks will be purchased for use in their classrooms. Curricular decision making is becoming more formally democratic; less power now resides in central curriculum offices or with select groups of administrators. Both teachers and parents are becoming more involved. Meanwhile, an increasing concern for accountability and for measurable achievement outcomes in a few "basic" areas will also bring a movement toward more standardized testing, more objectives, more focus on competencies, more centralized curricular control, and more teaching to the tests.

As this movement gains momentum, a vicious circle will develop. Publishers will further standardize content, basing it on competency tests and routinizing it as much as possible, so that their materials will produce measurable outcomes with little variability that will fit cost/control models.

Thus far, I have not been very optimistic about what will happen in the areas of curricular content, form, and decision making. I do not intend simply to be a nay-sayer. It is critically important to be realistic about the very difficult times that we educators will confront in the not-too-distant future. Only then can we begin to plan how to cope with what may happen. I would be remiss, however, if I did not point out some of the very beneficial tendencies that will become more visible by the year 2000.

Certain content areas — quite positive ones, in my opinion — will receive more emphasis than they do at present. Just as greater attention will be focused on mathematics and science (which, I hope, will be taught *not* as mere technical skills, but as creative and powerful ways of constructing meaning[10]), so, too, will teachers devote more time to the topics of ecology and peace. People from all walks of life, representing a variety of political persuasions, will coalesce around the topic of peace and urge that it be given more attention in the curriculum.

However, positive outcomes from additions to the curriculum will not be the dominant trend in a period of fiscal constraints. In fact, many school districts will be forced to save money by eliminating necessary programs. But this may prove beneficial, as well — especially in generating closer and more cooperative bonds between school personnel and the communities they serve. Teachers and parents will form coalitions to save programs that they see as essential. Difficult decisions will cause closer relationships to develop between community groups and the educators who must make those decisions. In a period of declining revenues and with the projected rise in enrollments, few outcomes will be more important. Funds will be needed to hire new teachers, to maintain and expand curricular offerings, to deal with students with special needs, and to carry on other essential tasks. Such funds can be generated only through greater cooperation with and increased support from the public. Even the scrutiny of the curriculum by conservative groups, to which I alluded earlier, should not be seen as merely a threat. The fact that parents — of whatever political persuasion — take a serious interest in their children's education suggests possible avenues for cooperation and fruitful discussion.

If we were freed from some of the tensions, conflicts, and pressures that will probably affect us as we strive to build or preserve a high-quality educational program for the children entrusted to us, what might we do about content, form, and decision making? Here I must be honest. A portion of what I will say has been recognized for years by knowledgeable educators. But such educators have seldom had the time, the resources, the support, or the freedom from contradictory pressures to act on this knowledge.

Let us look first at content. As attempts accelerate to redefine and to drastically limit what is taught to children, we should *broaden* our definitions of literacy and of the basics to include not only reading and writing — which are very important and must not be neglected — but also social, political, aesthetic, and technological literacy. Community action projects that provide curricular links between students and their local communities can help youngsters develop social and political responsibility and learn the necessary skills for active participation in the society.[11] At the same time, we should expose all students to beauty and form, aesthetics, and various ways of creating personal meanings — including research, poetry, dance, the visual arts, and film making. In other words, we should give equal weight to both "discursive" and "nondiscursive" subjects, so that each student has an opportunity to discover his or her talents and to develop the wide range of tools with which individuals control their own lives and their futures.[12] Thus we must define the "basics" very broadly.

Given the important role of technology in the future, *all* students — not just a select few who are "gifted and talented" — should be literate both in using computers and microcomputers *and* in analyzing their social implications. For example, computers and video-display equipment increase efficiency, but they may also cause untold thousands of workers (primarily women) to lose their jobs, become de-skilled, or work under stressful conditions. "Literacy" means the ability to analyze and deal with the social as well as the technical implications of this new technology.

In a recent column in the *New York Times*, Fred Hechinger noted that, if we approach computer literacy as a narrow vocational issue, we are bound merely to add one more relatively ineffective career education program to the many that already exist. As he put it:

The visions of brave new electronic worlds of microchips and robots raise simultaneous demands for a schooling that looks to the future by learning from the past. Yes, the computer must be mastered by all, regardless of race, sex, or economic condition. But at the same time . . . the computer must be mastered by young people who are secure in a broad understanding of what used to be called general education — including language, history, economics, mathematics, science, the arts; in short, the human condition.[13]

To focus on a broad and general education requires that we be sensitive to the fact that the curriculum must represent us all. A "selective tradition" has operated in curriculum to date. This tradition may be more visible in some subjects than in others, but it is quite clear that the knowledge of some groups is not represented adequately in the curriculum.[14] For instance, we tend to teach military history or the history of U.S. Presidents; we teach less rigorously the history of the U.S. working class. Obviously, we have made advances here, just as we have made advances in teaching the real histories, contributions, and cultures of ethnic minorities and of women. Our progress in eliminating sexism and racism and in recapturing the lost past of U.S. labor is too important to allow these advances to slip away in the next decade or two. We must continue to pursue curricular balance. The content that we teach cannot be determined solely by the needs of any one group, even in times of severe economic difficulty. That would be short-sighted.

The curriculum must simultaneously be both conservative and critical. It must preserve the ideals that have guided discourse in the U.S. for centuries: a faith in the American people, a commitment to expanding equality, and a commitment to diversity and liberty. Yet it must also empower individuals to question the ethics of their institutions and to criticize them when they fail to meet these ideals. Curricular content should give people the ability to interpret social change and to reflect critically on what is happening in their daily lives. This is not a formula for an "easy" curriculum. It requires hard work and discipline on the part of both teachers and students.

Moreover, participation in such a curriculum is not merely an individual act; it is a profoundly social act as well. In an interdependent society, the curriculum should encourage cooperation and the testing of each individual's ideas against those of others. This requires countering — at least to some degree — the individualized instructional models now widely practiced in schools. All too many children sit isolated from one another in the elementary grades, completing worksheet after worksheet with little or no opportunity for serious discussion, deliberation, debate, or cooperation. Individualization is important; however, to be truly meaningful, it must be balanced by a sense of social responsibility.

The issue of time looms large here. Educators must have time to consider the curriculum carefully. Too many curricular decisions today focus on *how* to teach, not on *what* to teach. Teachers and other educators must have opportunities to discuss in detail what they want to do and why they want to do it. Creative scheduling is essential, in order to make time available for frequent, in-depth discussions of curricular content among local educators.

Obviously, teachers are not the only ones who are affected by what is taught. As much as possible, all individuals who are affected by a curricular decision should be involved in making it.[15] This includes parents, concerned citizens, organized labor and other interest groups, and, when possible, the students themselves. I recognize that such broad participation can lead to political conflict and to interminable meetings, but it can also lead to a greater sense of trust and cooperation on the part of all those involved. Indeed, broad participation may be one way to bolster flagging community (and financial) support of public education.

Educators who act on this suggestion must be willing to take risks and to work hard. School officials must aggressively present their curricular proposals and programs to the community — especially to the most disenfranchised groups. They must show their publics what they offer and communicate the justifications for these offerings. They must take criticisms seriously and respond to them honestly.

I have good reasons for making these suggestions. Available evidence suggests that, unless participation in curricular planning is widely shared among teachers, principals, central office staff members, students, and parents, the amount of support for any program is significantly reduced.[16]

In addition, direct parental involvement in the classroom tends to foster both more and longer-lasting changes in the daily activities of teachers. And evidence suggests that *how* a program is carried out is just as important as the specific content of a program.[17] The prospect of a continued decline in educational funding will give impetus to broad participation in the classroom. Parents will have to become more deeply involved, since schools will be hard pressed to afford many of the programs essential to high-quality education. As parents (and the elderly, I hope) volunteer to serve as tutors, as resource people, as counselors, and in other capacities, they will become more knowledgeable and more skillful at dealing with curricular issues. This is an important step toward a genuinely cooperative effort to guarantee high-quality programs for children.

If parental participation in decision making is important, teacher participation is even more important. There tends to be a very high correlation between the involvement of teachers in decisions related to changes in the curriculum and "effective implementation and continuation" of such changes.[18] When we consider going from what *is* to what *should be*, there are few things we know for certain. However, we do have some guidelines for strategies that seem to foster more effective and lasting changes in the curriculum, in what teachers do, and in what students learn. The findings of several studies have suggested that "what should be" will be enhanced to the extent that there is: 1) concrete, extended, and teacher-specific training related to the curricular change; 2) continuing classroom assistance from the district; 3) opportunities for teachers to observe similar projects in other classrooms, schools, or districts; 4) frequent meetings among the people involved that focus on practical problems; 5) local development of materials, insofar as this is possible; and 6) emphasis on teacher participation in curricular decision making.[19] As the financial crunch worsens, these guidelines will become even more important, especially in larger school districts.

So far, I have suggested certain attitudes and activities that should guide our policies on curriculum content, form, and decision making. However, this article would be both incomplete and deceptively simplistic if I did not add that,

9. A LOOK TO THE FUTURE

just as many of the tensions and conflicts over the curriculum arise outside the school, so too do many solutions to these problems require changes in the larger society. The issues of raising students' achievement levels and preventing dropouts are cases in point; solving these problems will require coordinated efforts by the larger society.

Educators have given a good deal of attention to reforming the secondary school curriculum to prevent dropouts. These reforms have had mixed results, in part because focusing solely on internal curricular changes is too limited a strategy. As Christopher Jencks has recently shown, the economic benefits for students who complete secondary school are still *twice* as great for whites as for blacks.[20] Moreover, completing secondary school provides relatively few benefits to students from economically disadvantaged backgrounds. Jencks and his colleagues have summarized their findings thus: "Apparently, high school graduation pays off primarily for men from advantaged backgrounds. Men from disadvantaged backgrounds must attend college to reap large occupational benefits from their education."[21] Clearly, those minority and economically disadvantaged students who stay in secondary school longer receive few economic rewards for their efforts — regardless of what common sense tells us about the benefits of increased schooling.

I am *not* arguing against making the curriculum more responsive to the needs of such youngsters. Rather, I am saying that, without a societal commitment to altering the structure of the economic marketplace so that these more responsive programs pay off for participants, such efforts may be doomed to failure. Why should such students wish to take part even in well-designed programs, if the statistical probability that these programs will improve their lives is very low? We *do* need better secondary programs, but these programs will be successful only to the extent that students feel that the school has something to offer — both now and for the future.

Improving the achievement of students poses similar problems. We have spent many years and huge sums of money attempting to raise achievement — especially scores on reading tests — through better instructional materials and curricula, more intensive teaching strategies, and so on. Yet these efforts, too, have had mixed results. We may have to take seriously the evidence that suggests a marked relationship between socioeconomic status and achievement in schools. The answers to many of the curriculum questions we face now and will certainly face in the next two decades — such as how best to increase the achievement of minority and poor

The future context of education must broaden the student's educational experience. Literacy should be defined to include social, political, aesthetic, and technological literacy.

students — may be found as much in social policies as in better teaching and curricula. As I mentioned earlier, doing well in elementary and secondary school does not guarantee economic success in later life.

The implications of this fact are striking. If we are really serious about increasing student mastery of content, especially among economically disadvantaged groups, then we might consider embarking on a serious analysis of the prevailing patterns of educational financing, of the possibility of redistributing income, and of ways to create jobs that would make possible a decent standard of living for the many families who will suffer the most if the economy continues its downturn. However, such analysis must not serve as an excuse for failing to do the important work of revising the curriculum and teaching practices. My point is that we must take seriously the complications that hinder the schools from reaching their goals. If we are to reach these goals by the year 2000, we will have to consider how our ability to do so is linked to the existing distribution of resources in our society.

If our aim is a society in which all people are more equal in their opportunities to experience success and to exercise control over their own destinies, not a society in which the chasms between groups grow larger every day, then we must deal now with these larger social issues. Otherwise, the public will continue

to blame the school and its curriculum, its teachers, and its administrators for something over which they have much less control than do other social agencies.

If I am correct that the success of the schools is very much tied to conditions in the larger society, then the training of curriculum specialists, teachers, and administrators for the year 2000 cannot be limited to such things as techniques of teaching, management approaches, and methods of financial planning. We must focus more rigorously — starting now — on the skills of democratic deliberation about such questions as social goals, the proper direction for schools to take, and what we should teach and why.[22] We will never have a curriculum free of tensions and conflicts. And it would probably not be good if we did, since such conflicts demonstrate the vitality of democracy. We must learn to work creatively with conflicts, seeing them not as hindrances but as possibilities for cooperative improvement of education.

The results of the decisions we make today about curriculum policies and classroom practices will be with us in the year 2000, which is just around the corner. It is crucial that we debate now the questions of what we should teach, how it should be organized, who should make the decisions, and what we as educators should and can do about (and in) a society marked by large and growing disparities in wealth and power. I hope that I have stimulated such debate, because that is the necessary first step to taking seriously the question of what the curriculum should be in the year 2000.

NOTES

1. I have discussed this in much greater detail in Michael W. Apple, *Education and Power* (Boston: Routledge and Kegan Paul, 1982). See also Manuel Castells, *The Economic Crisis and American Society* (Princeton, N.J.: Princeton University Press, 1980); and Lester Thurow, *The Zero-Sum Society* (New York: Basic Books, 1980).

2. For a detailed analysis, see Martin Carnoy and Derek Shearer, *Economic Democracy* (White Plains, N.Y.: M.E. Sharpe, 1980).

3. See Michael W. Apple, *Ideology and Curriculum* (Boston: Routledge and Kegan Paul, 1979).

4. See, for example, Sheila Harty, *Hucksters in the Classroom* (Washington, D.C.: Center for Responsive Law, 1979); and Apple, *Education and Power*, esp. Ch. 5.

5. Castells, pp. 161-85.

6. For a review of the literature on tracking and differentiation, see Caroline H. Persell, *Education and Inequality* (New York: Free Press, 1977); and Thomas Good and Jere Brophy, *Looking in Classrooms* (New York: Harper and Row, 1978).

7. Michael W. Apple, "Work, Gender, and Teaching," *Teachers College Record*, in press.

8. See, for example, Seymour Sarason, *The Culture of the School and the Problem of Change* (Boston: Allyn & Bacon, 1971).

9. For an empirical analysis of what is happening to some teachers in elementary schools because of this separation, see Andrew Gitlin, "School Structure and Teachers' Work," in Michael W. Apple and Lois Weis, eds., *Ideology and Practice in Schooling* (Philadelphia: Temple University Press, forthcoming). See also Apple, *Education and Power*.

10. For an interesting discussion of various forms of meaning and "representation," see Elliot Eisner, *Cognition and Curriculum: A Basis for Deciding What to Teach* (New York: Longman, 1982).

11. Fred Newmann, Thomas Bertocci, and Ruthanne Landsness, *Skills in Citizen Action* (Skokie, Ill.: National Textbook Co., 1977). See also Fred Newmann, "Reducing Student Alienation in High Schools," *Harvard Educational Review*, Winter 1981, pp. 546-64.

12. Elliot Eisner, *The Educational Imagination* (New York: Macmillan, 1979).

13. 10 August 1982, Sec. 3, p. 7.

14. Apple, *Ideology and Curriculum*, pp. 6-7.

15. Joseph Schwab, "The Practical: A Language for Curriculum," in Arno Bellack and Herbert Kliebard, eds., *Curriculum and Evaluation* (Berkeley, Calif.: McCutchan, 1977), pp. 26-44.

16. Paul Berman and Milbrey W. McLaughlin, *Federal Programs Supporting Educational Change, Vol. VIII: Implementing and Sustaining Innovations* (Santa Monica, Calif.: Rand Corporation, May 1978), p. 14.

17. Ibid., p. 24.

18. Ibid., p. 29.

19. Ibid., p. 34.

20. Christopher Jencks et al., *Who Gets Ahead?* (New York: Basic Books, 1979), pp. 174-75.

21. Ibid., p. 175. It is unfortunate that most of this research has dealt only with men.

22. Kenneth Zeichner is doing some of the best work on helping teachers to develop the skills of deliberation and reflection. See his "Reflective Teaching and Field-Based Experience in Teacher Education," *Interchange*, vol. 12, no. 4, 1981, pp. 1-22.

Index

Credits/ Acknowledgments

Cover design by Charles Vitelli

1. Perceptions of Education in America
Facing overview—Dushkin Publishing Group/Richard Pawlikowski. 12—Illustration by Andrea Eberbach.
2. Continuity and Change in Education
Facing overview—United Nations photo by Marcia Weistein.
58—Photograph by John Schroeder, Ferndale Middle School, High Point, North Carolina.
3. The Struggle for Excellence
Facing overview—EPA-Documerica. 77—Chart by John McGuffin.
4. Morality and Values in Education
Facing overview—WHO photo by Paul Almasy. 102—Anna Kaufman Moon.
5. Discipline Problems in the Schools
Facing overview—Courtesy of Traver Steiner/Barbie Heid.

6. Equal Opportunity and American Education
Facing overview—United Nations.
7. Serving Special Needs and Individualizing Instruction
Facing overview—United Nations photo/S. Dimartini.
8. The Profession of Teaching Today
Facing overview—United Nations photo by Marta Pinter.
198-199—Illustration by Dan Sherbo.
9. A Look to the Future
Facing overview—United Nations/Y. Nagata. 224,226-229—From Informational Technology and Its Impact on American Education (Washington, D.C.:U.S. Congress, Office of Technology Assessment, OTA-CIT-187, November 1982). 240—Photo by Mattel Toys.

ANNUAL EDITIONS:
EDUCATION 87/88
Article Rating Form

We Want Your Advice

Here is an opportunity for you to have direct input into the next revision of this volume. We would like you to rate each of the 41 articles listed below, using the following scale:

1. **Excellent: should definitely be retained**
2. **Above average: should probably be retained**
3. **Below average: should probably be deleted**
4. **Poor: should definitely be deleted**

Your ratings will play a vital part in the next revision. So please mail this prepaid form to us just as soon as you complete it.
Thanks for your help!

Annual Editions revisions depend on two major opinion sources: one is our Advisory Board, listed in the front of this volume, which works with us in scanning the thousands of articles published in the public press each year; the other is you—the person actually using the book. Please help us and the users of the next edition by completing the prepaid article rating form on this page and returning it to us. Thank you.

Rating	Article	Rating	Article
	1. The Proper Study of Education		21. Good, Old-Fashioned Discipline: The Politics of Punitiveness
	2. False Premises, False Promises: The Mythical Character of Public Discourse About Education		22. Discipline Is Not the Problem: Control Theory in the Classroom
	3. The Fourth R: The Repatriation of the School		23. Help for the Hot-Tempered Kid
	4. Who Will Teach the Class of 2000?		24. The Courts and Education
	5. The 18th Annual Gallup Poll of the Public's Attitudes Toward the Public Schools		25. School Desegregation Since *Brown:* A 30-Year Perspective
	6. What Can Schools Become?		26. A Long-Term View of School Desegregation: Some Recent Studies of Graduates as Adults
	7. Education and the Sony War		27. The Bilingual Education Battle
	8. The Best Prep School in Town		28. Sexism in the Schoolroom of the '80s
	9. A National Survey of Middle School Effectiveness		29. "Appropriate" School Programs: Legal vs. Educational Approaches
	10. A Good School		30. Single-Parent Families: How Can Schools Help?
	11. Changing Our Thinking About Educational Change		31. Checking In: An Alternative for Latchkey Kids
	12. Sustaining the Momentum of State Education Reform: The Link Between Assessment and Financial Support		32. Student-Student Interaction: Ignored but Powerful
	13. The Carnegie Report: A Bold Beginning		33. Child Abuse and Neglect: Prevention and Reporting
	14. Educational Ideals and Educational Practice: The Case of Minimum Competency Testing		34. Kids and Drugs: Why, When, and What Can We Do About It
	15. Huffing and Puffing and Blowing Schools Excellent		35. The Making of a Profession
	16. The Great Tradition in Education: Transmitting Moral Values		36. On Stir-and-Serve Recipes for Teaching
	17. Moral Education in the United States		37. Teachers Aim at Turning Loose the Mind's Eyes
	18. Ethics Without Virtue: Moral Education in America		38. Profile of an Effective Teacher
	19. Reopening the Books on Ethics: The Role of Education in a Free Society		39. Schools of the Future
	20. Research Evidence of a School Discipline Problem		40. The Education of Children
			41. Curriculum in the Year 2000: Tensions and Possibilities

(continued on back)

ABOUT YOU

Name _____ Date _____

Are you a teacher? ☐   Or student? ☐

Your School Name _____

Department _____

Address _____

City _____ State _____ Zip _____

School Telephone # _____

▰▰▰▰▰▰▰▰▰▰▰▰▰▰▰▰▰▰▰▰▰▰▰▰▰

YOUR COMMENTS ARE IMPORTANT TO US!

Please fill in the following information:

For which course did you use this book? _____

Did you use a text with this Annual Edition?   ☐ yes ☐ no

The title of the text: _____

What are your general reactions to the Annual Editions concept?

Have you read any particular articles recently that you think should be included in the next edition?

Are there any articles you feel should be replaced in the next edition? Why?

Are there other areas that you feel would utilize an Annual Edition?

May we contact you for editorial input?

May we quote you from above?

▰▰▰▰▰▰▰▰▰▰▰▰▰▰▰▰▰▰▰▰▰▰▰▰▰

‖‖‖‖‖

EDUCATION 87/88

BUSINESS REPLY MAIL

First Class   Permit No. 84   Guilford, CT

Postage will be paid by addressee

**The Dushkin Publishing Group, Inc.
Sluice Dock
Guilford, Connecticut 06437**

‖‖‖‖‖‖‖‖‖‖‖‖‖‖‖‖‖‖‖‖‖‖‖‖‖‖‖‖‖‖‖